Tropical Snappers and Groupers

About the Book and Editors

Snappers (Lutjanidae) and groupers (Serranidae) are among the most widely distributed fish taxa, yet most studies of these ecologically and commercially important families have been region-specific. This book presents an international perspective on snappers and groupers, including both research on their biology and discussions of fisheries management.

The first half of the book is devoted to biological reviews covering taxonomy, reproductive biology, early life history, growth, mortality, and community-trophic interactions. Surveys of the literature and extensive bibliographies provide a comprehensive perspective on current work on these two important fish groups.

Four more chapters examine assessment and management of fisheries for snappers and groupers in Australia, Hawaii and the Marianas, the southeastern United States, and the Gulf of Mexico and the Caribbean. They discuss historical trends within the fisheries, briefly describe methods of harvest, and evaluate and apply analytical methods to provide estimates of population and yield parameters. A final synthetic chapter takes a comparative approach to pursue general biological conclusions and explores future research needs.

Jeffrey J. Polovina is a mathematical statistician with the Southwest Fisheries Center (SWFC) Honolulu Laboratory, National Marine Fisheries Service (NMFS), NOAA. Stephen Ralston is a research fisheries biologist with the NMFS Honolulu Laboratory.

Tropical Snappers and Groupers

Biology and Fisheries Management

edited by
Jeffrey J. Polovina
and Stephen Ralston

Westview Press / **Boulder and London**

Ocean Resources and Marine Policy Series

This Westview softcover edition is printed on acid-free paper and bound in
softcovers that carry the highest rating of the National Association of State
Textbook Administrators, in consultation with the Association of American
Publishers and the Book Manufacturers' Institute.

Published in 1987 in the United States of America by Westview Press, Inc.;
Frederick A. Praeger, Publisher; 5500 Central Avenue, Boulder, Colorado 80301

Library of Congress Cataloging-in-Publication Data
Tropical snappers and groupers.
   (Ocean resources and marine policy series)
   1. Lutjanidae.   2. Groupers.   3. Lutjanidae
fisheries--Tropics.   4. Grouper fisheries--Tropics.
5. Fishery management--Tropics.   6. Fishes--Tropics.
I. Polovina, Jeffrey.   I. Ralston, Stephen.
III. Series.
QL638.L9T76   1987   639.3'758   86-1698
ISBN 0-8133-7179-1

Composition for this book was provided by the editors.
This book was produced without formal editing by the publisher.

Printed and bound in the United States of America

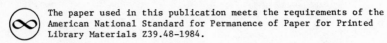

The paper used in this publication meets the requirements of the
American National Standard for Permanence of Paper for Printed
Library Materials Z39.48-1984.

6   5   4   3   2   1

Contents

Preface   ix

Biological Reviews

1 Systematics of the fishes of the   1
   family Lutjanidae (Perciformes: Percoidei),
   the snappers
   William D. Anderson, Jr.

2 Synopsis of the circumtropical fish genus   33
   <u>Lutjanus</u> (Lutjanidae)
   Gerald R. Allen

3 A preliminary synopsis of the groupers   89
   (Perciformes: Serranidae: Epinephelinae) of
   the Indo-Pacific Region
   John E. Randall

4 Review of the early life history of tropical   189
   groupers (Serranidae) and snappers (Lutjanidae)
   Jeffrey M. Leis

5 Reproductive biology of the Lutjanidae: 239
   A review
   Churchill B. Grimes

6 Reproduction in groupers   295
   Douglas Y. Shapiro

7 Age and growth of snappers and groupers   329
   Charles S. Manooch, III

8 Mortality rates of snappers and groupers   375
   Stephen Ralston

9 The trophic biology of snappers and groupers   405
   James D. Parrish

Fishery Management

10   Assessment and management of the demersal   465
fishery on the continental shelf of
northwestern Australia
    K. J. Sainsbury

11   Assessment and management of deepwater bottom   505
fishes in Hawaii and the Marianas
    Jeffrey J. Polovina

12   Development of management plans for reef   533
fishes--Gulf of Mexico and U.S. South
Atlantic
    Gene R. Huntsman and James R. Waters

13   Reproductive strategies and the management   561
of snappers and groupers in the Gulf of
Mexico and Caribbean
    **Scott P. Bannerot, William W. Fox, Jr.,
and Joseph E. Powers**

14   Demand considerations in fisheries   605
management--Hawaii's market for bottom fish
    Samuel G. Pooley

15   Workshop synthesis and directions for   639
future research
    John L. Munro

Preface

Snappers and groupers are important fishery resources throughout the tropical and subtropical regions of the world. These large apex predators are highly esteemed for their flavor and command high prices in virtually every society where they are found. Due in part to their non-migratory nature, geographic differences in species composition, and regional variation in methods of harvest, the literature concerning the biology and fisheries management of these fishes has been largely "region specific." This has been an unfortunate historical development. Clearly, much can be gained by comparing the experiences of researchers working on taxonomically similar resources that are harvested in differing localities.

In May of 1985 the Honolulu Laboratory of the Southwest Fisheries Center, National Marine Fisheries Service, sponsored a workshop which brought together researchers working on the biology and fisheries management of regional snapper and grouper stocks. Papers were presented that summarized our knowledge of these two groups, each written with the idea of developing a "resource specific" perspective on either their biology or fisheries management.

This book is the result of that workshop. The first nine chapters represent review papers that provide up-to-date summaries of our understanding of the biology of snappers and groupers. Included are papers dealing with taxonomy, early life history, reproductive biology, age and growth, mortality, and trophics. The next five chapters represent fisheries experience papers treating assessment, economic, and management aspects of snapper and grouper stocks. A final chapter synthesizes the main points and identifies critical information gaps. Regional coverage ranges from fisheries in the western Pacific Ocean to the Caribbean Sea. It is our hope that the results presented here will be of particular use in managing snapper and grouper fisheries to their fullest potential.

Many people contributed significantly to the completion of this volume. Izadore Barrett, Director of the Southwest Fisheries Center, and Richard S. Shomura, Director of the Honolulu Laboratory, provided the financial support and encouragement that we needed to see the project through. The talents of Elizabeth Young, Louise Lembeck, Virginia Ishida, Kathleen Repollo, and Gaylene Yoneda were used extensively in typing, editing, and preparing all the manuscripts for publication. Mary Lynne Godfrey technically edited each paper, Tom Weber prepared illustrations, and Josie Herr completed the layout for the book. Bill Walsh did a beautiful job preparing the cover gyotaku. We are particularly indebted to all these people for their dedicated work on this project. Lastly, we wish to thank each of the contributing authors for their patience and continued assistance as the volume approached completion.

Jeffrey J. Polovina
Stephen Ralston
Honolulu, Hawaii

1
Systematics of the Fishes of the Family Lutjanidae (Perciformes: Percoidei), the Snappers

William D. Anderson, Jr.
Grice Marine Biological Laboratory
College of Charleston
Charleston, South Carolina 29412

ABSTRACT

Seventeen genera and about 103 species are included in the snapper family (the Lutjanidae). Snappers are found throughout the world in tropical and subtropical seas, being largely confined to continental shelves and slopes and to corresponding depths around islands; some, however, enter estuaries and even fresh water. In this review descriptions of the family and subfamilies and keys to the genera and to the species of Pristipomoides and Paracaesio are furnished. In addition, descriptive information for genera and species, except those of Lutjanus, and geographic distributions are provided. In order to clarify the nomenclature, the status of numerous synonyms is presented.

INTRODUCTION

Fishes of the family Lutjanidae are found throughout the world in warm seas. Adults are mostly bottom-associated, feed chiefly on fishes and crustaceans, and occur from shallow inshore areas to depths of about 550 m. Some species enter estuaries and even fresh water. Early developmental stages are unknown for most species, but those stages that have been described are pelagic. The Lutjanidae include 17 genera and about 103 species. Herein I follow Johnson (1981) in excluding the Caesionidae from the Lutjanidae. Verilus and Symphysanodon, previously treated as members of the Lutjanidae by a number of

authors including Anderson (1967, 1970), are not members
of that family (Johnson 1975). Allen (1985) presents a
catalogue of lutjanid fishes. Some lutjanids reach sizes
as great as 100 to 120 cm. Many are important to sport
and/or commercial fishermen, and many are fine food
fishes, although some are ciguatoxic in certain areas.

No synapomorphic character is known that distin-
guishes the Lutjanidae from other percoid families. Johnson (1981) treated the Lutjanidae as a natural group
because of "the obvious intermediacy of the Apsilinae
between the Etelinae and Lutjaninae."

Gill-raker counts are of those on the first gill arch
and include rudiments. Counts of lateral-line scales are
of tubed scales. Abbreviations used include: GMBL (Grice
Marine Biological Laboratory, College of Charleston), SL
(standard length), and USNM (National Museum of Natural
History, Smithsonian Institution, Washington, D.C.).

FAMILY LUTJANIDAE

Mouth terminal. Two nostrils on each side of snout.
Maxilla slipping for most or all of its length under
lachrymal when mouth closed. Supramaxilla absent. Premaxillae usually moderately protractile (fixed in Aphareus
and Randallichthys). No bony suborbital stay. Subocular
shelf on third infraorbital. Opercle with two small flat
spines. Tubes in lateral-line simple; lateral line
complete, not extending far onto caudal fin. Scales
ctenoid; cheek and operculum scaly; maxilla with or without scales; snout, lachrymal, and lower jaw naked. Upper
and lower jaws usually with more or less distinct canines
(canines absent in Aphareus, Parapristipomoides, and
Pinjalo; molariform teeth present in Hoplopagrus). Vomer
and palatines usually with teeth. Pterygoids usually
toothless (pterygoid teeth present in Ocyurus and Rhomboplites). Gill membranes separate, free from isthmus.
Gill arches four, a slit behind fourth. Pseudobranchiae
well developed. Branchiostegal rays seven. Body moderately elongate to deep. Dorsal fin single, spinous
portion sometimes deeply incised; dorsal-fin rays IX to
XII, 9 to 18. Anal-fin rays III,7 to 11. Pectoral-fin
rays 14 to 19. Pelvic fins thoracic, I, 5; pelvic axillary process usually well-developed. Caudal fin truncate
to deeply forked; principal caudal-fin rays 17 (9 + 8);
procurrent caudal-fin rays 8 to 13 dorsally and ventrally;
posteriormost ventral procurrent caudal-fin ray without a

spur (Johnson 1975). Vertebrae 24 (10 precaudal + 14 caudal). Epipleural ribs 7 to 13, first articulating with first vertebra. Pleural ribs usually 8 (in **Apsilus fuscus** 11 or 12), first articulating with third vertebra. Predorsal bones usually three (two in **Aprion**). First dorsal and first anal pterygiophore each supporting two supernumerary spines. Posteriormost two to seven complete pterygiophores of dorsal fin and posteriormost one to six complete pterygiophores of anal fin trisegmental (i.e., proximal and middle elements not fused). A crescent-shaped bony stay posterior to last complete dorsal and anal pterygiophore. Three epurals; two pairs of uroneurals; five hypurals (hypurals 1-2 and 3-4 frequently fused); one parhypural with well-developed hypurapophysis. Adductor mandibulae with or without separate upper division of A_1 (i.e., A_1') originating on subocular shelf.

The limits and relationships of the family Lutjanidae have been studied in detail recently by Johnson (1981). The preceding descriptive material is largely derived from Johnson's study. Four subfamilies (Etelinae, Apsilinae, Paradicichthyinae, and Lutjaninae) are currently recognized.

KEY TO THE GENERA OF LUTJANIDAE

1a. Dorsal and anal fins without scales. Dorsal-fin rays X,10 or 11 (rarely X,9) 2
1b. Soft dorsal and anal fins with scales or sheathed with scales basally. Dorsal-fin rays IX-XII,10-18 11

2a. Maxilla with scales 3
2b. Maxilla without scales 5

3a. Spinous portion of dorsal fin deeply incised at its junction with soft portion. Dorsal-fin rays X,11 (very infrequently X,10) . . . . Etelis
3b. Spinous portion of dorsal fin not deeply incised at its junction with soft portion. Dorsal-fin rays X,10 4

4a. Ultimate soft ray of dorsal fin
     and anal fin shorter than
     penultimate soft ray . . . . Paracaesio
4b. Ultimate soft ray of dorsal fin
     and anal fin about equal to or
     slightly longer than penultimate
     soft ray . . . . Parapristipomoides

5a. Premaxillae essentially
     non-protractile, attached to
     snout at symphysis by a frenum 6
5b. Premaxillae protractile, not
     attached to snout by frenum 7

6a. Vomer without teeth. Teeth in
     jaws minute, no caniniform teeth.
     Pectoral fin somewhat shorter
     than head. Lateral surface of
     maxilla smooth . . . . Aphareus
6b. Vomer with teeth. Jaws with some
     caniniform teeth. Pectoral fin
     about one-half to two-thirds
     length of head. Lateral surface
     of maxilla with a series of well-
     developed longitudinal ridges . . . Randallichthys

7a. Ultimate soft ray of dorsal fin
     and anal fin longer than
     penultimate soft ray 8
7b. Ultimate soft ray of dorsal
     fin and anal fin about equal
     to or shorter than penultimate
     soft ray 9

8a. Groove present on snout below
     nostrils. Pectoral fin less
     than one-half length of head . . . . Aprion
8b. No groove on snout. Pectoral
     fin about two-thirds length
     of head to somewhat longer
     than head . . . . Pristipomoides

9a. Upper lip with a median
     fleshy protrusion,
     well-developed in adults.
     Spines of dorsal and anal

fins strong, very robust
in large adults . . . . **Lipocheilus**
9b. Upper lip without a median
fleshy protrusion 10

10a. Adductor mandibulae section
A_1 with a well-developed
anterodorsal extension.
Ultimate dorsal and
ultimate anal soft rays
86-113% length of respective
penultimate soft rays.
Atlantic . . . . **Apsilus**
10b. Adductor mandibulae section A_1
without an anterodorsal
extension. Ultimate dorsal
and ultimate anal soft rays
<90% length of respective
penultimate soft rays. Indo-
Pacific . . . . **Paracaesio**

11a. Vomer without teeth. Dorsal-fin
rays X,14-18. Some of anterior
dorsal soft rays produced as
filaments (at least in juveniles) 12
11b. Vomer with teeth. Dorsal-fin
rays IX-XII,10-16. None of
anterior dorsal soft rays
produced as filaments 13

12a. Anterior profile quite steep
(see Plate 1.2f). Upper and
lower pharyngeals enlarged
and bearing large molariform
teeth . . . . **Symphorichthys**
12b. Anterior profile sloping more
gently (see Plate 1.3a and 1.3b).
Upper and lower pharyngeals not
particularly enlarged, not
bearing molariform teeth . . . . **Symphorus**

13a. Pterygoid teeth present 14
13b. Pterygoid teeth absent 15

14a. Dorsal-fin rays XII,11 (rarely
XII,10 or XII,12) . . . . **Rhomboplites**

14b. Dorsal-fin rays X,12 or 13
     (rarely with IX or XI spines
     or 14 soft rays) . . . .   Ocyurus

15a. Teeth in jaws and on vomer
     molariform. Anterior nostril
     opening through a tube above
     upper lip . . . .   Hoplopagrus
15b. Teeth conical. Anterior nostril
     not opening through a tube above
     upper lip   16

16a. First gill arch with 60 or more
     gill rakers on lower limb . . . .   Macolor
16b. First gill arch with 20 or fewer
     gill rakers on lower limb   17

17a. Mouth rather small, somewhat
     upturned. Teeth in jaws small . . . .   Pinjalo
17b. Mouth larger, usually not upturned.
     Some caniniform teeth in jaws . . . .   Lutjanus

SUBFAMILY ETELINAE

Nostrils on each side close together; posterior flap
of anterior nostril, when reflected, typically reaching
anterior border of posterior nostril. Vomerine teeth
present (except in Aphareus). Body moderately elongate.
Dorsal and anal fins scaleless. Dorsal-fin rays X,11
(infrequently X,10). Anal-fin rays III,8 or 9 (very infrequently III,7). Anterior dorsal and anterior anal soft
rays not produced into filaments. Ultimate soft ray of
dorsal fin and anal fin produced, longer than penultimate
soft ray (except in Randallichthys where ultimate soft ray
about equal to penultimate). Caudal fin lunate to deeply
forked. Procurrent caudal-fin rays 10 to 13 dorsally, 9
to 13 ventrally. Interorbital region flattened. Configuration of predorsal bones, anterior neural spines, and
anterior dorsal pterygiophores (using the symbolization of
Ahlstrom et al. 1976) usually 0/0+0/2/1+1/ (Aprion with
0/0/2/1+1/). Posteriormost four to seven complete
pterygiophores of dorsal fin and posteriormost three to
six complete pterygiophores of anal fin trisegmental.
Adductor mandibulae typically simple, section A_1 with
anterodorsal extension only in Pristipomoides and Aprion;
division A_1' absent. (See Johnson 1981.)

Five genera: <u>Etelis</u>, <u>Randallichthys</u>, <u>Aphareus</u>, <u>Pris</u>-<u>tipomoides</u>, and <u>Aprion</u>.

GENUS <u>ETELIS</u> CUVIER, 1828

Maxilla with scales, but without a series of longi-tudinal bony ridges on lateral surface. Premaxillae protractile. Dorsal fin continuous, but spinous portion of fin deeply incised at its junction with soft portion. Pectoral fin fairly long; in specimens more than about 160 mm SL, length of pectoral fin about 80 to 90% of head length. Dorsal-fin rays X,11 (very infrequently X,10). Anal-fin rays III,8. Pectoral-fin rays 15 to 17 (usually 16). Species of <u>Etelis</u> are reddish dorsally and dorso-laterally, paler ventrolaterally and ventrally. Four species. Type species <u>Etelis carbunculus</u>. Anderson and Fourmanoir (1975) relegated <u>Erythrobussothen</u> Parr, 1933, to the synonymy of <u>Etelis</u>. (See Anderson 1981.)

Species of <u>Etelis</u> (Plate 1.1a)

<u>Etelis carbunculus</u> Cuvier, 1828. Gill rakers 5 to 8 + 11 to 14—total 17 to 22. Lateral-line scales 48 to 50. Length of pelvic fin 18 to 20% SL. Length of upper lobe of caudal fin 26 to 30% SL. Jaws each with several enlarged needlelike canine teeth. Widespread in the Indo-Pacific. <u>Etelis marshi</u> (Jenkins, 1903) is a junior synonym of <u>E. carbunculus</u>.
<u>Etelis coruscans</u> Valenciennes, 1862. Gill rakers 8 to 10 + 15 to 18—total 23 to 28. Lateral-line scales 47 to 50. Length of pelvic fin usually 21 to 23% SL. Length of upper lobe of caudal fin 33 to 75% SL. Widespread in the Indo-Pacific.
<u>Etelis oculatus</u> (Valenciennes, 1828). Gill rakers 7 to 11 + 14 to 18—total 23 to 28. Lateral-line scales 47 to 50. Length of pelvic fin 18 to 21% SL. Length of upper lobe of caudal fin 27 to >40% SL. Western Atlantic. Anderson and Fourmanoir (1975) showed that <u>Erythrobus</u>-<u>sothen gracilis</u> Parr, 1933, is a junior synonym of <u>Etelis</u> <u>oculatus</u>.
<u>Etelis radiosus</u> Anderson, 1981. Gill rakers 12 to 15 + 20 to 22—total 33 to 36. Lateral-line scales 50 or 51. Length of pelvic fin 17 to 18% SL. Length of upper lobe of caudal fin 31 to 34% SL. Tropical Indo-Pacific.

GENUS RANDALLICHTHYS ANDERSON, KAMI, AND JOHNSON 1977 (PLATE 1.1b)

Maxilla without scales, but with a well-developed series of longitudinal bony ridges on lateral surface. Premaxillae not protractile, fixed by a frenum. Gill openings extending anterior to orbit. Dorsal fin continuous, indented just anterior to junction of spinous and soft portions, but not as deeply incised as in Etelis. Pectoral fin short, about one-half to two-thirds length of head. Dorsal-fin rays X,11. Anal-fin rays III,9. Pectoral-fin rays 16 or 17. Gill rakers 5 to 9 + 14 to 16--total 19 to 23. Lateral-line scales 48 or 49. Ground color rosy to dull orange. The single species, Randallichthys filamentosus (Fourmanoir, 1970), is widespread in the central and western Pacific and may be antequatorial in distribution (Randall 1982). Etelis filamentosus Fourmanoir, 1970, and E. nudimaxillaris Yoshino and Araga, 1975, are synonyms of R. filamentosus.

GENUS APHAREUS CUVIER, 1830

Maxilla without scales; no well-developed series of longitudinal bony ridges on lateral surface of maxilla. Premaxillae not protractile, fixed by a frenum. Gill openings extending far anterior to orbit. Dorsal fin continuous, not deeply incised near junction of spinous and soft portions. Pectoral fin somewhat shorter than head. Dorsal-fin rays X,11 (infrequently X,10). Anal-fin rays III,8. Pectoral-fin rays 15 or 16. Lateral-line scales 69 to 75. Two species. Type species Aphareus furca.

Species of Aphareus (Plate 1.1c)

Aphareus furca[1] (Lacepède, 1801). Gill rakers 6 to 10 + 16 to 18--total 22 to 27. Color steel blue. Widely distributed in the Indo-Pacific.

Aphareus rutilans Cuvier, 1830. Gill rakers 16 to 19 + 32 to 35--total 49 to 52. Head and body brick red or pink dorsally; inside of mouth, gill chamber, and gills shining silver. Widely distributed in the Indo-Pacific.

GENUS PRISTIPOMOIDES BLEEKER, 1852

Maxilla without scales; no well-developed series of longitudinal bony ridges on lateral surface of maxilla. Premaxillae protractile. Gill openings not extending far anterior to orbit. Dorsal fin continuous, not deeply incised near junction of spinous and soft portions. Pectoral fin fairly long, about two-thirds length of head to somewhat longer than head. Dorsal-fin rays X,11 (rarely X,10). Anal-fin rays III,8 (rarely III,7 or III,9). Pectoral-fin rays 15 to 17. Eleven species. Type species *Pristipomoides typus*. *Tropidinius* Gill, 1868, a junior synonym of *Apsilus* Valenciennes, 1830, has been used incorrectly as the generic name for some species of *Pristipomoides*.

Key to the Species of *Pristipomoides*

1a. Western Atlantic species 2
1b. Indo-Pacific species 4

2a. Depth of body at origin of
dorsal fin 3.5-4.2 times in SL
(23.9-28.2% SL). Total number
of gill rakers 28-32. Lateral-
line scales 49-51 . . . . **P. freemani**
2b. Depth of body at origin of
dorsal fin 2.5-3.2 times in SL
(31.1-40.5% SL). Total number
of gill rakers 19-28. Lateral-
line scales 48-57 3

3a. Lateral-line scales 48-52. Total
number of gill rakers 24-28 . . . . . **P. aquilonaris**
3b. Lateral-line scales 54-57. Total
number of gill rakers 19-25 . . . **P. macrophthalmus**

4a. Lateral-line scales 48-50 5
4b. Lateral-line scales 57-71 6

5a. No golden bands on snout and
cheek; longitudinal vermiculations
on dorsum of head. Suborbital
narrow--8.4 times in length of
head at 150 mm SL, 7.3 at 250 mm,

	5.8 at 400 mm. (See Senta and Tan 1975:68.) . . . . P. typus
5b.	Two golden bands bordered with dark blue on snout and cheek; transverse vermiculations on dorsum of head. Suborbital wide—7.0 times in length of head at 150 mm SL, 5.5 at 250 mm, 4.0 at 400 mm. (See Senta and Tan 1975:68.) . . . . P. multidens
6a.	Total gill rakers 28–33. Lateral-line scales 67–71 7
6b.	Total gill rakers 17–25. Lateral-line scales 57–67 8
7a.	Vomerine tooth patch triangular in shape, without backward prolongation in midline; no teeth on tongue . . . . P. auricilla
7b.	Vomerine tooth patch with backward prolongation in midline (vomerine tooth patch sometimes diamond-shaped); patch of teeth on tongue . . . P. sieboldii
8a.	Lateral-line scales 63–67. Side of body with alternating oblique red and yellow bars . . . . P. zonatus
8b.	Lateral-line scales 57–62. Side of body without red and yellow bars 9
9a.	Total gill rakers 17–21. Side of body with numerous irregular dark markings, including zigzag line that runs at about level of lateral line anteriorly and then onto dorsolateral part of caudal peduncle posteriorly . . . P. argyrogrammicus
9b.	Total gill rakers 22–25. Side of body without irregular dark markings 10
10a.	Length of upper jaw 2.4–2.7 times in head length. Pyloric caeca 7–9 (usually 8). Canine teeth near symphysis of lower jaw

not greatly enlarged. (See Kami
1973a:99.) . . . . **P. filamentosus**
10b. Length of upper jaw 2.1–2.4 times
in head length. Pyloric caeca
4–6 (usually 5). Canine teeth
near symphysis of lower jaw
greatly enlarged. (See Kami
1973a:99.) . . . . **P. flavipinnis**

Species of Pristipomoides (Plate 1.1d, 1.1e, and 1.1f)

Pristipomoides aquilonaris (Goode and Bean, 1896).
Gill rakers 7 to 9 + 16 to 20—total 24 to 28. Lateral-
line scales 48 to 52. Western Atlantic. Pristipomoides
andersoni Ginsburg, 1952, is a junior synonym of P.
aquilonaris.
 Pristipomoides argyrogrammicus (Valenciennes, 1832).
Gill rakers 5 or 6 + 12 to 15—total 17 to 21. Lateral-
line scales 59 to 61. Indo-Pacific. Pristipomoides
amoenus (Snyder, 1911) is a junior synonym of P.
argyrogrammicus.
 Pristipomoides auricilla (Jordan, Evermann, and
Tanaka, 1927). Gill rakers 9 to 11 + 18 or 19—total 28
to 30. Lateral-line scales 67 to 71. Mainly purplish
with numerous yellow chevron-shaped bars; dorsal lobe of
caudal fin mainly yellow. Indo-Pacific. May be antiequatorial in distribution (Randall 1982). (See Kami
1973a.)
 Pristipomoides filamentosus (Valenciennes, 1830).
Gill rakers 7 or 8 + 15 to 17—total 23 to 25. Lateral-
line scales 57 to 62. Indo-Pacific. Pristipomoides
microlepis (Bleeker, 1869b) is a junior synonym of P.
filamentosus. (See Kami 1973a.)
 Pristipomoides flavipinnis Shinohara, 1963. Gill
rakers 6 to 8 + 16 to 17—total 22 to 25. Lateral-line
scales 59 to 62. Central and western Pacific. (See Kami
1973a.)
 Pristipomoides freemani Anderson, 1966. Gill rakers
8 to 10 + 19 to 23—total 28 to 32. Orange to rosy.
Lateral-line scales 49 to 51. Western Atlantic. (See
Anderson 1972.)
 Pristipomoides macrophthalmus (Müller and Troschel,
1848). Gill rakers 6 to 8 + 13 to 17—total 19 to 25.
Lateral-line scales 54 to 57. Western Atlantic.
 Pristipomoides multidens (Day, 1870). Gill rakers 6
to 8 + 13 to 15—total 20 to 22. Lateral-line scales 48

to 50. Ground color more or less yellowish. Indo-
Pacific. (See Senta and Tan 1975.)

Pristipomoides sieboldii (Bleeker, 1857). Gill
rakers 9 to 12 + 21 or 22--total 30 to 33. Lateral-line
scales 69 to 71. Indo-Pacific; eastern Atlantic (Vema
Seamount). Pristipomoides microdon (Steindachner, 1877)
is apparently a junior synonym of P. sieboldii. (See Kami
1973a.)

Pristipomoides typus Bleeker, 1852. Gill rakers 6 to
9 + 11 to 16. Lateral-line scales 48 to 50. Ground color
rosy. Indo-west Pacific. (See Senta and Tan 1975.)

Pristipomoides zonatus (Valenciennes, 1830). Gill
rakers 5 to 8 + 12 to 14--total 17 to 21. Lateral-line
scales 63 to 67. Indo-Pacific. Rooseveltia brighami
(Seale, 1901) is a junior synonym of P. zonatus.

GENUS APRION VALENCIENNES, 1830 (PLATE 1.2a)

Maxilla without scales; no well-developed series of
longitudinal bony ridges on lateral surface of maxilla.
Premaxillae protractile. Dorsal fin continuous, not
deeply incised near junction of spinous and soft portions.
Pectoral fin short, less than one-half length of head.
Dorsal-fin rays X,11. Anal-fin rays III,8. Pectoral-fin
rays 16 to 18. Gill rakers 7 or 8 + 14 to 16--total 21 to
24. Lateral-line scales 48 or 49. Dark green, bluish, or
gray-blue. The single species, Aprion virescens
Valenciennes, 1830, is widely distributed in the Indo-
Pacific.

SUBFAMILY APSILINAE

Nostrils on each side closely approximated; posterior
flap of anterior nostril when reflected typically reaching
anterior border of posterior nostril. Vomerine teeth
present. Body moderately elongate to moderately deep.
Dorsal and anal fins scaleless. Dorsal-fin rays X,10
(rarely X,9). Anal-fin rays III,8 (rarely III,9). Anterior dorsal and anterior anal soft rays not produced into
filaments. Ultimate soft ray of dorsal fin and anal fin
not produced or produced only slightly, shorter than
penultimate soft ray (except in Parapristipomoides and
Apsilus fuscus where ultimate soft ray about equal to or
slightly longer than penultimate). Caudal fin lunate to
well forked. Procurrent caudal-fin rays 11 to 13 dorsally,

13

10 to 13 ventrally. Interorbital region transversely
somewhat flattened to strongly convex. Configuration of
predorsal bones, anterior neural spines, and anterior
dorsal pterygiophores (using the symbolization of Ahlstrom
et al. 1976) usually 0/0/0+2/1+1/ (Apsilus occasionally
0/0+0/2/1+1/). Posteriormost 4-7 complete pterygiophores
of dorsal fin and posteriormost 5 or 6 complete pterygiophores of anal fin trisegmental. Adductor mandibulae
typically simple, Section A$_1$ with anterodorsal extension
only in Apsilus; division A$_1$' absent. (See Johnson 1981.)
    Four genera: Parapristipomoides, Paracaesio,
Lipocheilus, and Apsilus.

GENUS PARAPRISTIPOMOIDES KAMI, 1973b

    Maxilla with scales. Anterior end of upper lip with-
out a thick fleshy protrusion. Dorsal fin continuous, not
deeply incised near junction of spinous and soft portions.
Pectoral fin fairly long, about as long as head. Dorsal-
fin rays X,10. Anal-fin rays III,8. Pectoral-fin rays
16. Gill rakers 10 to 12 + 22 to 24--total 32 to 36.
Lateral-line scales 54 or 55. Ground color pink; "upper
lobe of caudal fin bright yellow" (Kami 1973b). The
single species, Parapristipomoides squamimaxillaris (Kami,
1973b), is known from Rapa and Easter Island in the South
Pacific.

GENUS PARACAESIO BLEEKER, 1875

    Maxilla with or without scales, but without a well-
developed series of longitudinal bony ridges on lateral
surface. Anterior end of upper lip without a thick fleshy
protrusion. Premaxillae protractile. Gill openings not
extending far anterior to orbit. Dorsal fin continuous,
not deeply incised near junction of spinous and soft
portions. Pectoral fin long, about 85 to 125% of head
length. Dorsal-fin rays X,10 (occasionally X,9 or X,11).
Anal-fin rays III,8 (rarely III,9). Pectoral-fin rays 15
to 18. Six species. Type species Paracaesio xanthura.
Vegetichthys Tanaka, 1917, and Aetiasis Barnard, 1937, are
junior synonyms of Paracaesio.

Key to the Species of Paracaesio[2]

This key is based in part on the one in Abe and Shinohara 1962.

1a. Lateral-line scales 68-73 2
1b. Lateral-line scales 47-50 3

2a. Caudal fin, upper part of caudal
    peduncle, and upper side of body
    to anterior end of dorsal fin
    yellow; remainder of body mostly
    blue. Maxilla with or without
    scales . . . . P. xanthura
2b. General color dark violet; fins
    reddish-brown. Maxilla without
    scales . . . . P. sordida

3a. Scales present on maxilla 4
3b. No scales on maxilla. 5

4a. Yellow band running from origin
    of lateral line obliquely to
    about middle of dorsal fin . . . . . . P. gonzalesi
4b. No oblique yellow band on
    side of body . . . . P. kusakarii

5a. General color cerulean blue . . . . P. caerulea
5b. Four or five broad brown to
    dark gray vertical bars on
    body extending from dorsal
    surface to midline or below
    midline laterally . . . . P. stonei

Species of Paracaesio (Plate 1.2b and 1.2c)

Paracaesio caerulea (Katayama, 1934). Gill rakers 10 to 12 + 19 or 20. Lateral-line scales 47 to 50. Western Pacific.

Paracaesio gonzalesi Fourmanoir and Rivaton, 1979. Gill rakers 11 + 20--total 31. Lateral-line scales 48 or 49. (Data taken by the author from the holotype, Museum National d'Histoire Naturelle Cat. No. 1978-691, 221 mm SL.) Western Pacific. Despite a statement to the contrary by Raj and Seeto (1983), P. gonzalesi (based on examination of the holotype) does have a scaly maxilla.

Fourmanoir and Rivaton (1979) stated that living P.
gonzalesi has eight broad dark vertical bars. Raj and
Seeto (1983) wrote that their freshly caught specimens of
P. gonzalesi from Fiji lack vertical bars. Remnants of
dark vertical bars were seen on the holotype of Paracaesio
gonzalesi in December 1982. Both Fourmanoir and Rivaton
(1979) and Raj and Seeto (1983) describe P. gonzalesi as
having a yellow band running from origin of lateral line
obliquely to about middle of dorsal fin.

Paracaesio kusakarii Abe, 1960. Gill rakers 8 to 11
+ 16 to 19. Lateral-line scales 47 to 50. Several broad
dark vertical bars on upper side of body. Central and
western Pacific.

Paracaesio sordida Abe and Shinohara, 1962. Gill
rakers 9 to 11 + 19 to 22--total 28 to 33. Lateral-line
scales 68 to 73. Indo-west Pacific.

Paracaesio stonei Raj and Seeto, 1983. Gill rakers
10 + 17 or 18--total 27 or 28. Lateral-line scales 48 or
49. Central and western Pacific.

Paracaesio xanthura (Bleeker, 1869a). Gill rakers 9
to 11 + 20 to 23--total 29 to 34. Tubed lateral-line
scales 68 to 72. Indo-west Pacific. Paracaesio pedleyi
McCulloch and Waite, 1916, P. tumida (Tanaka, 1917), and
P. cantharoides (Barnard, 1937) are here considered as
junior synonyms of P. xanthura.

GENUS LIPOCHEILUS ANDERSON, TALWAR, AND JOHNSON, 1977 (PLATE 1.2d)

Maxilla without scales; no well-developed series of
longitudinal bony ridges on lateral surface of maxilla.
Anterior end of upper lip of adults with thick fleshy
protrusion (see Chan 1970:23, plate 1). Premaxillae
protractile. Gill openings extending somewhat anterior to
vertical from anterior border of orbit. Dorsal fin
continuous, not deeply incised near junction of spinous
and soft portions. Pectoral fin about 70 to 80% of head
length in specimens less than about 225 mm SL, about 90 to
100% of head length in specimens more than about 285 mm
SL. Dorsal-fin rays X,10. Anal-fin rays III,8. Pectoral-
fin rays 15 or 16. Gill rakers 5 to 7 + 11 to 14--total
17 to 21. Lateral-line scales 49 to 54. Juveniles with
about five dark vertical bars on body; adults mainly
yellow. The single species, Lipocheilus carnolabrum
(Chan, 1970), is widespread in the Indo-west Pacific.
Lipocheilus is a replacement name for Tangia Chan, 1970,
preoccupied by Tangia Stål, 1859, a genus of Hemiptera.

GENUS _APSILUS_ VALENCIENNES, 1830

Maxilla without scales; no well-developed series of longitudinal bony ridges on lateral surface of maxilla. Anterior end of upper lip without a thick fleshy protrusion. Premaxillae protractile. Gill openings extending somewhat anterior to vertical from anterior border of orbit. Dorsal fin continuous, not deeply incised near junction of spinous and soft portions. Dorsal-fin rays X,10 (occasionally X,9). Anal-fin rays III,8. Two species. Type species _Apsilus_ _fuscus_. Tropidinius Gill, 1868, a junior synonym of _Apsilus_, has been used incorrectly as the generic name for some species of _Pristipomoides_.

Species of _Apsilus_ (Plate 1.2e)

Apsilus _dentatus_ Guichenot, 1853. Pleural ribs 8. Pectoral-fin rays 15 or 16. Gill rakers 7 or 8 + 15 or 16--total 22 to 24. Lateral-line scales 58 to 63. In specimens more than about 200 mm SL, depth of body at origin of dorsal fin 35 to 39% SL. In specimens more than about 200 mm SL, length of pectoral fin about equal to length of head. "Color in life, dusky violet, paler below" Jordan and Evermann (1898:1279). Western Atlantic.

Apsilus _fuscus_ Valenciennes, 1830. Pleural ribs 11 or 12. Pectoral-fin rays 17 or 18. Gill rakers 8 to 10 + 20 to 23--total 28 to 33. Lateral-line scales 62 to 66. Depth of body at origin of dorsal fin 28 to 34% SL. Pectoral fin two-thirds to four-fifths length of head. "Generally brown, lighter on ventral surface" (Allen 1981). Eastern Atlantic. Reports of this species from the western Indian Ocean appear to be based on misidentifications, perhaps of _Paracaesio_ _sordida_ and/or _P._ _xanthura_.

SUBFAMILY PARADICICHTHYINAE

Nostrils on each side not close together; posterior flap of anterior nostril, when reflected, falling well short of anterior border of posterior nostril. Vomer toothless. Body moderately deep. Soft dorsal and anal fins sheathed in scales basally. Dorsal-fin rays X,14 to 18. Anal-fin rays III,9 to 11. Some of anterior dorsal soft rays produced as filaments (at least in juveniles).

Ultimate soft ray of dorsal fin and anal fin not produced. Caudal fin truncate to lunate. Procurrent caudal-fin rays 9 or 10, dorsally and ventrally. Interorbital region transversely convex to somewhat flattened. Configuration of predorsal bones, anterior neural spines, and anterior dorsal pterygiophores (using the symbolization of Ahlstrom et al. 1976) 0/0/0+2/1+1/. Posteriormost 5-7 complete pterygiophores of dorsal fin and posteriormost 3 or 4 complete pterygiophores of anal fin trisegmental. Adductor mandibulae distinctive; section A_1 with well-developed, partially separate anterodorsal bundle inserting on maxilla, but not originating on subocular shelf, instead originating on heavy tendinous strap from preopercle and strongly associated with large tendinous sheet lying lateral to much of adductor mandibulae. (See Johnson 1981.)

Two genera: Symphorichthys and Symphorus.

GENUS SYMPOHORICHTHYS MUNRO, 1967 (PLATE 1.2f)

Head extremely blunt (i.e., anterior profile quite steep). Maxilla without scales; no well-developed series of longitudinal bony ridges on lateral surface of maxilla. Premaxillae protractile. Gill openings extending to about a vertical from anterior border of orbit. Dorsal fin continuous, incised slightly near junction of spinous and soft portions. Pectoral fin somewhat longer than head. Dorsal-fin rays X,17 or 18. Anal-fin rays III,11. Pectoral-fin rays 16. Gill rakers 6 + 14--total 20. Lateral-line scales 53 to 56. (Munro (1967) gave dorsal-fin rays as X,14 to 16, anal-fin rays as III,8 to 10, gill rakers as 5 + 15, and lateral-line scales as 50 or 51.) Munro (1967:311) described the coloration as: "Lemon-yellow with blue undulating longitudinal lines. A reddish-brown ocellated saddle on caudal peduncle superiorly. An orange transverse band across nape. Fins yellow or orange." The single species, Symphorichthys spilurus (Günther, 1873), is known from the western Pacific.

GENUS SYMPHORUS GÜNTHER, 1872 (PLATE 1.3a and 1.3b)

Head not blunt as in Symphorichthys. Maxilla without scales; no well-developed series of longitudinal bony ridges on lateral surface of maxilla. Premaxillae protractile. Gill openings extending somewhat anterior to

vertical from anterior border of orbit. Dorsal fin continuous, incised slightly near junction of spinous and
soft portions. Pectoral fin about 70 to 90% of head
length. Dorsal-fin rays X,14 to 16. Anal-fin rays III,9.
Pectoral-fin rays 16 or 17. Gill rakers 5 or 6 + 14 or
15--total 19 to 21. Lateral-line scales 50 to 52 (Munro
(1967) gave 49 to 55). Munro (1967:293) described the
coloration as: "Reddish with irregular brownish cross
bands. Juveniles with 6-13 bluish wavy longitudinal
stripes from snout to tail base." The single species,
Symphorus nematophorus (Bleeker, 1860), is known from the
Indo-west Pacific. Glabrilutjanus nematophorus (Bleeker,
1860) and Paradicichthys venenatus Whitley, 1930, are
synonyms of Symphorus nematophorus.

SUBFAMILY LUTJANINAE

Nostrils on each side usually not close together
(close together only in certain species of Lutjanus);
posterior flap of anterior nostril, when reflected,
typically falling well short of anterior border of
posterior nostril (in Hoplopagrus, anterior nostril in
tube above upper lip). Vomerine teeth present. Body
moderately elongate to moderately deep. Soft dorsal and
anal fins with scales basally. Dorsal-fin rays IX to
XII,10 to 16. Anal-fin rays III,7 to 11. Anterior dorsal
and anterior anal soft rays not produced into filaments.
Ultimate soft ray of dorsal fin and anal fin not produced,
shorter than penultimate soft ray. Caudal fin truncate to
forked. Procurrent caudal-fin rays 8 to 12 dorsally, 8 to
11 ventrally. Configuration of predorsal bones, anterior
neural spines, and anterior dorsal pterygiophores (using
the symbolization of Ahlstrom et al. 1976) 0/0/0+2/1+1/.
Posteriormost 2-7 complete pterygiophores of dorsal fin
and posteriormost 1-5 complete pterygiophores of anal fin
trisegmental. Adductor mandibulae section A_1 with
separate anterodorsal bundle, A_1', originating on
subocular shelf and inserting on dorsomedial surface of
maxillary shaft just posterior to head. (See Johnson
1981.)
    Six genera: Hoplopagrus, Rhomboplites, Macolor,
Pinjalo, Ocyurus, and Lutjanus.

GENUS HOPLOPAGRUS GILL, 1861 (PLATE 1.3c)

Anterior nostril in tube above upper lip. Maxilla without scales; no well-developed series of longitudinal bony ridges on lateral surface of maxilla. Molariform teeth on jaws and vomer. Premaxillae protractile. Gill openings not extending far anterior to vertical from anterior border of orbit. Dorsal fin continuous, but spinous portion of fin incised at its junction with soft portion. Pectoral fin 80 to 90% of head length. Dorsal-fin rays X,14. Anal-fin rays III,9. Pectoral-fin rays 16 or 17. Gill rakers 5 to 7 + 11 or 12--total 16 to 19. Lateral-line scales 47 to 49. "Color greenish above, belly coppery pink; head olive, sides with 8 cross-bands of warm brown, unequally placed; fins dusky olive, shaded with pinkish and brown; a round dusky blotch near base of last rays of soft dorsal..." Jordan and Evermann (1898: 1245). The single species, _Hoplopagrus guentherii_[3] Gill, 1862b, is known only from the eastern Pacific. Walford (1974:85) reported it as occurring "along the coast of Lower California, through the Gulf of California, and southward to Panama."

GENUS RHOMBOPLITES GILL, 1862A

Maxilla without scales; no well-developed series of longitudinal bony ridges on lateral surface of maxilla. Premaxillae protractile. Gill openings extending somewhat anterior to vertical from anterior border of orbit. Dorsal fin continuous, not deeply incised near junction of spinous and soft portions. In specimens more than about 70 mm SL, pectoral fin 70 to 90% of head length. Dorsal-fin rays XII,11 (rarely XII,10, very rarely XII,12). Anal-fin rays III,8 (very rarely III,9). Pectoral-fin rays 17 or 18 (very rarely 16 or 19). Gill rakers 8 to 10 + 19 to 21 (very rarely 22)--total 28 to 31 (rarely 27, very rarely 32). Lateral-line scales 47 to 51 (rarely 52, very rarely 46). "Color in life, vermilion; paler below; faint brown lines running obliquely forward and downward from dorsal along the rows of scales; sides with narrow sinuous streaks of golden yellow, some of them longitudinal, others oblique..." Jordan and Evermann (1898: 1277-1278). The single species, _Rhomboplites aurorubens_ (Cuvier, 1829), is widely distributed in the western Atlantic in tropical and warm temperate waters.

GENUS MACOLOR BLEEKER, 1860 (PLATE 1.3d)

Maxilla without scales; no well-developed series of longitudinal bony ridges on lateral surface of maxilla. Premaxillae protractile. Preopercle with deep notch (or gash) receiving elongate interopercular knob (or spine). Gill openings extending fairly far anterior to vertical from anterior border of orbit. Dorsal fin continuous. Pectoral fin fairly long, about equal to head length. Dorsal-fin rays X,13 or 14. Anal-fin rays III,10 or 11. Pectoral-fin rays 16 to 18. Gill rakers 29 to 41 + 63 to 78--total 96 to 115. Lateral-line scales 48 to 55. Young with striking black and white pattern; adults mostly black. Two nominal species. Type species Macolor niger (Forsskål, 1775). Macolor is widely distributed in the Indo-Pacific.

Allen (1985) recognized two species of Macolor based in part on numbers of lower-limb gill rakers on the first gill arch--M. niger (Forsskål, 1775) with 60 to 70 and M. macularis Fowler, 1931, with 70 to 80.

GENUS PINJALO BLEEKER, 1845

Maxilla without scales; no well-developed series of longitudinal bony ridges on lateral surface of maxilla. Premaxillae protractile. Mouth rather small, somewhat upturned. Teeth in jaws small. Gill openings about reaching vertical through anterior border of orbit. Dorsal fin continuous, not deeply incised near junction of spinous and soft portions. Scale rows dorsal and ventral to lateral line ascending obliquely towards dorsal contour. Pectoral-fin rays 17 to 19. Gill rakers 6 to 8 + 15 to 18--total 22 to 26. Tubed lateral-line scales 47 to 51. Species of Pinjalo are mainly reddish. Two species. Type species Pinjalo pinjalo.

Species of Pinjalo

Pinjalo pinjalo (Bleeker, 1850). Dorsal-fin rays XI,14 (infrequently XI,15). Anal-fin rays III,10 (infrequently III,9). Pelvic and anal fins yellow; no white saddle on dorsal half of caudal peduncle. Indo-west Pacific.

Pinjalo sp. Dorsal-fin rays XII,13. Anal-fin rays III,9. Pelvic and anal fins white or pinkish; pearly white saddle on dorsal half of caudal peduncle (faint or absent in preserved specimens). Indo-west Pacific.

GENUS OCYURUS GILL, 1862A (PLATE 1.3e)

Maxilla without scales; no well-developed series of longitudinal bony ridges on lateral surface of maxilla. Premaxillae protractile. Gill openings extending somewhat anterior to vertical from anterior border of orbit. Dorsal fin continuous, not deeply incised near junction of spinous and soft portions. Pectoral fin 80 to 90% of head length. Dorsal-fin rays X,12 or 13 (rarely with IX or XI spines or 14 soft rays). Anal-fin rays III,9 (rarely III,8). Pectoral-fin rays 15 or 16 (rarely 17). Gill rakers 9 to 11 + 21 to 23--total 30 to 34. Lateral-line scales 46 to 49. "A prominent mid-lateral yellow stripe beginning on snout, broadening as it passes posteriorly on body, the color continuous with the all-yellow caudal fin; yellow spots on back above yellow band and narrow yellow stripes below" (Randall 1968:128). The single species, Ocyurus chrysurus (Bloch, 1791), is widely distributed in the western Atlantic in tropical and warm temperate waters and has been reported from the Cape Verde Islands in the eastern Atlantic.

GENUS LUTJANUS BLOCH, 1790 (PLATE 1.3f)

Maxilla without scales; no well-developed series of longitudinal bony ridges on lateral surface of maxilla. Premaxillae protractile. Gill openings not extending far anterior to anterior border of orbit. Dorsal fin continuous. Dorsal-fin rays X to XII,11 to 16. Anal-fin rays III,7 to 11. Pectoral-fin rays 14 to 18. Lateral-line scales 40 to 53. Gill rakers 4 to 10 + 7 to 20--total 13 to 30. (Data for counts obtained from Jordan and Evermann 1898; Hildebrand 1946; Anderson 1967; Allen 1981; and Allen and Talbot 1985.) Sixty-five species (39 species in the Indo-Pacific, 9 in the eastern Pacific, 12 in the western Atlantic, and 5 in the eastern Atlantic). Type species Lutjanus lutjanus Bloch, 1790.

The genus Lutjanus is treated in detail by G. R. Allen in a separate chapter in this volume.

ACKNOWLEDGMENTS

I am indebted to the curators and their assistants at the numerous museums at which I have been allowed to examine specimens or from which I have borrowed material. Four other people have been especially helpful: James F. McKinney (GMBL) took data and provided radiographs; G. David Johnson (USNM) took data and spent many hours discussing the systematics of lutjanid fishes; Gerald R. Allen (Western Australian Museum) furnished data on Pinjalo; and Carole C. Baldwin (GMBL) typed the manuscript and helped in other ways. A number of the plates were reproduced, with permission, from color transparencies provided by John E. Randall of the Bernice P. Bishop Museum, Honolulu (Plates 1.1b–1.1d, 1.2b, 1.2d, 1.3d, 1.3f) and Richard C. Wass, U.S. Fish and Wildlife Service, Honolulu (Plate 1.2c). Permission to reproduce published illustrations was granted by A. Asher and Co., Amsterdam (Plates 1.2a, 1.2e); John E. Randall and Walter A. Starck, II, Daintree, Queensland (Plate 1.3e); and Victor G. Springer (USNM) (Plate 1.3c). The illustrations in Plates 1.2f, 1.3a, and 1.3b are reproduced from the book Guide to Fishes (The Department of Harbours and Marine, Brisbane, 1982) by permission of the Queensland Government. George C. Steyskal (Systematic Entomology Laboratory, USNM), Associate Editor for Classical Languages, Proceedings of the Biological Society of Washington, apprised me of the proper spellings of the names of a number of species. G. David Johnson read the manuscript and made some helpful suggestions. This is GMBL contribution No. 67.

NOTES

1. The spelling usually given is furcatus, but that with the original description is furca. George C. Steyskal informed me that furca is a noun in apposition and properly retains the original spelling in whatever genus it is placed.

2. George C. Steyskal advised me that Paracaesio is a feminine noun. Accordingly, adjectival names of species of Paracaesio that have been spelled with the –us ending must be emended to end in –a. This means that caeruleus, sordidus, tumidus, and xanthurus are properly spelled caerulea, sordida, tumida, and xanthura.

3. The spelling usually given is guntheri, but that with the original description is guentherii.

BIBLIOGRAPHY

Abe, T. 1960. Description of a new lutjanid fish of the genus *Paracaesio* from Japan. Jpn. J. Ichthyol. 8:56–62.

Abe, T., and S. Shinohara. 1962. Description of a new lutjanid fish from the Ryukyu Islands. Jpn. J. Ichthyol. 9:163–171.

Ahlstrom, E. H., J. L. Butler, and B. Y. Sumida. 1976. Pelagic stromateoid fishes (Pisces, Perciformes) of the eastern Pacific: Kinds, distributions, and early life histories and observations on five of these from the northwest Atlantic. Bull. Mar. Sci. 26:285–402.

Allen, G. R. 1981. Family Lutjanidae. In W. Fischer, G. Bianchi, and W. B. Scott (editors), FAO species identification sheets for fishery purposes, eastern central Atlantic fishing areas 34, 37 (in part). Vol. 2. FAO, Rome.

_____. 1985. FAO species catalogue. Snappers of the world. An annotated and illustrated catalogue of lutjanid species known to date. FAO Fish. Synop. (125) 6, 208 p.

Allen, G. R., and F. H. Talbot. 1985. Review of the snappers of the genus *Lutjanus* (Pisces: Lutjanidae) from the Indo-Pacific, with the description of a new species. Indo-Pac. Fish. 11:1–87 (Bernice P. Bishop Mus., Honolulu).

Anderson, W. D., Jr. 1966. A new species of *Pristipomoides* (Pisces: Lutjanidae) from the tropical western Atlantic. Bull. Mar. Sci. 16:814–826.

_____. 1967. Field guide to the snappers (Lutjanidae) of the western Atlantic. U.S. Fish Wildl. Serv., Bur. Commer. Fish. Circ. 252:1–14.

_____. 1970. Revision of the genus *Symphysanodon* (Pisces: Lutjanidae) with descriptions of four new species. Fish. Bull., U.S. 68:325–346.

_____. 1972. Notes on western Atlantic lutjanid fishes of the genera *Pristipomoides* and *Etelis*. Copeia 1972:359–362.

_____. 1981. A new species of Indo-west Pacific *Etelis* (Pisces: Lutjanidae), with comments on other species of the genus. Copeia 1981:820–825.

Anderson, W. D., Jr., and P. Fourmanoir. 1975. The status of *Erythrobussothen gracilis*, a percoid fish. Copeia 1975:181–182.

24

Anderson, W. D., Jr., H. T. Kami, and G. D. Johnson.
1977. A new genus of Pacific Etelinae (Pisces:
Lutjanidae) with redescription of the type species.
Proc. Biol. Soc. Wash. 90:89-98.

Anderson, W. D., Jr., P. K. Talwar, and G. D. Johnson.
1977. A replacement name for Tangia Chan (Pisces:
Perciformes: Lutjanidae) with redescriptions of the
genus and type-species. Proc. Biol. Soc. Wash. 89:
509-518.

Barnard, K. H. 1937. Further notes on South African
marine fishes. Ann. S. Afr. Mus. 32 (Part 2):41-67.

Bleeker, P. 1845. Bijdragen tot de geneeskundige topo-
graphie van Batavia. Generisch overzicht der fauna.
Natuur-en Geneeskundig Archief voor Neerland's Indie
2:505-528.

_____. 1850. Bijdrage tot de kennis der maenoiden
van den Soenda-Molukschen Archipel. Verhandelingen
van het Bataviaasch Genootschap van Kunsten en
Wetenschappen 23:1-13.

_____. 1852. Diagnostische beschrijvingen van
nieuwe of weinig bekende vischsoorten van Sumatra.
Tiental I-IV. Natuurkundig Tijdschrift voor Neder-
landsch Indie 3:569-608.

_____. 1857. Nieuwe nalezingen op de ichthyologie
van Japan. Verhandelingen van het Bataviaasch
Genootschap van Kunsten en Wetenschappen 26:1-132.

_____. 1860. Dertiende bijdrage tot de kennis der
vischfauna van Celebes, (visschen van Bonthain,
Badjoa, Sindjai, Lagoesi en Pompenoea). Acta
Societatis Scientarium Indo-Neederlandicae 8:1-60.

_____. 1869a. Description d'une espece inedite de
Caesio de l'ile de Nossibe. Versl. Akad. Amsterdam,
3, Ser. 2, p. 78-79.

_____. 1869b. Description d'une espece inedite de
Chaetopterus de l'ile d'Amboine: C. microlepis.
Versl. Akad. Amsterdam, 3, Ser. 2, p. 80-85.

_____. 1875. Recherches sur la faune de Madagascar
et de ses dependances, d'apres les decouvertes de
Francois P. L. Pollen et D. C. van Dam. 4th part.
Poissons de Madagascar et de l'ile de la Reunion des
collections de MM. Pollen et van Dam. E. J. Brill,
Leiden, The Netherlands.

Bloch, M. E. 1790. Naturgeschichte der auslandischen
Fische. 4. Berlin.

_____. 1791. Naturgeschichte der auslandischen
Fische. 5. Berlin.

Chan, W. L. 1970. A new genus and two new species of commercial snappers from Hong Kong. Hong Kong Fish. Bull. 1:19-38.

Cuvier, G. 1828. In G. Cuvier and A. Valenciennes. Histoire naturelle des poissons. 2. Reprint ed. 1969. A. Asher and Co., Amsterdam, The Netherlands.

_____. 1829. In G. Cuvier and A. Valenciennes. Histoire naturelle des poissons. 3. Reprint ed. 1969. A. Asher and Co., Amsterdam, The Netherlands.

_____. 1830. In G. Cuvier and A. Valenciennes. Histoire naturelle des poissons. 6. Reprint edition, 1969. A. Asher and Co., Amsterdam, The Netherlands.

Day, F. 1870. On the fishes of the Andaman Islands. Proc. Zool. Soc. Lond. 1870:677-705.

Forsskål, P. 1775. Descriptiones animalium, avium, amphibiorum, piscium, insectorum, vermium; quae in itinere orientali observavit. Post mortem auctoris edidit Carsten Niebuhr. Hauniae, 164 p.

Fourmanoir, P. 1970. Notes ichtyologiques (I). Cah. ORSTOM, Ser. Oceanogr. 8(2):19-33.

Fourmanoir, P., and J. Rivaton. 1979. Poissons de la pente recifale externe de Nouvelle-Caledonie et des Nouvelles-Hebrides. Cah. de l'Indo-Pacifique 1(4):405-443.

Fowler, H. W. 1931. Contributions to the biology of the Philippine Archipelago and adjacent regions. The fishes of the Families Pseudochromidae, Lobotidae, Pempheridae, Priacanthidae, Lutjanidae, Pomadasyidae, and Teraponidae, collected by the United States Bureau of Fisheries steamer "Albatross," chiefly in Philippine Seas and adjacent waters. Bull. U.S. Natl. Mus. 100 (Vol. 11):i-xi + 1-388.

Gill, T. 1861. On several new generic types of fishes contained in the museum of the Smithsonian Institution. Proc. Acad. Nat. Sci. Phila. 13:77-78.

_____.1862a. Remarks on the relations of the genera and other groups of Cuban fishes. Proc. Acad. Nat. Sci. Phila. 14:235-242.

_____. 1862b. Catalogue of the fishes of Lower California, in the Smithsonian Institution, collected by Mr. J. Xantus. Part 3. Proc. Acad. Nat. Sci. Phila. 14:249-262.

_____. 1868. In F. Poey. Synopsis piscium cubensium. Catalogo razonado de los peces de la isla de Cuba, extractado del repertorio fisico-natural de la isla de Cuba. Habana.

Ginsburg, I. 1952. Eight new fishes from the Gulf coast of the United States, with two new genera and notes on geographic distribution. J. Wash. Acad. Sci. 42:84-101.

Goode, G. B., and T. H. Bean. 1896. Oceanic ichthyology, a treatise on the deep-sea and pelagic fishes of the world, based chiefly upon the collections made by the steamers Blake, Albatross, and Fish Hawk in the northwestern Atlantic, with an atlas containing 417 figures. Spec. Bull., U.S. Natl. Mus., var. pag.

Grant, E. M. 1982. Guide to fishes. 5th ed. Department of Harbours and Marine, Brisbane, Queensland.

Guichenot, A. 1853. Histoire naturelle. Poissons. In Ramon de la Sagra. Histoire physique, politique et naturelle de Cuba. Part 2. Paris, 206 p.

Günther, A. 1872. Notice of two new fishes from Celebes. Ann. Mag. Nat. Hist. 4th Ser. 9:438-440.

_____. 1873. Andrew Garrett's Fische der Sudsee, beschrieben und redigirt von Albert C. L. G. Gunther. Band 1, Heft 1. J. Mus. Godeffroy 2(3):i-iv + 1-128.

Hildebrand, S. F. 1946. A descriptive catalog of the shore fishes of Peru. Bull. U.S. Natl. Mus. 189:i-xi + 1-530.

Jenkins, O. P. 1903. Report on collections of fishes made in the Hawaiian Islands, with descriptions of new species. Bull. U.S. Fish Comm. 22:417-511.

Johnson, G. D. 1975. The procurrent spur: An undescribed perciform caudal character and its phylogenetic implications. Occas. Pap. Calif. Acad. Sci. 121:1-23.

_____. 1981. The limits and relationships of the Lutjanidae and associated families. Bull. Scripps Inst. Oceanogr. 24:1-114.

Jordan, D. S., and B. W. Evermann. 1898. The fishes of North and middle America: A descriptive catalogue of the species of fish-like vertebrates found in the waters of North America, north of the Isthmus of Panama. Bull. U.S. Natl. Mus. 47 (Part 2):i-xxx + 1241-2183.

Jordan, D. S., B. W. Evermann, and S. Tanaka. 1927. Notes on new or rare fishes from Hawaii. Proc. Calif. Acad. Sci. 4th Ser. 16:649-680.

Kami, H. T. 1973a. The Pristipomoides (Pisces: Lutjanidae) of Guam with notes on their biology. Micronesica 9(1):97-117.

_____. 1973b. A new subgenus and species of Pristipomoides (Family Lutjanidae) from Easter Island and Rapa. Copeia 1973:557-559.

Katayama, M. 1934. On the external and internal characters of the bony fishes of the genus Vegetichthys, with a description of one new species. Proc. Imperial Acad. 10(7):435-438.

Lacepède, B. G. E. 1801. Histoire naturelle des poissons. 3. Paris.

McCulloch, A. R., and E. R. Waite. 1916. Additions to the fish fauna of Lord Howe Island. No. 5. Trans. Proc. R. Soc. S. Aust. 40:437-451.

Muller, J., and F. H. Troschel. 1848. In R. H. Schomburgk. The history of Barbados.... Longman, Brown, Green, and Longmans, London, England.

Munro, I. S. R. 1967. The fishes of New Guinea. Victor C. N. Blight, Sydney, Australia.

Parr, A. E. 1933. Deep sea Berycomorphi and Percomorphi from the waters around the Bahama and Bermuda Islands. Bull. Bingham Oceanogr. Collect. Yale Univ. 3(6):1-51.

Raj, U., and J. Seeto. 1983. A new species of Paracaesio (Pisces: Lutjanidae) from the Fiji Islands. Copeia 1983:450-453.

Randall, J. E. 1968. Caribbean reef fishes. T.F.H. Publications, Inc., Jersey City, New Jersey.

_____. 1982. Examples of antitropical and antiequatorial distribution of Indo-west Pacific fishes. Pac. Sci. 35:197-209.

Seale, A. 1901. New Hawaiian fishes. Occas. Pap. Bernice P. Bishop Mus., Polynesian Ethnol. Nat. Hist. 1(4):3-15.

Senta, T., and S.-M. Tan. 1975. On Pristipomoides multidens and P. typus (Family Lutjanidae). Jpn. J. Ichthyol. 22:68-76.

Shinohara, S. 1963. Description of the new lutjanid fish of the genus Pristipomoides from the Ryukyu Islands. Bull. Arts Sci. Div., Univ. Ryukyus, Math. Nat. Sci. 6:49-53.

Snyder, J. O. 1911. Descriptions of new genera and species of fishes from Japan and the Riu Kiu Islands. Proc. U.S. Natl. Mus. 40:525-549.

Stal, C. 1859. Novae quaedam fulgorinorum formae speciesque insigniores. Berliner Entomologische Zeitschrift 3:313-328.

Steindachner, F. 1877. Ichthyologische Beitrage. (5). 5. Uber einige neue oder seltene Fischarten aus dem atlantischen, indischen und stillen Ocean. Sitzungsberichte der Akademie der Wissenschaften,

Wien. Mathematische-Naturwissenschaftliche Klasse. Abteilung 1. 74:203-234.

Tanaka, S. 1917. Eleven new species of Japanese fishes. Zool. Mag. 29(339):7-12 (Engl. transl. of Jpn.)

Valenciennes, A. 1828. In G. Cuvier and A. Valenciennes. Histoire naturelle des poissons. 2. Reprint ed. 1969. A. Asher and Co., Amsterdam, The Netherlands.

_____. 1830. In G. Cuvier and A. Valenciennes. Histoire naturelle des poissons. 6. Reprint ed. 1969. A. Asher and Co., Amsterdam, The Netherlands.

_____. 1832. In G. Cuvier and A. Valenciennes. Histoire naturelle des poissons. 8. Reprint ed. 1969. A. Asher and Co., Amsterdam, The Netherlands.

_____. 1862. Description de quelques espèces nouvelles de poissons envoyees de Bourbon par M. Morel, directeur du museum d'histoire naturelle de cette île. Compte Rendu des Seances de l'Academie des Sciences 54:1165-1170.

Walford, L. A. 1974. Marine game fishes of the Pacific coast from Alaska to the Equator. Reprint edition. T.F.H. Publications, Inc., Neptune, New Jersey.

Whitley, G. P. 1930. Ichthyological miscellanea. Mem. Queensl. Mus. 10:8-31.

Yoshino, T., and C. Araga. 1975. In H. Masuda, C. Araga, and T. Yoshino. Coastal fishes of southern Japan. Tokai University Press, Tokyo.

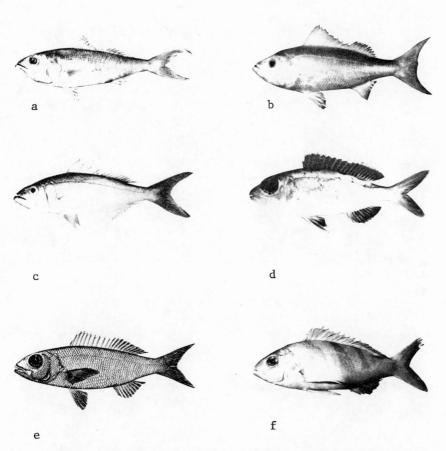

PLATE 1.1. (a) <u>Etelis radiosus</u>, holotype, USNM 220073, 380 mm SL, Sri Lanka. (b) <u>Randallichthys filamentosus</u>, USNM 216255, 487 mm SL, Hawaiian Islands. (c) <u>Aphareus furca</u>, 247 mm SL, Enewetak. (d) <u>Pristipomoides argyrogrammicus</u>, 199 mm SL, Mauritius. (e) <u>Pristipomoides freemani</u>, holotype, USNM 199391, 157 mm FL, Colombia (from Anderson 1966). (f) <u>Pristipomoides zonatus</u>, Hawaiian Islands.

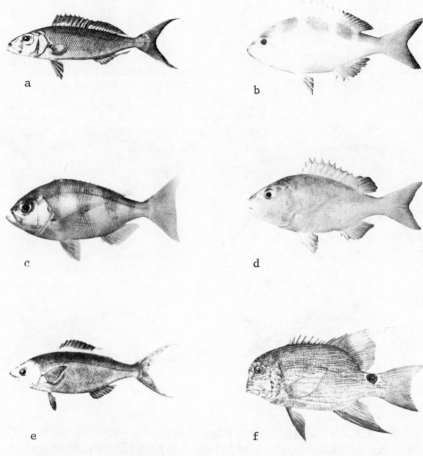

PLATE 1.2. (a) <u>Aprion virescens</u> (from Valenciennes 1830).
(b) <u>Paracaesio kusakarii</u>, 196 mm SL, Okinawa. (c)
<u>Paracaesio stonei</u>, 440 mm SL, Samoa. (d) <u>Lipocheilus
carnolabrum</u>, 380 mm SL, Cochin, India. (e) <u>Apsilus fuscus</u>
(from Valenciennes 1830). (f) <u>Symphorichthys spilurus</u>
(from Grant 1982).

PLATE 1.3. (a) <u>Symphorus</u> <u>nematophorus</u>, juvenile (from Grant 1982). (b) <u>Symphorus</u> <u>nematophorus</u>, adult (from Grant 1982). (c) <u>Hoplopagrus</u> <u>guentherii</u> (from Walford 1974). (d) <u>Macolor</u>, probably <u>Macolor</u> <u>niger</u>, 319 mm SL, Enewetak. (e) <u>Ocyurus</u> <u>chrysurus</u>, 160 mm SL, Florida Keys (from Randall 1968). (f) <u>Lutjanus</u> <u>buccanella</u>, 262 mm SL, Puerto Rico.

2
Synopsis of the Circumtropical Fish Genus
Lutjanus (Lutjanidae)

Gerald R. Allen
Western Australian Museum
Perth, Western Australia 6000

ABSTRACT

The snapper genus Lutjanus (Family Lutjanidae) is represented by 65 species in tropical and subtropical seas. They are primarily inhabitants of shallow coral reefs, although some species range into deeper water to at least 265 m, and three species are mainly confined to freshwater. This synopsis contains a generic synonymy and diagnosis, key to species according to major geographic region, and a list of the 225 nominal species assigned to Lutjanus. Illustrations for each species and a bibliography, which includes references for all nominal species, are also provided.

INTRODUCTION

The snapper family Lutjanidae contains 17 genera and 103 species, which are mainly confined to tropical and subtropical seas. Lutjanus Bloch is by far the largest genus with 65 species currently recognized as valid. Despite their abundance and importance as food fishes, the taxonomy of snappers has been poorly understood. Much of the confusion stems from the similar appearance of closely related species and frequent misidentifications in references utilized by scientists and fishery workers. Another contributing factor is the large number of nominal species (Appendix A).

The genus was reviewed by Allen (1985) as part of a comprehensive study of the Lutjanidae. Therefore detailed diagnostic information is omitted in the present synopsis.

In addition, the 39 species inhabiting the Indo-west
Pacific region were recently reviewed by Allen and Talbot
(1985). Other important regional reviews, containing keys
and diagnoses, are those of Rivas (1966), Anderson (1967),
and Allen (1981) for Atlantic species, and Jordan and
Swain (1885) and Jordan and Evermann (1898) for those from
the eastern Pacific Ocean.

SYSTEMATICS

Genus Lutjanus Bloch

Lutjanus Bloch 1790:108 (type species Lutjanus lutjanus
    Bloch 1790 by absolute tautonymy).
Lutjanus Bloch 1790:pl. 245 (type species Lutjanus lut-
    janus Bloch 1790 by monotypy).
Diacope Cuvier 1815:360 (type species Holocentrus bengal-
    ensis Bloch 1790 by subsequent designation of Jordan
    1917:94).
Mesoprion Cuvier (in Cuvier and Valenciennes) 1828:441
    (type species Lutjanus lutjanus Bloch 1790 by subse-
    quent designation of Jordan 1917:124).
Genyoroge Cantor 1849:994 (substitute name for Diacope
    Cuvier 1815 and therefore taking the same type
    species Holocentrus bengalensis Bloch 1790).
Neomaensis Girard 1859:167 (type species Lobotes emargina-
    tus Baird and Girard 1855 by monotypy).
Evoplites Gill 1862:236 (type species Mesoprion poma-
    canthus Bleeker 1855 by monotypy).
Hypoplites Gill 1862:236 (type species Mesoprion retro-
    spinis Cuvier (in Cuvier and Valenciennes) 1830 by
    monotypy).
Neomesoprion Castelnau 1875:8 (type species Neomesoprion
    unicolor Castelnau 1875 by monotypy).
Raizero Jordan and Fesler 1893:432, 438 (type species
    Mesoprion aratus Günther 1864 by monotypy).
Bennettia Fowler 1904:525 (type species Anthias johnii
    Bloch 1792 by original designation).
Parkia Fowler 1904:525 (type species Lutianus furvi-
    caudatus Fowler 1904 by original designation).
Rhomboplitoides Fowler 1918:33 (type species Rhombo-
    plitoides megalops Fowler 1918 by original designa-
    tion).
Loxolutjanus Fowler 1931:165 (type species Lutjanus
    erythropterus Bloch 1790 by original designation).

Diagnosis: dorsal rays X to XII,11-16; anal rays
III,7-10; pectoral rays 15-18; lateral-line scales 42-51;
gill rakers on first arch 4-10 + 7-20 = 13-30. Body
oblong to relatively elongate, laterally compressed. Head
more or less pointed; interorbital convex; mouth relatively large, protractile; pointed, conical teeth in jaws
arranged in one or more rows, with an outer series of
canine teeth, some of which, particularly at front of
jaws, are generally enlarged and fanglike; villiform teeth
on vomer in a crescentic band or triangular patch with or
without a median, posterior prolongation, or in a diamond-
shaped patch; tongue sometimes with one or more patches of
villiform teeth. Preoperculum serrate, its lower margin
with a shallow-to-deep notch, and opposite portion of
interoperculum sometimes with bony knob, most strongly
developed in species with deep preopercle notch. Body,
including bases of dorsal and anal fins, covered with
ctenoid scales, aligned in horizontal rows or those above
lateral line and sometimes below the lateral line oblique;
lateral line continuous, gently curved along upper sides,
predorsal scales extending forward to between posterior
part of eyes or behind this point; snout, preorbital,
suborbitals, and jaws scaleless. Dorsal fin continuous,
the anterior portion composed of stout spines; anal fin
small, rounded to pointed posteriorly; caudal fin truncate
or emarginate, rarely forked; pectoral fins relatively
long and pointed; pelvic fins usually shorter than
pectorals, with axillary scale process present.

KEY TO EASTERN PACIFIC SPECIES OF LUTJANUS (Table 2.1, Plate 2.1)

1a. Longitudinal scale rows above lateral line
     obliquely positioned (Figure 2.1A) 5
1b. Longitudinal scale rows above lateral line
     entirely horizontal (Figure 2.1B) 2

2a. Vomerine tooth patch diamond-shaped or having
     medial posterior extension (Figure 2.2A) 3
2b. Vomerine tooth patch without medial
     posterior extension (Figure 2.2B) 4

3a. Vomerine tooth patch diamond-shaped; color
     mainly red . . . . jordani

TABLE 2.1
Species of _Lutjanus_ from the eastern Pacific Ocean

Species	Author	Approximate Distribution
L. argentiventris	Peters, 1869	Southern California to Peru
L. aratus	Günther, 1864	Mexico to Ecuador
L. colorado	Jordan and Gilbert, 1881	Southern California to Panama
L. guttatus	Steindachner, 1869	Mexico to Peru
L. inermis	Peters, 1869	Mexico to Panama
L. jordani	Gilbert, 1897	Southern Mexico to Peru
L. novemfasciatus	Gill, 1862	Mexico to Panama
L. peru	Nichols and Murphy, 1922	Mexico to Peru
L. viridis	Valenciennes, 1845	Mexico to Ecuador

3b. Vomerine tooth patch V-shaped or
crescentic, sometimes triangular,
with medial posterior extension;
color mainly yellow . . . .   argentiventris

4a. Dorsal spines XI or XII; color dark
gray-green to red with alternating
dark and light stripes on sides . . . . aratus
4b. Dorsal spines X; color mainly red . . . . .colorado

5a. Body slender, the greatest depth
about 3.5 in standard length (SL);
soft anal rays 11 . . . . inermis
5b. Body deeper, the greatest depth
about 2.5-3.0 in SL; soft anal
rays 8. 6

6a. Vomerine tooth patch with medial
posterior extension (Figure 2.2A). 7
6b. Vomerine tooth patch without medial
posterior extension (Figure 2.2B). 8

7a. Vomerine tooth patch roughly diamond-
shaped; color uniformly reddish . . . . peru

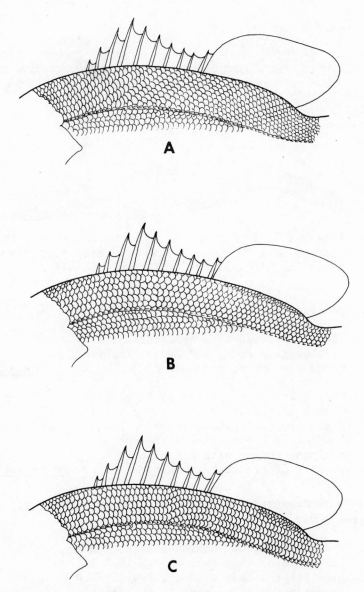

Figure 2.1   Scale alignment patterns on   upper
back   for   species   of   **Lutjanus:**   (A)   rising
obliquely   above   lateral   line,   (B)   parallel   to
lateral   line,   (C)   parallel   anteriorly   and   some
rows rising obliquely posteriorly

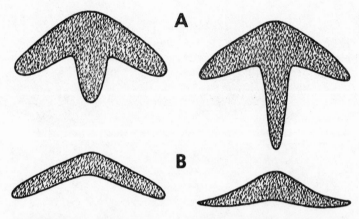

Figure 2.2 Shape of vomerine tooth patches in
species of _Lutjanus_: (A) with medial posterior
extension, (B) without posterior extension

7b. Vomerine tooth patch triangular with
     a relatively short backward prolonga-
     tion; color red with horizontal rows
     of blue-gray spots and large blackish
     blotch on upper side . . . . <u>guttatus</u>

8a. Body color pale (yellow in life) with
     5 dark-margined bluish stripes on
     sides; tongue without teeth . . . . <u>viridis</u>
8b. Body color brown or reddish without
     stripes; tongue with one or more
     patches of granular teeth . . . . . . <u>novemfasciatus</u>

**KEY TO INDO-PACIFIC SPECIES OF <u>LUTJANUS</u> (Table 2.2,
Plates 2.2-2.6)**

1a. Preorbital space (distance between upper
     jaw and eye) very narrow, 9.2-16.3 in
     head length; body slender, usually 3.0
     (sometimes 2.9) or more in SL; dorsal
     spines usually XI, occasionally X
     or rarely XII, soft dorsal rays 12 2
1b. Preorbital space wider, 3.3-8.9 in head
     length; body deeper, 2.1-3.1, but usually
     <3.0 in SL; dorsal spines variable,
     X-XII; soft dorsal rays, occasionally
     12, usually 13 or more 3

2a. Body depth 3.5–3.8 in SL; tongue
smooth without teeth; a dark band
from snout to caudal fin base and 2
pearly spots above lateral line, one
below spinous portion and the other
below soft portion of dorsal fin
(central Indian Ocean to Melanesia). . . . __biguttatus__

2b. Body depth 2.9–3.3 in SL; tongue
with patch of fine granular teeth;
color generally silvery white with
broad yellow stripe along middle of
side to caudal fin base and narrow
yellowish lines, corresponding with
longitudinal scale rows (eastern
Africa to western Pacific) . . . . __lutjanus__

3a. Ground color pale (mainly yellow in
life) with series of 4–8 longitudinal
stripes (blue in life, often brownish
in preservative) on side 4

3b. Color not as in 3a 8

4a. Dorsal spines X 5

4b. Dorsal spines XI or XII 7

5a. Stripes on side 6–8; a large
black spot on upper side below
soft dorsal fin; soft dorsal rays
usually 12 or 13; preopercular notch
weak or absent (southern Red Sea
to Gulf of Oman) . . . . __coeruleolineatus__

5b. Stripes on side 4 or 5; black spot
on upper side below soft dorsal
present or absent; soft dorsal
rays usually 14 or 15, occasionally
13; preopercular notch prominent 6

6a. Four stripes on side, belly more
or less abruptly whitish,
frequently with thin gray lines;
scale rows on cheek 5 or 6; upper
pectoral rays darkish (Indo-west
Pacific) . . . . __kasmira__

6b. Five stripes on side, belly not
abruptly whitish and without
thin lines; scale rows on cheek
10 or 11; upper pectoral rays

TABLE 2.2
Species of *Lutjanus* from the western Pacific and Indian Oceans

Species	Author	Approximate Distribution
L. adetii	Castelnau, 1873	Eastern Australia and New Caledonia
L. argentimaculatus	Forsskål, 1775	Samoa to East Africa
L. bengalensis	Bloch, 1790	Indian Ocean and Indonesia
L. biguttatus	Valenciennes, 1830	Palau and Solomon Islands to Sri Lanka
L. bitaeniatus	Valenciennes, 1830	Indonesia and off northwestern Australia
L. bohar	Forsskål, 1775	Society Islands to East Africa
L. boutton	Lacepède, 1803	Samoa to northwest Australia
L. carponotatus	Richardson, 1842	East Australia to India
L. coeruleolineatus	Rüppell, 1838	Southern Red Sea and western Arabian Sea
L. decussatus	Cuvier, 1828	Indonesia and northwestern Australia to India
L. dodecacanthoides	Bleeker, 1854b	Indonesia, Philippines, and Ryukyu Islands
L. ehrenbergii	Peters, 1869	Mariana and Caroline Islands to East Africa
L. erythropterus	Bloch, 1790	Eastern Australia to Gulf of Oman
L. fulviflamma	Forsskål, 1775	Samoa to East Africa
L. fulvus	Schneider, 1801	Line and Marquesas Islands to East Africa
L. fuscescens	Valenciennes, 1830	New Guinea, Indonesia, Philippines, and China (fresh water)
L. gibbus	Forsskål, 1775	Line and Tuamotu Islands to East Africa

Species	Author	Distribution
L. goldiei	Macleay, 1882	Southern New Guinea (fresh water)
L. guilcheri	Fourmanoir, 1959	Bangladesh to Madagascar
L. johnii	Bloch, 1792	Fiji Islands to East Africa
L. kasmira	Forsskål, 1775	Line and Marquesas Islands to East Africa
L. lemniscatus	Valenciennes, 1828	Australia to East Africa
L. lunulatus	Park, 1797	New Guinea to Sri Lanka
L. lutjanus	Bloch, 1790	Solomon Islands to East Africa
L. madras	Valenciennes, 1831	Indonesia and Philippines to East Africa
L. malabaricus	Schneider, 1801	Fiji Islands to East Africa
L. maxweberi	Popta, 1921	New Guinea, Indonesia, Philippines (fresh water)
L. mizenkoi	Allen and Talbot, 1985	Samoa and Indonesia
L. monostigma	Cuvier, 1828	Marquesas to East Africa
L. notatus	Cuvier, 1828	Southwest Indian Ocean (Mauritius to South Africa)
L. quinquelineatus	Bloch, 1790	Fiji Islands to Persian Gulf
L. russelli	Bleeker, 1849	Samoa to East Africa
L. rivulatus	Cuvier, 1828	Society Islands to East Africa
L. sanguineus	Cuvier, 1828	India to Persian Gulf and Red Sea
L. sebae	Cuvier, 1828	New Caledonia and East Australia to East Africa
L. semicinctus	Quoy and Gaimard, 1824	Society and Gilbert Islands to Indonesia and Philippines
L. stellatus	Akazaki, 1983	Hong Kong to southern Japan
L. timorensis	Quoy and Gaimard, 1824	Samoa to Andaman Sea
L. vitta	Quoy and Gaimard, 1824	Marshall Islands to Seychelles

pale (central Indian Ocean to
western Pacific) . . . . <u>quinquelineatus</u>

7a. Large black spot usually present on
upper side below spinous-soft dorsal
junction; 3 uppermost stripes slanting
obliquely toward dorsal fin; gill
rakers on lower limb of first gill
arch 10-13; total rakers 20 (south-
western Indian Ocean) . . . . <u>notatus</u>
7b. Black spot absent; uppermost stripes
more or less parallel to body axis
or only slanting gently toward
dorsal profile; gill rakers on
lower limb of first gill arch 17-19;
total rakers 26-28 (Indian Ocean to
Indo-Malayan Archipelago) . . . . <u>bengalensis</u>

8a. Longitudinal scale rows above
lateral line obliquely positioned
(Figure 2.1A) 9
8b. Longitudinal scale rows above
lateral line entirely horizontal
(Figure 2.1B) or some rows rising
obliquely from below middle part
of dorsal fin (Figure 2.1C) 34

9a. Vomerine tooth patch triangular or
diamond-shaped with medial posterior
extension (Figure 2.2A) 10
9b. Vomerine tooth patch crescentic or
triangular without posterior
extension (Figure 2.2B) 15

10a. Axil of pectoral fin with distinct
black spot on upper portion; a
series of 8 or 9 relatively broad
orange or yellow stripes on side;
soft dorsal rays usually 15
(occasionally 14, rarely 16);
soft anal rays 9 (India to
Melanesia and Australia) . . . . <u>carponotatus</u>
10b. Axil of pectoral fin without black
spot; color not as in 7a; soft
dorsal rays usually 13 or 14
(rarely 12); soft anal rays 8
(rarely 9) 11

11a. Large black spot usually present
     on upper side, juveniles sometimes
     with ocellated spot and/or series
     of 4-7 broad dark stripes on side 12
11b. Black spot absent, series of narrow,
     yellowish longitudinal lines on side,
     those on upper back slanting upward
     toward dorsal fin base, sometimes an
     enlarged darker stripe from eye to
     middle of caudal fin base 13

12a. Soft dorsal rays usually 14; a
     relatively wide gap on forehead
     between temporal scale band of
     each side (Figure 2.3B); spot on
     upper side situated mainly above
     lateral line; young specimens
     with series of 4-7 broad stripes
     (blackish to orange or yellow-
     brown in life) on side, these
     persisting as thin stripes in
     adults from the western Indian
     Ocean (eastern Africa to western
     Pacific) . . . . russelli

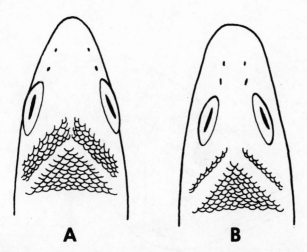

Figure 2.3   Dorsal view of head showing temporal
scalation: (A) _Lutjanus fulviflamma_,   (B) _L._
russelli

12b. Soft dorsal rays usually 13;
     little or no gap on forehead
     between temporal scale band
     of each side (Figure 2.3A);
     spot on upper side situated
     mostly below lateral line or
     bisected by it (spot sometimes
     elongate); young specimens
     without series or 4-7 broad
     dark stripes on side (eastern
     Africa to central South Pacific) . . . . <u>fulviflamma</u>

13a. Midlateral stripe usually
     broader and darker than other
     stripes on side; transverse
     scale rows on cheek 7-10
     (western Indian Ocean to
     western Pacific) . . . . <u>vitta</u>
13b. Midlateral stripe not broader
     or darker than other stripes
     on side, yellow in life and
     faint or absent in preserved
     specimens; transverse scale
     rows on cheek usually 6 or
     7, occasionally 8 14

Figure 2.4 <u>Lutjanus</u> <u>madras</u>, lateral view of head

14a. Predorsal scales extending to
     mid-interorbital level
     (Figure 2.4); a blunt,
     flattened spine on upper
     margin of opercle, above the
     main centrally located spine
     (Figure 2.4); interorbital
     width 4.4–6.5 in head length;
     total gill rakers on first
     arch 18–21 (eastern Africa to
     Indonesia and Philippines) . . . . **madras**
14b. Predorsal scales extending to
     level of rear part of orbit
     (Figure 2.5); blunt spine above
     central opercular spine absent
     (Figure 2.5); interorbital width
     6.5–6.9 in head length; total
     gill rakers on first arch 15 or
     16 (Indonesia to Samoa) . . . . **mizenkoi**

15a. Total gill rakers on first arch
     25–30 16
15b. Total gill rakers on first
     arch 14–23 17

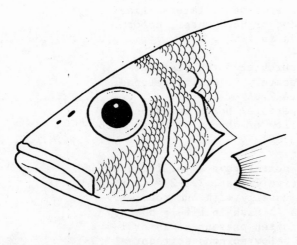

Figure 2.5 _Lutjanus mizenkoi_, lateral view of head

16a. Dorsal rays XI,14; longitudinal
scale rows below lateral line
parallel to axis of body; caudal
fin emarginate; color generally
pale with golden brown midlateral
stripe, slightly narrower than eye,
and series of oblique golden brown
lines ascending from lateral line
to base of dorsal fin (eastern
Australia and New Caledonia) . . . . **adetii**

16b. Dorsal rays X,13 or 14; scale
rows below lateral line ascending
obliquely; caudal fin distinctly
forked with rounded lobes; color
deep red to gray, fins red or
dark brown to blackish (Indo-west
Pacific) . . . . **gibbus**

17a. Soft anal rays 10; dorsal rays
XI,16 (rarely 15); scale rows
below lateral line ascending
obliquely; color pattern
consisting of 3 dark brown to
red transverse bands, which may
be indistinct in large adults
(eastern Africa to western
Pacific) . . . . **sebae**

17b. Soft anal rays 8 or 9; dorsal
rays variable, X or XI,12-16;
scale rows below lateral line
oblique or horizontal; color
not as in 17a 18

18a. Preopercular notch distinct
(moderately to well developed,
Figure 2.6A) 19

18b. Preopercular notch indistinct
(shallow or absent, Figures 2.6B
and 2.6C) 22

19a. Soft dorsal rays 15 or 16; body
relatively deep, 2.1-2.4 in SL;
head usually with numerous wavy
lines (bluish in life); chalky
spot often present on lateral
line below spinous-soft dorsal
junction, bordered with black

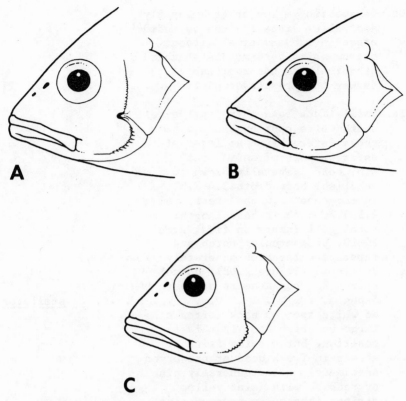

Figure 2.6 Lateral view of head showing variation in preopercle notch for species of _Lutjanus_: (A) well developed, (B) shallow, (C) absent

in juveniles, but lost with
age; lips thick in large adults
(eastern Africa to central
South Pacific) . . . . _rivulatus_
19b. Soft dorsal rays 13 or 14; body
usually more slender, 2.3-2.8 in
SL; color not as in 19a; lips
not thick in adults 20

20a. Caudal fin and distal third of
dorsal fin blackish or dusky
brown with narrow white border
(Indo-west Pacific) . . . . _fulvus_

20b. Caudal fin yellow or gray basally
and yellow distally (tan to medium
brown in preservative) without
narrow white border; distal third
of dorsal fin not noticeably
darker than remainder of fin 21

21a. Small (much less than pupil size)
chalk-white spot on back just
above lateral line at level of
anterior part of soft dorsal
fin; color generally brown to
purplish; body depth 2.4–2.5
in SL; snout 2.6 and preorbital
4.1–5.2, both in head length;
total gill rakers on first arch
16–19; preopercular notch and
interopercular knob moderately
developed (Figure 2.6B); dorsal
spines X (Hong Kong to southern
Japan) . . . . **stellatus**

21b. No white spot on back (often a
large brownish spot in this
position, but usually faint or
absent in fresh dead or preserved
specimens); color generally pink
or reddish with faint yellow
stripes (absent in preservative)
on side, margin of dorsal fin
sometimes blackish; snout 2.8–3.2,
preorbital 5.3–6.6, both in head
length; total gill rakers on first
arch 20–23; preopercular notch and
interopercular knob strongly
developed (Figure 2.6A); dorsal
spines X or XI (eastern Indian Ocean
to central South Pacific) . . . . **boutton**

22a. Broad transverse bands or saddles
on upper half of body and large
black blotch in center of caudal
peduncle (Indonesia to central
South Pacific) . . . . **semicinctus**

22b. Color pattern not as in 22a 23

23a. Color pattern consisting of series
of 5 dark stripes on whitish

ground color; 2 to 3 upper-most
stripes crossed by dark vertical
bars, thus forming a series of
light squares; large dark spot
at base of caudal fin (central
Indian Ocean to western Pacific) . . . . <u>decussatus</u>
23b. Color pattern not as in 23a 24

24a. Nostrils set in prominent groove
running forward from eye in
specimens >200 mm SL; specimens
under this size frequently with
2 whitish spots on upper back,
the anterior spot below last 4
dorsal spines and posterior one
under last 6 dorsal rays, meeting
that of other side across top of
caudal peduncle; color generally
dark brown on upper back, grading
to tan or light brownish (white or
pink in life) ventrally; dorsal and
caudal fins dusky; outer portion of
anal and pelvic fins distinctly
blackish; upper third of pectoral
fin dusky brown; tongue with patch
of fine granular teeth (Indo-west
Pacific) . . . . <u>bohar</u>
24b. Nostrils never set in a groove;
color pattern not as in 24a;
tongue smooth or with patch of
granular teeth 25

25a. Caudal fin with distinctive
crescentic black marking
(Figure 2.7), remainder of
body and fins uniformly
yellowish tan (yellow in life)
with silvery sheen on lower
sides (central Indian Ocean
to Melanesia) . . . . <u>lunulatus</u>
25b. Caudal fin base without
distinctive black marking
(although dark smudge or
blotch present on middle
caudal rays of <u>bitaeniatus</u>
<200 mm SL; color of body
and fins variable 26

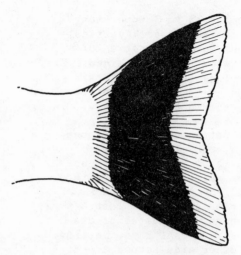

Figure 2.7 Caudal fin of _Lutjanus lunulatus_

26a. Black spot on upper side at
     level of lateral line below
     soft dorsal fin (faint or
     occasionally absent in large
     adults); remainder of body
     and fins mainly pale (fins
     yellow, body pink or yellow
     in life); tongue with patch
     of fine granular teeth,
     although sometimes absent in
     juveniles (Indo-west Pacific) . . . . . . <u>monostigma</u>
26b. Black spot on upper side of
     body absent, although saddle
     or spot sometimes present on
     upper portion of caudal
     peduncle; tongue smooth 27

27a. Dorsal spines XII; series of
     5 or 6 dusky stripes (yellow
     in life, may be faint in
     preservative); longitudinal
     rows of scales below lateral
     line rising obliquely
     (Indonesia and Philippines) . . . . <u>dodecacanthoides</u>
27b. Dorsal spines X or XI; color
     not as in 27a; longitudinal
     rows of scales below lateral

line parallel to axis of body
or rising obliquely 28

28a. Axil of pectoral fin black;
     color overall deep red in life;
     posterior dorsal and anal fin rays
     elongated to form pointed fins;
     soft anal rays 8 (eastern Indian
     Ocean to western Pacific) . . . . _timorensis_
28b. Axil of pectoral without black
     marking; color variable, although
     often red in life; posterior
     dorsal and anal rays low and
     rounded or tall and pointed, but
     specimens having latter condition
     usually with soft anal rays 9 29

29a. Dorsal spines X; soft anal rays
     usually 8, rarely 9; tongue with
     patch of fine, granular teeth;
     color variable, pink to gray-brown
     (tan to brown in preservative);
     juveniles without black saddle on
     upper caudal peduncle 30
29b. Dorsal spines usually XI, rarely X,
     soft anal rays usually 9, occasion-
     ally 8, tongue smooth; color largely
     reddish (brown in preservative);
     juveniles usually with black saddle
     on upper caudal peduncle 31

30a. Interorbital 4.9-5.2 in head length;
     body relatively deep, the depth
     2.3-2.5 in SL; snout-forehead
     profile straight or convex; color
     generally red or pink (brown to
     yellowish in preservative); fins
     pale except juveniles may have
     crescentic blotch in middle of
     caudal fin (eastern Indian Ocean
     and Indonesia) . . . . _bitaeniatus_
30b. Interorbital 5.5-7.6 in head length;
     body generally more slender, the
     depth 2.5-2.8 in SL; snout-forehead
     concave in specimens >150-200 mm
     SL; color generally gray-brown,
     reddish or pink ventrally, dorsal

and caudal fins dusky brown or
black, frequently with narrow
white border posteriorly;
juveniles with broad, black
midlateral stripe (eastern Africa
to western Pacific) . . . . <u>lemniscatus</u>

31a. Dorsal profile of head concave
(Figure 2.8A); longitudinal scale

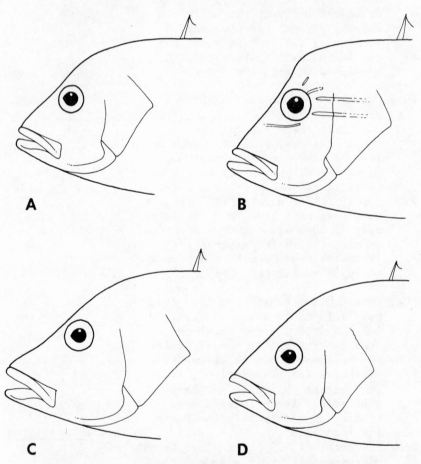

A

B

C

D

Figure 2.8 Head shapes of members of the red
snapper complex: (A) <u>Lutjanus guilcheri</u>, (B) <u>L.</u>
<u>sanguineus</u>, (C) <u>L. malabaricus</u> and <u>L. timoren-
sis</u>, (D) <u>L. erythropterus</u>

rows below lateral line horizontal;
hump on forehead absent; interorbital relatively narrow, about
5.8-6.0 in head length; length of
maxilla significantly less than
distance between bases of last
dorsal and anal rays; pectoral
fins yellow in life (central
and western Indian Ocean) . . . .   __guilcheri__

31b. Dorsal profile of head straight,
concave, or convex (Figures 2.8B-
2.8D); longitudinal scale rows
below lateral line horizontal
or oblique; hump on forehead
present or absent; interorbital
width variable, 3.5-6.6 in head
length; length of maxilla variable,
about equal to or distinctly less
than distance between bases of
last dorsal and anal rays;
pectoral fins reddish or pink
in life 32

32a. Prominent hump on forehead and
series of shallow, horizontal
grooves behind eye in specimens
>200-250 mm SL (Figure 2.8B);
anterior and posterior nostrils
widely separated, the distance
between them much greater than
length of posterior nostril
opening (Red Sea and western
Indian Ocean) . . . .   __sanguineus__

32b. Hump on forehead and grooves
behind eye always absent;
anterior and posterior
nostrils close set, the
distance between them about
equal or less than length of
posterior nostril opening 33

33a. Mouth relatively small, the
maxilla length much less than
distance between bases of last
dorsal and anal rays; interorbital 3.5-4.8 in head length
(specimens >150 mm SL); some

longitudinal scale rows below
lateral line slanting obliquely
in posterior direction toward
dorsal profile; head profile
convex (in specimens >150 mm SL)
(northwest Indian Ocean to
western Pacific) . . . . __erythropterus__

33b. Mouth larger, the maxilla length
about equal to distance between
bases of last dorsal and anal
rays; interorbital 5.1-6.6 in
head length (specimens >120 mm
SL); longitudinal scale rows
below lateral line horizontal,
although some rows may slant
obliquely in juveniles <100 mm SL;
head profile straight (eastern
Africa to western Pacific) . . . . __malabaricus__

34a. Color pattern consisting of 4
relatively wide dusky brown or
blackish stripes on pale ground;
only juveniles to 107 mm SL
known (freshwater streams of
the Philippines, Indonesia, and
New Guinea) . . . . __maxweberi__

34b. Color pattern not as in 34a 35

35a. Vomerine tooth patch triangular
with medial posterior extension
(Figure 2.2A); preorbital narrow,
8.6-10.3 in head length; prominent black spot, larger than eye
bisected by lateral line below
posterior part of spinous dorsal
fin (eastern Africa to western
Pacific) . . . . __ehrenbergii__

35b. Vomerine tooth patch crescentic
or triangular without medial
posterior extension (Figure 2.2B);
preorbital wider, 4.7-4.9 in head
length; black spot on back present
or absent 36

36a. Large black spot on upper back
usually present, if absent ground
color pale 37

36b. Black spot on upper back absent,
ground color dark 38

37a. Ground color pale, each scale on
side often with brownish spot,
thus forming longitudinal rows
on side; large spot on back, if
present, mainly above lateral
line; interorbital 5.6-7.3 in
head length; preorbital 4.9-6.0
in head length; tongue with
patch of fine granular teeth
(eastern Africa to central
South Pacific) . . . . _johnii_
37b. Ground color dusky brown; large
spot on back bisected by lateral
line; interorbital 5.0-5.6 in
head length ; preorbital about
6.8 in head length; tongue smooth
(fresh waters of China, Philippines,
Indonesia, and New Guinea) . . . . _fuscescens_

38a. Body depth 2.5-2.9 (average about
2.7) in SL; least depth of caudal
peduncle 3.0-3.5 in head length;
longitudinal scale rows on upper
back parallel to lateral line
anteriorly and some rows usually
ascending obliquely below
posterior dorsal spines
(Figure 2.1C); a marine species
also occurring in brackish
estuaries and lower reaches of
freshwater streams (eastern
Africa to central Pacific) . . . . . _argentimaculatus_
38b. Body depth 2.2-2.6 in SL;
least depth of caudal peduncle
2.5-3.0 in head length;
longitudinal scale rows on
upper back entirely parallel
to lateral line (Figure 2.1B);
a freshwater species (southern
New Guinea) . . . . _goldiei_

KEY TO EASTERN ATLANTIC SPECIES OF LUTJANUS (Table 2.3, Plate 2.7)

1a. Longitudinal scale rows above
lateral line obliquely positioned
(Figure 2.1A); vomerine tooth
patch without a narrow, elongate
posterior extension, usually
crescentic to triangular, often
with a short, medial posterior
extension 2
1b. Longitudinal scale rows above
lateral line entirely horizontal
(Figure 2.1B); vomerine tooth
patch with a narrow, elongate
posterior extension 4

2a. Transverse scale rows on cheek
5 or 6; forehead profile
distinctly angular; juveniles
with narrow, pale bars (or
vertical rows of spots),
narrower than dark interspaces . . . . *agennes*
2b. Transverse scale rows on cheek
8-10; forehead profile variable,
rounded to angular; juveniles
with either alternating light
and dark bars of approximately
the same width or 6-8 vertical
rows of spots on side 3

TABLE 2.3
Species of Lutjanus from the eastern Atlantic Ocean

Species	Author	Approximate Distribution
L. agennes	Bleeker, 1863b	Senegal to Angola
L. dentatus	Duméril, 1858	Gulf of Guinea
L. endecacanthus	Bleeker, 1863b	Ghana to mouth of Congo River
L. fulgens	Valenciennes, 1830	Nigeria to Senegal and Gulf of Guinea
L. goreensis	Valenciennes, 1830	Senegal to the Congo

3a. Longitudinal scale rows above
lateral line (below middle of
spinous dorsal fin) 4 or 5;
forehead profile evenly curved;
juveniles with alternating light
and dark bars of approximately
the same width . . . . **dentatus**
3b. Longitudinal scale rows above
lateral line (below middle of
spinous dorsal fin) 6; forehead
profile angular; juveniles often
with 6-8 vertical rows of white
spots on sides . . . . **endecacanthus**

4a. Total gill rakers (excluding
rudiments) on first arch 7 or
8; blue stripe from snout to
edge of opercle . . . . **goreensis**
4b. Total gill rakers (excluding
rudiments) on first arch 16; no
blue stripe from snout to edge of
opercle . . . . **fulgens**

KEY TO WESTERN ATLANTIC SPECIES OF LUTJANUS (modified from Anderson 1967 and Rivas 1966) (Table 2.4, Plates 2.7-2.8)

1a. Dorsal fin rays usually X,12
(rarely 11 or 13 soft rays); a
black spot below anterior part
of soft dorsal fin, persisting
throughout life 2
1b. Dorsal fin rays usually X,14
(rarely IX or XI spines and 13
or 15 soft rays, except 13 rays
in **ambiguus**); black spot
below anterior part of soft
dorsal fin present or absent 3

2a. About one-fourth to one-half of
black lateral spot extending
below lateral line; gill rakers
7 or 8 + 15 to 17 including
rudiments . . . . **mahogoni**

TABLE 2.4
Species of _Lutjanus_ from the western Atlantic
Ocean

Species	Author	Approximate Distribution
L. ambiguus	Poey 1860	Cuba and S. Florida
L. analis	Cuvier 1828	Massachusetts to Brazil
L. apodus	Walbaum 1792	Massachusetts to Brazil
L. buccanella	Cuvier 1828	North Carolina to Brazil
L. campechanus	Poey 1860	Gulf of Mexico and east coast of the United States
L. cyanopterus	Cuvier 1828	Massachusetts to Brazil
L. griseus	Linnaeus 1758	Massachusetts to Brazil
L. jocu	Bloch and Schneider 1801	Massachusetts to Brazil
L. mahogoni	Cuvier 1828	North Carolina to Venezuela
L. purpureus	Poey 1867	Cuba to Brazil
L. synagris	Linnaeus 1758	North Carolina to Brazil
L. vivanus	Cuvier 1828	North Carolina to Brazil

2b. Less than one-fourth or none of
black lateral spot extending below
lateral line in specimens >60 mm
SL; gill rakers 6 or 7 + 13 or 14
(rarely 11 or 15) including
rudiments . . . . synagris

3a. A large, pronounced black spot at
base and in axil of pectoral fin;
black spot below anterior part of
soft dorsal fin absent; anal fin
rounded; a dark area of scales at
base of soft dorsal fin (not always
obvious on preserved specimens) . . . buccanella

3b. Black spot at base and in axil of
pectoral fin absent; black spot
below anterior part of soft dorsal
fin present or absent; anal fin
rounded or angulated; dark area
at base of soft dorsal fin absent 4

4a. Anal fin rounded at all sizes, the
     middle rays considerably less than
     half length of head; no black spot
     below anterior part of soft dorsal
     fin 5
4b. Anal fin angulated in larger
     specimens, the middle rays produced,
     the longest almost half to greater
     than half length of head (anal fin
     rounded in <u>analis</u> <40 mm SL, in
     <u>campechanus</u> and <u>purpureus</u> <50 mm SL,
     and in <u>vivanus</u> <60 mm SL); a black
     spot below anterior part of soft
     dorsal fin, at least in young (this
     spot present in large analis, to at
     least 465 mm SL but disappearing by
     about 200-300 mm SL in <u>campechanus,</u>
     <u>purpureus,</u> and <u>vivanus</u>) 9

5a. Vomerine tooth patch without a
     distinct medial posterior extension
     (Figure 2.2B); upper and lower
     canines very strong, about equally
     developed; cheek scales in 8-10,
     usually 9 rows . . . . <u>cyanopterus</u>
5b. Vomerine tooth patch anchor-shaped,
     with a medial posterior extension
     (Figure 2.2A); upper canines usually
     larger than lower; cheek scales in
     5-9, usually 7 or 8 rows 6

6a. Body relatively slender (depth
     about 3.0 in SL); soft anal
     rays 9; gill rakers on lower
     limb (including rudiments) 16-18 . . . . <u>ambiguus</u>
6b. Body deeper, 2.3-2.8 in SL
     except 2.6-3.2 in <u>griseus</u>; soft
     soft anal rays 7-9; gill rakers
     on lower limb (including rudiments)
     11-17 (11-16 in most species) 7

7a. Pectoral fin length about equal
     to distance from tip of snout
     to posterior edge of preopercle,
     3.7-4.2 in SL; body comparatively
     slender, greatest depth 2.6-3.2,
     usually 2.7-3.1 in SL . . . . <u>griseus</u>

7b. Pectoral fin longer than distance
from tip of snout to posterior
edge of preopercle, 3.0-3.5 in SL
(in _apodus_ of 75-96 mm SL,
pectoral fin length approximately
equal to that of _griseus_ of
similar size); body comparatively
deep, greatest depth 2.3-2.8,
usually 2.4-2.7 in SL 8

8a. Scales relatively large, 39-44,
usually 40-43 transverse rows
between upper edge of opercle
and caudal base; 5-7 scales
between dorsal origin and
lateral line in a posteroventrally directed row (i.e.,
counting downward and backward);
no whitish bar below eye . . . . _apodus_

8b. Scales of moderate size, 45-49,
usually 46-48, transverse rows
between upper edge of opercle and
caudal base; 8-11 scales between
dorsal origin and lateral line in a
posteroventrally directed row (i.e.,
counting downward and backward);
whitish bar between eye and area
immediately posterior to maxillary
(not obvious in some preserved
specimens) . . . . _jocu_

9a. Vomerine tooth patch without a
distinct medial posterior extension
(Figure 2.2B); soft anal rays usually
8 (rarely 7); iris red in life; spot
below anterior part of soft dorsal
fin relatively large in small
specimens, small but distinct in
large specimens . . . . _analis_

9b. Vomerine tooth patch triangular or
anchor-shaped, with medial posterior
extension (Figure 2.2A); soft anal
rays 7-10 (usually 8 or 9) 10

10a. Soft anal rays 9 (rarely 8); lateral
line scales 46-50, usually 47-49;
scales above lateral line 7-10,

usually 8 or 9; scales on anterior
part of body, below lateral line,
conspicuously larger than those on
posterior part; suborbital width
8-9% of SL . . . . __campechanus__

10b. Soft anal rays 8 (rarely 7 or 9);
lateral line scales 49-53, usually
50 or 51; scales above lateral line
9-12, usually 10-12; scales on
anterior part of body, below lateral
line, not conspicuously larger than
those on posterior part; suborbital
width 6-7% of SL 11

11a. Scales below lateral line 16-19;
scales above lateral line 9-11,
usually 10; cheek scale rows 6,
rarely 5 or 7; scales above
lateral line, on anterior part of
body, smaller than those below;
pelvic fin length 53-62% of body
depth; lateral spot on upper side
of young about equal to, or larger
than, eye; iris red in live and
freshly preserved specimens . . . . . . __purpureus__

11b. Scales below lateral line 20-24,
usually 21-23; scales above lateral
line 10-12, usually 11 or 12; cheek
scale rows 7, rarely 8; scales above
lateral line, on anterior part of
body, about equal to those below;
pelvic fin length 63-76% of body
depth; lateral spot on upper side
of young smaller than eye; iris
yellow in live and freshly preserved
specimens . . . . __vivanus__

ACKNOWLEDGMENTS

Fieldwork and museum visits were greatly facilitated
by financial assistance of the Food and Agriculture Organ-
ization of the United Nations, Rome, under the auspices of
W. Fischer. Additional fieldwork in the Indian Ocean and
New Guinea was funded by grants from the Australian
National Parks and Wildlife Service and Papua New Guinea
Biological Research Foundation. Financial assistance and

study facilities during a research visit in 1984 were
provided by the California Academy of Sciences. The work
there was greatly facilitated by staff members L. Demp-
ster, W. N. Eschmeyer, T. Iwamoto, S. G. Poss, P. Sinoto,
and F. H. Talbot. I am especially indebted to J. E.
Randall (Bernice P. Bishop Museum, Honolulu) who collected
in my behalf from numerous localities throughout the Indo-
Pacific region and endeavored to obtain high quality
photographs of Lutjanus.

Illustrations were prepared by R. Swainston and M.
Thompson of Perth, Australia and are reproduced herein
through the courtesy of the Food and Agriculture Organization of the United Nations. Mrs. C. J. Allen compiled the
bibliography and prepared the typescript. W. D. Anderson,
Jr. and W. Fischer kindly read the manuscript and offered
suggestions.

BIBLIOGRAPHY

Akazaki, M. 1983. A new lutjanid fish, Lutjanus stel-
     latus, from southern Japan and a related species, L.
     rivulatus (Cuvier). Jpn. J. Ichthyol. 29:365-373.
Allen, G. R. 1981. Family Lutjanidae. In W. Fischer, G.
     Bianchi, and W. B. Scott (editors), FAO species iden-
     tification sheets for fishery purposes, eastern cen-
     tral Atlantic fishing areas 34, 37 (in part), Vol. 2.
     FAO, Rome.
_____. 1985. FAO species catalogue. Snappers of the
     world. An annotated and illustrated catalogue of
     lutjanid fishes known to date. FAO Fish. Synop.
     (125), Vol. 6:1-208.
Allen, G. R., and F. H. Talbot. 1985. Review of the
     snappers of the genus Lutjanus (Pisces: Lutjanidae)
     from the Indo-Pacific, with the description of a new
     species. Indo-Pac. Fishes 11:1-87 (Bernice P. Bishop
     Mus., Honolulu).
Alleyne, H. G., and W. M. Macleay. 1877. The ichthyology
     of the Chevert Expedition. Proc. Linn. Soc. N.S.W.
     1:261-281.
Anderson, W. D. 1967. Field guide to the snappers (Lut-
     janidae) of the western Atlantic. U.S. Fish. Wildl.
     Serv. Circ. 252:1-14.
Baird, S. F., and C. Girard. 1855. Report on the fishes
     observed on the coasts of New Jersey and Long Island
     during the summer of 1854. In S. F. Baird (editor),
     Smithson. Inst. 9th Annu. Rep. 1854:317-337.

Bennett, E. T. 1831. Observations on a collection of fishes from the Mauritius, with characters of new genera and species. Proc. Zool. Soc. Lond. p. 126-128.

_____. 1832. Characters of new species of fishes from Ceylon. Proc. Zool. Soc. Lond., p. 182-184.

Bleeker, P. 1845. Iden. continuatio. Nat. Geneesh. Arch. Ned. Ind. 2:505-528.

_____. 1849. Bijdrage tot de kennis der Percoiden van den Malajo-Molukschen Archipel, mit beschrijving von 22 nieuwe soorten. Verh. Batav. Genootsch. 22:1-64.

_____. 1851. Nieuwe bijdrage tot de kennis der Percoidei, Scleroparei, Sciaenoidei, Maenoidei. Chaetodontoidei en Scomberoidei van den Soenda-Molukschen Archipel. Nat. Tijdschr. Neder.-Indie 2:163-179.

_____. 1852a. Bijdrage tot de kennis der ichthyologische fauna van de Moluksche eilanden. Visschen van Amboina en Ceram. Nat. Tijdschr. Neder.-Indie 3:229-309.

_____. 1852b. Derde bijdrage tot de kennis der ichthyologische fauna van Celebes. Nat. Tijdschr. Neder.-Indie 3:739-782.

_____. 1853. Derde bijdrage tot de kennis der ichthyologische fauna van Amboina. Nat. Tijdschr. Neder.-Indie 4:91-130.

_____. 1854a. Bijdrage tot de kennis der ichthyologische fauna van Halmaheira (Gilolo). Nat. Tijdschr. Neder.-Indie 6:49-62.

_____. 1854b. Vijfde bijdrage tot de kennis der ichthyologische fauna van Amboina. Nat. Tijdschr. Neder.-Indie 6:455-508.

_____. 1855. Zesde bijdrage tot de kennis der ichthyologische fauna van Amboina. Nat. Tijdschr. Neder.-Indie 8:391-434.

_____. 1859. Enumeratio specierum piscium hucusque in Archipelago Indico observatarum. Acta Soc. Sci. Indo-Neerl. 6:1-276.

_____. 1860. Achtste bijdrage tot de kennis der vischfauna van Sumatra, Visschen van Benkoelen, Priaman, Tandjong, Palembag en Djambi. Acta Soc. Sci. Indo-Neerl. 8:1-88.

_____. 1863a. Douxieme notice sur la faune ichthyologique de l'île d'Obi. Ned. Tijdschr. Dierk. 1:239-245.

_____. 1863b. Mémoire su les poissons de la côte de Guinée. Nat. Verh. Holl. Maatsch. Wetensch. 2. Verz. Deel. 18:1-136.

_____. 1873. Revision des espèces indo-archipélagiques des genres Lutjanus et Aprion. Verh. Akad. Amsterdam 13:1-102.

Bloch, M. E. 1790. Naturgeschichte der auslandischen Fische. Part 4. J. Morino, Berlin, 128 p.

_____. 1792. Naturgeschichte der auslandischen Fische. Part 6. J. Morino, Berlin, 126 p.

Bloch, M. E., and J. G. Schneider. 1801. Systema Ichthyologiae iconibus cx illustratum. Berlin, 584 p.

Bocourt, F. M. 1868. Descriptions de quelques acantho-ptérygiens nouveaux appartenant aux genres Serranus et Mesoprion recueillis dans l'Amérique centrale. Ann. Sci. Nat. (Zool.) 5 Ser. 10:222-224.

Cantor, T. E. 1849. Catalogue of Malayan fishes. J. Roy. Asiat. Soc. Bengal 18:983-1042.

Castelnau, F. L. 1873. Contribution to the ichthyology of Australia. Proc. Zool. Acclim. Soc. Victoria 2:37-158.

_____. 1875. Researches on the fishes of Australia. Intercolonial Exhibition Essays 2:1-52. In Philadelphia Centennial Exhibition of 1876. Official record. Melbourne.

_____. 1878. Australian fishes, new or little known species. Proc. Linn. Soc. N.S.W. (1)2(3):225-248.

Chan, W. L. 1970. A new genus and two new species of commercial snappers from Hong Kong. Hong Kong Fish. Bull. 1:19-38.

Cope, E. D. 1871. Contribution to the ichthyology of the Lesser Antilles. Trans. Am. Philos. Soc. 14:445-483.

Cuvier, G. 1815. Observations et recherches critiques sur différents poissons de la Méditerranée et à leur occasion sur des poissons d'autres mers, plus ou moins liés avec eux. Mem. Mus. Natl. Hist. Nat. 1:353-363.

Cuvier, G., and A. Valenciennes. 1828. Histoire naturelle des poissons. Levrault, Paris, Vol. 2, 490 p.

_____. 1829. Histoire naturelle des poissons. Levrault, Paris, Vol. 3, 500 p.

_____. 1830. Histoire naturelle des poissons. Levrault, Paris, Vol. 6, 559 p.

_____. 1831. Histoire naturelle des poissons. Levrault, Paris, Vol. 7, 531 p.

_____. 1833. Histoire naturelle des poissons. Levrault, Paris, Vol. 9, 512 p.

Day, F. 1869. Remarks on some of the fishes in the Calcutta Museum, Part 1. Proc. Zool. Soc. Lond., p. 511-527.

_____. 1870. On the fishes of the Andaman Islands. Proc. Zool. Soc. Lond., p. 677-705.

_____. 1875. The fishes of India; being a natural history of the fishes known to inhabit the sea and fresh waters of India, Burma, and Ceylon. Lond., 168 p.

Desmarest, A. G. 1823. Premiere decade ichthyologique, ou description complete de dix especes de poissons nouvelles ou imparfaitement connues, habitant la mer qui baigne les cotes de l'île de Cuba. Mem. Soc. Linn. Paris, 2, 50 p.

De Vis, C. W. 1884. Fishes from South Sea islands. Proc. Linn. Soc. N.S.W. (1883) 8(4):445-457.

_____. 1885a. New Australian fishes in the Queensland Museum. Proc. Linn. Soc. N.S.W. 9(2):389-400.

_____. 1885b. On a new fish from Moreton Bay. Proc. Roy. Soc. Queensl. 1(3):144-147.

Duméril, A. 1860. Reptiles et Poissons de l'Afrique occidentale. Etude précédée de considerations générales sur leur distribution geographique. Arch. Mus. Hist. Nat. (Paris) 10:137-268.

Evermann, B. W., and M. C. Marsh. 1900. The fishes of Porto Rico. Bull. U.S. Fish Comm. p. 51-350.

Evermann, B. W., and A. Seale. 1907. Fishes of the Philippine Islands. Bull. U.S. Bur. Fish. (1906) 26:49-110.

Forsskål, P. 1775. Descriptiones animalium avium, amphibiorum, piscium, insectorum, vermium; quae in itinere orientali observavit. Post morten auctoris edidit Carsten Niebuhr. Molleri: Havinae, 164 p.

Fourmanoir, P. 1957. Poissons téléostéens des eaux malgaches du Canal de Mozambique. Mem. Inst. Rech. Sci. Madagascar, Sér. F Oceanogr. 1:1-316.

_____. 1959. Lutjanus guilcheri, nouvelle espèce de Lutjanidae capturée dans le Nord-Quest de Madagascar. Nat. Malgalche, 10:129-130.

Fowler, H. W. 1904. A collection of fishes from Sumatra. J. Acad. Nat. Sci., Phila. (2) 12:495-560.

_____. 1918. New and little-known fishes from the Philippine Islands. Proc. Acad. Nat. Sci. Phila. 70:1-71.

_____. 1931. Contributions to the biology of the Philippine Archipelago and adjacent regions. The fishes of the families Pseudochromidae, Lobotidae, Pempheridae, Priacanthidae, Lutjanidae, Pomadasyidae,

and Teraponidae collected by the United States Bureau
Fisheries Steamer "Albatross;" chiefly in Philippine
seas and adjacent waters. Bull. U.S. Natl. Mus.
100(11):1-388.

Gilbert, C. H. 1897. Descriptions of twenty-two new
species of fishes collected by the steamer "Albatross," of the United States Fish Commission. Proc.
U.S. Natl. Mus. 19:437-457.

Gilchrist, J. D. F., and W. W. Thompson. 1908. Descriptions of fishes from the coast of Natal. Ann. S.
Afr. Mus. 6:145-206.

Gill, T. N. 1862. Remarks on the relations of the genera
and other groups of Cuban fishes. Proc. Acad. Nat.
Sci., Phila. 14:235-242.

Girard, C. F. 1859. Ichthyology. In United States and
Mexican boundary survey, under the order of Lieut.
Col. W. H. Emory, Major First Cavalry and United
States Commissioner 2(2):1-85.

Gmelin, J. F. 1788-93. Systema naturae per regna tria
naturae, secundum classes, ordines, genera, species,
cum characteribus, differentiis, synonymis, locis.
Tomus I-III. Editio decimo tertia, acuta, reformata.
Cura Jo Fred Gmelin. Lipsiae 3 vols.

Goode, G. B., and T. H. Bean. 1878. Descriptions of two
new species of fishes, Lutjanus blackfordii and Lutjanus stearnsii, from the coast of Florida. Proc.
U.S. Natl. Mus. 1:176-181.

Guichenot, A. 1862. Fauna ichthyologique. In L. Mail-
lard (editor), Notes sur l'île de la Réunion, Paris,
32 p.

Günther, A. 1859. Catalogue of the acanthopterygian
fishes in the collection of the British Museum. Br.
Mus. Lond. Vol. 1, 524 p.

_____. 1864. Report of a collection of fishes made
by Messrs. Dow, Godman, and Salvin in Guatemala.
Proc. Zool. Soc. Lond., p. 144-154.

_____. 1873. Andrew Garrett's Fische der Sudsee.
Heft I. J. Mus. Godeffroy 2(3):1-24.

Hamilton, F. 1822. An account of the fishes found in the
River Ganges and its branches. Archibald Constable,
Edinburgh, 405 p.

Hombron, J., and H. Jacquinot. 1853. Poissons. In Gide
et J. Baudry (editors), Voyage au Pole Sud et dans
l'oceanie sur les corvettes, L'Astrolabe' et la
'Zelee', p. 29-56, 7 pls. Zoologie. Vol. 3, Paris.

Jordan, D. S. 1917. Genera of fishes. Part 1. Stanford
Univ. Publ. Univ. Ser. 27:1-151.

Jordan, D. S., and B. W. Evermann. 1898. The fishes of North and Middle America: A descriptive catalogue of the species of fish-like vertebrates found in the waters of North America, north of the Isthmus of Panama. Bull. U.S. Natl. Mus. 47(1):1-1240.

Jordan, D. S., and B. Fesler. 1893. A review of the sparoid fishes of America and Europe. Rep. U.S. Fish Comm. 1889-1891, 27:421-544.

Jordan, D. S., and C. H. Gilbert. 1882. Descriptions of thirty-three new species of fishes from Mazatlan, Mexico. Proc. U.S. Nat. Mus. 1881, 4:338-365.

Jordan, D. S., and S. Swain. 1885. A review of the species Lutjaninae and Hoplopagrinae found in American waters. Proc. U.S. Nat. Mus. 1884, 7:427-474.

Kendall, W. C., and E. L. Goldsborough. 1911. The shore fishes. In Reports on the scientific results of the expedition to the tropical Pacific, in charge of Alexander Agassiz, by the U.S. Fish Commission steamer "Albatross," from August, 1899, to March, 1900. Mem. Mus. Comp. Zool. Harvard Coll. 26:239-343.

Kent, W. S. 1893. The Great Barrier Reef of Australia; its products and potentialities. Lond.

Lacepède, B. G. 1802. Histoire naturelle des poissons. Chez Plassan, Paris, Vol. 4, 728 p.

_____. 1803. Histoire naturelle des poissons. Chez Plassan, Paris, Vol. 5, 803 p.

Lesson, R. P. 1830. Poissons. In L. I. Duperrey (editor), Voyage autour de monde éxecuté sur la corvette de la majesté "La Coquille" pendant les années 1822, 1823, 1824, et 1825. Bertrand, Paris 2(1):66-238.

Liénard, R. P. 1839. Poissons. Ann. Rapp. Soc. Hist. Nat. Maurice 10:31-47.

Linnaeus, C. 1758. Systema naturae. Holmiae, Salvii 10th ed., Vol. 1, 824 p.

Macleay, W. 1879. Notes on some fishes from the Solomon Islands. Proc. Linn. Soc. N.S.W. 4:60-64.

_____. 1881. Descriptive catalogue of the fishes of Australia. Part 1. Proc. Linn. Soc. N.S.W. (1)5(3):302-444.

_____. 1882. Contribution to the knowledge of the fishes of New Guinea. No. 1. Proc. Linn. Soc. N.S.W. (1)7(2):224-250.

_____. 1883. Contribution to the knowledge of the fishes of New Guinea. No. 4. Proc. Linn. Soc. N.S.W. (1)8(2):252-280.

Nichols, J. T., and R. C. Murphy. 1922. On a collection of marine fishes from Peru. Bull. Am. Mus. Natl. Hist. 46(9):501-516.

Park, M. 1797. Descriptions of eight new fishes from Sumatra. Trans. Linn. Soc. Lond. 3:33-38.

Peters, W. C. H. 1869. Über neue oder weniger bekannte Fische des Berliner Zoologischen Museums. Monatsber. Akad. Wiss. Berl., p. 703-711.

Poey, F. 1851. Memorias sobre la historia natural de la isla de Cuba, acompañadas de sumarios latinos y extractos en francés. Habana, Vol. 1, 441 p.

_____. 1860. Memorias sobre la historia natural de la isla de Cuba, acompañadas de sumarios latinos y extractos en francés. Habana, Vol. 2, 442 p.

_____. 1867. Revista de las peces descritos por Poey. Rep. Fisico-nat. Isla de Cuba 2:153-174.

_____. 1868. Synopsis piscium cubensium. Rep. Fisico-nat. Isla de Cuba 2:279-484.

_____. 1870. New species of Cuban fishes. Ann. Lyc. Nat. Hist. N.Y. 9:317-322.

_____. 1871. Genres des poissons de la faune de Cuba, appartenant, à la famille Percidae, avec une note d'introduction par J. Carson Brevoort. Ann. Lyc. Nat. Hist. N.Y. 10:27-79.

_____. 1875. Enumeratio piscium cubensium. Anal. Soc. Espanola Hist. Nat. 4:75-161.

Popta, C. M. L. 1921. Dritte Fortsetzung der Beschreibung von neuen Fischarten der Sunda-Expedition. Zool. Meded. (Leiden) 6:203-214.

Postel, E. 1965. Deux Lutjanidés nouveaux des environs de Nouméa (Nouvelle-Caledonie). Bull. Mus. Natl. Hist. Nat., Paris, 2d Ser. 37(2):244-251.

Quoy J. R. C., and J. P. Gaimard. 1824. Voyage autour du monde, entrepris par ordre du roi, exécuté sur les corvettes de S. M. "L'Uranie" et La "Physicienne" pendant les annees 1817, 1818, 1819 et 1820, par M. Louis de Frecinet. Zoologie. Poissons. Paris, p. 183-401.

Ramsay, E. P. 1884. Description of some new Australian fishes. Proc. Linn. Soc. N.S.W. (1883), (1) 8:177-179.

Richardson, J. 1842. Contributions to the ichthyology of Australia. Ann. Mag. Nat. Hist. (1), 9(55):15-31.

_____. 1846. Report on the ichthyology of the Seas of China and Japan. Rep. Br. Assoc. Adv. Sci. 15th Meet. (1845):187-320.

Rivas, L. R. 1966. Review of the Lutjanus campechanus complex of red snappers. Q. J. Fla. Acad. Sci. 29:117-136.

Rüppell, W. P. E. 1829. Atlas zu der Reise im nordlichen Afrika. Fische Rothen Meeres, Frankfurt 2:27-94.

_____. 1838. Neue wirbelthiere zu der fauna von Abyssinien gehorig. Fische Rothen Meeres, Frankfurt 4:81-148.

Seale, A. 1906. Fishes of the South Pacific. Occas. Pap. Bernice P. Bishop Mus. 4(1):1-89.

_____. 1909. New species of Philippine fishes. Phillip. J. Sci. 4(6):491-543.

Shaw, G. 1803. Pisces. In General zoology or systematic natural history, 4(Part 2):187-632, 67 pls. Lond.

Smith, H. M., and T. C. B. Pope. 1906. List of fishes collected in Japan in 1903, with descriptions of new genera and species. Proc. U.S. Natl. Mus. 31:459-499.

Steindachner, F. 1869. Ichthyologische Notizen (9). Sitzber. Akad. Wiss. Wien 60(1):290-318.

_____. 1882. Beitrage zur Kenntniss der Fische Afrika's und Beschreibung einer neuen Sargus-Art von den Galapagos-Inseln. Denkschr. Akad. Wiss. Wien 1882, 44:19-58.

Steindachner, F., and L. Doderlein. 1883. Beitrage zur Kenntniss der Fische Japan's, I-IV. Denkschr. Akad. Wiss. Wien 47:211-242.

Swainson, W. 1839. The natural history and classification of fishes, amphibians and reptiles, or mono-cardian animals. Lond. Vol. 2, 448 p.

Thiollière V. J. 1856. Essai sur faune de l'île de Woodlark ou Moiou. Ann. Sci. Phys. Nat. Agric. Ind. Soc. Imp. Agric. Lyon, 2e Sér. 8:393-504.

Valenciennes, A. 1845. Voyage autour du monde sur la frégate Venus. Zoologie, 351 p.

Walbaum, J. J. 1792. Petri Artedi renovati. In Petri Artedi Sueci Genera piscium in quibus systema totum ichthyologiae proponitur cum classibus, ordinibus, generum characteribus, specierum differentiis, obser-vationibus plurimis, ichthyologiae. Part 3. Grypes-waldiae, 723 p.

Whitley, G. P. 1928. Studies in ichthyology, No. 2. Rec. Aust. Mus. 16(4):211-239.

_____. 1934. A new fish, reputed to be poisonous, from Queensland. Mem. Queensl. Mus. 10(4):175-179.

_____. 1937. Studies in ichthyology, No. 10. Rec. Aust. Mus. 20(1):3-24.

APPENDIX A

The following list of nominal species of _Lutjanus_ gives in order (1) the scientific name, as it originally appeared in alphabetical order according to the specific or subspecific name; (2) the author or authors (Cuvier and Valenciennes is abbreviated CV and Bloch and Schneider BS); (3) date of publication; (4) present identification (although identifications of species residing outside the Indo-west Pacific should be considered provisional pending formal revision); (5) general distribution code in parentheses: EP = eastern Pacific, IP = Indo-west Pacific, EA = eastern Atlantic, WA = western Atlantic

Species, Author, and Date	Present Identification	Distribution
Lutjanus acutirostris Desmarest, 1823	_L. apodus_	WA
Diacope adetii Castelnau, 1873	_L. adetii_	IP
Lutjanus agennes Bleeker, 1863b	_L. agennes_	EA
Diacope alboguttata Valenciennes (in CV), 1828	_L. rivulatus_	IP
Bodianus albostriatus BS, 1801	_L. apodus_	WA
Lutjanus altifrontalis Chan, 1970	_L. erythropterus_	IP
Genyoroge amabilis De Vis, 1885	_L. adetii_	IP
Mesoprion ambiguus Poey, 1860	_L. ambiguus_	WA
Diacope amboinensis Bleeker, 1852a	_L. boutton_	IP
Diacope analis Valenciennes (in CV), 1830	_L. fulvus_	IP
Mesoprion analis Cuvier (in CV), 1828	_L. analis_	WA
Diacope angulus Bennett, 1831	_L. notatus_	IP
Mesoprion annularis Cuvier (in CV), 1828	_L. erythropterus_	IP
Perca apoda Walbaum, 1792	_L. apodus_	WA
Mesoprion aratus Günther, 1864	_L. aratus_	EP

Sciaena argentata Gmelin,1789	L. argentimaculatus	IP
Mesoprion argenteus Hombron and Jacquinot,1853	L. fulvus	IP
Sciaena argentimaculatus Forsskål,1775	L. argentimaculatus	IP
Mesoprion argentiventris Peters,1869	L. argentiventris	EP
Lutjanus aubrieti Desmarest,1832	L. synagris	WA
Diacope aurantiaca Valenciennes (in CV),1830	L. fulvus	IP
Mesoprion aureovittatus Macleay,1879	L. fulviflamma	IP
Mesoprion auro-lineatus Cuvier (in CV),1830	L. fulviflamma	IP
Diacope axillaris Valenciennes (in CV),1830	L. gibbus	IP
Holocentrus bengalensis Bloch,1790	L. bengalensis	IP
Genyoroge bidens Macleay,1883	L. gibbus	IP
Serranus biguttatus Valenciennes (in CV),1830	L. biguttatus	IP
Diacope bitaeniatus Valenciennes (in CV),1830	L. bitaeniatus	IP
Lutjanus blackfordii Goode and Bean,1878	L. campechanus	WA
Lutjanus blochii Lacepède,1802	L. lutjanus	IP
Sciaena bohar Forsskål,1775	L. bohar	IP
Diacope borensis Cuvier (in CV),1828	L. gibbus	IP
Diacope bottonensis Cuvier (in CV),1828	L. boutton	IP
Holocentrus boutton Lacepède,1803	L. buccanella	WA
Mesoprion buccanella Cuvier (in CV),1828	L. buccanella	WA
Anthias caballerote BS,1801	L. griseus	WA
Diacope calveti Cuvier (in CV),1828	L. timorensis	IP
Mesoprion campechanus Poey,1860	L. campechanus	WA
Lutjanus campechianus Poey,1875	L. campechanus	WA
Mesoprion caroui Cuvier (in CV),1831	L. lutjanus	IP
Mesoprion carponotatus Richardson,1842	L. carponotatus	IP
Lutjanus castelnaui Whitley,1928	L. adetii	IP
Coius catus Hamilton 1822	L. johnii	IP
Mesoprion caudalis Valenciennes (in CV) 1830	L. lunulatus	IP

(Continued)

APPENDIX A (Cont.)

Species, Author, and Date	Present Identification	Distribution
Mesoprion caudanotatus Poey 1851	L. buccanella	WA
Sparus caxis BS 1801	L. apodus	WA
Mesoprion chirtah Cuvier (in CV) 1828	L. erythropterus	IP
Mesoprion chrysotaenia Bleeker 1851	L. carponotatus	IP
Diacope civis Valenciennes (in CV) 1831	L. sebae	IP
Lutjanus coatesi Whitley 1934	L. bohar	IP
Diacope coccinea Cuvier (in CV) 1828	L. gibbus	IP
Diacope coeruleo-lineata Rüppell 1838	L. coeruleolineata	IP
Diacope coeruleo-punctata Cuvier (in CV) 1828	L. rivulatus	IP
Diacope coeruleovittata Valenciennes (in CV) 1830	L. notatus	IP
Lutjanus colorado Jordan and Gilbert 1881	L. colorado	EP
Lutjanus comoriensis Fourmanoir 1957	L. gibbus	IP
Lutjanus cubera Poey 1871	L. cyanopterus	WA
Mesoprion cyanopterus Cuvier (in CV) 1828	L. cyanopterus	WA
Lutjanus cynodon Poey 1868	L. cyanopterus	WA
Mesoprion cynodon Cuvier (in CV) 1828	L. apodus	WA
Diacope decemlineata Valenciennes (in CV) 1830	L. quinquelineatus	IP
Mesoprion decussatus Cuvier 1828	L. decussatus	IP
Mesoprion dentatus Dumeril 1858	L. dentatus	EA
Mesoprion dodecacanthoides Bleeker 1854b	L. dodecacanthoides	IP
Mesoprion dodecacanthus Bleeker 1853	L. malabaricus	IP

Diacope duodecemlineata Valenciennes (in CV) 1830	L. notatus	IP
Lutjanus ehrenbergii Peters 1869	L. ehrenbergii	IP
Mesoprion elongatus Hombron and Jacquinot 1853	L. biguttatus	IP
Lobotes emarginatus Baird and Girard 1855	L. griseus	WA
Lutjanus endecacanthus Bleeker 1863b	L. endecacanthus	EA
Mesoprion enneacanthus Bleeker 1849	L. vitta	IP
Diacope erythrina Rüppell 1838	L. sanguineus	IP
Mesoprion erythrognathus Valenciennes (in CV) 1831	L. lutjanus	IP
Lutjanus erythropterus Bloch 1790	L. erythropterus	IP
Mesoprion etaape Lesson 1830	L. kasmira	IP
Lutjanus eutactus Bleeker 1863b	L. dentatus	EA
Bodianus fasciatus BS 1801	L. apodus	WA
Mesoprion flavescens Cuvier (in CV) 1828	L. apodus	WA
Diacope flavipes Valenciennes (in CV) 1830	L. fulvus	IP
Mesoprion flavipinis Cuvier (in CV) 1828	L. argentimaculatus	IP
Mesoprion flaviroseus De Vis 1884	L. bouton	IP
Mesoprion fulgens Valenciennes (in CV) 1830	L. fulgens	EA
Sciaena fulviflamma Forsskål 1775	L. fulviflamma	IP
Holocentrus fulvus BS 1801	L. fulvus	IP
Lutjanus furvicaudatus Fowler 1904	L. lemniscatus	IP
Mewsoprion fuscescens Valenciennes (in CV) 1830	L. fuscescens	IP
Mesoprion gaimardi Bleeker 1859	L. fulvus	IP
Mesoprion garretti Günther 1873	L. argentimaculatus	IP
Alphestes gembra Schneider (in BS) 1801	L. argentimaculatus	IP
Sciaena gibba Forsskål 1775	L. gibbus	IP
Mesoprion goldiei Macleay 1882	L. goldiei	IP
Mesoprion goreensis Valenciennes (in CV) 1830	L. goreensis	EA

(Continued)

APPENDIX A (Cont.)

Species, Author, and Date	Present Identification	Distribution
Genyoroge grammica Day 1870	L. quinquelineatus	IP
Mesoprion griseoides Guichenot 1862	L. argentimaculatus	IP
Labrus griseus Linneaus 1758	L. griseus	WA
Lutjanus guilcheri Fourmanoir 1959	L. guilcheri	IP
Lutjanus guineensis Bleeker 1863b	L. goreensis	EA
Mesoprion guttatus Steindachner 1869	L. guttatus	EP
Centropomus hober Lacepede 1803	L. fulviflamma	IP
Mesoprion hoteen Richardson 1846	L. fuscescens	IP
Diacope immaculata Cuvier (in CV) 1828	L. fulvus	IP
Mesoprion immaculatus Cuvier (in CV) 1828	L. lemniscatus	IP
Mesoprion inermis Peters 1869	L. inermis	EP
Mesoprion isodon Valenciennes (in CV) 1833	L. analis	WA
Mesoprion janthinuropterus Bleeker 1852b	L. lemniscatus	IP
Mesoprion janthinurus Bleeker 1854a	L. gibbus	IP
Anthias jocu BS 1801	L. jocu	WA
Anthias johnii Bloch 1792	L. johnii	IP
Lutjanus jongarah Day 1875	L. argentimaculatus	IP
Neomaensis jordani Gilbert 1897	L. jordani	EP
Mesoprion kagoshima Steindachner and Doederlein 1883	L. fulvus	IP
Sciaena kasmira Forsskal 1775	L. kasmira	IP
Diacope labuan Thiolliere (in Montrouzier) 1856	L. bohar'	IP

Species		Region
Serranus lemniscatus Valenciennes (in CV) 1828	L. lemniscatus	IP
Sparus lepisurus Lacepède 1802	L. bohar	IP
Mesoprion linea Cuvier (in CV) 1828	L. apodus	WA
Diacope lineata Quoy and Gaimard 1824	L. gibbus	IP
Diacope lineolata Rüppell 1829	L. lutjanus	IP
Lutjanus lioglossus Bleeker 1873	L. monostigma	IP
Mesoprion litura Cuvier (in CV) 1828	L. jocu	WA
Lutjanus longmani Whitley 1937	L. erythropterus	IP
Perca lunulata Park 1797	L. lunulatus	IP
Lutjanus lutjanus Bloch 1790	L. lutjanus	IP
Lutjanus luzonius Evermann and Seale 1906	L. boutton	IP
Genyoroge macleayana Ramsay 1884	L. erythropterus	IP
Mesoprion madras Valenciennes (in CV) 1831	L. madras	IP
Mesoprion mahogoni Cuvier (in CV) 1823	L. mahogoni	WA
Sparus malabaricus Schneider (in BS) 1801	L. malabaricus	IP
Lutjanus maltzani Steindachner 1882	L. fulgens	EA
Diacope marginata Cuvier (in CV) 1828	L. fulvus	IP
Lutjanus marginatoides Kendall and Goldsborough 1911	L. fulvus	IP
Mesoprion marginipinnis Macleay 1883	L. fulvus	IP
Mesoprion maus Thiollière (in Montrouzier) 1856	L. fulvus	IP
Lutjanus maxweberi Popta 1921	L. maxweberi	IP
Neomaenis megalopthalmus Evermann and Marsh 1900	L. synagris	WA
Rhomboplitoides megalops Fowler 1918	L. lutjanus	IP
Mesoprion melanospilos Bleeker 1852b	L. boutton	IP
Lutjanus melanotaenia Bleeker 1863	L. lemniscatus	IP

(Continued)

APPENDIX A (Cont.)

Species, Author, and Date	Present Identification	Distribution
Diacope melanura Rüppell 1838	L. gibbus	IP
Lutjanus mizenkoi Allen and Talbot, In press	L. mizenkoi	IP
Lutjanus modestus Bleeker 1863b	L. agennes	EA
Mesoprion monostigma Cuvier (in CV) 1828	L. monostigma	IP
Mesoprion myriaster Liénard 1839	L. rivulatus	IP
Genyoroge nigricauda De Vis 1885	L. fulvus	IP
Lutjanus nishikawae Smith and Pope 1906	L. russelli	IP
Diacope notatus Cuvier (in CV), 1828	L. notatus	IP
Serranus nouleny Valenciennes (in CV), 1828	L. lutjanus	IP
Lutjanus novemfasciatus Gill, 1862	L. novemfasciatus	EP
Lutjanus nukuhivae Seale, 1906	L. bohar	IP
Mesoprion obscurus Macleay, 1881	L. argentimaculatus	IP
Diacope octolineata Cuvier (in CV), 1828	L. bengalensis (in part)	IP
Lutjanus octolineatus Fourmanoir, 1957	L. notatus	IP
Diacope octovittata Cuvier (in CV), 1830	L. bengalensis	IP
Mesoprion ojanco Poey, 1860	L. ehrenbergii	IP
Lutjanus oligolepis Bleeker, 1873	L. ehrenbergii	IP
Mesoprion olivaceus Cuvier (in CV), 1828	L. argentimaculatus	IP
Mesoprion ophuysenii Bleeker, 1860	L. vitta	IP
Lutjanus orientalis Seale, 1909	L. russelli	IP
Mesoprion pacificus Bocourt, 1868	L. novemfasciatus	EP
Lutjanus paravitta Postel, 1966	L. adetii	IP
Mesoprion pargus Cuvier (in CV), 1828	L. cyanopterus	WA

Mesoprion parvidens Macleay,1883	L. rivulatus	IP
Serranus pavoninus Valenciennes (in CV),1828	L. johnii	IP
Neomaenis peru Nichols and Murphy,1922	L. peru	EP
Mesoprion phaiotaeniatus Bleeker,1849	L. vitta	IP
Mesoprion pomacanthus Bleeker,1855	L. bengalensis (in part)	IP
	L. kasmira (in part)	IP
Lutjanus prieto Jordan and Gilbert,1881	L. novemfasciatus	EP
Mesoprion profundus Poey,1860	L. vivanus	WA
Lutjanus purpureus Poey,1867	L. purpureus	WA
Diacope quadriguttata Cuvier (in CV),1828	L. bohar	IP
Mesoprion quadripunctatus Günther,1859	L. rivulatus	IP
Holocentrus quinquelinearis Bloch,1790	L. quinquelineatus	IP
Holocentrus quinquelineatus Bloch,1790	L. quinquelineatus	IP
Mesoprion rangus Cuvier (in CV),1828	L. bohar	IP
Genyoroge regia De Vis,1885	L. sebae	IP
Mesoprion retrospinis Valenciennes (in CV),1830	?	EA
Diacope revulina Swainson,1839	L. rivulatus	IP
Mesoprion ricardi Cuvier (in CV),1828	L. mahogoni	WA
Diacope rivulata Cuvier (in CV),1828	L. rivulatus	IP
Mesoprion rosaceus Poey,1870	L. analis	WA
Diacope rosea Valenciennes (in CV),1830	L. gibbus	IP
Mesoprion roseigaster Macleay,1881	L. argentimaculatus	IP
Mesoprion rubellus Cuvier (in CV),1828	L. erythropterus	IP
Mesoprion rubens Macleay,1882	L. bohar	IP
Diacope rufolineata Valenciennes (in CV),1828	L. boutton	IP
Mesoprion russelli Bleeker,1849	L. russelli	IP
Lutjanus salmonides Gilchrist and Thompson,1908	L. argentimaculatus	IP
Diacope sanguinea Cuvier (in CV),1828	L. sanguineus	IP

(Continued)

APPENDIX A (Cont.)

Species, Author, and Date	Present Identification	Distribution
Diacope sebae Cuvier (in CV), 1828	L. sebae	IP
Lutjanus semicinctus Quoy and Gaimard, 1824	L. semicinctus	IP
Mesoprion sexfasciatus Macleay, 1883	L. argentimaculatus	IP
Genyoroge notata var. Sexlineata Kent, 1893	L. quinquelineatus	IP
Diacope siamensis Valenciennes (in CV), 1830	L. sebae	IP
Diacope sinal Thiollière (in Montrouzier), 1857	L. rivulatus	IP
Mesoprion sobra Cuvier (in CV), 1828	L. analis	WA
Diacope spilura Bennett, 1832	L. quinquelineatus	IP
Lutjanus stearnsii Goode and Bean, 1878	L. griseus	WA
Lutjanus stellatus Akazaki, 1983	L. stellatus	IP
Diacope striata Cuvier (in CV), 1828	L. gibbus	IP
Bodianus striatus BS 1801	L. apodus	WA
Genyoroge notata var. sublineata De Vis,1885a	L. quinquelineatus	IP
Diacope superbus Castelnau,1878	L. argentimaculatus	IP
Sparus synagris Linnaeus,1758	L. synagris	WA
Mesoprion taeniops Valenciennes (in CV), 1830	L. argentimaculatus	IP
Lutjanus tahitiensis Seale,1906	L. gibbus	IP
Mesoprion terubuan Thiollière (in Montrouzier),1856	L. fulviflamma	IP
Sparus tetracanthus Bloch,1791	L. griseus	WA
Mesoprion therapon Day,1869	L. decussatus	IP
Diacope tiea Lesson,1830	L. gibbus	IP

Diacope timorensis Quoy and Gaimard,1824	L. timorensis	IP
Lutjanus torridus Cope,1871	L. vivanus	WA
Sparus tranquebaricus Shaw,1803	L. johnii	IP
Genyoroge unicolor Alleyne and Macleay,1877	L. adetii	IP
Lutjanus unimaculatus Quoy and Gaimard,1824	L. fulviflamma	IP
Mesoprion uninotatus Cuvier (in CV),1828	L. synagris	WA
Diacope vaigiensis Guoy and Gaimard,1824	L. fulvus	IP
Sparus vermicularis BS,1801	L. synagris	WA
Diacope viridis Valenciennes,1845	L. viridis	EP
Diacope vitianus Hombron and Jacquinot,1853	L. boutton	IP
Serranus vitta Quoy and Gaimard,1824	L. vitta	IP
Bodianus vivanet Lacepède,1803	L. griseus	WA
Mesoprion vivanus Cuvier (in CV),1828	L. vivanus	WA
Mesoprion xanthopterygius Bleeker,1849	L. lutjanus	IP
Diacope xanthopus Cuvier (in CV),1829	L. fulvus	IP
Diacope xanthozona Bleeker,1845	L. johnii	IP
Mesoprion yapilli Cuvier (in CV),1828	L. johnii	IP

PLATE 1
Eastern Pacific <u>Lutjanus</u> 1) <u>L</u>. <u>argentiventris</u>,
2) <u>L</u>. <u>aratus</u> (shallow water), 3) <u>L</u>. <u>aratus</u> (deep
water), 4) <u>L</u>. <u>colorado</u>, 5) <u>L</u>. <u>guttatus</u>, 6) <u>L</u>.
<u>jordani</u>, 7) <u>L</u>. <u>novemfasciatus</u>, 8) <u>L</u>. <u>peru</u>, 9) <u>L</u>.
<u>viridis</u>

PLATE 2
Indo-west Pacific _Lutjanus_ (1-5 are red snappers), 1) _L. erythroperus_, 2) _L. guilcheri_, 3) _L. malabaricus_, 4) _L. sanguineus_, 5) _L. timorensis_, 6) _L. gibbus_, 7) _L. bohar_

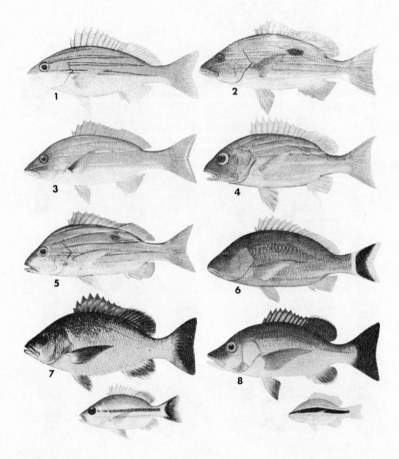

PLATE 3
Indo-west Pacific _Lutjanus_ (1-5 are blue-lined
snappers), 1) _L._ _bengalensis_, 2) _L._ _coeruleo-_
lineatus, 3) _L._ _kasmira_, 4) _L._ _notatus_, 5) _L._
quinquelineatus, 6) _L._ _lunulatus_, 7) _L._
bitaeniatus (juvenile below), 8) _L._ _lemniscatus_
(juvenile below)

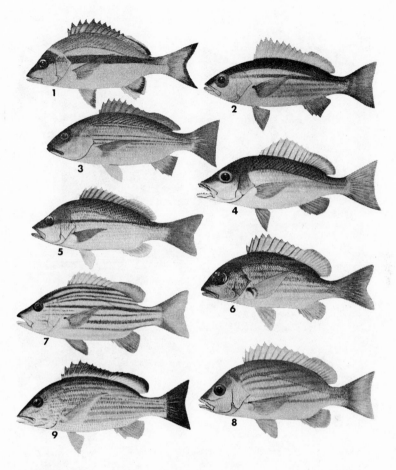

PLATE 4
Indo-west Pacific Lutjanus (1-5 are yellow-lined
snappers, 1) L. adetii, 2) L. lutjanus, 3) L.
madras, 4) L. mizenkoi, 5) L. vitta, 6) L.
boutton, 7) L. carponotatus, 8) L. dodecacan-
thoides, 9) L. fulvus

84

PLATE 5
Indo-west Pacific _Lutjanus_ (1-6 complete or partly inhabiting freshwater) 1) _L. argenti-maculatus_ (juvenile below), 2-4) _L. goldiei_ (adult color varieties), 5) _L. fuscescens_ (juvenile below), 6) _L. maxweberi_ (juvenile), 7) _L. rivulatus_, 8) _L. stellatus_, 9) _L. sebae_ (juvenile below)

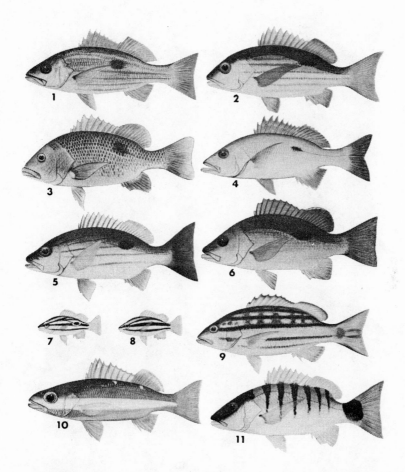

PLATE 6

Indo-west Pacific Lutjanus (1-8 are spotted
snappers), 1) L. enrenbergii, 2) L. fulviflamma,
3) L. johnii, 4) L. monostigma, 5) L. russelli
(Indian Ocean), 6) L. russelli (western
Pacific), 7-8) L. russelli (juveniles, western
Pacific), 9) L. decussatus, 10) L. bitaeniatus,
11) L. semicinctus

PLATE 7
West African (1-5) and western Atlantic Lutjanus (6-8 are red snappers), 1) L. agennes, 2)
L. dentatus 3) L. endecacanthus, 4) L. fulgens,
5) L. goreensis, 6) L. buccanella, 7) L. campechanus, 8) L. purpureus, 9) L. vivanus, 10) L.
ambiguus

PLATE 8
Western Atlantic _Lutjanus_, 1) L. _analis_, 2) L.
apodus, 3) L. _cyanopterus_, 4) L. _griseus_, 5) L.
jocu, 6) L. _mahogoni_, 7) L. _synagris_ (shallow
water), 8) L. _synagris_ (deep water)

3

A Preliminary Synopsis of the Groupers (Perciformes: Serranidae: Epinephelinae) of the Indo-Pacific Region

John E. Randall
Bernice Pauahi Bishop Museum
Honolulu, Hawaii 968617

ABSTRACT

The subfamily Epinephelinae (popularly known as groupers) of the family Serranidae consists of the following 11 genera in the Indo-Pacific region: Plectropomus, Saloptia, Cromileptes, Variola, Anyperodon, Aethaloperca, Gracila, Cephalopholis, Epinephelus, Dermatolepis, and "Trisotropis." Plectropomus contains 7 species, Variola 2 species, Gracila 2 species, Cephalopholis 19 species (plus 3 undescribed), and Epinephelus 63 species (plus 7 undescribed). The remaining genera are monotypic. Keys are provided for the genera with two or more species. A brief diagnosis and remarks are given for each species.

INTRODUCTION

The fishes of the serranid subfamily, Epinephelinae, popularly known as groupers, are among the most important benthic fishes of warm seas. They are of moderate to large size. Most are shallow-water species, but a few occur to depths as great as 300 m. All are carnivorous, feeding mainly on fishes, larger crustaceans, and occasionally on cephalopods. They are highly esteemed as food fishes, but some species, particularly those of the genera Plectropomus, Variola, Mycteroperca, and the larger species of Epinephelus, have frequently been implicated in ciguatera fish poisoning. Groupers are generally at or near the top of food chains of tropical and subtropical marine habitats and thus play a major role in the population structure of the animal communities of these environments.

In their volumes II and VI of "Histoire naturelle des poissons," Cuvier and Valenciennes (1828, 1830) were the first to review the serranid fishes of the world. Günther (1859) also attempted to include all the species of the family in his volume I of "Catalogue of the acanthopterygian fishes in the collection of the British Museum." He was followed by Boulenger (1895). Since Boulenger, systematic studies of the Serranidae have been restricted to certain geographical areas: (1) the Philippines by Fowler and Bean (1930); (2) Indonesia by Weber and de Beaufort (1931); (3) South Africa by Smith (1949); (4) the Marshall and Mariana Islands by Schultz in Schultz and collaborators (1953); (5) Japan by Katayama (1960); (6) the Seychelles by Smith and Smith (1963); (7) the Society Islands by Randall (1964); (8) the western Atlantic and eastern Pacific by Smith (1971); (9) Tanzania and Kenya by Morgans (1982); (10) the Red Sea by Randall and Ben-Tuvia (1983); and (11) the western Indian Ocean by Heemstra and Randall (1984).

Smith's (1971) review of the 35 American species of Epinephelus and allied genera appears to be definitive at the species level, though his broad generic classification might be questioned. Our knowledge of the systematics of Indo-Pacific species, however, is insufficient to complete a revision of the group in this vast region. The present review summarizes what is currently known of the classification of the Epinephelinae in the central and western Pacific and Indian Oceans.

The taxonomy of the Epinephelinae has been impeded by the paucity of museum specimens for many of the species. Some species are rare, particularly the larger ones. Most lots in museums consist of only one or two specimens. Also there has been a tendency by field workers to retain only small specimens of the larger species. This is due to the higher cost of larger specimens (if purchased from fishermen or markets), the difficulty in preserving big fishes, and the awareness that proper museum containers for storing large specimens may not be available. This results in a bias of data for proportional measurements that change with growth. The color of most groupers changes with age. Spotted species invariably have fewer and relatively larger spots when young. Some have markings that disappear with growth and vice versa.

The groupers are very generalized perciforms that can only be diagnosed collectively by a number of characters such as a large mouth with the maxilla exposed on the cheeks, 3 flat opercular spines, a single dorsal fin with 7-12 strong spines, and an anal fin with 3 stout spines and 7-10 soft rays.

In making counts of dorsal and anal rays, the last two rays are counted as one if their bases are adjacent and share the same pterygiophore. Pectoral-ray counts include the short, slender upper ray. Lateral-line scale counts are made from the upper end of the gill opening to the base of the caudal fin. Counts are also often made of the oblique scale rows just above the lateral line from the upper end of the gill opening to the caudal-fin base, hereinafter referred to as longitudinal scale series. Gill-raker counts include rudiments unless otherwise stated (fusion of rudimentary rakers may make their counts impossible, in which case only elevated rakers--i.e., those higher than their base--are counted); intercalary rakers (low rakers between the principal ones found in some species) are not counted; upper-limb gill-raker counts are given first; the raker at the angle is included in the lower-limb count. Standard length (SL) is taken from the front of the upper lip in the median plane to the midbase of the caudal fin (end of hypural plate). Adjustment in SL is made if the jaws are protruded. Body depth is the maximum depth but adjusted for malformation due to preservation or gross abdominal distention from very enlarged ovaries or a very full stomach. Head length is measured from the front of the upper lip to the posterior end of the opercular flap. In reference to the orientation of bands of color on specimens, bars are vertical markings and stripes are horizontal. The maximum length of a species given in remarks is the total length (TL) in centimeters. For many species this is an approximation.

When a distribution of a species is given below as Indo-Pacific, it implies a broad range from East Africa to at least French Polynesia. It may or may not include the Red Sea and Persian Gulf. Except for two species, it will not include the Hawaiian Islands.

The genera and species are presented alphabetically after the respective keys.

SUBFAMILY EPINEPHELINAE

Body robust to slightly elongate and somewhat compressed; mouth large, oblique, the lower jaw usually protruding, the maxilla fully exposed on cheek; a band of

small, slender, sharp, inwardly depressible teeth in jaws;
usually a few stout canine teeth anteriorly in jaws;
opercle with 3 flat spines; edge of preopercle serrate; a
single dorsal fin with VII–XI spines and 10–21 soft rays;
anal fin with III spines and 7–13 soft rays; pelvic rays
I,5; branched caudal rays usually 15; head and body fully
scaled; scales small, ctenoid or secondarily cycloid; a
single complete lateral line; branchiostegal rays 7;
vertebrae 24.

KEY TO THE INDO-PACIFIC GENERA OF EPINEPHELINAE

1a. Dorsal spines VIII; lower margin
     of preopercle with three strong
     antrorse spines 2
1b. Dorsal spines IX–XI; lower margin
     of preopercle without large antrorse
     spines (Epinephelus septemfasciatus
     with one to four moderate spines) 3

2a. Large canine teeth on side of lower
     jaw . . . . Plectropomus
2b. No large canine teeth on side of
     lower jaw . . . . Saloptia

3a. Dorsal spines X; dorsal profile of
     head strongly concave; posterior nostril
     a long vertical slit . . . . .Cromileptes
3b. Dorsal spines IX or XI; dorsal profile
     of head not concave; posterior nostril
     round or oblong 4

4a. Caudal fin lunate; developed gill
     rakers short . . . . Variola
4b. Caudal fin emarginate to rounded;
     developed gill rakers not short 5

5a. Palatine teeth absent; body depth
     3.3–3.7 in SL. . . . . Anyperodon
5b. Palatine teeth present; body depth
     2.1–3.7 in SL (rarely more than 3.3 in SL) 6

6a. Fifth or sixth pectoral rays longest;
     body depth 2.1–2.5 in SL; caudal fin
     truncate; dorsal spines IX . . . . Aethaloperca

6b. Middle pectoral rays longest; body depth
2.3-3.6 in SL (except the deep-bodied
Cephalopholis igarashiensis); caudal
fin emarginate to rounded (truncate in a
few species); dorsal spines IX or XI 7

7a. Dorsal spines IX 8
7b. Dorsal spines XI 9

8a. Caudal fin truncate to slightly
emarginate; head small, its length
contained 2.8-3.2 in SL . . . . Gracila
8b. Caudal fin rounded; head not small,
its length 2.3-2.8 in SL . . . . Cephalopholis

9a. Well-developed frontoparietal crests
on skull; body depth 2.3-2.8 in SL;
body strongly compressed; anal
soft rays 9-10 10
9b. Parietal crests not extending forward
onto frontal bones; body depth 2.5-3.7
in SL; body not strongly compressed;
anal soft rays 7-10 (usually 8) . . . . Epinephelus

10a. No canine teeth in jaws; scales with
greatly reduced ctenii, hence smooth
to the touch (except beneath pectoral
fins); dorsal profile of head straight
to slightly concave . . . . Dermatolepis
10b. Two short canine teeth on each side
anteriorly in jaws; scales ctenoid;
dorsal profile of head convex . . . . "Trisotropis"[1]

GENUS AETHALOPERCA FOWLER 1904

Diagnosis. Dorsal rays IX,17 or 18 (usually 18);
anal rays III,9 (rarely 8); pectoral rays 17 or 18
(usually 18); lateral-line scales 48-55; numerous small
platelets on side of first gill arch; body deep, the depth
2.1-2.5 in SL, and compressed, the width 2.25-2.8 in
depth; dorsal profile of head straight to eye, becoming
convex on nape; caudal fin truncate; fifth or sixth
pectoral rays longest; 1.5-1.6 in head; pelvic fins long,
extending beyond anus, 1.4-1.6 in head. Dark brown, often
with a whitish bar centered on abdomen.
Remarks. The genus is monotypic.

Aethaloperca rogaa (Forsskål 1775)

Diagnosis. See that of genus.
Remarks. Largest reported, 61 cm total length.
Ranges from the Red Sea and East Africa to the western
Pacific. A coral reef species often found in the vicinity
of caves.

GENUS ANYPERODON GÜNTHER 1859

Diagnosis. Dorsal rays XI,14-16; anal rays III,8-9;
pectoral rays 15-17; lateral-line scales 63-71; body
elongate, the depth 3.3-3.7 in SL; no palatine teeth; head
pointed, its length 2.4-2.5 in SL; caudal fin rounded.
Greenish gray with numerous orange-red spots smaller than
pupil on head, body, dorsal fin, and basally on caudal
fin; usually with two to four longitudinal whitish streaks
on head and body. Juveniles with blue and red stripes and
a blue-edged black spot or two spots at the caudal-fin
base.
Remarks. Monotypic.

Anyperodon leucogrammicus (Valenciennes 1828)

Diagnosis. See that of genus.
Remarks. Reported to attain 50 cm total length.
Ranges from the Red Sea and East Africa to the Phoenix and
Marshall Islands in the central Pacific. Serranus
urophthalmus Bleeker 1855 is a synonym based on the
juvenile stage.

GENUS CEPHALOPHOLIS SCHNEIDER 1801

Diagnosis. Dorsal rays IX,14-17; anal rays III,8-10
(rarely 10, 5 species with 8); pectoral rays 16-20, the
middle rays longest; no antrorse spines on ventral edge of
preopercle; body depth 2.3-3.2 in SL (except the deep-
bodied C. igarashiensis with a depth of 1.95-2.2 in SL);
membranes of spinous portion of dorsal fin moderately to
deeply incised; caudal fin rounded.
Remarks. Nineteen Indo-Pacific species are recognized in Cephalopholis, though C. igarashiensis is only
provisionally placed in the genus. Three species appear
to be undescribed: (1) a small reef grouper from the

Philippines allied to C. xanthoptera; (2) another reef
species from the Philippines and New Guinea; and (3)
Cephalopholis sp. of Allen (1985:figure 118).

KEY TO THE SPECIES OF CEPHALOPHOLIS

1a. Body very deep, the depth 2.0-2.3 in
    SL, and strongly compressed, the width
    2.5 to more in depth; lateral line
    strongly arched above pectoral fin;
    red with yellow bars, the pelvics
    tipped with black (young with a large
    black spot anteriorly in soft portion
    of dorsal fin) (central and western
    Pacific, in deep water) . . . . C. igarashiensis
1b. Body not deep, the depth 2.3-3.2 in SL,
    and not strongly compressed, the width <2.5
    in depth; lateral line not strongly arched
    above pectoral fin; color not as in 1a 2

2a. Anal soft rays 8; ground color brown
    to dark brown 3
2b. Anal soft rays 9 (rarely 10); ground
    color primarily red or reddish yellow
    (except C. argus) 7

3a. Numerous small dark spots (blue in life)
    on head and at least anteriorly on body 4
3b. No small dark spots on head or body 5

4a. Dorsal soft rays usually 16; dorsal
    spines short, the longest 3.25-3.65 in
    head; head, body, and fins with small,
    dark-edged blue spots in life; pectoral
    fins with a blackish posterior margin
    and a very broad, pale submarginal zone
    (orange in life) (Philippines, Indonesia,
    and northern Queensland) . . . . C. cyanostigma
4b. Dorsal soft rays usually 15; dorsal
    spines not short, the longest 2.7-3.2
    in head; head and anterior body with
    very small blue spots, none on rest
    of body or fins (except a few basally
    on pectorals of some specimens);
    pectoral fins brown without a dark
    margin and pale submarginal zone

(Philippines to Great Barrier Reef
and New Caledonia) . . . . **C. microprion**

5a. Pectoral fins short, 1.55–1.75 in head;
brown with narrow, dark blue stripes
on head, body, and fins (East Africa
to western Pacific) . . . . **C. formosa**

5b. Pectoral fins not short, 1.3–1.6 in
head; color not as in 5a 6

6a. Brown with eight slightly irregular,
dark brown bars on body and dark
brown bands radiating from eye; fins
dark brown, the caudal and portions of
the dorsal and anal fins with a narrow
bluish white margin (East Africa to
western Pacific) . . . . **C. boenack**

6b. Head and body uniform dark brown;
median and pelvic fins pale (bright
orange-yellow in life) except bases
of dorsal and anal, which are brown
like body (Indonesia, Solomon Islands,
and Great Barrier Reef) . . . . **C. xanthoptera**

7a. Dorsal soft rays 16 or 17; lower-limb
gill rakers 17–19; auxiliary scales
present on body; dark brown with
numerous black-edged blue spots on
head, body, and fins in life; 5 or 6
broad pale bars often present on
posterior half of body (Indo-Pacific) . . . **C. argus**

7b. Dorsal soft rays usually 14 or 15;
lower-limb gill rakers 13–16; auxiliary
scales not present on body; color not
as in 7a 8

8a. Ventral margin of preopercle serrate;
orange-red with widely scattered light
blue spots on body and fins in life,
and elongate spots or short lines on
head (Red Sea) . . . . **C. oligosticta**

8b. Ventral margin of preopercle smooth,
the edge fleshy; color not as in 8a 9

9a. Lateral-line scales 66–75; longitudinal scale series 122–140;
pectoral rays 18–20; body relatively

deep, the depth 2.3–2.75 in SL; red to
reddish brown in life (the young and
occasional large adults may be dark
brown) with widely scattered small
whitish blotches (Indian Ocean) or
numerous dark red to reddish brown
spots on body (Pacific) (East Africa
to central Pacific) . . . . <u>C</u>. <u>sonnerati</u>

9b. Lateral-line scales 46–68; longitudinal scale series 79–121;
pectoral rays 16–19 (rarely 19);
body depth 2.6–3.5 in SL; color not
as in 9a 10

10a. Lateral-line scales 54–68; caudal
fin darker than body 11
10b. Lateral-line scales 45–56; caudal
fin not darker than body (except
<u>C</u>. <u>hemistiktos</u>) 12

11a. Caudal fin blackish without white
bands; pectoral fins blackish
(Indian Ocean; absent from Red
Sea and Persian Gulf) . . . . <u>C</u>. <u>nigripinnis</u>
11b. Caudal fin blackish red centrobasally
in life, the corners broadly red,
each set off by a diagonal white band;
pectoral fins red basally, shading
to orange–yellow distally (central
and western Pacific) . . . . <u>C</u>. <u>urodeta</u>

12a. Longitudinal scale series 79–90; a
saddlelike, dark brown spot anteriorly on caudal peduncle separated
by a pale spot from a second, smaller,
dorsal, dark brown spot; a diagonal
dark streak on upper posterior part
of caudal fin (Indo–Pacific) . . . . . . <u>C</u>. <u>leopardus</u>
12b. Longitudinal scale series 90–121;
color not as in 12a 13

13a. Dorsal soft rays usually 14; caudal
fin and posterior part of dorsal
and anal fins blackish, darker than
body; numerous, small, dark-edged
blue spots on lower half of head
and body in life, very few on

upper half (Red Sea to Persian
Gulf) . . . . , . . . <u>C</u>. <u>hemistiktos</u>
13b. Dorsal soft rays usually 15; caudal
fin and posterior dorsal and anal
fins not blackish; small blue spots,
if present, uniformly distributed
on head and body 14

14a. Numerous, small, dark-edged blue
spots on head, body, and fins in life 15
14b. No blue spots present 16

15a. Dorsal spines relatively short,
the longest 3.2–3.5 in head; no
series of dark blotches along back
(Indo-Pacific) . . . . <u>C</u>. <u>miniata</u>
15b. Dorsal spines not short, the
longest 2.95–3.2 in head; a
series of six large, quadrangular,
dark brown blotches dorsally on
body (four along base of dorsal
fin and two on caudal peduncle)
(Indo-Pacific) . . . . <u>C</u>. <u>sexmaculata</u>

16a. Two rows of teeth on midside of
lower jaw; brownish yellow in
life with very small orange-red
dots on head, body, and median
fins (Indonesia) . . . . <u>C</u>. <u>miltostigma</u>
16b. Three to five rows of teeth on
midside of lower jaw; color not
as in 16a 17

17a. Subopercle and interopercle smooth
(rarely with a few small serrae
on interopercle); pelvic fins not
reaching anus, their length 1.9–2.1
in head; light red in life, mottled
with brownish red; caudal fin with
a bluish white posterior margin that
becomes submarginal as it approaches
upper and lower corners of fin (Indo-
Pacific, in moderate depths) . . . . . <u>C</u>. <u>spiloparaea</u>
17b. Subopercle and interopercle finely
serrate; pelvic fins usually reaching
anus, their length 1.8–1.9 in head;
orange-yellow to light orange-red

in life with red to orange-yellow
dots on head, dorsally on body, and
basally on dorsal fin; caudal fin
not colored as in 17a 18

18a. Anal fin pointed, the tip extending
posterior to a vertical at caudal fin
base; gill rakers 21-22; caudal fin
with a very narrow bluish white margin
that is not preceded by a black line
(western Pacific to Society Islands,
in deep water) . . . . *C. analis*
18b. Anal fin rounded (when fully spread),
not extending posterior to caudal
fin; gill rakers 24-26; caudal fin
with a narrow bluish white margin
(or it may be slightly submarginal
to orange ray tips) preceded by a
black line (western Indian Ocean,
in deep water) . . . . *C. aurantia*

Cephalopholis analis (Valenciennes 1828)

Diagnosis. Dorsal rays IX,14-15 (rarely 14); anal
rays III,8-9 (usually 9); pectoral rays 17-18; lateral-
line scales 48-53; scales in longitudinal series 95-109;
gill rakers 7-8 + 14-15; interopercle and subopercle
finely serrate; fleshy upper margin of operculum strongly
convex; body depth 2.55-2.85 in SL; anal fin pointed, the
tip extending posterior to a vertical at caudal-fin base;
pelvic fins reaching or nearly reaching anus, 1.75-2.05 in
head.

Orange-red to yellow with red to yellow dots on head,
nape, and basally on dorsal fin; a faint dark spot may be
present distally on posterior part of dorsal fin; a pale
bluish margin posteriorly on caudal fin and often on soft
portion of dorsal and anal fins (may persist as a dusky
edge on anal fin, hence the basis for the name analis).

Remarks. Largest specimen examined, 25 cm. A deepwater species known from Sumatra, Philippines, Ryukyu
Islands, Guam, and Tahiti. Bodianus indelebilis Fowler
1904 and C. obtusaurus Evermann and Seale 1907 are synonyms. Closely related to C. aurantia of the western
Indian Ocean. Illustrated in color as C. obtusaurus in
Masuda et al. (1984:plate 113, figure J).

Cephalopholis argus Schneider 1801

Diagnosis. Dorsal rays IX,15-17 (usually 16); anal rays III,9; pectoral rays 16-18 (usually 17, rarely 18); lateral-line scales 46-51; longitudinal scale series 95-110; auxiliary scales present; gill rakers 9-11 + 17-19; interopercle serrate and a few irregular serrae on subopercle; body depth 2.7-3.2 in SL; pectoral fins 1.6-2.05 in head; pelvic fins not reaching anus, 2.05-2.35 in head.

Dark brown with numerous black-edged blue spots on head, body, and fins; five or six broad pale bars often present posteriorly on body.

Remarks. Attains 50 cm. The most wide-ranging of the groupers, occurring from the northern Red Sea south to Natal and east to French Polynesia and the Pitcairn Group. Has been introduced to the Hawaiian Islands. About 80% of its food consists of fishes, the rest mainly crustaceans. Has caused ciguatera. The earliest name for this species is Bodianus guttatus Bloch 1790. Randall, Bauchot, Ben-Tuvia, and Heemstra (1985) have petitioned the International Commission of Zoological Nomenclature to suppress this name and conserve Cephalopholis argus.

Cephalopholis aurantia (Valenciennes 1828)

Diagnosis. Dorsal rays IX,14-15 (usually 15); anal rays III,9; pectoral rays 17-18 (usually 18); lateral-line scales 48-53; longitudinal scale series 103-117; gill rakers 8-9 + 16-17; subopercle and interopercle finely serrate; body depth 2.7-2.95 in SL; posterior part of anal fin just reaching a vertical at caudal fin base; pelvic fins reaching or nearly reaching anus, their length 1.8-1.9 in SL.

Orange-yellow to light orange-red with yellow to orange dots on head and anterodorsally to body; caudal fin with a narrow bluish white margin (though it may be submarginal to orange fin ray tips) and black submarginal line.

Remarks. Largest examined, 28.5 cm. Known from only a few specimens from Mauritius, Réunion, Seychelles, and East Africa, but doubtlessly more widespread. A deep-water species, generally found in over 100 m.

Cephalopholis boenack (Bloch 1790)

Diagnosis. Dorsal rays IX,15-17 (rarely 17); anal rays III,8; pectoral rays 16-18; lateral-line scales 47-51; longitudinal scale series 86-100; gill rakers 7-8 + 14-17; body depth 2.6-3.0 in SL; pectoral fins 1.3-1.6 in head; pelvic fins approaching or reaching anus, 1.6-2.1 in head.

Brown with eight slightly irregular, dark brown bars on body that are broader ventrally, and dark bands radiating from eye; a large black spot on opercular membrane between the two upper spines; fins dark brown, the distal margin of the caudal fin and soft portions of the dorsal and anal fins narrowly bluish white.

Remarks. One of the smallest of groupers; attains about 22 cm. Indian Ocean and western Pacific; generally found on dead reefs in protected waters. Serranus pachycentron Valenciennes 1828 and S. boelang Valenciennes 1828 are synonyms. Most authors have identified this species as Cephalopholis pachycentron.

Cephalopholis cyanostigma (Valenciennes 1828)

Diagnosis. Dorsal rays IX,16-17; anal rays III,8; pectoral rays 16-18 (rarely 18); lateral-line scales 47-49; longitudinal scale series 94-106; gill rakers 8-9 + 15-17; body depth 2.6-3.0 in SL; pectoral fins 1.6-1.8 in head; pelvic fins 1.75-2.1 in head.

Brown to reddish brown with numerous small blue spots on head, body, and fins, usually with pale bars or vertical rows of pale spots forming bars on body; caudal fin and soft portions of dorsal and anal fins darker than body, with light blue posterior margins.

Remarks. Reported to 35 cm. Known only from Philippines, Indonesia, southwest Thailand, New Guinea, New Ireland, and northern Queensland. Few specimens in collections. Cephalopholis kendalli Evermann and Seale 1907 is a synonym.

Cephalopholis formosa (Shaw 1804)

Diagnosis. Dorsal rays IX,15-17 (usually 16); anal rays III,8 (rarely 7); pectoral rays 16-18; lateral-line scales 47-52; longitudinal scale series 96-109; gill rakers 8-10 + 15-18; body depth 2.55-2.9 in SL; pectoral fins 1.55-1.75 in head; pelvic fins approaching or reaching anus, 1.75-1.95 in head.

Dark brown with slightly irregular, narrow, dark blue stripes on head, body, and fins (stripes may be lost on preserved specimens); a black spot on opercular membrane between upper two spines.

Remarks. Reaches about 33 cm. Indian Ocean (to about lat. 8° S on East African coast) to western Pacific, where it ranges from southern Japan to northern Queensland. Often misidentified as _C. boenack_ (Bloch 1790).

Cephalopholis hemistiktos (Rüppell 1830)

Diagnosis. Dorsal rays IX,14-15 (rarely 15); anal rays III,9; pectoral rays 16-18; lateral-line scales 47-52; longitudinal scale series 95-121; gill rakers 6-8 + 14-16; body depth 2.7-3.0 in SL; outer rear tips of soft portions of dorsal and anal fins extending posterior to a vertical at caudal-fin base; pelvic fins nearly or just reaching anus, their length 1.6-2.0 in head.

Dark brown to red (specimens from deeper water red) with dark-edged blue spots on lower half of head and body (those on thorax largest) and only a few on upper head and body; caudal fin and soft portions of dorsal and anal fins darker than body; pectoral fins brown, the outer margin broadly yellow.

Remarks. Largest examined, 32 cm. Red Sea to Persian Gulf; Day (1875) reported it (as _Serranus guttatus_) from the seas of India (hence probably Pakistan). Occurs in the depth range of 4-55 m. Red Sea individuals are smaller, have fewer scales in longitudinal series (96-104) compared to Oman and Persian Gulf specimens (109-121), and modally 17 instead of 18 pectoral rays.

Cephalopholis igarashiensis Katayama 1957

Diagnosis. Dorsal rays IX,14; anal rays III,9; pectoral rays 18; lateral-line scales 59-64; scales in longitudinal series 107-116; lateral line strongly arched above pectoral fins; body very deep, the depth 2.0-2.3 in SL, and compressed, the width 2.5 or more in depth.

Light red with yellow bars that become orange or orange-red ventrally, and broad yellow bands radiating from eye; pelvic fins distally edged in black. Young with

a large round black spot anteriorly in soft portion of
dorsal fin.

Remarks. Reaches 35 cm. A deepwater species known
from southern Japan to the South China Sea, with records
from Guam and Tahiti. Few specimens in museums.

Cephalopholis leopardus (Lacepède 1802)

Diagnosis. Dorsal rays IX,14-15 (rarely 15); anal
rays III,9-10 (rarely 10); pectoral rays 16-18; lateral-
line scales 46-53; longitudinal scale series 79-90; gill
rakers 7-8 + 14-16; body depth 2.5-2.9 in SL; pelvic fins
not reaching anus, 2.0-2.25 in head.

Reddish brown, shading to whitish ventrally, with
numerous red-orange spots (more evident on lower half of
head and body); a large, saddlelike, dark brown spot
anteriorly on caudal peduncle and a similar smaller spot
behind it; a diagonal red streak containing black pigment
on upper posterior part of caudal fin and a less distinct
one on lower part of fin.

Remarks. A small, secretive, coral-reef species.
Maximum length, 20 cm. Indo-Pacific, but absent from the
Red Sea and Persian Gulf. Cephalopholis urodelops Schultz
1943 is a synonym.

Cephalopholis microprion (Bleeker 1852)

Diagnosis. Dorsal rays IX,15; anal rays III,8;
pectoral rays 15-16 (usually 16); lateral-line scales 46-
50; longitudinal scale series 86-98; gill rakers 7-8 + 14-
17; body depth 2.5-2.8 in SL; pelvic fins approaching or
just reaching anus, 1.85-2.1 in head.

Dark brown, the basal half of scales darker than
outer half; numerous small, dark-edged, bright blue spots
on head and anteriorly on body; opercular flap dark brown;
fins dark brown, the median fins edged posteriorly with
dull blue; dark bars on body present or absent.

Remarks. A small species, the largest examined, 15.2
cm. Bishop Museum has specimens from the Philippines,
Indonesia, New Guinea, Solomon Islands, and Great Barrier
Reef; these were collected on reefs in the depth range of
2-23 m. Fourmanoir and Laboute (1976) recorded it (as C.
hemistiktos) from New Caledonia. Fowler and Bean (1930),
Weber and de Beaufort (1931), and Katayama (1960) all
regarded this species as a synonym of C. pachycentron (=

C. boenack); however, it is clearly distinct with blue
dots on its head and 15 dorsal soft rays.

Cephalopholis miltostigma (Bleeker 1874)

Diagnosis. Dorsal rays IX,15; anal rays III,9;
pectoral rays 18; lateral-line scales 48; longitudinal
scales series 99; body depth 2.9 in SL; median fins fleshy
at base; pelvic fins not reaching anus, 1.8 in head; 2
rows of teeth at middle of side of lower jaw, 5 to 6 rows
anteriorly.
Brownish yellow with very small orange-red spots on
head, body, and median fins; paired fins light yellow.
Remarks. Known only from the type specimen, 220 mm
total length, in the Rijksmuseum van Natuurlijke Historie
in Leiden. It was collected at Ambon, Indonesia.

Cephalopholis miniata (Forsskål 1775)

Diagnosis. Dorsal rays IX,14–15 (usually 15); anal
rays III,9; pectoral rays 17–18 (usually 18); lateral-line
scales 47–54; longitudinal scale rows 99–115; gill rakers
7–8 + 14–16; body depth 2.7–3.05 in SL; dorsal spines
short, the longest 3.25–3.5 in head; pelvic fins not
reaching anus, 1.9–2.3 in head.
Orange-red to reddish brown with numerous blue spots
(usually dark-edged), smaller than pupil, on head, body,
and median fins.
Remarks. Reported to 41 cm. A common coral-reef
species of the Indo-Pacific. Present in the Red Sea but
absent from the Persian Gulf. Cephalopholis formosanus
Tanaka 1911 and C. boninius Jordan and Thompson 1914 are
synonyms.

Cephalopholis nigripinnis (Valenciennes 1828)

Diagnosis. Dorsal rays IX,14–16 (nearly always 15);
anal rays III,9; pectoral rays 17–19 (usually 18);
lateral-line scales 54–68; longitudinal scale series 88–
109; gill rakers 8–9 + 15–17; body depth 2.7–3.2 in head;
pelvic fins not reaching anus, 1.85–2.1 in head.
Orange-red to brownish red with numerous, small,
orange-red spots on head (where most evident), dorsally on
body, and on median fins; two dark spots at tip of lower

jaw; caudal and pectoral fins dark brown (except specimens from deeper water, which do not have much dark pigment).

Remarks. Attains 28 cm. Indian Ocean, but absent from Red Sea and Persian Gulf. A coral-reef species known from the depth range of 5 to at least 40 m.

Cephalopholis oligosticta Randall and Ben-Tuvia 1983

Diagnosis. Dorsal rays IX,15; anal rays III,9; pectoral rays 16-18; lateral-line scales 60-71; longitudinal scale series 107-123; preopercular margin completely serrate and exposed (the ventral margin of other species fleshy, the bony edge smooth); body depth 2.6-3.0 in SL; longest dorsal spine 3.1-3.4 in head; pelvic fins nearly or just reaching anus, 1.6-1.95 in head.

Orange-red with a few light blue spots on head, body, and fins.

Remarks. Largest specimen, 27 cm. Known only from the Red Sea in the depth range of 24.5-43 m. Generally found in a dead reef environment with silty bottom.

Cephalopholis sexmaculata (Rüppell 1830)

Diagnosis. Dorsal rays IX,14-16; anal rays III,9; pectoral rays 16-18 (usually 17); lateral-line scales 49-56; longitudinal scale series 99-109; gill rakers 7-8 + 14-17; body depth 2.65-3.05 in SL; longest dorsal spine 2.95-3.2 SL; pelvic fins not reaching anus, 2.0-2.25 in head.

Orange-red with numerous small blue spots on head, body, and median fins (often with blue lines as well on head) and six large, squarish, blackish blotches on back, the first four extending basally onto dorsal fin, the last two on caudal peduncle; faint, double dark bars usually extending ventrally from each of the blackish spots at dorsal-fin base, and single bars from the peduncular spots.

Remarks. Largest examined, 47 cm. Indo-Pacific, including the Red Sea. A coral-reef species known from depths of <10 to 150 m; often found in caves. A good-eating fish. The oldest name for this species is Serranus zanana Valenciennes 1828; however, it has not been used (except in synonymy) since it was proposed. Randall, Bauchot, Ben-Tuvia, and Heemstra (1985) have petitioned the International Commission on Zoological Nomenclature to

suppress this name and conserve Cephalopholis sexmaculata.
Cephalopholis coatesi Whitley 1937 and C. gibbus Fourmanoir 1954 are synonyms.

Cephalopholis sonnerati (Valenciennes 1828)

Diagnosis. Dorsal rays IX,14-16 (usually 15); anal
rays III,9; pectoral rays 18-20 (usually 19); lateral-line
scales 66-76; longitudinal scale series 115-140; body
depth 2.3-2.75 in SL; nape of adults prominently convex;
median fins fleshy at their base; pectoral fins 1.45-1.7
in head; pelvic fins usually reaching or extending beyond
anus, 1.55-1.7 in head.

Body orange-red to reddish brown (juveniles may be
dark brown), often with scattered small whitish blotches;
head purplish to reddish brown with numerous close-set,
orange-red spots; fins usually darker than body, especially the caudal and posterior part of dorsal and anal
fins (Indian Ocean). In the Pacific, light reddish to
yellowish brown with numerous, small, brownish red spots
on head (where most close-set), body, and fins (spots
generally only basally on paired fins).

Remarks. Reported to 57 cm. East Africa to the
central Pacific (Marshall Islands and Gilbert Islands).
Adults usually found at depths >30 m and may be taken as
deep as 100 m. Epinephelus janthinopterus Bleeker 1874
and Cephalopholis purpureus Fourmanoir 1966 are synonyms.
The specimens from Onotoa, Gilbert Islands (Kiribati)
tentatively identified as C. hemistiktos by Randall (1955)
are C. sonnerati.

Cephalopholis spiloparaea (Valenciennes 1828)

Diagnosis. Dorsal rays IX,15-16 (rarely 16); anal
rays III,9 (rarely 10); pectoral rays 17-19 (rarely 19);
lateral-line scales 48-53; longitudinal scale series 87-
100; gill rakers 7-8 + 14-16; subopercle and interopercle
smooth or with a few serrae on interopercle; body depth
2.75-3.1 in SL; pelvic fins not reaching anus, their
length 1.9-2.1 in head.

Light red, mottled with darker red or brownish red;
caudal fin with a bluish white posterior margin that
becomes submarginal as it approaches corners; distal
margin of soft portions of dorsal and anal fins usually

pale bluish (often persisting as a dusky edge in preservative, especially on anal fin).

Remarks. Attains 22 cm. Ranges from East Africa to
French Polynesia and the Pitcairn Group. A common reef
species below depths of about 30 m. Specimens have been
taken in the depth range of 15-108 m. Misidentified as C.
analis (Valenciennes) by Heemstra and Randall in Fischer
and Bianchi 1984. Illustrated in color as C. aurantius in
Masuda et al. (1984:plate 113, figure I).

Cephalopholis urodeta (Schneider 1801)

Diagnosis. Dorsal rays IX,15; anal rays III,9;
pectoral rays 17-18; lateral-line scales 54-64; longitudinal scale rows 94-107; body depth 2.85-3.05 in SL;
pelvic fins approaching or just reaching anus, 1.9-2.05 in
head.

Reddish brown to brownish red, darker posteriorly,
with or without five faint, broad, dark bars on body;
very small brownish red spots may or may not be present on
head and body; two converging, diagonal white bands in
caudal fin, the area of fin proximal to bands dark reddish
brown, the broad corner zones distal to bands deep red;
median fins finely blotched with light orangish; broad
outer part of pectoral fins yellow.

Remarks. Largest collected, 23 cm. Western Pacific
to French Polynesia and the Pitcairn Group. A common
coral-reef species which has been taken from depths of 1-
35 m. Most closely related to C. nigripinnis of the
Indian Ocean. Serranus perguttatus De Vis 1883 is a
synonym. Most authors have called this fish C. urodelus;
however, Schneider in Bloch and Schneider (1801), after
Forster, first named it Percam urodetam. R. Melville
(Pers. com., Inter. Comm. on Zool. Nomenclature, 1984) has
advised the author that the correct combination with
Cephalopholis is urodeta.

Cephalopholis xanthoptera Allen and Starck 1975

Diagnosis. Dorsal rays IX,16; anal rays III,8;
pectoral rays 17; lateral-line scales 45-48; longitudinal
scale rows 95-100; body depth 2.8-2.9 in SL; pelvic fins
approaching or just reaching anus, 1.9-2.1 in head.

Head, body, and pectoral fins dark brown; remaining fins yellow except basal part of dorsal, which is dark brown like body.

Remarks. Probably the smallest species of the genus; largest examined, 14.2 cm. Described from eight specimens from the Solomon Islands, New Britain, Indonesia, and the Great Barrier Reef, from the depth range of 1.5-15 m. One was taken on a wreck in a silty bay and the others from coral reefs. Reported from the Philippines by Schroeder (1980:153, figure 142) as Cephalopholis sp.

GENUS CROMILEPTES SWAINSON 1839

Diagnosis. Dorsal rays X,17-19; anal rays III,10; pectoral rays 17-18; lateral-line scales 53-55; scales cycloid; dorsal profile of head markedly concave (anterior part of head to behind orbit small and pointed, the profile of nape rising steeply); body depth 2.6-3.0 in SL; no canine teeth; posterior nostril a large crescentic vertical slit; caudal fin rounded.

Light greenish gray with round black spots on head, body, and fins. The young with fewer and larger black spots.

Remarks. Monotypic.

Cromileptes altivelis (Valenciennes 1828)

Diagnosis. See that of genus.

Remarks. Maximum length about 70 cm. East Africa to the western Pacific. The young are sold in the aquarium trade as "panther fish."

GENUS DERMATOLEPIS GILL 1861

Diagnosis. Dorsal rays XI,17-20; anal rays III,9-10; pectoral rays 18-19; scales small, the ctenii greatly reduced, hence smooth to the touch (except beneath pectoral fins); canine teeth absent or very small; supra-occipital and parietal crests of skull continue forward onto frontal bones to interorbital space; body moderately deep, the depth 2.2-2.8 in SL, and compressed, the width 2.6-3.6 in depth; dorsal profile of head straight to slightly concave; third dorsal spine longest; caudal fin rounded to slightly emarginate.

Remarks. Three species known, one western Indian Ocean, one eastern Pacific, and one western Atlantic.

Dermatolepis striolatus (Playfair and Günther 1867)

Diagnosis. Dorsal rays XI,17-19; anal rays III,9-10; pectoral rays 18; scales smooth to touch; auxiliary scales present; no canine teeth; body deep, the depth 2.4-2.8 in SL, and compressed; caudal fin rounded to nearly truncate. Yellowish to reddish brown with small, round, dark spots on head, body, and fins. Juveniles with irregular pale blotches; many of the dark spots joined to form short horizontal streaks.

Remarks. Attains 85 cm. Western Indian Ocean from the Gulf of Oman to the Natal coast, including the Seychelles, Aldabra, and the Comoro Islands. Dermatolepis aldabrensis Smith 1955 is a synonym.

GENUS EPINEPHELUS BLOCH 1793

Diagnosis. Dorsal rays XI,12-19; anal rays III,7-10 (rarely 7 or 10; 3 species with 9); pectoral rays 15-20, the middle rays longest; parietal crests on skull not extending forward onto frontal bones; no antrorse spines on ventral edge of preopercle (E. septemfasciatus may have 1-4 ventrally directed spines); body depth 2.6-3.7 in SL; body not strongly compressed; membranes of spinous portion of dorsal fin varying from unindented to deeply incised; caudal fin rounded to slightly emarginate.

Remarks. Sixty-three named species are recognized herein in the genus Epinephelus from the Indo-Pacific region, including E. lanceolatus, which is usually classified in Promicrops. At least seven more remain to be described: one from the Gulf of Oman allied to E. chlorostigma is known from photos sent by Gabriella Bianchi (no specimens retained); another allied to chlorostigma but with 66-68 lateral-line scales (the Epinephelus sp. of the following key); two from northwestern Australia (Epinephelus sp. of Gloerfelt-Tarp and Kailola, 1984 and one being described by Last, Randall, and Whitelaw); one from 130 m at Dillon Shoals, Timor Sea; Epinephelus sp. of Okamura et al. (1982), a single specimen, 95 cm SL, taken in over 360 m from the Kyushu-Palau Ridge east of the Philippines; and a yellow-spotted species with slightly emarginate caudal fin from deep water off Fiji, Samoa Islands, and Phoenix Islands. A few nominal Bleeker species of Epinephelus from Indonesian waters now in synonymy need to be reexamined. Serranus lebretonianus Hombron and Jacquinot (1853) was described from a single specimen 24.8 cm SL from an unknown locality. It represents a valid species unique in possessing 17 dorsal soft rays, 20 pectoral rays, and 73 lateral-line scales. Additional descriptive data are given by Bauchot et al. (1984). The voyage to the South Pole by the corvettes l'Astrolabe and la Zélée, resulting in the collection of this specimen, went to all southern oceans.

KEY TO THE INDO-PACIFIC SPECIES OF EPINEPHELUS

1a. Caudal fin emarginate to truncate, at least in adults (fin may be slightly rounded when spread) 2
1b. Caudal fin rounded[2]. 13

2a. Membranes of spinous portion of dorsal fin not incised 3
2b. Membranes of spinous portion of dorsal fin incised 7

3a. Gill rakers 12-14 + 20-22; dorsal soft rays 17-19; purplish to brownish gray with yellowish brown dots on head and wavy longitudinal brown lines on upper two-thirds of body (lines disappear on large adults) (western Pacific to Indian Ocean) . . . . undulosus
3b. Gill rakers 6-11 + 13-18; dorsal soft rays 15-17; color not as in 3a 4

4a. Second dorsal spine of adults prolonged, its length 1.85-2.4 in head; upper-limb gill rakers 6 or 7 (one at angle not included in count); three rows of teeth on midside of lower jaw; body depth 2.7-3.2 in SL; reddish brown with a white dot on each scale; a broad, deep red margin on spinous portion of dorsal fin (Marquesas Islands and Marcus Island) . . . . . . irroratus
4b. Second dorsal spine not prolonged (3rd or 4th spines longest); upper-limb gill

rakers 8-11; 2 rows of teeth on midside
of lower jaw; body depth 2.4-2.8 in SL;
color not as in 4a 5

5a. Color in life deep blue without black
     spots, the caudal peduncle (at least
     posteriorly) and fins bright yellow
     (large adults may lose yellow colora-
     tion) (Indian Ocean) . . . . flavocaeruleus
5b. Color not as in 5a (numerous dark
     or whitish spots present) 6

6a. Dark purplish gray with scattered
     whitish blotches and/or numerous
     small dark spots (dark spots, if
     present, generally confined to
     lower half of head and body); serrae
     at corner of preopercle not enlarged
     or only slightly enlarged (Indian
     Ocean) . . . . multinotatus
6b. Light bluish gray with numerous
     blackish dots on head, body, median
     and pelvic fins (large adults
     developing, in addition, scattered
     irregular blackish blotches, most
     of which are smaller than pupil);
     serrae at corner of preopercle
     moderately enlarged (central to
     western Pacific) . . . . cyanopodus

7a. Lateral-line scales 48-54; body
     depth 2.9-3.4 in SL; corner of pre-
     opercle without enlarged serrae 8
7b. Lateral-line scales 58-76; body
     depth 2.6-3.1 in SL; corner of
     preopercle with moderately
     enlarged serrae 10

8a. Brownish gray with numerous small
     yellow spots; lower two-thirds of
     caudal fin blackish (India to the
     Philippines) . . . . bleekeri
8b. Pale with numerous, close-set, dark
     brown spots on head, body, and fins,
     the caudal with a white posterior
     margin 9

9a. Anal fin rounded to slightly
angular, the longest rays 2.0–2.6
in head; dorsal soft rays usually
16; pectoral fins relatively long,
1.6–1.8 in head; lower-limb gill
rakers 14–16 usually 15 (Red Sea
and East Africa to the western
Pacific) . . . . __areolatus__

9b. Anal fin angular, the longest rays
1.85–2.3 in head; dorsal soft rays
usually 17; pectoral fins not long,
1.70–2.0 in head; lower-limb gill
rakers 15–18, usually 16 or 17 (Red
Sea and East Africa to the western
Pacific) . . . . __chlorostigma__

10a. Anal soft rays 9; posterior
nostrils of adults three to four
times larger than anterior;
grayish brown with indistinct
dark blotches on back (no small
dark spots or dark bars) (Kenya to
South Africa) . . . . __chabaudi__

10b. Anal soft rays 8; nostrils subequal;
color not as in 10a 11

11a. Dorsal soft rays 14; lateral-line
scales 56–64; upper three-fourths
of body and postorbital head with
well-separated, small, dark brown
spots; a prominent dark brown
streak on upper edge of maxillary
groove; triangular outer part of
interspinous membrane of dorsal fin
orange-yellow (southern Mozambique
and east coast of South Africa) . . . __albomarginatus__

11b. Dorsal soft rays 16–17; lateral-
line scales 64–76; color not as
in 11a (brown spots, if present,
very close-set) 12

12a. Head, body, and fins with numerous,
very close-set, mainly polygonal,
dark brown spots; outer triangular
part of interspinous membranes of
dorsal fin not deep red or black;
pectoral rays 18 (rarely 19); 2

rows of teeth on midside of lower
jaw; small scales present on maxilla
(Gulf of Aden to India) . . . . undescribed species

12b. Head, body, and fins without dark
spots; outer triangular part of
interspinous membranes of dorsal
fin deep red or black; pectoral rays
19 (rarely 20); 3 rows of teeth
on midside of lower jaw; no small
scales on maxilla (Indo-Pacific,
usually in moderately deep water) . . . . . <u>retouti</u>

13a. Anal soft rays 9 (rarely 8 or 10) 14
13b. Anal soft rays 8 (rarely 7 or 9) 16

14a. Scales cycloid and embedded, the
longitudinal series about 95; dorsal
soft rays 16; nostrils subequal;
lower-limb gill rakers 9-10; pale
with numerous, close-set, reddish
brown spots on head and body;
spinous portion or dorsal fin with
slightly diagonal, narrow, alternating stripes of dark brown and white
(Madagascar, Mozambique, and Natal) . . . . <u>posteli</u>
14b. Scales ctenoid and not embedded, the
longitudinal series 107-139; dorsal
soft rays usually 14 or 15; posterior
nostrils of adults notably larger
than anterior; lower-limb gill rakers
14-18; color not as in 14a 15

15a. One to four spines on lower margin
of preopercle separated from the
enlarged spinules of the preopercular
angle; longitudinal scale series
107-116; suborbital depth 9.4-12.2
in head; brown with 7 or 8 broad
dark bars on body, the one on caudal
peduncle broadest and darkest,
especially dorsally (dark bars lost
on large individuals) (western
Pacific and Indian Ocean, in deep
water) . . . . <u>septemfasciatus</u>
15b. No spines on lower margin of pre-
opercle; longitudinal scale series
122-139; suborbital depth 7.5-9.2

in head; dark brown, the young and
sometimes small adults with vertical
rows of white spots on body (Hawaiian
Islands, in deep water) . . . . quernus

16a. Dorsal soft rays 12–13; young with
two broad, longitudinal, black-edged,
whitish bands that disappear in adults,
the dark edges in adults breaking into
dashes and spots (Red Sea to southern
Japan) . . . . latifasciatus

16b. Dorsal soft rays 14–18; color not as
in 16a 17

17a. Lateral-line scales with branched tubules;
eyes very small, varying from about 8 in
head of 20-cm SL individuals to about 9
for 35-cm ones and 13 for 145-cm fish;
maximum total length about 270 cm (Indo-
Pacific) . . . . lanceolatus

17b. Lateral-line scales with a single tubule
(except large E. malabaricus and E.
suillus); eye not very small, <7 in head
for 200-mm individuals and <8 for 35-cm
ones; maximum total length <150 cm 18

18a. Discrete dark spots on head and all of
body (spots brownish red to black in
life, persisting in preservative) 19

18b. No dark spots on head and all of body
(there may be yellow or orange spots
but these usually do not persist in
preservative) 41

19a. Lateral-line scales 46–53 20

19b. Lateral-line scales 55–74 (except
E. fuscoguttatus with 52–58) 29

20a. Scales cycloid, at least on adults
(may be ctenoid beneath pectoral
fin) 21

20b. Scales of body largely ctenoid 23

21a. Dorsal profile of anterior head
nearly straight; numerous, small,
close-set, dark spots on head, body,
and median and pelvic fins;

brownish red in life; no blackish
streak at upper edge of maxillary
groove; three or four prominent
black spots dorsally on body, the
first (and largest) at base of
middle of dorsal fin, the last on
caudal peduncle (southern Japan to
China) . . . . **trimaculatus**

21b. Dorsal profile of head convex; spots
on head, body, and fins dark brown
in life; a blackish streak at upper
edge of maxillary groove; three or
four prominent black spots dorsally
on body present or absent 22

22a. Dark spots present on pectoral fins,
progressively smaller distally;
dorsal soft rays usually 17; pelvic
fins short, 2.2–2.65 in head (India,
Sri Lanka, and Indonesia) . . . . **faveatus**

22b. No dark spots on pectoral fins or
present only basally; dorsal soft
rays usually 16; pelvic fins not
short, 1.85–2.35 in head (at standard
lengths <25 cm) (Indo-Pacific) . . . . . **macrospilos**

23a. Pectoral rays 18–19 (usually 19);
five, near-vertical, dark bars on body,
the edges with small black spots
(Taiwan to Indonesia, Fiji, and
western Australia) . . . . **amblycephalus**

23b. Pectoral rays 16–18; no dark bars
on body (dark spots numerous, but
not arranged in vertical rows) 24

24a. Longitudinal scale series 86–96;
pectoral fins relatively long,
1.2–1.5 in head; two diagonal dark
bands on thorax anterior to pectoral-
fin base (uppermost band may consist
of two elongate dark spots) (western
Pacific to southwest coast of Thailand) . . . **quoyanus**

24b. Longitudinal scale series 94–118;
pectoral fins 1.5–1.9 in head; no
diagonal dark bands on thorax 25

25a. Dark spots on body diagonally
elongate and much more numerous
posteriorly; dark spots on head
scattered, separated by more than
two-spot diameters (Indonesia and
Indian Ocean) . . . . **longispinis**
25b. Dark spots on body not diagonally
elongate and not more numerous
posteriorly; dark spots on head
close-set, separated by less than
a spot diameter 26

26a. Longest dorsal spine 2.3-2.5 in
head 27
26b. Longest dorsal spine 2.7-3.3 in
head 28

27a. Maxilla reaching beyond a vertical
at posterior edge of orbit; longitudinal scale series 103-120; dorsal
soft rays usually 16; spots on body
brown to black, about size of pupil;
pectoral fins of adults with more
than 15 dark spots (central and
western Pacific) . . . . **maculatus**
27b. Maxilla not reaching a vertical at
posterior edge of orbit; longitudinal scales series 92-108; dorsal
soft rays usually 17; spots on body
yellowish brown, much smaller than
pupil; pectoral fins of adults with
10-15 large black spots (Samoa and
Gilbert Islands to East Africa) . . . . . . **miliaris**

28a. Dorsal soft rays 15-17 (usually 16);
gill rakers 21-24; no black, saddlelike spot on caudal peduncle; spots
on body dark brown, larger than pupil,
round to hexagonal, and close-set
(some merging to form short bands)
(Indo-Pacific) . . . . **merra**
28b. Dorsal soft rays 14-15; gill rakers
24-27; a black, saddlelike spot
dorsally on caudal peduncle; numerous
very small, blackish spots on body
superimposed on a pattern of large
brown blotches (Indo-Pacific) . . . . **microdon**

29a. Most dark spots on body polygonal
and very close-set, only narrow
pale lines or white dots separating
individual spots 30
29b. Most dark spots on body round or
oblong and well-separated 32

30a. Second anal spine relatively long,
2.1-2.35 in head; longest dorsal
spine 2.55-2.9 in head; dorsal soft
rays usually 16; polygonal dark spots
of head and body merging or tending
to merge on sides, separated mainly
by white dots at angular corners of
spots; a large yellow-brown spot
behind eye, sometimes linked to but
usually separate from another horizontally elongate spot of the same
color on opercle (Indo-Pacific) . . . . **hexagonatus**
30b. Second anal spine not long, 2.5-
3.55 in head; longest dorsal spine
3.0-3.5 in head; dorsal soft rays
usually 15, polygonal dark spots of
head and body fully separated by a
network of pale lines; no large
yellow-brown spot behind eye or
on opercle 31

31a. A single large black spot on back
at rear base of spinous portion
of dorsal fin; no black spot
dorsally on caudal peduncle; dark
spots anteriorly on head about half
diameter of pupil or larger; gill
rakers 25-28 (East Africa to the
Line Islands and Phoenix Islands) . . . **melanostigma**
31b. Three or four large black spots
(or groups of spots much darker
than others, thus appearing as
large spots) along base of dorsal
fin; a saddlelike black spot (or
a partial merging of black spots)
dorsally on caudal peduncle; very
small dark brown to black spots
anteriorly on head (the spots much
smaller than half pupil diameter);

gill rakers 23-26 (East Africa to
the Line Islands) . . . . _spilotoceps_

32a. Longitudinal scale series 82-86;
dorsal soft rays 16-17; spots on
body small, scattered, many horizontally elongate; three longitudinal rows of diagonally elongate
dark spots in spinous portion of
dorsal fin (Indonesia to Taiwan) . . . . . _bontoides_
32b. Longitudinal scale series 97-135;
dorsal soft rays 14-16; dark spots
on body small to large, scattered
or close-set, but not horizontally
elongate; no rows of diagonally
elongate dark spots in dorsal fin 33

33a. Lateral-line scales 52-65 34
33b. Lateral-line scales 65-74 38

34a. Gill rakers 29-31; posterior
nostril subtriangular, more than 4
times larger than anterior nostril
in large adults; body depth 2.6-3.1
in SL; light yellowish brown with
large, irregular, dark brown spots
on head and body and numerous,
small, close-set, dark brown spots
on head, body, and fins; a saddlelike
black spot on caudal peduncle (Indo-
Pacific) . . . . _fuscoguttatus_
34b. Gill rakers 23-29; nostrils sub-
equal; body depth 2.7-3.7 in SL;
dark spots on head and body not
very small and not close-set; no black
spot dorsally on caudal peduncle 35

35a. Maxilla naked; no dark spots on
anal or paired fins and few on
caudal fin; two diagonal rows of
dark spots on head from eye to
above pectoral base (East Africa
to New Caledonia, in deep water) . . . . _magniscuttis_
35b. Maxilla with tiny scales; fins
with dark spots; dark spots on
head not arranged in two diagonal
rows from eye to above pectoral base 36

36a. Pectoral fins 1.5–1.75 in head; no
small platelets on side of first
gill arch; posterior nostril of
adults vertically elongate, its
length two to three times longer
than diameter of anterior nostril;
body depth 2.7–3.2 in SL; more than
two rows of teeth on midside of
lower jaw of adults; no obvious
dark bars on body (a large dusky
to blackish spot containing two
or more black spots on back below
rear of spinous dorsal fin and two
lesser dusky spots at base of soft
portion of fin); maximum length 32
cm (Indonesia and the Philippines) . . . <u>corallicola</u>

36b. Pectoral fins 1.75–2.25 in head;
small platelets on side of first gill
arch; posterior nostril round and not
enlarged; body depth 3.1–4.0 in SL;
two to five rows of teeth on midside
of lower jaw; body with five diagonal
dark bars (may be broken, sometimes
faint) that bifurcate ventrally;
maximum length at least 100 cm 37

37a. Spots on head and body black and
small (smaller at any given size
than the dark spots of <u>suillus</u>);
scattered, small, roundish, pale
spots (larger than black spots)
usually present on head and body;
pectoral rays modally 19; large
adults with 4 or 5 rows of teeth
on midside of lower jaw (Red Sea
and coast of East Africa to
western Pacific) . . . . <u>malabaricus</u>

37b. Spots on head and body brownish
orange and moderate in size; no
small pale spots on head and body;
pectoral rays modally 20; large
adults with 2 or 3 rows of teeth on
midside of lower jaw (East Africa
to western Pacific) . . . . <u>suillus</u>

38a. Longitudinal scale series 117–135;
five longitudinal rows of large dark

120

brown to black spots on body, those
in upper 3 or 4 rows larger than
eye; reaches 150 cm (East Africa to
western Pacific) . . . . tukula
38b. Longitudinal scale series 97–110;
dark spots smaller than eye; not
exceeding 100 cm 39

39a. Two rows of teeth on midside of lower
jaw; interorbital space moderately
convex; head with three, diagonal,
narrow, dark brown bands from behind
and below eye to end of operculum,
with only a few dark spots posteriorly
(southern Mozambique and east coast
of South Africa) . . . . andersoni
39b. Three or more rows of teeth on
midside of lower jaw; interorbital
space flat to slightly convex; head
with numerous small dark spots and
no dark bands 40

40a. Pelvic fins not short, 1.85–2.1 in
head; dorsal spines not short, the
longest 2.65–3.3 in head; dark spots
on body small and very close-set,
those posteriorly becoming confluent
to form irregular, horizontal, dark
bands; caudal fin and soft portions
of dorsal and anal fins dark brown
with small white spots (French
Polynesia and the Pitcairn Group to
the Marshall and Samoa Islands) . . . . . . socialis
40b. Pelvic fins short, 2.3–3.0 in head;
dorsal spines short, the longest
3.15–4.6 in head; dark spots on body
not very small and close-set; fins
pale with brown spots (Indo–Pacific) . . . . tauvina

41a. Membranes of spinous portion of
dorsal fin not incised; solid brown
or with a coarse dark brown reticular
pattern; one or two dark streaks on
cheek and operculum, the lowermost
from lower edge of eye to just above

corner of preopercle (East Indies to
Pakistan) . . . . __townsendi__

41b. Membranes of spinous portion of dorsal
fin incised; color not as in 41a (__E.__
__heniochus__ is light brown with two
diagonal brown streaks on cheek and
operculum but the lowermost extends
posteriorly from mouth) 42

42a. Body with four to six, slightly diagonal,
broad, dark bars that reach ventrally
(bars may be faint on large adults of
__E. bruneus, E. fasciatomaculatus,__ and
__E. rivulatus__) 43

42b. Body without dark bars (irregular dark
bands may be present on __E. damelii,__
__E. radiatus,__ and __E. caeruleopunctatus,__
but they are more diagonal--closer to
45°--than vertical) 50

43a. Corner of preopercle with one to five
greatly enlarged serrae (at least
twice as long as those above corner) 44

43b. Corner of preopercle with only slightly
to moderately enlarged serrae 46

44a. Longitudinal scale series 84-86;
lateral-line scales 46-51; dorsal
soft rays 14-16 (usually 15);
small blackish spots on median
fins (northern Australia,
Indonesia, Southeast Asia, and
the Philippines) . . . . __sexfasciatus__

44b. Longitudinal scale series 98-
120; lateral-line scales 50-60;
dorsal soft rays 15-17 (usually
16); no blackish spots on median
fins 45

45a. Maxilla scaled; lateral-line scales
53-60; longest dorsal spine 3.0-3.5
in head; no yellow spots on head
and body; no yellow margin on median
fins (Sri Lanka to Oman) . . . . __diacanthus__

45b. Maxilla naked; lateral-line scales
49-55; longest dorsal spine 2.35-
3.0 in head; small yellow spots on

head and body; dorsal and caudal
fins with a yellow margin (Japan
to South China Sea) . . . . **awoara**

46a. Lateral-line scales 64-67; dorsal
soft rays 14-15; body with six,
irregular, somewhat diagonal, brown
bars that contain large pale spots
or bars, the first on nape passing
to eye (bars faint in large adults,
which may be nearly uniform dark
brown); triangular outer portion
of interspinous membranes of dorsal
fin yellow or orange (southern Japan
to South China Sea) . . . . **bruneus**
46b. Lateral-line scales 48-58; dorsal
soft rays 15-17 (usually 16); color
not as in 46a 47

47a. Color pattern a combination of
brown bars and brownish yellow or
dark reddish brown spots 48
47b. No brownish yellow or dark reddish
brown spots 49

48a. Dorsal soft rays 15-17 (usually 16);
gill rakers 23-24; scales on body
largely ctenoid; six, slightly diagonal,
brown bars on body (the first on nape,
the last on caudal peduncle) that tend
to bifurcate ventrally, the second and
third bars more darkly pigmented (bars
faint in large adults), second to fourth
bars extending well into dorsal fin,
the first two bars black in young; head
and body with small brownish yellow
or orange spots (often not persisting
in preservative) (southern Japan to
Vietnam) . . . . **fasciatomaculatus**
48b. Dorsal soft rays 16-18 (usually 17);
gill rakers 19-22; scales on body
largely cycloid; four, broad, dark
brown bars on body, the first below
rear of spinous portion of dorsal
fin, the second and third close
together below soft portion of

dorsal, the last on caudal peduncle;
head and anterior half to two-thirds
of body with numerous dark reddish
brown spots smaller than pupil (Red
Sea to Gulf of Oman) . . . . stoliczkae

49a. Scales on nape and dorsoanteriorly on
body not very small; longitudinal
scale series 92-135; dorsal soft rays
15-17 (usually 16); outer triangular
part of interspinous membranes of
dorsal fin black (red on specimens from
deep water); orbit with a prominent dark
brown edge (except anteriorly); scales
without a pale dot (though scattered
small whitish spots often present on
body) (Indo-Pacific) . . . . fasciatus
49b. Scales on nape and anteriorly on body
above lateral line very small; longitudinal scale series 86-102; dorsal
soft rays 16-18 (usually 17); outer
triangular part of interspinous membranes of dorsal fin not black; orbit
without a prominent dark brown edge;
scales of body with a whitish dot (may
not persist in preservative) (Indian
Ocean and western Pacific) . . . . rivulatus

50a. Whitish spots (red to orange in life
in E. akaara) and/or blotches present
on body (may be lost in preservative,
particularly on E. damelii, E. guaza,
and adults of E. polystigma) 51
50b. No whitish spots or blotches on body 57

51a. Lateral-line scales 48-62 52
51b. Lateral-line scales 66-73 56

52a. Teeth on midside of lower jaw in two
or three rows; posterior nostrils not
enlarged (except large adults of
polystigma) 53
52b. Teeth on midside of lower jaw in three
to five rows; posterior nostrils of
adults vertically elongate and enlarged,
two times or more larger than anterior 55

53a. Dorsal soft rays usually 16; pectoral rays
17-19; spots on head and body red-
orange in life, about as large as pupil;
median fins without a narrow white or
orange-red margin; no conspicuous black
streak in maxillary groove (southern
Japan, Korea, and China) . . . . <u>akaara</u>

53b. Dorsal soft rays usually 15; pectoral
rays 15-18; spots on head and body
white in life, smaller than pupil;
posterior margin of median fins with a
narrow white or orange-red margin; a
blackish streak in upper part of
maxillary groove 54

54a. Pectoral rays 15-17 (rarely 17);
lower-limb gill rakers 15-17;
longitudinal scale series 90-109;
snout not short, 4.2-4.75 in head;
body with small white spots that
merge in adults to form irregular
longitudinal bands; median fins
with a narrow, white margin posteriorly and a broad, blackish submarginal band; pectoral fins without
a narrow, pale posterior margin
(Caroline Islands and western
Pacific to western Indian Ocean) . . . . <u>ongus</u>

54b. Pectoral rays 16-18 (usually 17);
lower-limb gill rakers 14-16;
longitudinal scale series 85-94;
snout short, 4.8-5.5 in head;
white dots present on body that
do not merge to form bands (dots
often not persisting in preserved
specimens); median fins with a
narrow, pale posterior border
(orange-red in life); pectoral
fins with a narrow, pale posterior
border (orange-red) in life)
(Indonesia, Philippines, and
northern Australia, in fresh to
brackish water) . . . . <u>polystigma</u>

55a. Dorsal margin of opercle slightly
convex; dorsal soft rays usually
16; pectoral rays usually 18;

lateral-line scales 51-62; body
depth 2.9-3.4 in SL; anal, caudal,
and paired fins without white
spots (except a few basally)
(central and western Pacific to
western Indian Ocean but not Red
Sea) . . . . caeruleopunctatus
55b. Dorsal margin of opercle strongly
convex; dorsal soft rays usually
15; pectoral rays usually 17;
lateral-line scales 49-54; body
depth 2.75-3.1 in SL; all fins
with white spots (Red Sea) . . . . summana

56a. Dorsal soft rays 14; posterior
nostril of adults 3-4 times
larger than anterior; gill rakers
27-29; a black saddlelike spot
on caudal peduncle; four, irregular,
oblique, dark brown bars on body
below dorsal fin that bifurcate
ventrally, and one on nape
(southern Queensland, New South
Wales, Lord Howe Island, and
Norfolk Island) . . . . damelii
56b. Dorsal soft rays 15-16 (usually
15); posterior nostril not
notably larger than anterior;
gill rakers 23-25; no black spot
on caudal peduncle and no oblique,
dark bars on body (though pale
blotches may form near-vertical
rows on some specimens, thus tending
to divide the brown body into zones)
(Mediterranean Sea, west coast of
Africa, and east coast of southern
Africa north to Mozambique) . . . . guaza

57a. Dorsal soft rays 15-17;
auxiliary scales present
on body; no dark bands
extending posteriorly from
eye across head 58
57b. Dorsal soft rays 13-15 (rarely 13);
no auxiliary scales on body; two
dark bands extending posteriorly
from eye across head 59

58a. Dorsal soft rays 17; upper-limb
gill rakers 8; body depth 3.4 in SL;
seven or eight stripes on body,
alternately greenish brown and
yellow-orange (Tonga Islands) . . . . __chlorocephalus__

58b. Dorsal soft rays 15-16; upper-limb
gill rakers 9-10; body depth 2.45-
2.95 in SL; body with irregular,
slightly oblique, longitudinal,
alternating lines of pale bluish
and brownish orange, the orange
twice as broad and appearing as
a merging of small spots; head
grayish brown with numerous, small,
close-set, brownish orange spots;
median fins edged with yellow
(southern Queensland to New
South Wales) . . . . __undulostriatus__

59a. Longitudinal scale series 88-95;
upper-limb gill rakers 7 to 8; no
dark markings on body (though 3
diagonal dark bands on postorbital
head) (Indonesia and northern
Australia, north to southern
Japan) . . . . __heniochus__

59b. Longitudinal scale series 100-136;
upper-limb gill rakers 8-11; dark
bars and/or small dark spots
present on body 60

60a. No dark bands on body; upper half
to two-thirds of body with very
small dark brown spots not in
regular rows (spots relatively
larger and in three longitudinal
rows in juveniles) (western Pacific
to western Indian Ocean) . . . . __epistictus__

60b. Body with curved, dark brown bands
(may divide into series of spots
with growth); dark spots, if
present, in rows paralleling dark
bands 61

61a. Dark bands (or rows of spots) on
head and body forming long, hori-

zontally oriented curves (the
middle of each band lower than the
ends) 62
61b. Dark bands on body not forming long,
horizontally oriented curves 63

62a. An isolated, broad, dark brown spot
(or group of smaller spots) below
middle of spinous portion of dorsal
fin, not joined to a diagonal dark
band; a curved, dark brown band or
double row of dark spots from nape to
anterior soft portion of dorsal fin
paralleling the curve of the broad
spot at base of spinous part of fin
(western Pacific to South Africa;
adults in deep water) . . . . <u>poecilonotus</u>
62b. A broad, dark brown spot at base
of middle of spinous portion of
dorsal fin joined to a diagonal
band passing to upper edge of
opercle; no continuous curved band
from nape to anterior soft portion
of dorsal fin (western Pacific to
western Indian Ocean, in deep water) . . . . <u>morrhua</u>

63a. Five dark brown bands (with age,
only the edges of these bands
remain dark) passing diagonally
downward and anteriorly from upper
edge of body, the first from nape
to eye, the second from midbase
of spinous portion of dorsal fin
to upper edge of opercle, the third
and fourth from soft portion of
dorsal fin, both branching as they
pass ventrally, and the fifth on
caudal peduncle (western Pacific to
western Indian Ocean, in deep water) . . . . <u>radiatus</u>
63b. Dark bands on postorbital head and
body forming a coarse reticulum,
none passing diagonally to ventral
part of body (French Polynesia, in
deep water) . . . . <u>tuamotuensis</u>

Epinephelus akaara (Temminck and Schlegel 1842)

Diagnosis. Dorsal rays XI,15-17; anal rays III,8; pectoral rays 17-19 (usually 18); lateral-line scales 50-53; longitudinal scale series 92-103; scales on body largely ctenoid; numerous auxiliary scales present; no scales on maxilla; gill rakers 8-9 + 15-17; 2 rows of teeth on midside of lower jaw; maxilla nearly reaching or extending slightly beyond a vertical at rear edge of orbit; serrae at corner of preopercle slightly enlarged; margins of subopercle and interopercle smooth; dorsal profile of head nearly straight; interorbital space flat to slightly convex; body depth 2.8-3.2 in SL; membranes of spinous portion of dorsal fin incised; longest dorsal spine 2.45-3.25 in head; pectoral fins 1.55-2.05 in head; pelvic fins 1.9-2.25 in head; caudal fin rounded.

Brown with numerous, close-set, red-orange spots about the size of pupil on head and body; a large dark blotch on back beneath last few dorsal spines and extending basally into fin; four lesser dark spots may be present dorsally on body.

Remarks. Largest specimen examined, 37.5 mm. Southern Japan, Korea, Taiwan, and China. The species from Taiwan identified as E. akaara by Shen (1984:figure 289-11a) is E. rivulatus. His figure 289-23c, identified as E. diacanthus is a juvenile akaara. A species of rocky bottom. Few specimens in museums.

Epinephelus albomarginatus Boulenger 1903

Diagnosis. Dorsal rays XI,14; anal rays III,8; pectoral rays 17-18; lateral-line scales 56-64; longitudinal scale series 102-116; scales on body strongly ctenoid (except anterodorsally); auxiliary scales present; no scales on maxilla; gill rakers 8-10 + 14-16; 2 rows of teeth at midside of lower jaw; maxilla usually reaching a vertical at rear edge of orbit; nostrils subequal; prominent rounded corner of preopercle with 3 or 4 acutely pointed, enlarged serrae; margins of subopercle and interopercle smooth or with one or a few serrae; interorbital space slightly convex; body depth 2.6-3.0 in SL; membranes of spinous portion of dorsal fin incised; pectoral fins 1.75-2.0 in head; pelvic fins not reaching anus, 1.85-2.1 in head; caudal fin truncate (the corners slightly rounded) to very slightly rounded.

Light brown with numerous, small, dark brown spots of variable size (none half the size of pupil) on upper three-fourths of body and on postorbital head; a prominent dark brown streak on upper edge of maxillary groove; dorsal fin with dark brown spots basally, the outer triangular part of each interspinous membrane bright yellow, this color continuing as a band in outer soft portion of fin; caudal fin brown with a few dark spots basally; remaining fins unspotted, the paired fins yellow; caudal fin and soft portions of dorsal and anal fins with a white margin and dark submarginal band.

Remarks. Attains 90 cm. Known from southern Mozambique to East London, South Africa in 10 to at least 70 m.

Epinephelus amblycephalus (Bleeker 1857)

Diagnosis. Dorsal rays XI,15-16; anal rays III,8; pectoral rays 18-19 (usually 19); lateral-line scales 46-52; longitudinal scale series 90-121; scales ctenoid; auxiliary scales present; maxilla scaled; gill rakers 8 + 15-16; 2 rows of teeth on midside of lower jaw; maxilla nearly or just reaching a vertical at rear margin of orbit; posterior nostril of adults about 3 times larger than anterior; preopercle with 4-6 strong serrae at angle; interopercle with a few feeble serrae; interorbital space flat to slightly convex; body depth 2.65-2.95 in SL; membranes of spinous portion of dorsal fin incised; dorsal spines short, the longest 2.8-3.65 in head; pectoral fins 1.75-2.0 in head; pelvic fins may reach anus, 1.9-2.3 in head; caudal fin rounded.

Light gray-brown with five brown bars on body (four extending into dorsal fin, the fifth on caudal peduncle), with small dark brown spots along their margins; a large, saddlelike, dark spot on nape and one or two diagonal dark bands on check, also with dark spots on edges; upper edge of maxillary groove dark brown.

Remarks. Reported to attain 45 cm. The author has examined specimens from Taiwan, Philippines, Vietnam, Indonesia, and Fiji, the largest 35 cm. Also known from southern Japan and the east Andaman Sea; G. R. Allen (Pers. com. Western Australian Museum, 1985) has examined material from Shark Bay, Western Australia. Apparently a deepwater species; few specimens are present in museums.

Epinephelus andersoni Boulenger 1903

Diagnosis. Dorsal rays XI,14-15; anal rays III,8; pectoral rays 17-19; lateral-line scales 66-74; longitudinal scale series 100-106; scales of large adults cycloid except midlaterally on anterior half of body where ctenoid (ctenoid scales extend more posteriorly on smaller fish); auxiliary scales present on body; tiny scales on maxilla; lower-limb gill rakers 14-17; 2 rows of teeth on midside of lower jaw; maxilla extending beyond a vertical at posterior edge of orbit; nostrils subequal; upper and lower opercular spines poorly developed; prominent rounded corner of preopercle with 3-7 enlarged serrae; no serrae on subopercle or interopercle; interorbital space convex; body depth 3.2-4.15 in SL; membranes of spinous portion of dorsal fin incised; dorsal spines short, the longest 3.5-3.65 in head; caudal fin broadly rounded.

Brown with numerous, round to somewhat irregular, dark brown spots on body (spots smaller than orbit diameter) and a few small dark spots posteriorly on head; three, narrow, diagonal, dark brown bands on head from behind and below eye to end of operculum; anal and paired fins unspotted.

Remarks. Attains 80 cm. Known only from the east coast of southern Africa from Mozambique to Knysna, South Africa. Occurs on reefs or rocky bottom to depths of at least 50 m.

Epinephelus areolatus (Forsskål 1775)

Diagnosis. Dorsal rays XI,15-17 (usually 16); anal rays III,8; pectoral rays 17-19 (most often 17, rarely 19); lateral-line scales 50-53; longitudinal scale series 97-115; auxiliary scales present on body; maxilla with tiny scales; gill rakers 8-9 + 14-16; teeth on midside of lower jaw in 2 rows; maxilla reaching a vertical between posterior edge of pupil and posterior edge of orbit; rounded corner of preopercle with 2-5 enlarged serrae; subopercle and interopercle partially serrate; interorbital space slightly convex; body depth 3.0-3.3 in SL; membranes of spinous portion of dorsal fin incised; outer posterior part of anal fin rounded to slightly angular, the longest ray 2.0-2.6 in head; pectoral fins 1.6-1.8 in head; caudal fin slightly emarginate (maximum caudal concavity 5 in head) to truncate.

Whitish with numerous, close-set, brown or brownish yellow spots on head, body, and fins (largest spots on adults approaching size of pupil); a distinct whitish border posteriorly on caudal fin.

Remarks. Reaches 35 cm. Western Pacific and Indian Ocean, including the Red Sea and Persian Gulf. Depth range 6-200 m; the typical inshore habitat is small coral heads in silty sand areas or sea grass beds. Serranus waandersii Bleeker is a synonym.

Epinephelus awoara (Temminck and Schlegel 1842)

Diagnosis. Dorsal rays XI,15-16 (usually 16); anal rays III,8; pectoral rays 17-19 (usually 18); lateral-line scales 49-55; longitudinal scale series 92-109; scales on body largely ctenoid; auxiliary scales absent; maxilla naked; gill rakers 8-9 + 16-18; 2 rows of teeth on midside of lower jaw; maxilla reaching a vertical at rear edge of orbit (or falling slightly short of or extending slightly beyond this line); nostrils subequal; 2-5 serrae at corner of preopercle greatly enlarged, generally more than twice as long as those above corner; margins of subopercle and interopercle smooth; interorbital space slightly convex; body depth 2.7-3.3 in SL; membranes of spinous portion of dorsal fin incised; longest dorsal spine 2.35-3.0 in head; pectoral fins 1.55-1.9 in head; pelvic fins not reaching anus, their length 1.8-2.2 in head; caudal fin slightly rounded.

Whitish to pale gray with six dark bars on body (one on nape, four beneath dorsal fin, and one on caudal peduncle), the second and third and the fourth and fifth much closer together than the third and fourth; small yellow spots on head and body; posterior edge of caudal fin with a broad yellow border; soft portion of dorsal fin with a narrow yellow margin; a faint dark streak at upper edge of maxillary groove.

Remarks. Attains 40 cm. Southern Japan to South China Sea. Occurs from the shallows (as young) to depths of at least 50 m. May be taken in trawls from sandy mud grounds or by handlining on rocky bottom.

Epinephelus bleekeri (Vaillant 1877)

Diagnosis. Dorsal rays XI,16-18; anal rays III,8; pectoral rays 17-19 (rarely 17); lateral-line scales 49-53; longitudinal scale series 99-115; auxiliary scales present on body; tiny scales on maxilla; gill rakers 10-11 + 16-18; 2 rows of teeth on midside of lower jaw; maxilla reaching to or slightly beyond a vertical at rear edge of orbit; rounded corner of preopercle with 3-9 moderately enlarged serrae; subopercle and interopercle smooth or with a few serrae; interorbital space slightly convex to flat; body depth 3.0-3.4 in SL; membranes of spinous portion of dorsal fin incised; pelvic fins short, not reaching anus, 1.95-2.25 in head; caudal fin truncate to very slightly rounded.

Brownish to purplish gray with numerous, small, orange-yellow spots (the largest about half pupil diameter) on head, body, dorsal fin, and upper third of caudal fin; lower two-thirds of caudal fin dark purplish gray.

Remarks. Attains about 70 cm. China and the Philippines to the Persian Gulf. Not known from coral reefs. Serranus coromandelicus Day 1878 is a synonym.

Epinephelus bontoides (Bleeker 1855)

Diagnosis. Dorsal rays XI,16-17 (usually 17); anal rays III,8; pectoral rays 18-20 (rarely 18 or 20); lateral-line scales 47-50; longitudinal scale series 82-86; auxiliary scales present; maxilla with small embedded scales; gill rakers 7 + 13-15; 2 rows of teeth on midside of lower jaw; maxilla reaching to or slightly beyond a vertical at posterior edge of orbit; serrae at corner of preopercle moderately enlarged; margins of subopercle and interopercle smooth or with a few serrae; interorbital space flat to slight convex; body depth 2.85-3.0 in SL; spinous portion of dorsal fin incised; pectoral fins 1.65-1.8 in head; pelvic fins reaching or nearly reaching anus, 1.9-2.15 in head; caudal fin rounded.

Grayish brown with or without faint dark bars; numerous dark reddish brown to black spots, smaller than pupil of eye, many horizontally elongate, in about 9 or 10 irregular rows on upper three-fourths of head and body; spinous portion of dorsal fin with 3 rows of diagonally elongate black spots; remaining fins dark brown to blackish with faint, small, dark spots, the soft portion of dorsal fin, pectoral fin, and caudal fin with a narrow, pale yellowish posterior margin.

Remarks. Largest specimen examined, 21 cm. Previously known only from Indonesia, the range here extended to the Philippines and Taiwan. Three speared by the author at Ambon were from a cobble bottom in 2-3 m in strong current; one from the east coast of Taiwan was taken on a rocky bottom off a cobble beach in only 2 m.

Epinephelus bruneus Bloch 1793

Diagnosis. Dorsal rays XI,13-15; anal rays III,8; pectoral rays 17-18; lateral-line scales 64-71; longitudinal scale series 93-120; scales on body largely ctenoid; no auxiliary scales; small scales on maxilla; gill rakers 9-11 + 16-17; 2 rows of teeth on midside of lower jaw; maxilla extending slightly to well beyond a vertical at rear edge of orbit; serrae at corner of preopercle enlarged; interopercle with 0 to 3 serrae at juncture with subopercle; interorbital space flat to slightly convex; body depth 2.95-3.45 in SL; membranes of spinous portion of dorsal fin incised; longest dorsal spine 3.1-3.7 in head; pectoral fins 1.8-2.05 in head; pelvic fins not reaching anus, 2.2-2.5 in head; caudal fin rounded.

Pale yellowish brown with six, irregular, somewhat diagonal, broad, dark brown bars that contain pale spots, the first on nape (where it curves and passes obliquely to eye), and the last on caudal peduncle; three dark brown bands radiating from lower part of eye (dark bars and bands obscure on large adults); triangular outer part of interspinous membranes of dorsal fin yellow or orange.

Remarks. Reaches 80 cm. Southern Japan to South China Sea. Few specimens in museums. Serranus moara Temminck and Schlegel 1842 appears to be a synonym (the lectotype of moara, a stuffed skin 333 mm SL, examined by author at the Rijksmuseum van Natuurlijke in Leiden).

Epinephelus caeruleopunctatus (Bloch 1790)

Diagnosis. Dorsal rays XI,15-17 (usually 16); anal rays III,8; pectoral rays 17-19 (usually 18); lateral-line scales 51-61; longitudinal scale series 86-106; scales on body largely ctenoid; auxiliary scales present on body of adults; a patch of tiny embedded scales on maxilla; gill rakers 8-10 + 15-17; 3-5 rows of teeth on midside of lower jaw (there may be 2 rows at sizes <15 cm SL); maxilla reaching to or slightly posterior to a vertical at rear edge of orbit; posterior nostril of adults vertically elongate and enlarged, its length 2-4 times that of diameter of anterior nostril; upper margin of opercle slightly convex; serrae at corner of preopercle slightly enlarged; margins of subopercle and interopercle smooth; dorsal profile of head nearly straight; interorbital space flat; body depth 2.9–3.4 in SL; membranes of spinous portion of dorsal fin incised; longest dorsal spine 2.55–3.6 in head; pectoral fins 1.55–2.1 in head; pelvic fins not reaching anus, their length 2.0–3.0 in head; caudal fin rounded.

Gray-brown, the body, posterior head, and dorsal fin with scattered large white spots (some as large or larger than pupil) and numerous small pale spots; a series of indistinct dark blotches on back at base of dorsal fin and one on caudal peduncle; a broad, dark brown to black streak on upper edge of maxillary groove; remaining fins dark brownish gray without pale spots except a few small ones basally on caudal and pectoral fins of some specimens.

Remarks. Reaches 60 cm. Gilbert Islands (two specimens in the Bishop Museum) and Caroline Islands west to East Africa. A shallow-water species of coral reefs and rocky substrata. Stays close to the shelter of caves and crevices. Serranus hoevenii Bleeker 1849 is a synonym. Epinephelus matterni Fowler 1918 also appears to be a synonym.

Epinephelus chabaudi (Castelnau 1861)

Diagnosis. Dorsal rays XI,14–15; anal rays III,9; pectoral rays 17–18; lateral-line scales 62–69; longitudinal scale series 104–114; body largely without auxiliary scales (a few above lateral line); lower-limb gill rakers 15–17; posterior nostril 3–4 times larger than anterior; maxilla generally reaching to below rear margin of eye; serrae at corner of preopercle not enlarged (only slightly coarser than those on vertical margin); body depth 2.6–2.8 in SL; membranes of spinous portion of dorsal fin incised; caudal fin truncate. Grayish brown with vague dark blotches on back; a prominent black streak along upper edge of maxillary groove.

Remarks. Reported to 137 cm. Known only from Kenya south to Algoa Bay, South Africa. Usual fishing depths, 30–180 m. No specimens examined by author. Epinephelus modestus Gilchrist and Thompson 1909 is a synonym.

Epinephelus chlorocephalus (Valenciennes 1830)

Diagnosis. Dorsal rays XI,17; anal rays III,8; pectoral rays 18; lateral-line scales 52–54; gill rakers 8 +

15; scales on body largely ctenoid; 2 rows of teeth on midside of lower jaw; maxilla reaching a vertical at rear edge of pupil; nostrils subequal; 5 serrae at corner of preopercle moderately enlarged; body depth 3.4 in SL; head 2.6 in SL, the opercular flap angling dorsally; membranes of spinous portion of dorsal fin incised; fourth dorsal spine longest, 2.45 in head; pectoral fins 1.75 in head; pelvic fins 2.65 in head; caudal fin rounded, 1.55 in head.

Color in preservative uniform brown. Valenciennes gave the color when fresh as follows: upper part of head and snout dark green, the cheeks light green, the body greenish, striped with seven to eight longitudinal bands that are alternately greenish brown and yellow-orange; dorsal and anal fins greenish, spotted with reddish brown at the base; paired fins light greenish without spots; ground color of caudal fin the same as that of the dorsal, faintly banded transversely with reddish.

Remarks. Known from only a single specimen, MNHN 7543, 171 mm SL, 209 mm total length (TL) from Tongatapu, Tonga Islands, which is in the Museum National d'Histoire Naturelle in Paris. The author spent nearly a month collecting fishes in the Tonga Islands and observing the catches of fishermen. No specimens of this grouper were found.

Epinephelus chlorostigma (Valenciennes 1828)

Diagnosis. Dorsal rays XI,16–18 (most often 17, rarely 18); anal rays III,8; pectoral rays 17–19 (rarely 19); lateral-line scales 49–53; longitudinal scale series 96–119; auxiliary scales present on body; maxilla with tiny scales; gill rakers 8–10 + 15–18; teeth on side of lower jaw in 2 rows; maxilla reaching from below center of eye to slightly posterior to rear of orbit; body depth 2.9–3.3 in SL; head moderately pointed, the lower jaw strongly projecting; rounded corner of preopercle with 4–7 enlarged serrae; subopercle and interopercle partially serrate; interorbital space slightly convex; membranes of spinous portion of dorsal fin incised; outer posterior portion of anal fin angular, the longest ray 1.85–2.3 in head; pectoral fins 1.70–2.0 in head; caudal fin slightly emarginate to truncate, the maximum caudal concavity 6.4 in head.

Whitish with numerous, close-set, round to hexagonal, brown to dark brown spots on head, body, and fins; posterior border of caudal fin usually with a narrow white margin.

    Remarks. Largest examined, 75 cm. Western Pacific and Indian Ocean, including the Red Sea and Persian Gulf. Known from the depth range of 4 to at least 150 m; usually associated with coral reefs. There appears to be some variation in this species over its range. In the Red Sea the anal fin is more distinctly angular; in Japan the caudal fin is truncate.

Epinephelus corallicola (Valenciennes 1828)

    Diagnosis. Dorsal rays XI,15–16; anal rays III,8; pectoral rays 18–20; lateral-line scales 54–63; longitudinal scale series 96–107; auxiliary scales present on body; very small scales on maxilla; gill rakers 9–10 + 15–17; 3 or 4 rows of teeth on midside of lower jaw; maxilla usually reaching to or slightly beyond a vertical at rear edge of orbit; posterior nostril of adults (over about 14 cm) vertically elongate, 2–3 times longer than diameter of anterior nostril; serrae at corner of preopercle not enlarged; no serrae on margins of subopercle and interopercle; dorsal profile of head nearly straight; interorbital space flat; body depth 2.7–3.2 in SL; membranes of spinous portion of dorsal fin incised; longest dorsal spine 2.65–3.35 in head; posterior dorsal rays reaching to or beyond a vertical at caudal-fin base; pectoral fins 1.5–1.75 in head; pelvic fins may reach anus, their length 1.95–2.25 in head; caudal fin rounded, 1.5–1.65 in head.

    Brownish to greenish gray with widely scattered black spots smaller than pupil on head, body, and fins; three dusky to blackish spots on back at base of rear half of dorsal fin, the most anterior (at base of last two or three spines) largest and most distinct. Juveniles with round, dark-edged, pale spots larger than pupil in about four rows on body.

    Remarks. Largest examined, 31 cm. Eastern and northern Australia to the Philippines and Taiwan. Shen (1984:figures 289–14; 289–21) misidentified this species as E. caeruleopunctatus and E. tauvina, respectively: the 305.5 mm SL given for the juvenile of figure 289–14b is obviously an error; it should be about 80 mm). A shallow-water species typically found on silty reefs; occurs in estuarine areas. The name corallicola has often been misapplied to other species such as E. macrospilos (Bleeker).

Epinephelus cyanopodus (Richardson 1846)

Diagnosis. Dorsal rays XI,16-17; anal rays III,8; lateral-line scales 63-75; longitudinal scale series 130-147; auxiliary scales present on body of adults; maxilla with tiny scales; gill rakers 8-11 + 15-17; 2 rows of teeth on posterior half of lower jaw; maxilla reaching to or slightly beyond a vertical at rear edge of eye; serrae at corner of preopercle somewhat enlarged; margins of subopercle and interopercle smooth; interorbital space moderately to strongly convex; body depth 2.4-2.65 in SL; longest dorsal spine 2.2-2.8 in head (mean length 2.5); membranes of spinous portion of dorsal fin not incised; caudal fin truncate.

Light bluish gray in life with numerous very small black spots and scattered larger blackish spots (usually less than pupil in size) on head, body, and fins (only basally on pectorals); subadults and large juveniles lack the larger dark spots and may have a broad submarginal black band posteriorly on the caudal fin and black-tipped pelvic fins; small juveniles may be mainly yellow.

Remarks. Reaches a maximum of about 100 cm. Western Pacific to the Marshall Islands and Gilbert Islands, often around isolated coral heads in lagoons. Reported from depths of 2 to 150 m. Closely related to the Indian Ocean species E. flavocaeruleus and E. multinotatus. Epinephelus hoedtii Bleeker 1855 and E. kohleri Schultz 1958 are synonyms (Randall and Whitehead 1985). Masuda et al. (1984:figures A and B of plate 114), identified as E. hoedtii and E. flavocaeruleus, respectively by Katayama, are E. cyanopodus.

Epinephelus damelii (Günther 1876)

Diagnosis. Dorsal rays XI,14; anal rays III,8; pectoral rays 18; lateral-line scales 66-75; longitudinal scale series 110-130; scales cycloid (ctenoid in young); auxiliary scales present; a short, narrow band of tiny scales dorsally on maxilla; gill rakers 11 + 16-18; maxilla reaching posterior to a vertical at rear edge of orbit; posterior nostril of adults 2 to 4 times larger than anterior; serrae at corner of preopercle slightly enlarged; margins of subopercle and interopercle smooth; interorbital space moderately convex; body depth 2.9-3.3 in SL; longest dorsal spine 2.9-3.7 in head; pectoral fins

1.85-2.15 in head; pelvic fins short; 2.2-2.5 in head; caudal fin rounded.

Grayish brown with scattered small whitish spots and a large, saddlelike, black spot on caudal peduncle (narrower dorsally) that extends nearly to midlateral line; four, irregular, oblique, dark brown bars on body beneath dorsal fin that bifurcate ventrally, and one on nape; fins largely without markings except extensions of brown bars into dorsal fin.

Remarks. Largest examined, 78.5 cm, but larger individuals have been observed. Southern Queensland, New South Wales, Lord Howe Island, and Norfolk Island. Occurs on rocky substrata and reefs from near shore to depths of at least 50 m.

Epinephelus diacanthus (Valenciennes 1828)

Diagnosis. Dorsal rays XI,15-17 (usually 16); anal rays III,8; pectoral rays 18-20 (usually 19); lateral-line scales 53-60; longitudinal scale rows 105-121; scales on body largely ctenoid; auxiliary scales present; maxilla with very small scales; gill rakers 8-10 + 15-16; 2 rows of teeth on midside of lower jaw; maxilla reaching to or slightly beyond a vertical at rear edge of orbit; nostrils subequal; 1-5 very large serrae at corner of preopercle, the largest more than twice as long as serrae above corner; margins of subopercle and interopercle smooth; interorbital space slightly convex; body depth 2.8-3.25 in SL; membranes of spinous portion of dorsal fin incised; longest dorsal spine 3.0-3.5 in head; pectoral fins 1.8-2.1 in head; pelvic fins short, 2.25-2.7 in head; caudal fin slightly rounded.

Whitish with five grayish brown bars broader than pale interspaces (four below dorsal fin and one on caudal peduncle); a dark brown streak on upper edge of maxillary groove, continuing posteriorly across cheek; fins without spots.

Remarks. Reported to 52 cm. Sri Lanka to Oman. A continental-shelf species known from the depth range of 2 to at least 50 m.

Epinephelus epistictus (Temminck and Schlegel 1842)

Diagnosis. Dorsal rays XI,14-15 (usually 14); anal rays III,8; pectoral rays 17-19 (rarely 19); lateral-line

scales 57-66; longitudinal scale series 100-120; scales of
body largely ctenoid; no auxiliary scales on body; maxilla
naked; gill rakers 8-10 + 15-18; 2 rows of teeth on midside of lower jaw; maxilla not reaching, just reaching, or
extending slightly posterior to a vertical at rear edge of
orbit; nostrils subequal; 3-5 greatly enlarged serrae at
corner of preopercle; margins of subopercle and interopercle smooth or with a few serrae; body depth 2.8-3.3 in
SL; longest dorsal spine 2.9-3.7 in head; pectoral fins
1.65-2.05 in head; pelvic fins short, not reaching anus,
their length 2.15-2.7 in head; caudal fin slightly to
moderately rounded.

Light brown, shading ventrally to lavender -brown,
with irregular rows of small dark brown spots on body
(spots relatively smaller and less distinct in larger
individuals; juveniles with spots in three longitudinal
rows); a faint, broad, dark band extending from orbit to
opercular flap, and two, narrower, diagonal, dark bands on
cheek and operculum, the lowermost passing from edge of
maxillary groove to below corner of preopercle; small dark
spots may be present basally in dorsal fin, but other fins
unmarked (except Japanese specimens where spots may be
present on caudal fin).

Remarks. Reaches 80 cm. Western Pacific to western
Indian Ocean, including the Red Sea and Persian Gulf.
Known from the depth range of 90-290 m. May be taken in
trawls, indicating its occurrence over sedimentary
bottoms. Serranus praeopercularis Boulenger 1887, and E.
stigmogrammacus Cheng and Wang 1983 are synonyms.

Epinephelus fasciatomaculatus (Peters 1865)

Diagnosis. Dorsal rays XI,15-17; anal rays III,8;
pectoral rays 17-18; lateral-line scales 48-53; longitudinal scale series 90-106; a few auxiliary scales
present on body; maxilla scaled (naked in juveniles); gill
rakers 7-8 + 14-16; 2 or 3 rows of teeth on midside of
lower jaw; maxilla nearly reaching a vertical at rear edge
of orbit or extending slightly posterior; prominent
rounded corner of preopercle with enlarged serrae; body
depth 2.85-3.3 in SL; membranes of spinous portion of
dorsal fin incised; pectoral fins 1.5-1.75 in head; pelvic
fins 1.9-2.25 in head, usually reaching anus; caudal fin
rounded.

Gray-brown with numerous, small, brownish yellow to
orange spots on head and body; juveniles and subadults

with five, slightly diagonal, broad, dark brown bars on body that bifurcate ventrally, and one on nape; first four bars on body extending well into dorsal fin, the first two very darkly pigmented on juveniles; bars faint in adults (may be lost in preservative except for dorsal part of first two body bars); fins of adults yellowish gray-brown, the dorsal with dull orange-yellow spots.

Remarks. Although reported to attain only 20 cm, Bishop Museum has a 37.5-cm specimen from Hong Kong that is believed to be this species. Also tentatively identified as E. fasciatomaculatus are figures 289-11b, 289-23a, and 289-23b in Shen (1984). Japan to South China Sea. A shallow-water species of rocky bottom. Few specimens in museums.

Epinephelus fasciatus (Forsskål 1775)

Diagnosis. Dorsal rays XI,15-17 (usually 16); anal rays III,8; pectoral rays 18-20 (rarely 20); lateral-line scales 50-58 (61-75 in Oceania); longitudinal scale series 92-125 (114-135 in Oceania); scales of body largely ctenoid; auxiliary scales numerous on body; maxilla with very small scales; gill rakers 6-9 + 15-18; 2 or 3 rows of teeth on midside of lower jaw; maxilla reaching to or slightly beyond a vertical at rear edge of orbit; nostrils subequal; serrae at corner of preopercle moderately enlarged; margins of subopercle and interopercle smooth; interorbital space flat; body depth 2.9-3.3 in SL; membranes of spinous portion of dorsal fin incised; longest dorsal spine 2.7-3.05 in head; pectoral fins 1.7-1.9 in head; pelvic fins not reaching or just reaching anus, their length 1.9-2.25 in head; caudal fin slightly rounded to rounded (slightly rounded to truncate in Oceania).

Light gray to pale yellowish red with five broad, dusky to dark orange-red bars on body (more evident on dorsal half); large dusky to dark reddish blotches on postorbital head and a broad orange-red streak across cheek; orbit edged with dark brown; triangular outer part of interspinous membranes of dorsal fin black (or red in deeper water specimens); occasional individuals from the Pacific with a black line at dorsal-fin base and short side branches into the spinous portion of the dorsal fin.

Remarks. Maximum length reported as 40 cm. Largest collected by author, 35 cm, from Rapa. Common and wide-ranging in the Indo-Pacific. A species of coral reefs and rocky bottoms from the shallows to 160 m. Serranus tsirimenara Temminck and Schlegel 1842 from Japan and E. zapyrus Seale 1906 from the Austral Islands are synonyms. Schultz and collaborators (1953) described Epinephelus emoryi from one specimen from Bikini and six from Rota, distinguishing it from E. fasciatus on the basis of a black streak at the base of the dorsal fin, the black margin only posteriorly on orbit, and higher counts of the longitudinal scale series than fasciatus. Katayama (1960) found intermediate specimens from Japan, so referred emoryi to the synonymy of fasciatus. The number of lateral-line scales and scales in longitudinal series are higher in specimens from the islands of Oceania (except the Palau Islands), and the caudal fin is less rounded. If one wishes to recognize the Pacific island populations as a species or subspecies, the first available name is Serranus variolosus Valenciennes in Cuvier and Valenciennes 1828, based on a Forster drawing. Valenciennes gave the locality as Tahiti, but Heemstra believes that two specimens in the British Museum (Natural History) from the Marquesas were the ones seen by Forster (Bauchot et al. 1984).

Epinephelus faveatus (Valenciennes 1828)

Diagnosis. Dorsal rays XI,16–18 (usually 17); anal rays III,8; pectoral rays 17–19 (usually 18); lateral-line scales 47–52; longitudinal scale series 83–98; scales on body cycloid; auxiliary scales present on body; gill rakers 7–9 + 14–16 (usually 8 + 15 or 16); teeth on mid-side of lower jaw in 2 rows; nostrils subequal; serrae ventrally on posterior margin of preopercle slightly enlarged; margin of subopercle and interopercle smooth; body depth 2.9–3.5 in SL; dorsal profile of head convex; snout 4.65–5.2 in head; maxilla extending well posterior to eye; pectoral fins 1.7–2.1 in head; pelvic fins 2.1–2.65 in head; caudal fin rounded, 1.65–1.9 in head.

Whitish with numerous roundish brown spots of unequal size on head, body, and fins, most of those on body larger than pupil, some approaching size of eye; four groups of two or three spots at base of dorsal fin and adjacent back darker than other spots, and one spot middorsally on caudal peduncle also darker; a narrow blackish streak on upper edge of maxillary groove; an elongate dark spot basally on pectoral fins linked to a dark band along edge of gill opening, the lower part of which connects to a dark band that extends to lower edge of pectoral base; posterior margin of caudal fin narrowly whitish.

Remarks. Largest of 27 specimens examined, 30.6 cm. West coast of India to Sri Lanka, the type locality. Collected by author in shallow water along rocky shore of southwest India and from fishermen in Tuticorin, southeast India. One specimen from Lombok, Indonesia tentatively identified as E. faveatus.

Epinephelus flavocaeruleus (Lacepède 1802)

Diagnosis. Dorsal rays XI,16-17; anal rays III,8; pectoral rays 18-19; lateral-line scales 61-74; longitudinal scale series 129-148; auxiliary scales present on body of adults, but not numerous; tiny scales on maxilla; 2 rows of teeth on posterior half of lower jaw; gill rakers 9-10 + 15-17; maxilla reaching to or slightly posterior to a vertical at rear edge of eye; posterior nostrils of large adults notably larger than anterior; serrae at corner of preopercle not enlarged; margins of subopercle and interopercle smooth; interorbital space moderately to strongly convex; body depth 2.45-2.8 in SL; membranes of spinous portion of dorsal fin not incised; longest dorsal spine 2.5-3.0 in head (mean length 2.7); caudal fin truncate.

Deep blue (dark brown in preservative) without black or white spots (but there may be scattered pale blue flecks), becoming yellow on caudal peduncle and fin; remaining fins yellow except basally on dorsal, anal, and pectorals; posterior margin or corners of caudal fin and tips of pelvic fins often black; yellow areas more extensive on juveniles; large adults may lose the yellow coloration.

Remarks. Reported to attain 90 cm. Indian Ocean, but not reported from the Red Sea. The juvenile reported by Randall and Whitehead (1985:36) as a first record from the Persian Gulf is a misidentification of E. multinotatus. Juveniles may occur in shallow water, but adults are usually found at moderate depths (to a maximum of about 150 m).

Epinephelus fuscoguttatus (Forsskål 1775)

Diagnosis. Dorsal rays XI,14-15 (usually 14); anal rays III,8; pectoral rays 18-20 (usually 19); lateral-line scales 52-58; longitudinal scale series 102-115; scales cycloid (ctenoid in juveniles); auxiliary scales present on body; small scales on maxilla; gill rakers 10-12 + 18-21; teeth on midside of lower jaw in 3 rows; maxilla reaching well posterior to eye; posterior nostril subtriangular, more than 4 times larger than anterior in specimens 30 cm or more SL; serrae at corner of preopercle not notably enlarged; margin of subopercle and interopercle smooth; interorbital space flat to slightly concave; dorsal profile of head of adults above interorbital space distinctly convex; body depth 2.6-2.9 in SL; membranes of spinous portion of dorsal fin incised; pelvic fins not reaching anus, 2.05-2.75 in head.

Light yellowish brown with large, irregular, brown blotches on head and body, the darkest along back; a black, saddlelike spot on caudal peduncle; head, body, and all fins with numerous, close-set, small, dark brown spots.

Remarks. Attains at least 90 cm. Red Sea and East Africa to the central Pacific (but not reaching French Polynesia). Randall (1964) described a neotype from Jeddah. A species of coral reefs and rocky bottom. Serranus horridus Valenciennes 1828 and S. lutra Valenciennes 1831 are synonyms.

Epinephelus guaza (Linnaeus 1758)

Diagnosis. Dorsal rays XI,15-16 (rarely 16); anal rays III,8; pectoral rays 17-19 (usually 18); lateral-line scales 66-73; longitudinal scale series 106-123; scales ctenoid on adults except anterolaterally on body; auxiliary scales present on body; scales not evident on maxilla; gill rakers 8-9 + 14-16; 2 rows of teeth on midside of lower jaw (3 in large adults); maxilla reaching to or posterior to a vertical at rear edge of orbit; nostrils subequal; serrae at corner of preopercle slightly to moderately enlarged; margins of subopercle and interopercle smooth; interorbital space slightly convex; body depth 2.65-3.0 in SL; membranes of spinous portion of dorsal fin incised; longest dorsal spine about 2.4-3.0 in head; pectoral fins 1.6-1.8 in head; pelvic fins may reach anus, their length 1.75-2.1 in head; caudal fin rounded.

Brown to dark brown, shading to yellow or whitish ventrally, with scattered whitish blotches on body and a few, narrow, irregular, whitish bands on head; a dark brown streak at upper edge of maxillary groove; upper triangular part of interspinous membranes of dorsal fin yellow to brownish yellow; caudal fin with a narrow whitish to pale yellowish margin.

Remarks. Reported to reach 150 cm. Mediterranean Sea, coast of west Africa and east coast of southern Africa north to Mozambique at lat. 25°S. Also reported from Brazil (Smith 1971). Occurs on rocky bottoms to depths of at least 50 m.

Epinephelus heniochus Fowler 1904

Diagnosis. Dorsal rays XI,15; anal rays III,8; pectoral rays 16-18; lateral-line scales 54-60; longitudinal scales series 91-95; scales of body largely ctenoid; no auxiliary scales; no scales on maxilla; gill rakers 7-9 + 14-15; 2 rows of teeth on midside of lower jaw; maxilla usually reaching to or slightly posterior to a vertical at rear edge of orbit; nostrils subequal; corner of preopercle with 2 or 3 greatly enlarged serrae; margins of subopercle and interopercle smooth or with a few serrae; interorbital space moderately convex; body depth 2.75-3.2 in SL; membranes of spinous portion of dorsal fin incised; longest dorsal spine 2.7-3.5 in head; pectoral fins 1.55-1.85 in head; pelvic fins not reaching anus, their length 1.9-2.2 in head; caudal fin rounded.

Light brown, whitish ventrally, with two slightly diverging brown bands passing posteriorly and diagonally downward from lower part of eye, the upper to base of the lower two opercular spines; a third brown band on head from upper edge of maxillary groove, paralleling second band and ending at lower part of corner of preopercle; no spots or bands on body or fins; lower part of caudal fin, anal fin, and pelvic fins dusky, the last two with a pale margin.

Remarks. Only five specimens examined, the largest 27.5 cm. The holotype, from Sumatra, is in the Academy of Natural Sciences of Philadelphia; it measures 18 cm SL. Two Bishop Museum specimens were collected by trawling in 60 and 78 m off the northern coast of Australia; Katayama (1953) described E. hata from Nagasaki, Japan. Katayama in Masuda et al. (1984) placed hata in the synonymy of heniochus. Although these two nominal species exhibit the same general morphology and color pattern, their conspecificity should be investigated further. Katayama gives an upper-limb, gill-raker count of 9-11 for his Japanese specimens.

Epinephelus hexagonatus (Schneider 1801)

Diagnosis. Dorsal rays XI,15-16 (usually 16); anal rays III,8; pectoral rays 18-19 (usually 18); lateral-line scales 61-68; longitudinal scale series 93-109; scales on body largely ctenoid; auxiliary scales present on body; very small scales on maxilla; gill rakers 7-9 + 16-19; midside of lower jaw with 3-5 rows of teeth; maxilla reaching to or beyond a vertical at rear edge of orbit; nostrils subequal; serrae at corner of preopercle only slightly enlarged; margins of subopercle and interopercle smooth; interorbital space flat; body depth 2.8-3.4 in SL; membranes of spinous portion of dorsal fin incised; longest dorsal spine 2.55-2.9 in head; posterior part of dorsal fin nearly reaching a vertical at caudal-fin base; second anal spine longer than third, 2.1-2.35 in head; pelvic fins nearly reaching or just reaching anus, their length 1.8-2.35 in head; caudal fin rounded.

Head and body with brown to dark brown polygonal spots (about as large as pupil of eye) that merge or tend to merge on their sides, separated mainly by a triangular white dot at each angular corner of the spots; groups of spots darker than others, forming a series of five dark blotches along back (four at base of dorsal fin and one dorsally on caudal peduncle); irregular bars on side of body below these spots; a large yellow-brown spot behind eye sometimes linked to a second horizontally elongate spot of the same color on opercle; all fins dark-spotted.

Remarks. Reaches about 30 cm. Indo-Pacific, but absent from the Red Sea and Persian Gulf. Usually found on exposed outer-reef areas in relatively shallow water.

Epinephelus irroratus (Schneider 1801)

Diagnosis. Dorsal rays XI,16; anal rays III,8; pectoral rays 19-20 (rarely 20); lateral-line scales 70-73; longitudinal scale series 117-136; scales on body largely ctenoid; auxiliary scales present on body; maxilla naked; gill rakers 6-7 + 13-16; 3 rows of teeth on midside of lower jaw of adults; maxilla reaching or extending slightly posterior to a vertical at rear edge of orbit; nostrils subequal; serrae at corner of preopercle slightly enlarged; margins of subopercle and interopercle smooth; interorbital space slightly convex; body depth 2.7-3.2 in SL; membranes of spinous portion of dorsal fin not incised

(or very slightly indented); second dorsal spine of adults
prolonged, 1.85-2.4 in head, the remaining spines three-
fourths or less second spine length; caudal fin truncate
to very slightly rounded.

Reddish brown with a white dot on each scale; a
conspicuous dark reddish brown streak at upper edge of
maxillary groove; spinous portion of dorsal fin with a
broad, deep red border; posterior margins of median and
pectoral fins with a narrow white margin.

Remarks. Largest specimen examined, 34 cm. Known
only from the Marquesas Islands and one specimen from
Marcus Island (Minami Tori Shima). A shallow-water fish
of coral reefs or rocky substrata. As will be shown by
Randall and Wheeler (Unpub.) Serranus spiniger (Günther
1859) and E. albopunctulatus Boulenger 1895 are synonyms.

Epinephelus lanceolatus (Bloch 1790)

Diagnosis. Dorsal rays XI,14-16 (usually 15); anal
rays III,8; pectoral rays 18-19; lateral-line scales 53-
67, the tubes branched; longitudinal scale series 89-110;
scales of body cycloid; gill rakers 9-10 + 14-16; side of
gill arches with numerous small platelets; body depth 2.5-
3.4 in SL; body thick, the width 1.55-1.75 in depth; eye
very small, its diameter contained 5.8 in head of a
specimen 12.2 cm SL, 6.9 in head of 17-cm specimen, 8.1 in
25-cm specimen, 8.7 in 33.5-cm specimen, and 13.0 in 145-
cm specimen; dorsal spines short, the longest (on adults,
the most posterior spines) 3.2-4.8 in head; caudal fin
rounded.

Juveniles and subadults irregularly barred and
mottled with dark brown and yellow, the fins yellowish
with dark brown spots; adults dark grayish brown, mottled
with pale.

Remarks. Reported to 270 cm TL and weights of over
400 kg, hence one of the largest of bony fishes. Indo-
Pacific. Although reported to depths of 100 m, it may be
encountered in only a few meters. There are reports of
fatal attacks on humans, but none fully documented. This
species is usually classified in Promicrops; however, the
characters given by Schultz in Schultz and collaborators
(1966) for this genus are either found in species of
Epinephelus (such as branched lateral-line tubules in
large E. malabaricus and E. suillus) or they are allo-
metric such as the small eye, broad interorbital space,
and short dorsal spines of large adults of this species.

Schultz pointed out that the posterior dorsal spines are longest, but this is true only of large individuals.

Epinephelus latifasciatus (Temminck and Schlegel 1842)

Diagnosis. Dorsal rays XI,12-13 (one of 17 examined with X,14); anal rays III,8; pectoral rays 18-19; lateral-line scales 58-63; longitudinal scale series 94-106; scales of adults cycloid; auxiliary scales may be present on body of adults; a small patch of tiny scales sometimes present posteriorly on maxilla; gill rakers 8-10 + 15-17; 2 rows of teeth on midside on lower jaw; maxilla extending posterior to eye; corner of preopercle with 3-7 greatly enlarged serrae; subopercle and interopercle smooth; membranes of spinous portion of dorsal fin incised; pelvic fins short, 2.2-2.65 in head; caudal fin slightly to moderately rounded.

Lavender-gray, shading to whitish ventrally, with two, broad, pale, longitudinal bands edged in black, one from above eye to base of anterior soft portion of dorsal fin and the other from cheek to lower caudal peduncle; pale bands disappearing in large adults, the dark edges breaking into dashes and spots; dorsal and caudal fin with black spots.

Remarks. Reported to 70 cm. Korea and southern Japan to the Red Sea. A continental-shelf species not known from oceanic islands. Occurs at depths of 20 to at least 200 m. Large individuals seem to prefer coarse sand or rocky substrata but young fish have been taken from mud bottoms.

Epinephelus longispinis (Kner 1865)

Diagnosis. Dorsal rays XI,16-17 (usually 17); anal rays III,8; pectoral rays 17-19 (usually 18, rarely 19); lateral-line scales 49-52; longitudinal scale series 103-121; scales on body ctenoid; some auxiliary scales present on body; very small scales on maxilla; gill rakers 8-11 + 14-16; 2 rows of teeth on midside of lower jaw; maxilla usually just reaching a vertical at hind border of orbit; corner of preopercle with enlarged serrae; margin of subopercle and interopercle smooth; interorbital space convex; body depth 2.8-3.35 in SL; membranes of spinous portion of dorsal fin incised; dorsal spines long, the third (occasionally the fourth) longest, 2.1-2.5 in head;

pectoral fins 1.5-1.9 in head; pelvic fins 1.7-2.25 in head; caudal fin rounded.

Light brown with small dark brown spots that are widely scattered on head and anterior body but much more dense on posterior half of body where most are diagonally elongate; fins with small dark spots, though few present on anal and pelvics.

Remarks. Reaches 55 cm. Indonesia to the Indian Ocean (but absent from the Red Sea and Persian Gulf). Often misidentified as E. gaimardi (Valenciennes), a synonym of E. miliaris (Valenciennes). Smith (1949) and Smith and Smith (1963) misidentified E. longispinis as E. fario (Thunberg).

Epinephelus macrospilos (Bleeker 1855)

Diagnosis. Dorsal rays XI,15-17 (usually 16); anal rays III,8; pectoral rays 17-19; lateral-line scales 48-52; longitudinal scale series 88-103; scales of body cycloid (may be ctenoid beneath pectoral fins); auxiliary scales present on body; some very small scales on maxilla; gill rakers 7-9 + 14-17 (usually 8 + 15 or 16); teeth on midside of lower jaw in 2 rows; maxilla extending well beyond a vertical at posterior edge of orbit; serrae at corner of preopercle moderately enlarged; margin of subopercle and interopercle smooth; nostrils subequal; body depth 2.9-3.5 in SL; snout 4.2-5.2 in head; pectoral fins 1.6-2.0 in head; pelvic fins 1.85-2.4 in head; caudal fin rounded, 1.5-2.0 in head.

Dark brown to black spots on head, body, and fins except pectorals (though there may be spots basally on these fins), the spots on body large (may be as large as eye), close-set, and often polygonal on western Indian Ocean specimens; spots smaller, round and well-separated on specimens elsewhere in range; a series of four large black spots on back (or a dusky area surrounding existing black spots at these sites), the first three along base of posterior half of dorsal fin (and extending into fin), the last on caudal peduncle; a blackish streak on upper edge of maxillary groove; pectoral fins dark with a narrow white posterior margin; caudal fin with a whitish or yellowish posterior margin.

Remarks. Attains a maximum length of about 40 cm. Western Indian Ocean specimens may have such close set dark spots that the pale interspaces form a narrow network in a honeycomb pattern. Specimens of this form have been

examined from the east coast of Africa from Kenya to
Natal, Madagascar, Mauritius, Réunion, Aldabra, and the
Chagos Archipelago. This form was described by Günther
(1859) as S. cylindricus. At present it is believed the
name cylindricus is best retained as a subspecies. The
western Indian Ocean population appears separable only by
color from the species in Indonesia and the Pacific, which
would therefore be E. macrospilos macrospilos. Its spots
are smaller (pupil size or smaller) and well-separated,
the interspaces usually equal to or greater than the spot
diameters; there are no dark spots on the underside of the
lower jaw (present on western Indian Ocean specimens).
Serranus howlandi Günther (1883) and E. spilotus Schultz
(1953) are synonyms based on specimens from islands of
Oceania. Katayama in Masuda et al. (1984) misidentified
this species as E. corallicola Valenciennes, and Bagnis et
al. (1972) as E. melanostigma Schultz.

Epinephelus maculatus (Bloch 1790)

Diagnosis. Dorsal rays XI,15-17 (usually 16, rarely
17); anal rays III,8; pectoral rays 17-18 (rarely 17);
lateral-line scales 48-51; longitudinal scale series 103-
120; scales on body ctenoid; auxiliary scales present;
very small scales present on maxilla; gill rakers 8-10 +
15-17; 2 rows of teeth on midside of lower jaw; maxilla
reaching beyond a vertical at rear margin of orbit; serrae
at corner of preopercle enlarged; margin of subopercle and
interopercle smooth; interorbital space convex; body depth
2.75-3.1 in SL; membranes of spinous portion of dorsal fin
incised; spinous portion of dorsal fin high, the third or
fourth spines longest, 2.2-2.7 in head; pectoral fins 1.5-
1.75 in head; pelvic fins may reach anus, their length
1.7-2.0 in head; caudal fin rounded.

Light brown with numerous, close-set, dark brown to
black spots that are round to hexagonal, those on body
about size of pupil; two, very large, diffuse dusky areas
on back that extend broadly into dorsal fin, where they are
more heavily pigmented and separated by a whitish area (in
juveniles these dark and white areas are much more evident, and there are, in addition, large white spots on the
head, body, and median fins).

Remarks. Attains 50 cm. Western Pacific east to the
Marshall Islands and Samoa. At atolls it is usually seen
around coral knolls in lagoons. Serranus medurensis
Günther 1873 is a synonym.

Epinephelus **magniscuttis** Postel,
Fourmanoir, and Guézé 1964

Diagnosis. Dorsal rays XI,14-16; anal rays III,8;
pectoral rays 17-19; lateral-line scales 55-62; longitudinal scale series 103-122; scales on body largely
ctenoid; no auxiliary scales; no scales on maxilla; gill
rakers 9 + 16-17; 2 rows of teeth on midside of lower jaw;
maxilla not reaching posterior to a vertical at rear edge
of orbit; nostrils subequal; 3-4 enlarged serrae on prominent rounded corner of preopercle; a few small serrae on
margins of subopercle and interopercle; interorbital space
flat; body depth 2.7-3.2 in SL; membranes of spinous
portion of dorsal fin incised; pectoral fins 1.7-2.0 in
head; pelvic fins 2.1-2.35 in head; caudal fin slightly to
moderately rounded.

Light brown with small dark brown spots on about
upper three-fourths of head and body, those on head tending to form two parallel diagonal rows from behind eye to
end of operculum; dorsal fin with small dark brown spots;
a few small, dark brown spots on caudal fin (especially
dorsally); remaining fins without markings.

Remarks. Specimens have been examined from Mozambique, Natal, Mauritius, Réunion, New Caledonia, and the
Philippines, the largest, 47 cm; may reach 70 cm. Occurs
at depths of about 100-300 m. Epinephelus pseudomorrhua
Postel, Fourmanoir, and Guézé 1964 is a synonym.

Epinephelus **malabaricus** (Schneider 1801)

Diagnosis. Dorsal rays XI,14-16 (usually 15); anal
rays III,8; pectoral rays 18-20 (usually 19); lateral-line
scales 54-64; longitudinal scale series 102-117; scales on
body largely ctenoid; auxiliary scales present on body;
large adults with branched anterior lateral-line tubules;
very small scales on maxilla; gill rakers 8-11 + 15-18; 2
rows of teeth on midside of lower jaw in subadults,
increasing to 4 or 5 rows in large adults; maxilla
extending posterior to a vertical at rear of orbit;
nostrils subequal except in large adults in which the
posterior becomes larger; prominent rounded corner of
preopercle with 3-5 enlarged serrae; no serrae on margins
of subopercle and interopercle; interorbital space usually
slightly convex; body depth 3.1-3.7 in SL (4.0 in one
unusually elongate specimen); membranes of spinous portion
of dorsal fin incised; longest dorsal spine 3.1-4.0 in

head; posterior dorsal rays usually not reaching a
vertical at caudal-fin base; pectoral fins 1.75-2.15 in
head; pelvic fins not reaching anus, their length 2.05-2.6
in head; caudal fin rounded.

Light grayish to yellowish brown with five slightly
oblique, broad, dark bars on body that tend to bifurcate
ventrally and may contain pale areas; head and body with
numerous small (but well-separated) black spots and scattered larger (but still smaller than eye) pale spots and
blotches; a dark streak at upper edge of maxillary groove;
fins generally with small dark spots.

Remarks. Maximum length not known because of confusion with E. suillus, but probably to at least 100 cm.
Indian Ocean, including Red Sea, to the western Pacific.
Apparently absent from the Persian Gulf. Occurs in
various habitats including estuarine areas, but usually
not in well-developed coral reefs. Holocentrus salmoides
Lacepède 1802, Serranus bontoo Valenciennes 1828, S.
crapao Cuvier 1829, S. polypodophilus Bleeker 1849, and
Epinephelus cylindricus Postel 1965 are synonyms. Very
closely related to E. suillus Valenciennes 1828, which has
orangish brown instead of black spots; its spots are
larger than those of E. malabaricus at a given size.
Epinephelus suillus lacks small pale spots and has modally
20 pectoral rays. The species identified as E. salmo-
noides [sic] by Katayama in Masuda et al. (1984:plate 115,
figures J,K) is malabaricus.

Epinephelus melanostigma Schultz 1953

Diagnosis. Dorsal rays XI,14-16 (usually 15); anal
rays III,8; pectoral rays 17-19 (usually 18); lateral-line
scales 56-68; longitudinal scale series 83-98; scales on
body largely ctenoid; auxiliary scales present; very small
scales on maxilla; gill rakers 7-10 + 17-19; midside of
lower jaw with 3-5 rows of teeth; maxilla reaching posterior to a vertical at rear edge of orbit; nostrils
subequal; serrae at corner of preopercle not enlarged or
slightly enlarged; no serrae on margin of subopercle and
interopercle; interorbital space flat; body depth 2.95-3.4
in SL; membranes of spinous portion of dorsal fin incised;
longest dorsal spine 2.9-3.5 in head; posterior part of
dorsal fin nearly or just reaching a vertical at caudal-
fin base; second anal spine not long, 2.75-3.55 in head;
pelvic fins may reach anus, their length 2.05-2.45 in
head; caudal fin rounded.

Orangish to reddish brown, polygonal, very close-set spots on head and body, those on body larger than pupil (some larger than eye on small specimens); a large black spot on back and basal part of last four dorsal spines; all fins dark-spotted.

Remarks. Maximum length, 30 cm. East Africa to the Line Islands and Phoenix Islands, but not reported from many intervening areas. A shallow-water reef species.

Epinephelus merra, Bloch 1793

Diagnosis. Dorsal rays XI,15-17 (usually 16); anal rays III,8; pectoral rays 16-18; lateral-line scales 48-52; longitudinal scale series 100-114; scales of body ctenoid; auxiliary scales present on body; very small scales on maxilla; gill rakers 6-8 + 14-16 + 2 rows of teeth on midside of lower jaw; maxilla reaching to below or posterior to rear edge of eye; nostrils subequal; serrae at angle of preopercle slightly enlarged; margin of subopercle and interopercle smooth; interorbital space flat to slightly convex; body depth 2.9-3.2 in SL; membranes of spinous portion of dorsal fin incised; longest dorsal spine 2.7-2.95 in head; posterior part of dorsal fin reaching a vertical at caudal-fin base; pectoral fins 1.55-1.7 in head; pelvic fins usually not reaching anus, their length 1.75-2.2 in head; caudal fin rounded.

Light brown with numerous, close-set, round to hexagonal, dark brown spots, a few of which are fused to form short bands; fins with dark brown spots that are progressively smaller distally except those of pectorals, which are small throughout and largely confined to the rays; median fins often with narrow whitish or yellowish margins, sometimes with a submarginal dusky band (most evident on anal fin).

Remarks. This species is sometimes called the dwarf spotted grouper, in reference to its small size; largest examined, 27.5 cm. Very common and wide-ranging in the Indo-Pacific (though absent from the Red Sea and Persian Gulf). A coral-reef species usually found in protected waters such as lagoons or bays.

Epinephelus microdon (Bleeker 1856)

Diagnosis. Dorsal rays XI,14-15; anal rays III,8; pectoral rays 16-17 (usually 17); lateral-line scales 47-

52; longitudinal scale series 95–111; scales ctenoid in a broad region of side of body and posteriorly, cycloid elsewhere; auxiliary scales present on body; maxilla with very small scales; gill rakers 9–10 + 15–17; 2 or 3 rows of teeth on midside of lower jaw; maxilla extending well posterior to a vertical at rear edge of orbit; nostrils subequal; serrae at corner of preopercle moderately enlarged; margins of subopercle and interopercle smooth; interorbital space usually flat; body depth 2.7–3.1 in SL; membranes of spinous portion of dorsal fin incised; longest dorsal spine 2.65–3.3 in head; longest dorsal ray not reaching or just reaching a vertical at caudal-fin base; pectoral fin 1.65–1.95 in head; pelvic fins not reaching anus, 1.9–2.35 in head; caudal fin rounded.

Light brown with large, irregular, brown blotches on head and body; superimposed on this pattern numerous small, close-set, dark brown spots; a prominent, black, saddlelike spot dorsally on caudal peduncle; all fins with numerous, small, dark brown spots.

Remarks. Largest specimen examined, 61 cm. Wide-ranging in the Indo-Pacific region. Generally found on well-developed coral reefs. This species has been confused with E. fuscoguttatus (Forsskål); it was differentiated from fuscoguttatus by Randall (1964) on its lower pectoral-ray and gill-raker counts.

Epinephelus miliaris (Valenciennes 1830)

Diagnosis. Dorsal rays XI,16–18 (rarely 18); anal rays III,8; pectoral rays 17–18; lateral-line scales 48–51; longitudinal scale series 92–108; scales on body mainly ctenoid; some auxiliary scales present on body; very small scales on maxilla; gill rakers 8–9 + 15–16; 2 rows of teeth on midside of lower jaw; maxilla not reaching a vertical at rear edge of orbit; nostrils subequal; serrae at corner of preopercle enlarged; no serrae on margins of subopercle and interopercle; interorbital space slightly convex; body depth 2.85–3.2 in SL; membranes of spinous portion of dorsal fin incised; longest dorsal spine 2.35–2.7 in head; pectoral fins 1.55–1.8 in head; pelvic fins not reaching or just reaching anus, their length 1.7–2.1 in head; caudal fin rounded.

Whitish with numerous, small, close-set, polygonal, yellowish brown spots on head and body, and broad, irregular, diagonal dark bars, 3 of which extend into dorsal fin; dorsal fin with numerous, close-set, dark yellowish brown spots, the remaining fins with very large black spots (about 6-15 on pectoral fins).

Remarks. Reaches 45 cm. East Africa to Samoa, but known from relatively few localities. One specimen was speared by the author in 16 m on a mud bottom in Honiara Harbor, Guadalcanal. Another Bishop Museum specimen from Western Samoa is labeled "handlined from deep water." The specimen from the Gilbert Islands identified as Epinephelus sp. by Randall (1955) is E. miliaris. The name miliaris was restricted by lectotype designation by Randall and Ben-Tuvia (1983). Serranus dictiophorus Bleeker 1856 and Epinephelus fuscus Fourmanoir 1961 are synonyms.

Epinephelus morrhua (Valenciennes 1833)

Diagnosis. Dorsal rays XI,14-15; anal rays III,7-8 (rarely 7); pectoral rays 17-18; lateral-line scales 57-64; longitudinal scale series 108-123; scales of body largely ctenoid; no auxiliary scales on body; maxilla with a patch of tiny scales; gill rakers 8-10 + 15-17; 2 rows of teeth on midside of lower jaw; maxilla reaching a vertical at rear edge of orbit; posterior nostril of large adults enlarged (in a 34-cm specimen it is twice as large as anterior nostril); corner of preopercle with 2-5 greatly enlarged serrae; margins of subopercle and interopercle partially serrate; interorbital space slightly to moderately convex; body depth 2.85-3.1 in SL; membranes of spinous portion of dorsal fin incised; longest dorsal spine 2.65-3.2 in head; pectoral fins 1.9-2.3 in head; pelvic fins not reaching anus, 2.1-2.5 in head; caudal fin rounded.

Light brown with dark brown bands as follows: one from upper orbit to posterior nape; one from upper edge of opercle to base of fifth to ninth dorsal spines; one from orbit to midside of body where it bifurcates to an upper branch that ends at base of anterior soft portion of dorsal fin and a second branch that ends at rear base of fin; one from lower edge of orbit to upper pectoral base, continuing as a broken band from beneath pectoral fin to upper caudal peduncle; a last broad band from upper edge of maxillary groove to corner of preopercle.

Remarks. Reported to attain 90 cm. Western Pacific to western Indian Ocean, including the Red Sea. Occurs in the depth range of 120-370 m. This was the first of a complex of four intricately banded, deepwater species of

Epinephelus (last four in the key above) to be described.
The others have occasionally been misidentified as
morrhua. Epinephelus cometae Tanaka 1927 is a synonym.

Epinephelus multinotatus (Peters 1876)

Diagnosis. Dorsal rays XI,15-17; anal rays III,8;
pectoral rays 18-19; lateral-line scales 64-80; longitudinal scale series 135-162; auxiliary scales present on
body; tiny scales on maxilla; gill rakers 9-11 + 15-18;
posterior nostrils of large adults notably larger than
anterior; 2 rows of teeth on midside of lower jaw; maxilla
usually reaching to or slightly beyond a vertical at
posterior edge of eye; serrae at corner of preopercle not
enlarged; margins of subopercle and interopercle smooth;
interorbital space moderately to strongly convex; body
depth 2.6-3.0 in SL; membranes of spinous portion of
dorsal fin not incised; longest dorsal spine (third or
fourth) 2.3-2.9 in head; caudal fin truncate.
 In the Persian Gulf, Gulf of Oman, and eastern Indian
Ocean, dark purplish gray with scattered whitish blotches
of variable size (white blotches may fade after death).
In the western Indian Ocean, the lower half of head and
body with numerous small, dark reddish brown spots superimposed on the gray, white-blotched pattern.
 Remarks. Maximum length about 100 cm. Indian Ocean.
Occurs from the shallows to at least 90 m. Serranus
jayakari Boulenger 1889 from the Gulf of Oman, Epinephelus
rankini Whitley 1945 from Western Australia, and E.
leprosus Smith 1955 from Aldabra are synonyms.

Epinephelus ongus (Bloch 1790)

Diagnosis. Dorsal rays XI,15-16 (usually 15); anal
rays III,8; pectoral rays 15-17 (usually 16); lateral-line
scales 48-53; longitudinal scale series 90-109; scales on
body largely ctenoid; auxiliary scales present; very small
scales on maxilla; gill rakers 8-10 + 15-17; teeth small;
2 rows of teeth on midside of lower jaw; maxilla reaching
to or slightly posterior to a vertical at rear edge of
orbit; nostrils subequal; fleshy upper margin of opercle
very highly arched; serrae at corner of preopercle
slightly enlarged; margins of subopercle and interopercle
smooth; interorbital space flat to slight convex; body
depth 2.75-3.2 in SL; membranes of spinous portion of

dorsal fin incised; longest dorsal spine 2.7-3.4 in head; posterior part of dorsal fin extending beyond a vertical at caudal-fin base; pectoral fins long, 1.4-1.7 in head; pelvic fins short, not reaching anus, their length 2.05-2.35 in head; caudal fin rounded.

Juveniles of about 60 mm SL with rounded white spots on head and body; all fins with white spots, the pectorals yellow with white dots; juveniles of about 100 mm SL show a horizontal elongation of spots on the head and body; in adults the spots have coalesced to form very irregular, narrow, longitudinal stripes on body; only a few small spots remain dorsally on postorbital head; a series of indistinct dark blotches along back; white spots persisting (but more as short lines or elongate spots) on median fins but not on paired fins; soft portions of dorsal and anal fins and posterior border of caudal fin with a narrow white margin and a broad, blackish submarginal band.

Remarks. Reported to 40 cm. Caroline Islands and western Pacific to western Indian Ocean. A shallow-water species of coral reefs and rocky substrata. Most recent authors have identified this species as E. summana, but Randall and Ben-Tuvia (1983) have shown that the latter is a Red Sea endemic.

Epinephelus poecilonotus (Temminck and Schlegel 1842)

Diagnosis. Dorsal rays XI,14-15 (usually 15); anal rays III,8; pectoral rays 17-19 (rarely 19); lateral-line scales 56-65; longitudinal scale series 110-136; scales of body largely ctenoid; no auxiliary scales on body; gill rakers 8-9 + 16-18; 2 rows of teeth on midside of lower jaw; maxilla usually reaching a vertical at rear edge of eye or extending slightly posterior to it; posterior nostril of adults notably larger than anterior (2 times larger in a specimen 35 cm SL); 2 or 3 very large serrae at corner of preopercle; interorbital space moderately convex; body depth 2.5-3.1 in SL; membranes of spinous portion of dorsal fin incised; longest dorsal spine 2.55-3.1 in head; pectoral fins about 1.8 in head; pelvic fins may reach anus in small individuals, their length about 1.9-2.2 in head; caudal fin rounded.

Yellowish brown, the young with a large, isolated, oval black spot basally in dorsal fin between spines III and IX (with age this spot breaks up into a group of smaller spots); a concentric dark brown band below base of dorsal spot from nape, bifurcating above upper end of gill opening, one branch to anterior soft portion of dorsal fin and the other to midbase of fin (with age the band breaks into a series of spots); a second concentric band (or row of spots) from head above upper end of preopercular margin, branching below middle of soft portion of dorsal fin, the upper branch ending at rear base of dorsal fin and the lower on caudal peduncle; a third concentric band from orbit to lower caudal peduncle; a dark band from lower part of orbit to end of operculum at level of upper pectoral-fin base; fins brownish yellow, only the dorsal with dark markings.

    Remarks. Attains 65 cm. Western Pacific to western Indian Ocean (not recorded from Red Sea or Persian Gulf). Occurs at depths of about 60 to 200 m. Very few specimens in collections. Sometimes misidentified as E. morrhua.

Epinephelus polystigma (Bleeker 1853)

    Diagnosis. Dorsal rays XI,15–16 (usually 15); anal rays III,8; pectoral rays 16–18 (usually 17); lateral-line scales 50–58; longitudinal scale series 81–91; scales on body largely ctenoid (but weakly so); scales on head embedded; auxiliary scales present; maxilla with a patch of small scales; gill rakers 8–9 + 14–16; teeth very small (canines and villiform teeth), those on midside of lower jaw in 2 rows in juveniles and subadults and 3 rows in adults; maxilla reaching posterior to a vertical at rear edge of orbit; nostrils subequal except for large adults in which the posterior is enlarged; serrae at corner of preopercle slightly to moderately enlarged; interorbital space flat to slightly convex; body depth 2.6–2.95 in SL; snout short, 4.8–5.5 in head; membranes of spinous portion of dorsal fin incised; longest dorsal spine 2.95–3.35 in head; posterior rays of dorsal fin extending beyond a vertical at base of caudal fin; pectoral fins about 1.55–1.75 in head; pelvic fins about 2.0–2.2 in head; caudal fin rounded and moderately long, 1.65–1.80 in head.

    Dark brown with numerous small white dots on head, body, and fins (dots may be absent in adults and are often lost in smaller specimens in preservative); soft portions of dorsal and anal fins and posterior caudal and pectoral fins with a narrow orange-red margin (whitish in preservative). A juvenile of 8.8 cm SL has some horizontal white dashes on the body in addition to the white dots, and the margins of the fins are pale orangish. A 2.2-cm juvenile taken at the same location is dark brown with scattered white spots larger than the pupil on the body.

Remarks. Bleeker described E. polystigma from two specimens, one from Ambon and the other Sumatra, 142–245 mm TL, in 1853. Later he relegated it to the synonymy of E. summana (his summana is ongus). The species is here resurrected from synonymy. The type specimens have been examined, as well as others from Ambon (the juvenile mentioned above), Papua New Guinea, Solomon Islands, New Britain, and two localities in Luzon, all from fresh or brackish water habitats. Largest specimen, 28.5 cm. Serranus australis Castelnau 1875 from Cape York, Australia is a synonym.

Epinephelus posteli Fourmanoir and Crosnier 1964

Diagnosis. Dorsal rays XI,16; anal rays III,8–9 (rarely 8); pectoral rays 18; scales cycloid and embedded, difficult to count (count of longitudinal scales series of holotype by Fourmanoir and Crosnier, 95); lower-limb gill rakers 9–10; nostrils of equal size; maxilla not reaching posterior to a vertical at rear edge of orbit; serrae at corner of preopercle not notable enlarged; body depth 3.0–3.5 in SL; membranes of spinous portion of dorsal fin incised; caudal fin rounded.

Head and body covered with numerous, small, close-set, round to hexagonal, dark brown spots; spinous portion of dorsal fin with a series of slightly diagonal, narrow, dark brown stripes separated by pale bands of nearly equal width; other fins with small dark spots but these obscured distally where fins are dark brown.

Remarks. Reported to reach 100 cm. Known only from Madagascar, Mozambique, and Natal. No specimens in United States or European museums; none examined by author.

Epinephelus quernus Seale 1901

Diagnosis. Dorsal rays XI,14–15 (usually 15); anal rays III,9; pectoral rays 19–20 (rarely 20); lateral-line scales 66–73; longitudinal scale series 122–139; scales on body largely ctenoid; some auxiliary scales anteriorly on body; maxilla naked; gill rakers 8–9 + 15–16; 2 rows of teeth on midside of lower jaw; maxilla from below rear of pupil to a short distance posterior to eye; posterior nostril of adults vertically elongate and enlarged, 3 times or more larger than anterior; corner of preopercle with 3-4 enlarged serrae, the 2 lowermost angling downward; no spines on lower margin of preopercle; subopercle and interopercle usually with a few serrae; interorbital space slightly convex; body depth 2.3-2.65 in SL; spinous portion of dorsal fin incised; pectoral fins 1.7-2.1 in head; pelvic fins may reach anus, 1.7-2.1 in head; caudal fin slightly rounded.

Grayish brown to dark brown, with vertical rows of small white spots on body (more evident on young than adults); a dark streak on upper edge of maxillary groove.

Remarks. Attains about 80 cm. Endemic to the Hawaiian Islands. Occurs to depths of at least 280 m. The young are occasionally encountered in the principal Hawaiian Islands in scuba-diving depths, but adults appear confined to deeper water. In the Northwestern Hawaiian Islands, however, adults have been taken in as little as 20 m. The white-spotted pattern is similar to that of E. niveatus (Valenciennes), a deepwater species of the western Atlantic. The latter has, in addition, a black, saddlelike spot on the caudal peduncle. Also it has scales on the maxilla, and the membranes of the spinous portion of the dorsal fin are very deeply incised.

Epinephelus quoyanus (Valenciennes 1830)

Diagnosis. Dorsal rays XI,16-18; anal rays III,8; pectoral rays 17-19 (rarely 19); lateral-line scales 48-51; longitudinal scale series 86-96; scales on body ctenoid except anterodorsally and ventrally; auxiliary scales present on body but not numerous; very small scales present on maxilla; gill rakers 7-8 + 14-16; 2 rows of teeth on midside of lower jaw; maxilla extending to or slightly posterior to a vertical at rear edge of orbit; corner of preopercle with enlarged serrae; no serrae on margin of subopercle and interopercle; snout short, 4.3-5.6 in head; interorbital space flat; body depth 2.9-3.5 in SL; membranes of spinous portion of dorsal fin incised; longest dorsal spine (third to fifth) 2.35-2.85 in head; pectoral fins relatively long, 1.2-1.5 in head; pelvic fins may reach anus, their length 1.7-2.1 in head; caudal fin rounded, 1.35-1.6 in head.

Whitish with numerous, large, close-set, roundish to hexagonal, dark brown to black spots on head and body (many on body as large or larger than eye); two, dark brown to black, diagonal bands on thorax anterior to pectoral-fin base (the upper sometimes divided into two elongate spots); fins with dark brown to black spots, those on pectorals small; caudal and anal fins with a narrow white posterior margin, the anal with a blackish submarginal band.

Remarks. Attains 35 cm. Western Pacific to southwest coast of Thailand. Serranus megachir Richardson 1846 and S. gilberti Richardson 1842 are synonyms.

Epinephelus radiatus (Day 1867)

Diagnosis. Dorsal rays XI,13–15; anal rays III,8; pectoral rays 17–18; lateral-line scales 57–66; longitudal scale series 110–120; scales of body largely ctenoid; no auxiliary scales on body; gill rakers 8–9 + 16–18; 2 rows of teeth on midside of lower jaw; maxilla varying from just short of a vertical at rear edge of orbit to extending beyond it; posterior nostril of adults enlarged relative to anterior; 2–5 greatly enlarged serrae at corner of preopercle; margins of subopercle and interopercle partially serrate (may be smooth in juveniles); interorbital space slightly convex; body depth 2.5–3.1 in SL; membranes of spinous portion of dorsal fin incised; longest dorsal spine 2.65–3.05 in head; pectoral fins 1.7–2.25 in head; pelvic fins not reaching anus, their length 2.0–2.7 in head; caudal fin rounded.

Five dark brown bands (only the edges dark brown in adults) that pass diagonally downward and ventrally from dorsal edge of body: first band from nape to eye, second from midbase of spinous portion of dorsal fin to upper edge of opercle, third and fourth from soft portion of dorsal fin, both branching as they pass ventrally, and fifth on caudal peduncle; an irregular single or double row of small dark brown spots in pale interspaces between dark bands.

Remarks: Reported to reach 70 cm. Western Pacific to western Indian Ocean. Randall and Klausewitz (In press) will report it from the Red Sea and Gulf of Oman. Adults generally from depths of 80–160 m. The young have been taken in as little as 18 m. Often misidentified as E. morrhua (e.g., by Katayama in Masuda et al. 1984).

Epinephelus retouti Bleeker 1874

Diagnosis. Dorsal rays XI,16 or 17 (usually 16); anal rays III,8; pectoral rays 19–20 (rarely 20); lateral-

line scales 64–76; longitudinal scale series 120–141;
auxiliary scales numerous; no scales on maxilla; gill
rakers 6-8 + 15-16; 3 rows of teeth on midside of lower
jaw of adults; maxilla reaching to a vertical from below
middle of eye to posterior edge of eye; serrae at corner
of preopercle only slightly enlarged, if at all; no serrae
on subopercle or interopercle; interorbital space slightly
concave to nearly flat; body depth 2.6–3.15 in SL;
membranes of spinous portion of dorsal fin deeply incised;
longest dorsal spine (usually the fourth) 2.6–3.1 in head;
pectoral fins 1.6–1.75 in head; pelvic fins 1.8–2.15 in
head; caudal fin truncate.

Reddish yellow (scale centers greenish yellow, the
edges red) with or without six broad dark bars on body;
outer triangular part of each interspinous membrane deep
red (or black on individuals from relatively shallow
depths) with a submarginal zone of whitish or pink.

Remarks. Attains 45 cm. Indo-Pacific, generally
from depths greater than 70 m. The author, however, has
observed juveniles in as little as 30 m at Mauritius.
Randall and Heemstra (1986) have shown that E. truncatus
Katayama 1957 is a junior synonym.

Epinephelus rivulatus (Valenciennes 1830)

Diagnosis. Dorsal rays XI,16–18 (usually 17); anal
rays III,8; pectoral rays 17–19 (usually 18); lateral-line
scales 49–53; longitudinal scale series 86–102; scales on
body largely ctenoid; very small cycloid scales on nape
and anteriorly on body above lateral line; auxiliary
scales present on body of adults; maxilla naked or with a
small patch of tiny embedded scales; gill rakers 7–8 + 13–
16; 2 rows of teeth on midside of lower jaw; maxilla
reaching to or posterior to a vertical at rear edge of
orbit; nostrils subequal; serrae at corner of preopercle
enlarged; margins of subopercle and interopercle without
serrae; interorbital space flat to slightly convex; body
depth 2.6–3.3 in SL; membranes of spinous portion of
dorsal fin incised; longest dorsal spine 2.5–2.85 in head;
pectoral fins 1.6–1.8 in head; pelvic fins may reach anus,
their length 1.9–2.25 in head; caudal fin rounded.

Reddish to greenish brown with a white dot on each
scale of body; six, irregular, slightly to moderately
oblique, dark brown bars on body, the first on nape, the
last on caudal peduncle; fourth and fifth bars (below

soft portion of dorsal fin) may be partially joined
dorsally; a large, oblong, deep red spot at base of
pectoral fins; irregular, broad, dark brown bands on head
(Pacific); irregular, dark bluish lines and spots on head
(Indian Ocean); tips of interspinous membranes of dorsal
fin yellow.

Remarks. Attains 35 cm. Western Pacific and Indian
Ocean (but absent from Red Sea and Persian Gulf). A
species of coral reefs or rocky bottoms from the depth
range of 1-150 m. Serranus rhyncholepis Bleeker 1859,
Epinephelus grammatophorus Boulenger 1903, E. homosinensis
Whitley 1944, and E. spiramen Whitley 1945 are synonyms.
The illustration in Masuda et al. (1984: plate 115, figure
A) identified by Katayama as E. rhyncholepis is E.
rivulatus.

Epinephelus septemfasciatus (Thunberg 1793)

Diagnosis. Dorsal rays XI,13-16 (rarely 13 or 16);
anal rays III,9-10 (rarely 10); pectoral rays 17-19;
lateral-line scales 63-71; longitudinal scale series 107-
116; no auxiliary scales on body; maxilla naked; gill
rakers 8-10 + 13-18; 2 rows of teeth on midside of lower
jaw; maxilla to below rear half of orbit; posterior nostril larger than anterior, in adults more than twice as
large; serrae at corner of preopercle enlarged; lower
margin of preopercle with 1 or 2 downward-directed spines
separated from serrae at angle (usually obscured by fleshy
tissue); subopercle and interopercle usually with a few
serrae; interorbital space moderately to strongly convex;
body depth 2.5-3.1 in SL; membranes of spinous portion of
dorsal fin incised; caudal fin rounded.

Brownish gray with seven or eight broad dark bars on
body, the first on nape and the last on caudal peduncle
(the broadest and darkest; the upper part black on juveniles); penultimate bar may be divided into two narrow
bars, hence variation in bar number; dark bars extending
basally into dorsal fin; anal and pelvic fins dark brown.

Remarks. May exceed 100 cm TL. Southern Japan to
the Indian Ocean, in deep water (young may be found in
lesser depths). Boulenger (1895) regarded the American
species E. mystacinus (Poey) as a junior synonym of E.
septemfasciatus. Smith (1971), however, recognized mystacinus as distinct. Surprisingly, Katayama in Masuda et
al. (1984) has reported mystacinus from the Izu Islands to
the South China Sea. Epinephelus mystacinus is here

regarded as a probable synonym of <u>septemfasciatus</u>. <u>Epine-</u>
<u>phelus compressus</u> Postel, Fourmanoir, and Guézé 1964 also
appears to be a synonym.

<u>Epinephelus sexfasciatus</u> (Valenciennes 1828)

<u>Diagnosis</u>. Dorsal rays XI,14–16 (usually 15); anal
rays III,8; pectoral rays 17–19 (usually 18); lateral-line
scales 46–51; longitudinal scale series 84–96; scales on
body largely ctenoid; auxiliary scales present; maxilla
naked; gill rakers 7–8 + 13–15; 2 rows of teeth on midside
of lower jaw; maxilla reaching slightly posterior to a
vertical at rear edge of orbit; nostrils subequal; corner
of preopercle with 1–4 greatly enlarged, acute serrae
(usually 2, which are well-separated and diverging); no
serrae on margins of subopercle and interopercle; interorbital space slightly convex; body depth 2.65–3.2 in SL;
membranes of spinous portion of dorsal fin incised; longest dorsal spine 2.6–3.35 in head; pectoral fins 1.55–1.8
in head; pelvic fins not reaching anus, their length 1.95–
2.25 in head; caudal fin rounded.

Whitish with six, slightly diagonal, grayish brown
bars, the first on nape, the last on caudal peduncle (a
narrow, pale bar or broken bar may be present within the
dark bars, nearly dividing them to two); fins pale, the
caudal fin and soft portions of the dorsal and anal fins
with small blackish spots.

<u>Remarks</u>. A small species; largest examined, 26 cm.
Northern Australia, Indonesia, Southeast Asia, and the
Philippines. Taken mainly in trawls (two depth records,
55–70 m).

<u>Epinephelus socialis</u> (Günther 1873)

<u>Diagnosis</u>. Dorsal rays XI,14–15 (usually 15); anal
rays III,8; pectoral rays 18–19 (usually 19); lateral-line
scales 65–70; longitudinal scale series 97–111; scales on
body ctenoid except anterodorsally and ventrally where
cycloid; auxiliary scales present; maxilla with very small
scales; gill rakers 8–9 + 16–19; 3–4 rows of teeth on
midside of lower jaw; maxilla extending posterior to a
vertical at rear edge of orbit; nostrils subequal; serrae
at corner of preopecle enlarged; no serrae on margins of
subopercle and interopercle; interorbital space flat to
slightly convex; body depth 3.0–3.4 in SL; membranes of

spinous portion of dorsal fin incised; longest dorsal
spine 2.65-3.3 in head; posterior dorsal rays nearly or
just reaching caudal-fin base; pelvic fins not reaching
anus, their length 1.85-2.1 in head; caudal fin rounded.

Whitish with numerous, very small, dark brown to
black spots on head and body, those posteriorly on body
often merging to form irregular longitudinal bands;
usually five large blackish spots on back, four at base of
dorsal fin, and one dorsally on caudal peduncle; caudal
fin and soft portions of dorsal and anal fins dark brown
with small whitish spots.

Remarks. Largest reported (from Pitcairn by Randall
1980) 42 cm SL (= 52 cm TL). Known only from islands of
Oceania, including Society Islands, Tuamotu Archipelago,
Rapa, Pitcairn Group, Cook Islands, Samoa Islands, and
Marshall Islands. Occurs mainly in shallow, often turbu-
lent water of exposed outer reef areas.

Epinephelus spilotoceps Schultz 1953

Diagnosis. Dorsal rays XI,14-15 (rarely 14); anal
rays III,8; pectoral rays 18-19 (usually 18); lateral-line
scales 60-69; longitudinal scale series 86-100; scales on
body largely ctenoid; auxiliary scales present; very small
scales on maxilla; gill rakers 7-8 + 15-18; 3 or 4 rows of
teeth on midside of lower jaw; maxilla reaching beyond a
vertical at rear edge of orbit; nostrils subequal; serrae
at corner of preopercle not enlarged or only slightly
enlarged; margin of subopercle and interopercle smooth or
with a few small serrae; interorbital space flat; body
depth 3.1-3.5 in SL; membranes of spinous portion of
dorsal fin incised; longest dorsal spine 2.75-3.2 in head;
posterior part of dorsal fin nearly reaching caudal-fin
base; second anal spine 2.5-3.2 in head; pelvic fins not
reaching anus, their length 2.1-2.4 in head; caudal fin
rounded.

Numerous, polygonal, brown spots on head and body,
those on body mostly smaller than pupil of eye, the spots
so close together on head and body (especially on dorsal
half) that the intervening pale space is a network of
white lines; a large black spot on back at base of last
four dorsal spines and extending basally into fin (this
spot a result of merging and darkening of the polygonal
spots); two similar but smaller spots at base of soft
portion of dorsal fin (an ill-defined one sometimes apparent below fifth dorsal spine), and one dorsally on caudal

peduncle; dark spots on head progressively smaller and darker anteriorly, those on snout very small (about the size of nostrils); all fins dark-spotted.

Remarks. Reaches about 35 cm. East Africa to the Line Islands; few literature records. A coral-reef species generally found in shallow water. Epinephelus salonotus Smith and Smith 1963, named from Seychelles material, is a synonym.

Epinephelus stoliczkae (Day 1875)

Diagnosis. Dorsal rays XI,16-18 (usually 17); anal rays III,8; pectoral rays 17-19; lateral-line scales 48-53; longitudinal scale series 93-106; scales cycloid (ctenoid beneath pectoral fins); maxilla with very small scales; gill rakers 6-7 + 13-15; 2 rows of teeth on mid-side of lower jaw; maxilla extending posterior to a vertical at rear edge of orbit; nostrils subequal; serrae at corner of preopercle somewhat enlarged; margins of subopercle and interopercle usually smooth; interorbital space moderately convex; body depth 2.9-9.3 in SL; membranes of spinous portion of dorsal fin incised; longest dorsal spine 2.4-3.1 in head; pectoral fins 1.65-1.95 in head; pelvic fins not approaching anus, their length 2.1-2.45 in head; caudal fin rounded.

Yellowish gray with a broad, dark grayish brown bar on body below posterior spinous portion of dorsal fin, two more bars close together beneath soft portion of fin, and one on caudal peduncle; numerous, small, dark reddish brown spots on head (where very close-set) and anterior half to two-thirds of body; a large, elongate, dark spot at pectoral-fin base with a diagonal dark line anterior to it on thorax.

Remarks. Reported to 38 cm. Ranges from the Red Sea to the Gulf of Oman and coast of Pakistan. A shallow-water species; observed by the author around small coral heads on sandy substrata in the Gulf of Tadjoura.

Epinephelus suillus (Valenciennes 1828)

Diagnosis. Dorsal rays XI,14-16 (1 of 37 specimens with 13); anal rays III,8; pectoral rays 19-20 (26 of 37 specimens with 20); lateral-line scales 58-65; longitudinal scale series 100-118; auxiliary scales present on body; tiny scales on maxilla; anterior lateral-line scales

of adults branched; gill rakers 8-10 + 15-17; 2 rows of
teeth on midside of lower jaw (3 rows in large adults);
maxilla extending posterior to a vertical at rear edge of
orbit; nostrils subequal; enlarged serrae at corner of
preopercle; margins of subopercle and interopercle smooth;
interorbital space usually slightly convex; body depth
3.2-3.75 in SL (an unusually elongate specimen has a depth
of 3.9 in SL); membranes of spinous portion of dorsal fin
incised; longest dorsal spine 3.0-3.85 in head; posterior
dorsal rays usually not reaching a vertical at caudal-fin
base; pectoral fins 1.75-2.25 in head; pelvic fins not
reaching anus, 2.15-2.65 in head; caudal fin rounded.

Pale yellowish or whitish with five slightly diagonal
brown bars on body that bifurcate ventrally, and one on
nape (bars may be broken above lateral line into two
segments); numerous brownish orange spots about the size
of pupil or smaller on head and body, those on body tending to be arranged in rows parallel to brown bars; fins
with indistinct brown spots (generally only basally on
caudal and pectoral fins).

Remarks. Reaches at least 100 cm. Indian Ocean to
western Pacific. Not definitely known from the Red Sea,
but common in the Persian Gulf where it is among the most
important of commercial fishes. Occurs from coral reefs
to estuarine areas. Often misidentified as E. tauvina or
E. malabaricus (see remarks for malabaricus). Figures A
and B of plate 116 identified as malabaricus by Katayama
in Masuda et al. 1984 are suillus.

Epinephelus summana (Forsskål 1755)

Diagnosis. Dorsal rays XI,14-16 (usually 15); anal
rays III,8; pectoral rays 16-18 (usually 17); lateral-line
scales 49-54; longitudinal scale series 95-110; scales on
body largely ctenoid; auxiliary scales present on body;
very small scales on maxilla; gill rakers 89-10 + 15-17; 3
or 4 rows of teeth on midside of lower jaw; maxilla
reaching to or slightly posterior to a vertical at rear
edge of orbit; posterior nostril of adults vertically
elongate and enlarged, its length 2 to 4 times longer than
diameter of anterior nostril; dorsal margin of opercle
strongly convex; serrae at corner of preopercle slightly
enlarged; margins of subopercle and interopercle smooth or
with a few serrae; interorbital space usually flat; body
depth 2.75-3.1 in SL; membranes of spinous portion of
dorsal fin incised; longest dorsal spine 2.75-3.15 in

head; pectoral fins 1.7-2.1 in head; pelvic fins not
reaching anus, 2.3-2.7 in head; caudal fin rounded.

Dark brown to dark brownish gray with large, round,
pale blotches and numerous, small, white spots overlying
the entire pattern; irregular, broad, dark bands and a few
small white spots on head; a prominent dark brown to black
streak at upper edge of maxillary groove; all fins with
small white spots (though few on pectorals); a series of
indistinct dark brown blotches along back at base of
dorsal fin and one on caudal peduncle. Juveniles dark
gray with large white spots on head, body, and fins.

Remarks. Largest examined, 52 cm. Red Sea. Found
on reefs in protected waters; will enter estuarine areas.
The name summana has often been applied to E. ongus, a
related species that does not occur in the Red Sea.
Actually, summana is more closely related to E. caeruleopunctatus, sharing with it the numerous teeth on the lower
jaw, enlarged posterior nostril, and similarity in color
pattern. The two are differentiated in the Key.

Epinephelus tauvina (Forsskål 1775)

Diagnosis. Dorsal rays XI,14-16 (rarely 16); anal
rays III,8; pectoral rays 18-19; lateral-line scales 65-
74; longitudinal scale series 98-113; scales cycloid
except for a patch of variable size in pectoral region of
body; auxiliary scales present; tiny embedded scales
present on maxilla; gill rakers 8-10 + 18-20; no small
platelets on side of first gill arch; 3 or 4 rows of teeth
on midside of lower jaw; maxilla extending well posterior
to a vertical at hind border of orbit; posterior nostril
larger than anterior on adults greater than 30 cm SL;
serrae at corner of preopercle not greatly enlarged;
margins of subopercle and interopercle smooth; interorbital space usually flat; body elongate, the depth 3.1-
3.8 in SL; head large, 2.15-2.4 in SL, and pointed; membranes of spinous portion of dorsal fin incised; dorsal
spines short, the longest 3.15-4.6 in head; pectoral fins
1.85-2.4 in head; pelvic fins not reaching anus, 2.3-2.9
in head; caudal fin rounded.

Greenish gray to brown dorsally, shading to whitish
ventrally, with numerous, well-spaced, dull orange-red to
dark brown spots on head, body, and fins (spots relatively
smaller and more numerous on larger individuals); five
faint, diagonal dark bars on body (or rows of dark spots),
four below base of dorsal fin and one on caudal peduncle;

a large blackish spot often present on back at base of
last four dorsal spines and extending basally into fin
(this spot more evident on small individuals), a lesser
blackish spot (or group of darker spots) at base of fourth
and fifth dorsal spines, two at base of soft portion of
caudal peduncle, and one dorsally on caudal peduncle.

Remarks. Reported to attain 70 cm; largest collected
by the author, 62 cm. Found throughout most of the Indo-
Pacific region, including the Red Sea (type locality) and
the Pitcairn Group. Not known from the Persian Gulf
(previous records being E. suillus). One record from the
Hawaiian Islands is erroneous. Generally found on coral
reefs in clear water; has been taken at depths as shallow
as 1 m. Epinephelus elongatus Schultz 1953 and E. chewa
Morgans 1966 are synonyms.

Epinephelus townsendi Boulenger 1898

Diagnosis. Dorsal rays XI,16–17; anal rays III,8;
pectoral rays 18–19 (usually 18); lateral-line scales 56–
62; longitudinal scale series 99–107; scales on body
strongly ctenoid; auxiliary scales numerous; maxilla
naked; gill rakers 8–9 + 15–16; 2–3 rows of teeth on
midside of lower jaw; maxilla reaching slightly beyond a
vertical at rear edge of orbit; nostrils subequal; serrae
at corner of preopercle not enlarged; interorbital space
flat to slightly convex; body depth 2.75–2.8 in SL;
membranes of spinous portion of dorsal fin not incised;
longest dorsal spine 3.5–3.75 in head; posterior dorsal
rays reaching slightly beyond a vertical at caudal-fin
base; pectoral fins 1.75–2.1 in head; pelvic fins short,
2.3–2.5 in head; caudal fin rounded.

Brown with one or two dark streaks across cheek and
operculum, the most evident the lowermost, which extends
from orbit to just above corner of preopercle; a dark
streak at upper edge of maxillary groove; subadults may
exhibit a coarse dark reticular pattern on body as illustrated by Bleeker (1877:plate 339, figure 3).

Remarks. Largest examined, 26 cm. Described from
four specimens, 186–208 mm SL, from the coast of Pakistan,
now in the British Museum (Natural History). Other specimens were examined in this museum from India, Thailand,
and Borneo. Bleeker (1876:66) misidentified this fish as
Epinephelus nebulosus (Valenciennes); he recorded specimens from Sumatra, Java, Bangka, and Singapore.

Epinephelus trimaculatus (Valenciennes 1828)

Diagnosis. Dorsal rays XI,16-17; anal rays III,8; pectoral rays 16-18 (rarely 16); lateral-line scales 48-52; longitudinal scale series 89-100; auxiliary scales present on body; maxilla with very small scales; gill rakers 7-9 + 14-15; 2 rows of teeth on midside of lower jaw; maxilla reaching to or beyond a vertical at rear of orbit; no enlarged serrae at corner of preopercle; margin of subopercle and interopercle smooth; dorsal profile of head nearly straight; interorbital space flat; body depth 2.75-3.25 in SL; membranes of spinous portion of dorsal fin incised; longest dorsal spine (third or fourth) 2.75-3.45 in head; pectoral fins 1.7-1.9 in head; pelvic fins short, 2.0-2.5 in head; caudal fin rounded.

Whitish with numerous small, close set, brownish red spots on head and body; a black spot larger than eye on back and rear base of spinous portion of dorsal fin, a second, smaller spot on back and midbase of soft portion of fin, a third spot on back and rear base of soft portion of fin, and a fourth middorsally on caudal peduncle; no dark streak at upper edge of maxillary groove; median fins with small reddish brown spots; paired fins yellowish, the pelvics with a few small red spots on rays and the pectorals with a few faint red spots basally; median fins with a very narrow whitish margin posteriorly.

Remarks. Attains 40 cm. Southern Japan to China. Few specimens in museums. Some authors such as Katayama in Masuda et al. (1984) and Shen (1984) have used the name E. fario (Thunberg 1792) for this species. The description and figure of fario by Thunberg cannot be linked with any known species of Epinephelus and must be regarded as unidentifiable. No type of E. fario is extant (L. Wallin Pers. comm., Zoologiska Institutionen, Uppsala Universitet, Sweden 1978).

Epinephelus tuamotuensis Fourmanoir 1971

Diagnosis. Dorsal rays XI,14-15; anal rays III,8; pectoral rays 18; longitudinal scale series 118 (1 specimen); scales of body largely ctenoid; a small patch of very small scales on maxilla; gill rakers 9 + 15-16 (2 specimens); 2 rows of teeth on midside of lower jaw; maxilla nearly or just reaching a vertical at rear edge of orbit; nostrils subequal; margins of subopercle and inter-

opercle partially serrate; interorbital space slightly
convex; body depth 2.8-3.1 in SL; membranes of spinous
portion of dorsal fin incised; longest dorsal spine 3.1-
3.25 in head; pectoral fins 1.75-1.9 in head; pelvic fins
not reaching anus, their length 2.15-2.25 in head; caudal
fin slightly rounded.

Light yellowish brown with an irregular, coarse
reticulum of dark brown bands on upper three-fourths of
postorbital head and body (though some segments not inter-
connecting); no markings on fins.

Remarks. Largest examined, 80 cm. Known only from
the Tuamotu Archipelago, Pitcairn Group, and Rapa in the
depth range of 122-240 m.

Epinephelus tukula Morgans 1959

Diagnosis. Dorsal rays XI,14-15 (usually 15); anal
rays III,7-9 (usually 8); pectoral rays 18-20; lateral-
line scales 66-70; longitudinal scale series 113-135;
scales on body largely ctenoid; auxiliary scales not
present on body; gill rakers 7-10 + 16-19; 3-6 rows of
teeth on midside of lower jaw; maxilla reaching to or
beyond a vertical at rear edge of orbit; posterior nostril
at most 1.5 times larger than anterior; serrae at corner
of preopercle moderately enlarged; interorbital space
slightly convex; body depth 2.9-3.3 in SL; membranes of
spinous portion of dorsal fin incised; longest dorsal
spine 3.3-4.0 in head; caudal fin broadly rounded in
juveniles, slightly rounded in adults.

Grayish brown with large, widely spaced, round to
horizontally elliptical, dark brown spots in about five
longitudinal rows on body (most spots larger than eye);
head with small dark spots and short bands radiating from
posterior part of orbit; fins with small dark spots. Very
large fish may be nearly black.

Remarks. Largest specimen reported, 139 cm (Morgans
1982). Only one specimen examined, a juvenile 8.8 cm SL
collected by the author off southwestern India. Large
adults were observed off Kenya and Natal. Katayama (1975)
recorded E. tukula from Okinawa, and Katayama in Masuda et
al. 1984 from Wakayama Prefecture, Japan. Shen (1984)
illustrated two specimens from Taiwan, one correctly identified as tukula, the smaller one incorrectly as E. hexagonatus. This grouper has been observed underwater on the
northern Great Barrier Reef where it is known as the

potato cod (Grant 1982). It was first described and figures as <u>Serranus</u> <u>dispar</u> var. A by Playfair and Günther (1867) from Zanzibar. Morgans (1959) selected <u>S</u>. <u>dispar</u> var. B (= <u>E</u>. <u>microdon</u>) to retain the name <u>dispar</u>; thus he was free to describe var. A as his new species, <u>E</u>. <u>tukula</u>.

<u>Epinephelus</u> <u>undulostriatus</u> (Peters 1866)

<u>Diagnosis</u>. Dorsal rays, XI,15-16 (usually 16); anal rays III,8; pectoral rays 17-18 (usually 18); lateral-line scales 48-56 (a report of 60 lateral-line scales by Boulenger 1895 should be confirmed); longitudinal scale series 96-110; scales on body largely ctenoid; auxiliary scales present on body; very small scales on maxilla; gill rakers 9-10 + 15-16; 2 rows of teeth on midside of lower jaw; maxilla of adults reaching to or slightly posterior to a vertical at rear edge of orbit; nostrils subequal; 2-5 serrae at corner of preopercle enlarged; margins of subopercle and interopercle smooth or with a few serrae; dorsal profile of head nearly straight; interorbital space slightly to moderately convex; body of adults moderately deep, the depth 2.45-2.9 in SL, and compressed, the width 2.1-2.5 in depth; membranes of spinous portion of dorsal fin incised; longest dorsal spine 2.3-2.8 in head; pectoral fins 1.6-2.0 in head; pelvic fins reaching anus only in young, their length 1.8-2.05 in head; caudal fin rounded.

Body with alternating, irregular, slightly diagonal, longitudinal lines of pale bluish and brownish orange, the orange twice as broad and appearing as merging series of spots; head grayish brown with numerous, small, close-set, brownish orange spots; fins brown with faint brownish orange spots (only basally on paired fins), the soft portions of the median fins with a yellow margin, the pectorals diffusely yellow posteriorly; tips of interspinous membranes of dorsal fin yellow. Juveniles with fewer and relatively broader longitudinal bands on body.

<u>Remarks</u>. Only six specimens examined, including the holotypes of <u>Serranus</u> <u>undulostriatus</u> Peters (11.3 cm SL) and <u>S</u>. <u>guttulatus</u> Macleay (29 cm SL). Largest specimen seen, 39.3 cm TL. Grant (1982) reported the species to weights of 5.5 kg but did not give lengths. Known only from southern Queensland and New South Wales. Grant wrote, "commonly taken by line fishing on reefs off the South Queensland coastline at depths of 27-73 m...."

Epinephelus undulosus (Quoy and Gaimard 1824)

Diagnosis. Dorsal rays XI,17-19; anal rays III,8; pectoral rays 18-19 (usually 19); lateral-line scales 63-75; longitudinal scale series 125-155; auxiliary scales numerous on body; tiny scales on maxilla; gill rakers well-developed and numerous, 13-15 + 20-22; 2 rows of teeth on midside of lower jaw; maxilla usually reaching a vertical from below middle to rear edge of eye (occasionally slightly posterior to eye); nostrils subequal or posterior nostril slightly larger than anterior; serrae at corner of preopercle moderately enlarged; no serrae on subopercle or interopercle; interorbital space moderately convex; body depth 2.65-3.2 in SL; membranes of spinous portion of dorsal fin not incised; pectoral fins 1.7-2.15 in head; pelvic fins 1.7-2.15 in head; pelvic fins may reach anus, their length 1.7-2.1 in head; caudal fin truncate to slightly emarginate.

Purplish to brownish gray with yellowish brown dots on upper half of head and slightly wavy, longitudinal, yellowish brown lines on body (lines may be lost on large adults).

Remarks. Attains 75 cm. China and the Philippines to the northwestern Indian Ocean (but not reported from the Red Sea or Persian Gulf); a species of open sedimentary bottoms, usually in the depth range of 20-90 m.

GENUS GRACILA RANDALL 1964

Diagnosis. Dorsal rays IX,14-15, the spines slender; anal rays III,9; pectoral rays 17-19, the middle rays longest; lateral-line scales 67-75; body depth 2.6-4.0 in SL; head short, 2.8-3.2 in SL; preopercle broadly rounded at corner, the upper margin finely serrate, the lower broadly scalloped; membranes of spinous portion of dorsal fin incised; paired fins short; caudal fin slightly emarginate to truncate.

Remarks. As this goes to press, osteological work by William S. Smith-Vaniz has emerged showing that *Gracila polleni* belongs in the genus *Cephalopholis*, with the truncate caudal fin distinguishing it from its congeners.

KEY TO THE SPECIES OF GRACILA

1a. Caudal fin slightly emarginate; head
     length 2.9-3.2 in SL; interorbital

space strongly convex; adults with
four, diagonal, deep blue bands on
head, numerous dark bars on side of
body, and a round dark spot midlaterally at posterior end of caudal
peduncle; juveniles brown or violet
with an orange stripe in dorsal and
anal fins and on caudal lobes (Indo-
Pacific) . . . .   <u>albomarginata</u>

1b. Caudal fin truncate; head length
2.8–3.0 in SL; interorbital space
slightly convex; head and body
with alternating stripes of blue
and orange-yellow (Mariana Islands
to western Indian Ocean) . . . .   <u>polleni</u>

<u>Gracila albomarginata</u> (Fowler and Bean 1930)

   <u>Diagnosis</u>. Dorsal rays IX,14–15 (usually 15); anal
rays III,9; pectoral rays 18–19 (usually 19); lateral-line
scales 67–73; longitudinal scale series 101–117; scales on
body largely ctenoid (weakly so on adults); maxilla of
adults with numerous small scales; gill rakers 8–9 + 15–
17; 2 rows of teeth on midside of lower jaw; body depth
2.6–3.2 in SL; head small, its length 3.0–3.2 in SL;
maxilla extending posterior to a vertical at rear edge of
orbit; caudal fin slightly emarginate.
   Adults greenish to brownish gray with 16–20 dark bars
on side of body (of about equal width to pale interspaces)
and a round spot about the size of eye midlaterally at
posterior end of caudal peduncle; four or five, diagonal,
narrow, dark blue bands on head. In life, one transient
color phase exhibits a large white area in middle of back,
flanked by black areas, and the caudal peduncle is
whitish, thus making the black peduncular spot more evident. Juveniles are brown or violet with a broad, red-
orange stripe in dorsal and anal fins (more on soft than
spinous portions) and in each caudal lobe, extending forward onto dorsal and ventral edges of caudal peduncle
(more so dorsally).
   <u>Remarks</u>. Attains nearly 40 cm. Indo-Pacific, on
coral reefs, usually in exposed outer reef areas at depths
greater than 15 m. An actively swimming grouper not
inclined to come to rest on the bottom.

Gracila polleni (Bleeker 1868)

Diagnosis. Dorsal rays IX,15; anal rays III,9; pectoral rays 17-19; lateral-line scales 65-75; scales on body ctenoid; maxilla naked or with only a small patch of tiny scales; gill rakers 7-8 + 14-16; 2 rows of teeth on midside of lower jaw; maxilla reaching to or slightly beyond a vertical at rear edge of orbit; body depth 2.8-4.0 in SL; head 2.8-3.0 in SL; caudal fin truncate.

Body with alternating stripes of blue and orange-yellow (about 10-11 of each); head brownish orange with three dark-edged blue stripes; median and pelvic fins orange-yellow with blue bands.

Remarks. See remarks following diagnosis of genus. Attains 35 cm. Known from the Mariana Islands, Palau Islands, New Britain, Philippines, Ryukyu Islands, Christmas Island (eastern Indian Ocean), and islands of the western Indian Ocean. A reef species usually found lurking in or near caves on drop-offs. Cephalopholis virgatus Fourmanoir 1954 and G. okinawae Katayama 1974 are synonyms.

GENUS PLECTROPOMUS OKEN 1817

Diagnosis. Dorsal rays VIII,11; anal rays III,8, the spines slender; pectoral rays 14-18; lateral-line scales numerous, 86-115; a pair of very large canine teeth anteriorly in jaws, and 1-4 moderate to large fixed canines on posterior half of lower jaw; lower margin of preopercle with 3 antrorse spines; body elongate, the depth 2.9-3.75 in SL; paired fins short; caudal fin emarginate to truncate.

Remarks. The species of Plectropomus are less sedentary than those of the genera Cephalopholis and Epinephelus and seem to roam over a larger area, in general, than other groupers (G. albomarginata and the two Variola excepted). They are reef-dwellers and primarily piscivorous. Along with Variola, species of this genus cause more cases of ciguatera than other groupers. Hoese et al. (1981) wrote a preliminary revision of the Australian species of Plectropomus. Randall and Hoese (In press) have revised the genus. At present we recognize seven species, but one in the Red Sea may represent an eighth (see remarks for P. pessuliferus).

KEY TO THE SPECIES OF PLECTROPOMUS
(after Randall and Hoese In press)

1a. Anterior soft portions of dorsal and
anal fins distinctly elevated, the
longest dorsal ray 1.55–2.1 in head
length; pectoral rays modally 15;
adults with vertical dark lines
(blue in life) anteriorly on side of
body and long, horizontal to oblique,
dark lines on head (Philippines and
East Indies) . . . . oligacanthus

1b. Anterior soft portions of dorsal and
anal fins not distinctly elevated,
the longest dorsal ray 2.2–3.25 in head
length; pectoral rays modally 16 or 17;
no vertical dark lines on body
(pessuliferus may have vertically
elongate spots on side of body, but
these generally are no more than 3
times longer than wide), and no long
dark lines on head 2

2a. Body uniform brown or brown marbled
with pale without dark spots, the
young with pale horizontally elongate
spots or dashes; caudal fin slightly
emarginate to truncate; pectoral rays
modally 17 (western Indian Ocean) . . . . punctatus

2b. Body either with numerous small dark
spots (blue in life) or with black,
saddlelike bars and few small dark
spots; caudal fin emarginate (except
areolatus); pectoral rays modally
16 (except laevis) 3

3a. Caudal fin truncate to slightly
emarginate, the caudal concavity
contained 13 or more times in head
length; small embedded scales in
interorbital space; head and body
of adults with numerous, relatively
large, round (rarely slightly oval)
dark spots (blue with black edges
in life), most of which are within
a spot diameter of adjacent spots;
dark spots present on lower abdomen

(Red Sea to Phoenix and Samoa
Islands) . . . . **areolatus**

3b. Caudal fin emarginate, the caudal
concavity 4.6–12.0 in head length; no
embedded scales in interorbital space;
dark spots on head and body either
relatively smaller at a given length or
most of them not within a spot diameter
of adjacent spots; dark spots usually
not present on lower abdomen 4

4a. Pectoral rays modally 17; lateral-
line scales 92–115; caudal-fin length
1.45–1.75 in head; pectoral-fin length
2.15–2.45 in head; pelvic-fin length
2.05–2.45 in head; color pattern either
brown with numerous, relatively small,
dark spots (blue in life), with or without faint, broad, dark bars, or pale
with fewer small spots and distinct,
broad, saddlelike, dark brown to black
bars on body (Indo-Pacific) . . . . **laevis**

4b. Pectoral rays modally 16; lateral-
line scales 83–101; caudal-fin length
1.3–1.55 in head; pectoral-fin length
1.85–2.35 in head; pelvic-fin length
1.7–2.35 in head; dark spots either
smaller or larger than those of
laevis at a given size, without
broad, saddlelike, dark bars 5

5a. Head and body with very small dark
spots (blue in life), the largest
on body contained three times or
more in pupil diameter; all spots
on head and body round (western
Pacific and Western Australia) . . . . . . **leopardus**

5b. Head and body with dark spots of
moderate size, the largest on body
half pupil diameter or larger; some
spots on head and anterior body
elongate (except juveniles) 6

6a. Pelvic fins without dark spots;
some spots anteriorly on side of
body of adults horizontally
elongate; gill raker at angle

of first gill arch longer than
longest gill filaments at angle;
pelvic fins 1.7-2.1 in head;
nostrils subequal (Philippines,
East Indies, and eastern to
Western Australia) . . . . **maculatus**
6b.   Pelvic fins with dark spots (blue
in life); some spots on side of
body of adults vertically elongate;
gill raker at angle of first gill
arch shorter than longest gill
filaments at angle; pelvic fins
1.9-2.35 in head; posterior
nostrils of large adults (over
about 40 cm SL) distinctly
larger than anterior nostrils . . . . . **pessuliferus**

Plectropomus areolatus (Rüppell 1830)

Diagnosis. Dorsal rays VIII,11; anal rays III,8;
pectoral rays 15-16 (rarely 15); lateral-line scales 83-
97; small embedded scales on interorbital space; gill
raker at angle of first gill arch clearly shorter than
gill filaments at angle; body depth 3.15-3.7 in SL; soft
rays of dorsal and anal fins not prolonged to form an
anterior lobe; outer margin of anal fin slightly convex;
caudal fin truncate to slightly emarginate.

Reddish brown with numerous, round, dark-edged blue
spots of fairly uniform size on head and body (slightly
smaller on head and posteriorly on body) that reach the
lower parts of head and body; spots on head and body
close-set, often separated by about a spot diameter from
adjacent spots; median fins with small, dark-edged blue
spots (notably smaller than those of body); paired fins
without spots except basally on pectorals; caudal fin with
a narrow, white posterior margin and broad, blackish submarginal band.

Remarks. Largest reported, 53 cm, but probably
attains about 70 cm. Samoa Islands and Marshall Islands
to the Indian Ocean (Cocos-Keeling Islands and Maldive
Islands) and the Red Sea. _Plectropomus truncatus_ Fowler
and Bean 1930 is a synonym.

Plectropomus laevis (Lacepède 1802)

Diagnosis. Dorsal rays VIII,11; anal rays III,8;
pectoral rays 16-18 (28 of 32 specimens with 17, 2 with 16

and 2 with 18); lateral-line scales 92-115; interorbital space naked; body depth 2.95-3.65 in SL; gill raker at angle of first gill arch shorter than gill filaments at angle; soft rays of dorsal and anal fins not prolonged to form an anterior lobe; outer margin of anal fin straight; caudal fin slightly emarginate, the caudal concavity 4.8-10.0 in head.

Two color phases: One is white, the dorsal part of snout and front of lips yellow, with a diagonal, dark brown bar passing dorsoposteriorly from eye, and four, large, dark brown, saddlelike bars on body (one on nape and three passing ventrally from base of dorsal fin, the two middle ones reaching to at least midside of body); a few, small, dark-edged blue spots usually present on body, more numerous posteriorly (and those more anteriorly generally confined to upper half of body); fins bright yellow, the median fins with small, dark-edged blue spots. The second color phase is reddish brown with numerous, small, round, dark-edged blue spots on head, body, and fins; dark bars as in the former color phase usually present but less conspicuous.

Remarks. Reaches at least 100 cm. Ranges throughout most of the Indo-Pacific but absent from the Red Sea and Persian Gulf. This species has been called P. melanoleucus (Lacepède) by most recent authors, but P. laevis was named by Lacepède in volume 3 of his Histoire Naturelle des Poissons, hence earlier than melanoleucus in volume 4. The lack of any morphological differences in the two color forms, the finding of occasional individuals intermediate in color to the two, and reports of change in color from one phase to another have led Randall and Hoese (In press) to conclude that these represent a single species. Final proof could be provided by placing the white, yellow-finned, black-barred phase in a large aquarium for an extended period and observe it change to the reddish brown form with numerous small blue spots.

Plectropomus leopardus (Lacepède 1802)

Diagnosis. Dorsal rays VIII,11; anal rays III,8; pectoral rays 15-17 (2 of 36 with 17, 1 with 15, the rest with 16); interorbital space and top of snout naked; body depth 2.9-3.6 in SL; soft rays of dorsal and anal fins not prolonged to form an anterior lobe; outer margin of anal fin convex; caudal fin slightly emarginate, the caudal concavity 5.2-12.5 in head.

Greenish to reddish brown with numerous, dark-edged blue dots on head, body, and median fins, the dots generally not extending onto abdomen and thorax below level of lower edge of pectoral fins (dots on fish of 20-35 cm SL are <1 mm in diameter); caudal fin with a narrow whitish margin centroposteriorly, sometimes with a dark submarginal band.

Remarks. Reaches about 75 cm. Southern Japan through the Philippines and Indonesia to the Great Barrier Reef. The only confirmed Indian Ocean records are from Western Australia. The most common species of the genus on the southern Great Barrier Reef. Goeden (1978) has studied its biology in the Capricorn group.

Plectropomus maculatus (Bloch 1790)

Diagnosis. Dorsal rays VIII,11; anal rays III,8; pectoral rays 16 or 17 (1 of 30 with 17); lateral-line scales 88-101; interorbital space and top of snout naked; gill raker at angle of first gill arch distinctly longer than longest gill filaments at angle; body depth 3.15-3.7 in SL; soft rays of dorsal and anal fins not prolonged to form an anterior lobe; outer margin of anal fin straight to concave; caudal fin slightly emarginate, the caudal concavity 4.2-10.1 in head; pelvic fins 1.7-2.1 in head.

Brownish red with dark-edged blue spots (dark in preservative) of variable size, larger in general on head and anteriorly on body; some spots, particularly postorbitally on head and front of body, horizontally elongate; spots, especially anteriorly, widely separated (often fewer than 10 on operculum); spots not extending onto lower third to fourth of body; median fins with small blue spots; a single blue spot dorsally on pectoral base and one in axil of this fin; no spots on pelvic fins.

Remarks. Largest specimen examined, 53 cm; probably reaches at least 70 cm. Philippines, Southeast Asia, Indonesia, and Australia (Northern Territory, Queensland, and Western Australia). This species has been confused with P. pessuliferus (see discussion below).

Plectropomus oligacanthus (Bleeker 1854)

Diagnosis. Dorsal rays VIII,11; anal rays III,8; pectoral rays 14-16 (2 of 26 with 14, 2 with 16, the rest with 15); lateral-line scales 86-96; interorbital space naked; body depth 3.15-3.65 SL; 3rd to 5th soft rays of dorsal fin and 2nd to 4th of anal fin prolonged, thus forming an elevated anterior lobe to these fins (and giving a concave distal margin to anal fin); caudal fin emarginate, the caudal concavity 3.2-6.3 in head.

Brownish red with blue spots and lines, the lines on operculum diagonal, those anterodorsally on head and nape paralleling dorsal profile, and those on side of body vertical; median fins with irregular lines, dashes, and blue spots; pelvic fins with blue lines paralleling rays; pectoral fins with blackish rays on basal two-thirds, abruptly pale yellowish distally.

Remarks. Largest examined, 56 cm. Known only from the Philippines, Indonesia, New Guinea, and the Solomon Islands. One record from Australia, the specimen described by Castelnau as Plectropoma variegatum from Cape York. Fowler and Bean (1930) proposed the subgenus Pleuroperca for oligacanthus.

Plectropomus pessuliferus (Fowler 1904)

Diagnosis. Dorsal rays VIII,11; anal rays III,8; pectoral rays 15-16; lateral-line scales 85-104; inter-orbital space naked; gill raker at angle of first gill arch shorter than gill filaments at angle; body depth 3.3-3.6 in SL; soft rays of dorsal and anal fins not prolonged to form an anterior lobe; outer margin of anal fin convex; pelvic fins 1.9-2.35 in head; caudal fin slightly emarginate, the caudal concavity 5.3-10.0 in head.

Brownish red with well-separated, small, red-edged blue spots on head, body (including ventrally on head, thorax, and abdomen), and all fins except basally on pectorals; many spots on side of body vertically elongate, and spots on operculum diagonally elongate.

Remarks. This species was described from Padang, Sumatra; the holotype (32.4 cm SL) is in the Academy of Natural Sciences of Philadelphia. Other specimens have been examined from Fiji, Sri Lanka, St. Brandons Shoals, and the Red Sea. The author took an underwater photograph of an adult in the Maldive Islands. The Plectropomus from the Red Sea, which Randall (1983) and other authors have misidentified as P. maculatus, is here identified as P. pessuliferus. It differs from pessuliferus from outside the Red Sea in having many more blue spots on the head and blackish (instead of pale) pectoral rays, except for pale yellowish tips. The specimen from Fiji was collected at a depth of 147 m and was photographed in color by A. Lewis; the photograph is the basis for the above color note. It is expected that the red borders to the blue spots on this fish might be black in specimens from shallow water.

Plectropomus punctatus (Quoy and Gaimard 1824)

Diagnosis. Dorsal rays VIII,11; anal rays III,8; pectoral rays 16-18 (usually 17); lateral-line scales 88-95; interorbital space naked; body depth 3.1-3.7 in SL; soft rays of dorsal and anal fins not prolonged to form an anterior lobe; outer margin of anal fin convex; caudal fin very slightly emarginate to truncate.

Adults grayish to purplish brown, mottled with darker and lighter blotches of the same hue; no spots or bars on head or body. Juveniles with numerous pale dashes on body.

Remarks. Reported to 80 cm. Western Indian Ocean. The juvenile form with pale dashes was described as punctatus from a specimen 14.2 cm SL from Mauritius. Plectropomus marmoratus Talbot 1958 is a synonym based on the adult form without these dashes.

GENUS SALOPTIA SMITH 1963

Diagnosis. Dorsal rays VIII,11-12; anal rays III,8; pectoral rays 15; lateral-line scales 71-74; longitudinal scale series 127-133; scales on body largely ctenoid; maxilla naked; gill rakers 7-8 + 15-17; maxilla not reaching a vertical at posterior edge of orbit; a pair of stout canine teeth anteriorly in jaws; lower jaw with 2 rows of teeth, none as enlarged canines; posterior nostril larger than anterior, divided internally by a septum; three prominent antrorse spines on lower margin of preopercle; interorbital space flat; body depth 2.7-3.2 in SL; dorsal spines III-VIII subequal; caudal fin slightly emarginate.

Yellow in life, suffused with red, shading to pale pink ventrally.

Remarks. Monotypic.

Saloptia powelli Smith 1963

Diagnosis. See that of genus.
Remarks. Attains 40 cm. Known from the Cook Islands
(type-locality), Society Islands, Samoa Islands, and
Ryukyu Islands to the South China Sea. A deepwater fish
for an epinepheline. One of 32.7 cm SL from Samoa in the
Bishop Museum was caught from 140 m.

GENUS "TRISOTROPIS" GILL 1865

Diagnosis. Dorsal rays XI,19-21; anal rays III,10;
pectoral rays 18-19; lateral-line scales 66-68; longitudinal scale series 132-140; scales of body ctenoid;
well-developed frontoparietal crest on skull; maxilla not
reaching a vertical at rear edge of orbit; a pair of short
canine teeth anteriorly in jaws; body depth 2.3-2.6 in SL;
dorsal profile of head strongly convex; interorbital space
markedly convex; caudal fin very slightly rounded.
Uniform dark purplish black.
Remarks. Monotypic. As mentioned, Trisotropis is a
synonym of Mycteroperca; thus a new generic name is needed
for this fish. G. David Johnson, G. R. Lowe, and the
author are planning to name this genus.

"Trisotropis" dermopterus (Temminck and Schlegel 1842)

Diagnosis. See that of genus.
Remarks. Attains 45 cm. Has a disjunct north-south
distribution: southern Japan, Taiwan, and China in the
Northern Hemisphere and Australia in the Southern Hemisphere. Altiserranus woorei Whitley 1951 from New South
Wales appears to be a synonym. Allen (1985) has recorded
it (as E. woorei) from Western Australia.

GENUS VARIOLA SWAINSON 1839

Diagnosis. Dorsal rays IX,13-15; anal rays III,8;
pectoral rays 16-19; lateral-line scales 67-75; scales on
body largely ctenoid; no auxiliary scales; 1 or 2 large,
fixed canine teeth on midside of lower jaw, in addition to
the pair of large canines anteriorly in jaws; no spines on
lower margin of preopercle; body depth 2.85-3.2 in SL;
dorsal spines relatively short, the longest 3.0-3.65 in

head; caudal fin lunate, the caudal concavity 1.3-2.4 in head.

Remarks. Two species are known, though both often identified as V. louti.

KEY TO THE SPECIES OF VARIOLA

1a. Caudal fin with a narrow white margin centroposteriorly, preceded by a dark submarginal band; dorsal, anal, and pectoral fins without distinct yellow posterior borders (western Pacific to western Indian Ocean . . . . albimarginata

1b. Caudal fin with a broad yellow posterior margin; rear margins of dorsal, anal, and pectoral fins broadly yellow (Indo-Pacific) . . . . louti

Variola albimarginata Baissac 1953

Diagnosis. Dorsal rays IX,14; anal rays III,8; pectoral rays 18-19; lateral-line scales 68-75; longitudinal scale series 110-130; gill rakers 7-9 + 13-16; maxilla usually reaching to or posterior to a vertical at rear edge of orbit; spinous membranes of dorsal fin slightly incised; caudal fin of adults very lunate, the caudal concavity about 1.4 in head.

Light red with short, irregular, yellow lines and scattered, small, irregular, red-edged whitish spots on body; median fins light red with small pink and red spots, the caudal with a narrow white margin centroposteriorly and a blackish submarginal band; paired fins yellowish, suffused with light red.

Remarks. Attains 60 cm. Western Pacific to western Indian Ocean. In spite of an adequate description by Baissac (1956) from material from Mauritius, this species continued to be misidentified as V. louti by most authors.

Variola louti (Forsskål 1775)

Diagnosis. Dorsal rays XI,13-15 (nearly always 14); anal rays III,8; pectoral rays 16-19; lateral-line scales 64-78; longitudinal scale series 113-135; gill rakers 7-10 + 15-19; maxilla reaching to or posterior to a vertical at rear edge of orbit; spinous membranes of dorsal fin very slightly incised; caudal fin of adults very lunate.

Brownish red with numerous small spots that may vary from blue to violet or pink on head, body, and median fins; posterior edge of median and pectoral fins with a broad yellow margin. Juveniles with an irregular dark brown stripe from eye to rear base of dorsal fin, the body dull yellow to reddish above and whitish below the stripe.

Remarks. Reaches 80 cm. Wide-ranging throughout most of the Indo-Pacific region. A coral-reef species found from depths of a few to at least 100 m. Has been implicated in causing ciguatera. Labrus punctulatus Lacepède 1801 has long been listed as a synonym of V. louti. When the author examined the presumed type of punctulatus at the Museum National d'Histoire Naturelle in Paris, he was surprised to see it was the same as the species described by Baissac as V. albimarginata. Lacepède's description of punctulatus, however, was from a drawing by Commerson, not a specimen, and the drawing is clearly of louti. Randall, Bauchot, and Desoutter (1985) have designated the drawing as the lectotype of punctulatus, thus restricting this name to the synonymy of louti (instead of having it replace albimarginata).

ACKNOWLEDGMENTS

The manuscript was reviewed by G. R. Allen, P. C. Heemstra, and D. F. Hoese.

NOTES

1. As pointed out by Johnson (1983), the Japanese serranid fish currently identified as Trisotropis dermopterus needs a new generic name because Trisotropis is a junior synonym of the American genus Mycteroperca.

2. Occasional specimens of Epinephelus fasciatus from oceanic islands of the Pacific have truncate or near-truncate caudal fins.

BIBLIOGRAPHY

Allen, G. R. 1985. Fishes of Western Australia. Pacific Marine Fishes, Book 9, p. 2205-2534. T.F.H. Publications, Neptune City, New Jersey.

Bagnis, R., P. Mazellier, J. Bennett, and E. Christian. 1972. Fishes of Polynesia. Les Éditions du Pacifique, Papeete, Tahiti, 368 p.

Baissac, J. de B. 1956. Description d'un nouveau serranide de l'île Maurice. Proc. Roy. Soc. Mauritius 1(Pt. 4):395-396.

Bauchot, M. L., M. Desoutter, and J. E. Randall. 1984. Catalogue critique des types de poissons du Museum national d'Histoire naturelle (Famille des Serranidae). Bull. Mus. Natl. Hist. Nat., Sér. 4, 6(3)Suppl.:3-82.

Bleeker, P. 1876. Atlas ichthyologique des Indes Orientales Néêrlandaises. Vol. 6. Frédéric Muller, Amsterdam, 170 p.

_____. 1877. Atlas ichthyologique des Indes Orientales Néêrlandaises. Vol. 7. Frédéric Muller, Amsterdam, 126 p.

Bloch, M. E., and J. G. Schneider. 1801. Systema ichthyologiae iconibus cx illustratum. Post obitum auctoris opus inchoatum absoluit, correxit, interpolavit. Sanderiano Commissum, Berolini, x, 584 pp., 110 pl.

Boulenger, G. A. 1895. Catalogue of the perciform fishes in the British Museum. Vol. 1. Taylor and Francis, Lond., 2d ed., xiii + 394 p.

Cheng, C. T., and W. Yang. 1983. A new species of the family Serranidae--Epinephelus stigmogrammacus. [In Chin.] Oceanol. Limnol. Sin. 14(5):506-509.

Cuvier, G., and A. Valenciennes. 1828. Histoire naturelle des poissons. Vol. 2. Reprint 1969. A Asher & Co., Amsterdam, xxi + 490 p.

_____. 1830. Histoire naturelle des poissons. Vol. 6. Reprint 1969. A. Asher & Co., Amsterdam, xxiv + 559 p.

Day, F. 1875-1878. The fishes of India. Bernard Quaritch, Lond., 778 p.

Fourmanoir, P., and P. Laboute. 1976. Poissons de Nouvelle Calédonie et des Nouvelles Hébrides. Les Editions du Pacifique, Papeete, Tahiti, 376 p.

Fowler, H. W., and B. A. Bean. 1930. Contributions to the biology of the Philippine Archipelago and adjacent regions. Vol. 10. U.S. Natl. Mus., Bull. 100, Wash., D.C., ix + 334 p.

Gloerfelt-Tarp, T., and P. J. Kailola. 1984. Trawled fishes of southern Indonesia and northwestern Australia. Aust. Dev. Assist. Bur., Aust.; Dir. Gen.

Fish., Indonesia; German Agency Tech. Coop., Fed. Republ. Germany, xvi + 406 p.

Goeden, G. B. 1978. A monograph of the coral trout Plectropomus leopardus (Lacepède). Res. Bull. Queensl. Fish. Serv. 1:1–42.

Grant, E. M. 1982. Guide to fishes. Dep. Harbours Mar., Brisbane, Queensl., 896 p.

Gunther, A. 1859. Catalogue of the acanthopterygian fishes in the collection of the British Museum. Vol. 1. Taylor and Francis, Lond., xxxi + 524 p.

Heemstra, P. C., and J. E. Randall. 1984. Serranidae. In W. Fischer and G. Bianchi (editors), FAO species identification sheets for fishery purposes: Western Indian Ocean, p. 1–241. FAO, Vol. 4.

_____. Unpub. Review of the serranid fishes of the western Indian Ocean. Bull. J. L. B. Smith Inst., Ichthyol.

Hoese, D. F., J. Bowling, B. Russell, and J. E. Randall. 1981. A preliminary revision of Australian species of coral trout of the genus Plectropomus. Occas. Rep. Aust. Mus. 2, ii + 28 p.

Hombron, J. B., and H. Jacquinot. 1853. Reptiles et poissons. In J. Dumont d'Urville (editor), Voyage au Pole Sud et dans l'Océanie sur les corvettes "L'Astrolabe" et "La Zélée," p. 31–56. Vol. 3, Pt. 2, Paris.

Johnson, G. D. 1983. Niphon spinosus: A primitive epinepheline serranid, with comments on the monophyly and intrarelationships of the Serranidae. Copeia 1983:777–787.

Katayama, M. 1953. A new serranid fish, Epinephelus hata, found in Japan. Bull. Fac. Educ., Yamaguchi Univ. 3(1):52–56.

_____. 1960. Fauna Japonica: Serranidae (Pisces). Tokyo News Serv., Tokyo, viii + 189 p.

_____. 1975. Serranid fishes of the Okinawa Islands (III). Bull. Fac. Educ., Yamaguchi Univ. 25(2):161–178.

Masuda, H., K. Amaoka, C. Araga, T. Uyeno, and T. Yoshino (editors). 1984. The fishes of the Japanese Archipelago. Tokai University Press, Tokyo, xxii + 437 p.

Morgans, J. F. C. 1959. Three confusing species of serranid fish, one described as new, from East Africa. Ann. Mag. Nat. Hist., Ser. 13, 1:642–656.

_____. 1966. East African fishes of the Epinephelus tauvina complex, with a description of a new species. Ann. Mag. Nat. Hist., Ser. 13, 8:257–271.

_____. 1982. Serranid fishes of Tanzania and Kenya. Ichthyol. Bull., J. L. B. Smith Inst. Ichthyol. 46:1–44.

Okamura, O., K. Amaoka, and F. Mitani (editors). 1982. Fishes of the Kyushu–Palau Ridge and Tosa Bay. Jpn. Fish. Resour. Conserv. Assoc., Tokyo, 435 p.

Playfair, R. L., and A. Günther. 1867. The fishes of Zanzibar. John van Voorst, Lond., 153 p.

Randall, J. E. 1955. Fishes of the Gilbert Islands. Atoll Res. Bull. 47, xi + 243 p.

_____. 1964. Notes on the groupers of Tahiti, with description of a new serranid fish genus. Pac. Sci. 18(3):281–296.

_____. 1980. A survey of ciguatera at Enewetak and Bikini, Marshall Islands, with notes on the systematics and food habits of ciguatoxic fishes. Fish. Bull., U.S. 78:201–249.

_____. 1983. Red Sea reef fishes. IMMEL Publications, Lond., 192 p.

Randall, J. E., M. L. Bauchot, and M. Desoutter. 1985. The status of the Indo–Pacific serranid fish Variola punctulatus (Lacepède). Bull. Mus. Natl. Hist. Nat., Paris, Sér. 4, 7(2):475–478.

Randall, J. E., M. L. Bauchot, A. Ben–Tuvia, and P. C. Heemstra. 1985. Cephalopholis argus Schneider, 1801 and Cephalopholis sexmaculata (Rüppell, 1830) (Osteichthyes, Serranidae): Proposed conservation by suppression of Bodianus guttatus Bloch, 1790, Anthias argus Bloch, 1792, and Serranus zanana Valenciennes, 1828 Z.N. (S.) 2470. Bull. Zool. Nomencl. 42(4):374–378.

Randall, J. E., and A. Ben–Tuvia. 1983. A review of the groupers (Pisces: Serranidae: Epinephelinae) of the Red Sea, with description of a new species of Cephalopholis. Bull. Mar. Sci. 33:373–426.

Randall, J. E., and P. C. Heemstra. 1986. Epinephelus truncatus Katayama, a junior synonym of the Indo–Pacific serranid fish Epinephelus retouti Bleeker. Jpn. J. Ichthyol. 33:51–56.

Randall, J. E., and D. F. Hoese. In press. Revision of the groupers of the Indo–Pacific genus Plectropomus (Perciformes: Serranidae). Indo–Pac. Fishes.

Randall, J. E., and A. C. Wheeler. Unpub. Notes on six tropical Pacific fishes collected or observed by the

Forsters during the voyage of H. M. S. "Resolution,"
1772-1775.

Randall, J. E., and W. Klausewitz. In press. New records
of the serranid fish *Epinephelus radiatus* (Day) from
the Red Sea and Gulf of Oman (Pisces: Perciformes:
Serranidae). Senckenb. Marit.

Randall, J. E., and P. J. P. Whitehead. 1985. *Epine-
phelus cyanopodus* (Richardson), a senior synonym of
E. hoedtii (Bleeker), and comparison with the related
E. flavocaeruleus (Lacepède). Cybium 9(1):29-39.

Schroeder, R. E. 1980. Philippine shore fishes of the
western Sulu Sea. Natl. Media Prod. Cent., Manila,
266 p.

Schultz, L. P., and collaborators. 1953-1966. Fishes of
the Marshall and Marianas Islands. U.S. Natl. Mus.
Bull. 202, Vol. 1, xxxii + 685 p.; Vol. 2, ix +
438 p.; Vol. 3, vii + 176 p. Wash., D.C.

Shen, S.-C. 1984. Coastal fishes of Taiwan. Private
printing, Taipei, 190 p.

Smith, C. L. 1971. A revision of the American groupers:
Epinephelus and allied genera. Bull. Am. Mus. Nat.
Hist. 146(2):67-242.

Smith, J. L. B. 1949. The sea fishes of southern Africa.
Central News Agency, Cape Town, South Africa, 550 p.

Smith, J. L. B., and M. M. Smith. 1963. The fishes of
the Seychelles. Dep. Ichthyol., Rhodes Univ.,
Grahamstown, South Africa, 215 p.

Weber, M., and L. F. de Beaufort. 1931. The fishes of
the Indo-Australian Archipelago. E. J. Brill,
Leiden, Vol. 6, xii + 448 p.

Whitley, G. P. 1944. New sharks and fishes from Western
Australia. Aust. Zool. 10(3):252-273.

_____. 1945. New sharks and fishes from Western
Australia. Pt. 2. Aust. Zool. 11(1):1-42.

_____. 1951. Studies in ichthyology, No. 15. Rec.
Aust. Mus. 22(4):389-408.

4

Review of the Early Life History of Tropical Groupers (Serranidae) and Snappers (Lutjanidae)

Jeffrey M. Leis
Division of Vertebrate Zoology
The Australian Museum
Sydney NSW 2000 Australia

ABSTRACT

Taxonomic studies of eggs and larvae of groupers (epinepheline serranids) and snappers (lutjanids) are few relative to the numbers of species involved. Therefore, few larvae can be identified to species, although identification to subfamily is relatively easy. Eggs are small, spherical, and pelagic and hatch in about 24-45 h. Larvae develop elongate fin spines and extensive spination on the head.

Ecological information summarized here is based on relatively few studies. Snapper and grouper larvae are not abundant in plankton samples, but their abundance seems in accord with expectations based on adult community structure. However, their relative rarity makes ecological work on larvae difficult. Both snapper and grouper larvae are generally more abundant over the continental shelf than in oceanic waters. The eteline lutjanids are an exception, and are more abundant in slope and oceanic waters than over the continental shelf.

Snapper and grouper larvae avoid surface waters during the day, but are more evenly distributed vertically at night. Seasonality of abundance varies with species. Larvae of most species are least abundant in winter, but at least one species is most abundant in winter. Virtually nothing is known of feeding behavior of larvae. A small amount of information on growth is available from labora-

tory studies, but little from field studies. Size
at settlement varies among species but seems relatively constant within species. Laboratory studies
suggest that size may be more important than age in
determining competency for settlement.

More work is required on all aspects of the
early life history of groupers and snappers. In
particular, the following require attention: taxonomy; ecology of early life history stages around
oceanic islands; feeding, growth, and survival;
return of young stages to adult habitat from the
pelagic larval habitat; year-to-year variation in
spatial and temporal patterns.

INTRODUCTION

It is axiomatic that knowledge of the biology of
tropical marine fishes lags behind that of temperate
species, and the reasons for this are obvious. The situation regarding early life history information is even more
pronounced, and the groupers and snappers are no exception. This is exemplified by the fact that the first
lutjanid larva identified to species was not described
until the mid-1970s (Heemstra 1974).

The serious taxonomic study of eggs and larvae of
epinepheline serranids and lutjanids began less than 10
years ago and has involved only a few workers. Few taxa
have been described. A number of descriptions, particularly the older ones, are of dubious reliability and were
not done with identification of larvae from plankton
samples in mind. The situation is improving, but it will
still be some time before identification of larval epinepheline serranids and lutjanids will be routine. This, of
course, impedes ecological studies.

Recent reviews of reef fish biology (Sale 1980;
Warner 1984) have emphasized the importance of understanding the early life history of fishes in order to
progress in ecological study and management of the very
complex and diverse communities found in tropical waters.
To date, we have little more than the realization of the
importance of the early life history of these fishes.

Ecological information from field studies is limited,
not only because of taxonomic obstacles, but also because
ecological studies of the larvae of reef and shelf species
in tropical waters have been underway for only a relatively short time. Only the most basic kind of distribu-

tional information is available at present. At this point, investigations on larvae of tropical fishes are establishing where the early life is spent and are beginning to approach questions about larval dispersal and retention. Unfortunately, because epinepheline serranid and lutjanid larvae are relatively rare, much less is known about them than about other, more abundant, reef fish larvae (Leis and Goldman Unpub. 2). Field studies of grouper and snapper larvae have relied on conventional plankton and neuston nets, with the exception of studies made by Mori (1984), who also utilized a juvenile fish seine. There have been no studies involving epibenthic sampling. This means the epibenthos, which is an important habitat for some types of fish larvae, has not been examined to see if it is utilized by grouper and snapper larvae.

Because of their commercial importance and high market price, a number of epinepheline serranid species have been the subject of laboratory rearing experiments in Asia. These studies have provided virtually all the available information on growth, survival, and feeding during the larval stage. Much less laboratory rearing has been done on lutjanids.

An unexpected impediment to preparation of this review was the discovery that the results of a major study of fish larvae in the Persian Gulf (Houde et al. 1981) was unavailable because it was considered restricted material by the management of the Kuwait Institute for Scientific Research. Some of the more important studies cited herein are "gray literature," an unfortunate but unavoidable situation. Because so little ecological information on the early life history of lutjanids and epinepheline serranids was available, I have included information based on my own and collaborative studies in progress or in manuscript.

For the purposes of this review, I have considered the early life history stage to begin with spawning and be completed when all larval characters (specializations for pelagic life, see Leis and Rennis 1983) are lost shortly after settlement. Thresher (1984) reviews what is known of reproductive behavior of both groups.

I have limited discussion of groupers to the Tribe Epinephelini of the serranid subfamily Epinephelinae (Johnson 1983). I have treated as genera a number of taxa considered subgenera of Epinephelus by Smith (1971). This should be considered more a matter of convenience than a formal elevation of these taxa to the generic level. I have retained the nomenclature used by the authors of papers on epinepheline eggs and larvae rather than that of

Randall (1986). This was done because it is often not possible to determine just what species the original authors had, particularly when species formerly thought to be synonymous have been split.

I have considered the Lutjanidae to be equivalent to Johnson's (1980) Lutjanoidea (i.e., I have included Caesionidae as a subfamily of the Lutjanidae) for reasons both systematic and pragmatic. The caesionids are undeniably closely related to the lutjanids (Johnson 1980, 1984). Given the position of the Caesionidae in Johnson's cladogram (Johnson 1980:figure 1), it is not possible to justify his maintenance of Caesionidae as a separate family without elevating Etelinae, Apsilinae, Paradicichthyinae, and Lutjaninae to familial status. I favor lumping in this case. On the pragmatic side, it is not yet generally possible to separate small larvae of these groups from one another, so if I were limited to a discussion of the larvae of Lutjanidae (sensu Johnson 1980), not much could be included. Therefore, the discussion of lutjanids includes caesionines, but, where possible, the subfamilies are treated separately.

LUTJANIDAE—SNAPPERS

Description and Identification
of Eggs and Larvae

Relatively few lutjanid eggs have been described. Information is available for only 12 species distributed among 4 of the 21 genera of lutjanids (Johnson 1980), but the consistency of the available information gives some assurance that generalizations based on it will hold for other members of the family. Lutjanids spawn spherical, pelagic eggs ranging in diameter from 0.65 to 1.02 mm, with the majority being <0.85 mm (Table 4.1). Based on unfertilized eggs, Starck (1970) incorrectly concluded that Lutjanus griseus had demersal eggs. The chorion is smooth and the yolk is unsegmented. A single colorless-to-slightly-yellowish oil droplet of 0.12-0.20 mm diameter is present (Table 4.1). Incubation times range from 17 to 36 h depending on species and incubation temperature.

Newly hatched larvae are typical of those from small pelagic eggs and have a large yolk sac, unpigmented eyes, no mouth, and limited swimming abilities. The oil droplet is located at the anterior tip of the yolk sac. The yolk reserves are exhausted 3-4 days after hatching, at which

TABLE 4.1
Descriptions of eggs of lutjanid (P = pelagic)

Species	Egg Type	Diameter (mm)	No. Oil Droplets (Diameter)	Incubation Period in Hours (Temperature ° C)	Reference
Caesio teres	P	0.77-0.78	1 (0.14-0.15)	26 (27°), 31-32 (21°)	Bell and Colin 1986
Lutjanus campechanus	P	0.77-0.85	1 (0.15-0.19)	24-27 (23°-25°) 20 (27°)	Rabalais et al. 1980; Minton et al. 1983
L. erythropterus	P	0.90-1.02	--	24 (25°-26.5°)	Lu Suifen 1981
L. griseus	P	0.70-0.85	1 (0.12-0.18)	20 (27°), 18 (28°), 17 (30°)	Damas et al. 1978; Richards and Saksena 1980
L. kasmira	P	0.78-0.85	1 (0.13-0.14)	18 (22-25°)	Suzuki and Hioki 1979
L. lutjanus	P	0.75-0.79	1 (0.16-0.17)	17 (26.7°)	Lu Suifen 1981
L. stellatus	P	0.80-0.85	1 (0.15-0.16)	--	S. Hamamoto Pers. com.
L. synagris	P	0.65-0.80	1 (0.13-0.20)	23 (26°)	Borrero et al. 1978

(Continued)

TABLE 4.1 (Cont.)

Species	Egg Type	Diameter (mm)	No. Oil Droplets (Diameter)	Incubation Period in Hours (Temperature ° C)	Reference
L. vittus	P	0.78-0.84	1 (0.16-0.18)	26 (26.5°)	Lu Suifen 1981
Pristipomoides filamentosus	P	--	--	--	G. W. Boehlert Pers. com.
P. sieboldii	P	0.88-0.98	1-2 (0.05-0.17)	36 (23°-25°)	G. W. Boehlert Pers. com.
Pterocaesio diagramma	P	--	--	--	Thresher 1984

time the eyes are pigmented and the mouth is functional (references in Table 4.1).

Larvae of only three lutjanid genera have been described (Table 4.2), but I am currently working on larvae of one to several species of Lutjanus, Etelis, Pristipomoides, Aprion, Caesio, Dipterygonotus, and Pterocaesio, and information on these is included in the following.

Pigment is initially sparse, but Lutjanus larvae at the end of the yolk-sac stage have a ventral series of about 15 melanophores on the tail (this may not be true in other genera). These reduce in number with growth. A lateral melanophore on the caudal peduncle may form at about the time of caudal flexion. A pigment cap over the gut forms very early and is retained. The several melanophores which form over the brain are present much earlier in some eteline larvae than in other lutjanid larvae. A few melanophores may form ventrally on the gut, and pigment on the fins varies with species. With growth, pigment along the base of the dorsal fin is common, and as settlement approaches, elements of juvenile pigment appear.

Possibly the two most striking features of larval lutjanids are the spination of fins and head (Figures 4.1-4.4). The preoperculum in particular develops elongate spines, and the spine at the preopercular angle is particularly enlarged. These spines are smooth in all described lutjanids but Rhomboplites aurorubens and in all Indo-Pacific specimens I have examined. In R. aurorubens fine serrations are present on this spine in larvae as small as 4.0 mm (Laroche 1977). Interopercular and subopercular spines may be well developed in postflexion larvae. The supraocular ridge may be serrate or not, depending on species. Spines also develop on the posttemporal and supracleithral bones. These spines disappear shortly after settlement.

The spines of the dorsal fin, particularly the second, and the spine of the pelvic fin are the earliest fin elements to form and become extremely elongate (Figures 4.1-4.4). Maximal size of the spines is reached at about 7-8 mm standard length (SL). Thereafter, they decrease in relative size and are only slightly enlarged at settlement. Spines may be smooth to strongly serrate, and while this seems to be constant within a species, it varies widely between species. Contrary to generalization by Heemstra (1974) and Thresher (1984), not all Lutjanus larvae have smooth fin spines. Many of the Lutjanus

TABLE 4.2
Descriptions of larval lutjanids (Ys = yolk sac, Pre = preflexion,
Flex = flexion, Post = postflexion)

Species	Stage				Size Range (mm)	Reference
	Ys	Pre	Flex	Post		
Caesio cuning	--	X	X	X	2.8-7.8	Leis and Rennis 1983
Lutjanus aratus	--	--	--	X	18.2	Heemstra 1974
Lutjanus (bohar?)	--	--	--	X	12-14	Fourmanoir 1976
L. campechanus	X	X	X	X	2.2-4.0	Collins et al. 1979; Rabalais et al. 1980[a]
Lutjanus (fulvus or kasmira)	--	--	--	X	7.7	Leis and Rennis 1983
L. griseus	X	X	X	X	2.3-48.5	Starck 1970; Damas et al. 1978[a]; Richards and Saksena 1980[a]
L. jordani	--	--	--	X	19.9	Heemstra 1974
L. kasmira	X	X	--	--	1.8-3.2	Suzuki and Hioki 1979[a]

L. synagris	X	—	—	—	1.9-2.6	Borrero et al. 1978[a]
Lutjanus (synagris or mahogoni)	—	—	—	X	17.8	Heemstra 1974
L. vittus	X	X	X	X	1.5-34.8	Lu Suifen 1981[a]; Mori 1984
Lutjanus sp. (several)	—	—	X	X	5.5-27.2	Vatanachai 1972; Fahay 1975; Fourmanoir 1976; Musiy and Sergiyenko 1977
Rhomboplites aurorubens	—	X	X	X	4.0-14.2	Laroche 1977

The 5 mm larva illustrated by Uchida (1937) as Lutjanus appears to be an epinepheline serranid. Fourmanoir (1976) lists, but does not describe, larvae of Etelis ocularis, E. carbunculus, Pristipomoides multidens and Caesio sp. Johnson (1984) reviews the development and relationships of percoid larvae and includes information on lutjanids.

[a]Indicates laboratory reared larvae.

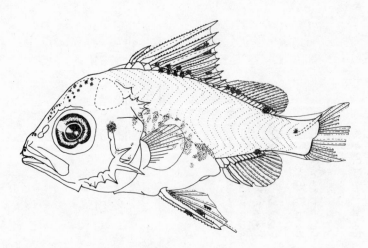

Figure 4.1 Larva of a lutjanine lutjanid. *Lutjanus* *sebae*, 6.13 mm standard length, from the Australian northwest continental shelf (original from a study in progress by J. M. Leis)

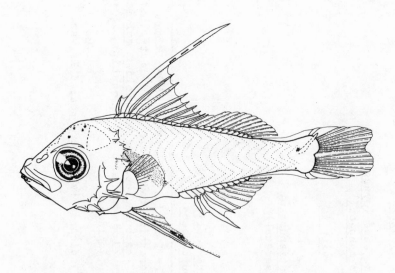

Figure 4.2 Larva of an eteline lutjanid. *Aprion* *virescens*, 7.06 mm standard length, from off Oahu, Hawaii (original from a study in progress by J. M. Leis)

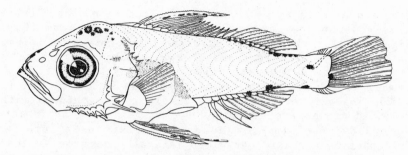

Figure 4.3 Larva of a caesionine lutjanid.
Dipterygonotus _balteatus_, 7.9 standard length,
from the Great Barrier Reef, Australia (original
from a study in progress by J. M. Leis)

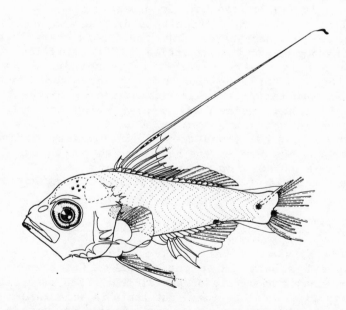

Figure 4.4 Larva of an apsiline lutjanid. An
unidentified species, 6.0 mm standard length,
from the Bismarck Sea (original from a study in
progress by J. M. Leis)

larvae available to me from Indo-Pacific waters have relatively strong serrations on the fin spines (Mori 1984; Figure 4.1), although none examined heretofore have spines as strongly serrate as those of epinepheline serranids.

Lutjanid larvae are relatively easy to identify to family using the above characters (see Leis and Rennis 1983). The only other families likely to be confused with lutjanid larvae are gempylids and epinepheline serranids. Gempylids have 31-67 myomeres while lutjanids have 24. Epinepheline serranids are less laterally compressed than lutjanids; the elongate dorsal fin spines of lutjanids are generally not as pronounced as they are in epinephelines (although there are exceptions); epinephelines have coarse serrations to large, recurved spinelets on the elongate fin spines, while lutjanids have smooth fin spines to moderately coarse serrations on the fin spines. The spine at the angle of the preopercle is serrate in epinephelines but smooth in all known lutjanids but Rhomboplites; pelvic rays are much shorter than the spine in epinephelines while the rays are about equal to or much longer than the spine in lutjanids (Figures 4.1-4.4); many epinephelines have a characteristic pigment pattern on the tail not found in lutjanids (see Leis In press).

It is much more difficult to distinguish species of lutjanids from each other. Once the fin rays are present, certain species can be identified by fin meristics alone, although this always leaves a large residue of larvae identified as Lutjanus spp. or Pterocaesio spp. However, the real problems lie in identification of larvae before their fins have formed (i.e., preflexion larvae), and numerous authors have commented on this (Powles 1977; Collins et al. 1979; Houde et al. 1979). I am currently working on this problem and have made some progress (Table 4.3), but much remains to be done before small lutjanid larvae can be identified beyond family with any assurance.

Ecological Information on Lutjanid Eggs and Larvae

There is relatively little published work on any ecological aspect of lutjanid early life history. No information is available on paradicichthyines or apsilines and very little on etelines, but there is some information on lutjanines and caesionines. There is nothing on lutjanid eggs, which is not surprising as lutjanid eggs are similar to the vast majority of pelagic fish eggs.

TABLE 4.3
Characters useful in separating larvae of four lutjanid subfamilies (from Leis
study in progress). Based on larvae of some species of _Lutjanus_, _Rhomboplites_,
Etelis, _Aprion_, _Pristipomoides_, _Caesio_, _Dipterygonotus_, _Pterocaesio_, and an unidentified apsiline. Larvae of the subfamily Paradicichthyinae are unknown

Character	Lutjaninae (Figure 4.1)	Etelinae (Figure 4.2)	Caesioninae (Figure 4.3)	Apsilinae (Figure 4.4)
Fin spines	Smooth to coarsely serrate	Smooth to slightly serrate	Finely to coarsely serrate	Smooth
Length second dorsal spine	Moderately to very long	Shorter than 3rd spine to moderately long	Moderately to very long	Very long
Body shape	Moderately to very deep and strongly compressed	Relatively elongate to moderately deep and moderately compressed	Relatively elongate and moderately compressed	Relatively elongate and moderately compressed
Dorsal fins	X-XII,11-17	X,11	IX-XV,9-22	X,10
Anal fin	III,8-11	III,8-9	III,9-14	III,8
Tail pigment in preflexion larvae	Ventral series of many melanophores	Ventral series of a few to one melanophores	Ventral series of two to five melanophores	?

(Continued)

TABLE 4.3 (Cont.)

Character	Lutjaninae (Figure 4.1)	Etelinae (Figure 4.2)	Caesioninae (Figure 4.3)	Apsilinae (Figure 4.4)
Pigment present on membrane of dorsal fin in preflexion larvae	Yes or no	Yes or no	No	?
Supraocular ridge serrate	Yes	No	Yes	No
Formation of third anal spine	Late	Early	Early	Early

Identification of lutjanid eggs from plankton samples is not likely to be possible in the foreseeable future.

Two factors make ecological study of lutjanid larvae difficult: low abundance and high diversity. A glance at Table 4.4 will reveal a major reason why so little ecological information is available on lutjanid larvae: They are rare compared with other larvae. Even if taxonomic problems are overcome (and they have only recently come under attack), and it proves possible to routinely identify lutjanid larvae from plankton samples, relative rarity of lutjanid larvae will make quantitative studies difficult. Even in the best cases represented in Table 4.4, lutjanid larvae constitute only a few percent of all the larvae taken, and in these cases (all from the Indo-Pacific), the majority of the lutjanid larvae were caesionines. The remaining Lutjanus or eteline larvae are split among so many species that numbers of any given species will be unlikely to be abundant enough for analysis. Given the immense effort involved in ichthyoplankton work, it is unlikely that studies aimed specifically at lutjanids will take place. We can expect, then, that ecological information on larval lutjanids will be provided only as a by-product of studies aimed at other, more abundant, species.

Lutjanid larvae, while relatively rare, do not appear to be underrepresented in plankton samples. Adult lutjanids are higher trophic level carnivores (Parrish 1986) and as such cannot be expected to form a major portion of the spawning biomass of any fish community. If one quite reasonably assumes that the smaller, lower trophic level and forage species of the fish community under study have a higher turnover rate than species at higher trophic levels, such as lutjanids, one would expect lutjanid larvae to constitute a small proportion of the total larval fish assemblage. In view of this, the numbers of lutjanid larvae found in ichthyoplankton surveys appear reasonable.

In most reports of ichthyoplankton surveys, lutjanid larvae are either not mentioned (e.g., Ahlstrom 1971, 1972) or mentioned only in passing with no real information provided other than the number of larvae caught. The few exceptions are summarized below.

Horizontal Distribution. Off the southeast coast of the United States (South Atlantic Bight), Powles (1977) discussed the horizontal distribution of the vermilion snapper (R. aurorubens) and of "unclassified snappers" (i.e., all lutjanids that could not be positively identified as R. aurorubens). The lutjanids captured were 2-8 mm

TABLE 4.4
Lutjanid and epinepheline serranid larvae (as percentage of total larvae captured) in ichthyoplankton studies of warm water areas which included coastal waters (-- indicates information not supplied). Two studies excluded: Leis and Miller (1976) caught no lutjanids and all serranids were anthiines; Dekhnik et al. (1966) confused some other types of larvae with their serranids and reported no lutjanids.

Area	Percent of Larvae That Were		Principal Sampling Environment	No. of Samples	Total No. of Larvae	Reference
	Epinepheline Serranids	Lutjanids				
Southeast coast, U.S.A.	0.10	0.25	Shelf	464	100×10^3	Powles 1977
Southeast coast, U.S.A.	0	0.03	Shelf	80	11×10^3	Fahay 1975
Eastern Gulf of Mexico	0.10	1.23	Shelf	756	143×10^3	Houde et al. 1979
Gulf of Mexico and Caribbean	0.11	0.07	Oceanic	109	9.5×10^3	Richards 1984
Caribbean	2.20[a]	--	Oceanic	10	--	Belyanina 1975
Gulf of California	1.46[a]	<0.01	Shelf/oceanic	628	252×10^3	Moser et al. 1975

Eastern Tropical Pacific	0.15[a]	—	Oceanic	837	218×10^3	Ahlstrom 1971, 1972
Hawaii	0	<0.5	Shelf	588	—	Leis 1978
Tuamotu Islands	0.21	0.21	Lagoon/oceanic	23	0.5×10^3	Bourret et al. 1979
South China Sea	0.10	0.16	Shelf	107	5×10^3	Vatanachai 1972
Great Barrier Reef/Coral Sea	0.07	3.11	Shelf/oceanic	36	23×10^3	Leis and Goldman 1984
Great Barrier Reef Lagoon (open water)	0.65–0.87	3.5–8.0	Shelf	112	76×10^3	Leis and Goldman Unpub. 1
Great Barrier Reef Lagoon (immediately around reefs)	<0.01–0.60	0.3–4.1	Shelf	144	81×10^3	Leis 1982b; 1986
Northwest Australian shelf	0.95	4.27	Shelf	355	53×10^3	Leis et al. Unpub.
Western Indian Ocean	1.53[a]	0.08	Shelf	327	49×10^3	Nellen 1973

[a]Includes all serranids (anthiines, serraniines, and epinephelines).

long and found primarily on the mid-to-outer continental
shelf in an irregular band. They were absent from stations
<20 m deep. Powles concluded that the distribution of the
larvae was similar to that of the adults. Bongo net
catches indicated similar distributions for small (2-3 mm)
and large (4-5 mm) lutjanid larvae, but neuston net
catches indicated spawning over the continental slope with
some movement onto the shelf with growth. Powles could
not determine if locally spawned lutjanid larvae were
transported out of the study area by the Gulf Stream or
retained in an eddy-like circulation.

Houde et al. (1979) studied lutjanid and other types
of larvae in the eastern Gulf of Mexico. Lutjanids were
the 19th most abundant family (0.25% of all larvae). Some
large larvae could be identified as Lutjanus sp. (3), R.
aurorubens (34), and Pristipomoides aquilonaris (41), but
more than 95% of the lutjanid larvae could not be identified beyond family level. Most unidentified lutjanid
larvae were taken between the 30 and 100 m isobaths, as
were most of the R. aurorubens larvae. The P. aquilonaris
larvae were captured mostly on the outer shelf between 50
and 200 m.

In the northwest Gulf of Mexico, Finucane et al.
(1979) captured 34 Lutjanus campechanus, 3 Pristipomoides
(probably P. aquilonaris, but identified as Etelis
oculatus) and 23 unidentified lutjanid larvae. This study
centered around oil platforms about 40 km off the Texas
coast in an area where the 200 m isobath is about 160 km
off the coast.

On the northwest continental shelf of Australia
(Young et al. In press; Leis et al. Unpub.), lutjanid
larvae were the eighth most abundant family, but still
constituted only 4.3% of all larvae. However, 68% of the
lutjanid larvae were Dipterygonotus or Pterocaesio
(Caesoninae). Based on preliminary analysis of the data,
the following summary was prepared. Dipterygonotus
balteatus larvae occurred primarily in the middle of the
shelf (58-110 m isobaths). Pterocaesio (chrysozona?)
larvae occurred primarily on the inner shelf (40-75 m
isobaths). Lutjanus larvae (many species, 31% of lutjanid
larvae) were found primarily on the inner shelf (40-75 m
isobaths). Larvae of eteline lutjanids (1% of all lutjanid
larvae, two species of Pristipomoides) were found only on
the outer shelf and slope (110-1,100 m isobaths).

In shallow (10-15 m) waters in the immediate vicinity
of the coral reefs at Lizard Island in the Great Barrier
Reef, lutjanids constituted 0.3-4.1% of all larvae

(depending on site), although virtually all were young (preflexion-stage) larvae (Leis 1982b, 1986). Most lutjanid larvae in this area were caesionines, and they were significantly less abundant inside the shallow reef-enclosed lagoon than outside it. There was no significant difference in abundance between windward and leeward sides of the island.

In the more open waters of the large Great Barrier Reef Lagoon, lutjanid larvae made up 3.5-8.0% of all larvae (again, all lutjanid larvae were treated as a group) (Leis and Goldman Unpub. 2). A much higher proportion of older (i.e., postflexion-stage) larvae were present in these samples than in the shallow water near Lizard Island. This led Leis and Goldman (1983, Unpub. 2) to conclude that these more open waters, rather than near-reef waters, are the nursery area for lutjanid larvae. Neither abundance nor concentration of lutjanid larvae was found to vary significantly along a transect across the Great Barrier Reef Lagoon (Leis and Goldman Unpub. 1).

In a preliminary comparison of concentrations of larvae in the Great Barrier Reef Lagoon with those in the Coral Sea, lutjanids constituted 3.1% of all larvae (Leis and Goldman 1984). Lutjanid larvae were present in greater concentrations in the Great Barrier Reef Lagoon than in the Coral Sea but did not differ in concentration between the two locations in the lagoon. A more comprehensive study of this same subject combined with an investigation of changes in abundance with distance seaward into the Coral Sea is underway (Leis study in progress). Initial results indicate that not only are lutjanids less abundant in the Coral Sea than in the lagoon, but that their abundance declines markedly with increasing distance from the reef. However, what applies to lutjanids when considered as a family may not apply to individual species. For example, only a few larvae of Pterocaesio tile have been collected, but all have come from the Coral Sea.

The early life history of Lutjanus vittus was investigated by Mori (1984) in Yuya Bay on the Sea of Japan. Mori concluded that larvae <7 mm were basically planktonic and spent this planktonic period in the open sea (i.e., outside Yuya Bay). Larvae of 7-16 mm began to migrate into the bay and concentrate in shallow water. At about 16 mm, the larvae entered the sea grass beds on the southern side of the bay but apparently remained pelagic. Mori concluded that L. vittus is "semi-benthic" from 24 mm but not fully demersal until 32 mm.

Young L. griseus entered the sea grass beds of southern Florida at about 10 mm (Starck 1970). These presumably
newly settled individuals were lightly pigmented and still
retained elongate dorsal and pelvic spines. Young L.
griseus moved out of the sea grass beds at about 80 mm and
concentrated around debris and channel edges in shallow
water. Lutjanus griseus larger than 170 mm were found in
channels and around reefs (Starck 1970). It remains to be
seen if the use of an intermediate nursery distinct from
the adult habitat is widespread among lutjanids.

The available information indicates that lutjanine
and caesionine larvae do not stay in the immediate
vicinity of shore or their natal reefs but spend the
pelagic period in more open continental shelf waters.
Lutjanine and caesionine larvae seem not to be present
over slope waters in large numbers and do not display the
tendency of so many reef fishes with specialized larvae to
spend the pelagic period of their life history in oceanic
waters (Leis and Miller 1976). In this sense, Powles
(1977) is probably correct in maintaining that the distribution of the larvae is similar to that of the adults.
However, how lutjanid larvae are distributed around
oceanic islands, which by definition lack continental
shelves, is not known.

Larvae of eteline lutjanids are found primarily over
the outer portion of the continental shelf and slope and
even into oceanic waters. There are no good quantitative
data on distribution of eteline larvae around oceanic
islands, but from incidental catches in Hawaii, they seem
to be more common in oceanic than in neritic or inshore
areas (sensu Leis 1982a).

There will surely be exceptions to these generalities
since they are based on the results of very few studies.
In fact, one apparent exception is already known: the
larvae of Pterocaesio tile have thus far been collected
only in oceanic (Coral Sea) waters, albeit within a few
nautical miles of the reef.

Vertical distribution.   Our only information on the
vertical distribution of lutjanid larvae comes from just
three studies, but it is consistent. Based on differences
between day and night catches of bongo and neuston nets,
Powles (1977) suggested that lutjanid larvae were largely
absent from the neuston during the day but moved upward
into the neuston at night.

In shallow (10–15 m), near-reef waters of the Great
Barrier Reef Lagoon, Leis (1986) found that concentrations
(number per m^3) of lutjanid larvae increased with depth

during the day. At night there was an apparent upward vertical migration, and no difference in concentration between depths was found.

Vertical distribution of lutjanid larvae was investigated in deeper (25 m), more open water by stratified bongo net samples at three depths plus neuston samples (Leis and Goldman Unpub. 3). Three taxa of lutjanids were abundant enough for analysis: Dipterygonotus balteatus, Caesio spp., and Lutjanus spp. All three types had highest concentrations in the deepest sampling stratum during the day and completely avoided the neuston. At night, distributions were uniform (i.e., no significant difference between depths) and all three types were found in the neuston.

Lutjanid larvae, at least in relatively shallow coastal waters, appear to prefer the greatest available depth during the day and to migrate upward at night for a uniform distribution, even entering the neuston.

Seasonality. Lutjanid larvae off the southeast coast of the United States were most abundant in summer, although they were present year-round (Powles 1977). Similarly, in the eastern Gulf of Mexico lutjanid larvae were taken in all seasons, but 79% were taken in summer (Houde et al. 1979).

In Hawaii, lutjanid larvae (primarily etelines) were found close to the leeward shore of Oahu and at other localities from May through December, but with highest concentrations in July and September (Leis 1978, Unpub. data). In a 15-month-long series of midwater trawl samples off leeward Oahu during 1977 and 1978, Lutjanus (kasmira?) larvae were found in June (1978), August (1977 and 1978), October (1977 and 1978), and November (1978), while Pristipomoides larvae were found in August (1977 and 1978) and October (1978) (T. A. Clarke Pers. com.).

On the northwest continental shelf of Australia, seasonality varied with species (Leis et al. Unpub.). Larvae of D. balteatus occurred year-round, but were most abundant by far in winter. Pteroceasio (chrysozona?) larvae also occurred year-round, but were most abundant in spring and early summer. Lutjanus spp. larvae were very rare in winter and most abundant in summer. Eteline lutjanid larvae were not captured in winter and were most abundant in summer.

In shallow waters in the immediate vicinity of reefs of the Great Barrier Reef Lagoon, lutjanid larvae were present year-round but were most abundant in spring and summer (Leis 1982b, 1986). In the more open, deeper waters of the large Great Barrier Reef Lagoon, samples were taken in spring, summer, and autumn, and highest abundances were found in summer (Leis and Goldman Unpub. 1).

Lutjanus vittus larvae appeared in Yuya Bay, Japan in August and moved into sea grass beds during late August and early September (Mori 1984). Juvenile L. vittus began to leave the sea grass beds in October and move into rocky reefs. They were completely absent from the sea grass beds by November. The juvenile fish leave the bay before they are 1 year old, and Yuya Bay contains no resident adults.

Based on available evidence of larval abundance, it seems that most lutjanids spawn to some degree year-round, but that reproductive activity is at a maximum in spring and summer. Dipterygonotus balteatus provides an exception to this in that it apparently has a winter spawning peak.

Feeding. The only available information on feeding of lutjanid larvae comes from laboratory rearing studies (Table 4.2). In the only successful rearing, wild zooplankton was fed to the larvae (Richards and Saksena 1980). Until we have field observations or laboratory rearings that compare what the larvae actually consume with what is offered, we will know little about what lutjanid larvae eat.

In his study of the early life history of L. vittus, Mori (1984) considered feeding, but examined only juveniles >60 mm.

Growth and Length of Larval Period. The only published information on growth of larval lutjanids comes from laboratory rearings, and only one of these was successful in keeping the larvae alive beyond yolk exhaustion. The laboratory rearings of various Lutjanus species (Borrero et al. 1978; Damas et al. 1978; Suzuki and Hioki 1979; Rabalais et al. 1980; and Lu Suifen 1981; Table 4.2) ended when the larvae died of starvation following exhaustion of the yolk, and so are of little use in estimating growth. Richards and Saksena (1980), however, were successful in rearing L. griseus for 36 days at 26°–28° C. Age (from hatching) and size of these larvae were: 4 days, 2.7–2.8 mm; 5 days, 3.0–3.1 mm; 7 days, 3.4 mm; 9 days, 4.1–4.2 mm; 15 days, 6.2–6.3 mm; 26 days, 9.6–12.5 mm; and 36 days, 15.4 mm.

Size at settlement seems to vary considerably with species. Thresher (1984) maintains that metamorphosis to the juvenile stage for most species occurs at a length of approximately 12–20 mm. Unfortunately, metamorphosis is not defined nor is any supporting evidence given for this statement. Fourmanoir (1976) has reported pelagic specimens of Etelis spp. as large as 44 mm; I have examined pelagic Pristipomoides sieboldii as large as 50 mm, E. carbunculus as large as 51 mm, and pelagic Lutjanus as large as 38 mm. Mori (1984) reports that L. vittus settles out at about 30 mm while Starck (1970) reports settled L. griseus as small as 10 mm from sea grass beds.

The duration of the pelagic period of lutjanids has been directly estimated only three times, and ranged from 25 to 47 days. Lutjanus griseus were 36 days old and fully scaled at the end of Richards and Saksena's (1980) rearing experiment, and were pelagic for "at least 26 days" (Richards 1982). Twenty-six-day-old larvae were 9.6-12.5 mm, agreeing with Starck's (1970) estimate of 10 mm at first appearance in sea grass beds. Lutjanus fulvus of an unstated length had an otolith-derived duration of pelagic period of 39-47 days (Goldman et al. 1983). Brothers et al. (1983) reported otolith ages of 25 days for two newly settled, unidentified lutjanids of 16.3 mm. Based on size, it seems likely that the duration of the pelagic period of eteline lutjanids is longer than that of Lutjanus spp.

Lutjanus vittus in Yuya Bay, Japan grew from about 18 to 110 mm during late summer and early autumn for a growth rate of 1.2-1.7 mm/day, depending on the year of the study (Mori 1984).

EPHINEPHELINE SERRANIDS—GROUPERS

Description and Identification of Eggs and Larvae

The larvae of epinepheline serranids provide striking examples of the types of specializations to pelagic life that are present in reef fishes. Unfortunately, except for larger individuals, relatively few have been described in enough detail in the literature to allow identification to species. Development of epinepheline serranids has recently been reviewed by Kendall (1984).

Eggs of 3 of the approximately 12 genera of epinepheline serranids have been described. All are pelagic, with a smooth chorion, unsegmented yolk, and a diameter of 0.75-1.20 mm (Table 4.5). A single colorless-to-slightly-yellowish oil droplet of 0.13-0.22 mm diameter is present. Incubation takes from 20 to 45 h.

Newly hatched larvae have a large yolk sac with the oil droplet located from the anterior to the posterior end of the yolk sac. Illustrations of the yolk-sac larvae of

TABLE 4.5
Description of eggs of epinepheline serranids (P = pelagic)

Species	Egg Type	Diameter (mm)	No. Oil Droplets (Diameter)	Incubation Period in Hours (Temperature ° C)	Reference
Chromileptes altivelis	P	0.80-0.83	1 (--)	22 (28.4°)	Tang et al. 1979
Epinephelus akaara	P	0.71-0.77	1 (0.13-0.16)	22-25 (25°-27°) 23 (25°-27°), 24 (22°-25°)	Ukawa et al. 1966; Tseng and Ho 1979
E. amblycephalus x E. tauvina (hybrid)	P	0.8-1.2	1 (--)	20 (28°)	Tseng and Poon 1983
E. fario	P	0.83-0.90	1 (0.17)	--	Mito 1963
E. gigas	P	0.75	--	38-43 (22°-26°)	Barnabe 1974
E. guaza	P	0.75-0.81	1 (0.18-0.20)	--	Raffaele 1888; Sparta 1935
E. morio	?	<1.0	1	--	Moe 1969
E. salmonoides	P	0.74-0.78	1 (0.16)	--	S. Hamamoto Pers. com.

E. striatus	P	1.02	1 (0.22)	40 (25°)	Guitart Manday and Juarez Fernandez 1966
E. tauvina	P	0.71–0.90	1 (0.16–0.20)	23–25 (27°), 26–35 (27°–30°)	Hussain et al. 1975; Chen et al. 1977; Hussain and Higuchi 1980
Mycteroperca microlepis	P	0.90–1.0	1 (ca. 0.20)	44.5 (21°)	Hardy 1978; Roberts and Schlieder 1983

TABLE 4.6
Descriptions of larval epinepheline serranids (Ys = yolk sac, Pre = preflexion, Flex = flexion, Post = postflexion)

Species	Stage				Size Range (mm)	Reference
	Ys	Pre	Flex	Post		
Alphestes afer	--	--	--	X	16.2-25.9	Johnson and Keener 1984
A. multiguttatus	--	--	--	X	8.4-31.2	Johnson and Keener 1984
Cephalopholis cruentatus	--	--	--	X	5.2-20.5	Johnson and Keener 1984
C. fulvus	--	--	--	X	5.5-25.2	Johnson and Keener 1984
C. panamensis	--	--	--	X	21.0-27.0	Johnson and Keener 1984
Cephalopholis spp.	--	X	X	X	2.0-33.0	Fourmanoir 1976?; Leis and Rennis 1983; Leis In press
Chromileptes altivelis	X	--	--	--	1.8-2.7	Tang et al. 1979[a]

Species						Reference
Dermatolepis inermis	--	--	--	X	6.8-10.5	Johnson and Keener 1984
Epinephelus aeneus	--	--	X	X	2.2-22.4	Aboussouan 1972
E. akaara	X	X	X	X	1.6-48.0	Mito 1966[a]; Ukawa et al. 1966[a]; Mito et al. 1967[a]; Tseng and Ho 1979[a]
E. analogus	--	--	--	X	26-34	Johnson and Keener 1984
E. acanthistius	--	--	--	X	22-27	Johnson and Keener 1984
E. guaza	--	--	--	X	6.5-53	Fage 1918; Bertolini 1933
E. itajara	--	--	--	X	6.2-17.4	Johnson and Keener 1984
E. labriformis	--	--	--	X	12-44	Johnson and Keener 1984
E. mystacinus	--	--	--	X	20	Johnson and Keener 1984
E. nigritus	--	--	--	X	9.1	Johnson and Keener 1984

(Continued)

TABLE 4.6 (Cont.)

Species	Stage				Size Range (mm)	Reference
	Ys	Pre	Flex	Post		
E. niveatus	--	--	X	X	5.5-19.0	Presley 1970; Johnson and Keener 1984
E. striatus	X	--	--	X	2.0-7.6	Guitart Manday and Juarez Fernandez 1966[a]; Kendall 1979
E. tauvina	X	X	X	X	1.7-70	Chen et al. 1977[a]; Hussain and Higuchi 1980
Epinephelus spp.	--	X	X	X	3-25	Uchida 1937; Smith 1971; Heemstra 1974; Fourmanoir 1976; Kendall 1979; Leis and Rennis 1983; Johnson and Keener 1984; Leis In press
Gonioplectrus hispanus	--	--	--	X	13-14	Kendall and Fahay 1979; Johnson and Keener 1984

Species				Size range	Reference
Mycteroperca microlepis	X	X	X	4.0-35.4	Kendall 1979; Roberts and Schlieder 1983
M. ruba [b]	--	X	X	3.6-58	Bertolini 1933; Sparta 1935
Mycteroperca spp.	--	--	X	3.5-24.0	Johnson and Keener 1984
Paranthias furcifer	--	--	X	7.7-34.0	Kendall 1979; Johnson and Keener 1984
Plectropomus leopardus	--	X	X	1.5-25	Leis In press
P. maculatus	--	X	X	1.8-37	Leis In press
P. areolatus	--	--	X	6.3-10.0	Leis In press
P. laevis	--	X	X	4.7-12.5	Leis In press

"Epinephelus" larvae illustrated by Nellen (1973) are in fact anthiine serranid larvae. Larvae described by Aboussouan (1972) as Epinephelus esonue and Epinephelus (goreensis?) are not epinepheline serranids (see Kendall 1979).

[a] Indicates laboratory-reared larvae.

[b] According to Tortonese (1973), the species described by Bertolini (1933) and Sparta (1935) as E. alexandrinus is in fact Mycteroperca ruba.

Epinephelus <u>akaara</u> and <u>E. tauvina</u> present some contradictions (references in Table 4.6). Curiously, photographs of
yolk-sac larvae of each species show the oil droplet along
the ventral edge of the yolk sac at about its middle (Chen
et al. 1977; Tseng and Ho 1979), while drawings of each
species show the oil droplet in the extreme posterior
portion of the yolk sac (Ukawa et al. 1966; Hussain and
Higuchi 1980). Based on recent studies (Randall 1986), it
is possible that two species were involved, and this could
explain the differences. At hatching, the larvae have
limited motility, the eyes are unpigmented, the jaws are
not functional, and little, if any, pigment is present.

Epinepheline larvae of nine genera have been
described (Table 4.6), and all possess a set of characters
that include "kite-shaped" body, elongate dorsal spine 2
and pelvic spine, extensive spiny ornamentation on these
spines, well-developed head spination particularly preopercular and supraocular spines, and pigment (Figure 4.5;
and see Kendall 1979, 1984).

The body of epinepheline larvae is much deeper at the
level of the pectoral base than at the anus until settlement is approached. This depth plus the very elongate
dorsal and pelvic spines that arise from the body at its
deepest point are responsible for kite shape of the body
(Figure 4.5).

Pigment in epinepheline larvae is dominated by an
extensive cap over the gut, melanophores on the elongate
fin spines, and pigment on the ventral surface of the
tail. Depending on species and stage of development, the
tail pigment varies from a series of 20 or more small
melanophores to a single, enlarged melanophore. The latter
migrates to a midlateral position on the caudal peduncle
in all genera but <u>Plectropomus</u> (references in Table 4.6).

A large, moderately serrate spine at the preopercular
angle is a characteristic of all epinepheline serranids
(Figure 4.5). This is accompanied by a number of smaller,
preopercular spines that may be serrate or not, depending
on species and stage of development. A prominent serrate
ridge develops over the eye and may have one or more
points. These head spines all begin to shrink in relative
length when the larvae reach about 7 mm but may be
retained in a reduced state following settlement.

The second spine of the dorsal fin and the pelvic fin
spines are the first fin elements to form and become very
elongate, reaching as much as 150% SL at about 7 mm. These
elongate spines are highly ornamented with species-
specific patterns which include ridges, serrations, and

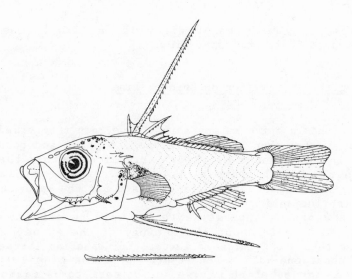

Figure 4.5 Larva of an epinepheline serranid. _Plectropomus laevis_, 12.5 mm standard length, from the Great Barrier Reef, Australia (after Leis In press). Pelvic spine shown below from different angle

recurved spinelets (Johnson and Keener 1984). The other spines of the dorsal and anal fins may also be ornamented. The spines shrink rapidly through an erosive process as settlement approaches, and in settled individuals the ornamentation and length of the spines are greatly reduced.

Epinepheline serranid larvae are relatively easy to distinguish from larvae of other groups with elongate spines (Leis and Rennis 1983 and this chapter, section on identification of lutjanid larvae).

Identification of epinepheline larvae beyond the subfamily level is more difficult and involves meristic characters, fin ornamentation, and pigment patterns (Johnson and Keener 1984; Leis In press). A fair amount of progress in identification of epinepheline larvae has been made since Kendall (1979) stated that "no larvae of epinephelines could be separated on the basis of any larval characters." The chief obstacles to advances in taxonomy of larval fishes (epinephelines included) are lack of material and the fact that most of the relatively few people who do taxonomic work on fish larvae are allowed to do it only part-time.

Ecological Information on Epinepheline Serranid Eggs and Larvae

Although epinepheline larvae have been recognized for a longer time than lutjanid larvae, no more, and possibly even less, is known of their early life history than of the early life history of lutjanids. Again, nothing is known of the ecology of the eggs and for the same reason as with lutjanids.

A second glance at Table 4.4 will reveal why even less can be said about the ecology of the epinepheline larvae than about lutjanid larvae: Epinepheline larvae are only about one-half to one-tenth as abundant as lutjanid larvae. Epinepheline larvae do not seem to be seriously underrepresented in plankton hauls. The same arguments advanced earlier to explain the relative rarity of lutjanid larvae apply also to epinepheline larvae, with the addition that adult groupers tend to be rarer than adult snappers and perhaps higher on the trophic scale (Parrish 1986). Therefore, one would expect epinepheline larvae to be less abundant than lutjanid larvae.

A second problem is that larvae of other serranid subfamilies are often much more abundant than the epinephelines, and published results are often given in terms of the family Serranidae as a whole (Table 4.4), therefore making information on epinephelines inaccessible. The available information on epinepheline larval ecology is summarized below.

Horizontal distribution. Off the southeast coast of the United States, Powles (1977) caught 106 epinepheline serranids (0.1% of all larvae). The larvae were not identified beyond subfamily and were 2-8 mm in length. The grouper larvae were found primarily on the outer continental shelf, with highest abundance in the northern portion of the study area off the South Carolina-North Carolina border. Powles (1977) concluded that distribution of larvae is generally similar to distribution of adults. In neuston samples, smaller larvae (2-3 mm) were caught only in waters over the continental slope, while larger larvae (>4 mm) were found in both slope and shelf waters. This suggests spawning offshore followed by shoreward movement and growth. As with the lutjanid larvae, it could not be determined whether locally produced grouper larvae were transported out of or retained in the study area by the currents (Powles 1977). However, Powles (1977) noted that grouper larvae may be primarily subject to northerly flow early in the spawning season and eddylike circulation later.

In the eastern Gulf of Mexico, epinepheline larvae constituted only 0.10% of all larvae and were found (with the exception of one larva) over depths of 10–200 m (Houde et al. 1979; Houde 1982). Epinepheline larvae were taken at least once at more stations between the 10 and 50 m isobaths than at stations between the 50 and 200 m isobaths. Only five Epinephelus morio larvae could be identified beyond the subfamily level (3.4% of all epinephelines). No difference in abundance of epinepheline larvae was detected between the northern and southern portions of the study area.

On the northwest continental shelf of Australia (Young et al. In press, Unpub. data), epinepheline larvae constituted nearly 1% of all larvae captured (507 larvae). Epinephelus spp. constituted 88.9% of all epinepheline larvae, while Cephalopholis spp. and Plectropomus spp. made up 2.6 and 8.5%, respectively. No epinepheline larvae were found over the continental slope or in oceanic waters. Based on preliminary analysis of the data, the following broad distributional patterns were discerned. Epinephelus spp. larvae were found primarily on the middle portions of the shelf (50–110 m isobaths). Cephalopholis larvae were rare and were found only at inner and midshelf areas (40–110 m isobaths). With the exception of one larva, Plectropomus larvae were found only on the inner half of the shelf (40–58 m isobaths). Plectropomus maculatus larvae were found only at the two stations near the coral reefs of the Montebello Islands, while all the P. areolatus larvae were found at a single inshore (40 m) station on 1 day.

In the shallow (10–15 m) waters immediately around the coral reefs at Lizard Island, epinepheline serranids constituted <0.01–0.06% of all larvae, depending on site, but were present on fewer than one-half of the sampling dates (Leis 1982b, 1986; Leis and Goldman Unpub. 2). Too few occurrences of epinepheline larvae were encountered to allow rigorous testing of distributional pattern, but 63 of the 65 Epinephelus larvae captured were taken off the downwind side of Lizard Island. No Cephalopholis or Plectropomus larvae were captured during the day, but two Plectropomus and eight Cephalopholis larvae were taken at night.

In the deeper (to 40 m) waters of the Great Barrier Reef lagoon, epinepheline larvae made up 0.65-0.87% of all larvae (Leis and Goldman Unpub. 2). Neither Epinephelus, Cephalopholis, nor Plectropomus (primarily P. leopardus) larvae had significant differences in concentration or abundance between stations along a transect across the Great Barrier Reef Lagoon (Leis and Goldman Unpub. 1). However, concentrations and abundances of all three were higher (although not significantly so) in the middle of the Lagoon. Abundances of epinepheline larvae, both young and old, were much higher in the lagoon than immediately adjacent to the Lizard Island reefs, and this led Leis and Goldman (Unpub. 2) to conclude that the nursery for epinepheline larvae was the open water of the lagoon rather than near-reef waters.

Epinepheline serranids made up 0.07% of all larvae in Leis and Goldman's (1984) preliminary study of concentrations of larvae in the Coral Sea and Great Barrier Reef Lagoon. Epinephelines were too rare for statistical testing, but all 17 larvae were taken in the Great Barrier Reef Lagoon. Initial results of a more comprehensive study of the larval fish faunas of these two areas were similar (Leis, study in progress). Epinephelines were rarely taken in the Coral Sea. Those that were taken there were primarily Plectropomus laevis (Leis In press).

Leis (In press) noted that the distribution of Plectropomus larvae was roughly similar to that of adults. Larvae of the inshore P. maculatus were found from near-shore to the middle of the Great Barrier Reef Lagoon. Larvae of the mid-to-offshore reef species P. leopardus overlap with those of P. maculatus but are found somewhat further from shore. Larvae of the offshore reef species P. laevis have so far been taken only in the Coral Sea.

It seems, based on the limited information reviewed above, that in spite of their conspicuous morphological adaptations for pelagic life, epinepheline larvae are not often found in high numbers in oceanic waters. In general, epinepheline larvae have been found either in highest numbers or exclusively over the continental shelf or within the large lagoon of the Great Barrier Reef. Exceptions are found: (1) in the study by Powles (1977), who found that in neuston samples, young larvae were found only over continental slope waters; and (2) for P. laevis larvae, which have been taken only in the Coral Sea (Leis In press). Epinepheline larvae do not appear to remain in the immediate vicinity (i.e., 100-200 m) of reefs or to disperse large distances in the offshore direction from the adult habitat. Of course, extensive longshore dispersal is possible. It may be that larvae of most species require the conditions found in relatively shallow waters for successful completion of the pelagic larval phase.

Vertical distribution. Knowledge of the vertical distribution of epinepheline larvae is derived from only three studies. Powles (1977) concluded, based on comparison of samples taken both day and night with a neuston net and an obliquely-towed bongo net, that epinepheline larvae avoided the surface during the day but not at night.

In the shallow (about 10 m) water in the immediate vicinity of Lizard Island in the Great Barrier Reef, only a few epinepheline larvae were taken (Leis 1986, Unpub. data). During the day, Epinephelus larvae were taken either exclusively (six occasions) or in much larger numbers (one occasion) in the deepest (6-7 m) stratum sampled. At night, only 11 Epinephelus larvae were captured: 7 at the surface, 2 at 3 m, and 2 at 6 m. Cephalopholis larvae were captured only at night: one at the surface, four at 3 m, and three at 6 m.

In the deeper (25 m), more open water of the Great Barrier Reef Lagoon, no Epinephelus larvae were captured, but 26 Cephalopholis and 14 Plectropomus larvae were captured in a study of vertical distribution (Leis and Goldman Unpub. 3). During the day Cephalopholis larvae seemed to prefer deeper water. No larvae were in the neuston or 0-6 m stratum samples, but eight larvae were present in samples from the 13-20 m stratum and three in the 6-13 m stratum. At night Cephalopholis larvae had a much more uniform distribution, with larvae present at all depths sampled. Plectropomus larvae, on the other hand, seemed to prefer middepths. During the day no Plectropomus larvae were found in the neuston and only one in the 0-6 m stratum, but eight were in the 6-13 m stratum and four in the 13-20 m stratum. Only a single Plectropomus larva was taken at night (6-13 m).

Epinepheline larvae do appear to avoid surface waters during the day, and while some taxa seem to prefer the greatest depth available, others opt for middepths. At night, epinepheline larvae appear to be more uniformly distributed vertically.

Seasonality. Off the southeast U.S. coast, Powles (1977) found epinepheline serranid larvae to occur in all seasons but to be by far most abundant in spring. Similarly, in the eastern Gulf of Mexico epinepheline larvae were present in all seasons but were most abundant in spring (Houde et al. 1979; Houde 1982).

On the Australian northwest continental shelf, Epinephelus larvae were present year-round, but were most abundant from late winter through late summer (Young et al. In press; Unpub. data). Plectropomus larvae were taken only in spring and early summer, and Cephalopholis larvae were present in the samples only from early summer through the beginning of winter.

In the shallow waters around Lizard Island, Epinephelus larvae were not present in winter, rare in autumn, but present in reasonably high numbers in spring and summer (Leis Unpub. data). In deeper, more open waters of the Great Barrier Reef Lagoon, Cephalopholis and Epinephelus larvae were more abundant in summer and autumn than in spring (Leis and Goldman Unpub. 1). Plectropomus larvae, however, were absent in autumn, and much more abundant in summer than in spring.

The only generality on seasonality that comes through the above studies is that epinepheline larvae are rare-to-absent in winter.

Feeding. As with the lutjanids, the only information on feeding in epinepheline larvae comes from laboratory rearing experiments. Tseng and Ho (1979) used Chlorella, bivalve eggs, cooked chicken egg yolk, and Brachionus plicatilis (rotifer) to rear Epinephelus akaara. Mito et al. (1967) fed E. akaara oyster larvae, rotifer, microzooplankton, brine shrimp, and minced fish. Marine yeast, trochophores, rotifers, and brine shrimp nauplii were fed to E. tauvina by Hussain et al. (1975). Hussain and Higuchi (1980) fed rotifers, copepods, and brine shrimp to larval E. tauvina, while Chen et al. (1977) used rotifer and a cladoceran (Diaphanosoma sp.). Tseng and Poon (1983) reared hybrids of E. amblycephalus and E. akaara and fed them cooked chicken egg yolk, oyster eggs, rotifers, brine shrimp, and mashed mollusc meat.

Obviously, the above bears little relevance to the field situation, but it might be expected that Epinephelus larvae will eat a variety of zooplankters.

Growth and Length of Pelagic Period. More attempts have been made to rear epinepheline serranids than lutjanids, and a number have been successful. This has resulted in a number of estimates of growth and duration of the pelagic period, but all are based on laboratory rearing. Growth rates in the laboratory vary among species, among different rearing experiments on a given species, and within a rearing experiment on a given species (Table 4.7). This is particularly true for larvae older than about 2 weeks. Survival rates are apparently less variable, with values varying by less than a factor of seven.

All the rearing experiments agree that size at settlement is about 25 mm for Epinephelus spp. However, in the laboratory, time to reach that size may vary from 35 to 50 days (Table 4.7). The largest pelagic Epinephelus larva to be reported from field samples is 27 mm (Heemstra 1974), while settled juveniles as small as 22.4 mm have been reported (Aboussouan 1972). On this point, then, there is agreement between laboratory and field. There is, therefore, an indication that in Epinephelus, settlement takes place at a fixed size (or developmental stage) rather than after a given period.

Teng et al. (1982) concluded that the optimal temperature range for rearing E. tauvina was 26°-29° C, and that optimal rearing density for growth and survival was 60 larvae per liter.

Data on other epinephelines are much more limited. Larvae of Plectropomus apparently settle out at about 20 mm and those of Cephalopholis at about 18 mm (Leis In press). Settled Mycteroperca microlepis as small as 22.6 mm have been reported (Kendall 1979). If larvae of these fishes have growth rates similar to those of Epinephelus, their pelagic period will be shorter than that of Epinephelus, but there are no data on this.

In laboratory rearing experiments, survival of larvae through settlement ranged from 0.14 to 1% (Table 4.7). The only estimate of mortality in the field is based on total serranids (i.e., all subfamilies) in the eastern Gulf of Mexico and is a loss of 56.7% of larvae per mm of growth (Houde et al. 1979). Estimates of this sort, based on the size frequency of larvae from plankton tows, must be treated with caution.

SUMMARY

Taxonomic studies of larval groupers and snappers are just beginning to provide enough information to allow ecological work to proceed at a level below family. However, much more work is needed. Progress in taxonomic research on larvae of these groups has been impeded in the past by taxonomic confusion at the adult level, lack of larval material, and too few larval fish taxonomists. The first impediment has been largely removed by the taxonomic

TABLE 4.7
Laboratory growth rates for Epinephelus species. Bold numbers are when settlement occurred, and percent survival refers to that age. Values are size as standard length (mm) unless noted

| Species | \multicolumn{11}{c}{Age (Days from Hatch)} | Rearing Temperature (° C) | Percent Survival |
	0	5	10	15	20	25	30	35	40	45	50		
Epinephelus tauvina (Chen et al. 1977)	1.7	--	3.8	5.0	--	--	--	**25**	--	--	--	27°	ca. 1.0
E. tauvina (Teng et al. 1982)	--	2.5	3.5–4.0	4.0–5.0	6.5–8.5	9–12	--	--	--	--	--	--	--
E. tauvina (Hussain and Higuchi 1980)	2.1	--	3.6	--	--	6–8	14	--	--	--	**26**	23°–28°	0.5
E. tauvina (Hussain et al. 1975)	--	--	--	--	--	7.5–17.0	--	--	--	--	--	27°–30°	--
E. akaara (Mito et al. 1967, 1973)	1.5	2.1	--	3.7–5.8	9.1–10.1	10–20	**23.4–25.6**	--	--	--	--	26°–31°	0.5

E. akaara (Tseng and Ho 1979)	1.6	2.4–2.7	3.2	--	--	--	--	--	25°	--
E. akaara x E. amblycephalus[a] hybrid Tseng and Poon 1983)	1.7–1.8	2.5–3.8	3.8–4.1	4.1–10.0	--	10.0–15.0	16–21	21–25	27°–28°	0.14

[a]Total length. A range of sizes was given for a range of ages (underlined).

papers in this volume, but the latter two impediments remain. Groupers and snappers spawn small, pelagic eggs that hatch in about 24 h. Larvae of both groups develop elongate, ornamented fin spines and extensive head spination but are easily separated by a variety of characters.

A major limitation in the study of the early life history of groupers and snappers is the relative rarity of the larvae of these relatively rare (in the sense of the whole community) fishes. This is further compounded by the high numbers of species found in these groups, thus ensuring that numbers of larvae of individual species will be low and that a high proportion of samples will contain no larvae of the species of interest. Therefore, quantitative studies are difficult, and the use of larval fish data to assess stock sizes of groupers and snappers in the future is unlikely to be possible. Our knowledge of the ecology of the early life history stages of groupers and snappers is, at present, based on only a few studies and rarely on studies at the species level.

Studies on larvae can provide valuable data on times and places of spawning and the mechanisms of recruitment. Questions regarding dispersal and retention of larvae as they pertain to the geographical extent of stocks can be answered in no other way. However, these questions require specific, intensive, problem-oriented sampling programs. Broad-scale surveys of distribution and abundance of rare types of larvae (such as groupers and snappers) should only be considered a first step. It may be possible to use the data from such surveys to identify times and locations for more intensive sampling. For example, it seems evident even at this early stage of our understanding that studies of eteline lutjanid larvae should omit sampling inshore of the outer shelf. Research on grouper and snapper larvae should be aimed at ecological questions rather than stock assessment.

The available information on distribution suggests that grouper, and caesionine and lutjanine snapper larvae are most abundant over continental shelves and are not found in high abundance seaward of the shelf break. Neither grouper nor snapper larvae (etelines excepted) seem to remain in the immediate vicinity of their natal reefs, but they don't seem to move very far away into oceanic conditions. A few species may be found primarily in oceanic conditions, but the major exception involves the larvae of eteline lutjanids, which have been found primarily in oceanic conditions. At present, the most significant of many gaps in our knowledge involves distribution of grouper and snapper larvae around oceanic islands. Studies by unconventional plankton sampling gear (e.g., diver-operated nets, epibenthic sleds) are needed to assess the importance to larvae of groupers and snappers of habitats that cannot be sampled by conventional plankton nets. P. J. Doherty of Griffith University, Nathan, Queensland (Pers. com.) has recently captured relatively large numbers of ready-to-settle epinepheline serranids (<u>Plectropomus</u>, <u>Cephalopholis</u>, <u>Epinephelus</u>) in trials with automated light traps at Lizard Island, Great Barrier Reef. This indicates that such devices may have considerable potential for sampling the larger pelagic stages of epinepheline serranids.

Both grouper and snapper larvae avoid the surface during the day, selecting middle-to-deep depth strata, at least in coastal waters. At night both are more uniformly distributed.

Lutjanid and epinepheline larvae can be found at least in low levels of abundance year-round, but distinct seasonal peaks in abundance are present, and these are primarily in summer. However, knowledge of temporal variation in seasonal patterns or in spatial patterns is essentially nonexistent, as most available studies are of 1-year duration at best.

The only information available on feeding by grouper and snapper larvae comes from laboratory rearing studies, as does most of the information on growth and duration of the pelagic period. The latter ranges from 25 to 50 days. Size at settlement varies considerably between species (10-50 mm), but seems relatively constant within a species. Rearing studies suggest that size rather than age may be more important in determining the duration of the pelagic stage.

Although all areas of the early life history of groupers and snappers require more work, the areas which are most in need of study are:

1. Taxonomy, for little can be done if the larvae can't be identified;
2. Ecological research at the species level;
3. Research comparing the very different situations on continental shelves with those around oceanic islands;
4. Research on return of young fishes to adult habitat, including possible intermediate nurseries, and retention versus dispersal of larvae;
5. Research on feeding and survival of larvae in the field; and

6. Assessment of year-to-year variation in spatial and temporal patterns.

ACKNOWLEDGMENTS

This review would have been far less complete but for N. Bain and C. Cantrell of the Australian Museum Library, who helped locate a number of obscure references. A. W. Kendall, Jr. provided assistance in locating literature on epinepheline larvae. P. L. Colin, P. J. Doherty, J. H. Finucane, S. Hamamoto, E. D. Houde, A. W. Kendall, Jr., K. Lindeman, W. J. Richards, and K. Suzuki provided access to unpublished results of their research or other assistance. T. Goh typed the manuscript. I was supported during the preparation of this review by Australian Commonwealth Marine Science and Technology (MST) Grant 83/1357. Much of the unpublished work cited in this review was supported by MST Grants 80/2016 and 83/1357. My thanks to all.

BIBLIOGRAPHY

Aboussouan, A. 1972. Oeufs et larves de Téléostéens de l'Ouest africain. XI. Larves serraniformes. Bull. de l'IFAN. 34A(2):485-502.

Ahlstrom, E. H. 1971. Kinds and abundance of fish larvae in the eastern tropical Pacific, based on collections made on EASTROPAC I. Fish. Bull., U.S. 69:3-77.

_____. 1972. Kinds and abundance of fish larvae in the eastern tropical Pacific on the second multi-vessel EASTROPAC survey, and observations on the annual cycle of larval abundance. Fish. Bull., U.S. 70:1153-1242.

Barnabe, G. 1974. La reproduction du merou Epinephelus gigas: Observations préliminaires de terrain. Aquaculture 4:363-367.

Bell, L. J., and P. L. Colin. 1986. Mass spawning of Caesio teres (Pisces: Caesionidae) at Enewetak Atoll, Marshall Islands. Environ. Biol. Fishes 15(1):69-74.

Belyanina, T. N. 1975. Preliminary results of the study of ichthyoplankton of the Caribbean Sea and the Gulf of Mexico. Tr. Inst. Okeanol. Akad. Nauk. S.S.S.R. 100:127-146. [Engl. transl. by Al Ahram Cent. Sci., 1981.]

Bertolini, F. 1933. Famiglia 2: Serranidae. In Uova, larve e stadi giovanili di Teleostei, p. 310-331. Fauna e Flora Golfo Napoli Monogr. 38.

Borrero, M., E. Gonzales, N. Millares, and T. Damas. 1978. Desarrollo embrionario y prelarval de la biajaiba (Lutjanus synagris, Linne 1758). Rev. Cubana Invest. Pesq. 3(3):1-28.

Bourret, P., D. Binet, C. Hoffschir, J. Rivaton, and H. Velayoudon.1979. Evaluation de "l'effet d'Ile" d'un Atoll: Plancton et micronecton au large de Mururoa (Tuamotus). Centre ORSTOM de Noumea, Nouvelle-Caledonie, 124 p.

Brothers, E. B., D. McB. Williams, and P. F. Sale. 1983. Length of larval life in twelve families of fishes at "One Tree Lagoon", Great Barrier Reef, Australia. Mar. Biol. (Berl.) 76:319-324.

Chen, F. Y., M. Chow, T. M. Chao, and R. Lim. 1977. Artificial spawning and larval rearing of the grouper, Epinephelus tauvina (Forskål) in Singapore. Singapore J. Primary Ind. 5(1):1-21.

Collins, L. A., J. H. Finucane, and L. E. Barger. 1979. Description of larval and juvenile red snapper, Lutjanus campechanus. Fish. Bull., U.S. 77:965-974.

Damas, T., M. Borrero, N. Millares, and E. Gonzales. 1978. Desarrollo embrionario y prelarval del caballerote (Lutjanus griseus, Linné, 1758). Rev. Cubana Invest. Pesq. 3(4):11-37.

Dekhnik, T. V., M. Haures, and D. Salabariya. 1966. Distribution of pelagic eggs and larvae of fishes in coastal waters of Cuba. In Investigations of the Central American Seas, p. 189-241. Instituta Biologiya Yuzhnikh Morei, Imperatorskagó Akad. A. O. Kovalevskogo. Akad. Nauk SSSR. [Engl. transl., U.S. Dep. Commer. TT70-57762, 1973.]

Fage, L. 1918. Shore fishes. Reports of the Danish oceanographic expedition to the Mediterranean. 2(A3).

Fahay, M. P. 1975. An annotated list of larval and juvenile fishes captured with surface-towed meter net in the South Atlantic Bight during four R.V. Dolphin cruises between May 1967 and February 1968. U.S. Dep. Commer., NOAA Tech. Rep. NMFS SSRF-685, 39 p.

Finucane, J. H., L. A. Collins, and L. E. Barger. 1979. Environmental assessment of an active oilfield in the northwestern Gulf of Mexico, 1977-78. In W. B. Jackson (editor), NOAA/NMFS Annu. Rep. to EPA, September 1979. EPA-JAG-D5-E693-EO. Work unit 2.3.6.

232

Fourmanoir, P. 1976. Formes post-larvaires et juvéniles de poissons cotiers pris au chalut pélagique dans le sud-ouest Pacifique. Cah. Pac. 19:47–88.

Fowler, H. W. 1944. The fishes. In Results of the fifth George Vanderbilt expedition (1941). Monogr. Acad. Nat. Sci. Phila. 6:57–581, 20 pls.

Goldman, B., G. Stroud, and F. Talbot. 1983. Fish eggs and larvae over a coral reef: abundance with habitat, time of day and moon phase. In J. T. Baker, R. M. Carter, P. W. Sammarco, and K. P. Stark (editors), Proceedings: Inaugural Great Barrier Reef Conference, p. 203–211. James Cook University Press, Townsville.

Guitart Manday, G., and M. Juarez Fernandez. 1966. Desarrollo embrionario y primeros estadios larvales de la cherna criolla, Epinephelus striatus (Bloch) (Perciformes: Serranidae). Acad. Cienc. Cuba. Estudios-Inst. Oceanol. 1:35–45.

Hardy, J. D. 1978. Development of fishes of mid-Atlantic Bight, an atlas of egg, larval, and juvenile stages. Vol. 3. Aphredoderidae through Rachycentridae. U.S. Fish Wildl. Serv., Biol. Serv. Prog. FWS/OBS-78/12, 394 p.

Heemstra, P. C. 1974. On the identity of certain eastern Pacific and Caribbean post-larval fishes (Perciformes) described by Henry Fowler. Proc. Acad. Nat. Sci. Phila. 126(3):21–26.

Houde, E. D. 1982. Kinds, distributions and abundances of sea bass larvae (Pisces: Serranidae) from the eastern Gulf of Mexico. Bull. Mar. Sci. 32:511–522.

Houde, E. D., and C. E. Dowd. 1976. Lutjanid and serranid larvae from the eastern Gulf of Mexico. Final Rep., Natl. Mar. Fish. Serv. Grant No. NOAA, NMFS P001-6042-11080, 12 p.

Houde, E. D., J. C. Leak, S. Al-Matar, and C. E. Dowd. 1981. Ichthyoplankton abundance and diversity in the western Arabian Gulf. Kuwait Inst. Sci. Res., Maricult. Fish. Dep. Final Rep. Proj. MB-16, 3 vol.

Houde, E. D., J. C. Leak, C. E. Dowd, S. A. Berkeley, and W. J. Richards. 1979. Ichthyoplankton abundance and diversity in the eastern Gulf of Mexico. Rep. Bur. Land Manage. Contract AA550-CT7-28. NTIS-PB-299-839, 546 p.

Hussain, N. A., and M. Higuchi. 1980. Larval rearing and development of the brown spotted grouper, Epinephelus tauvina (Forskål). Aquaculture 19:339–350.

Hussain, N., M. Saif, and M. Ukawa. 1975. On the culture of Epinephelus tauvina (Forskål). Kuwait Inst. Sci. Res., State of Kuwait, 14 p.

Johnson, G. D. 1980. The limits and relationships of the Lutjanidae and associated families. Bull. Scripps Inst. Oceanogr., Univ. Calif. 24, 114 p.

_____. 1983. Niphon spinosus: A primitive epinephe line serranid, with comments on the monophyly and interrelationships of the Serranidae. Copeia 1983:777-787.

_____. 1984. Percoidei: Development and relationships. In H. G. Moser, W. J. Richards, D. M. Cohen, M. P. Fahay, A. W. Kendall, Jr., and S. L. Richardson (editors), Ontogeny and systematics of fishes, p. 464-498. Am. Soc. Ichthyol. Herpetol. Spec. Publ. 1.

Johnson, G. D., and P. Keener. 1984. Aid to identification of American grouper larvae. Bull. Mar. Sci. 34:106-134.

Kendall, A. W., Jr. 1979. Morphological comparisons of North American sea bass larvae (Pisces: Serranidae). U.S. Dep. Commer., NOAA Tech. Rep. NMFS Circ. 428, 50 p.

_____. 1984. Serranidae: Development and relationships. In H. G. Moser, W. J. Richards, D. M. Cohen, M. P. Fahay, A. W. Kendall, Jr., and S. L. Richardson (editors), Ontogeny and systematics of fishes, p. 499-509. Am. Soc. Ichthyol. Herpetol. Spec. Publ. 1.

Kendall, A. W., Jr. and M. P. Fahay. 1979. Larva of the serranid fish Gonioplectrus hispanus with comments on its relationships. Bull. Mar. Sci. 29:117-121.

Laroche, W. A. 1977. Description of larval and early juvenile vermilion snapper, Rhomboplites aurorubens. Fish. Bull., U.S. 75:547-554.

Leis, J. M. 1978. Distributional ecology of ichthyoplankton and invertebrate macrozooplankton in the vicinity of a Hawaiian coastal power plant. Ph.D. Dissertation, Univ. Hawaii, Honolulu, 317 p.

_____. 1982a. Distribution of fish larvae around Lizard Island, Great Barrier Reef: Coral reef lagoon as refuge? Proc. 4th Int. Coral Reef Symp., Manila 2:471-477.

_____. 1982b. Nearshore distributional gradients of larval fish (15 taxa) and planktonic crustaceans (6 taxa) in Hawaii. Mar. Biol. (Berl.) 72:89-97.

_____. 1986. Vertical and horizontal distribution of fish larvae near coral reefs at Lizard Island, Great Barrier Reef. Mar. Biol. (Berl.) 90:505-516.

_____. In press. Larval development in four species of Indo-Pacific coral trout Plectropomus (Pisces: Serranidae: Epinephelinae) with an analysis of the relationships of the genus. Bull. Mar. Sci. 38(2).

Leis, J. M., and B. Goldman. 1983. Studies on the biology of larval fishes in the Lizard Island area, northern Great Barrier Reef. In J. T. Baker, R. M. Carter, P. W. Sammarco, and K. P. Stark (editors), Proceedings: Inaugural Great Barrier Reef Conference, p. 221-225. James Cook University Press, Townsville.

_____. 1984. A preliminary distributional study of fish larvae near a ribbon coral reef in the Great Barrier Reef. Coral Reefs 2(4):197-203.

_____. Unpub. 1. Horizontal distribution patterns of fish larvae in the outer portion of the Great Barrier Reef Lagoon near Lizard Island.

_____. Unpub. 2. Taxonomic composition and spatial distribution of larval fish assemblages and tentative location of larval nurseries in the Great Barrier Reef Lagoon near Lizard Island, Australia.

_____. Unpub. 3. Vertical distribution of fish larvae in the northern Great Barrier Reef Lagoon.

Leis, J. M., H. Hausfeld, and P. C. Young. Unpub. Distributional ecology of snapper and fusilier (Pisces, Lutjanidae) larvae on the Australian North West Continental Shelf.

Leis, J. M., and J. M. Miller. 1976. Offshore distributional patterns of Hawaiian fish larvae. Mar. Biol. (Berl.) 36:359-367.

Leis, J. M., and D. S. Rennis. 1983. The larvae of Indo-Pacific coral reef fishes. New South Wales University Press, Sydney, and University of Hawaii Press, Honolulu, 269 p.

Lu Suifen. 1981. Observations on the fish eggs and larvae of black-striped snapper, Lutjanus vitta (Quoy et Gaimard). [In Chin., Engl. abstr.] Trans. Chin. Ichthyol. Soc. 1:49-56.

Minton, R. V., J. P. Hawke, and W. M. Tatum. 1983. Hormone induced spawning of red snapper, Lutjanus campechanus. Aquaculture 30:363-368.

Mito, S. 1963. Pelagic fish eggs from Japanese waters-III. Percina. [In Jpn., Engl. resume.] Jpn. J. Ichthyol. 11 (1/2):39-64, 18 plates.

_____. 1966. Fish eggs and larvae. In S. Motoda (editor), Illustrations of the marine plankton of Japan. [In Jpn.] Vol. 7, Sôyô-sha, Tokyo, 74 p.

Mito, S., M. Ukawa, and M. Higuchi. 1967. On the larval and young stages of a serranid fish, Epinephelus akaara (Temminck et Schlegel). [In Jpn., Engl. abstr.] Bull. Nankai Reg. Fish. Res. Lab. 25:337-347.
_____. 1973. Growth of some marine fish larvae hatched out from pelagic eggs. J. Mar. Biol. Assoc. India 15(2):490-495.

Moe, M. A. 1969. Biology of the red grouper, Epinephelus morio (Valenciennes) from the eastern Gulf of Mexico. Fla. Dep. Nat. Resour., Mar. Res. Lab. Prof. Pap. Ser. 10:1-95.

Mori, K. 1984. Early life history of Lutjanus vitta (Lutjanidae) in Yuya Bay, the Sea of Japan. Jpn. J. Ichthyol. 30:374-392.

Moser, H. G., E. H. Ahlstrom, D. Kramer, and E. G. Stevens. 1975. Distribution and abundance of fish eggs and larvae in the Gulf of California. Calif. Coop. Oceanic Fish. Invest. Rep. 17:112-128.

Musiy, Yu. I. and V. A. Sergiyenko. 1977. Fingerlings of the genus Lutjanus (Lutjanidae, Perciformes) from the Gulf of Aden. J. Ichthyol. 17:151-154.

Nellen, W. 1973. Fischlarven des Indischen Ozeans. "Meteor" Forsch.-Ergebnisse, Reihe D 14:1-66.

Parrish, J. D. 1986. Trophic biology of snappers and groupers. In J. J. Polovina and S. Ralston (editors), Tropical snappers and groupers: Biology and fisheries management. Westview Press, Inc., Boulder. [See this volume.]

Powles, H. 1977. Larval distributions and recruitment hypotheses for snappers and groupers of the South Atlantic Bight. Proc. Annu. Conf. Southeast. Assoc. Fish. Wildl. Agencies 31:362-371.

Presley, R. F. 1970. Larval snowy grouper, Epinephelus niveatus (Valenciennes, 1828), from the Florida Straits. Fla. Dep. Nat. Resour., Leafl. Ser., Vol. IV, Part 1 (Pisces) No. 18, p. 1-6.

Rabalais, N. N., S. C. Rabalais, and C. R. Arnold. 1980. Description of eggs and larvae of laboratory reared red snapper (Lutjanus campechanus). Copeia 1980:704-708.

Raffaele, F. 1888. Le uova galleggianti e le larve dei Teleostei nel Golfo di Napoli. Mitth. Zool. Sta. zu Neapel 8:1-85, pls. I-V.

Randall, J. E. 1986. A preliminary synopsis of the groupers (Perciformes: Serranidae: Epinephelinae) of the Indo-Pacific region. In J. J. Polovina and S. Ralston (editors), Tropical snappers and groupers:

Biology and fisheries management. Westview Press, Inc., Boulder. [See this volume.]

Richards, W. J. 1982. Planktonic processes affecting establishment and maintenance of reef fish stocks. In G. R. Hunstman, W. R. Nicholson, and W. W. Fox (editors), The biological bases for reef fishery management, p. 92-100. U.S. Dep. Commer, NOAA Tech. Memo. NMFS, NOAA-TM-NMFS-SEFC-80.

_____. 1984. Kinds and abundances of fish larvae in the Caribbean Sea and adjacent waters. U.S. Dep. Commer., NOAA Tech. Rep., NMFS SSRF-776, 54 p.

Richards, W. J., and V. P. Saksena. 1980. Description of larvae and early juveniles of laboratory-reared gray snapper, Lutjanus griseus (Linnaeus) (Pisces, Lutjanidae). Bull. Mar. Sci. 30:515-521.

Roberts, D. E., and R. A. Schlieder. 1983. Induced sex inversion, maturation, spawning and embryogeny of the protogynous grouper, Mycteroperca microlepis. J. World Maricult. Soc. 14:639-649.

Sale, P. F. 1980. The ecology of fishes on coral reefs. Oceanogr. Mar. Biol. Annu. Rev. 18:367-421.

Smith, C. L. 1971. A revision of the American groupers: Epinephelus and allied genera. Bull. Am. Mus. Nat. Hist. 146(2), 241 p.

Sparta, A. 1935. Contributo alla conoscenza dello sviluppo nei Percidi. Uova ovariche mature di Epinephelus guaza L. e stadi post-embrionali e larvali di Epinephelus alexandrius. Cuv. e Val. Reale Comitato Talassografico Italino Memoria 224:1-12, 2 pls.

Starck, W. A., II. 1970. Biology of the gray snapper, Lutjanus griseus (Linnaeus), in the Florida Keys. In W. A. Starck, II and R. E. Schroeder (editors), Investigations on the gray snapper, Lutjanus griseus, p. 1-150. Stud. Trop. Oceanogr. (Miami) 10. (Copyright 1971.)

Suzuki, K., and S. Hioki. 1979. Spawning behavior, eggs, and larvae of the lutjanid fish, Lutjanus kasmira in an aquarium. Jpn. J. Ichthyol. 26:161-166.

Tang, H. C., J. Y. Twu, and W. C. Su. 1979. Experiment on artificial propagation of the high-finned grouper Cromileptes altivelis. China Fish. Monthly 324:25-31.

Teng, S. K., S. Akatsu, K. M. Abdul-Elah, A. Al-Marzouk, N. Downing, C. R. El-Zahr, and K. Al-Ghemlas. 1982. Spawning, fingerling production and market-size culture of Hamoor (Epinephelus tauvina) in Kuwait. Kuwait Inst. Sci. Res. Annu. Rep. 1981, p. 71-74.

Thresher, R. E. 1984. Reproduction in reef fishes. T.F.H. Publications, Neptune City, New Jersey, 399 p.

Tortonese, E. 1973. Serranidae. In J. C. Hureau and Th. Monod (editors), Checklist of the fishes of the north-eastern Atlantic and of the Mediterranean, p. 355-362. UNESCO, Paris.

Tseng, W.-Y., and S.-K. Ho. 1979. Egg development and early larval rearing of red grouper (Epinephelus akaara, Temminck and Schlegel). Q. J. Taiwan Mus. 32(3/4):209-219.

Tseng, W. Y., and C. T. Poon. 1983. Hybridization of Epinephelus species. Aquaculture 34(1/2):177-182.

Uchida, K. 1937. On floating mechanisms observed in pelagic larvae of fishes (1). [In Jpn.] Kagaku 7(13):540-546.

Ukawa, M., M. Higuchi, and S. Mito. 1966. Spawning habits and early life history of a serranid fish Epinephelus akaara (Temminck et Schlegel). [In Jpn., Engl. abstr.] Jpn. J. Ichthyol. 13(4/6):156-161.

Vatanachai, Sa-Nga. 1972. The identification of fish eggs and fish larvae obtained from the survey cruises in the South China Sea. In The 15th Session of the Indo-Pacific Fisheries Council, Wellington, New Zealand, October 1972, p. 111-130. FAO Reg. Off. Asia and Far East, Bangkok.

Warner, R. R. 1984. Recent developments in the ecology of tropical reef fishes. Arch. Fischereiwiss. 35(1):43-53.

Young, P. C., J. M. Leis, and H. Hausfeld. In press. Seasonal and spatial distribution of fish larvae in waters over the North West continental shelf of Western Australia. Mar. Ecol. Prog. Ser.

5
Reproductive Biology of the Lutjanidae: A Review

Churchill B. Grimes
Southeast Fisheries Center Panama City Laboratory
National Marine Fisheries Service, NOAA
Panama City, Florida 32407

ABSTRACT

Available information on the reproductive biology of over 40 species of the Lutjanidae found throughout the world's oceans is reviewed. The lutjanids are apparently gonochoristic, there being no histological evidence to the contrary. Population sex ratio as well as sex ratio at size is frequently skewed; however, evidence suggests this results from differential growth and mortality rates between the sexes.

Sexual maturity occurs at approximately 40–50% of maximum length. Analysis of covariance of length at maturity (with maximum length as a covariate) revealed that populations and species associated with islands mature at a significantly higher ($0.005 > P > 0.001$) proportion of maximum length (51%) than continental species and populations (43%). Deep (>91 m) dwelling species and populations mature at a significantly higher ($0.005 > P > 0.001$) proportion of maximum size (49%) than shallow (<91 m) species (43%).

Lutjanids are highly fecund, with large females producing $5-7 \times 10^6$ ova.

Two patterns of reproductive seasonality are apparent: Continental populations and species exhibit extended summer spawning, and insular populations and species reproduce year round with pulses in spring and fall.

Spawning appears to take place at night, sometimes timed to coincide with spring tides at new and full moons. Courtship behavior culminates in an upward spiral swim with gametes released at the apex.

Individual fish spawn more than once each reproductive season.

Many features of the reproductive biology of the lutjanids (e.g., spawning site preference, spawning seasonality, lunar periodicity, and spawning behavior) appear to be a strategy to introduce gametes into an environment where predation is relatively less intense. However, the strategy must also assure that young juveniles are returned to suitable, but patchy, habitat for settlement.

INTRODUCTION

The Lutjanidae is a large family consisting of about 17 genera and 103 species (Anderson 1986) found in the warmer regions of the world's oceans. Most species inhabit marine waters to depths of about 550 m, but a few occur in estuaries, particularly as juveniles and sometimes as adults. The family is speciose, with tropical members inhabiting a wide depth range. Temperate regions usually accommodate only the deeper-dwelling species. Snappers are highly substrate oriented and are usually associated with reefs and rock outcroppings.

Snappers can reach large size (>100 cm total length (TL) and 40 kg) and are important food fish in many parts of the world. Worldwide landings are estimated to be about 60,000 metric tons (FAO 1984). Commercial, recreational, and artisanal fishermen land snappers with bottom longlines, hook and line, traps, spears, and occasionally bottom trawls.

Despite their importance, the biology of many species is not well known. This paper presents a review of the state of knowledge of the reproductive biology of the Lutjanidae, with some general conclusions regarding similarities and differences among species throughout the tropical and temperate regions of the world. In some cases, this has been possible, but in others, obscure and inconsistent methodology make any general conclusions tentative at best.

SEXUALITY

Available information suggests that lutjanids are gonochoristic. Following sexual differentiation, sex remains fixed throughout life. Although studies utilizing histological techniques to examine the gonads are not numerous (Rodriguez Pino 1962; Alves 1971; Futch and Bruger 1976), only normal gonochoristic testicular and ovarian tissue features are reported. Standard histological evidence for hermaphroditism, including persistence of an ovarian lumen in the testis or testicular tissue embedded in the ovarian mass (Smith 1965; Fishelson 1975), has not been noted. Similarly, analyses of sex ratios in species from geographically diverse locations (Table 5.1) do not show a pattern of consistent variation in sex ratio with size that would suggest hermaphroditism (i.e., very high proportions of one sex at small size that gradually decrease with increasing size, eventually diminishing to near 0 (Wenner 1972)). Rather, the data show inconsistent variation of population and size-specific sex ratios. The more thorough studies, in which a wide range of sizes was sampled, suggest a tendency for females to be preponderant at larger sizes (Rodriguez Pino 1962; Erhardt 1977; Grimes and Huntsman 1980; Baez Hidalgo et al. 1982; Everson 1984). This predominance of females among large fish probably results from differential longevity of the sexes, as females have been shown to outlive males in at least a few species (Rodriguez Pino 1962; Grimes and Huntsman 1980). Also, if a species were hermaphroditic, both sexes should not be present at most ages. Rodriguez Pino (1962) has shown that Lutjanus synagris from Cuba has both males and females at every age up to 4 years, with only females present thereafter.

Sexual dimorphism is apparently rare among the Lutjanidae; it is reported in only two species (genus Pristipomoides) from the Indo-west Pacific (Kami 1973). The ventral lobe of the caudal fin of female P. auricilla from Guam is inconsistently tinged with yellow, but if tinged, never forms a distinct blotch. Large males (>270 mm fork length (FL)), however, usually have a distinct yellow blotch on the ventral lobe of the caudal fin. In P. filamentosus, males have dusky anal and pelvic fin membranes, and large specimens have a yellow-orange tinge between the first and second anal spines and last two rays. Occasionally, anal fins of large females are dusky, but never tinged in yellow-orange.

MATURITY

Review of the published literature concerning sexual maturity among the Lutjanidae (Table 5.2) showed that

TABLE 5.1
Sex ratio information on various lutjanid species arranged according to zoogeographic province. N = sample size, F = female, M = male, TL = total length, FL = fork Length, and SL = standard length

Species	Location	Population Ratio (F:M)	Ratio at Length	Reference
		Western Atlantic Species		
Rhomboplites aurorubens	North Carolina and South Carolina	1.6:1 (N = 874)	Size range 100-650 mm TL; biased in favor of F's above 150 mm, eventually reaching 100% F	Grimes 1976; Grimes and Huntsman 1980
	Puerto Rico	1:1.1 (N = 1,322)	About equal from 110 to 380 mm FL	Boardman and Weiler 1980
Lutjanus vivanus	Puerto Rico	1.3:1 (N = 3,235)	About 55-60% F from <210 to >530 mm FL	Boardman and Weiler 1980
	Jamaica	1:1.4 (N = 452)	Between 200 and 700 mm FL varies 25-60% with no pattern	Thompson and Munro 1974, 1983
	Virgin Islands	1:1.17 (N = 141)	No data	Sylvester et al. 1980

Species	Location	Sex ratio (N)		Reference
L. vivanus	Virgin Islands	1:1.04 (N = 265)	No data	Brownell and Rainey 1971
L. buccanella	Puerto Rico	1.8:1 (N = 672)	Between <140 and 500 mm FL decreases slowly from about 80 to 40% F	Boardman and Weiler 1980
	Virgin Islands	1:1.29 (N = 39)	No data	Sylvester et al. 1980
	Jamaica	1.5:1 (N = 756)	Between 190 and 510 mm FL decreases steadily from about 80 to 10% F	Thompson and Munro 1974, 1983
	Virgin Islands	1:1.2 (N = 91)	No data	Brownell and Rainey 1971
Apsilus dentatus	Jamaica	1:1.3 (N = 564)	Between 280 and 580 mm FL decreases steadily	Thompson and Munro 1974, 1983
L. apodus	Jamaica	1.03:1 (N = 75)	Between 200 and 500 mm FL varies between 33 and 75% F, with no pattern	Thompson and Munro 1974, 1983
Ocyurus chrysurus	Jamaica	1:1.3 (N = 695)	Between 200 and 580 mm FL varies erratically 10 to 60%, eventually attaining 100% F at large size	Thompson and Munro 1974, 1983

(Continued)

TABLE 5.1 (Cont.)

Species	Location	Population Ratio (F:M)	Ratio at Length	Reference
	Florida Keys	1:1.04 (N = 1,621)	No data	Collins and Finucane Unpub.
	Cuba	1:1.4 (N = 1,902)	No data	Piedra 1965
L. synagris	Trinidad	1.13:1 (trap) 1.6:1 (trawl) (N = ?)	No data	Manickchand-Dass In press
L. synagris	Cuba	1.3:1 (N = 1,640)	No data	Claro 1981
		1.9:1 (N = 1,441)	Between 80 and 420 mm FL 50% F initially, then 60-70% F to 300 mm, then 100% F	Rodriguez-Pino 1962
	Colombian Caribbean	1:1.3 (N = 2,472)	Size range 100-500 mm SL; about 40-60% F up to 400 mm, then increasing to 88% F above 400 mm	Erhardt 1977

Species	Location	Sex ratio (N)	Remarks	Reference
L. *griseus*	Florida Keys	1:1.1 (N = 722)	No data	Starck and Schroeder 1970
L. *griseus*	Florida Bay (Florida Everglades)	1.1:1 (N = 790)	No data	Croker 1962
L. *griseus*	Cuba	1.6:1 (N = 1,331)	Size range 140–530 mm FL; up to about 300 mm about 50% F, then slowly increases to 100% F by 450 mm	Baez Hidalgo et al. 1982
L. *campechanus*	Northwestern Gulf	1:1.3 (N = ?)	Size range 200–400 mm SL, M's predominate	Moseley 1966
	Campeche Banks	1.1:1 (N = 555)	Size range 250–800 mm FL; 1:1 up to about 600 mm then % F increases	Camber 1955
	South Atlantic Bight and Northeastern Gulf of Mexico	1.1:1 (N = 1,245)	Size range 230–858 mm FL	Collins et al. Unpub.
	Northwestern Gulf of Mexico	1.01:1 (N = 1,129)	No data	Bradley and Bryan 1975
L. *purpureus*	Northeastern Brazil	1:1.04 (N = 1,085)	No data	Ivo 1973

(Continued)

TABLE 5.1 (Cont.)

Species	Location	Population Ratio (F:M)	Ratio at Length	Reference
		Indo-West Pacific Species		
L. vaigiensis	Society Islands	1.7:1 (N = 56)	No data	Randall and Brock 1960
	Gulf of Aden	1:3.8 (N = 19)	Size range 225-315 mm SL	Druzhinin and Filatova 1980
L. sebae	Gulf of Aden	1:1.04 (N = 100)	Size range 215-745 mm SL	Druzhinin and Filatova 1980
L. rivulatus	Gulf of Aden	1.1:1 (N = 13)	Size range 555-715 mm SL	Druzhinin and Filatova 1980
L. lineolatus	Gulf of Aden	1.8:1 (N = 56)	Size range 175-325 mm SL	Druzhinin and Filatova 1980
L. kasmira	Gulf of Aden	1:1.5 (N = 5)	Size range 135-195 mm SL	Druzhinin and Filatova 1980
L. kasmira	Andaman Sea	1:1.16 (N = 1,122)	<99 mm TL M's pre-dominate; 100-169 mm F's dominant; >170 mm M's dominant; above 230 mm no F's	Rangarajan 1971

L. gibbus	Gulf of Aden	1:1.5 (N = 32)	Size range 265-475 mm SL	Druzhinin and Filatova 1980
L. duodecim-lineatus	Gulf of Aden	1.9:1 (N = 77)	Size range 225-365 mm SL	Druzhinin and Filatova 1980
L. fulviflamma	New Caledonia	1.1:1 (N = 68)	Size range 100-300 mm SL; about 50% F to 260 mm when increases to 100% F	Loubens 1980
	East Africa	2.04:1 (N = 76)	Size range 51-220 mm SL	Talbot 1960
L. quinquelineatus	Caledonia (N = 190)	1:1.2	Size range 100-219 mm SL; in favor of M's throughout	Loubens 1980
L. vitta	New Caledonia	1:1.1 (N = 147)	Size range 100->300 mm SL; about 40% F decreasing to 9% F by >300 mm	Loubens 1980
L. amabilis	New Caledonia	1:1.6 (N = 282)	Size range <200-520 mm SL; 40% F gradually becoming 0%	Loubens 1980
L. johni	Andaman Sea	1:1.4 (N = ?)	No data	Druzhinin 1970

(Continued)

TABLE 5.1 (Cont.)

Species	Location	Population Ratio (F:M)	Ratio at Length	Reference
L. malabaricus	Andaman Sea	1.2:1 (N = ?)	No data	Druzhinin 1970
L. malabaricus	Vanuatu, New Hebrides	2.7:1 (N = 78)	No data	Brouard and Grandperrin 1984
P. multidens	Andaman Sea/ South China Sea	1.2:1 (N = 301)	Size range about 200–600 mm SL	Min et al. 1977
	Vanuatu, New Hebrides	1.4:1 (N = 382)	No data	Brouard and Grandperrin 1984
P. typus	Andaman Sea/ South China Sea	1:1.4 (N = 730)	Size range about 200–600 mm SL	Min et al. 1977
P. filamentosus	Andaman Sea/ South China Sea	1.3:1 (N = 677)	Size range about 200–700 mm SL	Min et al. 1977
	Guam	1:1.4 (N = 183)	Size range 179–600 mm SL	Kami 1973
	Hawaiian Islands	1:1.02 (N = 449)		Ralston 1981

Species	Location (N)	Sex ratio	Size data	Reference
P. auricilla	Guam (N = 384)	1.3:1 mm SL	Size range 200-410	Kami 1973
P. sieboldii	Guam	1:1.1 (N = 110)	Size range 170-350 mm SL	Kami 1973
P. flavipinnis	Guam	1.1:1 (N = 180)	Size range 167-427 mm SL	Kami 1973
	Vanuatu, New Hebrides	1.26:1 (N = 165)	No data	Brouard and Grandperrin 1984
E. carbunculus	Vanuatu, New Hebrides	2.04:1 (N = 137)	No data	Brouard and Grandperrin 1984
	Hawaiian Islands	2.02:1 (N = 833)	Size range about 275-625 mm FL; biased in favor F's above 350 mm FL, eventually reaching >90% F's	Everson 1984
E. coruscans	Vanuatu, New Hebrides	1.7:1 (N = 135)	No data	Brouard and Grandperrin 1984

TABLE 5.2
Length at first sexual maturity and maximum length in the population for selected Lutjanidae according to location and sex. Length at maturity was determined by visual staging of gonads. Maximum length is as reported for that population except as noted

Species	Location	Sex	Length (mm) at First Maturity	Maximum Length in Population	Percent of Maximum Length at First Maturity	Reference
Western Atlantic Species						
Rhomboplites aurorubens	North Carolina and South Carolina	F	186 TL	627 TL	29.6	Grimes 1976; Grimes and Huntsman 1980
	Puerto Rico	M	140 FL	380 FL	36.8	Boardman and Weiler 1980
		F	170 FL		44.7	
Lutjanus synagris	Cuba	M	91[a]	300	22.8	Reshetnikov and Claro 1976
		F	91	400	22.8	
	Trinidad	M	225 TL	485 TL	46.4	Manickchand-Dass In press
		F	230 TL	431 TL	47.4	
	Cuba	M	85 FL	275 FL	30.9	Rodriguez-Pino 1962
		F	85 FL	310 FL	27.4	

Species	Location	Sex			%	Reference
L. synagris	Jamaica	M	183 FL	410 FL	44.6	Thompson and Munro 1974, 1983
		F	176 FL	410 FL	42.9	
Ocyurus chrysurus	Jamaica	M	260 FL	550 FL	47.3	Thompson and Munro 1974, 1983
		F	290 FL	560 FL	51.7	
	Florida Keys	F	200 FL	567 FL	35.3	Collins and Finucane Unpub.
L. griseus	Florida Keys	M	185 SL	489 SL	37.8	Starck and Schroeder 1970
		F	195 SL	489 SL	39.8	
	Cuba	M	245 FL	525 FL	46.7	Baez Hidalgo et al. 1982
		F	325 FL	525 FL	61.9	
L. campechanus	U.S. South Atlantic Bight and Gulf of Mexico	M	325 FL	970 FL[b]	33.5	Collins et al. Unpub.
		F	325 FL			
	Southwest Florida	M, F	334 FL	941 FL	35.5	Futch and Bruger 1976
	Campeche Banks	M, F	310 FL	778 FL	39.8	Camber 1955
	Northwestern Gulf of Mexico	M	230 FL	850 FL	27.1	Bradley and Bryan 1975
		F	255 FL	850 FL	30.0	
L. purpureus	Northeastern Brazil	M	400 TL	825 TL[c]	48.5	Alves 1971
		F	420 FL	825 TL	50.9	Gesteira and Ivo 1973

(Continued)

TABLE 5.2 (Cont.)

Species	Location	Sex	Length (mm) at First Maturity	Maximum Length in Population	Percent of Maximum Length at First Maturity	Reference
L. vivanus	Virgin Islands	M F	270 FL 240 FL	660 FL 660 FL	40.9 36.4	Brownell and Rainey 1971
L. vivanus	Jamaica	M F	525 FL 575 FL	720 FL 680 FL	72.9 84.5	Thompson and Munro 1974, 1983
	North Carolina and South Carolina	M F	270 TL 240 FL	660 TL 660 TL	40.9 36.4	Grimes et al. 1977
L. buccanella	Jamaica	M	260 FL 240 FL	490 FL 490 FL	53.1 48.9	Thompson and Munro 1974, 1983
	North Carolina and South Carolina	F	350 TL	627 TL	55.8	Grimes et al. 1977
	Virgin Islands	M F	380 FL 180 FL	540 FL	70.3 33.3	Brownell and Rainey 1971
L. apodus	Jamaica	M F	250 FL 250 FL	570 FL 570 FL	43.8 43.8	Thompson and Munro 1974, 1983

Species	Location	Sex				Reference
L. iocu	Jamaica	F	323 FL	720 FL	44.9	Thompson and Munro 1974, 1983
L. analis	Cuba	M, F	402 FL	690 FL	58.3	Rojas 1960
Apsilus dentatus	Jamaica	M	440 FL	560 FL	78.6	Thompson and Munro 1974, 1983
		F	400 FL	540 FL	74.1	
Pristipomoides macropthalmus	Jamaica	F	180 FL	350 FL	51.4	Thompson and Munro 1974, 1983
P. macropthalmus	Virgin Islands	M, F	230 FL	430 FL	53.5	Brownell and Rainey 1971
Indo-West Pacific Species						
L. bohar	East Africa	M, F	450 SL	660 SL	68.2	Talbot 1960
L. sebae	East Africa	M, F	490 SL	665 SL	73.7	Talbot 1960
L. amabilis	New Caledonia	M	186 SL	442 SL	42.1	Loubens 1980
		F	191 SL	382 SL	50	
L. fulviflamma	New Caledonia	M	185 SL	258 SL	71.7	Loubens 1980
		F	172 SL	285 SL	60.4	
	East Africa	M	145 SL	220 SL	65.9	Talbot 1960
		F	160 SL	220 SL	72.7	

(Continued)

TABLE 5.2 (Cont.)

Species	Location	Sex	Length (mm) at First Maturity	Maximum Length in Population	Percent of Maximum Length at First Maturity	Reference
L. quinquelineatus	New Caledonia	M	112 SL	189 SL	59.3	Loubens 1980
		F	113 SL	195 SL	57.9	
L. vitta	New Caledonia	M	128 SL	312 SL	41.0	Loubens 1980
		F	138 SL	264 SL	52.3	
L. rivulatus	East Africa	M	450 SL	640 SL	70.3	Talbot 1960
L. gibbus	East Africa	M	240 SL	355 SL	67.6	Talbot 1960
		F	223 SL	355 SL	62.8	
L. sanguineus	East Africa	M	480 SL	650 SL	73.8	Talbot 1960
		F	505 SL	650 SL	77.7	
L. kasmira	East Africa	M	155 SL	205 SL	75.6	Talbot 1960
		F	125 SL	205 SL	60.9	
L. monostigma	East Africa	M	350 SL	420 SL	Insufficient data	Talbot 1960
L. argenti-maculatus	East Africa	M	350 SL	630 SL	Insufficient data	Talbot 1960

Species	Location	Sex				Reference
Aprion virescens	East Africa	M	410 SL	800 SL	51.3	Talbot 1960
		F	465 SL	800 SL	58.1	
L. johni	Andaman Sea	M	301	913	32.9	Druzhinin 1970
		F	291		31.9	
L. ehrenbergi	East Africa	F	75 SL	228 SL[d]	32.9	Talbot 1960
L. vaigiensis	East Africa	M	190 SL	250 SL	76.6	Talbot 1960
P. filamentosus	Hawaiian Islands	F	456 FL	947 SL	48.1	Kikkawa 1984
P. multidens	South China Sea/ Andaman Sea	F	350 SL	700 SL	50	Min et al. 1977
P. multidens	South China Sea/ Andaman Sea	F	450 SL	680 SL	66.2	Min et al. 1977
P. typus	South China Sea/ Andaman Sea	F	280 SL	620 SL	45.2	Min et al. 1977
Etelis carbunculus	Hawaiian Islands	F	298 FL	650 FL	45.8	Everson 1984

[a] Length measurement not reported
[b] From Nelson and Manooch 1982
[c] Length from Ivo 1973
[d] From Druzhinin 1970, measurement not specified
[e] Not included in the statistical analysis

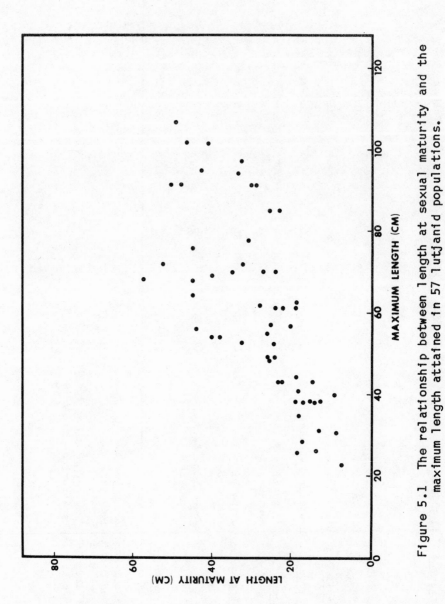

Figure 5.1 The relationship between length at sexual maturity and the maximum length attained in 57 lutjanid populations.

length at maturity ranges from 23 to 84% of the maximum length reported, that the relationship between maturity length and maximum length is linear (Figure 5.1), and that males mature at a slightly smaller size than females.

I used analysis of covariance to test the data in Table 5.2 for differences in size of maturity between (1) continental and insular habitats, (2) zoogeographic provinces, and (3) habitat depth. Because maturity length increases linearly with the maximum length reported for the population (Figure 5.1), the latter was used as a covariate to adjust the analysis for the possibility of different maximum sizes in the various species and populations.

There are consistent differences in the percentage of maximum length at which maturity is attained between continental and insular members of the fauna, as well as between deep (>91 m) and shallow (<91 m) components (Table 5.3). However, there are no apparent differences in relative size of maturity between western Atlantic and Indo-west Pacific lutjanids. Species and populations associated with islands mature at relatively larger size than those associated with continents (51 and 41% of maximum length, respectively). Similarly, populations and species associated with deep habitats mature at 49% of their maximum length, as compared to 43% for shallow species and populations (Table 5.3). Analysis of covariance testing for differences in length at maturity with regard to insular and continental habitats and habitat depth were significant (P<0.01), and there were no significant interactions (Table 5.4). Although an effect due to zoogeographic province was evident at the P = 0.05 level of significance, it was not as clear an effect as depth and habitat type.

I speculate that these differences in length at first maturity with regard to habitat depth and habitat type may be due to differences in the richness of food resources in insular versus continental and deep versus shallow habitats, coupled with the fact that sexual maturity in fish largely depends upon the allocation of energy between somatic and reproductive growth (Roff 1983). Fish have evolved a life history with an optimal balance between (1) rapid somatic growth to minimize predation while small and vulnerable, and (2) earliest possible reproduction to maximize the contribution of progeny to future generations. In young fish, energy resources are allocated more to somatic than gonadal growth, to obtain some minimum size where reproduction is physiologically possible and

TABLE 5.3
Length at maturity (MATLEN) and maximum length (MAXLEN) of selected lutjanid populations according to habitat type (insular or continental), zoogeographic province (western Atlantic or Indo-west Pacific), and habitat depth (deep $\geq$91 m or shallow $\leq$91 m). The % MAXLEN is the average percentage of maximum length at which sexual maturity occurs (SD = standard deviation)

		N	Mean	SD	Maximum	Minimum	% MAXLEN
Insular	MATLEN	38	245.6	120.5	575.0	85.0	51
	MAXLEN	38	477.0	164.3	947.0	189.0	
Continental	MATLEN	36	301.0	117.1	505.0	75.0	43
	MAXLEN	36	708.1	208.1	1066.0	228.0	
Western Atlantic	MATLEN	43	268.6	108.0	575.0	85.0	46
	MAXLEN	43	581.6	166.7	970.0	275.0	
Indo-west Pacific	MATLEN	31	277.9	139.4	505.0	75.0	46
	MAXLEN	31	600.3	278.6	1066.0	189.0	
Deep ($\geq$91 m)	MATLEN	33	333.7	118.2	575.0	140.0	49
	MAXLEN	33	682.3	185.7	1066.0	350.0	
Shallow ($\leq$91 m)	MATLEN	41	223.3	100.6	465.0	75.0	43
	MAXLEN	41	514.7	217.1	1015.0	189.0	

TABLE 5.4
Analysis of covariance of length at sexual maturity according to habitat type (insular or continental), zoogeographic province (western Atlantic or Indo-West Pacific), water depth (deep $\geq$91 m or shallow $\leq$91 m). Maximum length in the population is the covariate. All possible interactions between the main effects (i.e., habitat type, zoogeographic province, and habitat depth) and the covariate were tested, found nonsignificant, and dropped from the final model (df = degrees of freedom)

Effect	Sum of Squares	Mean Square	F-Value	df	P
Covariate	440732		85.01	1	0.0000
Overall	577.2		0.11	1	0.7396
Habitat type	59008		11.38	1	0.0012
Zoogeographic province	29385.8		5.67	1	0.0200
Habitat depth	43992.4		8.49	1	0.0048
Error	357745.8	5184.7			

the level of predation acceptable (Iles 1974; Roff 1982, 1983). Furthermore, fish growth is indeterminate, and maximum size is controlled (within genetic limitations) by food availability. Therefore, it may be that fish from relatively resource rich environments mature at a smaller proportion of final size than do fish from a poorer environment.

Habitats associated with continental margins and shallow depths are relatively rich in comparison to insular and deep habitats. Higher biological production is usually associated with large land masses for several reasons, such as opportunities for upwelling near continents (Cushing 1975), runoff of nutrient material into coastal waters (Gross 1972), and a greater amount of shallow continental shelf area providing habitat. Similarly, decreasing biological production is associated with increasing depth, primarily due to lower ambient light levels supporting primary production. A consequence of high production may be a greater food supply for the large predaceous fishes (e.g., lutjanids) in the community.

Another hypothesis to explain the effect of habitat on size at maturity relates to the physiological costs of reproduction over short versus long spawning seasons. Selection may have favored larger maturing fish on islands because the cost of spawning year round may be higher than the cost of more restricted spawning, as is typical of continental stocks. If true, maturation may be delayed until fish are able to sustain such costs. This explanation does not work as well for fish from deep versus shallow habitats, although the former do tend towards a less temporally restricted spawning season (see Seasonality section).

SEASONALITY

Numerous references to the seasonality of snapper reproduction suggest two fairly distinct seasonal patterns: (1) a restricted season (centered around summer) and (2) more or less continuous year-round spawning with peaks of reproductive activity in the spring and fall (Table 5.5). The pattern seems to depend more upon whether a population is found along a continental margin or on oceanic islands than upon latitude. Restricted spawning is more characteristic of continental species and populations, regardless of latitude. For example, continental populations (North Carolina, South

261

TABLE 5.5

Spawning seasons of selected Lutjanidae according to location and zoogeographic province. An X indicates ripe females were collected, XX indicates a peak spawning month, and dashed lines mean the author stated that spawning was continuous, or other types of analyses indicate spawning over the dashed period. Types of analyses are as follows: GSI = gonosomatic index, OD = ovum diameter distribution, VS = visual maturity staging, HS = histological sections, L = larval distribution, J = juvenile distribution, GW = gonad weights, MS = microscopic staging, and SR = sex ratio

Species	Location	Months J F M A M J J A S O N D	Analysis	Reference
Western Atlantic Species				
Apsilus dentatus	Jamaica	X--XX-X--XX-X-----X--X-XX-XX-XX	VS	Munro et al. 1973
	Northeastern Caribbean, including Virgin Islands	X X X	VS	Erdman 1976
Lutjanus analis	Northeastern Caribbean, including Virgin Islands	X	VS	Erdman 1976

(Continued)

TABLE 5.5 (Cont.)

Species	Location	Months (J F M A M J J A S O N D)	Analysis	Reference
L. apodus	Jamaica	X X X X	VS	Munro et al. 1973
	Jamaica	X X X X X X X X	VS	Thompson and Munro 1974, 1983
	Northeastern Caribbean, including Virgin Islands	X	VS	Erdman 1976
L. buccanella	Northeastern Caribbean including Virgin Islands	X X X	VS	Erdman 1976
	Jamaica	X------XX-X X--XX-----X	VS	Thompson and Munro 1974, 1983
	Jamaica	X--X--XX-X------------X--XX-----X	VS	Munro et al. 1973

263

	Puerto Rico	X————————————————X	VS	Boardman and Weiler 1980
L. campechanus	Southwest Florida	———XX–XX———	HS	Futch and Bruger 1976
	Northwestern Gulf of Mexico (Texas)	———XX———	VS, J	Moseley 1966
	Southeastern U.S. (North Carolina–East Florida)	X––X––X––X––X	VS, GSI, MS	Collins et al. Unpub.
	Northwestern Gulf of Mexico (Texas)	X––XX–XX–X––X––X––X	VS, J	Bradley and Bryan 1975
	Campeche Banks, Mexico	XX–XX–––X	VS	Camber 1955
	Northwestern Gulf of Mexico (Texas)	X———————	VS, J	Baughman 1943
	North Carolina and South Carolina	————————	VS	Grimes et al. 1977

(Continued)

TABLE 5.5 (Cont.)

Species	Location	J	F	M	A	M	J	J	A	S	O	N	D	Analysis	Reference
L. griseus	Northeastern Caribbean, including Virgin Islands					X			X	X				VS	Erdman 1976
	Venezuela						X		X					VS, GSI	Campos and Bashirullah 1975
	Cuba					X		X	X	X				VS, GSI	Baez Hidalgo et al. 1982
	Florida Keys					X	X	X	X	X				VS, J, GW	Starck and Schroeder 1970
L. jocu	Jamaica		X											VS	Munro et al. 1973
	Jamaica		X									X		VS	Thompson and Munro 1974, 1983

Months

Species	Locality				Reference
	Northeastern Caribbean, including Virgin Islands	X		VS	Erdman 1976
L. mahogoni	Northeastern Caribbean, including Virgin Islands		X	VS	Erdman 1976
L. purpureus	Northeastern Brazil	X--X--X--X	X--X--X	VS, GW	Gesteira and Ivo 1973
	Northeastern Brazil	X--X--X--X X	X	VS	Fonteles-Filho 1970, 1972
	Northeastern Brazil	X X X X		VS	Ivo 1973
	Northeastern Brazil	————	————	GW	De Moraes and DosSantos 1969
L. synagris	Northeastern Caribbean, including Virgin Islands	XX-X--X-----X-----		VS	Erdman 1976
	Jamaica	X X		VS	Munro et al. 1973

(Continued)

TABLE 5.5 (Cont.)

Species	Location	Months												Analysis	Reference
		J	F	M	A	M	J	J	A	S	O	N	D		
	Trinidad	X--X--X--XX-X--X--X--X--X------X--X												VS, J	Manickchand-Dass In press
	Cuba			X--X--XX-X--X--X--X									VS, HS	Rodriguez-Pino 1962
	Colombian Caribbean		X--X--XX-XX X	X	X		X			X		VS	Erhardt 1977
	Cuba			X	X	X	X	X					VS, GSI	Reshetnikov and Claro 1976
L. vivanus	Puerto Rico	X-------------------X												VS	Boardman and Weiler 1980
	Jamaica			XX-X--X-------X--XX----X									VS	Munro et al. 1973
	Northeastern Caribbean, including Virgin Islands	X	X						X		X	X		VS	Erdman 1976

Ocyurus **chrysurus**	North Carolina and South Carolina	X--X--X		Grimes et al. 1977
	Jamaica	XX-XX-XX-XX-X--X--X--X--XX-XX-X--X	VS	Thompson and Munro 1974, 1983
	Northeastern Caribbean, including Virgin Islands	X XX XX XX X XX	VS	Erdman 1976
	Jamaica	--XX------X--X-----XX-XX--X-----	VS	Munro et al. 1973
	Florida Keys	X X X--XX-XX-XX-XX X X X	VS, MS, GSI	Collins and Finucane Unpub.
	Cuba	X--X--XX-XX-X--X--X	VS	Piedra 1965
	North Carolina and South Carolina	X--X--X--X--X	GSI, OD, VS	Grimes 1976 Grimes and Huntsman 1980
Rhomboplites **aurorubens**	Northeastern Caribbean, including Virgin Islands	X-----X--X	VS	Erdman 1976

(Continued)

TABLE 5.5 (Cont.)

Species	Location	Months												Analysis	Reference
		J	F	M	A	M	J	J	A	S	O	N	D		
	Puerto Rico	X	—	—	—	—	—	—	—	—	—	—	X[a]	VS	Boardman and Weiler 1980
	Jamaica											X[b]			Munro et al. 1973
	North Carolina, South Carolina, Georgia							X	X[c]					L	Powles and Stender 1976
	Georgia							X	X					L	Fahay 1975
	Tortugas, Fla.								X[b]					VS	Longley and Hildebrand 1941
		Indo-West Pacific Species													
Aphareus rutilans	Vanuatu, New Hebrides	X	X	X	X			X	X	XX	XX			GSI, VS	Brouard and Grandperrin 1984
Aprion virescens	East Africa	X	—	X								—	X	VS	Talbot 1960

Species	Location		X^d		Method	Reference
Etelis carbunculus	East Africa	X			VS	Nzioka 1979
	Vanuatu, New Hebrides		X X X	X XX X	GSI, VS	Brouard and Grandperrin 1984
	Hawaiian Islands		X--X--X		VS, GSI, OD, MS	Everson 1984
E. coruscans	Vanuatu, New Hebrides	X	XX XX XX	X X X X X XX	GSI, VS	Brouard and Grandperrin 1984
L. amabilis	New Caledonia	XX-X		X--X--X--XX-XX	VS, GSI	Loubens 1980
L. argenti-maculatus	East Africa			X	VS	Talbot 1960
L. bohar	East Africa	---X-X------X------X-----X---		VS	Talbot 1960
	East Africa	X		X XX	VS	Nzioka 1979
L. duodecim-lineatus	Gulf of Aden	X			VS	Druzhinin and Filatova 1980
L. fulviflamma	New Caledonia	---X---	-X------X-		VS, GSI	Loubens 1980
	East Africa	------X	X------X------X-		VS	Talbot 1960

(Continued)

TABLE 5.5 (Cont.)

Species	Location	Months													Analysis	Reference
		J	F	M	A	M	J	J	A	S	O	N	D		
L. gibbus	East Africa								X	X			XX	VS	Nzioka 1979
	East Africa		------X						X-----		X--		X	VS	Talbot 1960
	East Africa	X	X										XX[b]	VS	Nzioka 1979
L. johni	Andaman Sea									X				VS	Druzhinin 1970
L. kasmira	East Africa		X								X			VS	Talbot 1960
	Andaman Sea	X	X	X					X		X	XX	XX	VS, GSI	Rangarajan 1971
	East Africa	X[d]												VS	Nzioka 1979
	Western Samoa	X	X	X	X	X	X	X	X	X	X	X	X	GSI, VS, SR	Mizenko 1984
L. lineolatus	Gulf of Aden	X								X				VS	Druzhinin and Filatova 1980
	East Africa											X[d]		VS	Nzioka 1979

271

Species	Location			Code	Reference
L. malabaricus	Andaman Sea		X	VS	Druzhinin 1970
	Vanuatu, New Hebrides	XX X X	X X X X XX XX		Brouard and Grandperrin 1984
L. monostigma	East Africa	X	X	VS	Talbot 1960
L. quinque-lineatus	New Caledonia	XX-X------X	X--XX-XX	VS	Loubens 1980
L. rivulatus	East Africa	---X--X--X	X X--X	VS	Talbot 1960
	Gulf of Aden	X^b		VS	Druzhinin and Filatova 1980
	East Africa	X X	XX X^d	VS	Nzioka 1979
L. rufolineatus	Western Samoa	XX XX XX XX X	X X X X X	GSI, VS, SR	Mizenko 1984
L. sanguineus	East Africa	X X	X X X	VS	Talbot 1960
	East Africa	X	X XX X^d	VS	Nzioka 1979
L. sebae	Gulf of Aden	X		VS	Druzhinin and Filatova 1980

(Continued)

TABLE 5.5 (Cont.)

Species	Location	Months J	F	M	A	M	J	J	A	S	O	N	D	Analysis	Reference
	East Africa	X--X--X										X--X		VS	Talbot 1960
	East Africa	X	X								X[d]			VS	Nzioka 1979
L. vaigiensis	Society Islands	X	X	X						X	X	X[b]		VS	Randall and Brock 1960
	Gulf of Aden				X[b]									VS	Druzhinin and Filatova 1980
L. vitta	New Caledonia	XX-XX----X							X--X--X--XX--XX--XX					VS, GSI	Loubens 1980
Pristipomoides argyrogrammicus	East Africa						X	X	X				X[d]	VS	Nzioka 1979
P. filamentosus	Hawaiian Islands	X	X	XX	XX	XX	XX	XX	XX	X	X	X	X	VS, GSI	Ralston 1981
	Hawaiian Islands								X	X	X			VS, GSI	Kikkawa 1984

Species	Location	J	F	M	A	M	J	J	A	S	O	N	D		Reference
	South China Sea and adjacent waters						X							GSI	Min et al. 1977
P. flavipinnis	Vanuatu, New Hebrides	XX	XX	X	X	X	X	X	X	X	X	X	X	XX	GSI, VS	Brouard and Grandperrin 1984
P. multidens	South China Sea and adjacent waters						X							GSI	Min et al. 1977
	Vanuatu, New Hebrides	XX	X	X	X	X	X	X	X	X	X	X	XX		VS, GSI	Brouard and Grandperrin 1984
	Western Samoa	X	X	X	X	X	X	X	X	X	X				GSI, VS, SR	Mizenko 1984
P. typus	South China Sea and adjacent waters	X	X		X		X								GSI	Min et al. 1977

a Monthly data not given
b Only months the species were collected
c Only summer months sampled
d No samples March-July

Carolina, Florida Keys) of <u>Rhomboplites aurorubens</u>, <u>L.</u> <u>vivanus</u>, and <u>Ocyurus chrysurus</u> are restricted spawners, while their insular counterparts (i.e., populations in Puerto Rico, Jamaica, and the northeastern Caribbean including the Virgin Islands) spawn year round. Strictly continental species such as <u>L. campechanus</u> from southeastern North America and Campeche Bank, Mexico, and <u>L.</u> <u>purpureus</u> from northeastern Brazil (3°–5° S) display the restricted pattern. Tropical East African populations (Tanzania and Kenya, 3°–7° S) of <u>L. sebae</u>, <u>L. fulviflamma</u>, <u>L. rivulatus</u>, <u>L. gibbus</u>, <u>L. sanguineus</u>, <u>L. kasmira</u>, <u>L. monostigma</u>, and <u>Aprion virescens</u> display the restricted continental pattern, as do <u>Pristipomoides multidens</u> and <u>P. typus</u> from the South China Sea and adjacent waters (20° N). Conversely, insular populations of <u>L. kasmira</u> (Western Samoa), <u>L. malabaricus</u> (New Hebrides), <u>P. multidens</u> (Western Samoa and New Hebrides), <u>Etelis carbunculus</u> (New Hebrides), <u>E. coruscans</u> (New Hebrides), <u>Aphareus rutilans</u> (New Hebrides), and <u>L. rufolineatus</u> (Western Samoa) do some spawning year round with peak activity during late spring, summer, and fall.

Several populations of lutjanids do not conform to this pattern. For example, snappers associated with large tropical islands such as Cuba (<u>L. synagris</u>, <u>L. griseus</u>, and <u>O. chrysurus</u>) and New Caledonia (<u>L. amabilis</u> and <u>L. fulviflamma</u>) do not display the typical insular pattern; they exhibit the continental pattern of restricted spawning. <u>Lutjanus kasmira</u> from the Andaman Sea and <u>Etelis carbunculus</u> from the Hawaiian Islands also do not conform to the pattern, as they are a continental population that spawns during fall and winter, and an insular population with restricted summer spawning, respectively.

The cause for the two patterns is not obvious. Presumably the patterns are adaptive and have survival value to their respective populations. Cushing (1975) and others have suggested that spawning cycles are timed to coincide with peaks in production cycles that provide food for the larvae. Nzioka (1979) suggested that peak spawning occurs among continental East African lutjanids at the time of highest productivity during the southeast monsoon, which speeds up the East African current, lowers the thermocline, and promotes vertical mixing. This also coincides with a period of low, but increasing, rainfall for that region (Dar es Salaam, Tanzania; Ruffner and Bair 1981). <u>Lutjanus purpureus</u>, a continental species from notheastern Brazil, also spawns during the season of lowest rainfall (Recife, Brazil; Ruffner and Bair 1981).

Similarly, L. kasmira in the Andaman Sea off Burma spawn during winter when rainfall is much lower than summer (Moidmein, Burma; Ruffner and Bair 1981). Continental snapper populations along the east coast of North America, from Venezuela and Campeche Banks, Mexico, spawn coincident with high summer rainfall (Wilmington, North Carolina; Miami, Florida; Pensacola, Florida; Caracas, Venezuela; and Mérida, Mexico; Ruffner and Bair 1981), warmest water temperatures, and peak production. Perhaps continental spawning is timed to introduce larvae into local production cycles created by oceanographic and meteorological conditions of high rainfall and subsequent nutrient runoff.

Populations on the large islands of Cuba and New Caledonia also reproduce during highest summer and fall rainfall (Havana, Cuba and Noumea, New Caledonia; Ruffner and Bair 1981). Perhaps these two large islands have the equivalent of continental production cycles, with peaks coincident with high rainfall.

Most island populations are in tropical and warm temperate areas where production is typically continuous and of low amplitude (Cushing 1975), and snapper reproduction there occurs more or less year round. Perhaps this is because there is no feeding advantage to be gained by restricting the spawning season, but predation can be avoided by spawning over an extended period. In contrast to continental and large island populations, reproductive cycles on islands are apparently not correlated with rainfall. In Trinidad, L. synagris spawn all year but peak during the dry spring (Manickchand-Dass In press). In contrast, peak spawning of many Indo-west Pacific island populations is reported to occur in late spring and summer when rainfall is frequently high (e.g., Guam, Mariana Islands, and Pago Pago, American Samoa (Ruffner and Bair 1981)).

The view that spawning in continental snapper populations may be timed to coincide with production cycles, while those associated with small islands reproduce year round because of low amplitude cycles, has support in the literature. Cushing (1975) has enunciated a very similar idea, based upon latitude, that summer spawning may be characteristic of fishes in low latitude steady-state production cycles, whereas spring and autumn spawning may be characteristic of the discontinuous high-amplitude production cycles of high latitudes. Lambert and Ware (1984) described reproductive strategies and suggested that pelagic and demersal spawning fish respond to the

major problems facing their larvae, i.e., finding food and
avoiding predation, in different ways. Pelagic spawners
use an "all at once" strategy to introduce larvae into a
rich food supply so that they may grow rapidly and escape
predators, which are swamped by great larval abundance.
Demersal spawners "bet hedge" and produce slow-growing
larvae in batches over an extended period. This insures a
more even distribution of scarce food to the larvae and is
a hedge against predation. Lutjanid reproductive strategies may fit the Lambert and Ware (1984) scheme because
they are fast growing (Richards 1982) and are produced in
batches (see Spawning section below) over an extended
period. If food for larvae is more abundant during a
season, then reproduction will be more seasonal (continental populations). If production is low and continuous
(islands) and food is always scarce, then spawning will be
continuous and in small batches as a hedge against predation.

SPAWNING

There is consistent evidence that lutjanids are batch
spawners. Distributions of ovum diameters from the
western Atlantic species L. synagris (Erhardt 1977), L.
purpureus (De Moraes 1970), L. griseus (Campos and
Bashirullah 1975), and R. aurorubens (Grimes and Huntsman
1980); and the Indo-west Pacific species P. multidens and
P. typus (Min et al. 1977; Kikkawa 1984), L. kasmira
(Rangarajan 1971), and E. carbunculus (Everson 1984) all
show marked polymodality, a characteristic generally taken
to indicate multiple or serial spawnings by individual
females during the reproductive season. Striking
variation in ovary lengths and weights of L. griseus
during the reproductive season indicated batch spawning to
Starck and Schroeder (1970). Similarly, marked variations
in gonosomatic indices (ovary weight/TL^3) of fish sampled
during the spawning season were interpreted to indicate
serial spawning in R. aurorubens (Grimes and Huntsman
1980), and Ralston (1981) suggested that the low standing
reproductive investment of P. filamentosus (ovaries of
ripe females about 4% of body weight) made it likely the
species was a multiple spawner. Everson (1984) found
spawned-out ovaries only at the end of the spawning
season, indicating fractional spawning in E. carbunculus.
Grimes and Huntsman (1980) and Everson (1984) also found
ovaries containing ova in various developmental stages in

R. aurorubens and E. carbunculus, which further suggested
fractional spawning.

Large females may spawn longer and perhaps more times
than small females. Grimes and Huntsman (1980) reported
that the gonosomatic indices of large female R. aurorubens
were high earlier and longer during the spawning season,
and Starck and Schroeder (1970) observed that large fish
with well-developed gonads remained on the reef longer
than small ones, and thus probably spawned more often.
Everson (1984) found that large E. carbunculus matured
earlier in the reproductive season and remained in
spawning condition longer than small fish.

The number of batches of eggs produced each spawning
season has not been conclusively determined. Arnold et
al. (1978) and Suzuki and Hioki (1979) reported several
spawnings of captive L. campechanus and L. kasmira over
periods of 1 month and 3 weeks, respectively. Each
spawning of L. campechanus consisted of a "few thousand"
small (0.8 mm diameter), nearly transparent eggs. It is
not known, of course, if these spawnings corresponded to
one or more size modes of developing ova, or how the
artificial conditions affected events.

Most authors (cited above) report two or three
distinct modes of developing ova from ripe females, but
how the number of modes relates to the actual number of
spawnings is not clear because the process of recruitment
of developing ova from the undifferentiated oocyte pool is
undescribed. Reshetnikov and Claro (1976) reported that
L. synagris females spawned two to three batches of eggs
in a spawning season, based upon temporal variation in
gonosomatic index for the same school of fish. The data
supporting this conclusion, however, are equivocal.

The timing of reproduction almost certainly involves
a number of environmental cues, for example, temperature,
photoperiod, and the lunar cycle. Temperature and
photoperiod influence the overall seasonality of reproduction, at least for some lutjanids. Grimes and Huntsman
(1980) showed that increasing gonad development and
preparation for spawning in R. aurorubens was correlated
with increasing water temperature and photoperiod off
southeastern North America (North Carolina). Similarly,
E. carbunculus spawned in the Hawaiian Islands when water
temperature and photoperiod were near the seasonal peak
(Everson 1984). Ripe R. aurorubens were found off North
Carolina when water temperature in the habitat was 20.6°-
24.8° C and photoperiod 13.5-14.5 h. When Arnold et al.
(1978) spawned L. campechanus in captivity, they simulated

normal temperature and photoperiod conditions for the
northwestern Gulf of Mexico (Port Aransas, Texas).
Natural spawning occurred under conditions of 15 h light
and 23°–25° C.

Lunar cycling of spawning activity appears to be
common among reef fishes (Johannes 1978; Lobel 1978; May
et al. 1979; McFarland 1982), apparently acting to align
spawning precisely with tidal conditions favoring
survival. The Lutjanidae are no exception. Based upon a
visual determination of maturation stages for gonads,
Randall and Brock (1960) reported spawning near full moon
for L. vaigiensis in the Society Islands. Starck and
Schroeder (1970) drew the same conclusion for L. griseus
by observing variation in gonad lengths and weights.
Occurrence of ripe gonads and regular cycling in gonosomatic index (gonad weight/body weight) indicated to
Mizenko (1984) that L. kasmira, L. rufolineatus, and P.
multidens spawned at or near full moon on Western Samoan
reefs. Reshetnikov and Claro (1976) also reported that
spawning of L. synagris in Cuba always coincided with full
moon. The fact that Suzuki and Hioki (1979) had successive spawnings of aquarium-maintained L. kasmira on dates
corresponding to new and full moon provides additional
evidence for lunar spawning periodicity. Although Grimes
and Huntsman (1980) could not demonstrate lunar reproductive cycling in R. aurorubens, very similar reproductive
condition (gonosomatic index) of fish caught from the same
school suggested that reproduction was synchronized within
the school.

Spawning of lutjanids has seldom been observed.
Wiklund (1969) gave the following account of L. synagris
spawning off southeast Florida. Courtship behavior began
during the crepuscular period (1930–2000 h) when fish
began to aggregate near the bottom in groups of 5–10 fish
and to chase each other. Most members of the group
(males) pursued a single lighter-colored female, and
different males nuzzled the vent of the female. The group
became more condensed and very active while moving slowly
off the bottom. At about 2 m (7 ft) off the bottom the
fish became extremely active, then swam suddenly in all
directions depositing eggs and milt in the water column.
The spawning was completed before dark.

Both L. campechanus (from the Gulf of Mexico) and L.
kasmira (from Japan) have spawned in captivity (Arnold et
al. 1978; Suzuki and Hioki 1979). The red coloration of
L. campechanus became noticeably deeper and more vivid,
and males nudged the bellies of females. In L. kasmira,

courtship behavior began among a small group of males and
females hovering near the bottom at 1800 to 1900, approximately 2 h before spawning. Pairs swam together in upward
spirals with males pecking and pushing the bellies of
females with their snouts. Spiral ascending movements
became more rapid and reached higher in the water column,
and were repeated 20-30 times over 2 h. Finally, spawning
occurred simultaneously among 10 or more fish spiraling
upward together, releasing their gametes just below the
surface.

FECUNDITY

Information in the published literature concerning
fecundity is fraught with inconsistency, and little
analysis was possible (Table 5.6). The data allow only
the general, and obvious, conclusion that the Lutjanidae
are highly fecund.

Maximum and minimum fecundity values reported for the
various species of Lutjanidae varied by about two orders
of magnitude. For example, maximum fecundity ranged from
9.3×10^6 ova for L. campechanus from the South Atlantic
Bight and Gulf of Mexico of North America to 2.03×10^5
ova for L. buccanella from the Virgin Islands. Minimum
values for ripe females were similarly variable among
species (1.8×10^6 ova in L. griseus from Venezuela to
8.17×10^3 ova in R. aurorubens from the North American
South Atlantic Bight).

Fecundity estimates for the same species from
different locations were also quite variable but were
within the same order of magnitude. For example, maximum
fecundity of L. synagris from northeastern Brazil was
estimated to be 2.28×10^5 for a 494 mm TL female, while
similar-sized animals from Trinidad (419 mm TL) and the
Colombian Caribbean (420 mm TL) had estimates of 5.95×10^5 and 2.67×10^5, respectively.

Fecundity is usually an exponential function of body
size, so if there were a consistent relationship between
body size (e.g., weight) and fecundity among the lutjanid
species, it would be indicated by the consistency of
exponents in predictive equations. No such relationship
is obvious, but the available data are clearly inadequate
to properly address the question. Consistency in the
relationship between fecundity and body size was also
examined by calculating maximum and minimum relative
fecundity (ova per gram of body weight, Table 5.6).

TABLE 5.6
Fecundity (F) of selected Lutjanidae. Lengths are in millimeters, weight in grams, and fecundity per gram body weight is in parentheses. TL = total length, FL = fork length, SL = standard length

Species	Location	Maximum F (10^5)	Length/Weight at Maximum F	Minimum F (10^4)	Length/Weight at Minimum F	Reference
		Western Atlantic Species				
Rhomboplites aurorubens	North Carolina and South Carolina	17.8 (776/g)	557 TL/2,293 g	0.817	229 TL/139 g	Grimes 1976; Grimes and Huntsman 1980
Lutjanus vivanus	Virgin Islands	2.99	630[a]	0.90	265[a]	Sylvester et al. 1980
L. buccanella	Virgin Islands	2.03	445[a]	1.15	290[a]	Sylvester et al. 1980
L. purpureus	Northeastern Brazil	9.0 (153/g)	780 TL/5,850 g	9.0	460 TL	Gesteira and Ivo 1973
L. synagris	Northeastern Brazil	2.28	494 TL	2.0	244 TL	Gesteira and Rocha 1976
	Trinidad	5.95	419 TL	2.87	294 TL	Manickchand-Dass In press

Species	Location					Reference
	Cuba	9.94 (1,875/g)	310 FL/530 g	34.7 (1,000/g)	225 FL/180 g	Rodriguez-Pino 1962
	Colombian Caribbean	2.67 (213/g)	420 TL/1,250 g	4.12 (206/g)	250 TL/200 g	Erhardt 1977
L. campechanus	South Atlantic Bight and Gulf of Mexico	93.2 (746/g)	605 FL/12,485 g	4.4 (4/g)	420 FL/1,100 g	Collins et al. Unpub.
L. griseus	Venezuela	58.4 (1,390/g)	660 TL/4,200 g	180.0 (1,440/g)	468 TL/1,250 g	Campos and Bashirullah 1975
	Florida Keys	5.48	354 SL			Starck and Schroeder 1970
L. analis	Colombian Caribbean	3.73 (162/g)	520 TL/2,300 g	13.8 (345/g)	320 TL/400 g	Erhardt and Meinel 1977
	Cuba	13.7 (603/g)	512 FL/2,270 g			Rojas 1960
Ocyurus chrysurus	Florida Keys	13.9 (779/g)	480 FL/1,784 g	3.8 (208/g)	212 FL/182 g	Collins and Finucane Unpub.
	Cuba	6.19 (672/g)	382 FL/920 g	9.97 (216/g)	302 FL/460 g	Piedra 1965

TABLE 5.6 (Cont.)

Species	Location	Maximum F (10^5)	Length/Weight at Maximum F	Minimum F (10^4)	Length/Weight at Minimum F	Reference
		Indo-West Pacific Species				
Pristipo-moides multidens	South China Sea/Andaman Sea	27.7 (769/g)	555 SL/3,600 g	49.0 (168/g)	484 SL/2,900 g	Min et al. 1977
P. typus	South China Sea/Andaman Sea	20.7 (828/g)	478 SL/2,500 g	76.0 (690/g)	356 SL/1,100 g	Min et al. 1977
P. fila-mentosus	South China Sea/Andaman Sea	21.4 (1,177/g)	425 SL/1,817 g	140.0 (1,125/g)	374 SL/1,244 g	Min et al. 1977
Etelis carbunculus	Hawaiian Islands	13.3 (534/g)	508 FL/2,490 g	34.9 (360/g)	383 FL/970 g	Everson 1984

[a] Length measurement unspecified

Maximum values ranged from 1,875 ova per gram for L.
synagris from Cuba to 153 ova per gram for L. purpureus
from northeastern Brazil. Minimum values were similarly
variable (1,900 ova per gram for L. synagris from Cuba to
60 per gram for R. aurorubens from the North American
South Atlantic Bight).

It seems likely that the large variation in the
fecundity results is mostly due to inconsistency of
method. The major methodological problem is in determining which ova to count in serial spawners, which have
several more or less distinct groups of developing ova.
It is difficult to distinguish small developing ova from
primary oocytes on the basis of size alone. How does one
easily determine if the developing ova present are all
that will develop during the current reproductive season,
or if more ova will be recruited later from the undifferentiated oocyte pool? Also, the fraction of the ovarian
egg complement actually spawned is usually unknown.
Another potential source of error in estimating the
fecundity of fractional spawners is using sample ovaries
from fish that have partially spawned. This results in
underestimation and can be avoided by careful selection of
ovarian samples early in the spawning season before any
spawning takes place. However, in populations that spawn
year round, or nearly so, this may be difficult.

Although problems of accurately estimating batch and
total fecundity have been addressed by De Silva (1973),
Macer (1974), Hunter and Goldberg (1979), Gale and Deutsch
(1985), and others, no clear and simple methods to resolve
them have been presented. The egg production process and
its relation to body size, fecundity estimation, realized
fertility, and other problem areas need thorough study.

REPRODUCTIVE STRATEGY

Lutjanids, like most species that reach large sizes
and are abundant enough to support fisheries, would be
considered r-strategists in the general parlance of life
history tactics. They are highly fecund (see Fecundity
section) broadcast spawners (see Spawning section) that
produce fairly typical pelagic eggs (approximately 0.8 mm
in diameter) and dispersive pelagic larvae (L. synagris,
Borrero et al. 1978; L. griseus, Damas et al. 1978,
Richards and Saksena 1980; L. campechanus, Arnold et al.
1978, Collins et al. 1980, Rabalais et al. 1980, and
Minton et al. 1983; R. aurorubens, La Roche 1977; L.

kasmira, Suzuki and Hioki 1979). However, lutjanids, like many other reef fishes, have evolved a number of reproductive mechanisms that help insure survival in a temporally constant, but patchy, habitat where predation is an important structuring force. In fact, Johannes (1978) has convincingly argued that predation is an overriding selective factor in the life history of most reef fish. He suggests that many aspects of reproduction, such as spawning site preference; seasonality, frequency and duration of spawning; and lunar and diel spawning periodicity, are all adaptations to reduce predation on the young.

The reproductive seasonality of lutjanids, as described earlier, displays two more or less distinct patterns, irrespective of latitude: (1) insular or year round, usually with spring and fall peaks, and (2) a continental or a restricted (centered around summer) spawning season. Johannes (1978) suggested that spawning seasonality of coastal marine tropical fishes is timed to coincide with periods when wind and current speed are at a minimum, to reduce loss of pelagic larvae from the patchy habitats of reef environments. Reshetnikov and Claro (1976) suggested that spawning is timed to coincide with periods of high rainfall, when increased runoff introduces nutrients into coastal waters and supports greater food production for early life stages. Periods of highest rainfall and reproductive activity are correlated for some continental and large island lutjanid populations, but the relationship is inconsistent for small islands (see Seasonality section). The hypothesis that spawning is timed to coincide with greater food availability is not supported, at least for small islands, by findings that show spawning intensity and larval fish density are not correlated with plankton density or productivity around Hawaii and Jamaica (Munro et al. 1973; Miller 1974).

Clearly the Lutjanidae are batch or serial spawners (see Spawning section). Johannes (1978) has suggested that batch reproduction over an extended period might increase recruitment under circumstances where random factors determine the availability of space suitable for settling by recruits (Sale 1978). However, McFarland (1982) has shown that recruitment of French grunts (Haemulon flavolineatum) is tightly coupled to lunar and tidal events, and there is order in the occupation of space because the same species repeatedly occupies the same settlement sites. A more plausible advantage for batch reproduction is offered by Lambert and Ware (1984), who suggested that batch spawning is a hedge against egg and larval predation and has the additional advantage of affording a more equitable distribution of scarce food.

Johannes (1978) speculated that spawning site preference, diel periodicity of spawning, and patterns of spawning behavior are also adaptations to reduce predation. He theorized that spawning offshore near the outer reef introduces gametes into more predator-free offshore waters, while nocturnal spawning reduces the threat of visually orienting predators to both gametes and spawning adults. The upward spawning rush described during the spawning ritual of many reef fish is also thought to help distribute gametes out of reach of benthic predators. The little information available on the Lutjanidae regarding site selection and spawning behavior indicates that they are typical of reef fish. Croker (1962) and Starck and Schroeder (1970) reported that L. griseus spawns on the outer reef. The upward spawning rush, culminating in the release of gametes, has been reported to occur at night for both L. synagris and L. kasmira (Wiklund 1969; Suzuki and Hioki 1979).

Many reef fish spawn according to a lunar rhythm on or around new or full moon (Johannes 1978; Lobel 1978; McFarland 1982), as if taking advantage of maximum tidal flows to flush propagules offshore to a more predator-free environment and ultimately to return them to inshore juvenile settlement sites (McFarland 1982). Lunar cycling of spawning is evidently the rule among the Lutjanidae (see Spawning section).

If spawning site preference, spawning seasonality, lunar and diel periodicity, etc., among the lutjanids are indeed adaptations to get propagules offshore to more predator-free waters, then egg and larval development rates should be rapid so that the young would not be swept away by oceanic currents before their development allowed return to suitable settlement sites by tidal flow. For example, McFarland (1982) demonstrated that H. flavolineatum spawn at about new or full moon and the larvae develop rapidly, returning to settle as juveniles 14 days later on the next spring tide. Data relevant to the length of the planktonic larval period of snapper are meager, but do suggest a similar rapid development rate. Fertilized eggs of L. synagris (Borrero et al. 1978), L. griseus (Damas et al. 1978), L. campechanus (Arnold et al. 1978; Rabalais et al. 1980; Minton et al. 1983) and L. kasmira (Suzuki and Hioki 1979) hatch in 19, 18, 20, and 18 h at ambient seawater temperatures; and the yolk is absorbed in 40-50,

45, 48, and 72 h. First feeding of larval L. campechanus
(Rabalais et al. 1980) and L. kasmira (Suzuki and Hioki
1979) occurred 72 h after hatching. The total duration of
the planktonic larval phase is unknown, however.

SUMMARY

The Lutjanidae are gonochoristic. Histological
studies have not revealed cellular or gross structural
evidence to indicate hermaphroditism. Population sex
ratios may be slightly unequal and skewed in favor of one
sex at larger size. Evidence suggests, however, that
skewed sex ratios probably result from differential growth
and mortality between the sexes.

Sexual maturation evidently occurs at a slightly
smaller size in males than females, and on average at
about 40-50% of maximum length for both sexes. Populations and species associated with islands mature at about
51% of their maximum length, while the figure for
continental stocks is 43%. Members of the deep reef fauna
(>91 m) mature at an average of 49% of maximum length, and
shallow forms (<91 m) at 43%.

Like most broadcast spawners, the Lutjanidae are
highly fecund, with large females (approximately 100 cm)
producing up to 5-7 x 10^6 ova. However, because they are
batch spawners with several size modes of developing ova
simultaneously present in ovaries, it has been difficult
to realistically estimate total egg production for one
spawning season.

Two patterns of reproductive seasonality emerge.
Continental populations and species have a spawning season
which is typically centered around summer, while populations and species associated with small oceanic islands
reproduce year round with pulses of activity in the spring
and fall.

Spawning evidently occurs at night near open water
and is timed to coincide with spring tides at new and full
moons. Distinct courtship behavior culminates in an
upward spiral swim toward the surface when gametes are
released. Individual fish are believed to spawn more than
once during a reproductive season (batch spawning).

Predation is apparently a strong selective factor for
reef fish; therefore, many aspects of the reproductive
biology of the lutjanids appear as adaptations to introduce gametes into an environment where predation is

reduced. At the same time, these adaptations must assure that young juveniles are returned to a suitable, but highly patchy, habitat for settlement.

ACKNOWLEDGMENTS

J. Polovina, S. Ralston, and the U.S. National Marine Fisheries Service (NMFS), Southwest Fisheries Center (SWFC), Honolulu, Hawaii, organized and financially supported the workshop that provided the impetus for this review. Grateful acknowledgment is tendered S. Ralston and A. Everson, NMFS, SWFC Honolulu Laboratory; J. Munro, International Center for Living Aquatic Resource Management; J. Ross, North Carolina (USA) Division of Marine Fisheries; S. Turner, NMFS, Southeast Fisheries Center (SEFC) Miami, Fla; and R. Thresher, Commonwealth Scientific and Industrial Research Organization, Hobart, Australia for their scientific criticism. C. Saloman, NMFS, SEFC, Panama City, Florida, prepared the figure.

BIBLIOGRAPHY

Alves, M. I. M. 1971. Sobre a maturacão sexual do pargo, Lutjanus purpureus Poey, do nordeste Brasileiro. Arq. Cienc. Mar 11:153–158.

Anderson, W. D. 1986. Systematics of the fishes of the family Lutjanidae (Perciformes: Percoidei) the snappers. In J. J. Polovina and S. Ralston (editors), Tropical snappers and groupers: Biology and fisheries management. Westview Press, Inc., Boulder. [See this volume.]

Arnold, C. R., J. M. Wakeman, T. D. Williams, and G. D. Treece. 1978. Spawning of red snapper (Lutjanus campechanus) in captivity. Aquaculture 15:301–302.

Baez Hidalgo, M., L. Alvarez-Lajonchere, and E. Ojeda Serrano. 1982. Reproducción del caballerote, Lutjanus griseus (Linnaeus) en Tunas de Zaza, Cuba. [In Span., Engl. abstr.] Rev. Invest. Mar. 3:43–85.

Baughman, J. L. 1943. The lutianid fishes of Texas. Copeia 1943:212–215.

Boardman, C., and D. Weiler. 1980. Aspects of the life history of three deepwater snappers around Puerto Rico. Proc. 32d Gulf. Caribb. Fish. Inst., p. 158–172.

Borrero, M., E. Gonzalez, N. Millares, and T. Damas. 1978. Desarollo embrionario y prelarval de la biajaiba (Lutjanus synagris Linne 1758). Rev. Cubana Invest. Pesq. 3(3):1-28.

Bradley, E., and C. E. Bryan. 1975. Life history and fishery of the red snapper (Lutjanus campechanus) in the northwestern Gulf of Mexico: 1970-1974. Proc. 27th Gulf Caribb. Fish. Inst., p. 77-106.

Brouard, F., and R. Grandperrin. 1984. Les poissons profonds de la pinta recifale externe a Vanatu. ORSTOM, Notes Doc. D'Oceanogr. 11:71-79.

Brownell, W. N., and W. E. Rainey. 1971. Research and development of deep water commercial and sport fisheries around the Virgin Islands Plateau. V. I. Ecol. Res. Sta., Caribb. Res. Inst. Contrib. 3, 88 p.

Camber, C. I. 1955. A survey of the red snapper fishery of the Gulf of Mexico, with special reference to the Campeche Banks. Fla. Board Conserv., Mar. Res. Lab., Tech. Ser. 12, 64 p.

Campos, A. G., and A. K. M. Bashirullah. 1975. Biología del pargo Lutjanus griseus (Linn.) de la Isla de Cubagua, Venezuela. II. Maduración sexual y fecundidad. Bol. Inst. Oceanogr. Univ. Oriente Cumana 14:109-116.

Claro, R. 1981. Ecología y ciclo de vida de la biajaiba Lutjanus synagris (Linnaeus), en la platforma Cubana. II. Biol. Pesq., Acad. Cienc. Cuba Inform. Cient.-Tec. 177, 53 p.

Collins, L. A., and J. H. Finucane. Unpub. Reproductive biology of the yellowtail snapper (Ocyurus chrysurus) from the Florida Keys, 15 p.

Collins, L. A., J. H. Finucane, and L. E. Barger. 1980. Description of larval and juvenile red snapper, Lutjanus campechanus. Fish. Bull., U.S. 77:965-974.

Collins, L. A., J. H. Finucane, and H. A. Brusher. Unpub. Reproductive biology of red snapper, Lutjanus campechanus (Poey), from three areas along the southeastern coast of the United States, 21 p.

Croker, R. A. 1962. Growth and food of the gray snapper, Lutjanus griseus in Everglades National Park. Trans. Am. Fish. Soc. 91:379-383.

Cushing, D. H. 1975. Marine ecology and fisheries. Cambridge University Press., Cambridge, 278 p.

Damas, T., M. Borrero, N. Millares, and E. Gonzalez. 1978. Desarrollo embrionario y prelarval del caballerote (Lutjanus griseus Linne 1758). Rev. Cubana Invest. Pesq. 3(4):11-37.

De Moraes, N. U. A. 1970. Sobre a desova e a fecundidade do Pargo, Lutjanus purpureus Poey no nordeste Brasileiro. Bol. Estud. Pesca 10(1):7-20.

De Moraes, N. U. A., and E. P. DosSantos. 1969. Sobre a curva de maturacão do pargo, Lutjanus purpureus Poey. Bol. Estud. Pesca 9(3):50-57.

De Silva, S. S. 1973. Aspects of the reproductive biology of the sprat, Sprattus sprattus (L.) in inshore waters of the west coast of Scotland. J. Fish Biol. 5:689-705.

Druzhinin, A. D. 1970. The range and biology of snappers (Family Lutjanidae). J. Ichthyol. 10:717-736.

Druzhinin, A. D., and N. A. Filatova. 1980. Some data on Lutjanidae from the Gulf of Aden area. J. Ichthyol. 20:8-14.

Erdman, D. S. 1976. Spawning patterns of fishes from the northeastern Caribbean. Puerto Rico Dep. Agric., Commer. Fish. Lab., Agric. Fish. Contrib. 8(2): 1-36.

Erhardt, H. 1977. Beitrage zur Biologie von Lutjanus synagris (Linnaeus 1758) an der Kolumbianischen Atlantikkuste. Zool. Beitr. 23(2):235-265.

Erhardt, H., and W. Meinel. 1977. Beitrage zur biologie von Lutjanus analis (Cuvier and Valenciennes 1828) (Lutjanidae, Perciformes, Pisces) an der Kolumbianischen Atlantikkuste. Int. Rev. Gesamten Hydrobiol. 62:161-171.

Everson, A. R. 1984. Spawning and gonadal maturation of the ehu, Etelis carbunculus, in the Northwestern Hawaiian Islands. In R. W. Grigg and K. Y. Tanoue (editors), Proceedings of the Second Symposium on Resource Investigations in the Northwestern Hawaiian Islands, Vol. 2, May 25-27, 1983, University of Hawaii, Honolulu, Hawaii, p. 128-148. UNIHI-SEAGRANT-MR-84-01.

Fahay, M. P. 1975. An annotated list of larval and juvenile fishes captured with surface-towed meter net in the South Atlantic Bight during four R/V Dolphin cruises between May 1967 and February 1968. U.S. Dep. Commer., Natl. Mar. Fish. Serv., Spec. Sci. Rep. Fish. 685, 39 p.

Fishelson, L. 1975. Ecology and physiology of sex reversal in Anthias squampinnis (Pisces, Teleostei, Anthiidae). In R. Reinboth (editor), Intersexuality in the animal kingdom, p. 284-294. Springer-Verlag, N.Y.

Fonteles-Filho, A. A. 1970. Estudo sobre a biología da pesca do pargo, Lutjanus purpureus Poey, no nordeste Brasileiro-dados de 1969. Arq. Cienc. Mar 10:73-78.
_____. 1972. Estudo sobre a biología da pesca do pargo, Lutjanus purpureus Poey, no nordeste Brasileiro-dados de 1970 e 1971. Arq. Cienc. Mar 12:21-26.

Food and Agricultural Organization. 1984. Yearbook of fishery statistics - 1982. Vol. 54. FAO, Rome, 393 p.

Futch, R. B., and G. E. Bruger. 1976. Age, growth and reproduction of red snapper in Florida waters. Proc. Colloq. on Snapper-Grouper Fish. Resour. West. Cent. Atl. Ocean, Fla. Sea Grant Rep. 17:165-184.

Gale, W. F., and W. G. Deutsch. 1985. Fecundity and spawning frequency of captive tessellated darters - fractional spawners. Trans. Am. Fish. Soc. 114:220-229.

Gesteira, T. C. V., and C. T. C. Ivo. 1973. Estudo da reprodução e fecundidade do pargo, Lutjanus purpureus Poey, no norte e nordeste do Brasil. Arq. Cienc. Mar 13:109-112.

Gesteira, T. C. V., and C. A. S. Rocha. 1976. Estudo sobre a fecundidade do ariaco, Lutjanus synagris (Linnaeus), da costa do estado do Ceara (Brasil). Arq. Cienc. Mar 16:19-22.

Grimes, C. B. 1976. Certain aspects of the life history of the vermilion snapper, Rhomboplites aurorubens (Cuvier) from North and South Carolina waters. Ph.D. Dissertation, Univ. North Carolina, Chapel Hill, 240 p.

Grimes, C. B., and G. R. Huntsman. 1980. Reproductive biology of the vermilion snapper, Rhomboplites aurorubens, from North Carolina and South Carolina. Fish. Bull., U.S. 78:137-146.

Grimes, C. B., C. S. Manooch III, G. R Huntsman, and R. L. Dixon. 1977. Red snappers of the Carolina coast. Mar. Fish. Rev. 39(1):12-15.

Gross, M. G. 1972. Oceanography - a view of the earth. Prentice-Hall, Inc., Englewood Cliffs, N.J., 581 p.

Hunter, J. R., and S. R. Goldberg. 1979. Spawning incidence and batch fecundity in northern anchovy, Engaulis mordax. Fish. Bull., U.S. 77:641-652.

Iles, T. D. 1974. The tactics and strategy of growth in fishes. In F. R. Harden Jones (editor), Sea fisheries research, p. 331-345. John Wiley & Sons, N.Y.

Ivo, C. T. C. 1973. Estudo sobre a biologia da pesca do pargo, Lutjanus purpureus Poey, no nordeste Brasileiro - dados de 1972. Arq. Cienc. Mar 13:39-43.

Johannes, R. E. 1978. Reproductive strategies of coastal marine fishes in the tropics. Environ. Biol. Fishes 3:65-84.

Kami, H. T. 1973. The Pristipomoides (Pisces:Lutjanidae) of Guam with notes on their biology. Micronesia 9(1):97-118.

Kikkawa, B. S. 1984. Maturation, spawning and fecundity of opakapaka, Pristipomoides filamentosus, in the Northwestern Hawaiian Islands. In R. W. Grigg and K. Y. Tanoue (editors), Proceedings of the Second Symposium on Resource Investigations in the Northwestern Hawaiian Islands, Vol. 2, May 25-27, 1983, University of Hawaii, Honolulu, Hawaii, p. 149-160. UNIHI-SEAGRANT-MR-84-01.

Lambert, T. C., and D. M. Ware. 1984. Reproductive strategies of demersal and pelagic spawning fish. Can. J. Fish. Aquat. Sci. 41:1565-1569.

LaRoche, W. A. 1977. Description of larval and early juvenile vermilion snapper, Rhomboplites aurorubens. Fish. Bull., U.S. 75:547-554.

Lobel, P. S. 1978. Diel, lunar and seasonal periodicity in the reproductive behavior of the pomacanthid fish, Centropyge potteri, and some other reef fishes in Hawaii. Pac. Sci. 32:193-207.

Longley, W. H., and S. F. Hildebrand. 1941. Systematic catalogue of the fishes of Tortugas, Florida, with observations on color, habits and local distribution. Pap. Tortugas Lab. 34, 331 p.

Loubens, G. 1980. Biologie de quelques especes de poissons du lagon Neo-Caledonien II. Sexualité et reproduction. Cah. Indo-Pac. 2:41-72.

Macer, C. T. 1974. The reproductive biology of the horse mackerel, Trachurus trachurus (L.) in the North Sea and English Channel. J. Fish Biol. 6:415-438.

Manickchand-Dass, S. In press. Reproduction, age and growth of the lane snapper, Lutjanus synagris (Linnaeus) in Trinidad, West Indies. Bull. Mar. Sci.

May, R. C., G. S. Akiyama, and M. T. Santerre. 1979. Lunar spawning of the threadfin, Polydactylus sexfilis, in Hawaii. Fish. Bull., U.S. 76:900-904.

McFarland, W. N. 1982. Recruitment patterns in tropical reef fishes. In G. R. Huntsman, W. R. Nicholson, and W. W. Fox, Jr. (editors), The biological bases for reef fishery management, p. 83-91. U.S. Dep. Commer., NOAA Tech. Memo. NMFS, NOAA-TM-NMFS-SEFC-80.

Miller, J. M. 1974. Nearshore distribution of Hawaiian marine fish larvae: effects of water quality, turbidity and currents. In J. H. S. Blaxter (editor), The early life history of fish, p. 217-243. Springer-Verlag, Berlin.

Min, T. S., T. Senta, and S. Supongpan. 1977. Fisheries biology of Pristipomoides spp. (Family Lutjanidae) in the South China Sea and its adjacent waters. Singapore J. Pri. Ind. 5(2):96-115.

Minton, R. V., J. P. Hawke, and W. M. Tatum. 1983. Hormone induced spawning of red snapper, Lutjanus campechanus. Aquaculture 30:363-368.

Mizenko, D. 1984. The biology of the Western Samoan reef-slope snapper populations of: Lutjanus kasmira, Lutjanus rufolineatus, and Pristipomoides multidens. M.S. Thesis, School Oceanogr., Univ. Rhode Island, Kingston, 66 p.

Moseley, F. N. 1966. Biology of the red snapper, Lutjanus aya Bloch, of the northwestern Gulf of Mexico. Publ. Inst. Mar. Sci. 11:90-101.

Munro, J. L., V. C. Gaut, R. Thompson, and P. H. Reeson. 1973. The spawning seasons of Caribbean reef fishes. J. Fish Biol. 5:69-84.

Nelson, R. S., and C. S. Manooch, III. 1982. Growth and mortality of red snappers in the west-central Atlantic Ocean and northern Gulf of Mexico. Trans. Am. Fish. Soc. 111:465-475.

Nzioka, R. M. 1979. Observations on the spawning seasons of East African reef fishes. J. Fish Biol. 14:329-342.

Piedra, G. 1965. Materials on the biology of the yellowtail snapper (Ocyurus chrysurus Bloch). In A. S. Bogdanov (editor), Soviet-Cuban fishery research, p. 251-269. All-Union Sci. Res. 'Inst. Mar. Fish. Oceanogr., Fish. Res. Cent. Nat. Pisc. Inst. Rep. Cuba.

Powles, H., and B. W. Stender. 1976. Observations on composition, seasonality and distribution of ichthyoplankton from MARMAP cruises in the South Atlantic Bight in 1973. South Carolina Mar. Res. Cent., Tech. Rep. Ser. 11, 47 p.

Rabalais, N. N., S. C. Rabalais, and C. R. Arnold. 1980. Description of eggs and larvae of laboratory reared red snapper (Lutjanus campechanus). Copeia 1980:704-708.

Ralston, S. V. D. 1981. A study of the Hawaiian deepsea handline fishery with special reference to the population dynamics of opakapaka, *Pristipomoides filamentosus* (Pisces: Lutjanidae). Ph.D. Dissertation, Univ. Wash., Seattle, 204 p.

Randall, J. E., and V. E. Brock. 1960. Observations on the ecology of epinepheline and lutjanid fishes of the Society Islands, with emphasis on food habits. Trans. Am. Fish. Soc. 89:9-16.

Rangarajan, K. 1971. Maturity and spawning of the snapper, *Lutjanus kasmira* (Forskål) from the Andaman Sea. Indian J. Fish. 18:114-125.

Reshetnikov, Y. S., and R. M. Claro. 1976. Cycles of biological processes in tropical fishes with reference to *Lutjanus synagris*. J. Ichthyol. 16:711-723.

Richards, W. J. 1982. Planktonic processes affecting establishment and maintenance of reef fish stocks. In G. R. Huntsman, W. R. Nicholson, and W. W. Fox, Jr. (editors), The biological bases for reef fishery management, p. 92-100. U.S. Dep. Commer., NOAA Tech. Memo. NMFS, NOAA-TM-NMFS-SEFC-80.

Richards W. J., and V. P. Saksena. 1980. Description of larvae and early juveniles of laboratory-reared gray snapper, *Lutjanus griseus* (Linnaeus) (Pisces, Lutjanidae). Bull. Mar. Sci. 30:515-521.

Rodriguez Pino, Z. 1962. Estudios estadísticos y biológicos sobre la biajaiba (*Lutjanus synagris*). Cent. Invest. Pesq., Notas Sobre Invest. 4, 91 p.

Roff, D. A. 1982. Reproductive strategies in flatfish: A first synthesis. Can. J. Fish. Aquat. Sci. 39:1686-1698.

_____. 1983. An allocation model of growth and reproduction in fish. Can. J. Fish. Aquat. Sci. 40:1395-1404.

Rojas, L. E. 1960. Estudios estadísticos y biológicos sobre el pargo criollo, *Lutjanus analis*. Cent. Invest. Pesq., Notas Sobre Invest. 2, 16 p.

Ruffner, J. A., and F. E. Bair. 1981. The weather almanac. Gale Research Co., Detroit, Michigan, 801 p.

Sale, P. F. 1978. Coexistence of coral reef fishes--a lottery for living space. Environ. Biol. Fishes 3:85-102.

Smith, C. L. 1965. The patterns of sexuality and the classification of serranid fishes. Am. Mus. Novit. 2207:1-20.

Starck, W. A. II, and R. E. Schroeder. 1970. Investigations on the gray snapper, Lutjanus griseus. Stud. Trop. Oceanogr. (Miami) 10, 224 p. + 44 figs. (Copyright 1971.)

Suzuki, K., and S. Hioki. 1979. Spawning behavior, eggs and larvae of the lutjanid fish, Lutjanus kasmira, in an aquarium. Jpn. J. Ichthyol. 26:161-166.

Sylvester, J. R., D. W. Drew, and A. E. Dammann. 1980. Selective life history of silk and blackfin snapper from the Virgin Islands. Caribb. J. Sci. 15:41-48.

Talbot, F. H. 1960. Notes on the biology of the Lutjanidae (Pisces) of the East African coast, with special reference to L. bohar (Forskål). Ann. S. Afr. Mus. 45:549-579.

Thompson, R., and J. L. Munro. 1974. The biology, ecology, exploitation and management of Caribbean reef fishes. Sci. Rep. OCA/UWI Fish. Ecol. Proj., Part V.d. Biology, ecology and bionomics of Caribbean reef fishes: Lutjanidae (Snappers). Res. Rep. No. 3, Univ. West Indies, 69 p. (Reprinted 1983 In J. L. Munro (editor), Caribbean coral reef fishery resources, in Chapter 9: The biology, ecology and bionomics of the snappers, Lutjanidae, p. 94-109. ICLARM Stud. Rev. 7.)

_____. 1983. The biology, ecology, and bionomics of the snappers, Lutjanidae. In J. L. Munro (editor), Caribbean coral reef fishery resources, p. 94-109. ICLARM Stud. Rev. 7, Manila.

Wenner, A. M. 1972. Sex ratio as a function of size in marine crustacea. Am. Nat. 106:321-350.

Wiklund, R. 1969. Observations on spawning of lane snapper. Underwater Nat. 6(2):40.

6
Reproduction in Groupers

Douglas Y. Shapiro
Department of Marine Sciences
University of Puerto Rico
Mayaguez, Puerto Rico   00708

ABSTRACT

All groupers that have been carefully studied
are protogynous, but fewer species are known to
change sex than is commonly thought. Populations
generally contain more females than males, and
spawning is usually restricted to less than half the
year. Many species spawn primarily during 1 to 2
months. Individuals whose gonads are thought to be
in the midst of sex reversal appear generally
throughout all seasons of the year. However, the
shortage of descriptions of the temporal sequence of
changes in the gonad during sex reversal renders the
interpretation of this absence of seasonality of
transitional individuals difficult. Some species
spawn in large aggregations at traditional sites
during short time periods. Fishermen tend to catch
large numbers of fish over such aggregations.
Evaluating the effect of aggregation fishing on
future reproductive yields in the population neces-
sitates study of the social and mating system, the
causes of sex change, the selectivity of fishing
techniques, and the proportion of the population's
annual reproduction that occurs at the time and
place of the aggregation.

INTRODUCTION

The salient feature of grouper reproduction is
protogynous hermaphroditism. In all carefully studied
grouper species, juveniles mature and then function as
adult females. Males are produced when adult females

change sex (Lavenda 1949; Smith 1959, 1965; McErlean and Smith 1964; Moe 1969; Bruslé and Bruslé 1976a; Nagelkerken 1979; Waltz et al. 1979; Chen et al. 1980). This form of sexuality is not uncommon among plants and invertebrates (Policansky 1982; Charnov 1984), as well as among marine fishes (Atz 1964; Reinboth 1970; Smith 1975; Chan and Yeung 1983), and serves as a focal point for a variety of issues.

Protogyny challenges our understanding of hypothalamic-pituitary-gonadal control of sexual function (Chan and O 1981), requires new approaches to evolutionary problems of sex allocation (Charnov 1982), and presents new possibilities for explaining the selective advantage of particular features of fish social behavior (Shapiro In press). In theory, protogyny can be expected to evolve whenever an individual can reproduce more successfully under particular environmental or social conditions by changing sex than by continuing as the same sex (Ghiselin 1969; Warner 1975; Shapiro 1984). This approach generally implies that a sex-change strategy has emerged histori- cally from gonochoristic forebears. Groupers, however, are thought more likely to have evolved from simulta- neously hermaphroditic ancestors (Smith 1965; Smith and Erdman 1973). The selective advantage of changing sex, if any, can be discovered by careful study of grouper social and mating systems.

Protogyny in groupers also presents dilemmas for rational fishery management (cf. management models for protandric pandalid shrimps, Fox 1972). Since males in protogynous species tend to be larger, older, and less numerous than females (Lavenda 1949; Moe 1969; Bruslé and Bruslé 1976a; Waltz et al. 1979), fishing may remove more males than females (e.g., Nagelkerken 1981). The repro- ductive consequence of selective fishing may differ in these fishes from the consequence of similar fishing in gonochoristic species. Similarly, predictive yield models for protogynous fishes will have to build upon different assumptions about life-history parameters than models applicable to gonochores (Bannerot 1984). Close study of social and mating systems is needed to provide the biolog- ical foundation for making such assumptions.

Some groupers restrict spawning to large aggregations at traditional sites during short periods of the year. The regularity and short duration of these aggregations raise intriguing problems concerning the way in which individuals assess the reproductive costs and benefits of changing sex at particular times, and the effect that intensive fishing over spawning aggregations has on the future reproductive potential of the population.

The purposes of this paper are to review the current state of knowledge of the reproductive biology of groupers, with particular attention to protogyny, and to discuss the types of information needed to resolve some of the outstanding issues surrounding grouper reproduction. In the first half of the paper, I discuss reproductive biology generally, including protogyny, sexual maturation, seasonality and periodicity of spawning, the expected relation between spawning aggregations and the timing of sex change, and fecundity and population sex ratios. In the second half of the paper, I focus attention on the type of information that we must have in order to determine how fishing over spawning aggregations influences the future reproductive potential of the population. This practical problem involves the nature of grouper social and mating systems, the causes of sex change and the size of the population contributing to a spawning aggregation, as well as the selectivity of fishing. Since the practical issues concerning spawning aggregations have been explored to date in only one species, the paper will move from a general, comparative perspective in the first half to a narrowed focus on one grouper in the second.

BIOLOGY OF REPRODUCTION

Evaluating Protogyny in Groupers

In the literature on fish hermaphroditism, criteria for diagnosing protogyny have seldom been discussed explicitly (Atz 1964; Smith 1982). In fact, at least 10 different features of gonadal histology and population structure have been used in various combinations in the past (Sadovy and Shapiro In press) to diagnose protogyny: (1) Bimodal size-frequency (or age-frequency) distributions, with males absent from small size (or age) ranges and predominating in large size (or age) ranges. Occasionally, differential size-frequency distributions between the sexes will be expressed as size- or age-specific sex ratios (e.g., Nagelkerken 1979). (2) Female-biased sex ratios. Presence within testes of features thought to be remnants of a prior ovarian state, namely (3) avitellogenic oocytes, (4) yellow-brown bodies (sometimes called atretic bodies or atretic follicles), (5) a central lumen not used for sperm transport and thought to represent a prior ovarian cavity, (6) organization of testicular tissues into lamellae reminiscent of ovarian lamellae. (7) A duct system for sperm transport located within the muscular wall of the gonad and morphologically dissimilar to sperm ducts in gonochoristic fishes. (8) Gonads containing degenerating ovarian tissue and proliferating spermatogenic tissue, thought to be typical of individuals in the midst of sex change. (9) Serial biopsies of gonads demonstrating ovarian function at one moment and testicular function later in identified individuals. (10) Gender-specific changes in spawning behavior, external coloration, or morphology in individuals observed over delimited time periods.

According to a recent appraisal of these features (Sadovy and Shapiro In press), protogyny can reliably be diagnosed by the presence of any combination of features (5)-(10) and atretic bodies in early stages of oocytic atresia within testes. Bimodal size- or age-frequency distributions, female-biased sex ratios (including size- or age-specific sex ratios), yellow bodies that are not clearly early stages of oocytic atresia, and oocytes in testes are nonspecific features that may have many causes, only one of which is protogyny.

Viewed from this perspective, reasonable evidence for protogyny has been published for 8 out of 28 groupers (Table 6.1) known in Atlantic and Pacific waters of the United States (Lavenda 1949; Smith 1959, 1965; McErlean and Smith 1964; Moe 1969; Nagelkerken 1979; Waltz et al. 1979; Robins et al. 1980), and for 4 groupers in other geographic areas (Bruslé and Bruslé 1976a; Chen et al. 1977; Chen et al. 1980). Explicit or implicit statements that all groupers are protogynous (Smith 1965, 1975) may or may not prove to be true, but run the risk of being misinterpreted. For example, Smith's (1959) histological description might be taken as evidence for concluding that Epinephelus striatus and Mycteroperca venenosa are protogynous (Thompson and Munro 1978). While Smith (1959) states that these species, along with eight others, were concluded to be protogynous based on two features of testis structure and the absence of males (which could only be identified by gonadal histology) from small size classes, in fact, no testis or male was identified in his samples of these two species (Smith 1959:Table 1). Thus, the description said to be a "composite" of features from all samples of all species apparently was not known to apply to these species in particular.

TABLE 6.1
Grouper species for which reasonable evidence of
protogyny has been published

Species	Gonadal Histology Sample Size	Source
Epinephelus aeneus	1,034	Bruslé and Bruslé 1976a
E. guaza	419	Bruslé and Bruslé 1976a
E. tauvina	53	Chen et al. 1977
E. diacanthus	380	Chen et al. 1980
E. morio	790	Moe 1969
E. guttatus	106	Smith 1959
Mycteroperca tigris	28	Smith 1959
M. bonaci	21	Smith 1959
M. microlepis	32	McErlean and Smith 1964
Centropristis striata	10	Lavenda 1949
C. striata	1,700	Waltz et al. 1979
Cephalopholis[a] fulva	41	Smith 1959[b]
	?	Smith 1965
C. cruentatus	670	Nagelkerken 1979
C. cruentatus	22	Smith 1959
C. cruentatus	?	Smith 1965

[a]Smith (1971) reduced Cephalopholis to a subgenus of Epinephelus for North American groupers (Robins et al. 1980). This change has not been recognized for Indo-Pacific species (Randall and Ben-Tuvia 1983). For consistency of usage in this chapter, Cephalopholis has been retained.

[b]Smith (1959) attributes protogyny to an additional five grouper species, but only had gonads of zero or one male for each species. Moore and Labisky (1984) examined gonads of 144 E. niveatus histologically but found no transitionals and did not describe features that, if present, would confirm a diagnosis of protogyny.

TABLE 6.2
Age and size (total length TL and standard
length SL) of sexual maturation in female
groupers

Species	Age Class	Size	Method	Source[a]
Epinephelus guttatus	3	--	Histology	1
E. guttatus	--	<250 mm TL	Macroscopic	2
E. striatus	--	<480 mm TL	Macroscopic	2
E. niveatus	3	--	Histology	3
E. morio	4-6	425-500 mm SL	Histology	4
E. areolatus	2	190 mm SL	GSI[b], squash	5
E. maculatus	5	310 mm SL	GSI, squash	5
E. rhyncholepis	3	230 mm SL	GSI, squash	5
E. microdon	--	340 mm SL	GSI, squash	5
E. diacanthus	--	125 mm SL	GSI, ova dia.	6
E. tauvina	2	412-500 mm SL	Histology	7
E. aeneus	--	5 kg	Histology	8, 9
E. aeneus	--	400 mm SL	GSI	10
E. guaza	--	360 mm SL	GSI	10
E. guaza	--	5 kg	Histology	8, 9
E. alexandrinus	--	270 mm SL	GSI	10
Cephalopholis fulva	--	<160 mm TL	Macroscopic	2
C. cruentatus	--	<160 mm TL	Macroscopic	2
C. cruentatus	2	140 mm TL	Histology	11
Centropristis striata	1	--	Histology	12
C. striata	1	100 mm SL	Histology	13
Mycteroperca venenosa	--	<510 mm TL	Macroscopic	2
Plectropomus leopardus	4	300 mm SL	GSI, squash	5

[a]Source: 1. Burnett-Herkes 1975; 2. Thompson and Munro 1978; 3. Moore and Labisky 1984; 4. Moe 1969; 5. Loubens 1980; 6. Chen et al. 1980; 7. Chen et al. 1977; 8, 9. Bruslé and Bruslé 1976a, 1976b; 10. Bouain 1980; 11. Nagelkerken 1979; 12. Waltz et al. 1979; 13. Mercer 1978.

[b]GSI = gonadosomatic index.

It is not true that all members of all genera with protogynous species are themselves protogynous (Robertson and Justines 1982). Thus, existence of several protogynous groupers is not sufficient to conclude that all groupers are protogynous, in spite of the fact that no grouper has yet been discovered to be gonochoristic. These observations emphasize the importance of analyzing and publishing complete histological series of gonads on any previously little-studied species.

Sexual Maturation

The age or size at which mature females first appear in samples has been reported for many grouper species (Table 6.2). The methods used for evaluating maturity have ranged from careful histological examination of gonads in a range of size- or age-classes (e.g., Nagelkerken 1979; Moore and Labisky 1984) through squash preparations of fresh material (Loubens 1980) to gonadosomatic indices, either alone (Bouain 1980) or in combination with microscopic measurements of the diameter of fresh ova (Chen et al. 1980).

If one presumes that all groupers are protogynous, then the size or age of sexual transition forms the male counterpart to size of maturation in females. One method of finding the size at sex change is to measure individuals whose gonads are histologically transitional between ovary and testis (see Sadovy and Shapiro In press for a review of the difficulties in defining "transitional"). The size or age classes in which transitional gonads appear can be taken to represent the range of sizes or ages of sex reversal (Table 6.3).

A second method of estimating the size at sex change is to examine the size range in which males overlap with females. The median value and its confidence limits can then be taken to represent the size at which sex change usually occurs within the population (Shapiro 1984). If the range of overlap is small, one may assume that females changed sex within a narrow range of ages or sizes. If the range of overlap is large, then females must have changed sex over a wide variety of sizes (or ages).

The extent of overlap can be compared among species attaining different sizes (or ages) by dividing the range of overlap by the maximum size (or age) observed for each species. The resulting ratio expresses the range over which sex change occurs as a proportion of the maximum

TABLE 6.3
Size (age) of sex change as judged by size (age) of transitional individuals, and variation in size (age) of sex change as judged by two ratios: (1) size (age) range of transitional fish divided by maximum size (age) of fish in population, and (2) range of overlap in size (age) of males and females divided by maximum size (age) of fish in population.

Species	Size (Age) of Transitionals	Maximum Fish Size (Age)	Ratio 1 (%)	Ratio 2 (%)	Source[a]
Epinephelus guttatus	--	405 mm SL	--	42	1
	--	28 otolith rings	--	75	2
E. guttatus	--	425 mm SL	--	47	3
E. guttatus	--	340 mm SL	--	44	4
E. guttatus	--	400 mm SL	--	25	5
E. guttatus	--	480 mm SL	--	42	2
E. striatus	--	640 mm SL	--	38	6
E. morio	301-676 mm SL	751 mm SL	50	60	
	3-13 age groups	30 age groups	37	77	
E. areolatus	--	300 mm SL	--	40	7
	--	15 years	--	47	
E. maculatus	--	440 mm SL	--	55	7
	--	15 years	--	73	
E. rhyncholepis	--	260 mm SL	--	15	7
	--	15 years	--	20	
E. microdon	--	440 mm SL	--	55	7
E. fasciatus	--	220 mm SL	--	36	7
	--	15 years	--	47	

Species / Location					Ref.
E. hoedti	--	520 mm SL	--	62	7
	--	15 years	--	100	7
E. merra	--	180 mm SL	--	0	8
	--	15 years	--	20	
E. diacanthus	--	240 mm SL	--	27	9
	2-6 age classes	7 age classes	71	86	
E. aeneus	--	890 mm SL	--	6	10
	3-6 age groups	6 age groups	67	67	
E. guaza	--	890 mm SL	--	0	9
	4-7 age groups	7 age groups	57	86	
Cephalopholis fulva	--	300 mm TL	--	23	10
C. cruentatus	135-255 mm TL	295 mm TL	41	41	5
	--	8 age groups	--	63	11
Centropristis striata					
New Jersey	--	400 mm SL	--	30	12
	--	12 years	--	42	
New York	--	480 mm SL	--	33	13
Middle Atlantic	100-360 mm SL	440 mm SL	59	55	13
	1-7 age groups	9 age groups	78	67	
South Atlantic	120-280 mm SL	320 mm SL	50	50	14
	1-5 age groups	8 age groups	63	75	
Florida	110-320 mm SL	420 mm SL	50	62	15
	1-8 age groups	10 age groups	80	100	
Georgia overall	--	905 gm	--	58	
<30 m depth	--	6 age groups	--	100	
>30 m depth	--	8 age groups	--	88	

(Continued)

TABLE 6.3 (Cont.)

Species	Size (Age) of Transitionals	Maximum Fish Size (Age)	Ratio 1 (%)	Ratio 2 (%)	Source[a]
Mycteroperca tigris	--	650 mm SL	--	0	4
M. microlepis	--	15 years	--	0	16
Plectropomus leopardus	--	520 mm SL	--	31	7
	--	15 years	--	7	

[a]Source: 1. Burnett-Herkes 1975; 2. Colin et al. In press; 3. D. Shapiro, Y. Sadovy, and G. Garcia-Moliner Unpub. data; 4. Smith 1959; 5. Thompson and Munro 1978; 6. Moe 1969; 7. Loubens 1980; 8. Chen et al. 1980; 9. Bouain 1980; 10. Bruslé and Bruslé 1976a; 11. Nagelkerken 1979; 12. Lavenda 1949; 13. Mercer 1978; 14. Waltz et al. 1979; 15. Low 1981; 16. McErlean and Smith 1964.

fish size (or age). A similar ratio can be constructed by dividing the range in which transitional fish appear by the maximum size (or age) of fish within the population.

In Table 6.3, both ratios are listed for all groupers for which evidence is available. In order to interpret these data as size (or age) ranges of sex reversal, one must assume that each species is a protogynous hermaphrodite. As judged by ratio 1 in the table, the size range of transitionals was 37-80% of the maximum size in six species, with median 58% (Table 6.3:column 4). As judged by ratio 2 in the table, in 19 species sex change occurred over 0-100% of the maximum size or age of fish in the population, with median 47% (Table 6.3:column 5).

Several points can be made about these data. First, extremely small ratios are probably erroneous and due to small sample size. For example, the four cases with 0% overlap (producing 0% on ratio 2 in column 5, Table 6.3) had sample sizes of 2, 5, 6, and 7 individuals, respectively, of one sex. With a larger sample size, overlap in size of males and females would likely have appeared in the data.

Second, the range of sizes and ages over which sex change can occur is apparently quite broad for many of these species. In 72% of the 46 calculations of ratio 2 in Table 6.3, sex change occurred over 33-100% of the size (age) range of fish in the population. Moreover, sex reversal fell within this broad range for at least 1 measurement in 13 of the 19 species represented, with 3 of the remaining 6 species suffering from the low sample sizes already mentioned.

These data are inconsistent with the idea that sex change occurs at a characteristic size or age for all members of a population. Thus, in my view, the data oppose any evolutionary explanation (e.g., the size advantage model (Warner 1975; Charnov 1982)) or proposed proximal mechanism for the causation of sex change (e.g., a developmental system in which females change sex upon attaining a characteristic age or size) that would predict sex change at approximately the same size, or age, for all members of the population.

Third, the data are consistent with a mechanism for behavioral induction of sex change, simply because behavioral control operates independently within social subdivisions of the population and, hence, may produce large differences in the time of life, and consequently in the size or age, at which particular females change sex (Shapiro 1984).

A few studies contain results that are difficult to interpret. Collections of some species contain males that are smaller than most immature females (e.g., Moe 1969). These small males may not have passed through a functional, adult female stage but may have developed through a juvenile phase in which the gonad contained primarily oogenic tissue, as occurs in some gonochoristic fishes (Takahashi 1977; Takahashi and Shimizu 1983). Additional work on early sexual development in groupers would resolve this problem.

Seasonality and Periodicity of Spawning

The relationship between spawning periods of groupers and water temperature, changes in water temperature, day length, plankton abundance, and latitude have been examined by several workers (Burnett-Herkes 1975; Nagelkerken 1979; Thresher 1984). No factor or combination of factors clearly explains the variability in time of year at which groupers spawn. There is some tendency for species to spawn between early spring and summer in low latitudes and somewhat later in the year in higher latitudes (Table 6.4), but this trend does not hold for all species (Thresher 1984).

All groupers for which there is evidence spawn during a restricted period (Table 6.4). Thus, the difference in duration of spawning periods, found for snappers, between species near continental land masses and species on islands (Grimes 1986) does not apply to groupers. Although some grouper species are known to spawn over 6-8 months (Nagelkerken 1979; Loubens 1980; Thompson and Munro 1983), most spawn over 1-5 months and many spawn primarily during 1-2 months (Randall and Brock 1960; McErlean 1963; Moe 1969; Munro et al. 1973; Burnett-Herkes 1975; Bruslé and Bruslé 1976a, 1976b; Johannes 1978; Manooch and Haimovici 1978; Bouain 1980; Chen et al. 1980; Loubens 1980; Nagelkerken 1981; Thompson and Munro 1983; Matheson et al. 1984; Moore and Labisky 1984). Since most of these estimates were based on fishery samples pooled on a monthly or bimonthly basis, it is not generally known whether fish spawn continually during these periods or at a few regular intervals each lasting only a few days. Epinephelus tauvina reportedly spawns only during days 27-13 of the lunar month, E. striatus during lunar days 14-18 (Johannes 1978), and E. merra for 3-4 days out of each reproductive month (Randall and Brock 1960).

Even less is known about frequency of spawning by individual males and females within general spawning periods. Bouain and Siau (1983) observed oocytes maturing in successive waves in E. aeneus. They concluded that oocytes maturing in waves not coincident with the "general ripening of the ovary" probably underwent atresia and were not spawned. Moe (1969) was unable to find evidence within maturing ovaries to suggest that individual E. morio females spawned more than once during a season. However, he sampled each female only once. One E. striatus female taken from a spawning aggregation contained both ripe and subripe oocytes, suggesting that females may spawn "repeatedly during the time when they are in the aggregation" (Smith 1972). Mercer (1978) inferred multiple spawning by Centropristis striata females during each reproductive period from bimodal frequency distributions of ova diameters. Male Cephalopholis cruentatus maintained high testis weight over a longer period than females maintained ovary weight, prompting the conclusion that "males can spawn several times during a season" (Nagelkerken 1979). Since actual spawning has only rarely been observed in groupers (Guitart and Juarez 1966 reported in Burnett-Herkes 1975; Neill 1966-67; Ukawa et al. 1966; Thresher 1984; Colin et al. In press), actual mating frequencies by individuals remain undescribed.

Spawning Aggregations and Timing of Sex Change

The most restricted spawning period known in groupers occurs when individuals aggregate at what seem to be traditional sites and spawn intensively for 1-2 weeks. Aggregations are thus far known for E. striatus in the Berry Islands, Bahamas, on Bermuda, in the Virgin Islands, off the end of three Cayman Islands, in Bimini, near Santa Lucia, Cuba, and off the coast of Belize; for E. guttatus in Bermuda, in the Virgin Islands, and off La Parguera, Puerto Rico; for M. venenosa in the Bahamas and off Belize; for Plectropomus leopardus and E. fuscoguttatus on Palau, Micronesia; for E. merra on Palau, Ponape, Truk, and Nukuoro; and purportedly for several other Pacific species at Losap Atoll (Smith 1972; Lee 1974; Burnett-Herkes 1975; Johannes 1978, 1981; Olsen and LaPlace 1978; Colin 1982; Bannerot 1984; Colin et. al In press; J. Carter, New York Zoological Society, Pers. com., 1985).

TABLE 6.4
Seasonality of reproduction in groupers

Species	Period with Ripe Gonads	Reproductive Peaks	Location	Source
Epinephelus guttatus	Dec.-Mar.	Jan.	Jamaica	Thompson and Munro 1978
E. guttatus	Dec.-Apr.	Feb.	Jamaica	Munro et al. 1973
E. guttatus	May-July	June	Bermuda	Burnett-Herkes 1975
E. striatus	Feb.-Apr.	--	Jamaica	Thompson and Munro 1978
E. striatus	Feb., Apr., May	--	Jamaica	Munro et al. 1973
E. niveatus	Apr.-July	--	Florida Keys	Moore and Labisky 1984
E. morio	Feb.-May	May	Eastern Gulf of Mexico	Moe 1969
E. areolatus	Sept.-Feb.	Dec.	New Caledonia	Loubens 1980
E. maculatus	Sept.-Feb.	Nov.-Dec.	New Caledonia	Loubens 1980
E. rhyncholepis	Sept.-Feb	Nov.-Dec.	New Caledonia	Loubens 1980
E. microdon	Sept.-Feb.	Nov.-Dec.	New Caledonia	Loubens 1980
E. fasciatus	Sept.-Feb.	Nov.-Dec.	New Caledonia	Loubens 1980
E. hoedti	Sept.-Feb	Nov.-Dec.	New Caledonia	Loubens 1980
E. merra	Sept.-Feb	Nov.-Dec.	New Caledonia	Loubens 1980
E. merra	Jan.-Apr.	--	Tahiti	Randall and Brock 1960
E. diacanthus	Apr.-June	--	Taiwan	Chen et al. 1980
E. aeneus	July-Aug.	July-Aug.	Tunisia	Bruslé and Bruslé 1976a, 1976b
E. aeneus	July	July	Tunisia	Bouain 1980
E. guaza	July-Aug.	July-Aug.	Tunisia	Bruslé and Bruslé 1976a, 1976b
E. guaza	June-July	June-July	Tunisia	Bouain 1980

E. alexandrinus	July-Aug.	July-Aug.	Tunisia	Bouain 1980
E. mystacinus	Nov.(average)	--	Jamaica	Thompson and Munro 1978; Munro et al. 1973
E. afer	Dec., May	--	Jamaica	Thompson and Munro 1978
Cephalopholis fulva	May-Oct.	--	Curacao	Nagelkerken 1979
C. fulva	Nov.-July	Jan.-Mar., June-July	Jamaica	Thompson and Munro 1978
C. fulva	Jan.-Apr., July	--	Jamaica	Munro et al. 1973
C. cruentatus	Apr.-May	--	Jamaica	Thompson and Munro 1978
C. cruentatus	Feb.-June	Mar.	Jamaica	Munro et al. 1973
C. cruentatus	May-Oct.	--	Curacao	Nagelkerken 1981
C. cruentatus	May-Oct.	Aug.-Sept.	Curacao	Nagelkerken 1979
C. miniata	June-Sept.	--	Sinai Peninsula	Shpigel 1985
C. argus	June-Sept.	--	Sinai Peninsula	Shpigel 1985
C. hemistiktos	June-Sept.	--	Sinai Peninsula	Shpigel 1985
Centropristis striata	May-June	May-June	New Jersey	Lavenda 1949
C. striata	Feb.-Oct.	July-Aug.	Virginia	Mercer 1978
C. striata	Feb.-May, Nov.	Mar.-May, Nov.	Carolinas	Mercer 1978
Mycteroperca venenosa	Feb.-Apr.	--	Jamaica	Thompson and Munro 1978
M. venenosa	Apr.-May	--	Jamaica	Munro et al. 1973
M. interstitialis	Apr.	Apr.	Jamaica	Thompson and Munro 1978
M. phenax	Apr.-Aug.	May-June	Carolinas	Matheson et al. 1984
M. microlepis	Feb.	Feb.	Carolinas	Manooch and Haimovici 1978
M. microlepis	Jan.-Mar.	--	Florida	McErlean 1963
Plectropomus leopardus	Sept.-Feb.	Nov.-Dec.	New Caledonia	Loubens 1980

Spawning aggregations are of particular interest. In theory, individuals should only change sex when it is to their reproductive advantage to do so (Ghiselin 1969; Warner 1975; Charnov 1982). The relative advantage to a female of changing sex depends on the reproductive success she can expect to have as a male. Reproductive success of males is determined by the number and fecundity of females with whom they spawn. The only direct place for a fish to assess male reproductive success is on the spawning ground. Thus, females of species that spawn in aggregations during only 1 or 2 weeks of the year must make crucial decisions about their future reproductive success during a short time.

This theoretical view implies that sex change should be initiated during or immediately after spawning aggregations. "Initiation" might include onset of changes in gonadal structure, hormonal secretions, and external coloration and behavior. If so, then we would primarily expect to find individuals in the process of sex change soon after spawning. Alternatively, "initiation" may imply only that the fish registers behavioral and social events internally, e.g., in memory, and these events are later translated into observable physiological changes. A fish responding in this way may present no clear evidence of sex change until the process of translating "memories" into physical sex change begins. In this case, fish in the midst of sex change might be found at some delay after the spawning aggregation had ended.

The only circumstance in which sex change might be initiated well after spawning is if spawning aggregations have an internal social structure that maps onto the social structure of the population during the remainder of the year. In that case, an alteration in the social system during the nonspawning months might enable a female to predict her future spawning potential during the coming aggregation.

What little is known about the timing of sex change in groupers is derived from plotting the occurrence of gonads presumed to be in transition from ovary to testis against time of year at which the fish were caught. Transitional gonads of E. diacanthus were found during all months of the year except during the 2 months of peak gonadal ripeness (Chen et al. 1980). The red grouper, E. morio, was said to change sex "immediately after spawning or vitellogenic activity in the female" (Moe 1969). In fact, transitional gonads were found during 7 months of

the year, including the 2 months of peak spawning (Moe
1969). The graysby, C. cruentatus, spawns from May to
October in Curacao, but primarily in August and September
(Table 6.4). Transitional gonads were found in March and
April, and from July to October (Nagelkerken 1979). In a
study based primarily on gonads of C. fulvus and C. cruentatus, but applied generally to all "Epinephelus-type"
gonads (Smith 1965), transitionals were said to appear
during the nonbreeding season, with sexual transformation
occurring soon after spawning. Data supporting this
conclusion were not presented. Transitional Centropristis
striata were found in the month following spawning, but no
other months were sampled (Waltz et al. 1979). In the
middle Atlantic region off the coast of Virginia, transitional C. striata were collected during all months of the
year except May and November, with highest incidence from
August to October, immediately after the peak spawning
from July to August (Table 6.4). However, in the South
Atlantic region off the Carolinas, where spawning peaked
twice, in March to May and again in November (Table 6.4),
transitionals of the same species were found throughout
the year, with highest frequency in November (Mercer
1978). In a study based on bimonthly collections of E.
guttatus over 29 months, transitionals examined to date do
not display any seasonal or other temporal pattern
(Shapiro et al. Unpub.).

There are several difficulties with defining the time
of sex change from the occurrence of transitionals in
monthly samples. The first difficulty is the lack of a
clear and uniformly applied criterion for defining a
transitional gonad (Sadovy and Shapiro In press).
Secondly, unless the duration required for a female to
complete sex change is known, the occurrence of transitionals within particular months may tell us little about
when the transitional individuals initiated sex change.
A third problem is the relatively small number of transitional gonads that are generally found. Although Moe
(1969), for example, examined 790 sets of gonads and
estimated the transition rate for female sex change to be
15% between 5 and 10 years of age, his total sample
consisted of only 19 transitional gonads. One reason for
finding small numbers of transitionals is that sex change
may be completed rapidly. In Anthias squamipinnis, a
small, protogynous serranid from the Indo-Pacific, a
female begins to change sex generally 3-10 days after
removal of a male from a social group, and gonadal sex
change is completed within 2 weeks (Shapiro 1981a, 1981b,

1981c). If sex change in groupers is equally rapid, most
sex changes throughout the year may be missed, and the
small numbers of transitionals appearing in collections
may not provide an adequate indication of time of occurrence. Of course, in species with known, rapid sex
changes, the appearance of transitionals in particular
months would provide accurate information on when sex
change was initiated.

Experimental studies on species in which sex change
is behaviorally induced (see below) have demonstrated that
females can be induced to change sex during all seasons of
the year by removing males from their social group
(reviewed in Shapiro 1984). Nothing is known about
induction of sex change in groupers. Nevertheless, it
would appear from the above findings that sex change in
groupers does occur throughout much of the year and is not
restricted to the immediate postspawning period. The
extent to which these preliminary observations agree or
disagree with evolutionary predictions will only become
clear when more is understood about grouper mating and
social systems, and when more detailed evidence is available on the timing and proximate causes of sex change.

Fecundity and Population Sex Ratios

Since groupers spawn over restricted periods, one
might expect females to release relatively large numbers
of eggs during the short breeding season. Fecundities
have generally fallen in the range of 100,000-5,000,000
eggs per female (Table 6.5). These estimates are potentially useful in evaluating the reproductive advantage of
remaining a female or of changing sex and becoming a male
(Warner 1975; Charnov 1982), but they will probably not be
employed in addressing this issue until more is known
about the mating system (so that male reproductive success
can be evaluated) and about the costs of changing sex
(Shapiro 1984).

Population sex ratios may provide clues to male
reproductive success, since the sex ratio estimates the
average number of females with whom the average male
spawns. Most estimates of sex ratio for most groupers
have differed from unity, with more females than males in
the sample (Table 6.6). Since most of these samples were
taken from commercial catches that employed fishing
techniques with unknown biases for selectively capturing
one sex more frequently than the other, the reliability of

TABLE 6.5
Fecundity estimates of groupers

Species	Fecundity (No. of Eggs x 1,000)	Source[a]
Epinephelus guttatus	90–3,365	1
E. guttatus	0.3–0.7/g ovary	2
E. morio	312–5,735	3
E. diacanthus	63–233	4
E. aeneus	404–12,589	5
E. guaza	258–606	5
E. alexandrinus	255–899	·5
E. afer	0.6–0.7/g ovary	2
Cephalopholis fulva	0.3–1.1/g ovary	2
C. cruentatus	0.6/g ovary	2
C. cruentatus	298	6
Centropristis striata	191–370	7
Mycteroperca microlepis	655–1,457	8

[a]Source: 1. Burnett-Herkes 1975; 2. Thompson and Munro 1978; 3. Moe 1969; 4. Chen et al. 1980; 5. Bouain and Siau 1983; 6. Nagelkerken 1979; 7. Mercer 1978; 8. McErlean 1963.

the estimates is not generally known (but see Selectivity and Aggregation Fishing, below).

EVALUATING THE EFFECT OF AGGREGATION FISHING

The most intensive fishing of grouper populations is over localized spawning aggregations (e.g., Olsen and LaPlace 1978). Aggregation fishing directly removes reproductively active fish from the spawning ground and thus may have severe detrimental effects on future fishery yields. The effect of intensive fishing on future reproductive potential depends on four factors: (1) the proportion of the total annual spawning that occurs in and during the aggregation; (2) the selectivity of aggregation fishing; (3) the causes of sex change; and (4) the nature of the social system before and after the spawning aggregation. In fact, information concerning these factors is

TABLE 6.6
Population sex ratios of groupers

Species	Sex Ratio (F/M)	Location	Source[a]
Epinephelus guttatus	5.6	Jamaica, Port Royal	1
E. guttatus	2.8	Jamaica, oceanic banks	1
E. guttatus	1.7	Bermuda, overall	2
E. guttatus	35	Bermuda, 1st sample	2
E. guttatus	3.2	Bermuda, 2d sample	2
E. guttatus	43	Puerto Rico, inshore	3
E. guttatus	4.5	Puerto Rico, aggregation	3
E. striatus	1.4	Jamaica, oceanic banks	1
E. striatus	1.9	Little Cayman, aggregation	4
E. niveatus	4.3	Florida Keys	5
E. morio	5.0	Eastern Gulf of Mexico	6
E. areolatus	2.9	New Caledonia lagoon	7
E. maculatus	4.8	New Caledonia lagoon	7
E. rhyncholepis	2.3	New Caledonia lagoon	7
E. microdon	2.9	New Caledonia lagoon	7
E. fasciatus	2.2	New Caledonia lagoon	7
E. hoedti	10	New Caledonia lagoon	7
E. merra	1.3	New Caledonia lagoon	7
E. diacanthus	2.6	Taiwan	8
E. aeneus	1.5–1.9	Tunisia	9, 10
E. aeneus	4.7	Tunisia	11
E. guaza	1.9–2.0	Tunisia	9, 10
E. guaza	14	Tunisia	11
E. alexandrinus	no M, N = 130F	Tunisia	11
Cephalopholis fulva	2.1	Jamaica, oceanic banks	1
C. cruentatus	6.0	Jamaica, Port Royal	1
C. cruentatus	2.5	Curacao	12
Centropristis striata	0.5–1.3	Georgia, Carolina	13
C. striata	0.9–1.2	Florida, Carolina	14
C. striata	1.5–2.2	Virginia	15
C. striata	2.8–5.0	Carolinas	15
Mycteroperca venenosa	1.2	Jamaica, oceanic banks	1
Plectropomus leopardus	7.7	New Caledonia lagoon	7

[a]Source: 1. Thompson and Munro 1978; 2. Burnett-Herkes 1975; 3. D. Shapiro, Y. Sadovy, and G. Garcia-Moliner, Unpub. data; 4. Colin et al. In press; 5. Moore and Labisky 1984; 6. Moe 1969; 7. Loubens 1980; 8. Chen et al. 1980; 9, 10. Bruslé and Bruslé 1976a, 1976b; 11. Bouain 1980; 12. Nagelkerken 1979; 13. Low 1981; 14. Waltz et al. 1979; 15. Mercer 1978.

necessary to evaluate the effect of   heavy fishing over
any localized portion of a spawning population of protogynous fish, whether aggregated or not. Focusing on aggregations simplifies the problem conceptually. Discussion
of these factors will be viewed, therefore, from this
perspective.

Distribution of Spawning Through Time and Space

Intensive fishing over aggregations will be much more
damaging to the population if most of the year's spawning
occurs there than if a large proportion of spawning is
spread over the remainder of the breeding season or in
areas outside of the aggregation. Assessing this proportion requires knowledge of the size of the population from
which fish are attracted and the area to which they
disperse subsequently as well as the relative amount of
spawning before, during, and after the aggregation.
Burnett-Herkes (1975) tagged 403 E. guttatus caught at
peak ripeness in two spawning aggregations in Bermuda,
relied on commercial catches for recovery of tagged fish,
and later retrieved 10 tagged individuals 0-13 km from the
aggregation site. His results suggest that fish joining
an aggregation subsequently disperse over a moderate-sized
area. Colin et al. (In press) argue that since only one
E. striatus aggregation is known for each of the three
Cayman Islands, E. striatus migrate 15-50 km along the
coast of each island to spawn. The presumption was that
individuals return to their point of origin at the
conclusion of spawning.

The size of an aggregation may be helpful in estimating the proportion of the population participating in it.
Unfortunately, estimates of aggregation size are scarce.
Smith (1972) estimated the two-dimensional extent of an E.
striatus aggregation in Bimini from the distribution of
fishing boats in the area. His estimate was 100 x 500 m.
During one dive over the aggregation, fish extended 3 m
off the bottom and were estimated to be present in a
density of one fish per 5 cubic meters of water. Thus, he
estimated the aggregation to contain 30,000-100,000 fish.

Along the southwest coast of Puerto Rico, E. guttatus
forms an unknown number of local aggregations within two
broad areas approximately 10 km apart along the edge of
the insular shelf. During January 1984, one of these
areas was estimated to contain four local aggregations,
one of which was studied intensively by four to eight

divers over a 10-day period. This aggregation measured 70
x 140 m and contained a maximum of 7.6 counted fish per
100 m² of bottom. If all four local aggregations were of
the same size and density, the number of fish in the
entire area totaled 2,979 fish (Shapiro et al. Unpub.).
Even assuming, as an example, that only 20% of the actual
number of fish were counted, the total number of fish at
the site was not large for the area of reef that it
presumably served. The possibility should be entertained
that fish do not remain for the duration of the aggregation. If so, turnover rate could substantially increase
the total number of fish spawning at any one site.

Gonadosomatic indices of 573 E. guttatus collected at
bimonthly intervals in Puerto Rico remained low over a 29-
month period except for a single, high peak during January
of each year. The peaks corresponded precisely with the
formation of the spawning aggregation in the week
preceding the full moon each January (Shapiro et al.
Unpub.) The virtual absence of ripe gonads outside of the
aggregation period suggests that most of the population's
annual spawning occurs at the time of aggregation.

With the limited evidence at hand, we can only
conclude that groupers concentrate their spawning during a
relatively short period of time, and that some groupers
aggregate at sites well-known to local fishermen and
probably migrate to the aggregation site over substantial
distances. Most of the spawning of such populations
probably is accomplished during the aggregation period,
but what proportion is done in the aggregation itself
rather than elsewhere in the population cannot yet be
ascertained.

Selectivity of Aggregation Fishing

Fishing is selective if it yields fish of particular
sizes or sex in numbers disproportionate to their presence
in the underlying population. Assessing selectivity
requires knowledge of the sizes and sexes in the actual
aggregation (or population) as well as in the fishing
catch. In theory, selective fishing can have a delete-
rious effect on reproductive output. For example, females
heavily outnumber males in an aggregation, but if fishermen take proportionately more males than females and if
individual males are limited in the number of ripe females
they can fertilize in a short period, then some females
may not be able to spawn for lack of males.

In the only study to date that has attempted to evaluate selectivity of aggregation fishing (Shapiro et al. Unpub.), both the sex ratio and size distribution of E. guttatus speared by divers within the aggregation were statistically indistinguishable from the sex ratio and sizes of specimens caught by fishermen on the surface (for sex ratio: chi-square = 0.063, df = 1, N = 190 males and females, NS; for size of females: chi-square = 0.263, df = 2, N = 186 females, NS; for size of males: chi-square = 0.017, df = 1, N = 41 males, NS). The sex ratio of this aggregation was 4.5 females per male. The handline techniques used by fishermen in this study were apparently sampling the aggregation nonselectively.

Causes of Sex Change

Nonselective fishing over aggregations of a protogynous grouper should influence the population's reproductive output in a manner dependent upon the cause of sex change. If sex change is developmentally induced, the addition of nonselective fishing mortality in the short term, i.e., over a period of months, will not alter the size structure or sex ratio of the population. In the long term, however, if the population is allowed to reach equilibrium, the size structure of the population will be altered, with a reduced proportion of large individuals. If fish change sex upon reaching a predetermined age or size, the result will be a higher female-to-male sex ratio in the population.

However, if sex change is controlled behaviorally, as it is in other protogynous fishes (reviewed by Shapiro In press), then nonselective fishing may only result in the loss of females. For example, if removal of a male stimulates a female to change sex, then catching one male and five females (assuming an aggregation sex ratio of five females per male) effectively removes six females and no male because the male is replaced by sex reversal of a remaining female. In this case, nonselective fishing may add, in effect, a highly selective fishing mortality and the population at equilibrium may respond differently from the case with developmental induction of sex change.

Females are induced to change sex, in all protogynous species for which there are data, including nongrouper serranids, by loss of a male from the social system or by alterations in behavioral interactions between the sexes (Fishelson 1970; Robertson 1972; Shapiro 1983; reviewed by

Shapiro In press). There is no direct evidence to suggest that females change sex upon attaining a particular size, age, or stage of development (Shapiro 1984).

Much of the literature on population structure in groupers contains bimodal size- or age-frequency distributions in which there are no or few males in small size (age) ranges and in which the proportion of males increases with size or age (e.g., Bruslé and Bruslé 1976a; Waltz et al. 1979; Thompson and Munro 1983). While this feature of population structure may suggest that sex reversal is triggered developmentally by attaining a particular size or age, in fact there are many possible causes for such a size (age) structure that are completely unrelated to protogyny (Sadovy and Shapiro In press). Furthermore, an identical population structure can be generated for species in which sex change is initiated behaviorally (Shapiro and Lubbock 1980). Thus, bimodal size- or age-frequency distributions constitute good evidence neither for protogyny nor for developmental induction of sex change. Unfortunately, no studies have yet been successfully completed testing whether sex change can be induced behaviorally in groupers.

Nature of Grouper Social Systems

Description of grouper social systems is important for at least two reasons. Firstly, the nature of the social system should be known to design realistic experiments on the proximal causes of sex change. Secondly, if, at the time spawning aggregations form, individual fish leave their usual social unit, travel to the aggregation, and subsequently return "home" and reestablish their prior social unit, heavy fishing on the aggregation will prevent or impede reestablishment of the social unit. If significant spawning or sex change occurs within that unit, reproductive yield in the population will be reduced to the extent that the social unit is delayed or prevented from restructuring itself. This effect will be in addition to the general reduction in reproductive yield that aggregation fishing will produce by alteration of overall sex ratio or by reduction of population size. Long delays in replacement of experimentally removed individuals have been reported in Red Sea groupers (Shpigel 1985).

Underwater observations of E. guaza and E. alexandrinus indicated that individuals of both species held poorly defined home ranges that were not defended against conspecifics (Neill 1966-67). Linear home range sizes were estimated as 20-70 m for E. guaza and much larger for E. alexandrinus. Two Red Sea groupers are said to form territorial harems of one male and two to three females in clear, shallow waters along the Sinai Peninsula (Shpigel 1985).

The locations of 20 tagged E. guttatus were plotted in a large grid during daily dives over a 148-day period on a shallow inshore-reef slope in southwest Puerto Rico. Home ranges of these individuals ranged from 70 to 4,707 m^2, with median 814 (Shapiro et al. Unpub.). The body size of a fish did not correlate significantly with its home range size. The home ranges of most fish overlapped heavily with the home ranges of others.

The most striking aspect of this shallow-water E. guttatus social system was that it consisted entirely of females (sex was determined by gonadal histology of tagged individuals). This result was checked by spearing all of the fish observed underwater on two other small, inshore patch reefs. All 46 of these fish were also female. Furthermore, the sex ratio of 323 fish caught by fishermen over similar inshore areas was 35 females per male. It was not likely that these results were the consequence of heavy selective fishing, partly because the study areas were intentionally sited away from heavy fishing zones, and partly because other data suggested that fishing techniques both in inshore areas and over the spawning aggregation sample the underlying population nonselectively. Thus, the entire inshore area seemed to be almost entirely female. These females did not differ in size from females speared or caught on lines from the spawning aggregation, and more than half of them were within the size range of males in the aggregation (Shapiro et al. Unpub.).

As has already been described (see Selectivity of Aggregation Fishing), the E. guttatus spawning aggregation in this area consisted of 4.5 females per male. The aggregation itself appeared to be organized internally into clusters of two to seven fish. Fish from 12 clusters were speared and later sexed. A male was found in each of four clusters, the balance consisting entirely of females (Shapiro et al. Unpub.). These data suggest that clusters may contain one male and several females and that spawning may involve only the male and females within a cluster. This explanation is consistent with previous observations of spawning and nonspawning behavior within red hind aggregations (Colin et al. In press). Nevertheless, no spawning behavior was observed during these aggregations.

Thus, any conclusions about the organization of the mating
system must remain tentative.

Epinephelus guttatus larvae probably settle and
develop in shallow inshore areas, as is known for other
groupers (McErlean 1963; Moe 1969; Burnett-Herkes 1975).
At spawning time, adult females almost certainly migrate
to aggregation sites where they encounter males and spawn.
The predominately female inshore social systems are reminiscent of all-female groups of another serranid, A.
squamipinnis (Shapiro 1984). It is conceivable, in both
cases, that females seldom change sex until they are
physiologically primed to do so by behavioral exposure to
males. Subsequent to such exposure, separation of females
from males might then induce sex change. There is solid
experimental evidence to support this idea for A. squamipinnis (D. Shapiro, Department of Marine Sciences, University of Puerto Rico Unpub. data). If this proves to be
true for E. guttatus, then aggregations would function in
at least three ways: (1) to congregate fish to spawn; (2)
to expose young adult females to males so that they become
capable of sex change; and (3) to allow females the opportunity to assess reproductive opportunities with a view
toward a possible future sex reversal. The third function
is stated in the language of evolutionary biology, i.e.,
in terms of individual strategies and ultimate causation.
This function might be stated also in terms of proximate
causation: During spawning aggregations, females are
exposed to reproductive interactions with males and other
females, such that if cues that trigger sex change are
present, females will be stimulated to change sex.

This postulated life history for E. guttatus involves
the migration of young adult females from inshore areas to
the edge of the insular shelf. Similar migrations are
thought to occur in a number of other groupers, although
little is known of their social systems (Moe 1969;
Burnett-Herkes 1975; Manooch and Haimovici 1978; Waltz et
al. 1979; Low 1981; Thompson and Munro 1983; Moore and
Labisky 1984).

CONCLUSION

Reproduction of groupers is of considerable interest
for many reasons. Restricted spawning periods, especially
in aggregations lasting 1-2 weeks, challenge behavioral
ecologists to harmonize apparently nonseasonal occurrence
of sex change with empirical observations that the only

opportunity for individuals to assess the balance between reproductive advantages and disadvantages of changing sex lies within the short period of spawning. Indeed, neither evolutionary functions for spawning aggregations nor proximate cues directing fish to traditional spawning sites are well understood. Whatever the proximal cause of sex change proves to be, it undoubtedly influences the structure of grouper social systems, at both the evolutionary and proximal levels. Similarly, much remains to be resolved before the effects of intensive fishing on grouper spawning aggregations can be evaluated. Fishery management plans will ultimately be based, in part, on yield models that have been especially designed for protogynous reproductive systems. More information about all aspects of grouper reproduction is needed to obtain applicable solutions from these models.

ACKNOWLEDGMENTS

Work on this paper has been supported variously by grants from the National Oceanic Atmospheric Administration, National Sea Grant College Program Office (NSGCPO), Department of Commerce, Grant UPR–SG R/LR–06–1, by N. I. H. Grant 2S06 RR–08103 and NSF Grant OCE 8410179. I thank R. Appeldoorn, C. Grimes, R. E. Johannes, J. E. Powers, S. Ralston, Y. Sadovy, and R. R. Warner for criticisms of the manuscript.

BIBLIOGRAPHY

Atz, J. W. 1964. Intersexuality in fishes. In C. N. Armstrong and A. J. Marshall (editors), Intersexuality in vertebrates including man, p. 145–232. Academic Press, Lond.

Bannerot, S. P. 1984. The dynamics of exploited groupers (Serranidae): An investigation of the protogynous hermaphroditic reproductive strategy. Ph.D. Dissertation, Univ. Miami, Coral Gables, 393 p.

Bouain, A. 1980. Sexualité et cycle sexuel des Mérous (Poissons, Teleosteèns, Serranidés) des côtes du sud tunisien. Bull. Off. Nature Pêche, Tunis. 4:215–229.

Bouain, A., and Y. Siau. 1983. Observations on the female reproductive cycle and fecundity of three species of groupers (Epinephelus) from the southeast Tunisian seashores. Mar. Biol. (Berl.) 73:211–220.

Bruslé, J., and S. Bruslé. 1976a. Contribution a l'etude de la reproduction de deux espèces de Mérous E. aeneus G. Saint-Hilaire, 1809, et E. guaza (Linne, 1758) des côtes de Tunisie. Rev. Trav. Inst. Pêches Marit. 39:313-320.

_____. 1976b. Contribution a l'étude de la reproduction de deux espèces de Mérous (Epinephelus aeneus et Ep. guaza) des côtes de Tunisie. Rapp. Comm. Int. Mer Mediterr. 23:49-50.

Burnett-Herkes, J. 1975. Contribution to the biology of the red hind, Epinephelus guttatus, a commercially important serranid fish from the tropical western Atlantic. Ph.D. Dissertation, Univ. Miami, Coral Gables, 154 p.

Chan, S. T. H., and W.-S. O. 1981. Environmental and non-genetic mechanisms in sex determination. In C. R. Austin and R. G. Edwards (editors), Mechanisms of sex determination in animals and man, p. 55-112. Academic Press, Lond.

Chan, S. T. H., and W. S. B. Yeung. 1983. Sex control and sex reversal in fish under natural conditions. In W. S. Hoar, D. J. Randall, and E. M. Donaldson (editors), Fish physiology, IXB, Reproduction: Behavior and fertility control, p. 171-222. Academic Press, N.Y.

Charnov, E. L. 1982. The theory of sex allocation. Princeton Univ. Press, Princeton, N.J., 335 p.

_____. 1984. Behavioural ecology of plants. In J. R. Krebs and N. B. Davies (editors), Behavioural ecology, p. 362-379. Sinauer Assoc., Sunderland, Massachusetts.

Chen, C.-P., H.-L Hsieh, and K.-H. Chang. 1980. Some aspects of the sex change and reproductive biology of the grouper, Epinephelus diacanthus (Cuvier et Valenciennes). Bull. Inst. Zool., Acad. Sin. (Taipei) 19:11-17.

Chen, F. Y., M. Chow, T. M. Chao, and R. Lim. 1977. Artificial spawning and larval rearing of the grouper, Epinephelus tauvina (Forskål) in Singapore. Singapore J. Primary Ind. 5:1-21.

Colin, P. L. 1982. Aspects of the spawning of western Atlantic reef fishes. In G. R. Huntsman, W. R. Nicholson, and W. W. Fox, Jr. (editors), The biological bases for reef fishery management, p. 69-78. U.S. Dep. Commer., NOAA Tech. Memo. NMFS, NOAA-TM-NMFS-SEFC-80.

Colin, P. L., D. Weiler, and D. Y. Shapiro. In press. Aspects of the reproduction of two species of groupers, Epinephelus guttatus and E. striatus in the West Indies. Bull. Mar. Sci.

Fishelson, L. 1970. Protogynous sex reversal in the fish Anthias squamipinnis (Teleostei, Anthiidae) regulated by the presence or absence of a male fish. Nature (Lond.) 227:90-91.

Fox, W. W., Jr. 1972. Dynamics of exploited pandalid shrimps and an evaluation of management models. Ph.D. Dissertation, Univ. Wash., Seattle, 194 p.

Ghiselin, M. T. 1969. The evolution of hermaphroditism among animals. Q. Rev. Biol. 44:189-208.

Grimes, C. B. 1986. Reproductive biology of the Lutjanidae: A review. In J. J. Polovina and S. Ralston (editors), Tropical snappers and groupers: Biology and fisheries management. Westview Press, Inc., Boulder. [See this volume.]

Guitart, D., and F. Juarez. 1966. Desarrollo embrionario y primeros estudios larvales de la cherna criolla, Epinephelus striatus (Bloch) (Perciformes: Serranidae). Acad. Cienc. Cuba, Estudios Inst. Oceanol. Havana 1:35-45.

Johannes, R. E. 1978. Reproductive strategies of coastal marine fishes in the tropics. Environ. Biol. Fishes 3:741-760.

_____. 1981. Words of the lagoon: Fishing and marine lore in the Palau District of Micronesia. Univ. Calif. Press, Berkeley, 245 p.

Lavenda, N. 1949. Sexual differences and normal protogynous hermaphroditism in the Atlantic sea bass Centropristes striatus. Copeia 1949:185-194.

Lee, A. S. 1974. Hábitos alimentarios de la cherna criolla Epinephelus striatus Bloch y algunos datos sobre su biología. Ser. Oceanol., Acad. Cienc. Cuba, 25:3-14.

Loubens, G. 1980. Biologie de quelques espèces de poissons du lagon Néo-Calédonien. II. Sexualité et reproduction. Cah. l'Indo-Pac. 2(1):41-72.

Low, R. A., Jr. 1981. Mortality rates and management strategies for black sea bass off the southeast coast of the United States. N. Am. J. Fish. Manage. 1:93-103.

Manooch, C. S., III, and M. Haimovici. 1978. Age and growth of the gag, Mycteroperca microlepis, and size-age composition of the recreational catch off the southeastern United States. Trans. Am. Fish. Soc. 107:234-240.

Matheson, R. H., III, G. R. Huntsman, and C. S. Manooch, III. 1984. Age, growth, mortality, foods and reproduction of the scamp, *Mycteroperca phenax*, collected off North Carolina and South Carolina. Second Southeast Stock Assessment Workshop, June 4-8, 1984, Miami. Southeast Fish. Cent., Natl. Mar. Fish. Serv., NOAA, SAW/84/RFR/8, 38 p.

McErlean, A. J. 1963. A study of the age and growth of the gag, *Mycteroperca microlepis* Goode and Bean (Pisces: Serranidae) on the west coast of Florida. Fla. Board Conserv., Mar. Res. Lab. Tech. Ser. 41:1-29.

McErlean, A. J., and C. L. Smith. 1964. The age of sexual succession in the protogynous hermaphrodite, *Mycteroperca microlepis*. Trans. Am. Fish. Soc. 93:301-302.

Mercer, L. P. 1978. The reproductive biology and population dynamics of black sea bass, *Centropristis striata*. Ph.D. Dissertation, Coll. William Mary, Williamsburg, 196 p.

Moe, M. A., Jr. 1969. Biology of the red grouper *Epinephelus morio* (Valenciennes) from the eastern Gulf of Mexico. Fla. Dep. Nat. Resour., Mar. Res. Lab. Prof. Pap. Ser. 10:1-95.

Moore, C. M., and R. F. Labisky. 1984. Population parameters of a relatively unexploited stock of snowy grouper in the lower Florida Keys. Trans. Am. Fish. Soc. 113:322-329.

Munro, J. L., V. C. Gaut, R. Thompson, and P. H. Reeson. 1973. The spawning seasons of Caribbean reef fishes. J. Fish Biol. 5:69-84.

Nagelkerken, W. P. 1979. Biology of the graysby, *Epinephelus cruentatus*, of the coral reef of Curacao. Stud. Fauna Curacao Other Caribb. Isl. 60:1-118.

_____. 1981. Distribution and ecology of the groupers (Serranidae) and snappers (Lutjanidae) of the Netherlands Antilles. Publ. Found. Sci. Res. Surinam Neth. Antilles 107:1-71.

Neill, S. R., St. J. 1966-67. Observations on the behaviour of the grouper species *Epinephelus guaza* and *E. alexandrinus* (Serranidae). Underwater Assoc. Rep. 101-106.

Olsen, D. A., and J. A. LaPlace. 1978. A study of a Virgin Islands grouper fishery based on a breeding aggregation. Proc. 31st Gulf Caribb. Fish. Inst., p. 130-144.

Policansky, D. 1982. Sex change in animals and plants. Annu. Rev. Ecol. Syst. 13:471-495.

Randall, J. E., and A. Ben-Tuvia. 1983. A review of the groupers (Pisces: Serranidae: Epinephelinae) of the Red Sea, with description of a new species of Cephalopholis. Bull. Mar. Sci. 33:373-426.

Randall, J. E., and V. E. Brock. 1960. Observations on the ecology of epinepheline and lutjanid fishes of the Society Islands, with emphasis on food habits. Trans. Am. Fish. Soc. 89:9-16.

Reinboth, R. 1970. Intersexuality in fishes. Mem. Soc. Endocrinol. 18:515-543.

Robertson, D. R. 1972. Social control of sex-reversal in a coral reef fish. Science 177:1007-1009.

Robertson, D. R., and G. Justines. 1982. Protogynous hermaphroditism and gonochorism in four Caribbean reef gobies. Environ. Biol. Fishes 7:137-142.

Robins, C. R., R. M. Bailey, C. E. Bond, J. R. Brooker, E. A. Lachner, R. N. Lea, and W. B. Scott. 1980. A list of common and scientific names of fishes from the United States and Canada. Am. Fish. Soc. Spec. Publ. 12:1-174.

Sadovy, Y., and D. Y. Shapiro. In press. Criteria for the diagnosis of hermaphroditism in fishes. Copeia.

Shapiro, D. Y. 1981a. Size, maturation and the social control of sex reversal in the coral reef fish Anthias squamipinnis (Peters). J. Zool. (Lond.) 193:105-128.

_____. 1981b. The sequence of coloration changes during sex reversal in the tropical marine fish Anthias squamipinnis (Peters). Bull. Mar. Sci. 31:383-398.

_____. 1981c. Behavioural changes of protogynous sex reversal in a coral reef fish in the laboratory. Anim. Behav. 29:1185-1198.

_____. 1983. Distinguishing direct behavioral interactons from visual cues as causes of adult sex change in a coral reef fish. Hormones Behav. 17:424-433.

_____. 1984. Sex reversal and sociodemographic processes in coral reef fishes. In G. W. Potts and R. J. Wotton (editors), Fish reproduction: Strategies and tactics, p. 103-118. Academic Press, Lond.

_____. In press. Sexual differentiation, social behavior and sex reversal in coral reef fishes. Bioscience.

Shapiro, D. Y., and R. Lubbock. 1980. Group sex ratio and sex reversal. J. Theor. Biol. 82:411-426.

Shpigel, M. 1985. Aspects of the biology and ecology of Red Sea grouper Cephalopholis (Serranidae, Teleostei). Ph.D. Dissertation, Tel-Aviv Univ., Tel-Aviv, Israel.

Smith, C. L. 1959. Hermaphroditism in some serranid fishes from Bermuda. Pap. Mich. Acad. Sci. Arts Lett. 44:111-118.

_____. 1965. The patterns of sexuality and classification of serranid fishes. Am. Mus. Novit. 2207:1-20.

_____. 1971. A revision of the American groupers: Epinephelus and allied genera. Bull. Am. Mus. Nat. Hist. 146:67-242.

_____. 1972. A spawning aggregation of Nassau grouper, Epinephelus striatus (Bloch). Trans. Am. Fish. Soc. 101:257-261.

_____. 1975. The evolution of hermaphroditism in fishes. In R. Reinboth (editor), Intersexuality in the animal kingdom, p. 295-310. Springer Verlag, Berl.

_____. 1982. Patterns of reproduction in coral reef fishes. In G. R. Huntsman, W. R. Nicholson, and W. W. Fox, Jr. (editors), The biological bases for reef fishery management, p. 49-66. U.S. Dep. Commer., NOAA Tech. Memo. NMFS, NOAA-TM-NMFS-SEFC-80.

Smith, C. L., and D. S. Erdman. 1973. Reproductive anatomy and color pattern of Bullicichthys caribbaeus (Pisces: Serranidae). Copeia 1973:149-151.

Takahashi, H. 1977. Juvenile hermaproditism in the zebrafish, Brachydanio rerio. Bull. Fac. Fish., Hokkaido Univ. 28:57-65.

Takahashi, H., and M. Shimizu. 1983. Juvenile intersexuality in a cyprinid fish, the Sumatra barb, Barbus tetrazona tetrazona. Bull. Fac. Fish., Hokkaido Univ. 34:69-78.

Thompson, R., and J. L. Munro. 1978. Aspects of the biology and ecology of Caribbean reef fishes: Serranidae (hinds and groupers). J. Fish Biol. 12:115-146.

_____. 1983. The biology, ecology, and bionomics of the hinds and groupers, Serranidae. In J. L. Munro (editor), Caribbean coral reef fishery resources, p. 59-81. ICLARM Stud. Rev. 7, Manila.

Thresher, R. E. 1984. Reproduction in reef fishes. T.F.H. Publications, Neptune City, N.J. 399 p.

Ukawa, M., M. Higuchi, and S. Mito. 1966. Spawning habits and early life history of a serranid fish, Epinephelus akaara (Temminck et Schlegel). Jpn. J. Ichthyol. 13:156-161.

Waltz, W., W. A. Roumillat, and P. K. Ashe. 1979. Distribution, age structure and sex composition of the black sea bass, Centropristes striata, sampled along the southeastern coast of the United States. South Carolina Mar. Resour. Cent. Tech. Rep. 43:1-18.

Warner, R. R. 1975. The adaptive significance of sequential hermaphroditism in animals. Am. Nat. 109:61-82.

7
Age and Growth of Snappers and Groupers

Charles S. Manooch, III
Southeast Fisheries Center Beaufort Laboratory
National Marine Fisheries Service, NOAA
Beaufort, North Carolina 28516-9722

ABSTRACT

Literature on the age and growth of lutjanids and serranids is reviewed. Analysis of rings formed on calcareous structures is the most frequently used method over length-frequency analysis or tag-recapture for determining the age and growth of tropical snappers and groupers. Worldwide studies indicate that these two groups of fish are long lived, slow growing, and have relatively low rates of natural mortality. Maximum ages generally exceed 10 years, and growth coefficients usually fall within a range of 0.10-0.25 per year. Discussions are presented on familial shared growth characteristics and on future research needs.

INTRODUCTION

Age and growth are of primary interest in fisheries research and yet the most basic analytical and laboratory procedures employed during study have seldom been standardized (but see van Oosten 1929). What may pass as simple differences in aging technique can lead to entirely different conclusions (Boehlert 1985). Moreover, rigorous attention to detail is essential in situations where the ultimate goal is to insure a level of accuracy that is sufficient to make important management decisions with confidence (Beamish 1979a, 1979b).

These concerns are particularly true of studies pertaining to tropical reef fishes. Biological and environmental conditions combine to make age and growth

determinations of tropical fishes difficult. Fishes like
the groupers (Serranidae) and snappers (Lutjanidae) share
biological characteristics such as extended reproductive
cycles and weakly expressed seasonality of growth, which
make age and growth rate determinations difficult at best.
Experience gained from research on temperate fishes,
however, can often be applied to tropical situations
although we must expect challenges in interpreting marks
in calcareous structures and in attempting to understand
the population dynamics of reef stocks. Obtaining large,
representative samples from fisheries that are typically
small or artisanal is a problem frequently encountered.

In general, age and growth data can be obtained using
one or more of the following three basic methods:

1. Counting regularly formed marks on hard parts
   such as scales, otoliths, vertebrae, spines, and
   urohyal bones. This approach is often referred
   to as the anatomical method.
2. Obtaining direct measurements of growth increment
   from specific individuals and extrapolating the
   data to the population as a whole. This may be
   accomplished by marking or tagging fish and later
   recapturing them, or by documenting the growth of
   fish of known age that have been held in
   captivity.
3. Measuring the modal progression of fish size
   classes, either statically or over some time
   interval. This method is referred to as length-
   frequency analysis.

All three approaches have been used to age tropical
fishes, yet each has its peculiar weaknesses. A major
problem with aging reef fish by counting regularly formed
marks on hard structures is due to uniform water temperatures in areas where these fish are collected. Large
variation in growth rate is not expected in the tropics,
at least not based on seasonal temperature fluctuations.
Nonetheless, bony structures in many tropical species
reveal an abundance of markings; discerning what they mean
is a challenge (Pannella 1980). Although tropical fishes
are more difficult to age anatomically than are temperate
species, many have been aged by this method. Scientists,
unable to explain the occurrence of periodic markings
based on fluctuating water temperature alone, are now
beginning to study less obvious genetic, physiological,
and environmental phenomena that may produce change in the
pattern of growth. Moreover, the study of daily growth

increments has provided a great new impetus to this type
of analysis (Campana and Neilson 1985).

The second method, obtaining direct measurements of
growth through marking, also has associated weaknesses.
Tagged and recaptured fish may reveal no growth or even
negative growth. This can result from injury or illness
to the fish that is a direct result of handling and
tagging. Error in measurements taken by fishermen at the
time of recapture is also often a problem. Furthermore,
the growth rate of most fish under confined conditions is
difficult to relate to that of natural populations.

Probably the most unreliable and yet widely used
method of aging tropical species is length-frequency
analysis (Schnute and Fournier 1980; Pauly and Ingles
1981). The analysis of length-frequency data from tropical systems is difficult because recruitment is usually
protracted, many species are slow growing and long lived,
and samples are often obtained on an irregular basis.
Interpretation of size structure is made difficult by
incomplete data and large overlap of adjacent age classes.
These problems often lead to unreliable or compromised
estimates of growth rate.

Nonetheless, scientists have successfully studied the
age and growth of reef fishes, including important species
of snapper and grouper, even when confronted with difficulties of sampling and interpretation of data. Following
is a three-part review of many of those studies, including: (1) methods and validation; (2) a review of general
results; and (3) new techniques with suggestions on
possible research needs for the future.

REVIEW OF METHODS AND VALIDATION

Calcareous Structures

Determination of age using regularly formed marks on
bony structures is clearly the preferred method of aging
tropical fishes. The only disadvantage of this technique
is that extreme care and extensive study are required to
establish the validity of marks providing a true indication of elapsed time. Scales, otoliths, spines, vertebrae, and hypural bones have all been used. The basic
assumption of this approach is that periodic (daily,
seasonal, annual) changes in growth rate are reflected in
these structures: i.e., circuli spacings are evident on

scales, and hyaline-opaque zone composition and spacings are observable on bones and otoliths.

Scales have been sometimes used to age tropical fish. They are easy to collect and prepare, a typical method being to remove 4 to 10 scales from beneath the tip of the posteriorly extended pectoral fin, soak them in a one-tenth aqueous solution of phenol to inhibit bacterial growth, and mount them dry between two glass slides. They are then viewed with a dissecting microscope or a scale projector and are measured in the anterior field along a line from the focus to the margin and also to each ring. However, of all the calcareous structures, scales are generally the least legible. They have seldom been used to age lutjanids and serranids.

In contrast, whole and sectioned otoliths have often been used to determine the age and growth of fishes from these two groups. Often ear stones, generally sagittae, are removed by splitting the cranium with a saw, thus exposing the structures. Alternatively, the skull can be entered from under the operculum by opening the otic bulla. The latter technique is usually done with a wood chisel and avoids disfiguring fish that are to be sold. Otoliths are best cleaned and stored dry in labeled vials or coin envelopes.

Whole otoliths immersed in clove oil or glycerine in a black-bottom watch glass are viewed with the aid of reflected light under a dissecting microscope. Measurements are typically made with an ocular micrometer from the otolith core to each ring and to the otolith margin. The optimum field (line) for measurement varies between species, however.

To determine the best plane for sectioning, otolith samples representing the full size range of fish collected should be examined microscopically to identify the area where rings are most legible and erosion of the otolith margin is minimal. Whole otoliths are then aligned and mounted to prevent movement, and sectioned with a low speed saw. Several thin sections are read and measured in the same manner described above for whole otoliths. If back-calculations to size at age are to be performed, great care must be taken to insure that all sections are made in the same plane.

Vertebral centra may be used to reveal the age of tropical fishes and to determine growth. Several vertebrae (usually the 13th and 15th) are dissected from the fish, cleaned by soaking in 7% sodium hypochlorite or 3% potassium hydroxide solution, and then dried and stained with 0.01% crystal violet solution. After drying, the stained vertebrae are cut in half along the lateral plane with a saw. The centrum depth and the distance from the centrum to each ring or ridge are measured with the aid of a dissecting microscope. Hypurals and other bones may be prepared and read in the same manner. The fact that vertebrae, hypurals, and skull bones are difficult to prepare often precludes their use in aging reef fish when alternative methods are available.

Dorsal spines have been used for aging species with very small otoliths and deeply embedded scales such as the triggerfishes (Balistidae). Usually, the first 5 mm of a spine shaft above the condyle are removed and serially sectioned. Sections are examined with a dissecting microscope illuminated by either transmitted or reflected light. Measurements along the spine radius and from the center of the spine to each ring are recorded.

The anatomical method has several advantages over other methods. First, it is not as dependent upon large-scale, representative sampling as are other techniques. Second, the scientist is able to retrieve historical data from the growth records of individuals through the process of back-calculation. Growth studies may then be extended into periods when environmental and population conditions were different from the present. This asset has been particularly useful in studying population trends with respect to different levels of fishing pressure. Third, it offers a simple way of aging individual fish, thus providing information on conspecific growth variation as well as establishing population growth parameters.

Validation

Aging tropical fish by calcareous structures is not an easy task. Marks referred to as false annuli or accessory checks often are found on hard parts, and these must be distinguished from marks that are formed at regular intervals. Also, some scales, otoliths, and bones are more legible than are others. Regardless of the structures used, it is extremely important to validate the periodicity of the marks. If rings are considered annuli, for example, they must be shown to form only once each year.

Validation of aging techniques has been important for many years. The early works of Graham (1929) and van Oosten (1929) outlined certain procedures for validating age marks, and these have since been enlarged upon. A revised list and brief discussion of the criteria used in validation studies follow. The first three criteria are perhaps the most widely used.

1. Marginal increment analysis involves determining the period and time of mark formation. This is accomplished by calculating the mean distance from the last ring to the edge of the structure (scale, otolith, bone) by time interval (usually months). A unimodal distribution results if one ring per annum is formed. Smaller (younger) fish are most often used in this analysis, since rings are more distinct and measurements more precise.

2. Compare ages obtained by examining different structures from the same fish, e.g., otoliths versus vertebrae. Since two different hard parts frequently are not available from the same fish, the researcher may calculate ages using two or more structures from the overall sample of fish.

3. Plot frequency distributions of focus-to-ring distances for different age groups. This analysis should reveal the occurrence of one mode for each ring and a consistent location of a specific mode on the x-axis for fish of different ages. Plotting focus-to-ring frequency distributions generally works well for about the first 10 age groups. Excessive overlap obscures the modes thereafter.

4. Compare length-age data obtained from laboratory studies with growth rate derived from tag-recapture data, or with growth rate data from fish confined in captivity.

5. Analyze length-frequency distributions of stationary population samples (i.e., Peterson method).

6. Perform modal progression analysis of a time series of several population samples.

7. Establish the proportionality between the growth of the whole fish and the increase in size of the aging structure. Once a relationship is derived, use measurements to previously formed marks to back-calculate growth history. A back-calculated growth curve should approximate that obtained from fish at the time of capture. Comparing theoretical growth curves with observed and back-calculated ones is also useful.

8. Have two or more examiners age the same fish and compare the results.
9. Implement criterion 4 by using chemicals such as calcium (Irie 1960), lead (Ichikawa and Hiyama 1954), or tetracycline (Weber and Ridgway 1967; Jones and Bedford 1968; Wild and Foreman 1980; Ralston and Miyamoto 1983; Hettler 1984). Compare the number of growth marks between the chemical label and the otolith margin to the amount of time elapsed.
10. Correlate ring formation with endogenous and exogenous cycles such as temperature, salinity, reproductive activity, rainfall, and feeding intensity. This step will help establish some biological basis for the formation of marks.

Estimating Growth with Calcareous Structures

Having selected a suitable aging structure, validated the aging technique, and counted time markers, the researcher typically calculates size- or age-specific growth rates. Generally, annual growth is referred to in three ways: observed, back-calculated, and theoretical. Observed growth is the difference in mean size at the date of capture of an age group relative to the mean size of the next largest group. Back-calculated growth is the difference in mean size of fish at the time of annulus formation relative to the mean size at the formation of the next annulus. Back-calculated size at age data are used to calculate theoretical growth.

To obtain back-calculated length at a specified age, one first determines the relationship between fish length and the radius of the aging structures by plotting fish length against, for example, otolith radius. Care should be taken to subsample fish size intervals more or less equally. The model regression equation should either be linear ($L = a+b(R)$, where L = fish length, R = radius of the aging structure, a = intercept, and b = slope) or the linearized form of the power function ($\log L = a+b(\log R)$). To back-calculate length at age, the means of the distances from the focus to each annulus are substituted for R in one of the above equations and the mean fish lengths at the time each annulus forms are calculated. Average growth increments between successive age groups are obtained by subtraction.

Theoretical growth models include parameters such as maximum attainable size (L_∞) and growth coefficient (K), which are used to specify a population growth model. The most frequently used theoretical growth curve is the von Bertalanffy equation:

$$\ell_t = L_\infty (1-e^{-K(t-t_0)}),$$

where ℓ_t = length at age t (usually in years) and t_0 = theoretical origin of the growth curve. The curve should be fitted to back-calculated lengths (Everhart et al. 1975; Ricker 1975). The growth parameter, L_∞, may be derived by fitting a Walford (1946) line:

$$\ell_{t+1} = L_\infty(1-k) + k\ell_t$$

to back-calculated data, where ℓ_t = length at age t and k = slope of the Walford line. An initial equation:

$$\ell_{t+1} = a+k\ell_t$$

is developed. The slope (k) is equal to e^{-K}, thus K = $-\ln(k)$.

Computers greatly facilitate estimating growth curve parameters. The SAS PROC NLIN (SAS Institute 1979) and BMDP P3R (Dixon 1977) are computer programs that can be used to fit the von Bertalanffy growth curve to length-at-age data. All use modified Gauss-Newton, steepest-descent, or Marquardt methods to regress the residuals on the partial derivatives of the model with respect to the relevant parameters. Iterations converge at the smallest possible error sum of squares. Advantages of these nonlinear curve-fitting procedures are that they are completely reproducible and estimates of the asymptotic variances of the parameter estimates are available for developing confidence intervals. As a statistical refinement, back-calculated lengths from each fish can be used in the regression. This reduces any bias induced by using average lengths at age with unequal sample sizes in the various age classes. Alternatively, weighting procedures are often part of these curve-fitting programs.

Length-Frequency Analysis

This technique is dependent upon large, representative samples from the population. Size structure of the sample, plotted as a length- or weight-frequency distribution, reveals various peaks that are assumed to represent modal lengths (weights) of discrete age classes. Computer programs are available to assist in the discrimination of modes (Mathews 1974; Skillman and Yong 1976; McNew and Summerfelt 1978; Schnute and Fournier 1980; Pauly and Ingles 1981). The utility of this method is largely governed by several conditions or assumptions. Length-frequency analysis works best for fishes that spawn over a relatively short period of time, have short lifespans, and are fast growing. Unfortunately, these biological characteristics are atypical of the lutjanids and serranids. Also, questions of gear selectivity and stock availability require careful consideration. Positive features of length-frequency analysis are that it is relatively inexpensive, requires minimal technical skills, and, under the right conditions, utilizes simple catch statistics as the basis for the age and growth studies. Length-frequency analyses are sometimes used to substantiate results produced by viewing hard parts. It is difficult, however, to compare K values without having complete information on such details as methods used to collect the fish, fish size distribution by depth, and fishing history. Moreover, it does seem that length-frequency analyses often yield unusually high growth coefficients. Recent studies (G. R. Huntsman and A. Chester Pers. com.) have compared length-at-age data and growth parameter estimates for several species of reef fish aged by reading calcareous structures and by length-frequency analysis (NORMSEP). While L_∞ estimates were about the same in both methods, K values were different. An example was the white grunt, Haemulon plumieri. Thirteen age classes were identified by reading otoliths, whereas only eight were identified by modal progression. Thus, L_∞ was approached faster in the latter method, resulting in a higher estimate of K.

Tag-Recapture and Rearing

Tagging has been used for many years to study fish movements, population sizes, exploitation rates, and growth. A variety of marking techniques are used, including fin clipping, attaching either internal or external tags, and labeling hard parts with chemicals. Individual fish are measured at the time of tagging and again upon recapture, thus providing direct information on the inter-

vening rate of growth. Age and growth information
obtained from individuals may be used to characterize
natural populations. The key assumption applied to any
tagging study is that capture, handling, and tagging will
in no way distinguish the tagged fish physically or
physiologically from the rest of the population. Movements, feeding, reproduction, growth, and survival should
be the same with or without the tag. This is an ambitious
assumption and biases frequently influence results. For
example, some tags cause lacerations that may become
infected, some alter natural movements of the fish, some
are more susceptible to fishing gear, and others are
easily shed. Another problem is measurement error,
usually magnified by the fact that many fish will have
relatively short (<1 year) release times. Precise
measurements are then a necessity for obtaining accurate
growth rates. Compounding the problem, recaptured fish
are often measured by persons who did not record the
initial length, with no growth or negative growth
frequently recorded. It is therefore imperative that the
researcher recognize potential sources of bias and
interpret the data accordingly. Several studies
pertaining to the tagging and growth of reef fish are
Randall (1962, 1963); Beaumariage (1969); and Holt and
Arnold (1982).

Growth of individual fish can also be documented when
reared in the laboratory, placed in a constructed enclo-
sure in the field, or introduced into man-made bodies of
water. Fish of known age can be monitored to ascertain
growth rates, specifically, size at age. Calcareous
structures removed from such individuals can be inspected
for growth marks, which can be compared with the known age
of the studied population. Physical effects of handling
and confinement, availability and types of foods, temperature, salinity, light intensity, and different population
levels and pressures are some of the factors that may
influence growth. Growth studies using reared lutjanids
and serranids are especially difficult, however, since
these species are typically slow growing and it is difficult to duplicate the very complex natural habitats of
reef fishes. Most research involved with rearing members
of these two families has concentrated on the young,
investigating the feasibility of mariculture (Teng et al.
1978; Thia-Eng and Teng 1978; Wakeman et al. 1979; Chua
and Teng 1980a, 1982; Mori 1984).

Otolith Microstructure

The study of otolith microstructure for age and growth analyses is relatively new. It has been applied most often for determining the ages and growth rates of young fishes. Since Pannella (1971) revolutionized fish growth research by concluding that certain lamellae of otoliths are formed daily, numerous authors have confirmed the presence of daily growth increments with a variety of methods (Pannella 1974; Brothers et al. 1976; LeGuen 1976; Methot and Kramer 1979; Brothers and McFarland 1981; Wild and Foreman 1980; Tsuji and Aoyama 1982; Warlen 1982; Ralston and Miyamoto 1983). Most studies involved temperate species, but many were tropical forms. Like some of their predecessors, several of these researchers felt that traditional methods of aging by calcareous structures were not applicable to reef fishes.

Research on the mechanisms of formation and occurrence of daily increments has revealed they are likely present in the otoliths of all bony fishes, at least through the juvenile phase. Complete daily growth records in tropical species are usually interpretable for the first 150 to 200 days; thereafter, the characteristics of the otolith and the biology of the subject species dictate the usefulness of daily growth increments for age and growth determination.

The growth units are simple bipartite structures composed of protein-rich and protein-poor layers embedded in calcium carbonate (aragonite) crystals. In temperate fishes, the protein-rich layer is formed at night and is influenced by falling water temperatures (Brothers 1982). For a detailed review of otolith microstructure and factors affecting accretion, see Campana and Nielson (1985).

At least three types of information may be obtained from the study of otolith microstructure. The first is merely a count of rings, a validation of their occurrence, and the determination of age and growth. The second type of information is derived from a detailed examination of each growth unit (i.e., its thickness, chemical content, and subdaily structure). Such information yields additional data on day-to-day growth. The third is obtained by back-calculating length at age, providing a historical growth record that may be compared with environmental and biological conditions (Brothers and MacFarland 1981).

This is particularly useful and is actually unique relative to traditional age and growth studies. This type of research can be used to predict the date and place of spawning, as well as to correlate spawning with water temperature, currents, tides, and phases of the moon. It can also be used to identify life history stages such as the pelagic phase, and residence times in freshwater or estuaries.

REVIEW OF RESULTS

Southeastern United States and Gulf of Mexico

Many of the reef species important to fisheries of this area have been aged, rates of growth have been measured, mortalities have been estimated, and yield-per-recruit models have been developed. Studies on 22 species have been or will soon be completed, including the following: red porgy, Pagrus pagrus (Manooch and Huntsman 1977; Nelson et al. 1985); knobbed porgy, Calamus nodosus (Horvath Unpub.); spottail pinfish, Diplodus holbrooki (Tardif and Manooch Unpub.); white grunt, Haemulon plumieri (Manooch 1977); cottonwick, H. melanurum (Nelson et al. 1985); tomtate, H. aurolineatum (Manooch and Barans 1982); blueline tilefish, Caulolatilus microps (Ross and Huntsman 1982); speckled hind, Ephinephelus drummondhayi (Matheson and Huntsman 1984); snowy grouper, E. niveatus (Matheson and Huntsman 1984); warsaw grouper, E. nigritus (Manooch Unpub. 2); black grouper Mycteroperca bonaci (Manooch Unpub. 1); gag, M. microlepis (Manooch and Haimovici 1978); scamp, M. phenax (Matheson et al. 1984); vermilion snapper, Rhomboplites aurorubens (Grimes 1978); red snapper, Lutjanus campechanus (Nelson and Manooch 1982; Nelson et al. 1985); gray snapper, L. griseus (Manooch and Matheson 1981); mutton snapper, L. analis (Mason and Manooch 1985); lane snapper, L. snyagris (Manooch and Mason 1984); creole-fish, Paranthias furcifer (Nelson et al. 1985); and the yellowtail snapper, Ocyurus chrysurus (Johnson 1983; Manooch and Drennon Unpub.).

Growth characteristics for the lutjanids and serranids are given in Table 7.1. Rings on calcareous structures, validated as annuli, were counted to determine age and growth. Otoliths, read whole or sectioned, were used most frequently, although scales and dorsal spines (singly or in combination with otoliths) were used for

some species. Specimens have typically been obtained from
hook-and-line fisheries, recreational head boats, and commercial handline vessels. Young fish, <2 years old, have
been sampled from a variety of sources: experimental and
commercial trawls, seines, channel nets, and powerplant
intake screens. The young fish were studied to verify the
time of annulus formation and to ascertain the location of
the first annulus on the hard part.

Research indicates that intrinsic biotic factors, in
addition to physical constraints by the environment,
affect populations of reef fish along the southeastern and
Gulf of Mexico coasts of the United States (Huntsman and
Manooch 1978). Reef fish attain maximum size slowly.
Growth coefficients (K) of the von Bertalanffy growth
equation for lutjanids and serranids from this area ranged
from 0.074 to 0.279 per year (Table 7.1). Several aspects
of these aging studies suggest that natural mortality
rates (M) of reef fish are also low (see Ralston 1986).
Maximum ages for many species are great, 10 to 27 years
(Table 7.1), and low K values indicate low natural mortality rates (Beverton and Holt 1959; see Ralston 1986). Data
obtained from the fishery and from basic age and growth
studies were used to develop yield-per-recruit models.

Other regional studies have made significant contributions to the understanding of the life histories of
lutjanids and serranids: Moe (1969) and Melo (1975), red
grouper, E. morio; Starck and Schroeder (1970) and Croker
(1962), gray snapper; Moore and Labisky (1984), snowy
grouper; Schlieder (Unpub.), gag; Godcharles and Bullock
(Unpub.), scamp; Bullock and Godcharles (Unpub.) yellowedge grouper, E. flavolimbatus; Hastings and Bortone
(1980), belted sandfish, Serranus subligarius; Bortone
(1971), sand perch, Diplectrum formosum; Burnett-Herkes
(1975), red hind, E. guttatus; Bradley and Bryan (1975),
Futch and Bruger (1976), Bortone and Hollingsworth (1980),
and Wade (1981), red snapper. Growth parameters, where
estimated, are given in Table 7.1 and were obtained by
aging the fish with calcareous structures. The above
studies, when taken as a whole, indicate that lutjanids
and serranids are slow growing, long lived, and have low
natural mortality rates.

Caribbean

There are more than 330 species of reef fish or reef-
associated species in the Caribbean region: about half are

TABLE 7.1
Estimates of maximum age and von Bertalanffy growth parameters for different
species of serranids and lutjanids (SL = standard length; TL = total length)

Species	Area	Method[a]	Maximum Age (in Yr)	L_∞ (mm)	K (per Yr)	t_0 (Yr)	Source(s)
Serranidae							
Epinephelus areolatus	New Caledonia	O	--	276 SL	0.330	--	Loubens 1980
Epinephelus cruentatus Graysby	Curacao	O	9	415 TL	0.130	-0.940	Nagelkerken 1979
	Jamaica	L	--	340 TL	0.340	--	Thompson and Munro 1974a
Epinephelus drummondhayi Speckled hind	North and South Carolina	O	15	967 TL	0.130	-1.01	Matheson and Huntsman 1984
Epinephelus fasciatus	New Caledonia	O	--	230 SL	0.160	--	Loubens 1980
Epinephelus flavolimbatus Yellowedge grouper	West coast Florida	O	27	800 SL	--	--	Bullock and Godcharles Unpub.
Epinephelus fulvus Coney	Jamaica	L	--	340 TL	0.630	--	Thompson and Munro 1974a
Epinephelus guttatus Red hind	Jamaica	L	--	520 TL	0.240	--	Thompson and Munro 1974a

Species	Locality	T				K	t_0	Reference
	Virgin Is.	T	--	--		0.180	--	Randall 1962
	Bermuda	L,O	17+	420 SL		0.180	-0.440	Burnett-Herkes 1975
Epinephelus hoedti	New Caledonia	O	--	581 SL		0.280	--	Loubens 1980
Epinephelus maculatus	New Caledonia	O	--	402 SL		0.280	--	Loubens 1980
Epinephelus merra	New Caledonia	O	--	179 SL		0.270	--	Loubens 1980
Epinephelus morio Red grouper	West coast Florida	O	25+	672 SL		0.179	0.449	Moe 1969
	Campeche Bank (Mexico)	O	14+	928 TL		0.113	0.091	Melo 1975
Epinephelus nigritus Warsaw grouper	South Atlantic Bight	O	24	1,629 TL		0.137	-0.142	Manooch Unpub.
Epinephelus niveatus Snowy grouper	North and South Carolina	O	17	1,255 TL		0.074	-1.920	Matheson and Huntsman 1984
	Florida Keys	O	27	1,320 TL		0.087	-1.013	Moore and Labisky 1984
Epinephelus rhyncholepis	New Caledonia	O	--	279 SL		0.490	--	Loubens 1980
Epinephelus sexfasciatus Banded grouper	Philippines	E	--	309 SL		0.510	--	Pauly and Ingles 1981

(Continued)

TABLE 7.1 (Cont.)

Species	Area	Method[a]	Maximum Age (in Yr)	L_∞ (mm)	K (per Yr)	t_0 (Yr)	Source(s)
Epinephelus striatus Nassau grouper	Virgin Is.	L,O	16	974 SL	0.183	0.488	Olsen and LaPlace 1978
	Virgin Is.	T	--	900 TL	0.090	--	Randall 1962, 1963
Epinephelus (tauvina?)	New Caledonia	O	--	307 SL	0.290	--	Loubens 1980
Mycteroperca bonaci Black grouper	South Florida	O	14	1,200 TL	0.160	-0.300	Manooch Unpub.
Mycteroperca microlepis Gag	West coast Florida	O	13	--	--	--	McErlean 1963
	North and South Carolina	O	13	1,290 TL	0.122	-1.127	Manooch and Haimovici 1978
	West coast Florida	O	16	1,014 SL	0.156	-1.407	Schlieder Unpub.
Mycteroperca phenax Scamp	West coast Florida	O	17	560 SL 720 TL	0.166	-1.487	Godcharles and Bullock Unpub.
	North and South Carolina	O	21	985 FL	0.092	-2.450	Matheson et al. 1984

Species / Common name	Location						Reference
Mycteroperca venenosa Yellowfin grouper	Jamaica	O	15	860 TL	0.100	--	Thompson and Munro 1974a
	Virgin Is.	T	--	--	0.170	--	Randall 1962, 1963
Paranthias furcifer	Gulf of Mexico	S,O	6+	372 FL	0.220	-0.250	Nelson et al. 1985
Pelectropomus leopardus Coral trout	Australia	E	--	647 TL	0.250	--	Pauly and Ingles 1981
Lutjanidae							
Aprion virescens	New Caledonia	O	--	656 SL	0.310	--	Loubens 1980
Lutjanus amabilis	New Caledonia	O(♂)	--	334 SL	0.260	--	Loubens 1980
	New Caledonia	O(♀)	--	293 SL	0.340	--	Loubens 1980
Lutjanus analis Mutton snapper	Cuba, zone B	O,U	9	880 FL	0.152	--	Claro 1981
	Cuba, zone C	O,U	8	1,178 FL	0.100	--	--
	Cuba	O,U	9	781 FL	0.246	--	Montes Unpub.
	Cuba	O,U	9	801-814 FL	0.120-0.143	--	Pozo 1979
	Cuba	O,U	9	1,178 FL	0.100-0.160	--	Claro 1976

(Continued)

TABLE 7.1 (Cont.)

Species	Area	Method[a]	Maximum Age (in Yr)	L_∞ (mm)	K (per Yr)	t_0 (Yr)	Source(s)
Lutjanus bohar	East coast Florida	O	14	862 TL	0.153	-0.579	Mason and Manooch 1985
	East coast of Africa	S	13	660 TL[b]	0.270[b]	--	Talbot 1960
	New Caledonia	O	--	520 SL	0.110	--	Loubens 1980
Lutjanus campechanus Red snapper	Southeastern United States	S,O	16	975 TL	0.160	0.000	Nelson and Manooch 1982
	Gulf of Mexico	S,O	13	941 TL	0.170	-0.10	Nelson and Manooch 1982
	Gulf of Mexico	O	10	925 TL	0.140	-0.10	Nelson et al. 1985
Lutjanus fulviflamma	New Caledonia	O	--	248 SL	0.300	--	Loubens 1980
Lutjanus griseus Gray snapper	Cuba	O	7	513 FL	0.240	-0.616	Baez Hidalgo et al. 1980
	Cuba	O	9	548 FL	0.228	-1.065	Claro 1983a
	East coast Florida	O	21	890 TL	0.100	-0.316	Manooch and Matheson 1981

Species	Location						Reference
Lutjanus kasmira	New Caledonia	O	--	211 SL	0.380	--	Loubens 1980
Lutjanus malabaricus Saddletail seaperch	Arafura Sea (Australia)	S,V	10	707 SL	0.168	0.418	Edwards 1985
Lutjanus purpureus Red snapper	Brazil	O	18?	977 TL	0.117	0.000	Lima 1965
	Brazil	S	12+	989 TL	0.090	0.000	Menezes and Gesteira 1974
Lutjanus quinquelineatus	New Caledonia	O	--	173 SL	0.370	--	Loubens 1980
Lutjanus sanguineus	Gulf of Tonkin (S. China Sea)	V	11	927 FL	0.142	-0.819	Lai and Liu 1974
	Northern Sunda (S. China Sea)	V	10	965 FL	0.148	-0.670	--
	Arafura Sea (Australia)	V	8	964 FL	0.120	-1.291	Lai and Liu 1979
	North West Shelf (Australia)	V	8	937 FL	0.126	-1.339	--
Lutjanus sebae	East coast of Africa (Gulf of Aden)	S	11	851[c]	0.157[c]	-1.015[c]	Druzhinin and Filatova 1980
Lutjanus synagris Lane snapper	Cuba	O,S,U?	6	475 FL[c]	0.200[c]	-0.500[c]	Claro and Reshetnikov 1981

(Continued)

347

TABLE 7.1 (Cont.)

Species	Area	Method[a]	Maximum Age (in Yr)	L_∞ (mm)	K (per Yr)	t_0 (Yr)	Source(s)
	Cuba	O, S, U?	6	350 FL[c]	0.350[c]	-0.900[c]	Rodriguez Pino 1962
	Trinidad	O(♂)	4	708 TL	0.220	-0.550	Manickchand-Dass Unpub.
		O(♀)	4	603 TL	0.200	-0.680	
	East coast Florida	O	10	501 TL	0.134	-1.490	Manooch and Mason 1984
Lutjanus vitta	New Caledonia	O(♂)	--	282 SL	0.320	--	Loubens 1980
		O(♀)	--	238 SL	0.300	--	--
Ocyurus chrysurus Yellowtail snapper	Cuba	V	8	500 FL[c]	0.150[c]	-0.800[c]	Piedra 1969
	Jamaica	L	--	600 FL	0.250	--	Thompson and Munro 1974b
	Cuba, SW	S,O	6	681 FL	0.159	--	Claro 1983b
	South Florida	O	14	451 FL	0.279	-0.355	Johnson 1983
Pristipomoides filamentosus Hawaiian snapper	Hawaii	O,D	18	780 FL	0.146	-1.670	Ralston and Miyamoto 1983

Pristipomoides multidens Sharp tooth snapper	Timor Sea (Australia)	V,S	14	591 SL	0.219	-0.073	Edwards 1985
Pristipomoides typus Sharp tooth snapper	Timor Sea (Australia)	V,S	11	515 SL	0.254	-0.515	Edwards 1985
Rhomboplites aurorubens Vermillion snapper	North and South Carolina	S,O	10	627 TL	0.198	0.128	Grimes 1978

aD = daily rings, E = ELEFAN I, L = length frequency, O = otoliths, S = scales, T = tag recapture, U = urohyals, V = vertebrae.
bCalculated by Munro (1983) from original data.
cCalculated by the author from original data.

marketed by fishermen. Lutjanids and serranids are included in the 10 families that are most important to these fisheries (Munro 1973). Unlike reef fishes found along the southeastern and Gulf of Mexico coasts of the United States, tropical species in the Caribbean are found almost exclusively on coral reefs and banks. The morphology and zonation of Caribbean reefs are highly variable, although relatively few species of hermatypic corals predominate in the reef communities. Much of the area is characteristically flat; depths seldom exceed 45 m and average about 30 m. At bank edges the depth increases abruptly, sometimes by a vertical drop to depths exceeding 400 m (Munro and Thompson 1973). Most Caribbean reefs are located adjacent to land. However, some of the best fishing sites for snappers and groupers are oceanic banks that occur well offshore, rising abruptly from depths in excess of 500 m to subsurface plateaus ranging from approximately 20 to 40 m in depth.

Caribbean reef fishes are tropical in the truest sense. As such, they have posed both real and imagined problems to biologists who age them. The fact that the environment is characterized by relatively stable water temperatures may lead one to question whether or not growth marks on calcareous structures, produced by alternating periods of accelerated and depressed growth, are typically formed. Some investigators have avoided using hard parts altogether to age Caribbean snappers and groupers, relying instead on length-frequency analysis (Thompson and Munro 1974a, 1974b; Olsen and LaPlace 1978). However, growth parameters (K and L_∞) for lutjanids and serranids obtained from length-frequency analyses often do not compare well with those obtained by other methods for similar species from the southeastern United States. It could be, as Pauly (1981) suggests, that a given species attains a larger asymptotic size (L_∞) and a lower growth coefficient (K) in cooler regions. While this may be true, many fishes aged by calcareous structures have similar growth parameters, whether they occur off Cuba or Jamaica, for example, or off the southeastern United States (Table 7.1). I suspect that much of the disparity between parameter estimates derived from length frequencies and from hard parts is due not so much to latitude as to the methods used to collect the fish, the representativeness of samples, and the interpretation of the data.

There have been a number of studies, published and unpublished, on the age and growth of Caribbean lutjanids and serranids. Some have appeared in journals that are

widely distributed, others in journals that are obscure
outside the region. Following is a list of species with
accompanying references: Nassau grouper, E. striatus
(Randall 1962, 1963; Olsen and LaPlace 1978); graysby, E.
cruentatus (Thompson and Munro 1974a; Nagelkerken 1979);
coney, E. fulva (Thompson and Munro 1974a; Stevenson
1976); red hind, E. guttatus (Randall 1962; Thompson and
Munro 1974a; Stevenson 1976); yellowfin grouper, M.
venenosa (Randall 1962, 1963; Thompson and Munro 1974a);
yellowtail snapper, O. chrysurus (Piedra 1969; Thompson
and Munro 1974b; Claro 1983b; Manooch and Drennon Unpub.);
mutton snapper, Lutjanus analis (Claro 1976, 1981; Pozo
1979; Montes Unpub.); gray snapper, L. griseus (Baez
Hidalgo et al. 1980; Claro 1983a); lane snapper, L.
synagris (Rodriguez Pino 1962; Claro and Reshetnikov 1981;
Manickchand-Dass Unpub.). Available growth parameters are
provided for each species in Table 7.1.

Of the 17 cited studies, 12 used hard parts to age
the fish, 2 used length-frequency analysis and otoliths, 1
used solely length-frequency data, and 2, tag-recapture.
Maximum ages for the species listed range from 6 to 17
years, although most are 8 to 10 years. Generally, the
growth coefficients are low, <0.20 per year. Obvious
exceptions are values that have been obtained by modal
progression or length-frequency analysis. Growth parameters of several species aged from the Caribbean may be
compared with those obtained from studies on the same
species along the southeastern United States. Maximum age
(years), L∞, and K for yellowtail snapper from the Caribbean are 6-17 years, 473-681 mm fork length (FL), and
0.139 to 0.332 per year; and from the southeastern United
States, 14 years, 451 mm FL, and 0.279 per year. The same
parameters for mutton snapper are 8-9 years, 781 to 1,178
mm FL, and 0.100 to 0.246 per year for the Caribbean; and
14 years, 862 mm total length (TL), and 0.153 per year for
the southeastern United States. Gray snapper growth
parameters are 7-9 years, 513-548 mm FL, and 0.228-0.240
per year from the Caribbean compared with 21 years, 890 mm
TL, and 0.100 per year. Finally, lane snapper growth
parameters are 4-6 years, 350 to 475 mm FL and 0.200 to
0.350 per year for Caribbean stocks and 10 years, 501 mm
TL, and 0.134 per year for the southeastern United States.
Thus, fish from cooler regions are typically larger and
generally have lower growth coefficients than those
inhabiting the tropics (Pauly 1981). However, I must
emphasize that most of the studies just cited used fish
that generally were captured in shallow water with fish

traps and trawls, so that a selection bias for smaller (younger) fish may have been in effect. The fish sampled for age and growth studies along the southeastern coast of the United States were collected primarily by hook and line over a wide range of water depths; larger (older) fish were not excluded by this gear. Although generally not as long lived, or as slow growing as reef fish studied off the continental United States, Caribbean lutjanids and serranids still reflect basic growth characteristics common to both familes no matter where they occur in the world.

South America

Age and growth papers from South America are diffi- cult to obtain. Two studies were conducted on lutjanids from Colombia, one by Erhardt (1977) on L. synagris, and the other by Erhardt and Meinel (1977) on L. analis. Both contain some growth data. Other studies have been conducted by Brazilian scientists (Lima 1965; Ivo and Gesteira 1974; Menezes and Gesteira 1974) on the age, growth, and mortality of the red snapper, L. purpureus. This large, commercially important species is long lived, possibly exceeding 18 years in age, and has a slow rate of growth (K = 0.09-0.117 per year) (Table 7.1).

East Coast of Africa

Druzhinin and Filatova (1980) conducted biological studies of eight species of lutjanids (L. duodecimlinea- tus, L. gibbus, L. kasmira, L. lineolatus, L. rivulatus, L. sanguineus, L. sebae, and L. vaigiensis) found in the Gulf of Aden. Snappers are commercially important fishes there and inhabit sand, coralline, and shell bottoms at depths ranging from 19 to 75 m. Using published lengths at ages obtained from reading scales, I was able to derive theoretical growth parameters for one species, L. sebae. This species lives for at least 11 years, attains a maximum length of 851 mm, and has a growth coefficient (K) of 0.157 per year (Table 7.1). Data for the other species were insufficient to calculate von Bertalanffy parameters.

Lutjanus bohar was one of 17 lutjanids studied by Talbot (1960) off Kenya, Tanzania, and Zanzibar along the east coast of Africa. Coral and other types of hard bottom are bathed throughout the year by the north-flowing

East African Coast Current. Fish collected in waters 25 to 65 fathoms deep were aged using scales and otoliths. Although only one in four scales was legible, they proved more useful in aging the species than otoliths. For L. bohar, Munro (1983) was able to estimate L_∞ (660 mm TL) and K (0.270 per year) from Talbot's data, concluding that this species lives at least 13 years.

Methods of validating ages were discussed by Samuel et al. (In press) for three species, including a serranid (E. tauvina) and a lutjanid (L. coccineus) from Kuwaiti waters in the Arabian Gulf. Rings on otoliths were determined to be annuli and were used to estimate maximum ages of 20-25 years for E. tauvina and 40-45 years for L. coccineus.

South China Sea

The red snapper, L. sanguineus, is one of the most important reef fishes in the Taiwanese trawler fishery that operates in the South China Sea off Vietnam, southward to the northern coast of Australia. Lai and Liu (1974) evaluated scales, opercle bones, and vertebrae for aging this species, and vertebrae were deemed most useful. These authors reported that specimens from the Gulf of Tonkin were aged to 11 years, with estimated von Bertalanffy growth parameters for L_∞, K, and t_0 of 927 mm FL, 0.142 per year, and -0.819 year. Fish from the North Sunda Shelf were aged to 10 years, with L_∞ = 965 mm FL, K = 0.148 per year, and t_0 = -0.670 year (Table 7.1).

Australia

There have been several studies pertaining to the age and growth of lutjanids and serranids from Australian waters (Goeden 1974; Lai and Liu 1979; Pauly and Ingles 1981; Edwards 1985). Goeden (1974) tried unsuccessfully to use scales to age the coral trout, Plectropomus leopardus. Aided by length-frequency analysis, he was able to identify five age classes with standard lengths (SL) of 145, 260, 340, 420, and 500 mm, respectively. The largest fish examined was 565 mm SL, indicating that an age >5 years is probably attained by this species.

Growth and natural mortality of exploited coral reef fishes was the subject of a paper by Pauly and Ingles (1981). The paper included length-frequency analysis (by

ELEFAN I microcomputer program) for coral trout collected
on the Great Barrier Reef. Data from this study, cited by
Munro (1983), indicated a K of 0.250 per year and L_∞ of
647 mm TL for P. leopardus (Table 7.1).

Rings on centra of vertebrae were examined by Lai and
Liu (1979) to describe the age and growth of red snapper,
L. sanguineus, collected from the Arafura Sea and North
West Shelf of Australia. Snappers from the Arafura Sea
were aged to 8 years, with von Bertalanffy growth parameter estimates for L_∞, K, and t_0 equal to 964 mm FL,
0.120 per year, and -1.291 years. Specimens obtained from
the North West Shelf were also aged to 8 years, with L_∞ =
937 mm FL, K = 0.126 per year, and t_0 = -1.339 years
(Table 7.1). No difference in growth between the two
geographical areas was found.

Taiwanese trawlers in the Arafura Sea and Japanese
drop line boats fishing the Timor Sea were used to obtain
samples of three lutjanids studied by Edwards (1985).
Lutjanus malabaricus, the saddletail seaperch, was found
to live for at least 10 years, attain a theoretical
maximum size of 707 mm SL, and have a growth coefficient
of 0.168 per year. By comparison, the sharp tooth
snappers, Pristipomoides multidens and P. typus, were
longer lived, 14 years for P. multidens and 11 years for
P. typus, and had higher growth coefficients, 0.219 and
0.254 per year, respectively (Table 7.1). The author
concluded that the relatively slow growth rates of the
three lutjanids favor a low rate of exploitation in the
management of the fishery.

Philippines

Munro (1983) cites a paper by Pauly and Ingles (1981)
that gives estimates of K (0.51 per year) and L_∞ (309 mm
SL) for the serranid, E. sexfasciatus. Length-frequency
analysis (ELEFAN I) was used to obtain the growth
parameters.

New Caledonia

Loubens (1980) conducted extensive research on the
growth of lutjanids and serranids around New Caledonia.
Growth parameters derived from reading otoliths for eight
serranids and seven lutjanids are provided, being also
cited by Munro (1983). The lutjanids were particularly

TABLE 7.2
Growth coefficients and maximum ages for lutjanids studied by geographic area
(data from Table 7.1.)

Area	Growth Coefficient (K)				Maximum Age (Yr)			
	N	Range	$\bar{X}$	σ	N	Range	$\bar{X}$	σ
Southeastern United States and Gulf of Mexico	8	0.10–0.279	0.167	0.054	7	10–21	14.00	3.78
Caribbean	14	0.10–0.35	0.197	0.066	13	4–9	7.23	2.42
Brazil	2	0.09–0.117	0.104	0.019	2	12–18	15.00	4.24
East coast Africa	2	0.157–0.270	0.214	0.080	2	11–13	12.00	1.41
Western Pacific	16	0.110–0.370	0.242	0.094	8	8–14	10.25	1.91
Hawaii	1	--	0.146	--	1	--	18.00	--
Weighted means	43	--	0.203	--	33	--	10.49	--

TABLE 7.3
Growth coefficients and maximum ages for serranids studied by geographic area
(data from Table 7.1.)

Area	Growth Coefficient (K)				Maximum Age (Yr)			
	N	Range	$\bar{X}$	σ	N	Range	$\bar{X}$	σ
Southeastern United States and Gulf of Mexico	13	0.074-0.220	0.140	0.042	15	6-27	17.73	5.96
Caribbean	9	0.09-0.63	0.229	0.168	3	9-16	13.33	3.79
Western Pacific	9	0.16-0.510	0.318	0.113	--	--	--	--
Weighted means	31	--	0.218	--	18	--	17.00	--

long lived. Two species, Lutjanus amabilis and L. bohar, were found to live for more than 30 years, and three, Aprion virescens, L. fulviflamma, and L. quinquelineatus, for more than 20. The range in values for maximum age, L_{∞}, and K were 8–38 years, 173–656 mm SL, and 0.112–0.380 per year for the lutjanids, and 15–26 years, 179–581 mm SL, and 0.158–0.331 per year for the serranids (Table 7.1).

Hawaii

The Hawaiian snapper, P. filamentosus, is a commercial deepwater lutjanid found around the Hawaiian Islands and elsewhere in the Pacific. Ralston and Miyamoto (1981, 1983) used otolith daily growth increments to provide basic growth data. This species was aged to over 18 years, attained a theoretical maximum fork length of 780 mm, and had a growth coefficient of 0.145 per year. Ralston (1985) used a somewhat different approach to study the age and growth of a small deepwater lutjanid, P. auricilla. The basic method was to estimate the average width of daily increments at various positions in the otolith. By recording fish length, otolith size, and subregional growth through time, he was able to follow growth for about 5 years of the fish's life.

Shared Growth Characteristics

Worldwide studies on the age and growth of lutjanids and serranids indicate that these taxa are long lived, slow growing, and have relatively low rates of natural mortality (Table 7.1). Maximum ages generally exceed 10 years, and growth coefficients usually fall within a range of 0.10–0.25 per year (Table 7.1). Observations on lutjanid maximum ages and growth coefficients had mean values of 10.49 years and 0.203 per year, respectively (Table 7.2). Mean maximum ages varied geographically from a low of 7.23 years in the Caribbean to a high of 18.00 years for the Hawaiian Islands, whereas K values ranged from a low of 0.104 per year in Brazil to a high of 0.242 in the western Pacific.

Eighteen maximum age and 31 K observations are listed for the serranids (Table 7.3). Mean values are 17.00 years and 0.218 per year, respectively. Growth coefficients were lowest for the southeastern United States

358

and highest for the western Pacific. Tables 7.2 and 7.3 summarize these findings.

Biologists have often discussed and evaluated the relationships of various growth parameters, especially as they relate to families and other taxa of fishes (Beverton and Holt 1959; Cushing 1968; Pauly 1980). Asymptotic weight ($W\infty$), K, and $L\infty$ have been related to derive constant familial characteristics. Pauly (1980) and Munro and Pauly (1983), for example, used the equations: $P = \log_{10} (KW\infty)$ and $\phi = \log K + 2/3 \log W_\infty$ as taxon-specific indices of growth performance. The calculation of P (or ϕ) may serve as a check to see if a growth estimate lies within an acceptable range. One would expect that an index value calculated for a species would fall within

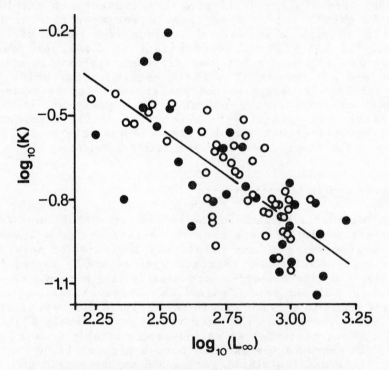

Figure 7.1 Growth performance expressed as the logarithmic relationship between the von Bertalanffy growth coefficient (K per year) and asymptotic length (L_∞, millimeters). Open symbols represent snappers while closed symbols indicate groupers

certain limits established for that family. Munro (1983)
includes an index of growth performance (ϕ) in a table
summarizing growth information on tropical fishes. The
serranids had a mean value of 1.66 (range of 1.35-2.26;
standard deviation (SD) = 0.36), whereas the lutjanids had
a mean value of 1.65 (range of 1.08-2.15; SD = 0.35).

I used the concept of the growth performance index
(Pauly and Munro 1983) to summarize graphically the data
presented in Table 7.1. Values of $\log_{10}(K)$ were regressed
against $\log_{10}(L\infty)$ for all species listed in the table.
The resulting plot (Figure 7.1) is linear with negative
slope. The y-intercept of the regression provides an
index of growth performance (ϕ'). Since the data from
snappers and groupers overlap quite broadly and there is
no statistical basis for separating the two (analysis of
covariance, P = 0.95 for equality of slopes and P = 0.71
on adjusted means), they have been pooled and analyzed
together. Inspection of the data also indicates that the
manner in which $L\infty$ was measured (i.e., TL, FL, or SL) has
no detectable effect on K.

The resulting regression line shown in Figure 7.1 is
given by $\log_{10}(K) = 1.098-0.658 \log_{10}(L\infty)$. Standard error
estimates for the slope and intercept are 0.066 and 0.183,
respectively, while the r^2 value is 0.57. As predicated,
there exists within these groups a clear inverse relationship between the theoretical maximum size ($L\infty$) and the von
Bertalanffy growth coefficient (K).

When the regression of $\log(K)$ on $\log(L_\infty)$ is
restricted to a number of distinct stocks within a
species, the slope should equal -2.0 (Pauly 1980). The
slope derived above for the various species of snapper and
grouper combined is significantly different from this
figure. This indicates the relationship of these growth
parameters alters as the taxonomic level of grouping
changes; however, it is unclear why this should be so.

FUTURE RESEARCH REQUIREMENTS

Future age and growth research on snappers and
groupers may continue successfully with ongoing studies of
species that are important to fisheries. There are
certainly many species for which we have no growth information, and there are geographic areas such as the Pacific
and south Atlantic where more effort is needed. The
techniques available to fishery biologists for estimating
the age and growth of tropical species have rapidly

expanded over the past decade, from the traditional use of calcareous structures to the use of biochemical techniques and instrumentation for analyzing instantaneous growth and growth that takes place on much smaller time frames, e.g., daily, hourly, or monthly.

The analysis of daily growth rings on otoliths has provided us with a means to study growth in the early life history stages. These stages are often the time when the biomass of recruiting cohorts is set. Once determined in the laboratory, daily growth can be evaluated in terms of impacts of environmental variation such as temperature, turbidity, and pollution. Studying daily increments may also prove effective in measuring the influence of reproductive cycles on fish growth. Fish held in the laboratory could have their otoliths labeled chemically, be induced to spawn, and have their daily growth measured before, during, and after spawning. Perhaps one of the most exciting uses of daily growth history is the corre-lation of spawning with environmental factors such as currents, moon phase, tides, and weather fronts. Thus, specific conditions could be evaluated as they relate to reproductive cycles. With an understanding of early growth characteristics, we have the opportunity to docu-ment changes in habitat, for example, pelagic-benthic and estuarine-marine phases.

Biochemical techniques, such as analyses of ^{14}C-labeled glycine uptake by scales (Ottaway and Simkiss 1977, 1979; Ottaway 1978), RNA/DNA, and ADP/ATP ratios (Bulow 1970; Haines 1973, 1980; Buckley 1979) in living tissues, give us the means to examine the instantaneous growth of fishes. This capability may become increasingly useful for monitoring stress and related effects on fishes. These biochemical techniques will probably become more prevalent in studies pertaining to the bioenergetics of fishes as related to food consumption, swimming, preda-tor avoidance, and reproduction. The usefulness of syner-gistic bioenergetic management models for multispecies assemblages of fishes will depend heavily on our ability to elaborate on interspecific relationships (competition, resource overlap, predation) in terms of their effect on the growth of individuals.

The continued development of elegant biochemical techniques at the tissue, and probably eventually the cellular, levels is expected. Integration of micro-processors with high-resolution video equipment will play an increasing role in the analysis of hard parts and growth marks in a more traditional mode. The most important point here, I believe, is that we must rigorously examine the limitations and biases inherent in new techniques and not be overwhelmed by their apparent elegance. No matter what technique is developed, its ultimate utility will be based on our ability to verify results of laboratory analyses in wild, natural populations.

Several concluding suggestions for future research pertaining to growth of tropical fishes are in order. Published studies should state clearly the methods used, the steps taken to validate the aging technique, and the types and units of measure used (i.e., total length, fork length, or standard length; millimeters or centimeters; whole weight or partial weight; grams or kilograms). Finally, researchers should provide as comprehensive a report as possible: age at size for all age groups identified, length-weight relationships, conversion equations for lengths (total, fork, standard), estimates of mortality, and yield equations. This information is vital for management, yet seldom appears in a single publication.

ACKNOWLEDGMENTS

Information from two papers (Brothers 1982; Manooch 1982) published as part of a workshop proceedings on reef fish were used extensively in preparing the introduction and methods sections of this paper. Special appreciation is due C. L. Drennon, who searched the literature and assisted with the preparation of the manuscript, and R. S. Nelson for his suggestions pertaining to future research directions. Both are with the Southeast Fisheries Center Beaufort Laboratory, National Marine Fisheries Service, NOAA.

BIBLIOGRAPHY

Baez Hidalgo, M., L. Alvarez-Lajonchere, and B. Pedrosa Tabio. 1980. Edad y crecimiento del caballerote Lutjanus griseus (Linné), en tunas de Zaza, Cuba. Rev. Invest. Mar. 1(3-5):135-150.

Beamish, R. J. 1979a. Differences in the age of Pacific hake (Merluccius productus) using whole otoliths and sections of otoliths. J. Fish. Res. Board Can. 36:141-151.

_____. 1979b. New information on the longevity of the Pacific ocean perch (Sebastes alutus). J. Fish. Res. Board Can. 36:1395-1400.

Beaumariage, D. S. 1969. Returns from the 1965 Schlitz tagging program including a cumulative analysis of previous results. Fla. Dep. Nat. Resour., Mar. Res. Lab., Tech. Ser. 59.

Beverton, R. J. H., and S. J. Holt. 1957. On the dynamics of exploited fish populations. Fish. Invest. Ser. II, Mar. Fish., G. B. Minist. Agric. Fish. Food 19:1-533

_____. 1959. A review of the lifespans and mortality rates of fish in nature, and their relation to growth and other physiological characteristics. In G. E. Wolstenholme and M. O'Connor (editors), The lifespan of animals, p. 142-177. CIBA Found. Colloq. Aging 5.

Boehlert, G. W. 1985. Using objective criteria and multiple regression models for age determination in fishes. Fish. Bull., U.S. 83:103-117.

Bortone, S. A. 1971. Studies on the biology of the sandperch, Diplectrum formosum (Perciformes: Serranidae). Fla. Dep. Nat. Resour., Mar. Res. Lab., Tech. Ser. 65, 27 p.

Bortone, S. A., and C. L. Hollingsworth. 1980. Ageing red snapper, Lutjanus campechanus, with otoliths, scales, and vertebrae. Northeast Gulf Sci. 4:60-63.

Bradley, E., and C. E. Bryan. 1975. Life history and fishery of the red snapper (Lutjanus campechanus) in the northwestern Gulf of Mexico, 1970-1974. Proc. 22d Gulf Caribb. Fish. Inst., p. 77-106.

Brothers, E. B. 1981. What can otolith microstructure tell us about daily and subdaily events in the early life history of fish? Rapp. P.-V. Reun. Cons. Int. Explor. Mer 178:393-394.

_____. 1982. Aging reef fishes. In G. R. Huntsman, W. R. Nicholson, and W. W. Fox, Jr., (editors), The biological bases for reef fishery management, p. 3-23. U.S. Dep. Commer., NOAA Tech. Memo. NMFS, NOAA-TM-NMFS-SEFC-80.

Brothers, E. B., C. P. Mathews, and R. Lasker. 1976. Daily growth increments in otoliths from larval and adult fishes. Fish. Bull., U.S. 74:1-8.

Brothers, E. B., and W. N. McFarland. 1981. Correlations between otolith microstructure, growth, and life history transitions in newly recruited French grunts

[Haemulon flavolineatum (Desmarest), Haemulidae].
Rapp. P.-V. Reun. Cons. Int. Explor. Mer 178:369-374.
Buckley, L. J. 1979. Relationships between RNA-DNA
ratio, prey density, and growth rate in Atlantic cod
(Gadus morhua) larvae. J. Fish. Res. Board Can.
36:1497-1502.
Bullock, L. H., and M. F. Godcharles. Unpub. Age, growth
and reproduction of the yellowedge grouper, Epinephe-
lus flavolimbatus (Pisces: Serranidae) from the
eastern Gulf of Mexico. Fla. Dep. Nat. Resour., Mar.
Res. Lab., St. Petersburg, FL 33701-5095.
Bulow, F. J. 1970. RNA-DNA ratios as indicators of
recent growth rates of a fish. J. Fish. Res. Board
Can. 27:2343-2349.
Burnett-Herkes, J. 1975. Contribution to the biology of
the red hind, Epinephelus guttatus, a commercially
important serranid fish from the tropical western
Atlantic. Ph.D. Dissertation, Univ. Miami, Coral
Gables, 154 p.
Campana, S. E., and J. D. Neilson. 1985. Microstructure
of fish otoliths. Can. J. Fish. Aquat. Sci. 42:1014-
1032.
Chua, T. E., and S. K. Teng. 1980a. Economic production
of estuary grouper, Epinephelus salmoides Maxwell,
reared in floating net-cages. Aquaculture 20:187-
228.
_____. 1980b. Relative growth and production of the
estuary grouper Epinephelus salmoides under different
stocking densities in floating net-cages. Mar. Biol.
(Berl.) 54:363-372.
_____. 1982. Effects of food ration on growth,
condition factor, food conversion efficiency, and net
yield of estuary grouper, Epinephelus salmoides Maxwell, cultured in floating net-cages. Aquaculture
27:273-283.
Claro, R. 1976. Ecologia y dinámica de algunos indices
biológicos en los lutianidos de Cuba. Tesis. Acad.
Cienc. URSS, Inst. Morfol. Evol. Ecol. Animal.
_____. 1981. Ecología y ciclo de vida del pargo
criollo, Lutjanus analis (Cuvier), en la plataforma
Cubana. Acad. Cienc. Cuba, Inf. Cient.-Tec. 186,
83 p.
_____. 1983a. Ecología y ciclo de vida del
caballerote, Lutjanus griseus (Linnaeus), en la
plataforma Cubana II. Edad y crecimiento, estructura
de las poblaciones y pesquerias. Acad. Cienc. Cuba,
Rep. Invest. Inst. Oceanol. 8, 26 p.

364

_____. 1983b. Ecología y ciclo de vida de la rabirrubia, Ocyurus chrysurus (Bloch), en la plataforma Cubana II. Edad y crecimiento, estructura de poblaciones, y pesquerias. Acad. Cienc. Cuba, Rep. Invest. Inst. Oceanol. 19, 33 p.

Claro, R., and Reshetnikov. 1981. Ecología y ciclo de vida de la biajaiba, Lutjanus synagris (Linnaeus), en la plataforma Cubana. Acad. Cienc. Cuba Ser. Oceanol. 174, 28 p.

Croker, R. A. 1962. Growth and food of the gray snapper, Lutjanus griseus, in Everglades National Park. Trans. Am. Fish. Soc. 91:379–383.

Cushing, D. H. 1968. Fisheries biology, a study in population dynamics. University of Wisconsin Press, Madison, Wis., 200 p.

Dixon, W. J. (editor). 1977. BMD biomedical computer programs, P-series. University of California Press, Los Angeles, 880 p.

Druzhinin, A. D., and N. A. Filatova. 1980. Some data on Lutjanidae from the Gulf of Aden area. J. Ichthyol. 20:8–14.

Edwards, R. R. C. 1985. Growth rates of Lutjanidae (snappers) in tropical Australian waters. J. Fish Biol. 26:1–4.

Erhardt, H. 1977. Beitrage zur biologie von Lutjanus synagris (Linnaeus, 1758) an der Kolumbianishen Atlantikkuste. Zool. Beitr. 23:235–265.

Erhardt, H., and W. Meinel. 1977. Contribution to the biology of Lutjanus analis (Cuvier and Valenciennes, 1818) (Lutjanidae, Perciformes, Pisces) on the Colombia Atlantic coast. Int. Rev. Gesamten Hydrobiol. 62:161–171.

Everhart, W. H., A. W. Eipper, and W. D. Youngs. 1975. Principles of fishery science. Cornell University Press, Ithaca, N.Y., 288 p.

Futch, R. B., and G. E. Bruger. 1976. Age, growth and reproduction of red snapper in Florida waters. In H. R. Bullis, Jr. and A. C. Jones (editors), Proceedings: Colloquium on snapper-grouper fishery resources of the western central Atlantic Ocean, p. 165–184. Texas A&M Univ. Sea Grant Coll. and Mississippi-Alabama Sea Grant Consortium. Fla. Sea Grant Coll. Rep. 17.

Godcharles, M. F., and L. H. Bullock. Unpub. Age, mortality and reproduction of the scamp, Mycteroperca phenax (Pisces: Serranidae). Fla. Dep. Nat. Res. Mar. Res. Lab., St. Petersburg, FL 33701-5095.

Goeden, G. B. 1974. Aspects of the biology and ecology of the coral trout, Plectropomus leopardus (Lacepède) (Serranidae) at Heron Island, Great Barrier Reef. Ph.D. Dissertation, Univ. Queensland, Australia.

Graham, M. 1929. Studies of age determination in fish. Pt. 2. A survey of the literature. Fish. Invest. Ser. II, Mar. Fish. G. B. Minist. Agric. Fish. Food 11:1-50.

Grimes, C. B. 1978. Age, growth, and length-weight relationships of vermilion snapper, Rhomboplites aurorubens from North Carolina and South Carolina waters. Trans. Am. Fish. Soc. 107:454-456.

Haines, T. A. 1973. An evaluation of RNA-DNA ratio as a measure of long term growth in a fish population. J. Fish Res. Board Can. 30:195-199.

_____. 1980. Seasonal patterns of muscle RNA-DNA ratio and growth in black crappie, Pomoxis nigromaculatus. Environ. Biol. Fishes 5:67-70.

Hastings, P. A., and S. A. Bortone. 1980. Observations on the life history of the belted sandfish, Serranus subligarius (Serranidae). Environ. Biol. Fishes 5:365-374.

Hettler, W. F. 1984. Marking otoliths by immersion of marine fish larvae in tetracycline. Trans. Am. Fish. Soc. 113:370-373.

Holt, S. A., and C. R. Arnold. 1982. Growth of juvenile red snapper, Lutjanus campechanus, in the northwestern Gulf of Mexico. Fish. Bull., U.S. 80:644-648.

Horvath, M. L. Unpub. Age, growth, and mortality of the knobbed porgy, Calamus nodosus, of the South Atlantic Bight, with notes on reproduction and possible gear selectivity of the recreational fishery. Cooke College, Rutgers Univ., New Brunswick, NJ 07102.

Huntsman, G. R., and C. S. Manooch, III. 1978. Coastal pelagic and reef fishes in the South Atlantic Bight. In H. Clepper (editor), Marine recreational fisheries 3, p. 97-106. Sport Fish. Inst., Wash., D.C.

_____. 1980. Minimum size limits for reef fishes. Proc. Ann. Conf. Southeastern Assoc. Fish Wildl. Agencies 32:509-513.

Huntsman, G. R., C. S. Manooch, III, and C. B. Grimes. 1983. Yield per recruit models of some reef fishes of the U.S. South Atlantic Bight. Fish. Bull., U.S. 81:679-696.

Ichikawa, R., and Y. Hiyama. 1954. Scale growth rate of the common goby assured by the lead-acetate injection method. Jpn. J. Ichthyol. 3:49-52.

Irie, T. 1960. The growth of the fish otolith. J. Fac. Fish., Anim. Husb., Hiroshima Univ. 3:203-229.

Ivo, C. T. C., and T. C. V. Gesteira. 1974. Estimacão preliminar das medidas de mortalidade do pargo, Lutjanus purpureus Poey, no norte e nordeste Brasileiros. Arq. Cienc. Mar 14:123-127.

Johnson, A. G. 1983. Age and growth of yellowtail snapper from South Florida. Trans. Am. Fish. Soc. 112:173-177.

Jones, B. W., and B. C. Bedford. 1968. Tetracycline labeling as an aid to interpretation of otolith structures in age determination—a progress report. Int. Counc. Explor. Sea, Com. Memo 1968/Gen, 11 p.

Jones, R. 1976. Growth of fishes. In D. K. Cushing and J. J. Walsh (editors), The ecology of the seas, p. 251-279. W. B. Saunders Co., Philadelphia, Pennsylvania.

Lai, H.-L., and H.-C. Liu. 1974. Age determination and growth of Lutjanus sanguineus (C and V) in the South China Sea. J. Fish. Soc. Taiwan 3:39-57.

_____. 1979. Age and growth of Lutjanus sanguineus in the Arafura Sea and North West Shelf. Acta Oceanogr. Taiwanica, Sci. Rep. Natl. Taiwan Univ. 10:164-175.

LeGuen, J. C. 1976. Utilization des otolithes pour la lecture de l'age de Sciaenides intertropicaux marques saisonnieres et journalieres. Cah. ORSTOM, Ser. Oceanogr. 14:331-338.

Lima, F. R. 1965. Crescimento do "pargo" (Lutjanus aya, Block, 1795): Aspectos quantativos. Bol. Estud. Pesca 5:33-42.

Loubens, G. 1980. Biologie de quelques espèces de poisson du lagon Néo-Calédonien III. Croissance. Cah. Indo-Pac. 2:101-153.

Manickchand-Dass, S. Unpub. Reproduction, age, and growth of the lane snapper, Lutjanus synagris (Linnaeus) in Trinidad, West Indies. Internal Rep., Inst. Mar. Affairs, Trinidad.

Manooch, C. S., III. 1977. Age, growth, and mortality of the white grunt, Haemulon plumieri Lacepède (Pisces: Pomadasyidae), from North Carolina and South Carolina. Proc. Ann. Conf. Southeastern Assoc. Game Fish Comm. 30:58-70.

_____. 1982. Aging reef fishes in the Southeast Fisheries Center. In G. R. Huntsman, W. R. Nicholson, and W. W. Fox, Jr., (editors), The biological bases for reef fishery management, p. 24-43. U.S. Dep. Commer., NOAA Tech. Memo. NMFS, NOAA-TM-NMFS-SEFC-80.

_____. Unpub. 1. Age and growth of the black grouper, Mycteroperca bonaci, from the southeastern and Gulf of Mexico coasts of the United States. Southeast Fish. Cent. Beaufort Lab., Natl. Mar. Fish. Serv., NOAA, Beaufort, NC 28516-9722.

_____. Unpub. 2. Age and growth of the warsaw grouper, Epinephelus nigritus, from the southeastern and Gulf of Mexico coasts of the United States. Southeast Fish. Cent. Beaufort Lab., Natl. Mar. Fish. Serv., NOAA, Beaufort, NC 28516-9722.

Manooch, C. S., III., and C. A. Barans. 1982. Distribution, abundance, and age and growth of the tomtate, Haemulon aurolineatum along the southeastern United States coast. Fish. Bull., U.S. 80:1-19.

Manooch, C. S., III, and C. L. Drennon. Unpub. Age and growth of the yellowtail snapper, Ocyurus chrysurus, from the Virgin Islands and Puerto Rico. Southeast Fish. Cent. Beaufort Lab., Natl. Mar. Fish. Serv., NOAA, Beaufort, NC 28516-9722.

Manooch, C. S., III, and M. Haimovici. 1978. Age and growth, of the gag, Mycteroperca microlepis, and size-age composition of the recreational catch off the southeastern United States. Trans. Am. Fish. Soc. 107:234-240.

Manooch, C. S., III, and G. R. Huntsman. 1977. Age, growth, and mortality of the red porgy, Pagrus pagrus. Trans. Am. Fish. Soc. 106:26-33.

Manooch, C. S., III, and D. L. Mason. 1984. Age, growth, and mortality of lane snapper from southern Florida. Northeast Gulf Sci. 7:109-115.

Manooch. C. S., III, and R. H. Matheson, III. 1981. Age, growth, and mortality of gray snapper collected from Florida waters. Proc. Ann. Conf. Southeastern Assoc. Fish Wildl. Agencies 35:331-344.

Mason, D. L., and C. S. Manooch, III. 1985. Age and growth of mutton snapper along the east coast of Florida. Fish. Res. 3:93-104.

Matheson, R. H., III, and G. R. Huntsman. 1984. Growth, mortality, and yield-per-recruit models for speckled hind and snowy grouper from the United States South Atlantic Bight. Trans. Am. Fish. Soc. 113:607-616.

368

Matheson, R. H., III, G. R. Huntsman, and C. S. Manooch, III. 1984. Age, growth, mortality, foods and reproduction of the scamp, Mycteroperca phenax, collected off North Carolina and South Carolina. Second Southeast Stock Assessment Workshop, June 4-8, 1984, Miami. Southeast Fish. Cent., Natl. Mar. Fish. Serv., NOAA, SAW/84/RFR/8, 38 p.

Mathews, C. P. 1974. An account of some methods of overcoming errors in ageing tropical and subtropical fish populations when the hard tissue growth markings are unreliable and the data sparse. In T. B. Bagenal (editor), Proceedings of an international symposium on the ageing of fish, p. 158-166. Unwin Brothers., Ltd., Surrey, Engl.

McErlean, A. J. 1963. A study of the age and growth of the gag, Mycteroperca microlepis Goode and Bean (Pisces: Serranidae), on the west coast of Florida. Fla. Board Conserv. Mar. Res. Lab. Tech. Ser. 41: 1-29.

McNew, R. W., and R. C. Summerfelt. 1978. Evaluation of a maximum likelihood estimator for analysis of length-frequency distributions. Trans. Am. Fish. Soc. 107:730-736.

Melo, A. M. 1975. Aspectos biológicos pesqueros de Epinephelus morio (Val.). M.S. Thesis, Univ. Nac. Autonoma Mexico, Mexico City, D.F., 68 p.

Menezes, M. F. de, and T. C. V. Gesteira. 1974. Age and growth of the paro, Lutjanus purpureus Poey, of the north and northeast of Brazil. Arq. Cienc. Mar 14:81-85.

Methot, R. D., Jr., and D. Kramer. 1979. Growth of northern anchovy, Engraulis mordax, larvae in the sea. Fish. Bull., U.S. 77:413-423.

Moe, M. A., Jr. 1969. Biology of the red grouper Epinephelus morio (Valenciennes) from the eastern Gulf of Mexico. Fla. Dep. Nat. Resour., Mar. Res. Lab. Prof. Pap. Ser. 10:1-95.

Montes, M. Unpub. Características peculiares del pargo en la zona D. Inst. Nac. Pesca Cent. Inf. Pesca Cuba (Mecanog.).

Moore, C. M., and R. F. Labisky. 1984. Population parameters of a relatively unexploited stock of snowy grouper, Epinephelus niveatus, in the lower Florida Keys, USA. Trans. Am. Fish. Soc. 113:322-329.

Mori, K. 1984. Early life history of Lutjanus vitta (Lutjanidae) in Yuya Bay, the Sea of Japan. Jpn. J. Ichthyol. 30:374-392.

Munro, J. L. 1973. Large-volume stackable fish traps for offshore fishing. Proc. 25th Gulf Caribb. Fish. Inst., p. 121-128.

_____. 1983. Epilogue: Progress in coral reef fisheries research, 1973-1982. In J. L. Munro (editor), Caribbean coral reef fishery resources, p. 249-265. ICLARM Stud. Rev. 7.

Munro, J. L., and D. Pauly. 1983. A simple method for comparing the growth of fishes and invertebrates. Fishbyte [ICLARM] 1(1):5-6.

Munro, J. L., and R. Thompson. 1973. The Jamaican fishing industry, the area investigated and the objectives and methodology of the ODA/UWI fisheries ecology research project. Res. Rep. Zool. Dep., Univ. West Indies 3(II):1-44. (Reprinted 1983 In J. L. Munro (editor), Caribbean coral reef fishery resources, in Chapter 2: The Jamaican fishing industry, p. 10-14, and in Chapter 3: Areas investigated, objectives and methodology, p. 15-25. ICLARM Stud. Rev. 7.)

Nagelkerken, W. P. 1979. Biology of the graysby, Epinephelus cruentatus, of the coral reef of Curacao. Stud. Fauna Curacao Other Caribb. Isl. 60:1-118.

Nelson, R. S., and C. S. Manooch, III. 1982. Growth and mortality of red snappers, Lutjanus campechanus, in the west central Atlantic Ocean and northern Gulf of Mexico. Trans. Am. Fish. Soc. 111:465-475.

Nelson, R. S., C. S. Manooch, III, and D. L. Mason. 1985. Ecological effects of energy development on reef fish of the Flower Garden Banks: Reef fish bioprofiles. Final report. Southeast Fish. Cent. Beaufort Lab., Natl. Mar. Fish. Serv., NOAA, Beaufort, NC 28516-9722.

Olsen, D. A., and J. A. LaPlace. 1978. A study of a Virgin Islands grouper fishery based on a breeding aggregation. Proc. 31st Gulf Caribb. Fish. Inst., p. 130-144.

Ottaway, E. M. 1978. Rhythmic growth activity in fish scales. J. Fish Biol. 12:615-623.

Ottaway, E. M., and K. Simkiss. 1977. "Instantaneous" growth rates of fish scales and their use in studies of fish populations. J. Zool. (Lond.) 181:407-419.

_____. 1979. A comparison of traditional and novel ways of estimating growth rates from scales of natural populations of young bass (Dicentrarchus labrax). J. Mar. Biol. Assoc. U.K. 59:49-59.

370

Pannella, G. 1971. Fish otoliths: Daily growth layers and periodical patterns. Science 173:1124–1127.

_____. 1974. Otolith growth patterns: An aid in age determination in temperate and tropical fishes. In T. B. Bagenal (editor), Proceedings of an international symposium on the ageing of fish, p. 28–39. Unwin Brothers., Ltd., Surrey, Engl.

_____. 1980. Growth patterns in fish sagittae. In D. C. Rhoads and R. A. Lutz (editors), Skeletal growth of aquatic organisms: Biological records of environmental change, p. 519–560. Plenum Press, N.Y.

Pauly, D. 1980. A new methodology for rapidly acquiring basic information on tropical fish stocks: Growth, mortality, and stock recruitment relationships. In S. B. Saila and P. M. Roedel (editors), Stock assessment for tropical small-scale fisheries, p. 154–172. Int. Cent. Mar. Resour. Dev., Univ. Rhode Island, Kingston.

_____. 1981. The relationships between gill surface area and growth performance in fish: A generalization of von Bertalanffy's theory of growth. Meeresforschung 28:251–282.

Pauly, D., and J. Ingles. 1981. Aspects of the growth and natural mortality of exploited coral reef fishes. In E. D. Gomez C. E. Birkeland, R. W. Buddemeier, R. E. Johannes, J. A. Marsh, Jr., and R. T. Tsuda (editor), Proc. 4th Int. Coral Reef Symp., Manila 1:89–98.

Pauly, D., and J. L. Munro. 1983. Once more on the comparison of growth in fish and invertebrates. Fishbyte (ICLARM) 2(1):21.

Piedra, G. 1969. Materials on the biology of the yellowtail snapper (Ocyurus chrysurus, Bloch). In A. S. Bogdanov (editor), Soviet-Cuban fishery research, p. 251–296. Isr. Progr. Sci. Trans. Jerusalem, Israel.

Pozo, E. 1979. Edad y crecimiento del pargo criollo (Lutjanus analis Cuvier 1928) en la plataforma nororientel de Cuba. Rev. Cubana Invest. Pesq. 4(2):1–24.

Ralston, S. 1976. Age determination of a tropical reef butterflyfish utilizing daily growth rings of the otoliths. Fish. Bull., U.S. 74:990–994.

_____. 1980. An analysis of the Hawaiian offshore handline fishery: a progress report. In R. W. Grigg and R. T. Pfund (editors), Proceedings of the Symposium on Status of Resource Investigations in the

Northwest Hawaiian Islands, April 24-25, 1980, University of Hawaii, Honolulu, Hawaii, p. 204-215. UNIHI-SEAGRANT-MR-80-04.

_____. 1985. A novel approach to aging tropical fish. ICLARM Newsl. Jan., p. 14-15.

_____. 1986. Mortality rates of snappers and groupers. In J. J. Polovina and S. Ralston (editors), Tropical snappers and groupers: Biology and fisheries management. Westview Press, Inc., Boulder. [See this volume.]

Ralston, S., and G. T. Miyamoto. 1981. Estimation of the age of a tropical reef fish using the density of daily growth increments. In E. D. Gomez, C. E. Birkeland, R. W. Buddemeier, R. E. Johannes, J. A. Marsh, Jr., and R. T. Tsuda (editor), Proc. 4th Int. Coral Reef Symp., Manila 1:83-88.

_____. 1983. Analyzing the width of daily otolith increments to age the Hawaiian snapper, Pristipomoides filamentosus. Fish. Bull., U.S. 81:523-535.

Randall, J. E. 1962. Tagging reef fishes in the Virgin Islands. Proc. Gulf 14th Caribb. Fish. Inst. p. 201-241.

_____. 1963. Additional recoveries of tagged reef fishes from the Virgin Islands. Proc. 15th Gulf Caribb. Fish. Inst., p. 155-157.

Ricker, W. E. 1975. Computation and interpretation of biological statistics of fish populations. Fish. Res. Board Can. Bull. 191, 382 p.

Rodriguez Pino, Z. 1962. Estudios estadísticos y biológicas sobre la biajaiba (Lutjanus synagris). Cent. Invest. Pesq. Habana. Nota Sobre Invest. 9, 99 p.

Ross, J. L., and G. R. Huntsman. 1982. Age, growth, and mortality of blueline tilefish from North Carolina and South Carolina. Trans. Am. Fish. Soc. 111:585-592.

Samuel, M., C. P. Mathews, and A. S. Bawazeer. In press. Aging and validation of age from otoliths for warm water species of fish from the Arabian Gulf. In R. C. Summerfelt and B. W. Menzel (editors), Proceedings of the Second International Symposium on age and growth of fish, June 9-12 1985, Des Moines, Iowa, 21 p.

SAS Institute. 1979. SAS user's guide. Statistical Analysis System, 494 p.

Schlieder, R. Unpub. Age, growth and reproduction of the gag grouper, Mycteroperca microlepis (Pisces:

Serranidae), from the eastern Gulf of Mexico. Fla. Dep. Nat. Res., Mar. Res. Lab., St. Petersburg, FL 33701-5095.

Schnute, J., and D. Fournier. 1980. A new approach to length-frequency analysis: Growth structure. Can. J. Fish. Aquat. Sci. 37:1337-1351.

Skillman, R. A., and M. Y. Y. Yong. 1976. Von Bertalanffy growth curves for striped marlin, Tetrapturus audax, and blue marlin, Makaira nigricans, in the central North Pacific Ocean. Fish. Bull., U.S. 74:553-566.

Starck, W. A., II, and R. E. Schroeder. 1970. Investigations on the gray snapper, Lutjanus griseus. Stud. Trop. Oceanogr. (Miami) 10, 224 p., + 44 figs. (Copyright 1971.)

Stevenson, D. K. 1976. Determination of maximum yield conditions from length frequency data for a tropical fish pot fishery. Ph.D. Dissertation, Univ. Rhode Island, Kingston, RI 02908.

Struhsaker, P., and J. H. Uchiyama. 1976. Age and growth of the nehu, Stolephorus purpureus (Pisces: Engraulidae), from the Hawaiian Islands as indicated by daily growth increments of sagittae. Fish. Bull., U.S. 74:9-17.

Talbot, F. H. 1960. Notes on the biology of the Lutjanidae (Pisces) of the East African coast, with species reference to L. bohar (Forskal). Ann. S. Afr. Mus. 65:549-573.

Tardif, C., and C. S. Manooch, III. Unpub. Age, growth and length-weight relationship of the spottail pinfish, Diplodus holbrooki, in the South Atlantic Bight. Southeast Fish. Cent. Beaufort Lab., Natl. Mar. Fish. Serv., NOAA, Beaufort, NC 28516-9722.

Taubert, B., and D. W. Coble. 1977. Daily rings in otoliths of three species of Lepomis and Tilapia mossambica. J. Fish. Res. Board Can. 34:332-340.

Teng, S. K., T. E. Chua, and P. E. Lim. 1978. Preliminary observation on the dietary protein requirement of estuary grouper, Epinephelus salmoides, cultured in floating net cages. Aquaculture 15:257-272.

Thia-Eng, C., and S. K. Teng. 1978. Effects of feeding frequency on the growth of young estuary grouper, Epinephelus tauvina, cultured in floating net cages. Aquaculture 14:31-48.

Thompson, R., and J. L. Munro. 1974a. The biology, ecology and bionomics of Caribbean reef fishes: Lutjanidae (snappers). Zoology Dep., Univ. West Indies, Kingston, Jamaica Res. Rep. 3, Pt. 5d.

_____. 1974b. The biology, ecology and bionomics of Caribbean reef fishes: Serranidae (hinds and groupers). Res. Rep. Zool. Dep., Univ. West Indies 3(V.b.):1-82. (Reprinted 1983 In J. L. Munro (editor), Caribbean coral reef fishery resources, in Chapter 7: The biology, ecology and bionomics of the hinds and groupers, Serranidae, p. 59-81. ICLARM Stud. Rev. 7.)

Tsuji, S., and T. Aoyama. 1982. Daily growth increments observed in otoliths of the larvae of Japanese red sea bream, Pagrus major. Bull. Jpn. Soc. Sci. Fish. 48:1559-1562.

Van Oosten, J. 1929. Life history of the lake herring (Leucichthys artedi Le Sueur) of Lake Huron as revealed by its scales with a critique of the scale method. U.S. Dep. Commer., Bull. U.S. Bur. Fish. 44:265-428 (1928).

Wade, C. W. 1981. Age and growth of spotted seatrout and red snapper in Alabama. Proc. Annu. Conf. Southeast. Assoc. Fish Wildl. Agencies 35:345-354.

Wakeman, J. M., C. R. Arnold, D. E. Wohlschlag, and S. C. Rabalais. 1979. Oxygen consumption, energy expenditure and growth of red snapper, Lutjanus campechanus. Trans. Am. Fish. Soc. 108:288-292.

Walford, L. A. 1946. A new graphic method for describing the growth of animals. Biol. Bull. (Woods Hole) 90:141-147.

Warlen, S. M. 1982. Age and growth of larvae and spawning time of Atlantic croaker in North Caroline. Proc. Annu. Conf. Southeast. Assoc. Fish Wildl. Agencies 34:204-214.

Weber, D., and G. J. Ridgway. 1967. Marking Pacific salmon with tetracycline antibiotics. J. Fish. Res. Board Can. 24:849-865.

Wild, A., and T. J. Foreman. 1980. The relationship between otolith increments and time for yellowfin and skipjack tuna marked with tetracycline. Inter-Am. Trop. Tuna Comm. Bull. 17:509-560.

8
Mortality Rates of Snappers and Groupers

Stephen Ralston
Southwest Fisheries Center Honolulu Laboratory
National Marine Fisheries Service, NOAA
Honolulu, Hawaii 96822-2396

ABSTRACT

Mortality concepts are briefly reviewed and
general methods of estimating mortality rates discussed. Special attention is devoted to techniques
used successfully in the study of snappers and
groupers. In particular, catch curves, Z/K ratio
estimates, and the Pauly equation are shown to
account for the majority of mortality estimates
reported from these two taxa. A review of the
snapper and grouper literature indicates that
instantaneous rates of natural mortality (M) can
simply be predicted with knowledge of the von
Bertalanffy growth coefficient (K)--the former being
roughly twice the latter. Reported agents responsible for natural deaths in these groups include
predation, parasitism, cold water shock, and red
tide poisoning. Examining levels of exploitation
suggests that snappers have been more intensively
harvested than groupers, although stocks characterized by high ratios of fishing to natural mortality
are known from both families. Based on the evidence
reviewed it is concluded that these species have a
relatively limited productive capacity and are
vulnerable to overfishing.

INTRODUCTION

In the tropical and subtropical waters of the world,
few demersal fishery resources are more important than the
snappers (Lutjanidae) and groupers (subfamily Epinephelinae of the Serranidae) (Bullis and Jones 1976; Pauly 1979;

375

Munro 1983). Yet in spite of their significance, yield assessments of these species have until recently been few (e.g., Ralston and Polovina 1982; Huntsman et al. 1983; Kunzel et al. 1983; Munro 1983; Powers 1983). Now, however, regional studies of snapper and grouper biology have proliferated to the extent that a review and synthesis of the information recently gained could considerably aid their management.

Estimation of mortality rates is central to demographic analyses and most types of stock assessment (Gulland 1955). This is because losses from exploited populations largely control the yields that can be obtained from them (Beverton and Holt 1957; Gulland 1971; Ricker 1975). Yet, biologists frequently regard the topic with apprehension because of preconceived ideas about its complexity. In truth, mortality concepts are quite simple, although statistical problems often do occur.

The organization of this chapter is, therefore, designed to first introduce several basic concepts which define what mortality is and in general terms how it is expressed mathematically. This leads to a discussion of specific methods and techniques for estimating mortality rates, especially those that have been successfully applied to snappers and groupers in tropical systems. Because natural mortality is of special significance when analyzing potential yield, and is usually difficult to determine, I present a brief discussion of factors correlating with it. From these ideas I develop a predictor of natural mortality and test it on data obtained from the snapper/grouper literature. This is followed by a review of factors known to be responsible for natural deaths in these two taxa. Finally, I briefly discuss the relationship between natural mortality and optimum rates of fishing mortality.

MORTALITY AND ITS ESTIMATION

When considered from the classical perspective of the Beverton and Holt (1957) dynamic pool model, there are three factors that uniquely determine the yield from a stock of fish. These factors are recruitment, growth, and mortality. The first two are renewal processes, which add biomass to the exploitable phase of the life history. Conversely, mortality represents the loss of individuals, and thus biomass, from the population. This loss process is usually subdivided into two separate categories:

deaths attributable to fishing, and deaths due to all other sources. Collectively the latter are termed natural mortality.

Jensen (1939) was among the first to argue that the force of mortality factors acts in a multiplicative fashion. He showed for a variety of stocks (including cod, haddock, plaice, and herring) that the number of individuals in a cohort or year class is diminished by a fixed percentage from year to year. Similarly, Beverton and Holt (1959) presented evidence for long-lived species demonstrating that a constant fraction of a cohort is removed each year by the various agents of natural mortality. Moreover, we know that when basic operational and statistical assumptions have been met, a fixed amount of fishing effort removes a fixed fraction of the fully vulnerable portion of a stock (Ricker 1975). Thus, at least in theory, fishing mortality operates in a multiplicative manner as well. In practice this may not be true.

The multiplicative nature of mortality factors lends itself to expression by the exponential function, especially in its differential form. Then the instantaneous total mortality rate from all causes (Z) can simply be defined as the proportionality constant that relates the rate of change (dN/dt) of a cohort to its absolute abundance (N). That is,

$$dN/dt = -ZN$$

It is a great convenience that, when mortality is expressed in this manner, fishing (F) and natural (M) mortality rates are additive; that is, $Z = F + M$. A necessary corollary is that total mortality equals natural mortality in the absence of fishing. When acting in concert, M and F compete for the individuals remaining in a year class, each responsible for a certain percentage reduction over time. Instantaneous mortality rates, as shown above, are by definition measured in units of inverse time, most frequently per year.

Given that mortality factors are related and expressed in this fashion, what methods are available to estimate these rates? Although a wide variety of techniques have been employed, most can be classified according to three fundamental types of estimation: (1) age-specific procedures for true cohorts; (2) time-specific methods for synthetic cohorts; and (3) mark-recapture methods. A very brief description of each follows.

Ideally, the total mortality rate of a cohort is estimated by determining the number of individuals of age x that are alive at time t, that is, $(N_{x,t})$, and also the number of individuals of age x+1 at time t+1 $(N_{x+1,t+1})$. If time is measured in years, the ratio of the latter to the former provides an estimate of the annual survivorship fraction (S_x) for fish aged x. Furthermore, the age-specific total instantaneous mortality rate (Z_x) is equal to $-\ln(S_x)$. Note that in this calculation an actual cohort is tracked in time and successively sampled. Thus, the measured mortality rate is the actual rate experienced by the cohort (Gulland 1955). An important practical adjustment often employed is to substitute properly subscripted catch per unit effort indices of abundance for the actual numbers of fish (Gray 1979; Paloheimo 1980; but see Butler and McDonald 1979). Age-specific mortality estimates are typically used in cohort and virtual population analysis (Ricker 1975) and result in the most compelling mortality assessments.

A second approach to the problem is through the use of synthetic cohorts. Rather than repetitively sampling a population through time, a single sample is taken and the numbers of fish aged x, x+1, x+2, ..., x+i determined. Often this entails developing an age-length key (Fridriksson 1934; Gulland 1955), a nontrivial problem in its own right, especially if the key is used on samples taken at different times or places (Kimura 1977; Westrheim and Ricker 1978; Clark 1981). If the sampled population is assumed to be age-stationary (i.e., the age distribution remains the same from year to year), one can estimate mortality rates by forming the ratios of successive age classes exactly in the manner outlined previously. Note that computing mortality rates from "synthetic" cohorts actually produces estimates that are time-specific, as opposed to age-specific.

To analyze these kinds of data, Chapman and Robson (1960) and Robson and Chapman (1961) derived a minimum-variance, unbiased estimator of S for single age-frequency distributions in the situation where mortality rate is uniform across all age groups. Alternatively, the analysis of catch or survivorship curves (Ricker 1975) permits visual inspection of the data to look for possible violations of assumptions, especially that of constant mortality rate. These are simply semi-logarithmic plots of abundance against age, where the slope of the descending right-hand limb provides an estimate of total mortality rate. An important variation on this theme is the analysis of single length-frequency distributions to estimate the ratio of total mortality rate to von Berta- lanffy growth coefficient (Z/K) (Beverton and Holt 1956; Ssentongo and Larkin 1973; Powell 1979; Wetherall et al. In press). With an independent estimate of K from the study of tag returns, otoliths, modal size progression, etc., it is possible to estimate Z by separating the ratio. Similarly, there are techniques that assume an underlying growth structure, which is then used to analyze length-frequency distributions. These methods produce mortality estimates after analytically reconstructing the unknown age-distribution (Olsen and LaPlace 1979; Pauly 1982; see also Schnute and Fournier 1980). Although all these various techniques are commonly used, each relies essentially on a single sample, be it age- or length- frequency, and each therefore suffers from the constraint of age stationarity, an assumption that frequently is not met.

A third class of mortality estimation techniques involves mark-recapture methods (Ricker 1975; Seber 1982). For example, it is generally possible to estimate exploi- tation fraction ($u = 1-\exp^{-F}$) in a marked population as the ratio of total marks in the catch to total marks in the population. From this, an estimate of fishing mortal- ity is obtained directly. Similarly, total mortality rate can be estimated by determining the extinction rate of marks in the population at large. Other fairly detailed methods exist to estimate M. Mark-recapture methods have not been used, however, to estimate mortality rates of snappers and groupers.

While these three general categories account for the majority of mortality estimations, several other tech- niques have been developed that differ from them sufficiently to warrant specific mention. Green (1970), and later Ebert (1973), presented a method for estimating growth and total mortality rates by graphical and numeri- cal means, respectively. Their method is restrictive in assuming age stationarity and full recruitment to the population over less than 1 month, but is appealing because it only requires estimates of average individual size at two times in the year. Saila and Lough (1981) derived an analytical solution to the same problem for an estimate of K, using this result in conjunction with the Z/K ratio method to separate the parameters. In yet another approach, Marten (1978) developed a procedure for determining total mortality rate from a length sample under conditions where fish growth can be considered

linear over the size range of interest. Also, regression
analysis has been used effectively to separate Z into its
constituent components (Beverton and Holt 1957; Cushing
1968). Here total mortality can be regressed against
nominal fishing effort, in which case the y-intercept
provides an estimate of M (see also Marten 1978). Similarly, Csirke and Caddy (1983) have suggested that a
parabolic nonlinear regression of yield on total mortality
rate (Z) allows estimation of M as the point of the left
hand or ascending x-intercept.

Another means of estimating mortality, particularly
natural mortality, is by comparative life history studies
of ecologically or taxonomically similar species (Adams
1980; Gunderson 1980). For example, Pauly (1980) suggests
predicting instantaneous natural mortality rate from a
multiple regression equation he derived from the study of
175 fish stocks. This equation incorporates three
independent variables: (1) mean annual water temperature;
(2) the von Bertalanffy growth coefficient K; and (3)
either the asymptotic weight or length parameter from the
von Bertalanffy growth model. Although the standard error
of the estimate (0.247) is too large to permit precise
estimation of natural mortality (estimated values of M
have sometimes exceeded measured values of Z), this
equation is still very useful when no historical information exists concerning the condition of a population in
its unexploited state. Similarly, Hoenig (1983) presented
an empirically derived equation which predicts total
mortality rate from maximum age data.

MORTALITY ESTIMATION IN TROPICAL SNAPPERS AND GROUPERS

The only study of a snapper species in which age-
specific mortality rates were determined for use in a
cohort or virtual population analysis was that of Mahmoudi
et al. (1984). The total catch of Rhomboplites aurorubens
by age class, determined over a 10-year period, was
estimated from size composition and total catch data from
three distinct segments of the fishery (recreational,
commercial hook-and-line, and commercial trawl). The data
were aggregated and then recursively analyzed to obtain
least squares estimates of age-specific fishing mortality
rates from 1973 to 1982. Natural mortality was estimated
from the Pauly (1980) equation. Given estimates of age-
specific fishing mortality and catch it was possible to
estimate the annual standing stock by age class and

recruit year-class strength. A graph relating the number of spawning females and recruitment was also presented. Thus a full history of the fishery was derived and a detailed assessment of the stock's response to exploitation was gained. They concluded that an increase in yield per recruit could be achieved by reducing fishing mortality on fish aged 1-3 years.

Without question catch curve analysis has been used more frequently on lutjanids and serranids than any other method of mortality estimation (Moe 1969; Manooch and Haimovici 1978; Nagelkerken 1979; Low 1981; Ivo and Hanson 1982; Nelson and Manooch 1982; Brouard and Grandperrin 1984; Matheson and Huntsman 1984; Moore and Labisky 1984; Ralston 1984; Witzig and Huntsman 1984). Studies have involved the following species: Epinephelus morio, E. cruentatus, E. niveatus, E. drummondhayi, Mycteroperca microlepis, Centropristis striata, Lutjanus purpureus, L. malabaricus, L. campechanus, Etelis carbunculus, E. coruscans, Pristipomoides flavipinnis, P. filamentosus, and P. multidens. Typically, investigators have used hard parts, sometimes scales but more often otoliths, to develop a von Bertalanffy growth curve (see Manooch 1986).

Age-length data have usually been used to construct age-length keys, although some investigators have developed an age sample which is sufficiently large to permit analysis of population age structure directly (Moe 1969; Nagelkerken 1979; Low 1981). Otherwise, the use of age-length keys has been widespread, a practice that can result in seriously biased mortality estimates. Kimura (1977) and Westrheim and Ricker (1978) have both shown that a key derived from one population that is applied to another, or even if applied to the same stock sampled at different times, can produce substantial errors. This is because a single key used on divergent length-frequency data sets results in projected age distributions that tend to mimic the age distribution from which the key was derived. Misapplication of this method is therefore likely if the same key is used repeatedly. Consequently, when mortality estimates appear to remain uniform through time (e.g., Nelson and Manooch 1982; Witzig and Huntsman 1984), it is difficult to conclude that no change has occurred if only one age-length key was used. Clark (1981), however, has proposed a method to circumvent this problem, employing least squares to determine the overall age distribution of the population given the distribution of lengths within each age class (see also Bartoo and Parker 1983).

Another popular technique that can lead to error in mortality estimates is that of directly transforming lengths to ages using the inverse form of the von Bertalanffy growth equation (e.g., Mahmoudi et al. 1984). Age-frequency distributions developed in this fashion need not represent the actual age structure of the population (Ricker 1975; Bartoo and Parker 1983). When the data resulting from this procedure are analyzed by catch curve methods or otherwise, mortality estimates are likely to be biased.

At least two studies have used a modified catch curve approach. Pauly and Ingles (1982) estimated the total mortality rate of Epinephelus sexfasciatus using ELEFAN I (Pauly 1982), a computer program that generates length-converted catch curves from length-frequency data. Olsen and LaPlace (1979) also estimated total mortality rate in E. striatus by first restructuring length samples using probit analysis, and then deriving a probability function to estimate age class abundance by size class.

A method used extensively to estimate mortality rates, and apparently with great success, is the Z/K ratio technique and its subsequent modifications (Beverton and Holt 1956; Powell 1979; Wetherall et al. In press). In its simplest form, this method calculates the ratio of mortality to growth parameters from a length-frequency distribution adjusted to provide: (1) the size at which fish become fully vulnerable to the gear (l_c), and (2) the mean size of fish in the catch larger than l_c. It is attractive for its simplicity of data requirements and robustness of estimates (Powell 1979; Wetherall et al. In press; but see Majkowski 1982).

Several researchers have estimated mortality with this technique. Thompson and Munro (1978) computed Z for five species of Jamaican grouper: E. guttatus, E. striatus, M. venenosa, Cephalopholis fulva, and Petrometopon cruentatum. Because some length-frequency samples were obtained from unfished areas, they were also able to estimate natural mortality (i.e., Z = M). Brouard and Grandperrin (1984) used the Z/K ratio approach to estimate total mortality rates (= natural mortality) for six lutjanids in Vanuatu: Etelis carbunculus, E. coruscans, L. malabaricus, Pristipomoides flavipinnis, P. filamentosus, and P. multidens. By comparison, estimates calculated from this approach averaged 24% higher than synoptic catch curve estimates for the same species. Ralston and Williams (Unpub.) also performed Z/K analyses for the same species (excluding L. malabaricus), as well as P. auricilla and P. zonatus sampled in the Mariana Archipelago. Because their samples typically came from virgin populations, estimates of M were derived.

Age-specific mortality estimates for L. purpureus and Plectropomus maculatus were derived by Ivo and Gesteira (1974) and Goeden (1977), respectively, although the mortality rate was effectively constant among age classes in the latter study. Similarly, Nagelkerken (1979) and Manooch and Haimovici (1978) reported nonlinear descending limbs in catch curve analyses of Epinephelus cruentatus and M. microlepis. As a result, neither study attempted to estimate mortality. In the three studies where grouper mortality rates have demonstrated clear age-specific variation, all showed an increase in age specific mortality rate with increasing age (i.e., an upwardly convex catch curve). This finding is in agreement with the suggestion of Cushing (1968) that the collective force of natural mortality among the smaller fishes is largely due to predation but is more the result of physiological events (e.g., senility) for the larger, predatory species like snappers and groupers.

Another important means of estimating natural mortality rate (M) in the snappers and groupers has been the Pauly (1980) equation, used by Pauly and Ingles (1982) on E. sexfasciatus, Nelson and Manooch (1982) on L. campechanus, Brouard and Grandperrin (1984) on the six species mentioned previously (Pauly equation estimates were 46% greater than comparable catch curve estimates), Matheson and Huntsman (1984) on E. niveatus and E. drummondhayi, and Ralston (1984) on Pristipomoides filamentosus (equation estimate was 45% greater than a catch curve estimate from an unfished stock).

The only other two methods that have been employed to estimate mortality in these two groups are the Robson and Chapman (1961) maximum likelihood estimator, used by Nelson and Manooch (1982) on L. campechanus, and a regression of total mortality rate (Z) on nominal fishing effort, used to estimate natural mortality in L. purpureus by Ivo and Gesteira (1974). In the former study, the Robson-Chapman estimator produced estimates approximately 8% greater than catch curve estimates from the same data.

From this brief review, it is evident that three methods have accounted for the great majority of snapper/grouper mortality estimations: catch curves, Z/K ratios, and Pauly equation estimates. In situations where more than one of these has been used (Brouard and Grandperrin 1984; Ralston 1984), the Pauly (1980) equation produced

estimates of M that were distinctly higher than catch
curve estimates derived from virgin stocks, while Z/K
ratio estimates lay midway between the two.

PREDICTING NATURAL MORTALITY

Estimating instantaneous natural mortality rate (M)
is of special significance in fisheries research (Ricker
1975). Although it is one of the most difficult parameters
in fisheries to estimate, virtually all age-structured
yield models require it. Once obtained, however, its uses
are multiple.

One particular application of natural mortality
estimates is to estimate maximum sustained yield (MSY).
Alverson and Pereyra (1969), based on the unpublished
ideas of Gulland (1971) and an earlier Soviet study
(Tiurin 1962), first proposed that at MSY the optimum
level of fishing mortality (F_{opt}) could be directly
estimated with the natural mortality rate. This particular
conclusion applied not only to surplus-production models
like the Graham-Schaefer formulation, but more loosely to
the Beverton and Holt (1957) constant recruitment model as
well (Gulland 1971). Saetersdal (1973) also advocated
using M as a direct estimate of F_{opt} when assessing
unexploited resources and catch statistics are unavailable. From these ideas a number of studies have estimated
MSY by the following relationship:

$$MSY = 0.5 \; M \; B_{o}$$

where B_{o} represents exploitable virgin biomass. Kunzel et
al. (1983), for example, estimated MSY for the lutjanids
of the Mahe Plateau, Seychelles using this relationship.

Francis (1974), Deriso (1982), and Beddington and
Cooke (1983) examined the theoretical basis for this
approximation and concluded that it should hold only in
situations where recruitment is constant over stock sizes
ranging from B_{o} to $0.5 \; B_{o}$. They showed on a purely
analytical basis that if an asymptotic form of spawner-
recruit curve were applicable, then $F_{opt} < M$, whereas if a
dome-shaped relationship were in effect, then $F_{opt} > M$.
Furthermore, optimum fishing mortality relative to MSY was
generally shown to be less than F_{opt} for yield/recruit
analyses.

Because of the biological importance of natural
mortality and its utility in yield assessment, a number of

studies have tried to determine factors that might correlate with M, allowing its prediction from some other more
easily estimated statistic. Beverton and Holt (1959) tabulated values of asymptotic size, K, maximum age, and M,
and showed that the von Bertalanffy growth rate parameter
K correlates well with M. Cushing (1968) summarized these
findings in the statement "a fish with a high growth rate
dies young" and presented plots of M versus K for the
clupeoidei, gadiformes, salmonoidei, and pleuronectoidei.

  More recently, Adams (1980) and Gunderson (1980) used
r-K selection theory (MacArthur and Wilson 1967) as a
basis for developing predictors of natural mortality.
They concluded that the von Bertalanffy growth coefficient
and the gonadosomatic index, respectively, were best
correlated with M, although in all cases their trial
predictors (size at maturity, asymptotic size, maximum
age, and age at maturity) agreed well with r-K selection
theory. Myers and Doyle (1983), under the assumption that
fish life histories are evolutionary stable strategies,
also estimated M from growth rate, fecundity, energy
expenditure per egg, age and size at maturity, and a value
of surplus energy available. Indeed, the Pauly (1980)
equation itself relies on values of K, asymptotic size,
and mean annual water temperature to predict M.

  Based on the presumption that K is a good predictor
of M, a survey of the snapper/grouper literature was
undertaken that was designed to locate populations in
which the von Bertalanffy growth coefficient (K) and the
natural mortality rate were jointly estimated. An added
appeal of K as a predictor of M is that both are measured
in identical units (per year). Moreover, asymptotic size
and mean annual water temperature are typically correlated
with K and provide little independent information regarding M (but see Pauly 1980).

  To determine if a more taxon-specific compilation of
K and M statistics would increase the precision of natural
mortality rate predictions, studies that used the Pauly
(1980) equation to estimate snapper/grouper M were
excluded unless an independent estimate was also given.
Nineteen snapper/grouper stocks were identified in which
the two parameters were both estimated. Table 8.1 summarizes the findings, including recent studies of 15
populations not incorporated in Pauly's original work.
Some discussion of these is warranted.

  Brouard and Grandperrin (1984) reported on six
lutjanid species from Vanuatu, estimating Z by two
independent means: catch curve and Z/K ratio. Growth was

TABLE 8.1
Summary information on growth and natural mortality
determinations in the snapper and grouper families

Species	K	M	Source
Lutjanidae			
Etelis carbunculus	0.07	0.08	Brouard and Grandperrin 1984
E. coruscans	0.13	0.12	Brouard and Grandperrin 1984
	0.16	0.36	Ralston and Williams Unpub.
L. malabaricus	0.31	0.42	Brouard and Grandperrin 1984
L. purpureus	0.09	0.35	Menezes and Gesteira 1974
			Ivo and Gesteira 1974
Ocyurus chrysurus	0.16	0.20	Piedra 1965
Pristipomoides auricilla	0.27	0.66	Ralston and Williams Unpub.
P. filamentosus	0.15	0.25	Ralston 1984
			Ralston and Miyamoto 1983
	0.22	0.55	Ralston and Williams Unpub.
	0.29	0.53	Brouard and Grandperrin 1984
P. flavipinnis	0.36	0.83	Brouard and Grandperrin 1984
P. multidens	0.24	0.42	Brouard and Grandperrin 1984
	0.19	0.63	Ralston and Williams Unpub.
P. zonatus	0.20	0.53	Ralston and Williams Unpub.
Serranidae			
Epinephelus guttatus	0.24	0.68	Thompson and Munro 1978
E. niveatus	0.09	0.18	Moore and Labisky 1984
E. striatus	0.09	0.23	Thompson and Munro 1978
Mycteroperca venenosa	0.13	0.29	Thompson and Munro 1978
Plectropomus maculatus	0.13	0.30	Goeden 1977

estimated by total counts of daily otolith increments. Because exploitation was negligible, each calculation can be considered an independent estimate of M. The value given in the table is the average of these two estimates (see discussion above). Ralston and Williams (Unpub.) studied six lutjanids from the Marianas as well as P. multidens from Papua New Guinea. With the single exception of P. flavipinnis, all their estimates of total mortality could be considered equivalent to natural mortality because of low or nonexistent levels of fishing. However, one of the remaining species (Etelis carbunculus) was excluded due to an aberrant population structure. Growth rates were determined by numerical integration of daily otolith increments. Of the five serranid species studied by Thompson and Munro (1978), reasonably reliable growth curves were developed from modal progressions and hard parts for the three species listed in the table. They estimated the ratio of total mortality to growth from a number of areas, one of which could be considered virgin fishing grounds, and separated the ratio using their growth estimates. Where parameter estimates were specified as a range, the interval midpoint was used here. Although age-specific mortality rates were given by Goeden (1977, see above) for Plectropomus maculatus, survivorship from age 2 to 3 is used here because the remaining estimates are unaccountably low.

Natural mortality rate is then plotted against the von Bertalanffy growth rate parameter in Figure 8.1, where, not surprisingly, it is seen that M is positively correlated with K (r = 0.82). Closed symbols in the figure represent the 14 lutjanid stocks while the 5 open circles depict the serranids. Among the former, the circles are from the study of Brouard and Grandperrin (1984) in Vanuatu, the squares from Ralston and Williams' (Unpub.) work on Marianas stocks, and the triangles represent the remaining four investigations of snappers (Piedra 1965; Menezes and Gesteira 1974; Ivo and Gesteira 1974; Ralston 1984; Ralston and Miyamoto 1983).

Analysis of covariance was used to determine whether the data from snappers and groupers could be pooled. The results showed that no differences were evident in either slope (P = 0.29) or adjusted means (P = 0.42), although clearly the size of the grouper sample was small. The data were then pooled and analyzed by linear regression (solid line in figure), with the following result:

$$M = 0.0189 + 2.06 \ K$$

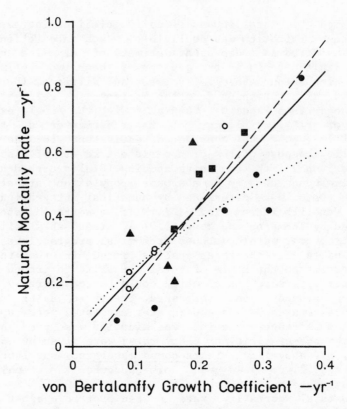

Figure 8.1 The relationship between natural mortality rate (M) and von Bertalanffy growth coefficient (K) for 19 stocks of snappers and groupers. See text for a detailed explanation of symbols

with standard errors for the intercept and slope equal to 0.0713 and 0.3528, respectively. The regression's slope was highly significant (P < 0.0001), although the estimate of intercept did not differ significantly from zero (P = 0.79). Thus, the ratio of natural mortality to growth rate within these two taxa is estimated to approximately 2, a simple rule of thumb that agrees with the data presented in Sylvester (1974). He presented length-frequency distributions for populations of L. vivanus, L. buccanella, and Pristipomoides macrophthalmus with negligible levels of exploitation, all of which had near linear descending (i.e., right-hand) limbs to the curves.

a characteristic of populations with mortality to growth ratios (Z/K) equal to 2 (Powell 1979). Similarly, highly skewed length-frequency distributions of L. campechanus (Bradley and Bryan 1975; Fable 1980) and Rhomboplites aurorubens (Fable 1980) are known from heavily exploited populations in which Z/K greatly exceeds 2.0.

The estimate of mean squared error for the regression in Figure 8.1 is 0.015, and thus the standard deviation of residuals is s = 0.12 per year. Although predictions of individual and population M values depend on specifying the level of K (Snedecor and Cochran 1967), one would expect the 95% confidence interval for a prediction to lie very roughly +0.24 per year above and below the regression line (i.e., two standard deviations). Similarly, approximately two-thirds of all observations are expected to lie within +0.12 per year of the regression.

Presented in the figure as a dashed line is the functional regression (Ricker 1973) of M on K, where:

$$M = -0.0666 + 2.52\ K$$

Due to the nature of functional regressions, no statistical inference can be drawn from this result, except to say that it provides the best estimates of natural mortality rate if K is measured with a level of error comparable to that of M, a likely situation. If necessary, Ricker (1973) suggests using the symmetrical regression error limits obtained from the predictive analysis.

The dotted line in Figure 8.1 is the fit of a modified form of the Pauly (1980) equation to the data presented in Table 8.1. A simple $\log_{10}$ power function was made to pass through the means of $\log(K)$ and $\log(M)$, with the coefficient on the $\log_{10} K$ independent variable (0.665) obtained from the Pauly multiple regression equation. The result is to fit the data to his model, but using only one of the three variables he used. The graph shows that over the available range of K values the Pauly equation performs reasonably well, but tends toward overestimation of M for slow-growing species and underestimation of M for the faster growing ones.

The results presented here demonstrate that one can predict the natural mortality rate of snapper and grouper stocks with some accuracy, possessing nothing more than an estimate of the von Bertalanffy growth coefficient. These predictions are appreciably better than those calculated from the Pauly (1980) equation, both in terms of the distribution of residuals and the precision of estimates.

Comparable correlation coefficients were derived in the
two studies (0.82 here versus 0.84 for Pauly's overall
multiple correlation coefficient, and 0.58 for the second
order partial correlation coefficient between M and K
after the effects of temperature and asymptotic size were
removed), although the range of available K values was 17
times greater in Pauly's study (0.04-4.92 per year). By
necessity, residual variation must have correspondingly
been reduced in Figure 8.1. Moreover, the standard
deviation of $\log_{10}$ M values about the regression line
(0.247) given in Pauly (1980) is indicative of a level of
variation substantially greater than that in Figure 8.1
(s = 0.12 per year on untransformed M values). The
improvement in predictive capability of the K variable is
likely due to restricting the analysis to more narrowly
defined taxa and habitats.

AGENTS OF NATURAL MORTALITY

A number of studies have reported incidental observations on factors actually or potentially responsible for
the natural deaths of snappers and groupers. There have
been four agents identified to date, including predation,
parasitism, cold water shock, and red tides.

Starck and Schroeder (1970) were among the first to
document predation on either of these groups, observing a
great barracuda, Sphyraena barracuda, strike a gray snapper, L. griseus, and also finding the remains of another
in the stomach of a cubera snapper, L. cyanopterus.
Additionally, they also believed green morays, Gymnothorax
funebris, were important predators of L. griseus. Bradley
and Bryan (1975) found juvenile red snapper, L.
campechanus, in the gut contents of a lizard fish, Syno-
dontidae, and a dolphin, Coryphaena hippurus, and
speculated that "sharks probably also prey on snappers."
Likewise, Olsen and LaPlace (1979) observed sharks
attacking Epinephelus striatus that had formed a breeding
aggregation, and Fable (1980) saw amberjack, Seriola
dumerili, and S. barracuda consume L. campechanus and R.
aurorubens that had recently been tagged and released.
From the available evidence it seems likely that predation
related mortality on snappers and groupers is strongly
size dependent, being most severe on the young.

Parasitism of lutjanids has been documented in
several investigations (Starck and Schroeder 1970; Skinner
1982; Brusca and Gilligan 1983), but was apparently only a

serious problem where pollutants (ammonia, pesticides, etc.) so severely irritated and stressed a population of L. griseus that physical and physiological changes were induced, including epithelial hyperplasia, fusion of gill lamellae, and aneurisms. These changes resulted in reduced resistance to parasite infestations, which on occasion were debilitating (Skinner 1982).

Cold water shock has been cited repeatedly as a source of natural mortality in Florida's snappers and groupers. Starck and Schroeder (1970) reported that reduced water temperatures (11-14° C) resulting from cold snaps were known to kill L. griseus. Gilmore et al. (1978) observed mortality of E. itajara, E. morio, Mycteroperca microlepis, L. griseus, L. analis, and L. synagris from 13° C seawater. They also cite cold water intolerance by E. striatus, M. bonaci, Diplectrum formosum, L. apodus, L. jocu, and Ocyurus chrysurus. Likewise, Bohnsack (1983) observed E. striatus, L. apodus, and M. bonaci either dead or stunned from the effects of cold water (11-14° C) and concluded that "larger fish species and larger individuals within a species were the most sensitive to cold stress." Although in each of these studies thermal stress was cited as a major mortality factor, it is unlikely that most snappers and groupers, coming from more tropical climes, are similarly exposed to the threat of cold water shock.

The same is probably true of mass mortalities attributable to red tides, which typically are associated more with continental waters than insular areas. Smith (1976), however, documented extensive mortality in Gulf of Mexico populations of E. morio, E. itajara, M. microlepis, M. phenax, and L. griseus due to the effects of the red tide dinoflagellate Gymnodinium breve.

THE RELATIONSHIP OF FISHING MORTALITY TO NATURAL MORTALITY

As discussed previously, empirical and some theoretical justification exists to suppose that the optimum level of fishing mortality (F_{opt}) that can be applied to a stock to maximize biological yield is reasonably estimated by the natural mortality rate of the unfished population (Alverson and Pereyra 1969; Gulland 1971). Without detailed knowledge of the shape of the spawner-recruit relationship, however, it would seem more prudent to employ the range $0.8 M < F_{opt} < 1.5 M$ as reasonable bounds on an estimate of optimum fishing mortality (Francis 1974;

Deriso 1982; Beddington and Cooke 1983; Polovina 1986).
Given this range for a target level of exploitation, what
does the literature tell us about the intensity with which
snapper/grouper stocks have been harvested?

A convenient means of expressing exploitation intensity is to scale fishing mortality by natural mortality,
i.e., to form the ratio F/M. The ratio goes to zero in
the absence of fishing and increases without bound as
fishing mortality increases. An F/M ratio of 1.0 would
correspond to the suggestion of Gulland (1971) that
fishing mortality was at an optimal level. When properly
scaled, comparisons become possible between stocks with
differing mortality schedules and/or yield potentials.

The results presented in Table 8.2 provide a representative sampling of studies that have estimated snapper/
grouper natural and fishing mortalities. The F/M ratio is
presented for each, but some additional information is
useful in interpreting the results.

The value for natural mortality used by Nelson and
Manooch (1982) was obtained from the Pauly (1980) equation
and equaled 0.20 per year. This estimate may be low since
they estimated K = 0.17 per year. The relationship derived
earlier would suggest that M = 0.36 per year may be a
better estimate. If true, the F/M ratios listed for their
study may be too high. The same is true of Matheson and
Huntsman (1984), who used a Pauly estimate of M = 0.20 per
year for E. drummondhayi when the von Bertalanffy growth
rate parameter was determined to be K = 0.13 per year.
For P. flavipinnis (Ralston and Williams Unpub.), the
total mortality rate was determined by the Z/K regression
method of Wetherall et al. (In press) and natural mortality from the relationship between K (0.20 per year) and M
derived earlier. Although McErlean (1963) did not calculate the von Bertalanffy growth rate parameter or the
mortality rate of M. microlepis, he presented information
concerning both age at length and abundance in the catch
by age class. These data were reanalyzed using a Walford
plot and catch curve, respectively, yielding K = 0.14 per
year and Z = 1.20 per year. Natural mortality was also
estimated from the K of this species (M = 0.30 per year).
One study that is not included is that of Moe (1969),
because he estimated total mortality rate to be 0.32 per
year with a K of 0.18 per year. These findings would
suggest that the stock was lightly fished, even though it
was believed to be heavily exploited for years.

The data from Table 8.2 were tabulated into a
frequency distribution of F/M values, which is presented

TABLE 8.2
Summary information on the ratio of natural and fishing mortality estimates (F/M) for the snapper and grouper families

Species	F/M	Source
Lutjanidae		
Lutjanus	1.25	Nelson and Manooch 1982
campechanus	1.63	Nelson and Manooch 1982
	1.26	Nelson and Manooch 1982
	3.30	Nelson and Manooch 1982
L. purpureus	1.66	Ivo and Gesteira 1974
	1.94	Ivo and Hanson 1982
	2.23	Ivo and Hanson 1982
	1.73	Ivo and Hanson 1982
Pristipomoides filamentosus	1.92	Ralston 1984
P. flavipinnis	1.33	Ralston and Williams Unpub.
Serranidae		
Centropristis	1.77	Low 1981
striata	1.00	Low 1981
Epinephelus	0.85	Matheson and Huntsman 1984
drummondhayi	0.35	Matheson and Huntsman 1984
E. guttatus	0.28	Thompson and Munro 1978
	0.32	Thompson and Munro 1978
E. niveatus	0.27	Matheson 1981
	1.80	Matheson 1981
	1.93	Matheson and Huntsman 1984
	0.67	Matheson and Huntsman 1984
E. sexfasciatus	0.71	Pauly and Ingles 1982
E. striatus	2.52	Olson and LaPlace 1979
Mycteroperca microlepis	3.00	McErlean 1963 (recalculated)
M. phenax	2.00	Matheson et al. 1984
	1.24	Matheson et al. 1984

in Figure 8.2. Snapper stocks are shown in crosshatch and grouper populations are stippled. The solid line represents the frequency polygon for the combined snapper/grouper data.

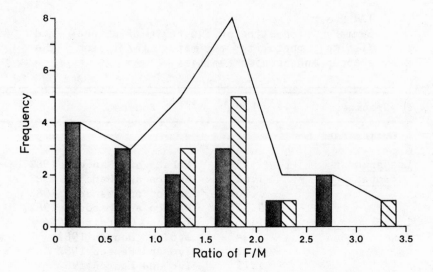

Figure 8.2 Exploitation intensity on snappers (crosshatch) and groupers (stiple). The figure presents the ratio of published values of fishing and natural mortality rates for 25 exploited stocks. The solid line represents the combined frequency polygon

At least two major trends are evident in the figure. It is clear that on a relative basis the lutjanid stocks reviewed here have been more intensely harvested than the groupers. Whether this conclusion is more generally warranted or whether it simply reflects a sampling or research bias is unknown. If, however, the pattern is real, it may reflect conservative fishing practices towards the epinephelines. This group is believed to be especially vulnerable to overexploitation, both because of their protogynous reproductive system and their tendency to aggregate during spawning (Johannes 1981; Shapiro 1986; but see Bannerot et al. 1986).

It is also apparent from the figure that many studies have determined fishing to natural mortality ratios far in excess of the 0.8 to 1.5 range suggested earlier. That some of these stocks are heavily exploited and have been so for years, is well documented (Camber 1955; Carpenter 1965; Ramirez 1970; Bradley and Bryan 1975; Tashiro and Coleman 1977). Nonetheless, the extreme levels of exploitation that seem to characterize some snapper and grouper stocks (e.g., the Louisiana stock of L. campechanus cited by Nelson and Manooch (1982), where F = 0.86 per year and F/M > 3.0) are reason to assess the situation and develop alternative explanations for these data, including the following: (1) The theoretical basis for of the $F_{opt} = M$ approximation is in error; (2) the approximation is not applicable to snapper and grouper stocks; (3) the amount of replenishment or exchange between "stocks" is often so poorly understood that analyses of population dynamics tell us very little; and (4) some stocks are simply over-fished due to lack of management action.

With regard to relative levels of exploitation, one observation by Adams (1980) is particularly relevant. So-called "K" selected species are those with late maturity, slow growth rate, large asymptotic size, low rates of natural mortality, and extended maximum age. Note that K here refers to carrying capacity, which should not be confused with the von Bertalanffy growth coefficient. Members of the Lutjanidae and Epinephelinae, when placed on an r-K continuum defined by the community of tropical species with which they are found, tend to fit this description well (Beverton and Holt 1959; Pauly 1980). Simulation studies (Adams 1980) and actual fisheries experience (Huntsman et al. 1983; Mahmoudi et al. 1984) have shown that for these kinds of species, maximum yield per recruit (sensu Beverton and Holt 1957) is obtained at lower levels of fishing mortality and higher ages of recruitment (i.e., entry to the fishery) than their ecological counterparts. Furthermore, the relatively low levels of natural mortality that characterize snappers and groupers indicate a low natural turnover ratio (Allen 1971) and thus a reduced productive capacity (Alverson and Pereyra 1969; Gulland 1971). Fisheries for these kinds of species are also likely to develop excessive harvesting capacity during the fishing-up process (Francis 1984; Leaman and Beamish 1984). Based upon these considerations and on the high economic value of snappers and groupers, it is important that future efforts to manage these resources show caution and appropriate restraint.

BIBLIOGRAPHY

Adams, P. B. 1980. Life history patterns in marine fishes and their consequences for fisheries management. Fish. Bull., U.S. 78:1-12.

Allen, K. R. 1971. Relation between production and biomass. J. Fish. Res. Board Can. 28:1573-1581.

Alverson, D. L., and W. T. Pereyra. 1969. Demersal fish explorations in the northwestern Pacific Ocean - An evaluation of exploratory fishing methods and analytical approaches to stock size and yield forecasts. J. Fish. Res. Board Can. 26:1985-2001.

Bannerot, S. P., W. W. Fox, Jr., and F. E. Powers. 1986. The biology and management of snappers and groupers in the tropics: Assessment and management in the Gulf of Mexico and Caribbean. In J. J. Polovina and S. Ralston (editors), Tropical snappers and groupers: Biology and fisheries management. Westview Press, Inc., Boulder. [See this volume.]

Bartoo, N. W., and K. R. Parker. 1983. Stochastic age-frequency estimation using the von Bertalanffy growth equation. Fish. Bull., U.S. 81:91-96.

Beddington, J. R., and J. G. Cooke. 1983. The potential yield of fish stocks. FAO Fish. Tech. Pap. 242, 47 p.

Beverton, R. J. H., and S. J. Holt. 1956. A review of methods for estimating mortality rates in exploited fish populations, with special reference to sources of bias in catch sampling. Rapp. P.-V. Reun. Cons. Int. Explor. Mer 140:67-83.

_____. 1957. On the dynamics of exploited fish populations. Fish. Invest. Ser. II. Mar. Fish., G. B. Minist. Agric. Fish. Food 19:1-533.

_____. 1959. A review of the lifespans and mortality rates of fish in nature, and their relation to growth and other physiological characteristics. In G. E. Wolstenholme and M. O'Connor (editors), The lifespan of animals, p. 142-177. CIBA Found. Colloq. Aging 5.

Bohnsack, J. A. 1983. Resiliency of reef fish communities in the Florida Keys following a January 1977 hypothermal fish kill. Environ. Biol. Fishes 9(1): 41-53.

Bradley, E., and C. E. Bryan. 1975. Life history and fishery of the red snapper (Lutjanus campechanus) in the northwestern Gulf of Mexico: 1970-1974. Proc. 27th Annu. Gulf Caribb. Fish. Inst. p. 77-106.

Brouard, F., and R. Grandperrin. 1984. Les poissons profonds de la pente recifale externe a Vanuatu. Notes et Documents d'Oceanographie No. 11, 131 p. Mission ORSTOM, Port-Vila, Vanuatu.

Brusca, R. C., and M. R. Gilligan. 1983. Tongue replacement in a marine fish (Lutjanus guttatus) by a parasitic isopod (Crustacea: Isopoda). Copeia 1983: 813–816.

Bullis, H. R., Jr., and A. C. Jones, (editors). 1976. Proceedings: Colloquium on snapper-grouper fishery resources of the western central Atlantic Ocean. Fla. Sea Grant Coll. Rep. 17, 333 p.

Butler, S. A., and L. L. McDonald. 1979. A simulation study of a catch-effort model for estimating mortality rates. Trans. Am. Fish. Soc. 108:353–357.

Camber, C. I. 1955. A survey of the red snapper fishery of the Gulf of Mexico, with special reference to the Campeche Banks. Fla. Board Conserv. Mar. Res. Tech. Ser. 12, 64 p.

Carpenter, J. S. 1965. A review of the Gulf of Mexico red snapper fishery. U.S. Fish Wildl. Serv., Circ. 208, 35 p.

Chapman, D. G., and D. S. Robson. 1960. The analysis of a catch curve. Biometrics 16:354–368.

Clark, W. G. 1981. Restricted least-squares estimates of age composition from length composition. Can. J. Fish. Aquat. Sci. 38:297–307.

Csirke, J., and J. F. Caddy. 1983. Production modeling using mortality estimates. Can. J. Fish. Aquat. Sci. 40:43–51.

Cushing, D. H. 1968. Fisheries biology, a study in population dynamics. University of Wisconsin Press, Madison, 200 p.

Deriso, R. B. 1982. Relationship of fishing mortality and growth at the level of maximum sustainable yield. Can. J. Fish. Aquat. Sci. 39:1054–1058.

Ebert, T. A. 1973. Estimating growth and mortality rates from size data. Oecologia (Berl.) 11:281–298.

Fable, W. A., Jr. 1980. Tagging studies of red snapper (Lutjanus campechanus) and vermilion snapper (Rhomboplites aurorubens) off the south Texas coast. Contrib. Mar. Sci. 23(Aug.):115–121.

Francis, R. C. 1974. Relationship of fishing mortality to natural mortality at the level of maximum sustainable yield under the logistic stock production model. J. Fish. Res. Board Can. 31:1539–1542.

_____. 1984. Fisheries research and its application to west coast groundfish management. In T. L. Frady (editor), Proceedings of the Conference on Fisheries Management: Issues and Options, p. 285–304. Alaska Sea Grant Program, Fairbanks.

Fridriksson, A. 1934. On the calculation of age distribution within a stock of cod by means of relatively few age-determinations as a key to measurements on a large scale. Rapp. P.-V. Reun. Cons. Int. Explor. Mer 86:1-5.

Gilmore, R. G., L. H. Bullock, and F. H. Berry. 1978. Hypothermal mortality in marine fishes off south-central Florida, January 1977. Northeast Gulf Sci. 2(2):77-97.

Goeden, G. B. 1977. The life and loves of the coral trout. Aust. Fish. 36(8):16-18.

Gray, D. F. 1979. Some extensions to the least squares approach to deriving mortality coefficients. Invest. Pesq. 43:241-243.

Green, R. H. 1970. Graphical estimation of rates of mortality and growth. J. Fish. Res. Board Can. 27:204-208.

Gulland, J. A. 1955. Estimation of growth and mortality in commercial fish populations. Fish. Invest. Ser., II Mar. Fish., G. B. Minist. Agric. Fish. Food 18(9):1-46.

_____ (compiler and editor). 1971. The fish resources of the ocean. Fishing News (Books) Ltd., Surrey, Engl., 225 p.

Gunderson, D. R. 1980. Using r-K selection theory to predict natural mortality. Can. J. Fish. Aquat. Sci. 37:2266-2271.

Hoenig, J. M. 1983. Empirical use of longevity data to estimate mortality rates. Fish. Bull., U.S. 82:898-903.

Huntsman, G. R., C. S. Manooch III, and C. B. Grimes. 1983. Yield per recruit models of some reef fishes of the U.S. South Atlantic Bight. Fish. Bull., U.S. 81:679-695.

Ivo, C. T. C., and T. C. V. Gesteira. 1974. Estimacão preliminar des medidas de mortalidade do pargo Lutjanus purpureus Poey, no norte e nordeste Brasileiros. Arq. Cienc. Mar 14(2):123-127.

Ivo, C. T. C., and A. J. Hanson. 1982. Aspectos da biologia e dinamica populacional do pargo, Lutjanus purpureus Poey, no norte e nordeste do Brasil. Arq. Cienc. Mar 22(1/2):1-41.

Jensen, A. J. C. 1939. On the laws of decrease in fish stocks. Rapp. P.-V. Reun. Cons. Int. Explor. Mer 110:86-96.

Johannes, R. E. 1981. Words of the lagoon: Fishing and marine lore in the Palau District of Micronesia. University of California Press, Berkeley, 245 p.

Kimura, D. K. 1977. Statistical assessment of the age-length key. J. Fish. Res. Board Can. 34:317-324.

Kunzel, T., V. Lowenberg, and W. Weber. 1983. Demersal fish resources of the Mahe Plateau/Seychelles. Arch. Fischereiwiss. 34(1):1-22.

Leaman, B. M., and R. J. Beamish. 1984. Ecological and management implications of longevity in some northeast Pacific groundfishes. Int. North Pac. Fish. Comm. Bull. 42:85-97.

Low, R. A. Jr. 1981. Mortality rates and management strategies for black sea bass off the southeast coast of the United States. N. Am. J. Fish. Manage. 1:93-103.

MacArthur, R. H., and E. O. Wilson. 1967. The theory of island biography. Princeton University Press, Princeton, New Jersey, 203 p.

Mahmoudi, B., J. E. Powers, and G. R. Huntsman. 1984. Assessment of vermilion snapper of the northern South Atlantic Bight. Second Southeast Stock Assessment Workshop, June 4-8, 1984, Miami. Southeast Fish. Cent., Natl. Mar. Fish. Serv., NOAA, SAW/84/RFR/2, 36 p.

Majkowski, J. 1982. Usefulness and applicability of sensitivity analysis in a multispecies approach to fisheries management. In D. Pauly and G. I. Murphy (editors), Theory and management of tropical fisheries, p. 149-165. Proceedings of the ICLARM/CSIRO Workshop on the Theory and Management of Tropical Multispecies Stocks, 12-21 January 1981, Cronulla, Australia. ICLARM Conf. Proc. 9.

Manooch, C. S. III. 1986. A review of age and growth of the Lutjanidae and Serranidae. In J. J. Polovina and S. Ralston (editors), Tropical snappers and groupers: Biology and fisheries management. Westview Press, Inc., Boulder. [See this volume.]

Manooch, C. S. III, and M. Haimovici. 1978. Age and growth of the gag, Mycteroperca microlepis, and size-age composition of the recreational catch off the southeastern United States. Trans. Am. Fish. Soc. 107:234-240.

Marten, G. G. 1978. Calculating mortality rates and optimum yields from length samples. J. Fish. Res. Board Can. 35:197-201.

Matheson, R. H. III. 1982. Age, growth, and mortality of two groupers, Epinephelus drummondhayi Goode and Bean and Epinephelus niveatus (Valenciennes), from North

Carolina and South Carolina. M.S. Thesis, North Carolina State Univ., Raleigh, 67 p.

Matheson, R. H. III., and G. R. Huntsman. 1984. Growth, mortality, and yield per recruit models for speckled hind and snowy grouper from the United States South Atlantic Bight. Trans. Am. Fish. Soc. 113:607–616.

Matheson, R. H. III., G. R. Huntsman, and C. S. Manooch III. 1984. Age, growth, mortality, foods and reproduction of the scamp, Mycteroperca phenax, collected off North Carolina and South Carolina. Second Southeast Stock Assessment Workshop, June 4–8, 1984, Miami. Southeast Fish. Cent., Natl. Mar. Fish. Serv., NOAA, SAW/84/RFR/8, 38 p.

McErlean, A. J. 1963. A study of the age and growth of the gag, Mycteroperca microlepis Goode and Bean (Pisces: Serranidae) on the west coast of Florida. Fla. Board Conserv., Mar. Res. Lab. Tech. Ser. 41: 1–29.

Menezes, M. F. De., and T. C. V. Gesteira. 1974. Age and growth of the pargo, Lutjanus purpureus Poey, in northern and northeastern Brasil. Arq. Cienc. Mar 14(2):81–85.

Moe, M. A., Jr. 1969. Biology of the red grouper Epinephelus morio (Valenciennes) from the eastern Gulf of Mexico. Fla. Dep. Nat. Resour., Mar. Res. Lab. Prof. Pap. Ser. 10:1–95.

Moore, C. M., and R. F. Labisky. 1984. Population parameters of a relatively unexploited stock of snowy grouper in the lower Florida Keys. Trans. Am. Fish. Soc. 113:322–329.

Munro, J. L. 1982. Estimation of biological and fishery parameters in coral reef fisheries. In D. Pauly and G. I. Murphy (editors), Theory and management of tropical fisheries, p. 71–82. Proceedings of the ICLARM/CSIRO Workshop on the Theory and Management of Tropical Multispecies Stocks, 12–21 January 1981, Cronulla, Australia. ICLARM Conf. Proc. 9.

_____ (editor). 1983. Caribbean coral reef fishery resources. ICLARM Stud. Rev. 7, 276 p.

Myers, R. A., and R. W. Doyle. 1983. Predicting natural mortality rates and reproduction—mortality trade-offs from fish life history data. Can. J. Fish. Aquat. Sci. 40:612–620.

Nagelkerken, W. P. 1979. Biology of the graysby, Epinephelus cruentatus, of the coral reef of Curacao. Stud. Fauna Curacao Other Caribb. Isl. 60:1–118.

Nelson, R. S., and C. S. Manooch III. 1982. Growth and mortality of red snappers in the west-central Atlantic Ocean and northern Gulf of Mexico. Trans. Am. Fish. Soc. 111:465-475.

Olsen, D. A., and J. A. LaPlace. 1979. A study of a Virgin Islands grouper fishery based on a breeding aggregation. Proc. 31st Annu. Gulf and Caribb. Fish Inst., p. 130-144.

Paloheimo, J. E. 1980. Estimation of mortality rates in fish populations. Trans. Am. Fish. Soc. 109:378-386.

Pauly, D. 1979. Theory and management of tropical multispecies stocks: A review with emphasis on the Southeast Asian demersal fisheries. ICLARM Stud. Rev. 1, Manila, 35 p.

_____. 1980. On the interrelationships between natural mortality, growth parameters, and mean environmental temperature in 175 fish stocks. J. Cons. Cons. Int. Explor. Mer 39:175-192.

_____. 1982. Studying single-species dynamics in a tropical multispecies context. In D. Pauly and G. I. Murphy (editors), Theory and management of tropical fisheries, p. 33-70. Proceedings of the ICLARM/ CSIRO Workshop on the Theory and Management of Tropical Multispecies Stocks, 12-21 January 1981, Cronulla, Australia. ICLARM Conf. Proc. 9.

Pauly, D., and J. Ingles. 1982. Aspects of the growth and natural mortality of exploited coral reef fishes. In E. D. Gomez, C. E. Birkeland, R. W. Buddemeir, R. E. Johannes, J. A. Marsh, Jr., and R. T. Tsuda (editors), Proc. 4th Int. Coral Reef Symp., Manila, 1:89-98.

Piedra, G. 1965. Materials on the biology of the yellowtail snapper (Ocyurus chrysurus Bloch). In A. S. Bogdanov (editor), Sovetsko-Kubinskie rybokhozyaistvennye issledovaniya. Izdatel'stvo "Pishchevaya Promyshlennost'." [Soviet-Cuban Fish. Res.] (Transl. IPST 5514, TT 69-59016, p. 251-269. 1969. Clearinghouse Fed. Sci. Tech. Inf., Springfield, Va.)

Polovina, J. J. 1986. Assessment and management of deepwater bottom fishes in Hawaii and the Marianas. In J. J. Polovina and S. Ralston (editors), Tropical snappers and groupers: Biology and fisheries management. Westview Press, Inc., Boulder. [See this volume.]

Powell, D. G. 1979. Estimation of mortality and growth parameters from the length frequency of a catch. Rapp. P.-V. Reun. Cons. Int. Explor. Mer 175:167-169.

Powers, J. E. 1983. Report of the Southeast Fisheries Center stock assessment workshop August 3-6, 1982. U.S. Dep. Commer., NOAA Tech. Memo. NMFS, NOAA-TM-NMFS-SEFC-127, 229 p.

Ralston, S. 1984. Biological constraints on production and related management issues in the Hawaiian deepsea handline fishery. In R. W. Grigg and K. Y. Tanoue (editors), Proceedings of the Second Symposium on Resource Investigations in the Northwestern Hawaiian Islands, Vol. 2, May 25-27, 1983, Univ. Hawaii, Honolulu, p. 248-264. UNIHI-SEAGRANT-MR-84-01.

Ralston, S., and G. T. Miyamoto. 1983. Analyzing the width of daily otolith increments to age the Hawaiian snapper, Pristipomoides filamentosus. Fish. Bull., U.S. 81:523-535.

Ralston, S., and J. J. Polovina. 1982. A multispecies analysis of the commercial deep-sea handline fishery in Hawaii. Fish. Bull., U.S. 80:435-448.

Ralston, S., and H. A. Williams. Unpub. Age, growth, and mortality of lutjanid and other deep slope fishes from the Mariana Archipelago. Southwest Fish. Cent., Honolulu Lab., Natl. Mar. Fish. Serv., NOAA, Honolulu, HI 96822-2396.

Ramirez, M. S. 1970. The red grouper fishery of Yucatan Peninsula, Mexico. Proc. 22d Gulf Caribb. Fish. Inst., p. 122-129.

Ricker, W. E. 1973. Linear regressions in fishery research. J. Fish. Res. Board Can. 30:409-434.

_____. 1975. Computation and interpretation of biological statistics of fish populations. Bull. Fish. Res. Board Can. 191, 382 p.

Robson, D. S., and D. G. Chapman. 1961. Catch curves and mortality rates. Trans. Am. Fish. Soc. 90:181-189.

Saetersdal, G. 1973. Assessment of unexploited resources. J. Fish. Res. Board Can. 30:2010-2016.

Saila, S. B., and R. G. Lough. 1981. Mortality and growth estimation from size data - an application to some Atlantic herring larvae. Rapp. P.-V. Reun. Cons. Int. Explor. Mer 178:7-14.

Schnute, J., and D. Fournier. 1980. A new approach to length-frequency analysis: Growth structure. Can. J. Fish. Aquat. Sci. 37:1337-1351.

Seber, G. A. F. 1982. The estimation of animal abundance. MacMillan Publishing Co., Inc., N.Y., 654 p.

Shapiro, D. Y. 1986. Reproduction in groupers. In J. J. Polovina and S. Ralston (editors), Tropical snappers and groupers: Biology and fisheries management. Westview Press, Inc., Boulder. [See this volume.]

Skinner, R. H. 1982. The interrelation of water quality, gill parasites, and gill pathology of some fishes from South Biscayne Bay, Florida. Fish. Bull., U.S. 80:269-280.

Smith, G. B. 1976. The impact of fish-killing phytoplankton blooms upon mideastern Gulf of Mexico reeffish communities. In H. R. Bullis, Jr. and A. C. Jones (editors), Proceedings: Colloquium on Snapper-Grouper Fishery Resources of the Western Central Atlantic Ocean, p. 185-191. Texas A&M Univ. Sea Grant Coll. and Mississippi-Alabama Sea Grant Consortium. Fla. Sea Grant Coll. Rep. 17.

Snedecor, G. W., and W. G. Cochran. 1967. Statistical methods. Iowa State Univ. Press, Ames, 593 p.

Ssentongo, G. W., and P. A. Larkin. 1973. Some simple methods of estimating mortality rates of exploited fish populations. J. Fish. Res. Board Can. 30:695-698.

Starck, W. A. II, and R. E. Schroeder. 1970. Investigations of the gray snapper, Lutjanus griseus. Stud. Trop. Oceanogr. (Miami) 10, 224 p., 44 figs. (Copyright 1971.)

Sylvester, J. R. 1974. A preliminary study of the length composition, distribution, and relative abundance of three species of deepwater snappers from the Virgin Islands. J. Fish Biol. 6:43-49.

Tashiro, J. E., and S. E. Coleman. 1977. The Cuban grouper and snapper fishery in the Gulf of Mexico. Mar. Fish. Rev. 39(10):1-6.

Thompson, R., and J. L. Munro. 1978. Aspects of the biology and ecology of Caribbean reef fishes: Serranidae (hinds and groupers). J. Fish Biol. 12:115-146.

Tiurin, P. V. 1962. Factor estestvennoi smertnosti ryb i ego znachenie pri regulirovanii rybolovstva (The natural mortality factor and its importance in regulating fisheries). Vopr. Ikhtiol. 2:403-427. (Fish. Res. Board Can. Transl. Ser. 558).

Westrheim, S. J., and W. E. Ricker. 1978. Bias in using an age-length key to estimate age-frequency distributions. J. Fish. Res. Board Can. 35:184-189.

Wetherall, J. A., J. J. Polovina, and S. Ralston.   In press.   Estimating growth and mortality in steady state fish stocks from length-frequency data.   In D. Pauly and G. R. Morgan (editors), Length-based methods in fishery research.   The ICLARM/KISR Conference on the Theory and Application of Length-Based Methods for Stock Assessments, Sicily, Italy, February 1985.   Vol. 1.

Witzig, J. F., and G. R. Huntsman.   1984.   Report: Mortality rates of South Atlantic reef fishes as determined from samples of the headboat fishery. Second Southeast Stock Assessment Workshop, June 4-8, 1984, Miami.   Southeast Fish. Cent., Natl. Mar. Fish. Serv., NOAA, SAW/84/RFR/6, 24 p.

9
The Trophic Biology of Snappers and Groupers

James D. Parrish
Hawaii Cooperative Fishery Research Unit
University of Hawaii
Honolulu, Hawaii 96822

ABSTRACT

Snappers and groupers are large, predacious fishes that occur commonly in benthic habitats throughout the tropics and subtropics of the world. Their trophic biology has been incompletely studied, but much new information has been added within the last two decades. Especially little is known about the deepwater species because of limited scientific collection and frequent loss of gut contents by regurgitation.

Snappers and groupers consume a broad range of prey dominated by fish, crabs, shrimp, and other benthic crustaceans, especially stomatopods and lobsters. Cephalopods are a common diet component, especially for snappers, which also eat large plankton, including particularly pelagic urochordates and gastropods. The importance of plant material, which has been found in the guts of a number of species, cannot be resolved from reports available.

Snapper and grouper species occur and apparently feed from the surface to depths of 400-500 m. Few snappers but many groupers feed only in shallow waters (to several tens of meters). Conversely, many snappers but few groupers (at least as adults) are restricted to feeding in water more than 100 m deep. Many species of both families forage at intermediate depths and sometimes in the shallows as well. Diets of the fully deepwater species are poorly known; results from all known sources are reported here. Fish are again the major prey group, but shrimp, planktonic urochordates and gastropods, and cephalopods are more important than in shallow-water species, while crabs are less important.

Habitat dependence appears stronger in the groupers, which generally lead more sedentary lives and feed more by ambush than do snappers. Snapper feeding usually involves widespread foraging, most often at night. Groupers seem to feed at all times of day, perhaps more actively near dawn and dusk. Most species take most of their prey at or very near the bottom.

Snappers and groupers exert a major predation pressure on many benthic fishes and invertebrates. The distribution and diversity of their prey suggest that most snappers and groupers can draw upon a broad base of food resources. This may reduce competition among these predator species and provide considerable resilience to alterations in their trophic environment. However, major reductions in populations (e.g., by fishing) of some snapper or grouper species can be expected to reduce predation pressure and feeding competition, thus enhancing populations and potential catches of other demersal, carnivorous fishes, including snappers and groupers.

INTRODUCTION

While the trophic literature on snappers and groupers is substantial, these fishes are much less studied than some other groups. A great deal of the extant literature is recent, and it seems appropriate that a summary and synthesis of the widely scattered information now be made. If snappers and groupers have escaped serious trophic study until recently, it may have been largely due to the combination of (1) their occurrence in the tropics (away from most fish scientists) and (2) the relatively diffuse nature of traditional fisheries for them. Both these factors have changed considerably within the last two decades.

The earliest (largely anecdotal) trophic reports on these fishes were made before the turn of the century (e.g., Collins 1887; Brice 1898) and were usually based on incidental observations on the catch of established fisheries. Additional results accumulated during the first half of the present century from similar sources and from a few natural history studies at a small number of tropical laboratories (e.g., Kluegel 1921; Breder 1925;

Beebe and Tee-Van 1928; Gudger 1929; Breder and Nigrelli 1934; Longley and Hildebrand 1941).

Beginning around 1960, several important multispecies studies were completed (e.g., Hiatt and Strasburg 1960; Randall and Brock 1960; Talbot 1960; Miles 1963; Randall 1967; Hobson 1968), as well as more detailed studies of individual species (especially by workers from Caribbean countries). Some trophic results also appeared as incidental ecological notes in popular monographs on fish identification, distribution, and species biology (e.g., Bohlke and Chaplin 1968; Randall 1968; Bagnis et al. 1972; Fourmanoir and Laboute 1976; Schroeder 1980; van der Elst 1981; Masuda et al. 1984).

The rate of publication has subsequently increased, with the addition of several works on groups of species in the early 1970s (e.g., Druzhinin [summary] 1970; Brownell and Rainey 1971; Starck 1971). Since about 1975, publication has been especially prolific, including new studies of individual species and of groups of species in a regional fishery, and summaries of available information for regional fisheries. The total information available on trophics of deeper species (away from coral reefs, immediate coastal areas, and shallow banks) has multiplied many times since the studies of Brownell and Rainey (1971), and especially over the last 10 years. Almost all data for the deepwater genera Etelis and Pristipomoides are from this period.

Diets of the truly deepwater fishes remain poorly known. This is partly a result of the remote fishing locations and inadequate funds for research. The situation is rapidly improving, however, because of recent attempts to expand and develop fisheries for deepwater snappers and groupers.

An equally serious problem is the loss of gut contents by regurgitation at the time of capture, caused by the rapid ascent from deep water. Regurgitation has been controlled with some success by raising the fish slowly to permit gradual decompression (e.g., Moseley 1966; Burnett-Herkes 1975; Oda and Parrish 1981). When regurgitation occurs, it is sometimes still possible to salvage food items retained in the mouth, gill rakers, or other structures, or spewed onto the deck when the fish are landed (e.g., Seki 1984; Parrish and Callahan Unpub. data; Ralston and Sorden Unpub. data) (Appendixes A and B). Most studies employ the reasonable assumption that, at least for sizable collections, what is recovered represents a fairly unbiased sample of what the guts contained at the time of capture.

CHARACTERISTICS OF THE DIET

Snappers and groupers have often been characterized as generalized, opportunistic carnivores. A review of the literature on their diets provides considerable support for this view (Appendix A). For snappers, at least 15 rather high level, nonoverlapping diet classes are represented in Appendix A, including 5 of the major column categories and a further breakdown of "benthic invertebrates" and "plankton" (see footnote abbreviations). For groupers, at least 13 classes are represented. Certainly a large variety of foods is included in terms of systematics, structure, size, texture, habitat, nutritional value, and means of capture and handling. The range of diet is, as a whole, broader for the snappers than for the groupers. This is partly because almost no feeding on planktonic animals has been reported for groupers, whereas it is perhaps surprisingly common in snappers. A wide range of noncrustacean benthos is also reported in the diets of snappers, much more so than in groupers. In addition, cephalopods are reported more often in snappers.

A crude measure of how widespread or pervasive the various food groups are in the diets of these fishes can be drawn from their frequency of occurrence among the various literature sources. For snappers, results from at least 199 reports (studies, collections, citations, or summaries) are included in Appendix A, counting only adults in reports where juveniles are recorded separately. There must be some repetition, since not all publications contained original data, but duplication was avoided when apparent. Similarly, there are results from at least 210 reports for groupers. A more restricted subset includes only those reports in which a specific, unique sample of about 10 specimens or more was clearly reported. There are results from at least 88 such reports for snappers and 60 for groupers.

If these materials are used as a basis of assessment, the dominant food groups for both families are clearly fish and decapod crustaceans (Table 9.1). For snappers, fish were recorded to compose more than about 10% of all prey in 90% of the more quantitative reports. Fish were the major diet category in 56% of these reports. For all

TABLE 9.1
Major diet categories of snappers and groupers based on percent frequency of occurrence in the literature (data from Appendix A)

Diet Category	Percentage of Studies in Which Category Was ≥10% of the Diet		Percentage of Studies in Which Category Was Dominant	
	Lutjanidae	Serranidae	Lutjanidae	Serranidae
Fish	90	95	56	72
Shrimp	30	23	2	0
Crabs	56	43	15	17
Other crustaceans	32	17	2	2
Other benthic invertebrates	13	8	0	0
Cephalopods	10	7	1	0
Plankton	17	0	3	0

groupers combined, the corresponding occurrences were 95 and 72%, respectively. These reports were usually unambiguous, although sometimes there was doubt about the extent to which larval fish may have been reported as fish or as plankton. Many sources reported some or all of the recognizable types of fish consumed; occasionally some breakdown by size was given. The systematic range was great, and few general trends seemed to emerge. In a few studies, the range of fish prey taxa reported was rather restricted, even when samples were sizable. However, many studies with large sample sizes indicated that the species have generalized tastes and can capture a variety of diverse fishes.

For a number of commercial species taken at intermediate depths in other than coral reef locations, small, schooling species such as clupeids and engraulids appeared prominently in the diets. Anguilliform fishes were rather common and sometimes fairly abundant in the diets of snappers and groupers. Predacious forms such as congrids and muraenids were included. Where snappers were taken on or near coral reefs, the diet included a variety of fishes that are often associated with reefs; however, fish that are not reef associated were also common.

Crabs were the second largest diet category, and it seems clear that a variety of adult crabs are important in the diets of fish from both families. Most were likely brachyurans, although anomurans were also cited. Most reports were not more specific. Portunids and calappids were mentioned in several reports; this may represent a positive reporting bias because these groups have conspicuous identifying characters. In some studies, larval forms of crabs and other crustaceans were reported explicitly. Any significant amounts reported are noted in Appendix A. However, it is likely that an additional undisclosed larval component was included in some of the totals. In many studies all crustaceans were reported together, and even when major groups such as crabs and shrimps were named, the quantities could not always be separated (hence the dotted lines across some columns of Appendix A). Crabs and shrimps are reported in Appendix A separately, as quantitatively as the available information permitted.

Shrimps were the next largest discrete diet category, followed by "other crustaceans"--defined as all benthic crustaceans other than crabs and shrimps. Major groups included stomatopods and lobsters; small forms such as amphipods were occasionally quantitatively significant.

Obviously planktonic forms such as copepods, euphausiids, and unidentified larvae were included in plankton where possible. Both shrimps and other benthic crustaceans represent important components of the diets of these fishes. Again, the composition of the prey was diverse, but the groups mentioned were the major constituents, although their relative importance varied among predator species.

No other groups of benthic invertebrates were broadly important in the diets of these fishes. Altogether a large variety of forms occurred, but usually only very few types were of any importance for particular species. The aggregate of all these benthic groups was never dominant in a sample, and the fraction of total food that they represented was nearly always rather small. No single group was particularly conspicuous. Molluscs were reported most often, usually as gastropods or unspecified. Benthic urochordates were mentioned in several reports, occurring primarily in deepwater species. Sometimes it was unclear whether urochordates were benthic or pelagic. Cephalopods occurred very widely (40% of all snapper reports, 30% of all grouper reports), although the quantity in a gut was often low. Both squid and octopus were well represented.

Planktonic forms may be fairly important for some snappers, both in frequency of occurrence and in bulk consumed, especially in the deepwater species. The major components were pelagic gastropods (pteropods and heteropods) and pelagic urochordates (Salpida, Pyrosomida, and Dolioda). These groups were reported from several geographic areas and several species. In some reports, they occurred in species that are believed to feed above the bottom. Often the quantities in a gut were substantial. The nutritional value of the gelatinous forms may be rather low, but the large quantities eaten at times suggest that they are important in the diet. The gastropods must be a valuable pelagic food resource for some species. For a very few snappers (e.g., Ocyurus chrysurus, Rhomboplites aurorubens, perhaps Macolor niger), traditional small plankton—primarily small crustaceans—appear to provide a significant part of the diets of adults (Appendix A) (Hiatt and Strasburg 1960; Schroeder 1980). Such plankton are also probably important for certain more pelagic lutjanids such as the Paracaesio species, which are not reviewed here.

Snappers and groupers are commonly considered to be entirely carnivorous, and clearly their diets are heavily dominated by animal food. However, on a number of

occasions plant material has been reported in the guts of
snappers: 17 reports involving 11 snapper species were
encountered in this review, plus 1 report for a grouper.
In several reports the amount of material was small or was
unspecified. A number of authors have suggested (always
without presenting evidence) that the plant material
present in their samples was probably ingested incidental
to capturing animal food. However, there are at least six
reports in which the plant material was quantified, with
occurrences ranging from 2 to 23% of all fish specimens
and amounts ranging from 0.1 to 15% of gut contents by
volume. Bagnis et al. (1972) reported that _Lutjanus_
kasmira in French Polynesia "also eat various species of
algae," and algae are reported in the guts of that species
in two other studies and once in the very similar _L._
quinquelineatus (Talbot 1960; Schroeder 1980; Mizenko
1984). Evidence in the literature to date does not establish whether plant material has any role in the nutrition
of snappers or groupers. Data on their consumption of
plant material must be taken and reported more fully,
carefully, and objectively if that possibility is to be
explored further.

FEEDING AND DEPTH

The depth at which feeding occurs is an important
aspect of fish trophic ecology. Available accounts of
snapper and grouper feeding indicate that depth is poorly
known. For many studies it is simply not reported, even
where a set of rather discrete, coherent collections is
involved. Often the range of capture depths reported
together is such that no detailed information on depth of
feeding can be extracted. Very few investigators appear
to have specifically considered feeding as a function of
depth in collecting samples and analyzing data. Thus,
there is often little basis for estimating depths in
association with diet information, other than (1) records
of the range of depths from which the species has ever
been reported or (2) generalized comments on the depths at
which it is commonly fished.

For several species, the reported depth range is very
great, even as adults, and preferred depth strata often
change with age. For example, _L. synagris_ is reported to
occur between 9 and 395 m, and _Epinephelus niveatus_ has
been collected from the shoreline to 395 m depth (Florida
Sea Grant College 1981). For such fishes, unless depths in

specific reports on feeding are well documented, there is little prospect of identifying the particular depth range that constitutes the important feeding habitat and determining what resource environments are important for support of these fishes. There appears to be a fairly general trend that young juveniles of most species are found shallower (i.e., inshore) than the adults (e.g., Randall 1967; Starck 1971; Schroeder 1980; Florida Sea Grant College 1981; van der Elst 1981; Masuda et al. 1984; Allen 1986). Except where otherwise stated, this discussion is restricted to the food and feeding ecology of adults.

Most of the species considered here probably have reported depth ranges of at least several tens of meters, which involve a variety of habitat types and available food resources. The groups most easily defined are those that are restricted rather strongly to very shallow or very deep waters (Table 9.2).

A small number of snapper species and a much larger number of groupers appear to be restricted to feeding almost entirely in waters several tens of meters deep. In contrast, many snappers but very few groupers appear to feed almost entirely in deep water. Of the remaining fishes, many species of both families seem to cover a range of intermediate depths. Several occur very shallow as well as fairly deep; others are limited to an inter-mediate range. In both families, a few species (the "mixed" group of Table 9.2) occur in shallow water commonly enough to be distinguished from the deepwater group; however, they are also commonly caught in deeper water (e.g., 150-200 m) than the intermediate-depth group. Species missing from Table 9.2 were: (1) not reviewed; (2) without trophic data; or (3) without sufficient informa-tion to estimate their depth ranges.

The species restricted to shallow water often seem to be associated with hermatypic coral reefs, sand/shell flats, grass beds, and mangrove lagoons. The depth dis-tribution of specific resources (food or shelter) peculiar to these environments may tend to limit the depth distri-bution of these fishes. However, many species occupy more than one shallow environment and probably also feed in more than one. There is much broad similarity, particu-larly at higher taxonomic levels of prey, between the diets of these fishes and those that also forage in deeper water.

The fully deepwater fishes are the group whose diet is least known. For Pacific _Etelis_, information exists

TABLE 9.2
Likely depth ranges for major feeding of some snapper and grouper species. (shallow only = several tens of meters; intermediate = shallow to over 100 m; mixed = intermediate to deep; and deep = mostly over 100 to 500 m)

LUTJANIDAE[a]

Shallow Only	Intermediate	Mixed	Deep
Lutjanus apodus	Lutjanus analis	Aphareus rutilans	Etelis carbunculus
L. fulviflamma <-----	L. argentimaculatus	Apsilus dentatus	E. coruscans
L. fulvus <-----	L. bohar	Lutjanus buccanella	E. oculatus
L. mahogoni	L. boutton[b]	L. vivanus	E. radiosus
L. russelli	L. campechanus[b]	Rhomboplites aurorubens	Pristipomoides amoenus
Macolor niger <-----	L. cyanopterus		P. aquilonaris
	L. gibbus		P. argyrogrammicus
	L. griseus		P. auricilla
	L. jocu		P. filamentosus
	L. johnii		P. flavipinnis
	L. kasmira -------->		P. macrophthalmus
	L. malabaricus		P. multidens
	L. monostigma		P. sieboldii
	L. purpureus		P. typus
	L. rivulatus		P. zonatus
	L. sanguineus		
	L. sebae		
	L. synagris -------->		
	Ocyurus chrysurus		

SERRANIDAE

Alphestes afer	Aethaloperca rogaa	Epinephelus	Epinephelus
Anyperodon	Centropristis striata	chlorostigma	epistictus
leucogrammicus	Cephalopholis aurantia	E. flavocaeruleus	E. morrhua
Cephalopholis argus	C. fulva	E. flavolimbatus	E. mystacinus
C. miniata	C. sexmaculata	E. modestus	E. quernus[c]
C. oligosticta	C. sonnerati	E. niveatus	E. tuamotuensis
C. urodela	Epinephelus		
Dinoperca petersii	albomarginatus		
Epinephelus	E. areolatus		
adscensionis <------	E. cruentatus		
E. andersoni	E. drummondhayi		
E. hemistiktos	E. fasciatus		
E. hexagonatus	E. guaza ------>		
E. itajara	E. guttatus		
E. malabaricus	E. morio		
E. merra	E. multinotatus		
E. striatus[d]	E. rivulatus		
E. summana	E. tauvina		
Mycteroperca rosacea	E. undulosus		
	Mycteroperca bonaci		
	M. interstitialis		
	M. microlepis		
	M. phenax		
	M. venenosa		
	Variola louti		

[a] Aprion virescens and Aphareus furcatus apparently feed shallow, i.e., high in the water column, as well as at greater depths.
[b] Although these species have been reported from quite shallow waters as adults, it seems unlikely that major feeding occurs there.
[c] Small numbers may occur much shallower in some locations.
[d] There may also be rather separate populations somewhat deeper (Smith 1961).

for 3 species from only 2 research studies based on a
total of 57 specimens, plus published general references
to diet of 1 species in the central Pacific, 1 in the west
Pacific, and 1 in the western Indian Ocean (Appendix A).
Results for 8 species of Pristipomoides from the Pacific
and Indian Oceans are based on only 6 reported research
studies, with sample sizes of 1 to 209 specimens each (a
total of 467 specimens), plus 3 published general references. For both genera combined, only one research study
is published, two are in theses, and the results of three
studies are otherwise unpublished. No diet information
was found for deepwater Atlantic snappers.

Diet data were found associated with records of deep
catches for only three deepwater grouper species. These
results came from 1 general reference and 6 research
studies involving sample sizes (where given) of 1 to 67
specimens (total of 89 specimens) (Appendixes A and B).
Three research studies are published, one is a thesis, and
two are otherwise unpublished. Brownell and Rainey (1971)
reported recovering two fish (one a Xanthichthys ringens)
and a squid from specimens of Epinephelus mystacinus
caught on the deep slopes around the Virgin Islands over
both hard and soft bottoms. The species occurred there at
depths of 100–300 m and was the dominant grouper caught,
especially at depths below 150 m. Thompson and Munro
(1978) reported that an E. mystacinus taken from a depth
of 200 m near Jamaica contained eight caridean shrimps and
one eel. The Florida Sea Grant College (1981) report that
"fish and squid have been found in stomachs" of this
species may have been based on these two reports. An E.
chlorostigma taken at 140 m near Papua New Guinea by
Richards (Unpub. data) (Appendixes A and B) contained 18
Parapandalus serratifrons, a deepwater shrimp.

Parrish (Unpub. data) found only traces of penaeid
shrimp in two specimens of E. quernus (26 and 27 cm standard length (SL)) taken in unusually shallow water (10–15
m) in Midway Atoll lagoon. Ralston (Unpub. data) (Appendixes A and B) collected and Sorden analyzed samples
regurgitated by 17 E. quernus taken by handline at depths
of 110–180 m at four locations in the Northwestern
Hawaiian Islands (NWHI). Seki (1984) collected and
analyzed 14 intact stomachs and the regurgitated contents
from 53 specimens of E. quernus caught in depths of 130–
220 m at 21 islands and banks of the NWHI (Appendixes A
and B).

Appendix B provides a detailed compendium of all
known diet results for the fully deepwater groupers and

snappers of the Pacific, including published and unpublished work. At the lower systematic levels, only certain
selected taxa are shown in the table. Many other
families, especially of fishes, occurred occasionally in
the samples.

The diets of deep and shallow-water predators
contained the same major prey groups, but the relative
importance of some groups was different. On the basis of
the number of reports and the number of different prey
taxa, fish were the dominant prey for the deepwater
predators also. On the same basis, a third or more of
this consumption was of fishes clearly belonging to
deepwater taxa. Most of the remainder consisted of fishes
of unknown depth range, including a sizable component of
anguilliform species. In contrast to the diets of
shallow-water predators, shrimps and planktonic forms were
next in importance (and these groups were about equal).
Fully deepwater shrimp taxa were prominent. Almost all the
planktonic forms were urochordates (most common) or
gastropods. "Other crustaceans" were next in importance,
somewhat as with shallow water predators. In contrast,
cephalopods (with octopus and squid both well represented)
were about as important as crustaceans. Crabs were of
similar importance in the diets of the deepwater predators, but much less prominent than in the shallow-water
species. The crabs were primarily deepwater forms,
especially galatheids such as <u>Munida</u>. Other benthic
invertebrates were only a minor component of the diets.

FEEDING HABITAT

Both the Lutjanidae and Serranidae are large, diverse
groups that show a considerable diversity in feeding
ecology. However, there are broad similarities across
many species, and relatively few narrow feeding specializations are reported.

Snappers

Most snappers lead a primarily demersal existence
(Hiatt and Strasburg 1960; Randall and Brock 1960; Talbot
1960; Randall 1967). They usually remain within a few
meters of the bottom, where most feeding seems to occur.
A large portion of the prey shown in Appendix A must be
captured at the substratum: certainly crabs, many of the

other crustaceans, other benthic invertebrates, and probably a good portion of the shrimp and octopus.

Almost all adult snappers in shallow water associate strongly with hard bottom or at least with bottom having some type of relief or cover. In addition to coral and rock reef areas, wrecks, discarded materials, artificial reefs, pilings, docks, and similar structures appear attractive. Some species, such as L. analis, L. apodus, L. griseus, L. fulviflamma, and L. mahogoni, also use other types of cover, e.g., grass and marl beds, tidal creek and canal banks, and mangroves (Croker 1962; Randall 1967; Bohlke and Chaplin 1968; Starck 1971; Florida Sea Grant College 1981; van der Elst 1981). A number of species frequent coastal lagoons. A few species (e.g., L. argentimaculatus, L. colorado, L. fulviflamma, young L. jocu, L. johnii, L. griseus, L. russelli, and L. synagris) are found in low salinity coastal environments or even in freshwater as well as at full oceanic salinity (Druzhinin 1970; Florida Sea Grant College 1981; van der Elst 1981; Allen 1986). Feeding seems to occur in all these habitats.

Although the requirement for some type of cover seems important, a common behavior pattern is loitering or sheltering at or near cover during part of the day and actively foraging over surrounding open areas, often at night (Randall and Brock 1960; Hobson 1965, 1968; Starck and Davis 1966; Randall 1967). It seems likely that most feeding occurs while dispersed abroad (e.g., Randall 1967; Starck 1971), but opportunistic feeding closer to shelter has also been reported (e.g., Ormond 1980; Fallows 1984). The range of bottom types (and prey habitats) used for feeding is consistent with the variety of prey consumed. Even where the range of available substrata is limited, as in some oceanic atolls, snappers commonly forage both on coral reefs and over lagoon sand flats (Hiatt and Strasburg 1960).

For species of "intermediate" and "mixed" depths, there is commonly a narrower range of feeding habitats available. There are fewer in situ observations, and inferences have usually been made from catches. Because the microtopography is usually unknown at the exact location where fish are caught, it is seldom possible to confirm whether small patches of hard substrate are present. Reports of snappers caught over extensive soft bottom (e.g., Bradley and Bryan 1975; South Atlantic Fishery Management Council 1981) are, therefore, hard to interpret. There is little doubt that many snapper species forage widely from shelter over soft bottoms at

intermediate depths on a diel basis (Croker 1962; Futch
and Bruger 1976). This activity probably meets most of
their food requirements (Moseley 1966; Futch and Bruger
1976). Usually, however, some type of hard substrate,
shelter, or bottom discontinuity is close by. Examples
are the well-documented concentrations of snappers at
sites such as the Galveston "Lumps" or "Western Grounds"
(Camber 1955; Johnston et al. 1976), the "snapper banks"
such as the Flower Garden and associated features of the
open Gulf of Mexico (Bright and Rezak 1976), and the rocky
areas along the shelf break of the South Atlantic continental shelf of the United States (Grimes et al. 1977;
Grimes 1979).

For the fully deepwater snappers such as the genera
Etelis and Pristipomoides (but see Wray 1979 for Pristipomoides typus), little is known of the type of substrate
where feeding occurs. Based on the results of fishing,
these species are usually sought in areas of rather high
relief, including steep slopes of islands located in deep
basins. Handlines are the favored gear, so there is
evidence that these species will feed actively on bait
over bottoms with high relief. Fishing over steep
terrain, the precise depth to bottom is often in doubt, as
is the depth of the fish when hooked. The general
impression from handline fishing for deep snappers in the
central and west Pacific is that they bite both at the
bottom and many meters above it. In light of their diets
and the little information available about the habitat of
the prey, it is unclear whether this environment presents
more favorable feeding opportunities or whether it has
other appeal. A few direct observations from a submersible at depths to about 350 m suggest that around some
Pacific islands (high islands and atolls), deepwater
snappers are more common in areas of high relief (Ralston
et al. 1986). Various bottom types are likely available
in these areas, including patches of sediment. Reed
(1964) reported that P. filamentosus in the Red Sea
inhabits mud bottom areas about 180 m deep near reefs.

Diet results (Appendixes A and B) indicate clearly
that some benthic food items are taken, and Kluegel (1921)
characterized P. filamentosus as a bottom feeder on the
basis of "compound ascidians, algae, foraminifera, and
gravel" found in 10 specimens with food. Other diet items
are pelagic, and for the most part, their vertical distributions are not well enough known to establish whether
they might have been taken at the bottom. There is little

or no evidence whether snappers migrate vertically to feed.

The exceptions to the general pattern of demersal habit and daily use of bottom cover are relatively few but interesting. Among the predominantly shallow-water species of commercial interest, Ocyurus chrysurus is perhaps least constrained in its feeding environment. It occurs over a variety of depths and forages freely throughout much of the water column (Longley and Hildebrand 1941; Randall 1967; Fallows 1984; Naughton and Saloman Unpub. 1). Midwater activity is reflected to some extent in its diet (Appendix A), which often contains considerable plankton. However, a variety of crustaceans appear to be taken from the substrate and the water column, and a number of studies show considerable amounts of other fully benthic prey groups. Piedra (1965) and Naughton and Saloman (Unpub. 1) found that fish predominated in the diet, and Naughton and Saloman suggested that progressively larger fish were increasingly piscivorous.

Aprion virescens is another species that appears to be little constrained by substrate association. It forages throughout the water column, apparently more often in the shallower portion (Ommanney 1953; Hiatt and Strasburg 1960; Talbot 1960; van der Elst 1981), and can even be caught with a surface lure (Talbot 1960). Reed (1964) reported capture of Aprion in the Red Sea using fish as bait in midwater at depths of 90-150 m. The diet is dominated by fish (Appendix A), with considerable quantities of cephalopods and pelagic urochordates. Some benthic invertebrates are also included.

Aphareus furcatus has somewhat similar habits but does not appear to forage as much near the sea surface. Hobson (1974) described its habit of swimming well above the reef and attacking demersal fishes from above. Its diet is poorly known (Appendix A), but fish are included.

A few other species of shallow and intermediate depths seem to practice mixed tactics of patrolling up to several meters off the bottom for nektonic prey and periodically foraging on the substrate for fully benthic forms. Hiatt and Strasburg (1960), Talbot (1960), and Ormond (1980) reported frequent observations of this behavior by L. bohar, and the broad range of items that appears in substantial quantities in its diet confirms this habit.

Among species living at greater depths, the depth at which natural feeding occurs is less certain and is based largely on estimates from captures by fishing gear. For most species, there is no reason to believe that major feeding occurs much above the substrate. However, Grimes (1979) believed that <u>Rhomboplites</u> <u>aurorubens</u> does much of its feeding several meters above the bottom. Almost all prey he found in a large sample consisted of "pelagic or epibenthic" forms, including many larval stages, pelagic gastropods, gelatinous invertebrates, and other holo-plankton (Appendix A). Gut analysis also led to the intriguing suggestion that the food of fish 100-175 mm long consisted largely of fish scales. Large samples obtained subsequently (South Carolina Wildlife and Marine Resources Department 1981/1984; Appendix A) confirmed the importance of pelagic food items, but indicated a larger proportion of fish and benthic invertebrates in the diet.

Groupers

In general, the groupers are considerably more seden-tary than the snappers and are more dependent on a hard substrate habitat (Hiatt and Strasburg 1960; Randall and Brock 1960; Smith 1961; Bohlke and Chaplin 1968). This characteristic results in more exact habitat requirements in terms of area, relief, and shelter size. Many groupers make frequent use of shelters, and even those that are usually exposed often rest on or remain close to large masses of hard substrate (Hiatt and Strasburg 1960; Randall and Brock 1960; Ormond 1980; Smale 1983). This behavior is consistent with the ambush mode of feeding practiced by most grouper species. They often lurk within shelters or rest motionless on the substrate until their prey venture close enough to be captured with a quick lunge and rapid ingestion through expansion of their large mouths (Breder 1925; Hiatt and Strasburg 1960; Burnett-Herkes 1975; Ormond 1980). They also forage in caves, cracks, crevices, and other openings within reefs and rock masses, sucking benthic invertebrates out of hiding with a similar oral action (Burnett-Herkes 1975). It is not surprising then that the fish in grouper diets are often demersal species rather than wide-ranging, schooling pelagics. For example, Menzel (1960) reported that nearly all the fish he found in guts of E. <u>guttatus</u> were benthic, reef-associated labrids.

A hard substrate of fairly high relief and complexity may be important as habitat for groupers' preferred foods. Smith (1961) believed that the rather unspecialized groupers may be in food competition with all local carnivores, particularly other groupers. However, he suggested that competition may be strongest for shelter and space, and that the distribution and abundance of groupers is largely determined by suitable hard substrate. He pointed out that, on a large scale, their spatial distribution in the western North Atlantic corresponds roughly to the distribution of reef building corals.

Consistent with their strongly demersal behavior, most groupers in shallower waters appear to take their prey—both fish and invertebrates—very near the bottom. This is particularly true within the genera Epinephelus and Cephalopholis. However, E. andersoni has been known to take a fishing lure at the surface (van der Elst 1981). Plectropomus leopardus (and/or P. laevis?), P. truncatus (= P. areolatus), and Variola louti have been observed to forage more widely in midwater (at least a few meters above the substrate), although P. leopardus is also known to hide in caves at times (Hiatt and Strasburg 1960; Randall and Brock 1960; Randall 1986). All three species are highly piscivorous (Appendix A). Gracila albomarginata appears to move about more openly and continually than most groupers (e.g., Randall 1986), but its feeding seems not to have been studied in detail.

The various species of Mycteroperca are basically demersal and form associations with hard substrate, but they seem less sedentary and less restricted in their foraging, both horizontally and vertically. For example, M. tigris has been seen hovering above a reef and making quick dashes to the sea surface after a trolled lure (Smith 1961). Hobson (1968) made extensive observations of M. rosacea congregating on the bottom beneath schools of herring, Harengula thrissina, and anchoveta, Cetengraulis mysticetus, and feeding on them by means of explosive rushes to the surface.

In general, the body form of Mycteroperca is more terete than that of Epinephelus or Cephalopholis. Mycteroperca tend to forage higher above the bottom and appear to be stronger, more agile swimmers. Their diets are more strongly dominated by fish (Appendix A), including some fast-swimming, wide-ranging species of the water column such as Caranx ruber, which the more sedentary groupers probably cannot capture (Randall 1967).

The Mycteroperca may range rather widely from shelter. Where shallow water permits observation, adults appear to maintain a diel association with cover. Catches at intermediate depths are not entirely consistent. Mycteroperca microlepis and M. phenax have been reported caught only over hard bottom (20-90 m deep), and M. venenosa mostly over hard bottom but occasionally over mud (full depth range 35-120 m). Mycteroperca interstitialis has been taken from both coral and sand substrata to depths of 150 m (Florida Sea Grant College 1981). All four species appear to be almost exclusively piscivorous (Appendix A). Other species of Mycteroperca are commonly reported from hard bottom areas in shallow water.

Plectropomus maculatus is reported to inhabit coral reefs off Saudi Arabia (Wray 1979), but leaves the reefs to forage more actively than most groupers for demersal prey. Epinephelus morio (Florida Sea Grant College 1981) and E. awoara (Randall 1986) have occasionally been reported from mud bottoms as well as from rocky or reef areas. Alphestes afer (Randall 1967) and E. areolatus (Randall 1986) have been seen in shallow grass beds as well as on reefs. At the extensive reef tract at Tulear, Madagascar, Harmelin-Vivien and Bouchon (1976) found most of the common groupers distributed over most of the range of depths and substrate types, from shallow grass beds out to the base of the outer reef slope at 60 m depth. The following species have been taken in trawls (Masuda et al. 1984; Randall 1986), which implies that they frequent soft bottom habitats: E. awoara, E. epistictus, E. heniochus, E. latifasciatus, E. morrhua, E. septemfasciatus, and E. sexfasciatus. Randall (1986) also reports E. undulosus as a species of open sedimentary bottoms. Of the fully deepwater groupers, E. mystacinus has been reported over both hard and soft bottoms at depths to 490 m (Florida Sea Grant College 1981), but the data are minimal.

Groupers in general may have a tendency to be less dependent upon hard bottom at greater depths, but this tendency has not been well established. As a group they are more strongly oriented to bottom cover than the snappers.

OTHER BIOLOGICAL AND ECOLOGICAL INFLUENCES

Diel feeding periodicity has been the subject of a number of isolated observations and reports, several field studies, and much literature discussion. Table 9.3 contains an incomplete list of published times of snapper and grouper feeding activity. The bases for these inferences are highly variable among studies: in situ observation of actual feeding or feeding attempts, observation of behavior clearly related to feeding, observation of active

TABLE 9.3
Reported periods of diel feeding activity for some snapper and grouper species (symbols used: X activity observed/implied, + major activity, ++ most activity, - some or minor activity, ? report reflects uncertainty)

Species/Group	Source	Dawn	Daytime	Dusk	Night
LUTJANIDAE					
Lutjanids generally	Hobson (1968), Randall (1967), Starck and Davis (1966)				X
Aphareus furcatus	Hobson (1974)		X?		
Aprion virescens	van der Elst (1981)		<------------------->		X
Lutjanus analis	Randall (1967), Starck (1971)		X		X
L. apodus	Randall (1967)		X		
L. apodus	Starck (1971)				++
L. argentiventris	Hobson (1968)		X		X
L. bohar	Ormond (1980)		-		
L. erythropterus	Vien (1968)				++
L. fulvus	Hobson (1974), Randall and Brock (1960)				X
L. gibbus	van der Elst (1981)				++
L. griseus	Longley (1924), Starck and Davis (1966)				X

Taxon	Reference			South Atlantic Fishery Management Council (SAFMC) (1981)
L. griseus		−		
L. griseus	Starck (1971)	+	+(Juv.)	+
L. jocu	Starck (1971)			++
L. kasmira	van der Elst (1981)			++
L. mahogoni	Randall (1967)			X
L. mahogoni	Starck (1971)			++
L. sanguineus	van der Elst (1981)			++
L. sebae	van der Elst (1981)		<—————————————>	
L. synagris	Starck (1971)		X	X
L. vivanus	SAFMC (1981)			X
Macolor niger	Ormond (1980)		−	
Ocyurus chrysurus	Collette & Talbot (1972), Starck (1971)		X	X
O. chrysurus	Fallows (1984)		−	++
Rhomboplites aurorubens	Grimes (1979)			X?

SERRANIDAE

Taxon	Reference			
Serranids generally	Thompson and Munro (1978)		X	X
Several species in Florida Keys	Starck and Davis (1966)		<————Same————>	
Several species in the Society Islands	Randall and Brock (1960)		++	+
Several species at Tulear, Madagascar, including: Cephalopholis argus, Epinephelus merra, E. fario, E. hexagonatus	Harmelin-Vivien and Bouchon (1976)		<————Same————>	

(Continued)

TABLE 9.3 (Cont.)

Species/Group	Source	Dawn	Daytime	Dusk	Night
Aethaloperca rogaa	Ormond (1980)		X		
Alphestes multiguttatus	Hobson (1968)				X
Cephalopholis spp.	Ormond (1980)		X		
C. argus	van der Elst (1981)		++		
Dinoperca petersii	van der Elst (1981)				++
E. flavocaeruleus	van der Elst (1981)				++?
E. guaza	van der Elst (1981)	?	++	?	
E. labriformis	Hobson (1968)		X		X
E. malabaricus	van der Elst (1981)		++		
E. morio	Longley and Hildebrand (1941)	<------Same------>			
E. striatus	Randall (1967)		X		X
Mycteroperca phenax	SAFMC (1981)	+?		+?	
M. rosacea	Hobson (1968)	+	X	+	-
Plectropomus maculatus	Choat (1968)	-	++		
P. maculatus	Ormond (1980)		X		
Variola louti	van der Elst (1981)		+		

versus dormant periods, and analysis of guts collected at various times of day. Details supplied by authors varied greatly; for most studies, little importance can be attached to differences in the meanings of symbols in Table 9.3.

Qualitative differences in time of feeding have occasionally been established or strongly implied. Harmelin-Vivien and Bouchon (1976) found that E. merra in Madagascar, Mauritius, and La Reunion contained mostly fish when collected well into the daytime or evening, but mostly brachyuran crabs when collected late at night or early in the morning. Hobson (1968) obtained somewhat similar results for E. labriformis and L. argentiventris in the Gulf of California. A variety of crustaceans was taken.

It is clear that there is considerable variability among species within each family, but the expected broad trends appear to hold. Snappers tend to feed more actively at night, although daytime feeding does occur. Most groupers seem to feed at all times of day, but tend to peak in activity at dawn and dusk (e.g., Starck and Davis 1966; Ormond 1980). Species that forage more in the water column may feed more actively during daylight, whereas those that depend more heavily on benthic invertebrates may be more active nocturnally (e.g., Starck and Davis 1966; Hobson 1968). In terms of the behavior of the prey, this seems a reasonable schedule. Some fish species may adjust their schedules to optimize both types of feeding.

No important diet trends emerge when examined on a large geographical scale. The major diet components seem much the same in all regions and are even fairly stable across major habitat types and over a considerable range of depths (discussed above). It is likely that both snappers and groupers are sufficiently adaptable to exploit local abundances of food, so that small-scale and short-term variations can be expected to occur (e.g., Talbot 1960).

Changes in diet with age have been discussed in the literature for many species, especially for snappers (e.g., Rangarajan 1970; Starck 1971; Bradley and Bryan 1975; Grimes 1979; Smale 1983; Naughton and Saloman Unpub. 1, Unpub. 2; Saloman and Naughton Unpub.). On the whole, from the recruited juvenile stage to large adult size, the changes are perhaps surprisingly small. Very young fish of course eat small plankton and other items not important in the adult diet. But from the smallest size included in most diet studies, the spectrum of major food items remains essentially the same. Many studies report some change in proportion of various food items--e.g., consumption of more fish and less crustaceans with increasing age. This may represent a fairly general trend, although some studies with adequate specimen size ranges fail to show it.

TROPHIC ECOLOGY AND FISHERY IMPLICATIONS

From the perspective of fishery management, several aspects of the trophics of snappers and groupers are of interest. These fishes tend to occur at rather high levels in the trophic web. Traditional ecological wisdom would predict that large changes in their populations might significantly alter other components of the community.

These predators and their prey organisms have a wide but patchy distribution. For most species of these fishes, the distribution seems most closely linked to suitable physical habitat, especially shelter. Hard bottom and high relief seem to be key elements, particularly for the groupers. It is not clear how strongly the occurrence of food items is controlled by this type of physical habitat. For a number of demersal/benthic prey species, this substrate dependence may be quite important. However, many of the snappers and the Mycteroperca species (at least) seem to forage rather far from cover. The breadth of diet shown by most groupers and particularly snappers also suggests that their habitat dependency is primarily based on shelter rather than on prey distributions.

There are probably no snappers or groupers so heavily dependent on such a narrow taxonomic range of prey that a major reduction in availability of one prey group would produce catastrophic effects on the predator population. The diet accepted by most species seems broad enough to permit shifts in feeding, even between rather diverse prey groups--e.g., pelagic fish, demersal fish, large or small benthic crustaceans, and a variety of invertebrate nekton or plankton. It, therefore, seems unlikely that large movements of snapper or grouper populations would occur in response to changes in abundance of one or a few components of their diet. For the same reasons, these species are expected to be resilient to changes in abundance of feeding competitors.

However, most of the major prey groups taken by most snappers and groupers are animals that must be hunted, captured, and to some extent manipulated after capture. They typically are not uniformly or densely distributed, nor extremely abundant. Thus, the rate of food consumption by the predators would be expected to show some direct (probably nonlinear) functional response to prey abundance. The aggregate consumption of prey by all snappers and groupers in a community may represent a significant source of mortality for these prey groups. If the predator populations are greatly reduced by fishing, the populations of fish that are their prey or that have diets that overlap theirs, might increase substantially. This mechanism could explain observations such as those of Goeden (1982), that in communities with similar habitat but different levels of "keystone" predator species populations (affected by fishing), there were widely divergent patterns in the abundance of other predators. This mechanism may also contribute to the phenomenon, sometimes observed in multispecies fisheries, in which total landings from a fishery persist at high levels over a fairly long period even though the catch changes sequentially from one species to another, usually moving to lower levels in the trophic web.

There also seem to be substantial predatory interactions among the snappers and groupers. There is considerable overlap (at least at the family level) of prey fish taken by the various species. Many benthic and some pelagic invertebrate taxa are also shared. Considering the overlap of distributions of some of these predators, some level of competition seems likely. Because of the predators' broad diets, it is probably diffuse and seldom severe. However, the effects of competition for shelter or space might be more serious (Smith 1961). There appears to be little or no direct evidence concerning the importance of food as a limiting factor in the growth, reproduction, or survival of wild populations of snappers or groupers.

There are ample reports to establish that snappers and groupers eat other snappers and groupers (e.g., Piedra 1965; Rodrigues 1974; Grimes 1979; Naughton and Saloman Unpub. 1, Unpub. 2; Saloman and Naughton Unpub.; Appendix B). The prey are usually rather young stages, but predation on adults does occur (Smith 1961; Randall 1980). Particularly for the deepwater predator genera, the prey seem to be primarily nonfishery species. However, undoubtedly some predation by harvested species upon other exploited species occurs. Thus, it is possible that an active fishery for one species of snapper or grouper may directly enhance the populations of others through reduced predation.

ACKNOWLEDGMENTS

The Hawaii Cooperative Fishery Research Unit (HCFRU) is supported jointly by the Hawaii Department of Land and Natural Resources, the U.S. Fish and Wildlife Service, and the University of Hawaii. M. W. Callahan and C. T. Sorden each analyzed large samples of fish guts at the HCFRU, the results of which are first reported here (see Appendix B). S. Ralston and M. P. Seki provided the samples from collections sponsored by the Southwest Fisheries Center Honolulu Laboratory, National Marine Fisheries Service, and the University of Hawaii Sea Grant College Program. A. H. Richards, K. J. Sainsbury, and R. E. Schroeder generously provided unpublished diet information from their studies for publication here. J. A. Fallows, R. H. Matheson III, G. R. Huntsman, C. S. Manooch III, D. Mizenko, S. P. Naughton, C. H. Saloman, and M. J. Smale all provided valuable, current information in the form of copies of their theses or other prepublication manuscripts for use and citation here. G. R. Allen, W. D. Anderson, Jr., and J. E. Randall gave of their personal time in helping to get the taxonomy in order. Dozens of other colleagues, fish workers, and agencies throughout much of the tropical and subtropical world supplied copies of documents, references, or other forms of information and encouragement. All these contributions have improved the quality and completeness of this review.

BIBLIOGRAPHY

Adams, A. C., and W. C. Kendall. 1891. Report upon an investigation of the fishing grounds off the west coast of Florida. Bull. U.S. Fish Comm. 9:289-312.

Allen, G. R. 1986. Synopsis of the circumtropical fish genus Lutjanus (Lutjanidae). In J. J. Polovina and S. Ralston (editors), Tropical snappers and groupers: Biology and fisheries management. Westview Press, Inc., Boulder. [See this volume.]

Bagnis, R., P. Mazellier, J. Bennett, and E. Christian. 1972. Fishes of Polynesia. Les Éditions du Pacifique, Papeete, Tahiti, 368 p.

Barroso, L. M. 1965. Regime alimentar do pargo (Lutianus aya Bloch, 1795) no nordeste Brasileiro. Bol. Estud. Pesca 5(3):7-16.

Basheeruddin, S., and K. N. Nayar. 1962. A preliminary study of the juvenile fishes of the coastal waters off Madras city. Indian J. Fish. 8(1):169-188.

Baughman, J. L. 1943. The lutjanid fishes of Texas. Copeia 1943:212-215.

_____. 1944. Notes on the Serranidae and Lobotidae of Texas. Copeia 1944:89-90.

Beebe, W., and J. Tee-Van. 1928. The fishes of Port-au-Prince Bay, Haiti, with a summary of the known species of marine fish of the Island of Haiti and Santo Domingo. Zoologica 10:1-279.

Bogdanov, D. V., Yu. A. Korzhova, N. P. Kornilov, L. I. Leonova, T. G. Lyubimova, A. L. Obvintsev, Ye. S. Prosvirov, N. Ye. Salnikov, Ye. S. Terekhin, and N. S. Khromd. 1967. Meksikanskiy zaliv. [The Gulf of Mexico]. Moscow.

Bohlke, J. E., and C. C. G. Chaplin. 1968. Fishes of the Bahamas and adjacent tropical waters. Livingston Publishing Co., Wynnewood, Pa., 771 p.

Bradley, E., and C. E. Bryan. 1975. Life history and fishery of the red snapper (Lutjanus campechanus) in the northwestern Gulf of Mexico: 1970-1974. Proc. 27th Gulf Caribb. Fish. Inst., p. 77-106.

Breder, C. M. 1925. On the feeding behavior of fishes with terminal mouths. Copeia 1925:89-91.

Breder, C. M., and R. F. Nigrelli. 1934. The penetration of a grouper's digestive tract by a sharp-tailed eel. Copeia 1934:162-164.

Brice, J. J. 1898. The fish and fisheries of the coastal waters of Florida. Rep. U.S. Fish Comm. 22:263-342.

Bright, T. J., and R. Rezak. 1976. Fishing banks of the Texas continental shelf. In H. R. Bullis, Jr. and A. C. Jones (editors), Proceedings: Colloquium on snapper-grouper fishery resources of the western central Atlantic Ocean, p. 248-288. Texas A&M Univ. Sea Grant Coll. and Mississippi-Alabama Sea Grant Consortium. Fla. Sea Grant Coll. Rep. 17.

Brownell, W. N., and W. E. Rainey. 1971. Research and development of deep water commercial and sport fisheries around the Virgin Islands plateau. Contrib. No. 3. Virgin Isl. Ecol. Res. Stn., 88 p.

Bullis, H. R., Jr., and A. C. Jones (editors). 1976. Proceedings: Colloquium on snapper-grouper fishery resources of the western central Atlantic Ocean. Texas A&M Univ. Sea Grant Coll. and Mississippi-Alabama Sea Grant Consortium. Fla. Sea Grant Coll. Rep. 17, 333 p.

Burnett-Herkes, J. 1975. Contribution to the biology of the red hind, Epinephelus guttatus, a commercially important serranid fish from the tropical western Atlantic. Ph.D. Dissertation. Univ. Miami, Coral Gables, 154 p.

Camber, C.I. 1955. A survey of the red snapper fishery of the Gulf of Mexico, with special reference to the Campeche Banks. Fla. Board Conserv., Mar. Res. Lab. Tech. Ser. 12, 63 p.

Cervigon M., F. 1966. Los peces marinos de Venezuela. Fundación La Salle de Ciencias Naturales Monografía No. 11 (Tomo 1), 436 p.

Choat, J. H. 1968. Feeding habits and distribution of Plectropomus maculatus (Serranidae) at Heron Island. Proc. R. Soc. Queensl. 80(2):13-18.

Collette, B. B., and F. H. Talbot. 1972. Activity patterns of coral reef fishes with emphasis on nocturnal-diurnal changeover. Nat. Hist. Mus. Los Ang. County, Sci. Bull. 14:98-124.

Collins, J. W. 1885. The red snapper grounds in the Gulf of Mexico. Bull. U.S. Fish Comm. 5:145-146.

_____. 1887. Notes on the red snapper fishery. Bull. U.S. Fish Comm. 6:299-300.

Croker, R. A. 1962. Growth and food of the gray snapper, Lutjanus griseus, in Everglades National Park. Trans. Am. Fish. Soc. 91:379-383.

Druzhinin, A. D. 1970. The range and biology of snappers (Family Lutjanidae). J. Ichthyol. 10:717-736.

Evermann, B. W., and M. C. Marsh. 1902. The fishes of Puerto Rico. U.S. Fish Comm., Wash., D.C., 400 p.

Fallows, J. A. 1984. The behavioural ecology of feeding in the yellowtail snapper, Ocyurus chrysurus (Family Lutjanidae). Ph.D Dissertation, Univ. Newcastle Upon Tyne, 157 p.

Florida Sea Grant College. 1981. Environmental impact statement and fishery management plan for the reef fish resources of the Gulf of Mexico. Prepared for Gulf of Mexico Fish. Manage. Counc.

Fourmanoir, P. 1968. La pêche au pagre, Lutianus aya, au large de la Guyane et du Brazil. La Pêche Maritime. An. 47, No. 1080.

Fourmanoir, P., and P. Laboute. 1976. Poissons de Nouvelle Caledonie et des Nouvelles Hebrides. Les Éditions du Pacifique, Papeete, Tahiti, 376 p.

Furtado-Ogawa, E., and M. Ferreira de Menezes. 1972. Alimentacão do pargo Lutjanus purpureus Poey, no nordeste brasileiro. Arq. Cienc. Mar 12:105-108.

Futch, R. B., and G. E. Bruger. 1976. Age, growth, and reproduction of red snapper in Florida waters. In H. R. Bullis, Jr. and A. C. Jones (editors), Proceedings: Colloquium on snapper-grouper fishery resources of the western central Atlantic Ocean, p. 165-184. Texas A&M Univ. Sea Grant Coll. and Mississippi-Alabama Sea Grant Consortium. Fla. Sea Grant Coll. Rep. 17.

Godcharles, M. F. 1970. Exploratory fishing for southern sea bass, Centropristes striatus melanus, in the northeastern Gulf of Mexico. Fla. Dep. Nat. Resour., Mar. Res. Lab. Tech. Ser. 63, 26 p.

Goeden, G. B. 1982. Intensive fishing and a "keystone" predator species: Ingredients for community instability. Biol. Conserv. 22:273-281.

Grimes, C. B. 1979. Diet and feeding ecology of the vermilion snapper, Rhomboplites aurorubens (Cuvier) from North Carolina and South Carolina waters. Bull. Mar. Sci. 29:53-61.

Grimes, C. B., C. S. Manooch III, G. R. Huntsman, and R. L. Dixon. 1977. Red snappers of the Carolina coast. Mar. Fish. Rev. 39(1):12-15.

Gudger, E. W. 1929. On the morphology, coloration and behavior of seventy teleostean fish of Tortugas, Florida. Carnegie Inst. Wash. Publ. 391. Pap. Tortugas Lab. 26, Part 5, p. 149-204.

Harmelin-Vivien, M. L., and C. Bouchon. 1976. Feeding behavior of some carnivorous fishes (Serranidae and Scorpaenidae) from Tulear (Madagascar). Mar. Biol. (Berl.) 37:329-340.

Helfrich, P., T. Piyakarnchana, and P. S. Miles. 1968. Ciguatera fish poisoning. 1. The ecology of ciguateric reef fishes in the Line Islands. Occas. Pap. Bernice P. Bishop Mus. 23:305-369.

Hiatt, R. W., and D. W. Strasburg. 1960. Ecological relationships of the fish fauna on coral reefs of the Marshall Islands. Ecol. Monogr. 30:65-127.

Hobson, E. S. 1965. Diurnal-nocturnal activity of some inshore fishes in the Gulf of California. Copeia 1965:291-302.

_____. 1968. Predatory behavior of some shore fishes in the Gulf of California. U.S. Fish Wildl. Serv., Bur. Sport Fish. Wildl. Res. Rep. 73, 92 p.

_____. 1974. Feeding relationships of teleostean fishes on coral reefs in Kona, Hawaii. Fish. Bull., U.S. 72:915-1031.

Hussain, N. A., and M. A. S. Abdullah. 1977. The length-weight relationship, spawning season and food habits of six commercial fishes in Kuwaiti waters. Indian J. Fish. 24:181-194.

Iversen, E. S., and F. H. Berry. 1969. Fish mariculture: Progress and potential. Proc. 21st Gulf Caribb. Fish. Inst., p. 163-176.

Johnston, J. B., J. K. Adams, and R. Foster. 1976. The red snapper resource of the Texas continental shelf. In H. R. Bullis, Jr. and A. C. Jones (editors), Proceedings: Colloquium on snapper-grouper fishery resources of the western central Atlantic Ocean, p. 237-247. Texas A&M Univ. Sea Grant Coll. and Mississippi-Alabama Sea Grant Consortium. Fla. Sea Grant Coll. Rep. 17.

Joubert, C. S. W., and P. B. Hanekom. 1980. A study of feeding in some inshore reef fish of the Natal Coast, South Africa. S. Afr. J. Zool. 15:262-274.

Kami, H. T. 1973. The Pristipomoides (Pisces: Lutjanidae) of Guam with notes on their biology. Micronesica 9:97-117.

Karplus, I. 1978. A feeding association between the grouper Epinephelus fasciatus and the moray eel Gymnothorax griseus. Copeia 1978:164.

Kluegel, E. 1921. The food of Hawaiian food fishes. M.S. Thesis. Univ. Hawaii, Honolulu, 18 p., 3 plates.

LaMonte, F. 1952. North American game fishes. Doubleday & Co., Inc., Garden City, N.Y., 202 p.

Longley, W. H. 1924. Observations upon submarine color photography, the food and rate of digestion of fishes, and the power of discrimination and association in the gray snapper. Carnegie Inst. Wash. Year Book 22:159-163.

Longley, W. H., and S. F. Hildebrand. 1941. Systematic catalogue of the fishes of Tortugas, Florida, with observations on color, habits and local distribution. Carnegie Inst. Wash. Publ. 535, Pap. Tortugas Lab. 34, p. 1-331.

Masuda, H., K. Amaoka, C. Araga, T. Uyeno, and T. Yoshino. 1984. The fishes of the Japanese archipelago. Tokai University Press, 437 p.

Matheson, R. H., III, G. R. Huntsman, and C. S. Manooch III. 1984. Age, growth, mortality, foods and reproduction of the scamp, Mycteroperca phenax, collected off North Carolina and South Carolina. Second Southeast Stock Assessment Workshop, June 4–8 1984, Miami. Southeast Fish Cent., Natl. Mar. Fish. Serv., NOAA. SAW/84/RFR/8, 38 p.

Menzel, D. W. 1960. Utilization of food by a Bermuda reef fish, Epinephelus guttatus. J. Cons. Cons. Int. Explor. Mer 25:216–222.

Miles, P. S. 1963. Seasonal and geographic variation in the diet of Lutjanus bohar (Forskål). M.S. Thesis. Univ. Hawaii, Honolulu, 84 p.

Misra, P. M. 1968. Die Ernahrungsgewohnheiten von Lutianus jahngarah Day ("marine snapper") an der Puri-Kuste. Z. Fisch. Hilfswiss 16(3–4).

Mizenko, D. 1984. The biology of Western Samoan reef-slope snapper (Pisces: Lutjanidae) populations of: Lutjanus kasmira, Lutjanus rufolineatus, and Pristipomoides multidens. M.S. Thesis. Univ. Rhode Island, Kingston, 66 p.

Moe, M. A., Jr. 1969. Biology of the red grouper, Epinephelus morio (Valenciennes) from the eastern Gulf of Mexico. Fla. Dep. Nat. Resour., Mar. Res. Lab. Prof. Pap. Ser. 10:1–95.

Montgomery, W. L. 1975. Interspecific associations of sea basses (Serranidae) in the Gulf of California. Copeia 1975:785–787.

Morgans, J. F. C. 1965. East African fishes of the Epinephelus tauvina complex, with a description of a new species. Ann. Mag. Nat. Hist. Ser. 13(8):257–271.

_____. 1982. Serranid fishes of Tanzania and Kenya. Ichthyol. Bull. J. L. B. Smith Inst. Ichthyol. 46, 37 p.

Moseley, F. N. 1966. Biology of the red snapper, Lutjanus aya Bloch, of the northwestern Gulf of Mexico. Publ. Inst. Mar. Sci., Univ. Texas 11:90–101.

Nagelkerken, W. P. 1979. Biology of the graysby, Epinephelus cruentatus, of the coral reef of Curacao. Stud. Fauna Curacao Other Caribb. Isl. 186, 118 p.

_____. 1980. Coral reef fishes of Aruba, Bonaire and Curacao. Island Territory of Curacao, 125 p.

_____. 1981. Distribution and ecology of the groupers (Serranidae) and snappers (Lutjanidae) of the Netherlands Antilles. Publ. Found. Sci. Res. Surinam Neth. Antilles 107, 71 p.

Naughton, S. P., and C. H. Saloman. Unpub. 1. Food of
yellowtail snapper (Ocyurus chrysurus) from the lower
Florida Keys, U.S.A. Southeast Fish. Cent. Panama
City Lab., Natl. Mar. Fish. Serv., NOAA, Tech. Memo.
_____. Unpub. 2. Stomach contents of red snapper,
Lutjanus campechanus, from the Gulf of Mexico and
U.S. South Atlantic. Southeast Fish. Cent. Panama
City Lab., Natl. Mar. Fish. Serv., NOAA, Tech. Memo.
Oda, D. K., and J. D. Parrish. 1981. Ecology of commer-
cial snappers and groupers introduced to Hawaiian
reefs. In E. D. Gomez, C. E. Birkeland, R. W. Budde-
meier, R. E. Johannes, J. A. Marsh, Jr., and R. T.
Tsuda (editors), Proc. 4th Int. Coral Reef Symp.,
Manila 1:59-67.
Ommanney, F. D. 1953. The pelagic fishes. In J. F. G.
Wheeler and F. D. Ommanney (editors), Report on the
Mauritius-Seychelles fisheries survey, 1948-49, p.
58-104. Fishery Publications, Lond. 1(3).
Ormond, R. F. G. 1980. Occurrence and feeding behaviour
of Red Sea coral reef fishes. In Proceedings of the
symposium on the coastal and marine environment of
the Red Sea, Gulf of Aden and tropical western Indian
Ocean, p. 329-371. The Red Sea and Gulf of Aden
Environmental Programme. Vol. 2, Jeddah (ALECSO).
Div. Mar. Sci. (UNESCO) and Saudi-Sudanese Red Sea
Comm. (RSC), 9-14 January 1980. Khartoum.
Piedra, G. 1965. Materials on the biology of the yellow-
tail snapper (Ocyurus chrysurus Bloch). In A. S.
Bogdanov (editor). Sovetsko-Kubinskie rybokhozyaist-
vennye issledovaniya. Izdatel'stvo "Pishchevaya
Promyshlennost'." [Soviet-Cuban Fish. Res.]
(Transl. IPST 5514, TT 69-59016, p. 251-269. 1969.
Clearinghouse Fed. Sci. Tech. Inf., Springfield, Va.)
Ralston, S., R. M. Gooding, and G. M. Ludwig. 1986. An
ecological survey comparison of bottom fish resource
assessments (submersible versus handline fishing) at
Johnston Atoll. Fish. Bull., U.S. 84(1). (In press.)
Randall, J. E. 1955. Fishes of the Gilbert Islands. Atoll
Res. Bull. 47, 243 p.
_____. 1967. Food habits of reef fishes of the West
Indies. Stud. Trop. Oceanogr. (Miami) 5:665-847.
_____. 1968. Caribbean reef fishes. T. F. H. Publica-
tions, Inc., Jersey City, N.J., 318 p.
_____. 1980. A survey of ciguatera at Enewetak and
Bikini, Marshall Islands, with notes on the systematics and food habits of ciguatoxic fishes. Fish.
Bull., U.S. 78:201-249.

_____. 1986. A preliminary synopsis of the groupers (Perciformes: Serranidae: Epinephelinae) of the Indo-Pacific region). In J. J. Polovina and S. Ralston (editors), Tropical snappers and groupers: Biology and fisheries management. Westview Press, Inc., Boulder. [See this volume.]

Randall, J. E., and A. Ben-Tuvia. 1983. A review of the groupers (Pisces: Serranidae: Epinephelinae) of the Red Sea, with description of a new species of Cephalopholis. Bull. Mar. Sci. 33:373-426.

Randall, J. E., and V. E. Brock. 1960. Observations on the ecology of epinepheline and lutjanid fishes of the Society Islands, with emphasis on food habits. Trans. Am. Fish. Soc. 89:9-16.

Rangarajan, K. 1970. Food and feeding habits of the snapper, Lutjanus kasmira (Forskål) from the Andaman Sea. Indian J. Fish. 17:43-52.

Rathjen, W., and K. Kawaguchi. 1969. Unpub. Progress report on exploratory fishing for snapper and related species in the Caribbean. UN/FAO Caribb. Fish. Dev. Proj., Barbados, West Indies, 13 p.

Reed, W. 1964. Red Sea fisheries of Sudan. Sudan Government Printing Press, Khartoum, 116 p.

Rivas, L. R. 1949. A record of lutjanid fish (Lutjanus cyanopterus) for the Atlantic coast of the United States, with note on related species of the genus. Copeia 1949:150-152.

Rodrigues, M. M. 1974. Alimentacão do ariaco, Lutjanus synagris Linnaeus, do Estado do Ceara (Brasil). Arq. Cienc. Mar 14:61-62.

Rodriguez Pino, Z. 1962. Estudios estadísticos y biológicos sobre la biajaiba (Lutjanus synagris). Cent. Invest. Pesq. Habana. Nota Sobre Invest. 4, 90 p.

Saloman, C. H., and S. P. Naughton. Unpub. Food of gag (Mycteroperca microlepis) from North Carolina and three areas of Florida. Southeast Fish. Cent. Panama City Laboratory, Natl. Mar. Fish. Serv., NOAA, Tech. Memo.

Schroeder, R. E. 1980. Philippine shore fishes of the western Sulu Sea. National Media Production Center, Manila, 266 p.

Seki, M. P. 1984. The food and feeding habits of the grouper, Epinephelus quernus Seale 1901, in the Northwestern Hawaiian Islands. In R. W. Grigg and K. Y. Tanoue (editors), Proceedings of the Second Symposium on Resource Investigations in the Northwestern Hawaiian Islands, Vol. 2, May 25-27, 1983, Univ.

Hawaii, Honolulu, p. 179–191. UNIHI–SEAGRANT–MR–84–01.

Senta, T., and C. Peng. 1973. Studies on the feeding habits of red snappers, Lutjanus sanguineus and L. sebae. In Proc. Tech. Semin. South China Sea Fish. Resour., p. 63–84. SEAFDEC/SCS.73:S–11.

Smale, M. J. 1983. Resource partitioning by top predatory teleosts in eastern Cape coastal waters (South Africa). Ph.D. Dissertation, Univ. Rhodes, Grahamstown, S. Afr.

Smith, C. L. 1961. Synopsis of biological data on groupers (Epinephelus and allied genera) of the western North Atlantic. FAO Fish. Biol. Synop. 23.

South Atlantic Fishery Management Council. 1981. Source document for the fishery management plan for the snapper-grouper complex of the South Atlantic region.

South Carolina Wildlife and Marine Resources Department. 1981/1984. South Atlantic OCS area living marine resources study. Phases II and III. Final reports to U.S. Miner. Manage. Serv. under Contract 14–12–0001–29/85 by Mar. Resour. Res. Inst.

Starck, W. A., II. 1971. Biology of the gray snapper, Lutjanus griseus (Linnaeus), in the Florida Keys. In W. A. Starck, II and R. E. Schroeder (editors), Investigations on the gray snapper, Lutjanus griseus, p. 1–150. Stud. Trop. Oceanogr. (Miami) 10. (Published 1970.)

Starck, W. A., II, and W. P. Davis. 1966. Night habits of fishes of Alligator Reef, Florida. Ichthyol. Aquarium J. 38:313–356.

Stearns, S. 1884. On the position and character of the fishing grounds of the Gulf of Mexico. Bull. U.S. Fish Comm. 4:289–290.

Sumner, F. B., R. C. Osburn, and L. J. Cole. 1911. A biological survey of the waters of Woods Hole. Part 2. Sect. 3. A catalogue of the marine fauna. U.S. Bur. Fish. Bull. 31:545–794.

Sylvester, J. R., D. W. Drew, and A. E. Dammann. 1980. Selective life history of silk and blackfin snapper from the Virgin Islands. Caribb. J. Sci. 15:41–48.

Talbot, F. H. 1960. Notes on the biology of the Lutjanidae (Pisces) of the East African coast, with special reference to L. bohar (Forskål). Ann. S. Afr. Mus. 45:549–573.

Thompson, R., and J. L. Munro. 1978. Aspects of the biology and ecology of Caribbean reef fishes:

Serranidae (hinds and groupers). J. Fish Biol. 12:115–146.

Van der Elst, R. 1981. A guide to the common sea fishes of southern Africa. C. Struik, Cape Town, South Africa, 367 p.

Vien, L. M. 1968. [Commercial ichthyofauna of the Tonkin Bay.] Vop. Ikhtiol. 8:817–833. (Transl.: Comm. ichthyofauna of the Gulf of Tonkin. Probl. Ichthyol. 8(5):655–667.)

Wheeler, J. F. G. 1953. The bottom fishes of economic importance. In J. F. G. Wheeler, and F. D. Ommanney, (editors), Report on the Mauritius–Seychelles fisheries survey, 1948–49, p. 1–57. Fishery Publications, Lond. 1(3).

Wheeler, J. F. G., and F. D. Ommanney (editors). 1953. Report on the Mauritius–Seychelles fisheries survey, 1948–49. Fishery Publications, Lond. 1(3), 145 p.

Wray, T. (editor). 1979. Commercial fishes of Saudi Arabia. Saudi Arabia Minist. Agric. Water Resour., 120 p.

APPENDIX A Summary of major diet studies and other trophic reports on some important species of snappers and groupers. (See footnotes for explanation of symbols).

SPECIES[a] & SOURCE	DIET						
	Fish	Shrimp	Crabs	Other Crustaceans	Other Benthic Inverts.	Cephalopods	Plankton
LUTJANIDAE							
Aphareus furcatus							
Bagnis & (1972)CP	F50						+
Hobson (1974)CP:2	X						
Miles (1963)CP:1	X						
Randall (1955)CP:1			F50(ML)	F50			
Aprion virescens							
Kluegel (1921)CP:4	F75	X				F11	
Ommanney (1953)WI:36		X		(ML) X			F31 PU
Randall (1980)CP:6	F67		F17	Sto F17		F17	
Talbot (1960)WI:<25[b]	V49	X		V12		V14	
van der Elst (1981)WI	-50%		+ ML	+ ML			V17 PU + ML
Apsilus dentatus							
Brownell & (1971)WA:1	ML				Tun		
Rathjen & (1969)WA[c]							
Etelis carbunculus							
Bagnis & (1972)CP							
Parrish & (unpub)WP:38[d]	F45 N47 V78	F8 N6 V2	F24 N18 V17	F3 N2 V.1			PU F32 N27 V3
Reed (1964)WI		X		+			
Richards (unpub)WP:17[d]	+			X Lob Sto			
E. coruscans							
Fourmanoir & (1976)WP[a]l	X						
Richards (unpub)WP:1[d]	X					X	
E. radiosus							
Richards (unpub)WP:1[d]	X						
Lutjanus analis							
Beebe & (1928)WA	+			X	Mol X		
Bohlke & (1968)WA	+ Grunt		X	X			
Florida Sea Grant (1981)GM	Grunt			+	Gas		
Gudger (1929)WA	Grunt						
LaMonte (1952)	X			X			
Longley & (1941)WA:<29	+	X					
Randall (1967)WA:53	V30	V2	V47	V3		Oct V3	
Starck (1971)WA:40	F42	F2	F50	+	Mol F>25	Oct F5	

L. apodus
Reference							
Beebe & (1928)WA:-25	F≥60						
Bogdanov & (1967)GM[e]	X		X			X Wor	
Florida Sea Grant (1981)GM	X	R2	X		+	X Wor	
Longley & (1941)WA:≤241	R3		R1				F1 X
Starck (1971)WA:70	F81	F6	F11	V22	+	Gas VT	V3 Squ
Randall (1967)WA:58	V61	V3			V10		

L. argentimaculatus
| Schroeder (1980)WP | X | | X | | | | |
| van der Elst (1981)WI | X | | X | | X | | |

L. argentiventris
| Hobson (1968)EP:13 | F30 | X | X | | + | X Mol | |

L. biguttatus
| Schroeder (1980)WP | X | X | | | | Gas Squ | |

L. bohar
Bagnis & (1972)CP	X		X			Mol	
Helfrich & (1968)CP:1789	V-57		X	V14(ML)		X Mol V19	
Hiatt & (1960)CP:1	100%	VT	V22(ML)	F69 V4		V27	F-5 V4
Miles (1963)CP:915	F58 V42	F4	F11				F9
Randall (1980)CP:35	F76		X	V4			X V4
Schroeder (1980)WP	X	V4	X	V9	V11	X Ech Biv	Squ +
Talbot (1960)WI:359b	V62		X	X	Sto	Wor	X
van der Elst (1981)WI	-50%	X	X	Sto Amp		X Gas	
Wheeler (1953)WI:827	F57		+	+			
Wray (1979)WI	+						

L. boutton a2
| Mizenko (1984)CP:335 | F25 | F17 | F-50 | F90 | F>10 | | F1 X |
| Schroeder (1980)WP | X | X | X | | | | |

L. buccanella
Brownell & (1971)WA:24[f]	F33 N12	F8 N6	F4 N1	F46 N79 Iso		Tun	F8 N2
Rathjen & (1969)WA[c]						Tun V12	
Sylvester & (1980)WA:10[f]	V48						V40

L. campechanus a3
Adams & (1891)GM[g]	X		X Calappa	X Squilla			
Barroso (1965)WA:<837	FR1 VR1			FR3 VR3		FR2&4 VR1&2	
Baughman (1943)GM:1	X						
Beebe & (1928)WA:2	F100						
Bogdanov & (1967)GM[e]	X	F46	V>50	X		X Tun	
Bradley & (1975)GM:J258 A190	V20 V52 V71	F-15 F33	F14 F10	V8 V6	F-13 V20 F8 V8		X Tun
Camber (1955)GM:A24 J14	F42	F93	F12			F4	F4
Collins (1885)GM[g]	+						

PU Clavelina

(CONTINUED)

APPENDIX A (Cont.)

SPECIES[a] & SOURCE	DIET						
	Fish	Shrimp	Crabs	Other Crustaceans	Other Benthic Inverts.	Cephalopods	Plankton
Collins (1887)WA	+ Scomber						
Cervigon (1966)GM	X		X	X			X
Florida Sea Grant (1981)GM	+	+				Squ +	
Fournanoir(1968)WAe	N46	N4	N13	N30	Wor N4 Mol		
Futch & (1976)GM:56	+	+	+				
Grimes & (1977)WA	+	X	X		X Tun	X	
Iversen & (1969)GM	X					X	+
Moseley (1966)GM:J73	V14	V26 V14	V3	V32 Sto			
A114	V55	V14	V3	X		X	PU
Naughton & (MSa)WA/GM:2431	F66	F9 .. V4	F20.. VI2..	X	X Uro Mol Pol	X	
SAFMC (1981)WA	V71	V4	V4 +	F36 V19 Sto	X Asc + Uro	Squ F16 V7	X PG
So. Car. (1981/4)WA:35	F69 N77 V95	X.	N6 V.6..	N20 V5			PG F3 N2 VT
Stearns (1884)GM:18					Sand worms		PG?
L. cyanopterus							
Bohlke & (1968)WA	X			X			
Randall (1967)WA:11	V100						
Rivas (1949)WA	X	X	X	X			
Starck (1971)WA:5	+						
L. decussatus							
Schroeder (1980)WP	X	X				Squ	
L. erythropterus[h]							
Senta & (1973)EI:≤276	F-50 W-35	X	F-35 W-20	X Sto	X	X Squ	
Vlen (1968)WP	+						
L. fulviflamma							
Schroeder (1980)WP	X	X			Mol		
Talbot (1960)WI:<126	X	X	+	X			
van der Elst (1981)WI	+	+	+	Sto +	Wor		+
L. fulvus[a4]							
Bagnis & (1972)CP	+						
Helfrich &(1968)CP:≤51	F50	F17	F50	+			
Hiatt & (1960)CP:6	F31	F8	F52	+			
Miles (1963)CP:51	F50		F25	+			
Randall (1955)CP:14	F32	F25	F-65 Calappids..	+ Sto	F>16 Hol F25	F2	
Randall (1980)CP:13	F42	F9 ..	F35	F68			
Randall & (1960)CP:50			X	F54 Sto	X	X	
Schroeder (1980)WP	X						

L. gibbus

Reference	Values (left → right)
Bagnis & (1972)CP	F4 · F-10 · X · Mo1 · X
Helfrich & (1968)CP:36	F40 · F5 · F-75 · + · + · X Mo1 Ech · F4
Hiatt & (1960)~CP:23	F56 · F40 · X · + · X
Miles (1963)CP:20	F56 · F56 · F-75 Sto
Randall &(1960)CP:9	F26 · F2 · F40 · F2
Randall (1980)CP:24	X Lob · X Ech Oph
Schroeder (1980)WP	X · X · + · X
Talbot (1960)WI:<126	X · X · + · X · X Lob · X · Squ
van der Elst (1981)WI	+ · +
Wray (1979)WI	+ · + · X

L. griseus

Reference	Values (left → right)
Bogdanov & (1967)GM[e]	X · F34 N38 V23 · + · X · Wor
Croker (1962)WA:146	+ · F42 N28 V25 · F27 N19 V13 · X · X
Florida Sea Grant (1981)GM	+ · + · X · X
Gudger (1929)WA	X · X
LaMonte (1952)	+ · +
Longley & (1941)WA:19	+ · + · + · Ann · X
Nagelkerken (1980)WA	V39 · V13 · V40 · X
Randall (1967)WA:28	V32 · F27 N22 V20 · F25 N17 V16 · X · Gas V7
Starck (1971)WA:636	F35 N19 V32 · F22 N42 V32 · X · F.8 N.4 V.5

L. jocu

Reference	Values (left → right)
Florida Sea Grant (1981)GM	61% · Lob V10 · Mo1 · Oct V7
Randall (1967)WA:56	V61 · V15 · F-24 Lob · Gas V4 · Oct F9
Starck (1971)WA:34	F65 · F6 · F24 · Mo1 · X

L. johnii

Reference	Values (left → right)
Druzhinin (1970)EI:26	42% · 58% · +
Wray (1979)WI	+ · +

L. kasmira

Reference	Values (left → right)
Bagnis & (1972)CP	+ · + · Pol +
Basheeruddin & (1962)EI:J-84	F29 · F10 · F-45 · F80 · F>10
Mizenko (1984)CP:311	F46 V48 · F20 V2 · F61 V16 · F-30 V-14 Sto · X V3
Oda & (1981)CP:115	F57 N-19 · F86 N-27 · F 43 N-54
Parrish (unpub)CP:7	F56 · F11 · F11 · F22 · F22
Randall & (1960)CP:9	F10 V4 · Crab F32 V12
Rangarajan (1970)EI:<792	NV>50 · NV~10 · NV>10 · X
Talbot (1960)WI:<77	X · + · X · +
van der Elst (1981)WI	X · X · X

L. lemniscatus[a5]

Reference	Values (left → right)
Misra (1968)EI:60[e]	X · (ML) X · X · X

L. lutjanus[a6]

Reference	Values (left → right)
Basheeruddin & (1962)EI:J-<137	X · (ML) · (ML)Biv Gas · Squ · Cop
Schroeder (1980)WP	X · X

(CONTINUED)

APPENDIX A (Cont.)

SPECIES[a] & SOURCE	DIET						
	Fish	Shrimp	Crabs	Other Crustaceans	Other Benthic Inverts.	Cephalopods	Plankton
L. mahogoni							
Florida Sea Grant (1981)GM:32	+	X	X				
Randall (1967)WA:8	V75	V12	V3			Oct V9	
Starck (1971)WA:17	F76	F12	F6			Oct F6	
L. malabaricus							
Druzhinin (1970)EI:49	37%			63%			
Sainsbury (pers comm)WP:19[1]	N56	N6	N25	N13			
L. monostigma							
Helfrich & (1968)CP:<29	F92			F23 Sto(ML)Lob			
Hiatt & (1960)CP:1	100%						
Miles (1963)CP:5	F80			F60			
Randall (1980)CP:18	V92		V8				
Randall & (1960)CP:14	100%						
Schroeder (1980)WP	X	X				Squ	
Talbot (1960)WI:<18	+	X					
L. novemfasciatus							
Hobson (1968)EP:<15	F>33			X Lob			
L. purpureus							
Evermann & (1902)WA[j]	X Selar		X		X		
Furtado- & (1972)WA:198	F41	F-12	F6	F40(ML)	X Asc	F-5	F-30 PG
Nagelkerken (1981)WA:Several	+						
L. quinquelineatus							
Schroeder (1980)WP[a7]	X	X	X	+	Mol	Squ	
L. rivulatus							
Bagnis (1972)CP	X						
Schroeder (1980)WP			X	+	Mol	X	
Talbot (1960)WI:<129	+		X		Ech Mol	X	
van der Elst (1981)WI	X		X		X Pol Ech Asc	X	
L. russelli							
Schroeder (1980)WP	X	X	X			Squs	
van der Elst (1981)WI			+	X			
L. sanguineus							
Talbot (1960)WI:<102	+	X	X	X		X	X rU PG
van der Elst (1981)WI	X	X	X	Sto		Squ	X

L. sebae							
Schroeder (1980)WP	X						
Senta & (1973)EI:<129	F-50 W-30	F-40 W-20	X Sto F25 W13	Mol X	X Squ F20 W30		
Talbot (1960)WI:<27	X	X	X	X	X		
van der Elst (1981)WI	X	+	+	Lob +	Squ		
L. synagris							
Beebe & (1928)WA:78	F38	F19	F19	F6	F8 Pol X		
Florida Sea Grant (1981)GM	+	X	X	+	X Ann Mol	X	
LaMonte (1952)	X						
Longley & (1941)WA:1	100%						
Randall (1967)WA:2		V50		Sto V50			
Rodriguez (1962)WA:207	F32	F-15 F30	F-15 F10	F27	F>12 Ann Mol		F1
Rodrigues (1974)WA:159	F62		F>15	F>16 Sto	X		
Starck (1971)WA:10	F20			+			
L. vitta							
Hiatt & (1960)CP:16	F~20	F38	F-50	X Sto	X	Oct V6	
L. vivanus							
Brownell & (1971)WA:73	F51 N55	F18 N16	F11 N11	N5	N2	N3	N2 PU
Florida Sea Grant (1981)GM	50%	17%	11%	4%	X Tun Mol Tun	X	
Grimes & (1977)WA							
Rathjen & (1969)WA[c]	X	X	X	X			
SAFMC (1981)WA	X						
Sylvester & (1980)WA:-37	V52	V10	V15	V8		Oct V6	
Ocyurus chrysurus							
Beebe & (1928)WA:16	X	X	X	X	X Pol		X Cop PG
Bohlke & (1968)WA	X	X	X	Sto	Ann		
Fallows (1984)WA:39	F44 N5	F36 N33	F13 Juv N2	F+ N23	N2	F-20 N30 PG	X
Florida Sea Grant (1981)GM	+		X	X	Mol	X	
LaMonte (1952)	X	X	X				
Longley & (1941)WA:1	X	X	X	Sto	Ann		
Nagelkerken (1981)WA:1	Jenkensia F88 V78	F6 V2	F4 V1 V-9	F12 V3 Sto	V1 Mol Wor	Squ F3 V2	
Naughton & (MSb)WA:2204	V84	X	X	X	Gas V2	V4	V32 PG PU
Piedra (1965)WA:<250	V15(ML)	V16(ML)	V23(ML)	X	X	F2	F56
Randall (1967)WA:42	F>29(ML)	F7	F12	X	X		
Starck (1971)WA:41				Sto	Ann		
Pristipomoides argyrogrammicus							
van der Elst (1981)WI	X			Sto X ML		Squ	X
P. auricilla							
Kami (1973)WP:5	F20						
Parrish & (unpub)WP:103[d]	F22 N5 V16	F11 N3 V2	F2 N.4 V.6	F>20 N10 V6	N9 V3	F5 N1 V5	PU F60 N74 V68 PU F39 N19 V36 PG F73 N50 V30

(CONTINUED)

APPENDIX A (Cont.)

SPECIES[a] & SOURCE	DIET						
	Fish	Shrimp	Crabs	Other Crustaceans	Other Benthic Inverts.	Cephalopods	Plankton
P. filamentosus							
Kami (1973)WP:5			F20	F20	F60	F60	PU F100 PG
Kluegel (1921)CP:10					Asc		
Ralston & (unpub)CP:17[d]	F65 N49 V40	F18 N9 V.7	F6 N1 V.4	F24 N6 V1 Amp		Oct F53 N13 V11	PU F59 N16 V43
Richards (unpub)WP:1[d]		X					
P. flavipinnis							
Fourmanoir & (1976)WP	F67	+					PU F17
Kami (1973)WP:6							
P. macrophthalmus							
Brownell & (1971)WA:3		X	X				
Florida Sea Grant (1981)GM		+					
P. multidens							
Mizenko (1984)CP:91	F69	F4	F15	F47		F6	PG F22
Richards (unpub)WP:19	+	+		X Lob Sto		Squ	PU
P. sieboldii							
Kami (1973)WP:1	+	X	X		Pol	X	X PU
P. typus							
Wray (1979)WI	X	. . . . . .			X		
P. zonatus							
Parrish & (unpub)WP:209[d]	F49 N29 V50	F6 N4 V4	F36 N16 V26	N9 V2	N.6 V.3	F4 N1 V1	N40 V18 PU
Rhomboplites aurorubens							
Florida Sea Grant (1981)GM	V8						V41 PG
Grimes (1979)WA:353 S	Scales V68		ML	V6 ML		V37	V78 Cop
M	V8					V9	V23 Cop PG
L			ML	V38	Pol	V37	V17 PG
So. Car. (1981/4)WA:253	F28 N7 V32	ML . . . Larval &	ML . . . Pelagic	+	X Pol Gas	F6 N.4 V44	+ PU
Symphorus nematophorus							
Fourmanoir & (1976)WP							
Schroeder (1980)WP	X	X	X Raninoides			Squ	

SERRANIDAE

Aethaloperca rogaa
Harmelin-Vivien & (1976)WI   W100
Morgans (1982)WI:6   F67   F33 Stσ   Oct
Randall & (1983)WI:1   100%
Schroeder (1980)WP   X

Alphestes afer
Beebe & (1928)WA:1   X   V2
Randall (1967)WA:30   V7   V7   V77   V7   Oct F14

A. multiguttatus
Hobson (1968)EP:7   F14   .... +

Anyperodon leucogrammicus
Hiatt & (1960)CP:3   F67   X
Morgans (1982)WI:2   100%
Randall & (1983)CP:1   100%
Schroeder (1980)WP   X   X   Mol

Centropristis striata
Baughman (1944)GM   +   +   Mol Amp
Godcharles (1970)GM   +   +   Squ
LaMonte (1952)WA   X   X   X
SAFMC (1981)WA   R2   .... R1   R3 Mol Ech   F4 N,3 V7
So. Car. (1981/4)WA:313   F29 N3 V42   .... + Amp   + Amp   X
Sumner & (1911)WA   X   X

Cephalopholis argus
Bagnis & (1972)CP   +   X   Lob
Harmelin-Vivien & (1976)WI:27   W96   W4   X
Helfrich & (1968)CP<51   F89   X   X
Hiatt & (1960)CP:9   F-40   F33   X
Hobson (1974)CP:4   100%
Miles (1963)CP:28   F89   F18   X
Morgans (1982)WI:7   +   X   X   Pol
Parrish (unpub)CP:10   F100 N91   F10 N9
Randall (1955)CP:2   F50   F50 Penaeid   Sto F8
Randall (1980)CP:13   F92   X
Randall & (1960)CP:98   F78   F10   F8   X
van der Elst (1981)WI   +   X   Lob

C. aurantia
Morgans (1982)WI:1   100%

C. boenack[a8]
Schroeder (1980)WP   X   X   X   Squ

(CONTINUED)

APPENDIX A (Cont.)

	DIET						
SPECIES[a] & SOURCE	Fish	Shrimp	Crabs	Other Crustaceans	Other Benthic Inverts.	Cephalopods	Plankton
C. fulva							
Beebe & (1928)WA							
Randall (1967)WA:29	V46	+ V21	V17	V16	X		
C. igarishiensis							
Schroeder (1980)WP	X			X			
C. leopardus							
Morgans (1982)WI:2	100%						
Randall (1955)CP:1	100%		F50	F50			
Randall & (1960)CP:1							
C. miniata							
Schroeder (1980)WP	X	X	X			X	X
van der Elst (1981)WI	+	+	+	X Sto ML			X
C. oligosticta							
Randall & (1983)WI:1	100%						
C. sexmaculata							
Morgans (1982)WI:1		100%					
Randall & (1960)CP:24	F42	F8					
C. sonnerati							
Harmelin-Vivien & (1976)WI:2			W99 Galatheid				
Morgans (1982)WI:13	W1	X	X	F38 Sto			
van der Elst (1981)WI	F54 X	X	X	X Lob			
C. urodela							
Bagnis & (1972)CP	X						
Hiatt & (1960)CP:13	F42	F28	F-20	X			
Randall & (1960)CP:25	F68	F12	F12	F8			
Schroeder (1980)WP	X	X	X		Mol	Squ	
Chromileptes altivelis							
Schroeder (1980)WP	X	X			Mol Ech	Squ	
Dermatolepis dermatolepis							
Montgomery (1975)EP:4	X		X	X			
D. striolatus							
Morgans (1982)WI:2	100%						

Species / Reference	1	2	3	4	5	6	7
Dinoperca petersii							
Joubert & (1980)WI:2			X	X			
van der Elst (1981)WI			X	X ML	Sto	Gas V5	X
Epinephelus adscensionis							
Nagelkerken (1980)WA							
Randall (1967)WA:31	V20		V4	V67	V4		
E. albomarginatus							
van der Elst (1981)WI			+		Lob		Oct + Squ
E. andersoni							
Joubert & (1980)WI:16	F69 V41 W49	F44 V5 W5	F56 V15 W16		Lob F6 V38 W30		
van der Elst (1981)WI	X		X		Lob		
E. areolatus							
Fourmanoir & (1976)WP		+ Penaeidae					X
Schroeder (1980)WP	X						
E. caeruleopunctatus							
Morgans (1982)WI:2	F50	F50					
E. chlorostigma							
Morgans (1982)WI:9	X	. . . .	X	X	X Sto	 X	
Richards (unpub) WP:1[d]		Pandalidae	X				
van der Elst (1981)WI:several	X	. . . .	. . . .				
Wray (1979)WI	X						
E. corallicola							
Randall (1955)CP:1					Lob 100%		
E. cruentatus							
Beebe & (1928)WA:1	F13	F80			Sto X		
Nagelkerken (1979)WA:J45 A239	F75	F>7	. . . .		F18		
Randall (1967)WA:26	V66	V17	V4		Sto V9	Gas V4	
E. cyanopodus							
Hiatt & (1960)CP:1[a9]	X						
Randall (1980)CP:6	F67	X	F33 Calappid			Mol	X
Schroeder (1980)WP:[a10]	X		X				
E. drummondhayi							
So. Car. (1981/4)WA:18	F~50 N-53 V-65	. . . .	X		X	Asc F-30 N-35 V~30	
E. epistictus							
Morgans (1982)WI:1all	X	. . . .	X		X		
E. fario (?)							
Harmelin-Vivien&(1976)WI:10	W22	W3	W74				

(CONTINUED)

APPENDIX A (Cont.)

SPECIES[a] & SOURCE	Fish	Shrimp	Crabs	DIET Other Crustaceans	Other Benthic Inverts.	Cepha-lopods	Plankton
E. fasciatus							
Harmelin-Vivien&(1976)WI:11	W34		W65				
Karplus (1978)WI:13	F23	....	....	F77			
Morgans (1982)WI:29	X		X	Sto	Oph	X	
Randall & (1983)WI:12	F67	F8 Alpheid	F25 Majid	X		X	
Schroeder (1980)WP	X			X			
van der Elst (1981)WI	X	X	+		Wor		
E. faveatus a12							
Harmelin-Vivien&(1976)WI:6	W16		W62	Sto W23	Pol		
Hiatt & (1960)CP:1k			F33	Lob F33			
Miles (1963)CP:3k	F33		X				
Schroeder (1980)WP	X					X	
E. flavocaeruleus							
Morgans (1982)WI:22	50%	X	F5 Calappid	Sto F5	F5	X	PU F5
van der Elst (1981)WI	+		X	Lob		Squ	
Wheeler (1953)WI	X	....	.... X Calappa	X Sto			
E. flavolimbatus							
Brownell & (197l)WA:1						Squ	
Florida Sea Grant (1981)WA		....	....	....		X	
E. fuscoguttatus							
Harmelin-Vivien&(1976)WI:2	W94		W6				
Randall (1980)CP:3	F33					Oct F≥33	
Schroeder (1980)WP	X	X	X			X	
E. guaza							
Joubert & (1980)WI:5	X		X	Lob			
Smale (1983)WI/EA:90	F-30 N25 W25	F6 N24 W2	F28 N17 W5	F26 N19 W21		F-20 N16 W48	
van der Elst (1981)WI/EA	X	....	X	Lob X			
E. guttatus							
Beebe & (1928)WA:2	F50	F50	F42				
Burnett- (1975)WA:56	F31	F38					
Florida Sea Grant (1981)GM	V21	V10 + Alpheid	V40 + Calappa	Lob Sto			
Menzel (1960)WA	+		+	V>17		Oct F7	
Nagelkerken (1980)WA	X				V-2	Oct V7	
Randall (1967)WA:50	V21	V10	V40	V20			
Thompson & (1978)WA	X		X	X Lob	X	Oct V7	

E. hexagonatus

Reference						
Harmelin-Vivien&(1976)WI:8	W74		W4	Sto W22	Pol F25	
Hiatt & (1960)CP:4	F75		F40	F17		
Miles (1963)CP:5	F60		F33			
Randall & (1960)CP:6	F50					

E. itajara [a13] (Clupea / Myrichthys)

Reference						
Beebe & (1928)WA:1	X					
Breder (1925)WA	X					
Breder & (1934)WA:1	+		X	Lob		
Brice (1898)WA			X	Lob +		
Florida Sea Grant (1981)GM				Lob		
LaMonte (1952)WA				Lob +		
Longley & (1941)WA	V13		V12	Lob V69 +		
Randall (1967)WA:9						
Smith (1961)						

E. labriformis

Reference						
Hobson (1968)EP:29	F-30	......		F-70		

E. longispinis

Reference						
Morgans (1982)WI:~10	F-10	......	+	R1 Sto	Biv F-10	F-10

E. malabaricus

Reference						
Randall & (1983)WI	X	X	X	Lob		X
van der Elst (1981)WI	+					

E. merra

Reference						
Bagnis & (1972)CP	+		+	+		
Harmelin-Vivien & (1976)WI:37	W63	W3	W27	Sto W2		W5
Hiatt & (1960)CP:25	F~50	F~8	F~35	X Sto		
Schroeder (1980)WP	X	X	X			

E. microdon

Reference						
Helfrich & (1968)CP:81	+	......	+ Portunid	V64 Lob	Gas	X
Hiatt & (1960)CP:5	F-80	F20	F20			
Miles (1963)CP:291	F62		F65			
Randall (1980)CP:14	F21		F57	Lob F7	Mol F17	F14
Randall & (1960)CP:101	F50	F10	F40			
Schroeder (1980)WP	X	X	X	X		X

E. miliaris

Reference						
Morgans (1982)WI:2 [a14]	X	X	Calappa	Sto	Gas	X

E. morio

Reference						
Florida Sea Grant (1981)GM	+	+	+	+		X
Gudger (1929)WA	X		X			
LaMonte (1952)	X	X				Oct
Longley & (1941)WA	X	X		X Sto Lob		Oct

(CONTINUED)

APPENDIX A (Cont.)

SPECIES[a] & SOURCE	DIET						
	Fish	Shrimp	Crabs	Other Crustaceans	Other Benthic Inverts.	Cephalopods	Plankton
Moe (1969)GM	X	+	+	+		X	X
Randall (1967)WA:2	V17	X	V33	V50			
SAFMC (1981)WA			X	X			
E. multinotatus							
Morgans (1982)WI:3[a15]	X		X				
E. mystacinus							
Brownell & (1971)WA	X						
Florida Sea Grant (1981)GM	X					Squ	
Thompson & (1978)WA:1	X	X				Squ	
E. niveatus							
So. Car. (1981/4)WA:2	X		X				
So. Car. (1981/4)WA:18	F-42 N-20 V-28		F-55 N-78 V-72				
E. quernus							
Kluegel (1921)CP:3	Scombroidei						
Ralston&(unpub)CP:17[d]	F65 N32 V40	F29 N42 V3		F35 N9 V4		F53 N17 V53	
Seki (1984)CP:67	F60 N14 V76	F36 N82 V9		F51 N84 V15		F6 N1 V8	T PU
E. quoyanus							
Morgans (1982)WI:$\leq$16[a16] [a17]	X		R1 *Calappa*		T	X	
E. rivulatus							
Morgans (1982)WI	X		X				
van der Elst (1981)WI	+	+	+				
E. sexfasciatus							
Schroeder (1980)WP	X		X				
E. socialis							
Randall (1980)CP:5	F40		F60			F20	
E. spilotus[m]							
Hiatt & (1960)CP:8	F75	F25	F25			Oct F12	
E. striatus							
Beebe & (1928)WA	X						
Florida Sea Grant (1981)WA	55%	X	22%	X	Mol	X	
Randall (1967)WA:153	V54	V5	V24	V10	Mol V2	V5	
Thompson & (1978)WA	X						

Species / Reference	N76	N7	N11	N7	N6
E. suillus Hussain & (1977)WI:55[n]					N6
E. summana Schroeder (1980)WP		X		Mol	Squ
E. tauvina					
Miles (1963)CP:9a18	F33		F33	+ Mol F22	Squ X
Morgans (1965)WI:2[o]	X		F7		
Randall (1980)CP&WI:15	F93		F33		
Randall & (1960)CP:3a18	F100				
Wray (1979)WI[p]	+	......		+	
E. tukula van der Elst (1981)WI	+	......		Lob	
E. undulosus					
Morgans (1982)WI:~30	R1	+	X	Sto +	Squ
Schroeder (1980)WP		X	X		
Mycteroperca bonaci					
Bohlke & (1968)WA	X		X		
LaMonte (1952)	X		X		
Randall (1967)WA:4	V100				
M. interstitialis Randall (1967)WA:5	V100		X		
M. microlepis					
LaMonte (1952)	X		X		
Longley & (1941)WA:1	X	X	X		
SAFMC (1981)WA	X	X	X		
Saloman & (MS)WA/GM:979	F-96 V-97			X Blv	F8 N4 V4
So. Car. (1981/4)WA:13	F85 N74 V96			F8 N9 V.2 X Gas	X N4 V4
M. phenax					
Matheson & (1984)WA:91	I99	......		I.5 X Ech	T / X Squ / F1 N1 V1
So. Car. (1981/4)WA:2	X				
So. Car. (1981/4)WA:91	F-87 N-97 V-90	X	X		
M. rosacea Hobson (1968)EP:J38 A<125	N>60 Harengula 100%	......		X X	
M. tigris Randall (1967)WA:34	V100				
M. venosoa					
Gudger (1929)WA	Grunt V95	V1			Squ V4
Randall (1967)WA:51					
Plectropomus areolatus[a19] Hiatt & (1960)CP:1	X				

(CONTINUED)

APPENDIX A (Cont.)

				DIET			
SPECIES[a] & SOURCE	Fish	Shrimp	Crabs	Other Crustaceans	Other Benthic Inverts.	Cephalopods	Plankton
P. laevis							
Bagnis & (1972)CP[q]	+						
Randall (1980)CP&WP:22[q]	100%						
Randall & (1960)CP:3[q]	100%						
Schroeder (1980)WP:[a]20	X			X	Mol	Oct	
P. leopardus							
Schroeder (1980)WP	X	X	X	X		X	
P. maculatus							
Choat (1968)WP:95	N97 V98	N2 V1				N1 V1.5	
Schroeder (1980)WP	X	X		X		X	
Wheeler (1953)WI	+						
Wray (1979)WI	+			+			
P. oligacanthus							
Schroeder (1980)WP	X			X			
P. punctatus [a1]							
Morgans (1982)WI:30	100%						
Promicrops lanceolatus							
Bagnis & (1972)CP	+			Lob +			
van der Elst (1981)WI	+		+				
Variola albimarginata							
Morgans (1982)WI:1	100%						
V. louti							
Bagnis & (1972)CP	W100						
Harmelin-Vivien & (1976)WI	F80			R1	Mol R2 Ech R4		
Helfrich & (1968)CP:≤44	X			F11			
Hiatt & (1960)CP:1	F75		F18		X		
Miles (1963)CP:16	+	X	X	X		X	
Morgans (1982)WI:90	F92		F4	F4			
Randall (1980)CP:24	100%						
Randall & (1960)CP:2			X				
Schroeder (1980)WP			X		Mol		
van der Elst (1981)WI	X			X Sto			
Wheeler (1953)WI	+					X	

Symbols for information sources:
& - Following an author's name [e.g., Longley &(1941)] indicates additional authors.

Geographical area of study:
EA - Eastern Atlantic
WA - Western Atlantic
GM - Gulf of Mexico
EP - Eastern Pacific
CP - Central Pacific
WP - Western Pacific
EI - Eastern Indian
WI - Western Indian

: - No. following indicates no. guts containing food in the sample.

J or A indicates no. from juvenile fish or no. from adult fish.

S,M,L - Small, medium, large size fish.

< indicates that the no. following may be the total no. of guts examined, including empty guts.

Symbols in category columns:
F - % of all specimens with food that contained the category.
N - % of all prey individuals that were of the category.
V - % of all prey volume that was of the category.
W - % of all prey weight that was of the category.
I - % of the sum of all values of Index of Relative Importance [IRI = F(N + V)] that was of the category.
% - Basis used to compute % not stated; or only one food category identified.
R - Rank among all food categories (may be combined with F, N, V, or W to indicate basis of ranking).

NV-Preponderance Index: $\dfrac{N \times V}{\Sigma(N \times V)}$

+ - Abundant, important or dominant.
x - Occurred (moderate or unknown quality).
T - Trace amount (may be combined with F, N, V or W)
ML - Much of the amount was larval forms.

Abbreviations for more specific diet items:
PG - Pelagic gastropods (e.g. pteropods, heteropods)
PU - Pelagic urochordates (e.g. Salpida, Doliolida, Pyrosomida)
Amp - Amphipods
Ann - Annelids
Asc - Ascidians
Biv - Bivalves
Cop - Copepods
Ech - Echinoids
Gas - Gastropods (probably mostly benthic)
Hol - Holothurians

Lob - Lobsters
Mol - Molluscs (probably excluding cephalopods)
Oct - Octopus
Oph - Ophiuroids
Pol - Polychaetes
Squ - Squid
Sto - Stomatopods
Tun - Tunicates
Uro - Urochordates
Wor - Worms

(CONTINUED)

APPENDIX A (Cont.)

Where a diet item appears alone, no other type food in that category was reported.
Where a diet item follows an abundance symbol, it was one of the items reported.
Where a diet item precedes an abundance symbol, it was the major item reported.
Dotted line connecting Other Crustaceans with Shrimp and/or Crabs columns indicates that "crustaceans" were reported as a
category, whether or not shrimp or crabs were separately specified.

Superscripted notes:

[a] Synonymy: In several cases a species was reported under a different name from that used in App. A. In most such cases, that
different name has been listed in the literature in synonymy with a Table 1 name, since the original report (see papers by Allen,
Anderson and Randall this volume). Such cases are listed below. Most are in the format: Synonym = Currently Accepted Name.

[a1] The authors' E. oculatus appears to be E. coruscans.

[a2] Lutjanus rufolineatus = L. boutton

[a3] Several names used. These reports all appear to refer to
L. campechanus.

[a4] Several authors:
Lutjanus vaigiensis = L. fulvus
[a5] Lutjanus rangus = L. lemniscatus
[a6] Lutjanus lineolatus = L. lutjanus
[a7] Lutjanus spilurus = L. quinquelineatus
[a8] Cephalopholis pachycentron = C. boenack
[a9] Epinephelus kohleri = E. cyanopodus
[a10] Epinephelus hoedtii = E. cyanopodus

[a11] Epinephelus praeopercularis = E. epistictus
[a12] Epinephelus macrospilos = E. faveatus
[a13] Several names used.
[a14] Epinephelus dictiophorus = E. miliaris
[a15] Epinephelus leprosus = E. multinotatus
[a16] Epinephelus gilberti = E. quoyanus
[a17] Epinephelus grammatophorus = E. rivulatus
[a18] Epinephelus elongatus = E. tauvina
[a19] Plectropomus truncatus = P. areolatus
[a20] Plectropomus melanoleucus = P. laevis
[a21] Plectropomus marmoratus = P. punctatus?

[b] Amounts for food categories probably given in volume %, but uncertain.

[c] Cited in Brownell and Rainey (1971).

[d] Unpublished results:
Parrish, James D. Hawaii Cooperative Fishery Research Unit, 2538 The Mall, University of Hawaii, Honolulu, Hawaii 96822, USA.
Material collected in Northwestern Hawaiian Islands and Island of Hawaii.
Parrish, James D. and Michael W. Callahan. Hawaii Cooperative Fishery Research Unit, 2538 The Mall, University of Hawaii,
Honolulu, Hawaii 96822, USA. Material supplied by National Marine Fisheries Service, Honolulu Laboratory, collected by
Michael P. Seki. Gut analyses by M.W. Callahan.
Ralston, Stephen V. and Carol T. Sorden. National Marine Fisheries Service, Honolulu Laboratory, 2570 Dole St., Honolulu,
Hawaii 96822. Gut analysis by C. T. Sorden.
Richards, Andrew H. Senior Fisheries Scientist. Fisheries Research, P.O. Box 101, Kavieng, Papua New Guinea.

[e] Cited in Druzhinin (1970).

[f] Some of the same specimens may be included in both collections.

[g] Cited in Camber (1955).

[h] *L. erythropterus* was probably the species studied in both cases (G.R. Allen, pers. comm.), but it may have been *L. malabaricus*.

[i] Collected off northwestern Australian shelf by K.J. Sainsbury, CSIRO Fisheries Research Division, Hobart, Australia.

[j] Cited in Brownell & Rainey (1971).

[k] *E. faveatus* does not occur in these localities. Per J.E. Randall (pers. comm.), the most similar species are *E. howlandi* and *E. maculatus*.

[l] Reported as *E. fuscoguttatus*. Per Randall (1980) probably *E. microdon*.

[m] *E. spilotus* is not a valid species. It is not clear what species was meant.

[n] Reported as *E. tauvina*.

[o] Cited in Randall & Ben-Tuvia (1983).

[p] May include *E. suillus*.

[q] Reported as *P. leopardus*. Per J.E. Randall (this volume), fish from these areas are most likely *P. laevis* or possibly an undescribed species of the central Pacific.

APPENDIX B Prey items collected from guts of 11 deep-water Pacific snapper and grouper species. Data source for each entry is indicated in parentheses. Where data permit, results within each source are cumulative in some higher systematic categories. There is no accumulation across sources. (See footnotes for explanation of symbols.)

DIET ITEM	Epinephelus chlorostigma	E. quernus	Etelis carbunculus	E. coruscans	E. radiosus	Pristipomoides auricilla	P. filamentosus	P. flavipinnis	P. multidens	P. sieboldii	P. zonatus
FISH		F60 N14 V76 (3) F65 N32 V40 (6)	F45 N47 V78 (8) F82 (1)	X/1 (1) G (4)	3/1 (1)	F22 N5 V16 (8) 2/5 (2)	F65 N49 V40 (6) X/5 (2)	4/6 (2)	F69 (7) F74 (1)	D/1(2)	F49 N29 V50 (8)
Anguilliformes		F29 N6 V3 (6) F12 N3 V1 (6)	F3 N2 V3 (8)						X/19 (1)a		N7 V13 (8)
Ophichthidae											F11 N4 V5 (8) X (8)
Congridae		F6 N1 V10 (3)				X (8)			X/19 (1)		
Muraenidae		F2 N.2 V.2 (3)	X (8)								F1 N.3 V3 (8)
Antigoniidae		F2 (3)	X/17 (1) X/17 (1) D/17 (1)						X/19 (1)		
Apogonidae											
Bramidae											
Bregmacerotidae			D/17 (1)b	X/1 (1)b		1/5 (2)b			D/19 (1)		
Echeneidae		F6 (3) F12 (3)									
Emmelichthyidae				G (4)c							
Gonostomatidae											
Holocentridae									F1 (7)		
Lutjanidae		F3 (3) F2 (3)	X/17 (1)								
Etelis carbunculus		F3 (3)									
Myctophidae				G (4)							
Paralepidae					3/1 (1)						
Priacanthidae		F2 (3) F2 (3)	D/17 (1)						F1 (7) D/19 (1)		
Priacanthus sp.							F6 N1 (6)				

Taxon										
Scombroidei										
Serranidae	3/3 (5)	F4 (3)	X/17 (1)					X/19 (1)		F1 N.5 V1 (8)
Pseudanthias thompsoni										
Symphysanodontidae[d]		F6 N1 V17 (6) F4 (3)	F11 N18 V4 (8)		F2 N.4 V6 (8)					F11 N10 V12 (8)
Tetraodontiformes										
Tetraodontidae		F2 (3)				N28 V12 (6)				
Canthigaster rivulatus		F12 N6 V1 (6)			F18 N24 V11 (6)					
Trachichthyidae		F6 (3)								
Paratrachichthys sp.		F3 (3)								
Triglidae			X/1 (1)[e]	X/1 (1)			X/6 (2)[e]	D/19 (1)		
SHRIMP	18/1 (1)	F36 N82 V9 (3) F30 N43 V2 (6)	F8 N6 V2 (8) D/17 (1)	X/1 (1)	F11 N3 V2 (8)	F18 N9 V.7 (6) 1/1 (1)	G (4)	F7 (7) D/19 (1)	X/1 (2)	F6 N4 V4 (8)
Caridea	18/1 (1)	N70 V8 (3) F18 N40 V2 (6)	F8 N6 V2 (8) D/17 (1)	X/1 (1)	F5 N1 V1 (8)	F12 N8 V.3 (6) 1/1 (1) F12 N8 V.3 (6)		F4 (7) D/19 (1)		N3 V1 (8)
Oplophoridae										
Oplophorus sp.										
Palaemonidae	18/1 (1)			X/1 (1)[f]						
Pandalidae		F>24 N64 V7 (3)	F8 N6 V2 (8) X/17 (1)			1/1 (1)		F3 (7) D/19 (1)		F3 N1 V.7 (8)
Parapandalus serratifrons	18/1 (1)		X/17 (1)			1/1 (1)				
Plesionika spp.[g]		F3 N1 V.5 (3)	X/17 (1)							
Heterocarpus spp.[h]		F12 N3 V.1 (6)	X/17 (1) D/17 (1)[i]			1/1 (1)		D/19 (1)		
Eugonatonotidae										
Penaeidae			F24 N18 V17 (8)			F6 N1 V.4 (6)		F15 (7)		F.5 N.2 V3 (8)
CRABS		F12 N2 V5 (3) F6 N1 V.2 (6) N1 V5 (3)			F2 N.4 V.6 (8)	F6 N1 V.4 (6) 1/5 (2)	X/6 (2)	F15 (7)	X/1 (2)	F36 N16 V26 (8)
Brachyura						F6 N1 V.4 (6)		F15 (7)		
Homolidae		F2 N.2 V.6 (3)								
Raninidae		F2 N.2 V1 (3)								

(CONTINUED)

APPENDIX B (Cont.)

PREDATOR SPECIES

DIET ITEM	Epinephelus chlorostigma	E. quernus	Etelis carbunculus	E. coruscans	E. radiosus	Pristipomoides auricilla	P. filamentosus	P. flavipinnis	P. multidens	P. sieboldii	P. zonatus
Galatheidae		N.6 V.2 (3) F6 N1 V.2 (6)	F21 N16 V17 (8)				1/5 (2)				F23 N10 V11 (8)
Munida sp.		F3 N.4 V.1 (3) F6 N1 V.2 (6)	D (8)								
OTHER CRUSTACEANS		N.6 V.2 (3) N8 V4 (6)	F3 N2 (8) X/17 (1)	X/1 (1)		F-20 N9 V4 (8)	F24 N6 V1 (6) X/5 (2)		X (7) X/19 (1)		F>10 N9 V2 (8)
Stomatopods		F2 N.2 V.2 (3)	X/17 (1)			F2 N.4 V.6 (8)	X/5 (2)		F2 (7) X/19 (1)		F.5 N.2 V.1 (8).
Odontodactylus japonicus		F12 N3 V1 (6)				F1 N.2 V.5 (8)					
Odontodactylus brevirostris		F12 N3 V.2 (3)				F1 N.2 V.5 (8)					
Lobsters		F2 N.2 V.2 (3) F12 N3 V1 (6)	X/17 (1)	X/1 (1)					X/19 (1)		
Palinuridae		F6 N1 V.3 (6)									
Scyllaridae		F6 N1 V1 (6)	X/17 (1)	X/1 (1)					X/19 (1)		
Isopods		F2 N.2 (3)					F6 N1 (6)		F1 (7)		
Amphipods		F2 N.2 (3)					F6 N3				
Hyperiidea							V.4 (6)				

OTHER BENTHIC INVERTS.	F2 N.2 (3)							
Polychaetes			F12 N8 V3 (8)				X/1 (2)	N.5 V.3 (8)
Hemichordates			F12 N8 V3 (8)				X/1 (2)	F.5 N.2 V.2 (8)
Benthic Urochordates								
Echinoderms	F2 N.2 (3)							F.5 N.2 (8)
Ophiuroids	F2 N.2 (3)							F.5 N.2 (8)
CEPHALOPODS	F6 N1 V8 (3) F53 N17 V53 (6)	X/1 (1) G (4)	F5 N1 V5 (8)	F53 N13 V11 (6) X/5 (2)	1/6 (2)	F6 (7) F21 (1)	X/1 (2)	F4 N1 V.7 (8)
Octopus	F4 N.8 V8 (3) F53 N17 V53 (6)			F35 N9 V9 (6)		F6 (7)		X (8)
Squid		X/1 (1) G (4)	X (8)	F6 N1 V1 (6) X/5 (2)	1/6 (2)	F21 (1)	X/1 (2)	X (8)
Sepioidea		X/1 (1)				1/19 (1)		
Sepiadariidae		X/1 (1)				1/19 (1)		
Teuthoidea		X/1 (1)				2/19 (1)		
Cycloteuthidae								
Loliginidae		X/1 (1)				1/19 (1) 2/19 (1)		
Ommastrephidae								X (8)
PLANKTON	F2 N.2 V.7 (3) F32 N27 V3 (8)		N74 V68 3/5 (2)	F59 N16 V43 (6) 5/5 (2)	1/6 (2)	F22 (7) X/19 (1)	X/1 (2)	N40 V18 (8)
Siphonophores			F16 N5 V2 (8)					
Ctenophores								F.5 N:2 V.1 (8)
Euphausiids			F4 N.7 V.5 (8) F73 N50 V29 (8)					F.5 N.2 (8)
Pelagic gastropods						F22 (7)		F5 N4 V.2 (8)
Heteropods			F>14 N5 V1 (8)	X/5 (2)		F7 (7)		F>1 N.6 (8)
Atlantidae			F14 N4 V1 (8)			F7 (7)		F1 N.5 (8)
Pteropods			F67 N45 V28 (8)			F19 (7)		F5 N3 V.1 (8)
Cavoliniidae								

APPENDIX B (Cont.)

	PREDATOR SPECIES										
DIET ITEM	Epinephelus chlorostigma	E. quernus	Etelis carbunculus	E. coruscans	E. radiosus	Pristipomoides auricilla	P. filamentosus	P. flavipinnis	P. multidens	P. sieboldii	P. zonatus
Pelagic Urochordates		F2 N.2 V.7 (3)	F32 N27 V3 (8)			F39 N19 V36 (8) 3/5 (2)	F59 N16 V43 (6) 5/5 (2)	1/6 (2)	X/19 (1)	X/1 (2)	F38 N36 V18 (8)
Pyrosomatidae											
Pyrosoma sp.		F2 N.2 V.7 (3)	F32 N27 V3 (8)			F39 N19 V36 (8) 2/5 (2) 1/5 (2)	F59 N15 V42 (6) 5/5 (2) 3/5 (2) F6 N1 V1 (6)	1/6 (2)		X/1 (2)	F38 N36 V18 (8)
Salpida											
Salpa sp.											
Predator Sample Size and Depth of Capture [m]:											
(1) Richards	(1) 1 [140]		(1) 17 [240-280]	(1) 1 [200]	(1) 1 [220]		(1) 1 [150]		(1) 19 [120-260]		
(2) Kami (1973)						(2) 5 [90-360]k	(2) 5 [90-360]k	(2) 6 [90-360]k		(2) 1 [180-360]	
(3) Seki (1984)		(3) 67 [130-220]									
(4) Fourmanoir & Laboute (1976)[1]				(4)m ·········	········· Unknown ········· (4)						
(5) Kluegel (1921)[1]		(5) 3					(5) 10				
(6) Ralston & Sorden		(6) 17 [110-180]					(6) 17 [110-185]				
(7) Mizenko (1984)									(7) 91 [90-160]		
(8) Parrish & Callahan			(8) 38 [165-275]			(8) 103 [165-240]					(8) 209 [130-275]

Sources:

(1) Richards, Andrew H. (see footnote d, App. A). Unpublished data from Papua New Guinea.

(2) Kami (1973). Data from Guam.

(3) Seki (1984). Data from the Northwestern Hawaiian Islands.

(4) Fourmanoir and Laboute (1976). Data from New Caledonia and New Hebrides.

(5) Kluegel (1921). Data from Hawaii.

(6) Ralston and Sorden (See footnote d, App. A). Unpublished data from the Northwestern Hawaiian Islands.

(7) Mizenko (1984). Data from Western Samoa.

(8) Parrish and Callahan (see footnote d, App. A). Unpublished data from Mariana Islands.

Codes:

F - % of all specimens with food that contained the category.

N - % of all prey individuals that were of the category.

V - % of all prey volume that was of the category.

D/19. - A dominant category in a sample of 19 guts with food.

X/17 - Present in a sample of 17 guts with food.

3/5 - Present in 3 of the 5 guts with food.

18/1 - 18 prey individuals present in the 1 gut with food.

G - The reference contains a general, nonquantified statement that the category was found in the diet.

Superscripted Notes:

[a] Includes leptocephalus larvae; likely anguilliform.

[b] Some were Bregmaceros spp.

[c] Argyripnus spp.

[d]

[e] Almost all were Symphysanodon, mostly Symphysanodon maunaloae.

[e] Some were Lepidotrigla sp; one was a Trigla sp.

[f] All Periclimenes sp.

[g] P. rostricrescentis in Pristipomoides filamentosus; P. longirostris in the other predators.

[h] H. ensifer dominant. H. gibbosus, H. dorsalis and H. sibogae also present in P. multidens.

[i] Eugonatonotus crassus.

[j] All 10 guts with contents "were almost entirely filled with tunicates." Also spoke of "compound ascidians" and reported algae, foraminifera and gravel.

[k] Probably all specimens were taken in the depth range 180-360 m.

[l] Depth of collections unknown.

[m] Reported as E. oculatus.

10

Assessment and Management of the Demersal Fishery on the Continental Shelf of Northwestern Australia

Keith J. Sainsbury
Commonwealth Scientific and
Industrial Research Organization
Hobart, Tasmania 7001, Australia

ABSTRACT

The diverse fish community on the continental shelf of northwestern Australia has been exploited since 1959. The history of exploitation is summarized, and concurrent changes in fish community are inferred from data collected during research surveys. Some possible reasons for the observed changes in fish community structure are provided, including the direct modification of the demersal habitat by trawling.

Assessments of the North West Shelf fishery have utilized surplus production models and multiple "dynamic pool" models of the Beverton and Holt type. These assessments are described, and their limitations discussed. Present management questions concern the extent of management control over the fish community and determination of the yield available from alternative configurations of the fish community. An approach to examination of these questions is described.

INTRODUCTION

The terms tropical snappers and groupers are commonly used in Australia to refer to large fishes of the families Lutjanidae, Lethrinidae, and Serranidae. These groups are exploited by three main fisheries: the commercial trawl fishery on the continental shelf of northern and northwestern Australia, which takes significant quantities of

465

<u>Lutjanus</u> and <u>Lethrinus</u>; the predominantly recreational
fishery on the Great Barrier Reef, which takes mostly
<u>Plectropomus</u>, <u>Lethrinus</u>, and <u>Lutjanus</u>; and the recrea-
tional fishery on Norfolk Island, which takes mostly
<u>Lethrinus</u>.

This paper describes the northern Australian trawl
fishery, and is presented in two main sections. The first
section describes the fishery and its resources, including
the gear employed, the history of exploitation, the
species taken, and some of the effects of exploitation on
the resources. The second section describes the methods
used for assessment of the fishery, examines some general
issues involved in the biological management of a multispecies resource, and illustrates these issues as they
apply to the North West (NW) Shelf fishery.

The continental shelf (to a depth of 200 m) of northern Australia is extensive (Figure 10.1), biologically
productive (Tranter 1962; Kabanova 1968; Motoda et al.
1978), has a tropical hydrographic regime (Wyrtki 1961,
1962), and supports a diverse fish fauna, mostly of Indo-
west Pacific affinity (Gloerfelt-Tarp and Kailola 1984;
Sainsbury et al. 1985). The substrate is mostly of calcareous sands (Van Andel and Veevers 1967; Jones 1973;
McLoughlin and Young 1985), although there are some areas

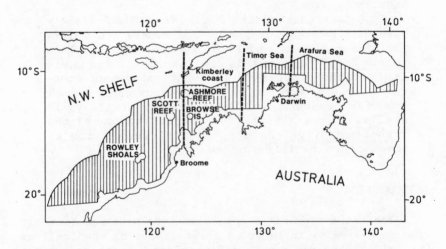

Figure 10.1 The 200-nmi Australian Fishing Zone
in northern Australia, and the major faunistic
boundaries identified by cluster analysis of
research survey species composition data

of coral reef. Classification of the species composition
of research trawl catches in 1978–1979 revealed four main
faunistic regions (Sainsbury Unpub. data; Figure 10.1).
The NW Shelf, extending from long. 114° to 123° E, has
provided most of the fishing yield from the northern
portion of the 200–nmi Australian Fishing Zone (AFZ) (Liu
et al. 1978; Edwards 1983), and the remainder of this
paper will deal only with the NW Shelf.

THE FISHERY AND ITS RESOURCE

The Fishery

The NW Shelf has been exploited by four commercial
fishing operations: Japanese stern trawlers from 1959 to

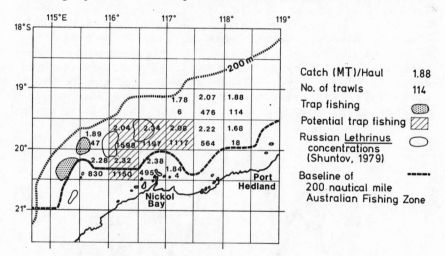

Figure 10.2 The western portion of the North
West Shelf showing the 200-m depth contour and
the Australian Fishing Zone (AFZ) coastal baseline. The upper and lower figures in each 30'
square give the catch rate (MT/h) and number of
trawls applied by the Japanese trawl fishery
(after Robins 1969), and the areas of high
Lethrinus concentration identified during
Russian surveys are indicated (after Shuntov
1979). Also shown are the areas in the AFZ
currently exploited by the trap fishery, and the
area in which development of a trap fishery may
be possible

1963, Taiwanese pair trawlers from 1972 to the present, Australian/Korean "feasibility fishing" stern trawlers in 1979, and a small Australian trap fishery since 1983.

The Japanese experimentally trawled the NW Shelf in 1935, and commenced commercial fishing in 1959 (Suzuki et al. 1964; Robins 1969). The fishery concentrated on the area between long. 116° and 117°30' E (Figure 10.2), and provided 7,517 metric tons (MT) of Lethrinus over 3 years at a catch rate of about 500 kg of Lethrinus per hour of trawling (Robins 1969). About 40-50% of the total catch consisted of Lethrinus (Suzuki et al. 1964; Robins 1969; Table 10.1), and there was no indication of a reduction of the catch rates of either Lethrinus or total fish during the period of the fishery (Figure 10.3). There was a considerable change in the size composition of Lethrinus, however, with animals larger than 0.6 kg disappearing from the catch after 8 months of fishing (Suzuki et al. 1964). Suzuki et al. (1964) described the species caught as L. ornatus. However, Masuda (Pers. com. 1978) reported that K. Amaoka (Hokkaido University) examined specimens and concluded that they were not L. ornatus but an unknown species of Lethrinus. A Japanese survey of the NW Shelf (Anonymous 1964) illustrated a specimen of L. choerorynchus as L. ornatus, and so it is possible that L.

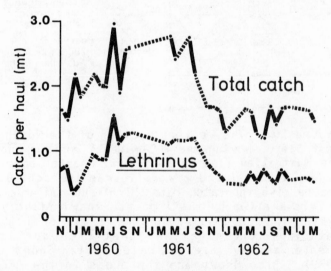

Figure 10.3 The catch rate of Lethrinus and total fish obtained by the Japanese fishery on the North West Shelf (after Suzuki et al. 1964)

TABLE 10.1
Summary of the catch composition, number of trawls, mean catch rate, and length of the trawl headrope for research surveys and commercial fishing on the North West Shelf. The rank correlation between year of observation and both percentage composition of species groups and total catch per hour trawling is calculated from surveys with compatible gear and spatial coverage (i.e., excluding commercial fishing ventures and the Russian survey data; see text). NA = not available; * = statistically significant at σ = 0.05

Vessel, Source and References	Year	Percent Composition by Weight								Number of Trawl Hauls	Mean Catch Rate (kg/h)	Trawl Headrope (m)
		Lethrinidae	Lutjanidae	Serranidae	Nemipteridae	Saurida	Sparidae	Haemulidae	Carangidae			
Japanese fishery Masuda et al. (1964) Suzuki et al. (1964) Robins (1969)	1960-1962	40-50	NA	NA	NA	NA	NA	NA	NA	7,616	1,100[a]	NA
Oshoro Maru survey 1 Anonymous (1964) Masuda et al. (1964)	1962	20.7	35.6	5.9	1.1	5.5	1.6	1.3	2.2	15	206	38.2
Oshoro Maru survey 7 Anonymous (1965) Masuda et al. (1964) Suzuki et al. (1964)	1963	16.3	19.8	5.4	6.5	2.6	2.1	1.7	4.4	20	564	38.2
Nagasaki Maru survey Abe et al. (1967)	1966	27.9	21.9	6.8	7.5	10.0	1.6	1.5	NA	14	316	33.6

Continued

470

TABLE 10.1 (Cont.)

Vessel, Source and References	Year	Percent Composition by Weight								Number of Trawl Hauls	Mean Catch Rate (kg/h)	Trawl Head-rope (m)
		Lethrinidae	Lutjanidae	Serranidae	Nemipteridae	Saurida	Sparidae	Haemulidae	Carangidae			
Russian survey Anonymous (1978) Shuntov (1979) Suzuki et al. (1964)	1962–1973	47.2	12.0	0.9	NA	2.9	3.5	NA	11.0	NA	2,100[a]	NA
Hai Ching survey Shu, Shoa, and Chun (1973)	1972	24.7	30.3	3.7	7.4	5.6	NA	1.0	NA	54	134	34
Hai Ching survey Shu, Shaur, and Tzong (1973)	1973	23.6	31.6	2.2	6.3	7.8	NA	NA	NA	73	92	34
Taiwanese fishery Liu et al. (1978)	1971–1976	9.8	6.3	0.8	21.1	12.3	1.7	4.4	3.1	15,124	1,000[a]	48
Feasibility fishing Anonymous (1980a)	1979	16.0	26.0	2.6	9.0	5.1	2.6	5.7	9.6	5,809	246	38.5
Oh Dae San Ho survey Anonymous (1980b)	1979	10.5	6.2	0.8	26.4	8.2	0	0.7	6.1	24	235	38.5
Hai-Kung survey Chen et al. (1979)	1979	6.9	17.8	1.8	12.7	35.9	NA	0	4.8	12	359	27.49

Soela (1/83) survey Original data	1983	6.8	11.6	3.0	12.5	9.2	1.4	2.6	7.7	62	327	25.9
Soela (4/83) survey Original data	1983	5.4	8.1	2.4	12.0	13.7	0.4	2.3	2.9	70	250	25.9
Spearman rank correlation coefficient (r_s)		-0.75*	-0.73*	-0.68*	0.73*	0.75*	-0.93	0.36	0.37		0.13	
Probability that $r_s = 0$		0.03	0.04	0.05	0.04	0.03	0.06	0.38	0.41		0.15	

[a] Approximate.

choerorynchus was the species taken by the Japanese fishery. Lethrinus nebulosus is also known from the area, has a history of confusion with L. choerorynchus, and was reported as comprising about 50% of Russian survey catches between 1962 and 1973 (Anonymous 1978; Shuntov 1979), and so this species also could have been taken by the Japanese fishery.

The Taiwanese began pair trawling on the NW Shelf in 1972 (Liu 1976; Liu et al. 1978; Edwards 1983). The fishery developed rapidly to provide a catch of 20,000–30,000 MT per year in the following 5 years (Table 10.1), mostly from the area between long. 115° and 120° E (Edwards 1983; Liu and Yeh 1984; Figure 10.4). Most trawling has been conducted between 30 and 140 m depth. All fishing vessels are pair trawlers (see Thompson 1978 for a general description) of 200–500 gross tons, and all have similar fishing power (Yeh and Chin 1982). The trawl has a headrope of about 30 m (measured by AFZ observers), and cod end mesh sizes were commonly about 45 mm until introduction of a 60-mm minimum mesh size in 1981 (Sainsbury 1984). The fishery initially operated in international waters but came under Australian management jurisdiction with the declaration of the 200-nmi AFZ in 1979. Since then, fishing operations on the NW Shelf have been restricted to the area north of lat. 21° S and beyond a "coastal baseline" (Figure 10.2), and from late 1985 operations will be further restricted to east of long. 116° E. Information from the fishery (catch by commercial categories of fish, fishing effort, and trawl location) was collected from logbooks of the National Taiwan University (Anonymous 1972–1979), and the Australian Department of Primary Industry has operated a similar logbook program since 1979. The proportion of logbooks returned by fishermen was variable between 1972 and 1978 (Table 10.2), but all have been returned since 1979. The average composition of the catch by main commercial categories, and the main species combined in those categories on the NW Shelf are given in Table 10.3. Nemipterus spp. form the single most abundant category, and the families Lethrinidae, Lutjanidae, and Serranidae together constitute 17% of the catch.

"Feasibility fishing" (short-term, trial commercial fishing involving a foreign fishing company) was attempted on the NW Shelf in 1979 (Anonymous 1980a). Five stern trawlers expended 5,808 h of trawling effort on the NW Shelf, and retained 1,427 MT of fish. Lethrinidae, Lutjanidae, and Serranidae together constituted 44.6% of this catch, with lutjanids providing 26% (Table 10.1). How-

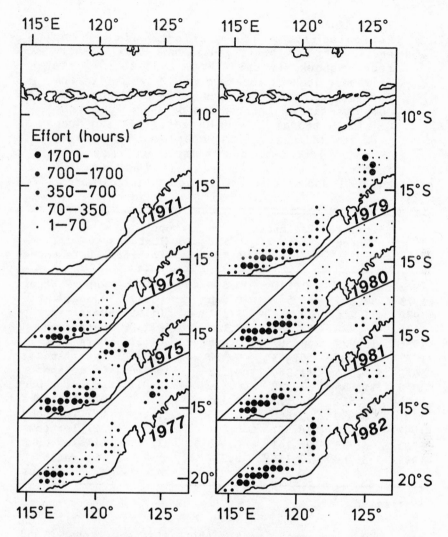

Figure 10.4 The spatial distribution of fishing
effort by the pair trawl fishery (after Liu and
Yeh 1984)

ever, the ventures were not economically successful and
were abandoned.

An Australian trap fishery began on the NW Shelf in
1984, although some trapping was conducted earlier (B.
Bowen and N. Hall, Western Australian Department of Fisheries and Wildlife, Pers. com. 1985). It is a small fish-

474

TABLE 10.2
Estimated catch, fishing effort, and catch per
unit effort for the Taiwanese pair trawl fishery
from logbook surveys. From 1972 to 1979 the
Taiwanese logbook data are used, available from
annual reports (Anonymous 1972-1979) and from
computer tape of unprocessed data provided by H.
C. Liu (National Taiwan University); and from
1980 to 1983 Australian Department of Primary
Industry logbook data are used. It is assumed
that trawls were of 2.5 h duration between 1972
and 1979 and catches are in metric tons (MT)

Year	Estimated Catch (MT)	Estimated Effort (h)	CPUE (MT/h)	Proportion of Logbooks Recovered	Data Source
1972	555	1,110	0.500	0.538	Annual report
1973	37,202	64,545	0.576	0.517	Annual report
1974	31,256	79,861	0.391	0.199	Data tape
1975	21,288	57,768	0.368	0.149	Data tape
1976	18,929	46,592	0.406	0.113	Data tape
1977	19,080	56,413	0.338	0.336	Data tape
1978	14,616	41,360	0.353	0.686	Data tape
1979	11,866	37,222	0.320	0.917	Annual report
1980	12,512	36,172	0.345	1.0	DPI logbooks
1981	10,930	30,666	0.356	1.0	DPI logbooks
1982	13,418	38,991	0.344	1.0	DPI logbooks
1983	8,735	26,161	0.333	1.0	DPI logbooks
1984	8,766[a]	33,178[a]	0.277	--	DPI radio reports

[a]Estimated.

ery, highly seasonal (mostly April through October), and
is localized in the western portion of the NW Shelf
(Figure 10.2) in areas lightly exploited by the pair
trawlers (presumably because of unsuitable bottom topog-
raphy). A cylindrical trap is used mostly (see Bowen 1961
for description), and fishing extends to a depth of about
80 m. Total catch for this fishery was about 200 MT in
1984, and it is expected to be about 300 MT in 1985 (N.
Hall Pers. com. 1985). The common names of the fish
forming the bulk of catches are northwest snapper, long-
nose emperor, red emperor, and cod (B. Bowen Pers. com.

TABLE 10.3
Percent composition by weight of North West
Shelf catches of the pair trawl fishery from
1971 to 1976 by some commercial categories (from
Liu et al. 1978), and the main species consti-
tuting each category (following the nomenclature
of Sainsbury et al. 1985)

Percent	Commercial Category	Main Species
21.1	Golden thread	_Nemipterus_ _furcosus_ _N._ _celebicus_ _N._ _peronii_ _N._ _bathybius_ _N._ _virgatus_
12.3	Lizardfish	_Saurida_ _undosquamis_ _Saurida_ sp. 1 _S._ _micropectoralis_
8.4	Porgies	_Lethrinus_ _choerorynchus_ _L._ _nematacanthus_ _L._ _lentjan_ _L._ _fraenatus_ _L._ _nebulosa_
4.9	Red snapper	_Lutjanus_ _malabaricus_ _L._ _erythropterus_ _L._ _sebae_
3.9	Small snapper	_Lutjanus_ _vittus_ _L._ _russelli_
1.4	Sharp-toothed snapper	_Pristipomoides_ _multidens_ _P._ _typus_
1.4	Large eye bream	_Gymnocranius_ _robinsoni_ _G._ _griseus_
0.6	Blue spotted grouper	_Plectropomus_ _maculatus_
0.5	Painted sweetlip	_Diagramma_ _pictum_
0.03	Emperor red snapper	_Lutjanus_ _sebae_

1985). These probably refer to <u>Lethrinus</u> spp. (possibly
<u>L. choerorynchus</u> and <u>L. nebulosus</u>), <u>L. microdon</u>, <u>Lutjanus</u>
spp. (probably including <u>L. sebae</u>), and <u>Epinephelus</u> spp.,
respectively. There is some indication that this fishery
could expand in the future.

The Resource

Catch composition data from commercial and research
trawler operations since 1960 provide indications of the
composition of the NW Shelf fish community during and
prior to development of the pair trawl fishery (Table
10.1). To allow comparison, percent composition by weight
is given for fish groups at the family level, although
some surveys identified fish to the specific or generic
level. Comparison of the commercial catch composition is
complicated by the variety of gears used (e.g., stern
trawling compared to pair trawling), the different markets
being supplied, and the likelihood that economic considerations strongly influenced the choice of fish retained and
hence included in catch compositions. Russian surveys
between 1962 and 1973 are also difficult to compare with
other data sets, because details of the surveys (e.g.,
trawl locations, trawl size and type, and catch composition) are unavailable. The other research surveys are
more comparable, however, as they were all conducted by
research stern trawlers using similar size nets (Table
10.1) and covered a similar geographic range. Sampling
designs did differ between surveys, however. The <u>Soela</u>
surveys (Table 10.1) conducted by Commonwealth Scientific
and Industrial Research Organization (CSIRO) (Young and
Sainsbury 1985) utilized a depth and sediment type stratified, random sampling design in the area between long.
116° and 119° E and from 20 to 200 m depth. Most of the
research surveys on the NW Shelf placed similar emphasis
on this area, although trawl locations were not random-
ized.

The relationship between the year of surveys and the
proportion of the catch made up of the families Lethrinidae (including <u>Gymnocranius</u>), Lutjanidae, Serranidae,
Nemipteridae, <u>Saurida</u>, Sparidae, Carangidae, and Haemulidae are shown in Figures 10.5 and 10.6. For the nine
comparable research surveys (excluding the commercial
fishery and Russian survey data), there is a significant
($\alpha = 0.05$) negative correlation between year of observation and the percentage of Lethrinidae, Lutjanidae, and

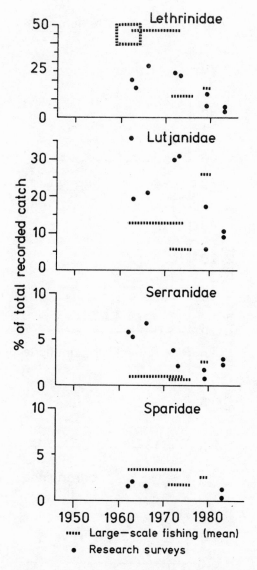

Figure 10.5 The percent abundance of Lethrinidae, Lutjanidae, Serranidae, and Sparidae in catches from the North West Shelf (data from Table 10.1). Large-scale fishing refers to commercial operations by the Japanese (1959-1962), Taiwanese (data shown are for 1971-1976) and feasibility fishing (1979) fleets, and to the Russian surveys (1962-1973)

478

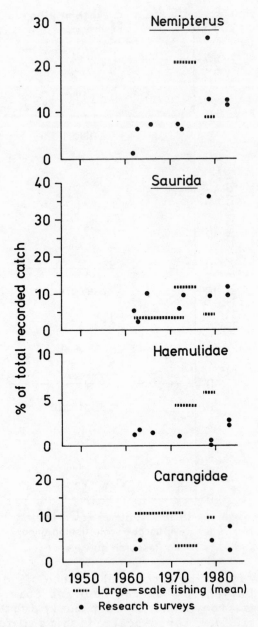

Figure 10.6 The percentage abundance of Nemipteridae, _Saurida_, Haemulidae, and Carangidae in catches from the North West Shelf (data from Table 10.1). Symbols are as for Figure 10.5

Serranidae in samples, while there is a significant positive correlation for Nemipteridae and Saurida. Sparidae
show a decline which is bordering on statistical significance, while Haemulidae, Carangidae, and total fish catch
show no trend.

The species represented in most families through the
time series of Table 10.1 is not well known. The uncertain identity of the lethrinid taken by the Japanese
fishery has already been mentioned. The lethrinid catches
of the Oshoro Maru and Nagasaki Maru were described as
Lethrinus spp. with a small component of Gymnocranius spp.
The Oshoro Maru listed L. miniatus, L. nematacanthus, L.
Ornatus (presently reidentified from the photograph in
Anonymous (1965) as L. choerorynchus), and L. nebulosus as
the dominant lethrinid, while the Hai Ching lists L.
reticulatus, L. ornatus, and L. miniatus, as occurring.
Lethrinid catches of Soela were strongly dominated by L.
choerorynchus (76 and 51% in cruises 1/83 and 4/83,
respectively) and L. nematacanthus (20 and 43%), with L.
nematacanthus restricted to depths <50 m. Lethrinus nebulosus was collected on the main trawl grounds during a
CSIRO survey in 1979, but has not been observed since.
Similarly the species composition of the lutjanid category
of Table 10.1 is not well known. From the published
species lists it would appear that Lutjanus sebae, L.
malabaricus, L. vittus, and L. janthinuropterus were
important and persistent components of the lutjanid catch,
with L. gibbus and L. varigensis also described as common
in the early Japanese surveys. Lutjanus vittus comprised
14% of the lutjanid catch of the Oshoro Maru catch in
1962, 17% of the Oshoro Maru catch in 1963, 17% of the
Nagasaki Maru catch in 1966, and made up 17 and 20% of the
lutjanid catches of the two Soela cruises in 1983. Pristipomoides spp. appear never to have been particularly
abundant on the NW Shelf. Serranids were mostly Epinephelus spp. (listed as E. areolatus, E. merra, E. tauvina, E.
diacanthus, and E. bleekeri) with some Plectropoma maculatus, and the sparids were predominately Argyrops spinifer
throughout the time series in Table 10.1. Similarly,
nemipterids has been composed predominantly of Nemipterus
peronii (now N. furcosus) throughout the time series.
Saurida undosquamis is consistently described in early
surveys as being the main species in Saurida catches.
However, there has been a rapid increase in the population
of a small-bodied lizardfish, Saurida sp. 2 (of Sainsbury
et al. 1985), since 1980, and this species is at present
the numerically dominant species of Saurida (Thresher et

480

al. In press; Figure 10.7). *Saurida undosquamis* has also
increased in abundance, but not to the extent of, or at
the rate of, *Saurida* sp. 2.

It would appear that there has been little change in
the species composition within the groups *Lutjanus,*

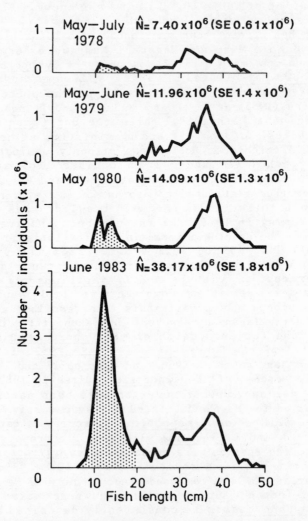

Figure 10.7 Size structure and total number of
Saurida undosquamis and *Saurida* sp. 2 together
as determined by CSIRO research surveys. Most
animals <20 cm are *Saurida* sp. 2, and all animals >25 cm are *Saurida undosquamis*

Epinephelus, Sparidae, and Nemipterus, but the abundance of each genus has increased or decreased as a whole. It is not clear whether there has been a major change within the Lethrinus, and Saurida has shown a marked change in species composition very recently.

From the research survey data and the catch composition of the Japanese fishery, there can be little doubt that during the 1960s and early 1970s the fish community was strongly dominated by Lethrinus, Lutjanus, and Epinephelus. These groups probably comprised 20–40%, 20–30%, and 5–7%, respectively, of the fish biomass in the midshelf area between about long. 115°30' and 118°30' E. Nemipterus and Saurida together constituted about 10% of fish biomass. Eleven years later, coinciding with the 1972–present period of the pair trawl fishery, the situation is almost reversed. Lethrinus, Lutjanus, and Epinephelus together now comprise about 15% of the fish biomass, while Nemipterus and Saurida comprise about 25%. Furthermore, the recent changes in the abundance and species composition of the genus Saurida suggest that the community is still undergoing major alteration.

Possible causes of these changes in fish community composition are:

1. Environmental changes (e.g., oceanographic conditions, pollution, sedimentation) independent of the operation of the fishery.
2. Direct alteration of the size of fish populations as a result of fishing, with the size of the alteration being determined by the fishing mortality exerted on the particular group and the basic population parameters of that group (independent, but different, single species responses).
3. Indirect effects of fishing via altered interspecific biological interactions (e.g., predator-prey relationships, competition for food, and altered habitat availability for adults and/or juveniles).

From the available data, none of these mechanisms of change can be excluded from a possible role in the observed changes to the fish community on the NW Shelf. Examining some aspects of each mechanism:

1. The oceanography of the NW Shelf and the mechanisms by which biological production in the water column affects the dynamics of the fish populations are poorly known. However, while it is unlikely that pollution and artificially

increased sedimentation have occurred to a pronounced extent in the sparsely inhabited region of the NW Shelf, the oceanography of the area is strongly influenced by the "southern oscillation" (Bye and Gordon 1982). Consequently, major episodic changes in oceanography are likely, which could greatly influence fish community structure.

2. Application of a given fishing mortality to a group of independent species with different, fixed, population parameters would alter the species composition of that group. For example, considering all population parameters to be constant and the natural mortality to be 0.7 for Saurida, 1.0 for Nemipterus, 0.4 for Lutjanus, 0.6 for Lethrinus, and 0.1 for Epinephelus (Sainsbury 1984), the percent reduction in equilibrium numbers in each group caused by a fishing mortality of 0.4 (Sainsbury 1984) is 25% for Saurida, 16% for Nemipterus, 40% for Lutjanus, 29% for Lethrinus, and 76% for Epinephelus. Further differences in response are expected due to differences in the fishing mortality applied. For example, introduction of the 60 mm minimum cod end mesh size in 1979 would have increased the mean length at which Saurida have a 50% chance of being retained in the cod end from 17.5 to 21.5 cm (Liu et al. 1985). Consequently Saurida sp. 2, which has a maximum length of about 25 cm, would have been subject to a much lower fishing mortality since 1979 relative to Saurida undosquamis, which reaches about 53 cm. This may have been responsible for the large increase in Saurida sp. 2 since 1980 (Figure 10.7). While changes in species composition as a direct result of the imposed fishing effort are to be expected, this mechanism alone does not generate changes of the magnitude observed between the Lethrinus, Lutjanus, Nemipterus, and Saurida groups without postulating very unlikely levels of group specific fishing mortality, or highly density-dependent population parameters for some groups. Similar conclusions were reached by Larkin and Gazey (1982) from attempts to simulate changes in the Gulf of Thailand fish community.

3. Habitat modification as a result of trawling appears to have influenced the species composition of the NW Shelf fish community, and may well have been the major influence. Large catches of large sponges were reported from the NW Shelf, and the area between long. 115° and 120° E in particular, by most of the pre-1972 research surveys (Anonymous 1965; Shu, Shaur, and Tzong 1973; Shu, Shoa, and Chun 1973), and large sponge catches were encountered during the early years of the pair trawl fishery (C. Ossel, Western Australian Department of Fisheries and Wildlife, Pers. com. 1983). Comparison of sponge catch rate recorded from 20 hauls of the <u>Oshoro Maru</u> in 1963 (Anonymous 1965) with that from 40 hauls during a CSIRO survey in 1979 (Sainsbury 1979) shows a significant reduction in sponge density during the 16-year interval (Figure 10.8;

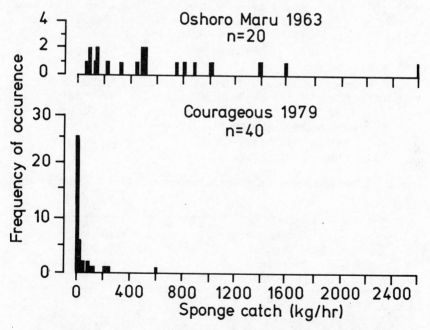

Figure 10.8 Sponge catch rate on the North West Shelf in 1963 (Anonymous 1965) and 1979 (original data from CSIRO research survey). Catch rates differ significantly (Mann-Whitney U = 763, P<0.01) between years

Mann-Whitney U = 763, P<0.01). The reduction is presumably a result of sponge removed incidentally during trawling. Even the relatively low level of fishing effort exerted in the past few years was sufficient to annually sweep an area equivalent to 10% of the total trawl grounds, and for the intensely trawled region (long. 116° to 117°30° E and depth 50–120 m), an area equivalent to 40% of the available seabed is swept by trawls per year.

Research to quantitatively determine the effect on the fish community composition of converting sponge/gorgonian-dominated habitat to more open habitat is currently in progress. However, preliminary analysis of data from a photographic survey of the demersal habitat and its associated fauna indicates that Nemipterus and Saurida occur predominantly in the open sand/sparse benthos habitat (Table 10.4), and so an increase in their proportionate abundance following increase in the area of this type of habitat would be expected. Lethrinus and Lutjanus (mostly L. vittus) occur mostly in areas of dense benthos,

TABLE 10.4
Frequency of observation of various fish genera in different demersal habitats, based on analysis of 2,720 frames of a photographic survey. Habitats were defined by cluster analysis, and the benthos consists mostly of sponges, gorgonians, and alcyonarians

		Habitat		
Genus	Number of Frames Containing this Genus	Open Sand	Patchy Benthos and Open Sand	Dense Benthos
Saurida	454	232(65%)	108(30%)	14(3%)
Nemipterus	232	124(53%)	78(33%)	30(13%)
Lethrinus	40	12(30%)	7(17%)	21(52%)
Lutjanus	40	12(30%)	6(15%)	22(55%)
Number of frames of this habitat		1,752	764	204

and so a reduction in <u>Lethrinus</u> and <u>Lutjanus</u> proportionate abundance would be expected following widespread elimination of the sponge-dominated habitat.

ASSESSMENT AND MANAGEMENT

Fishery Assessment: The Pair Trawl Fishery

The yield available to the pair trawl has been examined using three approaches.
1. Estimation of the unexploited fish biomass, and application of Gulland's (1971) approximation:
    $$Yield = 1/2 \, M \, B_0$$
    M = natural mortality rate
    B_0 = unexploited biomass.
2. Fitting of a surplus production model to the time series of catch and effort data.
3. Construction of noninteracting "dynamic pool" population models for the major species groups.

Estimation from unexploited biomass. Table 10.5 summarized the estimates of unexploited biomass of fish on the NW Shelf, and the resulting estimates of total yield. There is a threefold difference among the estimates of unexploited biomass, and the yield estimates differ by an order of magnitude. The variation in biomass estimates is due mainly to differences in the area to which early catch rates were considered to apply: Liu et al. (1978) considered them to be representative of the entire shelf area. White (1978) applied them to the area "commonly fished," Sainsbury (1982a) applied them to the area fished in 1973, and Edwards (1983) considered only "areas of concentration of effort." Research surveys have shown that the species of commercial interest are mostly limited to depths <120 m, and the commercial fishery has not extended its operation to the whole shelf, so the area used by Liu et al. (1978) may be regarded as an overestimate of the area occupied by the exploitable fish community. Variation in the yield estimates from a given biomass is mostly due to differences in the value of M used; Liu et al. (1978) and White (1978) used 1.0, Sainsbury (1982a) used 0.5, and Edwards (1983) used 0.3. Gulland (1979) considered M = 0.5 to be appropriate for a similar fishery in western Africa.

TABLE 10.5
Yield and unexploited biomass estimates for the North West Shelf (NA = not available)

Author	Data Source	Catch per Trawl (MT/h)	Area Swept per Trawl (km²)	Proportion of Fish Retained by Trawl	M	Exploitable Area (km²)	Exploitable Biomass (10⁶ MT)	Available Yield (10³ MT)
Anonymous (1978)	Russian survey 1962–1973	2.1	NA	NA	NA	NA	NA	0.22
Liu et al. (1978)	Taiwanese (1972–1974)	0.977/2.5	0.926	0.5	1	320,053	0.671	336
White (1978)	Taiwanese (1973)	1.44/2.5	0.926	0.5	1	93,240	0.290	145
Sainsbury (1982a)	Taiwanese (1973)	1.44/2.5	0.926	0.5	0.5	111,888	0.347	87
Edwards (1983)	DPI logbooks (1980)	0.865/2.5	0.820	0.4	0.3	86,000	0.239	36

Disparate estimates of yield from different applications of this method of assessment are to be expected, since the parameters necessary for the calculations are not well estimated. Besides a better understanding of the areal extent of the exploitable community and the appropriate value of M (for which there is no totally satisfactory answer in a multispecies application), calculations also require knowledge of the area swept by the trawl and the proportion of fish in that area which are retained. Neither of these quantities is known accurately and both contribute greatly to uncertainty in the resulting yield estimate.

There are also several theoretical grounds for expecting the estimate to be unreliable (and usually an overestimate), particularly when applied to multispecies fisheries. These are:

- Gulland's approximation is based on a simplification of the logistic surplus production model in which the optimum fishing mortality is assumed equal to the natural mortality. This is not always true, and applies only for a very restricted class of stock recruitment relationships (Francis 1974).

- The logistic surplus production model is often not a good description of the dynamics of production, and most other models indicate a maximum sustainable yield less than that of the logistic model (Shepherd 1982).

- Attempts to harvest the estimated yield from a population with varying recruitment will often cause recruitment overfishing, i.e., the yield is not really sustainable (Beddington and May 1977; Larkin 1977).

- The validity of Gulland's approximation depends critically on the age at recruitment and the M/K ratio, with overestimates of the maximum sustainable yield occurring for populations recruiting at a young age (Beddington and Cooke 1983).

- The Gulland approximation was developed for a single species fishery, and there is no theoretical justification for its application in a multispecies context (Pauly 1979; Sainsbury 1982b, 1982c).

Most of these difficulties are not readily overcome and their consequences are usually unknown in any particular application. However, the implications of the assumed age at recruitment in Gulland's approximation can be examined for the NW Shelf assessment following the recent discovery that species groups comprising a large proportion of community biomass (all <u>Nemipterus</u> spp., all <u>Saurida,</u> spp., <u>Parupeneus</u> <u>pleurospilus,</u> <u>Upeneus</u> spp., <u>Lutjanus</u> <u>vittus,</u> and <u>Abalistes</u> <u>stellaris</u>) recruit directly onto the trawl grounds (Young and Sainsbury 1985) and so are subject to fishing from a very early age. Beddington and Cooke (1983) have shown that for direct recruitment and $M = 0.5$, the potential yield is about 0.1 of the unexploited biomass, rather than 0.25 as given by Gulland's approximation. Taking a conservative view and applying this to the total community reduces the yield estimate of Sainsbury in Table 10.5 from 87,000 to 35,000 MT or from 0.78 to 0.31 MT/km^2.

Overall, this method of assessment provides a very crude estimate of the yield available; it is often useful in the very early stages of fishery assessment but is subject to many sources of large, and usually unknown, bias.

<u>Surplus production models.</u> The logistic surplus pro-production model was fitted to the time series of catch per unit effort and effort data by Sainsbury (1982a), and an exponential surplus production model was fitted by Liu and Yeh (1984). Sainsbury applied the time averaging technique suggested by Gulland (1968) in an attempt to compensate for lack of equilibrium conditions. In neither of these attempts was there a significant relation between catch per unit effort and effort, so explicit use of the surplus production models is not valid.

From the available time series (Table 10.2; Figure 10.9), it is clear that a simple surplus production model does not describe the data. A reasonable interpretation of the data is that accumulated stock was rapidly fished down between 1972 and 1974, with fish density being reduced to about two-thirds of its initial level (from about 0.55 to 0.35 MT per trawl hour, although the reduction may have been greater if the Russian and Japanese catch rates of 2.2 and 1.1 MT/h shown in Table 10.1 are comparable), and that fish density has slowly declined under the declining fishing effort exerted since 1974. It is clear that the catch rate–effort relationship being traversed during the decrease in effort is not the same as that traversed during the increase in effort. This could occur for a number of reasons, including a fundamental change in the means of production in the fish community, the existence of large time lags in the response of fish production to fish density, and confounding temporal

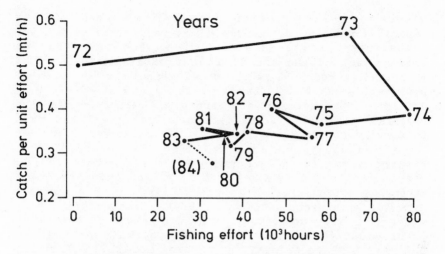

Figure 10.9 Relation between catch per unit effort and effort for the pair trawl fishery on the North West Shelf (data from Table 10.2)

trends within the logbook data (e.g., an increase in the discard rate).

Dynamic pool models. Sainsbury (1984) estimated optimal mesh size and yield from a set of noninteracting dynamic pool models of the Beverton and Holt (1957) type; 1 for each of 10 major species groups. The groups examined were: (1) Nemipterus spp.; (2) Saurida spp.; (3) large Lutjanus spp. (L. malabaricus, L. erythropterus, L. sebae); (4) small Lutjanus spp. (L. vitta, L. russelli, and L. lutjanus); (5) Lethrinus choerorynchus; (6) Priacanthus spp.; (7) Haemulidae; (8) Carangoides spp.; (9) small Serranidae (Epinephelus areolatus, E. maculatus, and Plectropoma maculatum), and 10) Pristipomoides spp. (P. multidens and P. typus), which together comprise about 60% of the total catch. The total yield (Y) was calculated from a simple extension of the Beverton and Holt (1957) model as

$$Y = \sum_i F_i R_i W_{\infty,i} \left(1 - \frac{S_i D}{L_{\infty,i}}\right)^{\frac{M_i}{K_i}} \left(1 - \frac{l_{r,i}}{L_{\infty,i}}\right)^{-\frac{M_i}{K_i}} \left(\sum_{n=0}^{n=3} \frac{U_n\left(1 - \frac{S_i D}{L_{\infty,i}}\right)^n}{F_i + M_i + nK_i}\right)$$

where, for the ith species, F is fishing mortality, M is natural mortality, K, L_∞ and W_∞ are parameters of the von Bertalanffy growth equation, l_r is the mean size at recruitment to the trawl grounds, R is the number of recruits per year, S is the trawl mesh "section factor," D is mesh size, and U takes values $U_0 = 1$, $U_1 = -3$, $U_2 = 3$, $U_3 = -1$. Estimates of the parameters except recruitment and fishing mortality were obtained from the literature comparative studies (e.g., Pauly 1980) or specific studies (e.g., Sainsbury and Whitelaw 1984; Liu et al. 1985). Fishing mortality and recruitment were estimated from research survey data and catch data, and from fitting a recursive catch equation to the fishery catch and effort data for each group (Sainsbury 1984). This equation provides a prediction of the catch each year from the catch in previous years in terms of the recruitment, catchability, fishing effort, and natural mortality. That is, the predicted catch in year k after inception of a fishery is

$$\hat{c}_k = qE_k\left[\frac{R}{\left(1-e^{-M}\right)} - \sum_{j=1}^{j=k-1} c_j e^{-M(k-j)} - \frac{C_k}{2}\right]$$

where q is catchability, E_k is fishing effort in year k, R is the recruitment, and C_j is the actual catch in year j. If natural mortality is known, this equation may be fitted to a time series of catch and effort data to provide estimates of "average" recruitment and catchability. Fishing mortality can then be obtained from $F = qE$. The yield curves for each species group and the total of all groups is shown in Figure 10.10. Maximum total annual yield for the groups considered was 10,767 MT, with a 90% confidence interval, determined by sensitivity analysis, of 7,800 to 16,000 MT. From this it was inferred that the total yield available from all groups of fish on the NW Shelf was approximately 18,000 MT (approximate 90% confidence interval 13,000–27,000 MT). The estimated yield available from each fish group and the average annual catch between 1980 and 1983 are given in Table 10.6. For most groups the estimated yield available has been exceeded.

While this analysis is the most thorough for the fishery so far, it has several important limitations. These include:

- Analysis is applied at the species group level, resulting in difficulty in interpretation of the

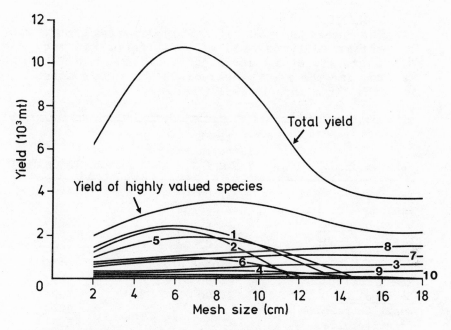

Figure 10.10 Relationship between mesh size and yield for all species groups, the total fishery, and highly valued species (large _Lutjanus_ spp., _Lethrinus_ spp., Pomadasyidae, and _Pristipomoides_ spp.) for a fishing mortality of 0.4 (after Sainsbury 1984)

1. _Nemipterus_ spp. 6. _Priacanthus_ spp.
2. _Saurida_ spp. 7. Pomadasyidae
3. _Lutjanus_ spp. (large) 8. _Carangoides_ spp.
4. _Lutjanus_ spp.(small) 9. Serranidae (small)
5. _Lethrinus_ spp. 10. _Pristipomoides_ spp.

growth, mortality, and recruitment parameters, which are usually regarded as species attributes.
• All parameters (including recruitment) are regarded as constant, and so the analysis must be repeated frequently with updated data to try to accommodate expected changes in parameters (particularly recruitment) with changes in the fishery, the biotic environment, and the physical environment. Furthermore, the recruitment esti-

TABLE 10.6
The sustainable annual yield by species group,
estimated by Sainsbury (1984) for a fishing
mortality of 0.4 and a cod end mesh size of 6
cm, and the mean annual catch (in metric tons
(MT)) from 1980 to 1983 (inclusive)

Species Group	Estimated Sustainable Yield (MT)	Actual Catch (MT)
Nemipterus	2,500	3,718
Saurida	2,600	629
Large Lutjanus	360	501
Small Lutjanus	320	630
Lethrinus	1,870	1,389
Priacanthus	1,000	262
Haemulidae	900	145
Carangoides	1,000	702
Small Serranidae	150	207
Pristipomoides	70	156

mates were obtained from catch and effort data
collected between 1973 and 1980, and so there is
considerable potential for temporal trends (in
recruitment, for example) during this period to
cause bias and mislead interpretation. This is
likely to cause overestimation of the yield
presently available from populations whose
recruitment was declining, and underestimation of
yield for populations whose recruitment was
increasing.

● All groups of species are considered to be independent, explicitly excluding biological interactions and associations thought to be important
in tropical communities.

● Few of the parameter values needed were available
for the NW Shelf populations, and most values
used in the analysis were taken from the literature.

Fishery Assessment: The Trap Fishery

The trap fishery has developed only recently, and there has been no biological assessment of its yield potential. There is insufficient information available to provide a detailed assessment, but a very crude indication of potential yield may be obtained from yield per unit area comparison with similar fisheries elsewhere. The sustainable yield of fisheries on tropical coastal and coral reefs was suggested to be 0.8-5 $MT/km^2/year$ by Marshall (1980) and 0.8-11 $MT/km^2/year$ by Marten and Polovina (1982). Australian catching and market conditions would probably dictate that relatively few species are economically harvestable so the appropriate productivity is uncertain, but it is likely to be low in the cited ranges. The area trapped, or available to be trapped, inshore of the 200 nmi "coastal base line" (Figure 10.2) is also presently unknown. However, a minimum estimate of the area available is that known to be utilized, shown in Figure 10.2. This is approximately 1,000 km^2, which with a productivity of 0.8 $MT/km^2/year$ could provide an annual yield of about 800 MT. It is interesting to note, however, that there is potential for the trap fishery yield to be considerably higher. The midshelf region between long. 116° and 117°30' E supported a Lethrinus and Lutjanus dominated fish community with a high fish density during the 1960s (Figure 10.2; Table 10.1), in a depth range similar to that presently being trapped farther west. If the change in the fish community composition which occurred during the 1970s was reversed, it is highly likely that this region could support a trap fishery. The area involved (Figure 10.2) is approximately 12,000 km^2, which, with a productivity of 0.8 $MT/km^2/year$, could provide an annual yield of about 10,000 MT. These estimates are, of course, very approximate, and take very little account of the economics of such a fishery.

Biological Management

Biological management at the single species level is primarily concerned with determination of the yield and catch rate sustainable from a population. Management at the community level involves these considerations for a number of species, and additionally most consider the species composition of the community and catch.

Changes in community species composition are to be expected whenever a fishery operates on a community. Because the population parameters are species specific, almost any fishery regime will overfish (in the simplest, growth-mortality, sense of the term) some species and underfish others. It is also likely to result in recruitment overfishing of some species (Sainsbury 1984). Ignoring for the moment all fishing effects other than the direct removal of individuals from their populations, a given fishing mortality (F) is expected to cause greatest decline in species with the lowest intrinsic growth rate (r). For example, the proportionate decline in population growing according to the logistic model is F/r. Because size is positively correlated with intrinsic growth rate (e.g., Pauly 1982), it is likely that large fish decrease proportionately more in abundance than small fish. Many other factors are also important in determining the response of a particular species to fishing, and in particular permitting some species to increase in both absolute and relative abundance. For example, there is considerable range in r for species of the same size, fishing does not impose an equal fishing mortality on all species, the intensity of biological interactions such as predation may not remain constant during fishery development, and the area suitable for habitation by the species may alter. But by whatever mechanism, change in the species mix (community structure) is to be expected and is a crucial parameter of fisheries management at the community level. The NW Shelf provides a good example of some consequent management issues and problems.

- The total catch rate on the NW Shelf, and presumably fish density of the community, has not altered greatly. The catch rate of commercially retained fish has declined by about one-third (Figure 10.9) for the pair trawl fishery, but this includes a decline in the retention of Saurida despite an increase in its absolute abundance, and there is no significant correlation between catch rate and year for the research surveys between 1962 and 1983 (Table 10.1). The species group composition has altered considerably, however, with dominance moving from the groups Lethrinus and Lutjanus to Nemipterus and Saurida. For the present trawl fishery, such a change may be economically acceptable, since the unit value of Nemipterus on the Taiwanese market is similar to that for Lethrinus or Lutjanus (Liu and Lai 1980), illustrating the point that changes in species composition are not necessarily detrimental. Indeed, Larkin (1982:314) suggested that the total yield available from a community may remain the same or increase as a fishery intensifies and exploits a succession of species, and that decrease in retained catch only occurs as an economic species mix is replaced by an uneconomic one or one unavailable to the fishing gear. Such an outcome would seem inevitable if a community was fished sufficiently intensely, and one task of biological management is to attempt to determine this intensity. The changes in species composition on the NW Shelf appear acceptable to the present fishery, but the fishing intensity at which further major changes in community structure would occur, and what those changes would be, cannot be predicted. Indeed, the recent increase in the abundance of low-valued Saurida under the relatively constant fishing effort exerted between 1978 and 1983 gives rise to some concern that persistent application of the present level of fishing effort could cause economically undesirable changes in the species mix.

Estimates of yield and catch rate for a multispecies fishery will differ greatly according to the species considered of interest to the fishery. For example, the yield available to the NW Shelf trawl fishery may be estimated as 10,700 MT for the fish groups listed in Table 10.6, 8,100 MT if Saurida is regarded as essentially noncommercial and 3,500 MT if only the large species (large Lutjanus, Lethrinus, Haemulidae, and Pristipomoides) are considered. These differences in yield estimates for the same fish community can cause confusion, and emphasize the strong linkage between community level fishery assessments and the economics of the fishery. Economic considerations enter into multispecies fishery assessments at an earlier stage than is usually the case for single species assessments. It is possible to estimate the yield and catch rate for a single species fishery without reference to the economics of the fishery, but even this is impossible in a multispecies context because a choice must be made of the species to include.

● Fishery assessment usually involves evaluation of a number of different resource usage options or fishing regimes. In multispecies fisheries, different options may be quite imcompatible in their species mix requirements, and it may prove very difficult either to evaluate or change options. On the NW Shelf the pair trawl fishery can utilize the present species mix, whereas development of the trap fishery (for example) would require the now historical species mix dominated by <u>Lethrinus</u>, <u>Lutjanus</u>, and Serranidae. The gross yield available from the two options may not be greatly dissimilar (approximately 18,000 MT for the trawl fishery and about 10,000 MT for the trap fishery), but their value to the Australian economy could differ considerably. Assessing these particular options gives rise to two difficult questions: (1) are the historical changes in species composition reversible (and if so what is the time required), and (2) how can the viability of a larger scale trap fishery be tested without disrupting the existing and known viable fishery? Similar questions of viability, species mix, and reversibility also arise from consideration of the trawl fishery alone. For example, should the trawl fishery be encouraged to intensify in an attempt to provide a higher yield and "economic rent," and would rotational strip-harvesting provide greater control of the catch rate and species mix?

Given these issues, how then should biological management proceed? At present it would seem imprudent to rely solely on ecological theory for biological management which risks major economic loss and persistent species composition changes (Sainsbury 1982b, 1982c). It would also seem imprudent to ignore it. Fishery management has usually involved a large empirical element, and the most fruitful approach to multispecies fishery management would appear to be (1) development of community dynamics models incorporating available knowledge of the biological processes affecting fish density and species mix; and (2) development of a sound empirical framework to explore the management options thought desirable for fishery development and predicted to be biologically feasible by the dynamics models. Emphasis here is placed on the need for a sound empiricism. Usually the selected management option is applied to the whole fishery, thereby placing the whole resource and fishery at risk and temporally confounding observations of the effects of the management measure. There is a need for management experiments, on a space scale of relevance to the fishery, to explore the commercially and biologically important features of the fish community's response to a changed fishing regime. Similar arguments for empirical, adaptive, or experimental management have been made by Hilborn (1979), Stocker and Hilborn (1981), Tyler et al. (1982), and Sainsbury (1982b, 1982c).

In applying this approach to the NW Shelf fishery, it is thought that a model of the fish community should incorporate at least the following features.

- The spatial distribution and abundance of benthic habitats primarily controls the spatial distribution and abundance of fish species assemblages.

- At moderate to low levels of fishing effort, the main effect of fishing on the fish community composition is via alteration of the relative frequency of habitat types and hence the relative abundance of fish species assemblages. In particular this refers to the conversion of areas with dense epibenthos (sponge, corals, hydroids, gorgonians) to areas with sparse epibenthos.

- At higher levels of fishing, the main effect of fishing on the fish community composition is via the direct effect of removals on the biotic balance within the (by now fewer) assemblages in simplified habitats. In particular this involves interspecific differences in vulnerability to fishing gear, growth overfishing, reduction of reproductive output due to low spawner biomass, and alteration of predator-prey interactions.

This outline of community control differs from that of Pauly (1979) who emphasized the importance of predator-prey interactions alone in determining the major changes in the exploited Gulf of Thailand fish community, although other interpretations were possible (e.g., Larkin 1982). The pretrawling fish community on the NW Shelf appears to have been very different from that of the Gulf of Thailand (dominated by Lethrinus and Lutjanus on the NW Shelf, and by Leiognathidae, Carangidae, Nemipteridae, Sciaenidae, and Mullidae in the Gulf of Thailand), and the same groups of fish behaved differently following exploitation in the two areas (Lutjanus and Lethrinus declined while Saurida and Nemipterus increased on the NW Shelf, but Saurida and Nemipterus declined while Lutjanus and Lethrinus showed no

498

significant change in the Gulf of Thailand). This suggests that the processes influencing community dynamics before and during development of the fisheries in the two areas were fundamentally different.

Construction of a simple mathematical model of the NW Shelf community incorporating the above features is currently being attempted, but even in qualitative form the above "word model" suggests potentially useful management measures for investigating the potential of the trap fishery. A suitable first step in investigating the extent of management control over the density and species mix of the community is to protect one area from trawling while continuing to trawl in other areas. From late 1985 the area west of long. 116° E will be closed to trawling, and so changes in the benthic habitat and fish community can be examined using an adjacent trawled area as a temporal control. This is not an ideal experiment. For example, it lacks replication and controls between areas for the numerous differences other than fishing intensity, and the area west of long. 116° E is not among the most productive areas of the Japanese and Taiwanese fisheries. However, it represents a considerable advance towards determining the best usage of the resource, since it both allows empirical examination of a possible harvesting option without greatly jeopardizing the existing fishery, and will improve biological understanding of the dynamics of the harvested community.

BIBLIOGRAPHY

Abe, S., S. Yada, S. Inove, and Y. Akishige. 1967. Survey on summer trawl grounds off the North West coast of Australia. Bull. Fac. Fish. Nagasaki Univ. 21-27:205-215.

Anonymous. 1964. The Oshoro Maru cruise 1 to the Indian Ocean. Data record of oceanographic observation and exploratory fishing 8:116-199.

_____. 1965. The Oshoro Maru cruise 7 to the Indian Ocean. Data record of oceanographic observations and exploratory fishing 9:32-105.

_____. 1972-1979. Annual report of effort and catch statistics by area on Taiwan demersal fish fisheries. Demersal Fish. Res. Cent. Inst. Oceanogr. Natl. Taiwan Univ., Taipei, Taiwan.

_____. 1978. The state of biological resources in waters off Australia on the results of TINRO

research. Document submitted to the Australian
Government by the Russian Government following
declaration of the Australian Fishing Zone. [Mimeo.]

_____. 1980a. Feasibility trawl fishing off W. A.
S. Aust. Fish. Ind. Counc. 4:28-30.

_____. 1980b. Investigations in fishing grounds of
northern waters of Australia. Fish. Res. Dev. Agency,
Korea Tech. Rep. 51, 287 p.

Beddington, J. R., and J. G. Cooke. 1983. The potential
yield of fish stocks. FAO Fish. Tech. Pap. FRs/T242,
47 p.

Beddington, J. R., and R. M. May. 1977. Harvesting natural
populations in a randomly fluctuating environment.
Science 197:463-465.

Beverton, F. J. H., and S. J. Holt. 1957. On the dynamics
of exploited fish populations. G. B. Minist. Agric.
Fish. Food, Dir. Fish. Res., Fish. Res. Invest.,
Lond. Ser. 2(19), 533 p.

Bowen, B. K. 1961. The Shoule Bay fishery on snapper
Chrysophrys unicolor. Dep. Fish. Wildl. Western
Aust. Rep. 1, 15 p.

Bye, J. A. T., and A. H. Gordon. 1982. Speculated cause of
interhemispheric oceanic circulation. Nature 296:52-
54.

Chen, S. C., C. H. Chen, T. N. Chi, K. C. Fan, D. C. Liu,
and R. Y. Tsay. 1979. Demersal fish resources investigation on trawl grounds off the North West coast of
Australia. Bull. Taiwan Fish. Res. Inst. Keelung,
Cruise Rep. 31.

Edwards, R. R. C. 1983. The Taiwanese pair trawler
fishery in tropical Australia waters. Fish. Res.
2:47-60.

Francis, R. C. 1974. Relationship of fishing mortality
to natural mortality at the level of maximum sustainable yield under the logistic stock production model.
J. Fish. Res. Board Can. 31:1539-1542.

Gloerfelt-Tarp, T., and P. J. Kailola. 1984. Trawled
fishes of southern Indonesia and northern Australia.
Aust. Dev. Assist. Bur. Canberra; Direct. Gen'l.
Fish. Jakarta; German Agency Tech. Coop. Hamburg, 406
p.

Gulland, J. A. 1968. Manual of methods for fish assessment. Pt. 1. Fish population analysis. FAO Fish.
Tech. Pap. FRs/T40, 154 p.

_____. (compiler and editor). 1971. The fish
resources of the ocean. Fishing News (Books) Ltd.,
Surrey, Engl., 255 p.

_____. 1979. Report of the FAO/IOP workshop on the fishery resources of the western Indian Ocean south of the Equator. FAO IOFC/DEV/79/45, 99 p.

Hilborn, R. 1979. Comparison of fisheries coastal systems that utilize catch and effort data. J. Fish. Res. Board Can. 36:1477-1489.

Jones, H. A. 1973. Marine geology of the North-West Australia continental shelf. Bur. Miner. Resour. Geol. Geophys. Bull. (Canberra) 136, 19 p.

Kabanova, Y. G. 1968. Primary production of the northern part of the Indian Ocean. Oceanology 8:214-224.

Larkin, P. A. 1977. An epitaph for the concept of maximum sustainable yield. Trans. Am. Fish. Soc. 106:1-11.

_____. 1982. Directions for future research in tropical multispecies fisheries. In D. Pauly and G. I. Murphy (editors), Theory and management of tropical fisheries, p. 309-328. Proceedings of the ICLARM/CSIRO Workshop on the Theory and Management of Tropical Multispecies Stocks, 12-21 January 1981, Cronulla, Australia. ICLARM Conf. Proc. 9.

Larkin, P. A., and N. Gazey. 1982. Application of ecological simulation models to management of tropical multispecies fisheries. In D. Pauly and G. I. Murphy (editors), Theory and management of tropical fisheries, p. 123-140. Proceedings of the ICLARM/CSIRO Workshop on the Theory and Management of Tropical Multispecies Stocks, 12-21 January 1981, Cronulla, Australia. ICLARM Conf. Proc. 9.

Liu, H. C. 1976. The demersal fish stocks of the waters of north and northwestern Australia. Acta Oceanogr. Taiwanica 6:128-134.

Liu, H. C., and H. L. Lai. 1980. Cost-revenue analysis of Taiwanese pair trawler operated in Australian waters. Acta Oceanogr. Taiwanica 11:217-227.

Liu, H. C., H. L. Lai, and S. Y. Yeh. 1978. General review of demersal fish resources in the Sunda Shelf and the Australian waters. Acta Oceanogr. Taiwanica 8:109-140.

Liu, H. C., K. J. Sainsbury, and T. S. Chin. 1985. Trawl cod end mesh selectivity for some fishes of northwestern Australia. Fish. Res. 3:105-129.

Liu, H. C., and S. Y. Yeh. 1984. Yield analysis of the groundfish resources in the Australian waters off north and northwestern Australia. Acta Oceanogr. Taiwanica 15:141-153.

Marshall, N. 1980. Fishery yields of coral reefs and adjacent shallow-water environment. In S. B. Saila and P. M. Roedel (editors), Stock assessment for tropical shell scale fisheries, p. 103-109. Int. Cent. Mar. Resour. Dev., Univ. Rhode Island.

Marten, G. G., and J. J. Polovina. 1982. A comparative study of fish yields from various tropical ecosystems. In D. Pauly and G. I. Murphy (editors), Theory and management of tropical fisheries, p. 255-289. Proceedings of the ICLARM/CSIRO Workshop on the Theory and Management of Tropical Multispecies Stocks, 12-21 January 1981, Cronulla, Australia. ICLARM Conf. Proc. 9.

Masuda, K., S. Nakane, S. Saito, and T. Fujii. 1964. Survey of trawl grounds off the north-west coast of Australia with special reference to hydrographical conditions on the grounds. Bull. Fac. Fish. Hokkaido Univ. 15-16:77-88.

McLoughlin, R. J., and P. C. Young. 1985. Sedimentary provinces of the fishing grounds of the North West Shelf of Australia: Grain-size frequency analysis of surficial sediments. Aust. J. Mar. Freshwater Res. 36:671-681.

Motoda, S., T. Kawamura, and A. Taniguchi. 1978. Differences in productivities between the Great Australian Bight and the Gulf of Carpentaria, Australia, in summer. Mar. Biol. (Berl.) 46:93-99.

Pauly, D. 1979. Theory and management of tropical multispecies stocks: A review with emphasis on the Southeast Asian demersal fisheries. ICLARM Stud. Rev. 1, Manila, 35 p.

_____. 1980. On the interrelationships between natural mortality, growth parameters, and mean environmental temperature in 175 fish stocks. J. Cons. Cons. Int. Explor. Mer 39:175-192.

_____. 1982. Studying single-species dynamics in a tropical multispecies context. In D. Pauly and G. I. Murphy (editors), Theory and management of tropical fisheries, p. 33-70. Proceedings of the ICLARM/CSIRO Workshop on the Theory and Management of Tropical Multispecies Stocks, 12-21 January 1981, Cronulla, Australia. ICLARM Conf. Proc. 9.

Robins, J. 1969. North-West trawl fishing. FINS (Fishing Ind. News Serv., Western Australia) 2:5-13.

Sainsbury, K. J. 1979. CSIRO defining fish stocks on North West Shelf. Aust. Fish. 38:4-12.

_____. 1982a. 1982 Assessment of the North West Shelf demersal fish stocks. Document submitted to the Department of Primary Industry, 9 p. [Mimeo.]

_____. 1982b. The ecological basis of tropical fisheries management. In D. Pauly and G. I. Murphy (editors), Theory and management of tropical fisheries, p. 167-188. Proceedings of the ICLARM/CSIRO Workshop on the Theory and Management of Tropical Multispecies Stocks, 12-21 January 1981, Cronulla, Australia. ICLARM Conf. Proc. 9.

_____. 1982c. The biological management of Australia's multispecies tropical demersal fisheries: A review of problems and some approaches. CSIRO Mar. Lab. Rep. 147, 16 p.

_____. 1984. Optimal mesh size for tropical multispecies trawl fisheries. J. Cons. Cons. Int. Explor. Mer 41:129-139.

Sainsbury, K. J., P. J. Kailola, and G. G. Leyland. 1985. Continental shelf fishes of northern and northwestern Australia. Clouston & Hall and Peter Pownall Fisheries Information Service, Canberra, Australia, 375 p.

Sainsbury, K. J., and A. W. Whitelaw. 1984. Biology of Peron's threadfin bream, Nemipterus peronii (Valenciennes), from the North West Shelf of Australia. Aust. J. Mar. Freshwater Res. 35:167-185.

Shepherd, J. G. 1982. A family of general production curves for exploited populations. Math. Biosci. 59:77-93.

Shu, F. W., S. C. Shaur, and S. C. Tzong. 1973. Investigation of bottom trawl grounds in the Arafura Sea. Taiwan Fish. Res. Inst., Keelung, Cruise Rep. 40.

Shu, F. W., S. C. Shoa, and H. C. Chun. 1973. Survey of bottom trawl grounds in the Arafura Sea. Taiwan Fish. Res. Inst., Keelung, Cruise Rep. 39.

Shuntov, V. P. 1979. Ichthyofauna of the Australian and New Zealand regions and its environments. Tr. Inst. Okeanol. Akad. Nauk SSSR 106:8-56.

Stocker, M., and R. Hilborn. 1981. Short term forecasting in marine fish stocks. Can. J. Fish. Aquat. Sci. 38:1247-1254.

Suzuki, T., K. Masuda, and S. Nakane. 1964. Variation of the catches and the volume of stomach contents of medium sized "Kuchinidai" (Lethrinus ornatus Cuvier & Valencienna) between day and night and observed in the trawl ground along the northwestern coast of Australia. Bull. Fac. Fish., Hokkaido Univ. 15-16:29-44.

Thompson, D. 1978. Pair trawling and pair seining. The technology of two-boat fishing. Fishing News (Books), Surrey, Engl., 168 p.

Thresher, R. E., K. J. Sainsbury, J. Gunn, and A. W. Whitelaw. In press. Life history strategies and recent changes in population structure in the lizardfish genus, Saurida, on the Australian North West Shelf. Copeia, 13 p.

Tranter, D. J. 1962. Zooplankton abundance in Australian waters. Aust. J. Mar. Freshwater Res. 13:106-129.

Tyler, A. V., W. L. Gabriel, and W. J. Overholtz. 1982. Adaptive management based on structure of fish assemblages of northern continental shelves. In M. C. Mercer (editor), Multispecies approaches to fisheries management advice, p. 149-156. Spec. Publ. Can. Fish. Aquat. Sci. 59.

Van Andel, T. H., and J. J. Veevers. 1967. Morphology and sediments of the Timor Sea. Aust. Bur. Miner. Resour. Geol. Geophys. Bull. 83, 72 p.

White, T. 1978. Interim report on investigations into potential development areas for the western Australian fishing industry, in relation to Australia's 200 mile fishing zone. Fishing and Allied Industries Committee Report 216 p. [Mimeo.]

Wyrtki, K. 1961. Scientific results of marine investigation of the South China Sea and the Gulf of Thailand 1959-1961. NAGA Rep. Vol. 2, 195 p.

_____. 1962. The upwelling in the region between Java and Australia during the southeast monsoon. Aust. J. Mar. Freshwater Res. 13:217-225.

Yeh, S. Y., and T. S. Chin. 1982. Standardization of fishing effort of the Taiwanese pair trawl fishery of northern Australia. Acta Oceanogr. Taiwanica 13:215-225.

Young, P. C., and K. J. Sainsbury. 1985. CSIRO's North West Shelf program. Aust. Fish. 44:16-20.

11

Assessment and Management of Deepwater Bottom Fishes in Hawaii and the Marianas

Jeffrey J. Polovina
Southwest Fisheries Center Honolulu Laboratory
National Marine Fisheries Service, NOAA
Honolulu, Hawaii 96822-2396

ABSTRACT

Stocks of deepwater snappers, groupers, and jacks in the Mariana Archipelago are just beginning to be exploited, and it is estimated from a 5-year fishery assessment program that the annual equilibrium yield for this resource will be 109 metric tons (MT). Stocks of deepwater bottom fishes in the Hawaiian Islands have a long history of exploitation and have been fished very heavily in recent years, especially around the populated islands. Commercial landings for 1984 are estimated at 414 MT from the populated islands and 662 MT for the entire archipelago. There is some evidence that the high fishing pressure at least around the populated islands has so substantially reduced the spawning stock biomass for at least one of the major species that the recent levels of yield may not be sustainable.

The Beverton and Holt yield equation is used to evaluate the impact of fishing mortality on spawning stock biomass, and some general guidelines are proposed: When the size of entry to the fishery exceeds the size of sexual maturity, fishing mortality should not exceed twice natural mortality; and when the size of entry to the fishery is less than or equal the size of sexual maturity, fishing mortality should not exceed natural mortality. The Beverton and Holt equation is also used to simulate multispecies interactions for a developing fishery that arise when fishing mortality applied to one species impacts another. As fishing mortality increases and concurrently the size of entry to the

fishery decreases, the catches of species with
higher natural mortality to growth ratios will
increase relative to those with lower natural
mortality to growth ratios.

INTRODUCTION

The Hawaiian and Mariana Archipelagos support
deepwater bottom fishes, which are a multispecies group
consisting principally of snappers (Lutjanidae) and
groupers (Serranidae), but also including jacks (Carangidae) in depths from 125 to 360 m. In Hawaii there is a
long history of fishing for deepwater bottom fishes;
currently the resource is fished throughout the archipelago and heavily fished around the populated islands
(Ralston and Polovina 1982). In the Marianas the fishery
for the deepwater bottom fishes is a much more recent
development, and the stocks around many of the islands and
banks are still unexploited. The first section of this
chapter presents an estimate of the potential yield of the
deepwater bottom fishes in the Marianas based on a
recently concluded 5-year fishery assessment program by
the Southwest Fisheries Center Honolulu Laboratory,
National Marine Fisheries Service, NOAA. The next section
treats the trends and estimated yield of the bottom fish
fishery in the Hawaiian Islands, based primarily on a time
series of commercial landings. The final section gives
general guidelines on assessment and management of the
deepwater bottom fishes for Pacific islands.

DEEPWATER BOTTOM FISH FISHERY IN THE
MARIANAS AND ITS POTENTIAL YIELD

The Mariana Archipelago consists of a chain of
islands and banks on a north-south axis, beginning with
Galvez Banks and Santa Rosa Reef at the southernmost end
and extending northward to Farallon de Pajaros, and a
chain of seamounts also on a north-south axis about 120
nmi west of the high island chain (Figure 11.1).
The fishery for deepwater bottom fishes in the
Marianas grew out of a program of exploratory fishing for
deepwater snappers and groupers initiated in 1968 (Ikehara
et al. 1970). The bottom fishing fleet consists of
vessels 6 to 15 m long based primarily in Guam or Saipan.
The vessels typically use electric or hydraulic gurdies

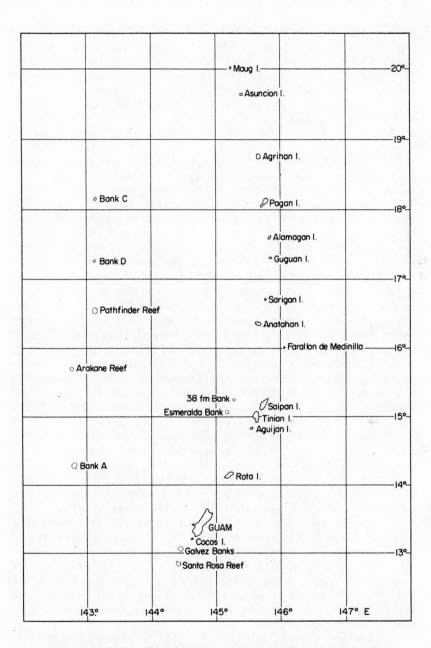

Figure 11.1   The Mariana Archipelago with the
22 islands and banks sampled

with a terminal rig consisting of a weight and four to six hooks, each attached to the mainline with a leader and spaced about a meter apart. From 1980 to 1984, the landings of deepwater bottom fishes in Guam have increased from 6 metric tons (MT) in 1980 to an estimated 20 MT in 1984. About 65 to 90% of the landings come from the waters around Guam.[1] The estimated commercial landings in Saipan for the period 1981 to 1984 ranged from 2 to 10 MT.[1]

In 1980, a 5-year fishery assessment was begun in the Marianas, and the deepwater snappers, groupers, and jacks were one of the resource groups targeted. A total of 7,621 deepwater bottom fishes were caught with handline gear during six assessment cruises. Pristipomoides zonatus accounted for 51.2% of the catch and three species (P. zonatus, P. auricilla, and Etelis carbunculus) accounted for 79.1% of the total catch (Table 11.1).

The resource is relatively unexploited except around a few of the islands and banks where the collection of catch and effort data has recently been initiated. Thus, any approach to yield assessment must be independent of catch and effort data. In recent years, there have been a number of new methods and modifications of existing methods to estimate growth and mortality parameters, standing stock, and yield for fish stocks particularly in the absence of a time series of commercial catch and effort data (Beddington and Cooke 1983; Munro 1983a; Pauly 1983; Polovina 1986; Wetherall et al. In press). A number of these methods have been combined to produce an integrated approach to yield assessment that was applied to the multispecies resource of deepwater bottom fishes in the Marianas (Polovina and Ralston In press) (Figure 11.2). This approach to equilibrium yield estimation assumes: (1) that growth follows the deterministic von Bertalanffy curve with parameters K and L_∞; (2) that the mortality of fish above the smallest length fully represented in the catch (L_c) occurs at a constant instantaneous rate (Z); (3) that recruitment is constant (R recruits entering the first age class annually); and (4) that the resource is essentially unexploited. Departures from some of these assumptions are discussed in Polovina and Ralston (In press).

The resource in the Marianas is essentially unexploited; thus an estimate for each species of the unexploited biomass that is recruited to the fishery and can be harvested with handline gear for each species was obtained from a systematic survey, and an estimate of

TABLE 11.1
List of species caught with bottom handline gear
in the Mariana Archipelago during the period
April 1982 to May 1984

Species	Number Caught	Percentage of Catch
Lutjanidae		
Aphareus rutilans	81	1.06
Aprion virescens	7	0.09
Etelis coruscans	202	2.65
E. carbunculus	952	12.49
Pristipomoides sieboldii	57	0.75
P. filamentosus	191	2.51
P. auricilla	1,170	15.35
P. flavipinnis	502	6.59
P. zonatus	3,904	51.23
P. amoenus	26	0.34
Carangidae		
Seriola sp.	60	0.79
Carangoides orthogrammus	9	0.12
Caranx lugubris	272	3.57
Serranidae		
Serranidae sp.	102	1.34
Epinephelus morrhua	15	0.20
Cephalopholis igarasihensis	11	0.14
Variola louti	13	0.17
Saloptia powelli	47	0.62
Total	7,621	100

catchability was obtained from an intensive fishing
experiment on a small isolated pinnacle (Polovina 1986).
For each of the major species, an estimate of the von
Bertlanffy growth parameter (K) was obtained from otolith
data (Ralston and Williams Unpub.). Estimates of natural
mortality (M) were obtained from large length-frequency
samples by applying a regression model to the standard
Beverton and Holt relationship for M/K in an unexploited
stock, expressed as:

$$M/K = (L_\infty - \bar{\ell}) / (\bar{\ell} - L_c) \quad ,$$

510

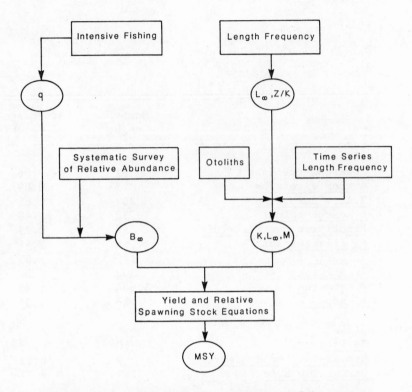

Figure 11.2 A schematic of the yield assessment approach--a more general approach to fishery assessment--which includes a treatment of catch and effort data as well is given in Munro (1983b); this figure represents a detailed subset of Munro's (1983b) figure 1

where L_c is the smallest length fully represented in the catch and $\bar{\ell}$ is the mean length of all fish greater than L_c (Beverton and Holt 1956). The regression approach constructs a series of L_c values at intervals beginning with the smallest L_c and going up to L_∞, together with the corresponding set of $\bar{\ell}$ values. By solving the M/K equation for $\bar{\ell}$ as a function of L_c, the following relationship is obtained:

$$\bar{\ell} = L_\infty \ / \ ((M/K) + 1) \ + \ L_c (M/K) \ / \ ((M/K) + 1) \ .$$

Thus, regressing a sequence of $\bar{\ell}$ values on the corresponding L_c values (with the appropriate weighting) produces estimates for the slope and intercept that can be solved for L_∞ and M/K (Wetherall et al. In press).

The yield assessment approach is based on the Beverton and Holt yield equations, where equilibrium yield (Y) can be expressed as a function of growth (K), natural mortality (M), age of entry to the fishery (T_r), and fishing mortality (F) as:

$$Y = RF \int_{T_r}^{\infty} e^{(-tM-(t-T_r)F)} w(t)\,dt \quad,$$

$$\text{with } w(t) = W(1-e^{(-Kt)})^a \quad,$$

where W is the asymptotic weight and a is the coefficient of allometry. The unexploited biomass recruited to the fishery (B_∞) can be expressed as:

$$B_\infty = R \int_{T_r}^{\infty} w(t)e^{(-tM)}\,dt \quad.$$

The ratio of equilibrium yield to unexploited recruited biomass (Y/B_∞) is independent of W and R and depends only on K, M, T_r, F, and a. Once an estimate of B_∞ is available, the equilibrium yield is estimated for a given level of fishing mortality as the product of Y/B_∞ and B_∞.

Further, if the age of the onset of sexual maturity (T_m) is known, the spawning stock biomass (SSB) that corresponds to a given level of fishing mortality is:

$$SSB = R \int_{T_m}^{\infty} w(t)e^{-(t-T_r)F}e^{-tM}\,dt \quad \text{where } T_m \geq T_r$$

and

$$SSB = R \int_{T_m}^{T_r} w(t)e^{-tM}\,dt + R \int_{T_r}^{\infty} w(t)e^{-(t-T_r)F}e^{-tM}\,dt$$

when $\quad T_m < T_r \quad.$

The ratio of the SSB for a specific level of F to the spawning stock biomass in the absence of exploitation (SSB_0) is a useful measure of the relative impact that F has on the SSB and under the assumption of constant recruitment is independent of R, depending only on T_m, K, T_r, M, F, and a.

In the systematic survey of the resource in the Marianas, seven species, one jack, Caranx lugubris, and six snappers, Pristipomoides zonatus, P. auricilla, P. filamentosus, P. flavipinnus, Etelis carbunculus, and E. coruscans, accounted for 92% of the catch (Table 11.1). Yield assessment was performed for each of these seven species plus an eighth group that consisted of all other species. For this latter group, the ratio (Y/B_∞) is estimated as the ratio of total yield for the seven species divided by their total unexploited recruited biomass. In this analysis, the age of entry for each species is the age that maximizes their yield per recruit.

The total equilibrium yield is computed as a function of F for the multispecies bottom fish complex fished with handline gear in the 125 to 275 m depth range for 22 islands and banks of the Mariana Archipelago. At each bank, the equilibrium yields are summed over the eight species groups to produce the bank equilibrium yield. The bank equilibrium yields then are summed over the 22 islands and banks surveyed. This archipelago yield increases rapidly as a function of fishing mortality to a

TABLE 11.2
Annual sustainable handline yield for the Marianas for the age at entry that maximizes the yield per recruit for each species in metric tons (MT)

Fishing Mortality (F)	Total Yield (MT)
0.1	35
0.5	91
1.0[a]	109[a]
1.5	114
2.0	116
2.5	116

[a]$F_{0.1}$ and $Y_{0.1}$ as defined by Gulland (1983).

level of about 100 MT, exhibits only a gradual increase
with increasing F (Table 11.2). The yield curve assumes
constant recruitment: of course when F is sufficiently
large, this assumption will no longer hold, the yield will
decline. Ideally, a spawner-recruit relationship is
needed to determine the sustainable yield curve. However,
in the absence of that relationship, the maximum level of
F that will be sustained before a serious reduction in
recruitment occurs can be estimated from the ratio of
spawning stock biomass under F relative to the unexploited
spawning stock biomass. In the absence of any species-
specific knowledge, it has been suggested that a substantial reduction in recruitment will occur if the spawning
stock biomass of a species is reduced below 20% of its
unexploited level (Beddington and Cooke 1983). With F of
1.0 and the age of entry that maximizes their yields per
recruit, the spawning stock biomasses for the seven
species are reduced to levels ranging from 20 to 42% of
their unexploited levels, suggesting that recruitment will
not be reduced significantly if the lower bound of 0.20

TABLE 11.3
The ratio of spawning stock biomass to
unexploited spawning stock biomass as a
function of F with the ages of entry for each
species taken at the age that maximizes the
yield per recruit[a]

Species	Spawning Stock Biomass Relative to Its Level in the Absence of Exploitation		
	$F = 0.5$	$F = 1.0$	$F = 1.5$
Caranx lugubris	0.44	0.26	0.17
Pristipomoides filamentosus	0.46	0.33	0.28
P. auricilla	0.45	0.29	0.23
P. flavipinnis	0.45	0.26	0.17
P. zonatus	0.39	0.24	0.18
Etelis coruscans	0.31	0.20	0.15
E. carbunculus	0.58	0.42	0.34

[a] Based on length of maturity (L_m) estimated as $L_m = 0.576$ L_{max} (Anonyme 1977 in Brouard and Grandperrin 1984).

suggested by Beddington and Cooke is valid for these species (Table 11.3). As an alternative approach, the maximum sustainable yield (MSY) from the Beverton and Holt yield equation can be taken as the yield corresponding to that level of fishing mortality where an increase of one unit of fishing mortality will increase the catch by .0.1 of the amount caught by the very first unit of fishing mortality (Gulland 1983, 1984). This fishing mortality and corresponding yield have been denoted as $F_{0.1}$ and $Y_{0.1}$, respectively. The value of $F_{0.1}$ for the bottom fish resource in the Marianas based on this marginal yield approach is also estimated to be $F = 1.0$.

The annual equilibrium yield corresponding to $F = 1.0$ is 109 MT (an approximate 95% confidence interval is 81 to 137 MT (Polovina and Ralston In press)). About 70% of this yield would come from the southern islands and banks that include Guam and Saipan, 27% would come from the northern islands and banks, and only 3% from the seamounts (Table 11.4). This yield estimate can be converted to a yield per unit of bottom fish habitat. It is difficult to compute an area measure for the steep-sloped Pacific islands, and since the bottom fishes are found along the steep dropoff zones centered around the 200-m isobath, the length of the 200-m contour around an island or bank has been used as an index of bottom fish habitat. The means of the annual sustainable yield per nautical mile of 200-m contour for the northern banks, southern banks, and western seamounts are 212.9, 228.5, and 264.4 kg, respectively; a ratio of total yield for the archipelago to the total length of the 200-m contour is 222.4 kg/nmi of 200-m contour (95% confidence interval of 165.3 to 279.6 kg/nmi 200-m contour) (Table 11.4; Polovina and Ralston In press). There is, however, detailed bathymetry data from Guguan Island, one of the Northern Mariana Islands, where it is estimated that 1 nmi of 200-m isobath corresponds to 0.23 nmi^2 of habitat in the 125 to 275 m depth range (Polovina and Roush 1982). Based on this correspondence the unit MSY of 222.4 kg/nmi of 200-m contour for the Marianas is equivalent to approximately 1.0 MT/nmi^2 or 0.3 MT/km^2, which is at the lower end of the sustainable yield estimates for the bottom fish resources of the northwest Australian shelf (Sainsbury 1986).

There are two approximations to estimate MSY that express it as a fraction of the unexploited recruited biomass. Gulland (1969) uses a formula that estimates MSY as 0.5 MB_∞, where M is the instantaneous natural mortality and B_∞ the unexploited biomass, and while Pauly (1983)

TABLE 11.4
Annual sustainable yield and yield per nautical
mile of 200-m contour for the age at entry that
maximizes the yield per recruit at a level of
fishing mortality of F = 1.0 (MT = metric tons)

Location	Total Yield (MT/Year)	Yield (kg/year)/nmi of 200-m Contour
Northern Islands and Banks		
Maug	2.7	262.2
Asuncion	2.1	188.4
Agrihan	5.6	303.6
Pagan	7.7	255.1
Alamagan	2.0	177.6
Guguan	1.7	179.0
Sarigan	1.6	193.8
Anatahan	2.5	144.2
38-Fathom	0.5	187.3
Esmeralda	2.9	237.4
Total	29.3	Mean 212.9
Southern Islands and Banks		
Farallon de Medinilla	16.7	216.6
Saipan	13.4	254.1
Tinian	8.8	303.9
Aguijan	4.2	266.7
Rota	6.1	192.2
Guam	17.2	201.6
Galvez and Santa Rosa	8.6	164.2
Total	76.0	Mean 228.5
Seamounts		
Bank C	0.9	288.2
Bank D	1.1	351.2
Pathfinder	0.9	303.5
Arakane	0.6	199.6
Bank A	0.6	179.7
Total	4.1	Mean 264.4
Total yield from all banks	109 MT/year	

estimates MSY as $(2.3w^{-0.26})$ B_∞ , where w is the mean of the weight at sexual maturity and the asymptotic weight. A comparison of both these approaches with the values of Y/B_∞ produced with the Beverton and Holt equation for the seven species shows that in four out of the seven the Y/B values estimated with the Beverton and Holt equation lie between the values obtained from the Pauly and Gulland approximations. For the other three species, the Y/B_∞ values fall slightly below the Pauly and Gulland estimates for two and substantially above for the third (Table 11.5). Thus, for at least six out of the seven species, the mean of the two estimates provides a useful approximation of Y/B_∞ computed from the Beverton and Holt equation. Further, the means of these estimates for Y/B_∞ are all in very close agreement.

Based on the estimate of catchability derived from the intensive fishing experiment, which represents lower bound for a commercial vessel, a fleet of 15 small vessels with two hydraulic or electric gurdies fishing 12 h a day, 200 days per year can produce the fishing effort approximately equal to the optimum fishing mortality of F = 1.0. The catch rate for this fleet would be about 1.5 kg per line-hour, and the average annual landing per vessel would be 7.3 MT.

TABLE 11.5
Annual maximum sustainable yield as a fraction of unexploited recruited biomass at F = 1.0 together with 0.5M and $2.3w^{-0.26}$

Species Groups	Y/B_∞	0.5M	$2.3w^{-0.26}$
Caranx lugubris	0.261	0.335	0.252
Pristipomoides filamentosus	0.262	0.270	0.296
P. auricilla	0.306	0.325	0.403
P. flavipinnis	0.680	0.475	0.348
P. zonatus	0.280	0.270	0.363
Etelis coruscans	0.201	0.175	0.226
E. carbunculus	0.375	0.515	0.289
Mean	0.338	0.338	0.311

DEEPWATER BOTTOM FISH FISHERY IN
HAWAII AND ITS POTENTIAL YIELD

The Hawaiian Archipelago stretches from the Island of Hawaii to Hancock Seamounts 1,500 nmi to the northwest. The populated islands in the southern portion of the chain are often referred to as the main Hawaiian Islands, and the small, uninhabited islands, atolls, and seamounts that begin north of Niihau and extend northwest to Kure Atoll and Hancock Seamounts are called the Northwestern Hawaiian Islands (NWHI) (Figure 11.3).

There are 13 species groups that are harvested with deep-sea handline gear by the fishery (Table 11.6). Opakapaka, P. filamentosus, is the single most important species by weight, and the other major species consist of ulua (Caranx and Carangoides spp.), kahala, Seriola dumerili, uku, Aprion virescens, and onaga, Etelis coruscans. In 1984 opakapaka constituted 23% of the catch, and together onaga, opakapaka, uku, and ulua accounted for almost 70% of the landings.

Unlike the situation in the Marianas, there is a long history of commercial fishing for deepwater bottom fish in the Hawaiian Islands. There was a fleet of vessels that fished the deepwater bottom fishes throughout most the archipelago at least as early as the 1930s. Catch records from 1945 to 1982 indicate that the commercial landings

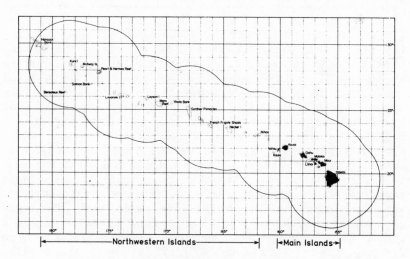

Figure 11.3   The Hawaiian Archipelago

TABLE 11.6
Principal species of fish landed in the Hawaiian
offshore handline fishery

Family	Species	Common Name	Range of Landed Weight (kg)
Lutjanidae	Aphareus rutilans	Lehi	3–8
	Aprion virescens	Uku	2–8
	Etelis coruscans	Onaga	2–8
	E. carbunculus	Ehu	0.5–2
	Lutjanus kasmira	Taape	0.5
	Pristipomoides filamentosus	Opakapaka	1–6
	P. sieboldii	Kalekale	0.5
	P. zonatus	Gindai	0.5–2
Carangidae	Caranx and Carangoides spp.	Ulua	1–10
	Seriola dumerili	Kahala	3–10
Serranidae	Epinephelus quernus	Hapuupuu	3–10
Labridae	Bodianus spp.	Aawa	1–3
Scorpaenidae	Pontinus macrocephala	Nohu	1–2

for the State began at about 450 MT after the hiatus
imposed by World War II, declined rapidly to a level of
about 180 MT by 1959, and remained relatively stable at
around 180 MT until 1974, when landings began steadily
increasing (Figure 11.4). These catch data come only from
fishermen with commercial fishing licenses and do not
include the catches from the recreational fishermen, which
may be substantial around the populated islands. An
estimate of the commercial landings for the State for 1984
is 662 MT, which indicates that commercial landings have
continued their rapid increase and are now greater than at
any time since World War II (Figure 11.4).[2] The high
catches from 1948 to 1953 correspond to catches for a
period when both the NWHI and main Hawaiian Islands were
fished. However, from the mid-1950s until about 1975,
when there was renewed interest in the stocks of the NWHI,

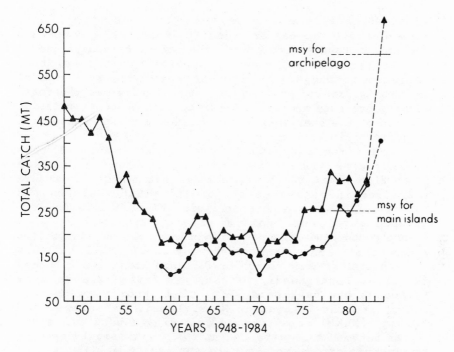

Figure 11.4   The annual commercial landings for deepwater bottom fishes from the main islands and the entire archipelago for 1948-1984.   Data reported by State of Hawaii, Division of Aquatic Resources.   ▲ = archipelago landings; ● = main island landings

most of the fishing was restricted to the main Hawaiian Islands.   Records of landings from the main Hawaiian Islands are available only since 1959.   Landings have fluctuated in the range of 100 to 200 MT from 1959 to 1978 while since 1978 have shown rapid growth.   The estimated catch for 1984 is 413.6 MT.   The rapid increase in landings from the main Hawaiian Islands and from the entire State since 1978 is a direct result of an expansion of the local market for fresh bottom fishes at a relatively stable and strong price (Pooley 1986).   In 1984 the wholesale prices for bottom fishes averaged $5.83/kg, and onaga and opakapaka commanded the highest prices at $8.80 and $7.37/kg, respectively.[2]

The species composition of the commercial landings from the main islands does not show any radical changes from 1959 to 1984, but some of the species do exhibit

substantial relative increases or decreases (Table 11.7).
Some of these changes are readily explainable, such as a
decline of kahala (grouped in the Others category) due to
its implication in ciguatera poisoning, the relative
increase of onaga, the deepest water species, due to
increasing fishing pressure in deeper habitat as the total
fishing pressure increases, and the corresponding relative
decline of the shallower water species ulua and uku due to
overfishing in shallow waters.

The first approach to yield assessment for this
multispecies fishery was fitting a Schaefer surplus
production model to the commercial catch and effort data
(measured in vessel days) for 1959-1978 (Ralston and
Polovina 1982). For this analysis the main islands were
grouped into four banks that are separated by deep
channels and hence assumed to represent closed populations
since adults and juveniles are not known to move across
deep channels. The Islands of Oahu and Hawaii each formed
their own bank; Kauai, Niihau, and Kaula Islands were
pooled as one bank because of their proximity to each
other; and the Islands of Maui, Lanai, Kahoolawe, and
Molokai (MLKM) were treated as a single bank since the
depths between them were <200 m. At first, single species
surplus production models were applied to all 13 species
for each of the 4 banks, but most of the fits were not

TABLE 11.7
Commercial landings of deepwater bottom fishes
from the main Hawaiian Islands (in metric tons)

Species	1964	(%)	1974	(%)	1984	(%)
Ehu	9.3	(5.2)	9.4	(6.3)	16.7	(4.0)
Gindai	0.7	(0.4)	0.5	(0.3)	2.1	(0.5)
Hapuupuu	4.0	(2.3)	8.5	(5.7)	25.1	(6.1)
Kalekale	7.1	(4.0)	2.2	(1.5)	10.8	(2.6)
Lehi	0.4	(0.2)	1.9	(1.3)	7.4	(1.8)
Onaga	21.7	(12.2)	17.7	(11.8)	86.7	(21.0)
Opakapaka	42.4	(23.9)	48.7	(32.4)	96.2	(23.2)
Uku	40.1	(22.6)	35.0	(23.3)	66.4	(16.1)
Ulua	13.8	(7.8)	12.0	(8.0)	27.1	(6.6)
Others	38.0	(21.4)	14.1	(9.4)	75.0	(18.1)
Total	177.5		150.0		413.6	

statistically significant. The poor fit of the single
species models was probably a result of using effort
measured in vessel-days, because a vessel-day produces a
multispecies catch; hence this represented a measure of
multispecies effort more than effort directed toward any
particular species. Next, 2 aggregated multispecies surplus production models were applied, 1 to the 13 species
pooled together, the total biomass Schaefer model, and the
other to 3 separate species groups formed by aggregating
the species according to their depth distribution.

The MLKM bank, which accounts for over 50% of the
State bottom fish landings, is the only bank where both
approaches produced statistically significant results.
The application of the Schaefer model to the three
aggregated species groups explained only slightly more of
the total variation in catch than the total biomass
Schaefer model. As a first approximation, treating the 13
species bottom fish resource with the total biomass model
is appealing. All the species occupy a very similar range
of habitat, all the species appear to be high level
carnivores with no evidence of prey-predator interactions
among them, and fishing for one species also exerts
pressure on other species.

The estimated MSY based on the total biomass Schaefer
model for the MLKM bank is 106 MT, which corresponds to a
unit MSY of 272 kg/nmi of 200-m contour (Ralston and
Polovina 1982). This estimate is a lower bound since it
includes only commercial landings and not the recreational
catch, which could be substantial.

The lengths of the 200-m contour for the main islands
and the NWHI are 977 and 1,231 nmi, respectively. Based
on the annual MSY estimate of 272 kg/nmi of 200-m contour,
the MSY is estimated at 266 MT for the main islands, 335
MT for the NWHI, and 601 MT for the entire archipelago.
Since 1979 the landings from the main islands have
exceeded the estimated MSY level, and the 1984 estimated
landings of 414 MT were 55% above the MSY. Landings from
the NWHI for 1984 were 74% of the MSY.

It is difficult to obtain an accurate measure of
fishing mortality for the resource. Over the period 1959-
1978, where a measure of effort in vessel-days is available, there was a threefold increase in vessel days
(Ralston and Polovina 1982). However, technological
changes such as electric or hydraulic gurdies, fathom-
eters, chromoscopes, and loran have increased the fishing
power of the vessel so that the trend in vessel days
underestimates the real trend in fishing mortality. In

addition to the considerable increase in fishing mortality in recent years, there is evidence, at least for opakapaka in the main islands, of substantial decrease in the age of entry to the fishery between 1980 and 1984 (Ralston and Kawamoto 1985). A yield-per-recruit analysis indicates that in 1980 the age of entry and fishing mortality for opakapaka on Penguin Bank were 4 years and 0.48/year, respectively, which placed it on the eumetric line of the yield-per-recruit isoplath (Ralston 1984). By 1984, however, a weight-frequency distribution for fish landed from the main Hawaiian Islands indicated that the age of entry was 1.8 years, which, with a fishing mortality of 0.48/year, results in a 17% reduction from the 1980 yield-per-recruit level (Ralston and Kawamoto 1985). When the approach used in the Marianas analysis to compute the ratio of the exploited to unexploited spawning stock biomass is applied to opakapaka stocks in the Hawaiian Islands with an age of entry of 1.8 years and a fishing mortality of 0.5/year, it is estimated that the spawning stock biomass is reduced to 10% of its unexploited level. This compares with 28% of its unexploited level when the age of entry is 4 years and the level of fishing mortality remains the same.

MANAGEMENT IMPLICATIONS

If the range of annual sustainable yield of 165 to 280 kg/nmi of 200-m contour estimated in the Marianas is taken as an archipelago range for Pacific islands and applied to the main Hawaiian Islands, an upper bound of sustainable yield is estimated at 274 MT annually. The landings from the main islands have exceeded this level since 1980, and by over 55% in 1984. This raises questions about the general nature of the range. However, given the evidence of growth overfishing, at least for opakapaka, and the reduction of its spawning stock biomass to as low as 10% of its unexploited level, it also suggests that these high levels of yield may not be sustainable.

Whereas the total biomass approach for multispecies bottom fish stocks is useful as a first step for assessment and management, it can be refined with a species specific approach based on the Beverton and Holt yield equation. This equation, appropriately formulated, requires only estimates of Z/K, F/M, L_c/L_∞ and L_m/L_∞ for yield-per-recruit and relative spawning stock analyses

(Beverton and Holt 1966; Beddington and Cooke 1983). Given that some of the recent length-based methods produce efficient estimators of Z/K when applied to large length-frequency samples, it is possible to develop species specific management of deepwater bottom fishes for Pacific islands based only on length-frequency samples. Even heavily fished archipelagos such as Hawaii have relatively unfished areas that can be sampled to estimate M/K. Fished banks will provide an estimate of Z/K that, together with M/K, provides an estimate of F/M. These estimates, together with estimates of L_c/L_∞ and L_m/L_∞, which are also easy to obtain from length-frequency samples and maturation studies, can be used to determine if the stock departs from the eumetric line and to estimate relative spawning stock biomass. Further, a time series of species specific estimates of Z or even Z/K obtained from length-frequency data, together with total catch data, can be used as the basis for single species production modelling (Csirke and Caddy 1983).

Based on the Beverton and Holt yield equation, upper bounds on F relative to M can be established as a function of L_c/L_∞. Consider the bottom fishes that have M/K values falling within the range of 1.0 to 4.0, which appears to include a large number of the snappers and groupers (Munro 1983b; Bannerot 1984; Ralston 1986; Polovina and Ralston In press). Further, suppose that the size of the onset of sexual maturity is estimated as $L_m = 0.5\ L_\infty$, which appears valid for most snappers (Grimes 1986). The ratio of spawning stock biomass under exploitation to the spawning stock biomass in the absence of fishing, computed as a function of F/M with the Beverton and Holt yield equation, is presented in Figure 11.5. Calculations were performed for two levels of M/K, 1.0 and 4.0, and for three levels of L_c/L_∞, 0.4, 0.5, and 0.6. When M/K is 4.0 and L_c/L_∞ is 0.6, the stock can sustain high levels of exploitation with minimal impact on the spawning stock. This is because when M/K is high and harvesting occurs above the size of sexual maturity, most of the contribution to the spawning stock comes from fish between the sizes L_m and L_c. However, when harvesting occurs at or below L_m, or if harvesting is above L_m and M/K is low, there is an exponential decline in the relative spawning stock biomass as a function of F/M. If L_c is greater than L_m, it appears that the relative spawning stock biomass for a fixed level of exploitation (F/M) increases with increasing M/K. Conversely, when L_c is less than L_m, the greater M/K, the lower the relative spawning stock biomass. If it is

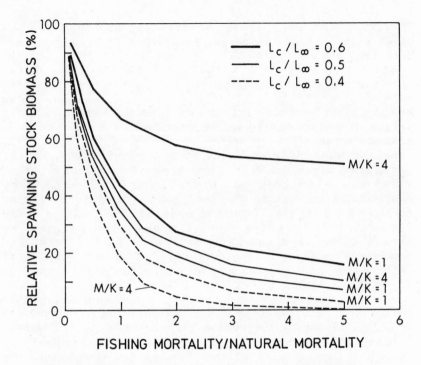

Figure 11.5   The ratio of spawning stock biomass as a function of fishing mortality to spawning stock biomass in the absence of exploitation for two levels of M/K and three levels of L_c/L_∞ when $L_m/L_\infty = 0.5$

determined that the exploited spawning stock biomass should not fall below about 20% of its unexploited level, then for fishes with M/K values in the range of 1 to 4 and when L_m is 0.5 L_∞, F should not exceed 2M if L_c is greater than or equal to L_m and F should not exceed M if L_c is below L_m.

    Prey-predator interactions do not appear to be strong for the bottom fish community (Parrish 1986), and hence multispecies interactions are probably negligible (Ralston and Polovina 1982). However, multispecies interaction in the form of changes in relative species abundance may occur. For example, based on the Beverton and Holt equation it can be shown that in a multispecies fishery as F increases from a lightly exploited situation to a heavily exploited situation and concurrently the age of entry decreases, the yield per recruit of those stocks

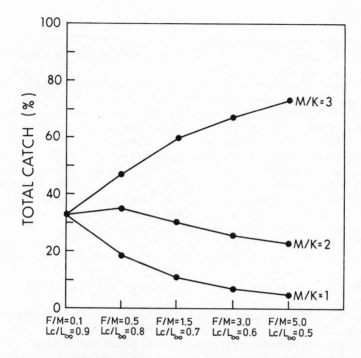

Figure 11.6   The relative contribution to the total catch for a multispecies group consisting of three species with different M/K values as a function of fishing mortality to natural mortality (F/M) and relative age of entry L_c/L_∞

with the higher M/K values will increase relative to the yield per recruit of those stocks with the lower M/K values. Simulation on a three-species group with M/K values of 1, 2, and 3, which represents a reasonable range for the bottom fishes in Hawaii, begins with F/M equal to 0.1, size of entry equal to 90% L_∞, and each species accounting for one-third of the landings. When F/M has increased to 3 and size of entry to 60% L_∞, (and assuming no change in recruitment for each species), the species with M/K of 3 will account for 67% of the landings while the species with M/K of 1 will only account for 7% (Figure 11.6). Further, the ratio of the exploited spawning stock biomass to unexploited spawning stock biomass will decline more rapidly for the species with low M/K values than for the species with higher M/K values (when L_c is greater than L_m), possibly adding further to the reduction of the relative contribution of low M/K species (Figure 11.5). It is the change in the age of entry more than the change in fishing mortality that is responsible for the change in relative yield.

Once the age of entry has been reduced substantially below the optimum value based on yield per recruit and relative spawning stock biomass analysis, as it appears to be for opakapaka in the main Hawaiian Islands, management recommendations that increase the age of entry must be sensitive to the dynamic or short-term response of the fishery. Even though yield-per-recruit analysis indicates that the long-term equilibrium yield will be increased with an increased age of entry, the short-term loss may exceed the long-term gain to the fishermen while the population structure of the stock is readjusting to the higher age of entry (Huntsman and Waters 1986). In such situations, management may find that a gradual increase in the age of entry through small annual increments is preferable to a single step increase to the optimal age of entry.

Although the mean level of the exploited spawning stock biomass relative to the unexploited level has been used to determine the level of exploitation that can be sustained, the variation in spawning stock biomass about this mean level has not been considered. If variation in recruitment is substantial, it may induce variation in the spawning stock biomass, which may have a greater impact on the sustainability of a level of yield than the mean value of the spawning stock biomass (Beddington and Cooke 1983). If it is assumed that recruitment is random and annual values are independent and identically distributed about a mean R with a coefficient of variation (standard deviation divided by mean) of s, and if it is assumed that the year-to-year variance in growth and mortality are negligible, then variances for annual yield, spawning stock biomass, and recruited biomass can be derived by computing the variance of yield, spawning stock, or biomass for a cohort of age t and integrating that variance with respect to t (Beddington and Cooke 1983). For example, the variance of the recruited biomass (V(B)) in the absence of exploitation is:

$$V(B) = R^2 s^2 W^2 \int_{T_r}^{\infty} \exp(-2tM)(1 - \exp(-Kt))^6 \, dt \quad .$$

Beddington and Cooke (1983) provide an approximation based on the Beverton and Holt equation that expresses the coefficient of variation (c.o.v.) of either the catch, the recruited biomass, or the spawning biomass as the same function of the coefficient of variation of recruitment (s) and total mortality (Z) as:

$$c.o.v. = (2/3)s(Z)^{0.5} \quad . \tag{1}$$

Thus, if catch data are available for a period where Z is relatively constant and known, the c.o.v. of recruitment can be estimated, and the c.o.v. of the spawning stock biomass determined as a function of Z. With this latter relationship, confidence intervals of the relative spawning stock biomass can be computed as a function of F. In a number of instances it appears that annual recruitment and hence spawning stock biomass has a lognormal distribution, so the appropriate transformation must be applied to the variance of the spawning stock biomass before confidence intervals based on normal theory can be used.

This approach will be applied to estimate the lower bound of a 90% confidence interval of the relative spawning stock biomass for opakapaka when F is 0.5/year, age of entry to the fishery is 1.8 years, and age of sexual maturity is 3.25 years (the parameters that appear to represent the condition of the stock around the main islands in 1984 (Ralston and Kawamoto 1985)). The c.o.v. of the catch for the opakapaka fishery was estimated at 0.23 by using annual landings from just the main island catch for 1959 to 1970, when fishing effort was relatively constant. From Equation 1 with Z estimated to be 0.5 (M = F = 0.25) over the period 1959–1970 and the c.o.v. for opakapaka catch of 0.23, s is estimated to be 0.49. An estimate of the c.o.v. for opakapaka spawning stock biomass (SSB) is then estimated from Equation 1 as:

$$c.o.v. (SSB) = (0.49)(2/3)\sqrt{0.25 + F} \quad .$$

When the mean spawning stock biomass is at 10% of the unexploited spawning stock biomass (SSB_0), which corresponds to F = 0.5, Equation 1 becomes:

$$c.o.v.(SSB) = 0.28$$

or standard deviation (SSB) = 0.28 mean (SSB)

$$= 0.28 \ (0.1)(SSB_0)$$

$$= 0.028 \ SSB_0 \quad .$$

Thus, variance $\left(\dfrac{SSB}{SSB_0} \right) = 7.84 \times 10^{-4} \quad .$

A confidence interval for the relative spawning stock biomass can be obtained by transforming the lognormally distributed spawning stock biomass into a normally distributed variable. When the mean value for the spawning stock biomass is 10% of its unexploited value, the lower bound of the 90% confidence interval is 6% of its unexploited level. Thus, when recruitment variation is not considered, it is estimated that the spawning stock biomass of opakapaka around the main islands in 1984 was at about 10% of its unexploited level, but when variation in recruitment is taken into account, the relative spawning stock biomass could have been as low as 6%. It is interesting that the c.o.v. of recruitment for opakapaka estimated at 0.49 is slightly less than most of the estimates of the c.o.v. of recruitment for 18 temperate species that typically exceeded 0.6 (Hennemuth et al. 1980).

Beyond the conventional management approaches such as regulating the age of entry to the fishery and the fishing pressure, fishery enhancement may provide opportunities to increase yields of deepwater bottom fishes around Pacific islands. One approach to fishery enhancement in Hawaii has been the introduction of species groups that were underrepresented among the native fauna of the Hawaiian Islands, with the idea that these groups would fill a niche in the ecosystem and add to the total fishery yield. Between 1955 and 1961, 11 species of Serranidae, Lutjanidae, and Lethrinidae were introduced. Only three species have established significant populations: the grouper, Cephalopholis argus, and a snapper, Lutjanus fulvus, which only constitute a minor component of the commercial landings, and taape, Lutjanus kasmira, which has spread widely throughout the archipelago. The commercial catch of taape is 30 MT, and most probably would be considerably greater if market prices were higher (Oda and Parrish 1981). Although the introduction of taape appears to have increased the total yield of the bottom fish fishery and there does not appear to be a major dietary overlap between taape and any native species, some fishermen complain that it competes aggressively and successfully for fishing gear so that catches of more desirable native species are reduced (Oda and Parrish 1981).

Artificial reefs represent another fishery enhancement approach that may increase the production of deepwater bottom fishes. In Hawaii, many banks that support populations of snappers and groupers along their perimeters have flat, sandy tops in the 50 to 90 m depth range that support very low densities of fish. If the low densities of fish over the tops of these banks are a result of the lack of suitable habitat, and recruitment is not limiting, artificial reefs placed on these banks can offer appropriate habitat to support an increased standing stock and hence a yield of commercially valuable bottom fishes. The total area of habitat utilized by deepwater snappers and groupers in the Hawaiian Archipelago is about 2,000 nmi^2. Penguin Bank alone offers an area of 500 nmi^2 of level, sandy habitat which currently supports only a very low density of commercially valuable fishes. If appropriate habitat is a limiting factor, artificial reefs placed on Penguin Bank alone can increase the productive bottom fish habitat in the State by 25%.

NOTES

1. Data on file with Western Pacific Fishery Information Network, Southwest Fisheries Center Honolulu Laboratory, National Marine Fisheries Service, NOAA, Honolulu, HI 96822-2396.

2. Data from Western Pacific Regional Fishery Management Council.

BIBLIOGRAPHY

Bannerot, S. P. 1984. The dynamics of exploited groupers (Serranidae): An investigation of the protogynous hermaphroditic reproductive strategy. Ph.D Dissertation, Univ. Miami, Coral Gables, 393 p.

Beddington, J. R., and J. G. Cooke. 1983. The potential yield of fish stocks. FAO Fish. Tech. Pap. 242, 47 p.

Beverton, R. J., and S. J. Holt. 1956. A review of methods for estimating mortality rates in fish populations, with special reference to sources or

bias in catch sampling. Rapp. P.-V. Reun. Cons. Int.
Explor. Mer 140:67-83.

_____. 1966. Manual of methods for fish stock
assessment. Part 2. Tables of yield functions. FAO
Fish. Tech. Pap. 38, Rev. 1, 67 p.

Brouard, F., and R. Grandperrin. 1984. Les poissons
profonds de la pente recificale externe a Vanuatu.
Mission ORSTOM, Vanuatu, Notes Doc. Oceanogr. 11,
131 p.

Csirke, J., and J. F. Caddy. 1983. Production modeling
using mortality estimate. Can. J. Fish. Aquat. Sci.
40:43-51.

Grimes, C. B. 1986. Reproductive biology of the Lutjanidae: A review. In J. J. Polovina and S. Ralston
(editors), Tropical snappers and groupers: Biology
and fisheries management. Westview Press, Inc.,
Boulder. [See this volume.]

Gulland, J. A. 1969. Manual of methods for fish stock
assessment. Part 1. Fish populations analysis. FAO
Fish. Tech. Pap. 38, Rev. 1, 67 p.

_____. 1983. Fish stock assessment. A manual of
basic methods. John Wiley & Sons, N.Y., 223 p.

_____. 1984. Advice on target fishery rates.
Fishbyte [ICLARM] 2(1):8-11.

Hennemuth, R. C., J. E. Palmer, and B. E. Brown. 1980. A
statistical description of recruitment in eighteen
selected fish stocks. J. Northwest Atl. Fish. Sci.
1:101-111.

Huntsman, G. R., and J. R. Waters. 1986. Development of
management plans for reef fishes—Gulf of Mexico and
U.S. South Atlantic. In J. J. Polovina and S.
Ralston (editors), Tropical snappers and groupers:
Biology and fisheries management. Westview Press,
Inc., Boulder. [See this volume.]

Ikehara, I. I., H. T. Kami, and R. K. Sakamoto. 1970.
Exploratory fishing survey of the inshore fisheries
resources of Guam. In Proc. 2d CSK Symp., p. 425-
437, Tokyo.

Munro, J. L. 1983a. A cost-effective data acquisition
system for assessment and management of tropical
multitispecies multi-gear fisheries. Fishbyte
[ICLARM] 1(1):7-11.

_____ (editor). 1983b. Caribbean coral reef fishery
resources. ICLARM Stud. Rev. 7, Manila, 276 p.

Oda, D. K., and J. D. Parrish. 1981. Ecology of commercial snappers and groupers introduced to Hawaiian
reefs. In E. D. Gomez, C. E. Birkeland, R. W.

Buddemeier, R. E. Johannes, J. A. Marsh, Jr., and R. T. Tsuda (editors), Proc. 4th Int. Coral Reef Symp., Manila 1:61-67.

Parrish, J. D. 1986. The trophic biology of snappers and groupers. In J. J. Polovina and S. Ralston (editors), Tropical snappers and groupers: Biology and fisheries management. Westview Press, Inc., Boulder. [See this volume.]

Pauly, D. 1983. Some simple methods for the assessment of tropical fish stocks. FAO Fish. Tech. Pap. N(234), 52 p.

Polovina, J. J. 1986. A variable catchability version of the Leslie model with application to an intensive fishery experiment on a multispecies stock. Fish. Bull., U.S. 84(2).

Polovina, J. J., and S. Ralston. In press. An approach to yield assessment for unexploited resources with application to the deep slope fishes of the Marianas. Fish. Bull., U.S.

Polovina, J. J., and R. C. Roush. 1982. Chartlets of selected fishing banks and pinnacles in the Mariana Archipelago. Southwest Fish. Cent. Honolulu Lab., Natl. Mar. Fish. Serv. NOAA, Honolulu, HI 96812, Admin. Rep. H-82-19, 15 p.

Pooley, S. G. 1986. Demand considerations in fisheries management—Hawaii's market for bottom fish. In J. J. Polovina and S. Ralston (editors), Tropical snappers and groupers: Biology and fisheries management. Westview Press, Inc., Boulder. [See this volume.]

Ralston, S. 1984. Biological constraints on production and related management issues in the Hawaiian deepsea handline fishery. In R. W. Grigg and K. Y. Tanoue, (editors), Proceedings of the Second Symposium on Resource Investigations in the Northwestern Hawaiian Islands, Vol. 1, May 25-27, 1983, University of Hawaii, Honolulu, p. 248-264. UNIHI-SEAGRANT-MR-84-01.

_____. 1986. Mortality rates of snappers and groupers. In J. J. Polovina and S. Ralston (editors), Tropical snappers and groupers: Biology and fisheries management. Westview Press, Inc., Boulder. [See this volume.]

Ralston, S., R. M. Gooding, and G. M. Ludwig. In press. An ecological survey and comparison of bottom fish resource assessments (submersible versus handline fishing) at Johnston Atoll. Fish. Bull., U.S.

Ralston, S., and K. Kawamoto. 1985. A preliminary analysis of the 1984 size structure of Hawaii's commercial opakapaka landings and a consideration of age at entry and yield per recruit. Southwest Fish. Cent. Honolulu Lab., Natl. Mar. Fish. Serv., NOAA, Honolulu, HI 96812, Admin. Rep. H-85-1, 9 p. .

Ralston, S., and J. J. Polovina. 1982. A multispecies analysis of the commercial deep-sea handline fishery in Hawaii. Fish. Bull., U.S. 80:435-448.

Ralston, S., and H. A. Williams. Unpub. Age, growth, and mortality of lutjanid and other deep slope fishes from the Mariana Archipelago. Southwest Fish. Cent. Honolulu Lab., Natl. Mar. Fish. Serv., NOAA, Honolulu, HI 96822-2396.

Sainsbury, K. J. 1986. Assessment and management of the demersal fishery on the continental shelf of north-western Australia. In J. J. Polovina and S. Ralston (editors), Tropical snappers and groupers: Biology and fisheries management. Westview Press, Inc., Boulder. [See this volume.]

Wetherall, J. A., J. J. Polovina, and S. Ralston. In press. Estimating growth and mortality in steady state fish stocks from length-frequency data. In D. Pauly and G. R. Morgan (editors), Length-based methods in fishery research. The ICLARM/KISR Conference on the Theory and Application of Length-Based Methods for Stock Assessment, Sicily, Italy, 11-16 February 1985. Vol. 1.

12
Development of Management Plans for Reef Fishes--
Gulf of Mexico and U.S. South Atlantic

Gene R. Huntsman and James R. Waters
Southeast Fisheries Center Beaufort Laboratory
National Marine Fisheries Service, NOAA
Beaufort, North Carolina 28516

ABSTRACT

After a brief overview of the reef fisheries
of the southeastern United States, the chapter
describes the problems faced by the South Atlantic
and Gulf of Mexico Fishery Management Councils
(Council) in developing snapper-grouper management
plans for the two regions. While a principal
feature of both plans is the use of size limits to
increase yield per recruit, special concerns of each
Council required development of new models. For the
South Atlantic Council, a model predicting the time-
path of losses and gains in yield per recruit after
the establishment of a size limit allowed evaluation
of the annual mean net gain resulting from various
proposed size limits and objective selection and use
of only those limits whose long-term gains exceeded
a previously established criterion for a minimum
internal rate of return. For the Gulf Council,
concern about the effects of imperfect survival of
released undersized fish resulted in a modified
Beverton and Holt yield per recruit model incorporating mortality from catch and release. This new
model suggested that for red snapper a 330-mm (13-
inch) total length size limit would increase yield
per recruit if the probability of survival of
released fish were >0.6 if instantaneous natural
mortality (M) = 0.35, or >0.5 if M = 0.25. However,
as the probability of survival decreases, restrictions on fishing mortality are increasingly important to maintaining yield.

534

PREFACE

"But the sweet vision of the Holy Grail...the
phantom of a cup that comes and goes...and if a man
could touch or see it he was healed at once, by
faith, of all his ills"

Tennyson 1939

So might we describe the goal of those wide-eyed
innocents zealous for resource protection, armed with the
blood-tempered blade of stock assessment and mounted on
the frothing charger of the Magnuson Fishery Conservation
and Management Act of 1976, who set forth in the late
1970s to pursue the healing grail of management for
America's abused ocean fisheries. But the managers-
courageous quickly found that it was White's, not
Tennyson's, Arthurian saga that told their tale and that,
to their dismay, their quarry was not Percivale's
ephemeral grail but Pellinore's horrific Questing Beast
with "the head of a serpent, ah and the body of a libbard,
the haunches of a lion, and he is footed like a hart.
Wherever he goes he makes a noise in his belly as it had
been the noise of thirty couple of hounds questing...a
dreadful monster." And most especially our knights of
extended jurisdiction learned they shared poor Pellinore's
complaint that it "gets a bit lonely...following the beast
about and never knowing where one is" (White 1939).

INTRODUCTION

In this paper we trace the evolution of thought and
process in the establishment of management plans for reef
fish in the U.S. South Atlantic and Gulf of Mexico.
Although the fish, fisheries, environment, and obstacles
to plan development in the two areas were very similar,
there were two fishery management councils involved, and
each took a different path to management. Eventually both
councils adopted the same device for management, but the
rationales by which they decided whether or not to implement the device were markedly different. Both to record
for posterity the meanderings of management scheme development and to forewarn others of fruitless side paths, we
present this discourse based upon the recollections of

those closely associated with the plan development and upon various contemporary documents.

Upon passage of the Magnuson Fishery Conservation and Management Act of 1976, the newly established Gulf of Mexico and South Atlantic Councils (Councils) quickly identified their reef fisheries as requiring management plans. Given that reef fisheries of the southeast contribute a relatively small amount of weight (unknown but approximately 22,000-45,000 metric tons (MT) (50-100 million pounds) to the total U.S. catch, some might be surprised by the immediacy of the move toward management. But in the warm offshore waters of the Fishery Conservation Zone (FCZ) of the southeastern United States, relatively few fisheries are large and important enough to warrant attention by management agencies. Among those few, the reef fisheries were prominent. The impetus for management arose not so much from vigorously documented arguments about deterioration of the fishery as it did from commonly agreed upon perceptions of fishermen, scientists, and managers that fishing was poorer (at least in some areas), that major changes in the amount or kinds of fishing effort had recently taken or were about to take place, and that an allocation problem between recreational and commercial users could conceivably occur.

At the inception of management efforts, we apparently believed that a proactive plan was needed to protect a resource that gave evidence of fragility. At least in the Atlantic, probably the greatest evidence forcing the Council towards management measures was the history of reef fisheries elsewhere. Both in the Gulf of Mexico and on many insular shelves, it appeared that reef stocks were quickly depleted after initial large catches of old, large fish, and that subsequent catches were much smaller and, especially, that the fish taken later were much smaller. In the Atlantic there was hope that the harvest of the then new fisheries could be balanced to production so that the size of fish remained large. In the Gulf there was hope that a semblance of the original fishery could be created.

THE FISHERY SYSTEM

Given that reef fisheries in the southeastern continental United States extend from Cape Hatteras to Key West and around the Gulf of Mexico (with a small gap associated

with the discharge of the Mississippi River) to Mexico,
and that the continental shelf is sometimes as much as 167
km (100 mi) wide, it is understandable that reef habitat
types are numerous, that the overall fauna is complex, and
that the intensity and kinds of fishing vary widely.
Nonetheless we shall attempt a brief description of the
fisheries to furnish a context for our later discussions.
Throughout the discussion we hope, despite the great
variability, to reveal the overriding similarity of the
Gulf and South Atlantic regions.

Habitat Types

Three major kinds of natural reef systems exist in
the area. The most abundant, and probably most important
to fisheries, are the "live bottom" reefs which are scattered at depths of 20 to 100 m over the continental shelf
from Cape Hatteras, North Carolina to Ft. Pierce, Florida,
and from Naples, Florida westward around the Gulf of
Mexico (with a gap from Cape San Blas to Texas). Having
horizontal dimensions ranging from meters to kilometers,
live bottom reefs usually are associated with outcropped
sedimentary rocks, have relief ranging up to several
meters, and, are richly overgrown with macrobenthos:
sponges, sea fans, soft and diminutive hard corals, etc.
(Struhsaker 1969; Huntsman and Macintyre 1971; Wenner
1983). Live bottom reefs occupy approximately 57,000 km^2
in the Gulf and South Atlantic, an area three times that
occupied by the State of Hawaii land mass and about equal
to that of West Virginia (Parker et al. 1983). While the
distribution of live bottom reefs is approximately uniform
in the South Atlantic, that in the Gulf of Mexico is
heavily skewed. More than 37% of the west Florida shelf,
but only about 2% of the remaining Gulf shelf, is reef
(Parker et al. 1983).

True high-relief, hermatypic coral reefs become
common south of Jupiter, Florida and occupy most of the
narrow shelf south through the Florida Keys and Dry Tortugas. Hermatypic corals occur rarely outside southeast
Florida at such places as the Flower Gardens off Texas
(Bright and Pequegnat 1974) and occasionally on the
Carolina Shelf (Huntsman and Macintyre 1971), where
normally large species form stunted colonies seldom
exceeding 1 m in height. The third reef type, deep shelf
edge and shelf break reefs (Struhsaker 1969), occurs in a
narrow band from about 100 to 250 m of depth throughout

the region. Like live bottom, deep reefs are rock outcroppings overgrown with macrobenthos, but submergence at
greater depths where conditions are more uniform and
cooler has resulted in a distinct fauna remarkable for its
uniformity throughout the western Atlantic (Chester et al.
1984).

Of the three types of reef systems, live bottom
reefs, probably due to area alone, are the most significant producers of commercial and recreational catches of
reef fishes for the eastern United States and have
received the most attention from the Councils. Indeed, not
until relatively late in the planning process (September
1980) was jurisdiction over fisheries of most of the true
coral reefs, those in the Florida Keys, conditionally
granted to the South Atlantic Council by a proposed NOAA
rule based on a previous Supreme Court decision. Because
of the numerous problems associated with the Keys' reefs
that result both from biological complexity and intense
use by the large south Florida population, we believe that
the court case winners may actually have been the losers,
headache-wise. Nonetheless, ambiguity of jurisdiction,
among other reasons, resulted in less attention to true
coral reefs than to other types. Deep reefs also received
more attention late in the planning process as fishermen,
in about 1980, began intense exploitation of the shelf
edge fauna for the first time. Bottom longlining, though
successful for Nelson and Carpenter (1968) as early as
1967, was not adopted widely until transplanted New Jersey
longline fishermen introduced with great success the techniques of tilefishing to Gulf waters. Subsequently bottom
longlining on deep reefs was introduced to the South
Atlantic in about 1982.

Finally artificial reefs have importance in the
southeastern United States as nowhere else in the country.
While the area of such reefs in the Atlantic is insignifi-
cant, there are over 3,000 offshore platforms (Ditton and
Falk 1981) associated with petroleum development in the
Gulf of Mexico. Platforms support a specialized portion
of the live bottom fauna and are immensely important to
both recreational and commercial fisheries.

Ichthyofauna

As there are three reef types, there are three
distinct faunas: (1) one associated with live bottom and
platforms, which has been subdivided into several communi-

ties (Miller and Richards 1980; Grimes et al. 1982; Chester et al. 1984); (2) one associated with deep reefs (Chester et al. 1984); and (3) one characteristic of true coral reefs (Starck 1968; Gilbert 1972). Four families and nine genera of fishes, Lutjanidae (Lutjanus, Rhomboplites, and Ocyurus), Serranidae (Mycteroperca and Epinephelus), Sparidae (Pagrus, Calamus, and Diplodus), and Haemulidae (Haemulon), are common to all three faunas and provide the bulk of the catch. Over 500 reef species are known from Florida's true coral reefs (Starck 1968) and over 300 from the live bottom reefs (Steven Ross Pers. com. North Carolina Division of Marine Fisheries, Moorehead City, NC 28557).

The availability and desirability of different species vary by region. Unquestionably red snapper (L. campechanus, and to a lesser extent, L. vivanus and L. buccanella) are the most popular species region-wide. Red snapper are distributed throughout the live bottom reef region, but they are dependably abundant only in the Gulf of Mexico west of Cape San Blas and the Cape Canaveral area of the South Atlantic. Nonetheless, headboat fishing from Cape Canaveral to Cape Hatteras is advertised as red snapper fishing. The relative scarcity of L. campechanus to the north is obviated by the abundance of large vermilion snapper, Rhomboplites aurorubens, which, in truth, are red (colored) snapper.

The most important groupers of live bottom reefs are gag, Mycteroperca microlepis, and scamp, M. phenax, and to a lesser extent speckled hind, Epinephelus drummondhayi, in the Atlantic, and red grouper, E. morio, in the Cape Canaveral area and off Florida's west coast. White grunt, Haemulon plumieri, are abundant on live bottom reefs from Cape Hatteras to Georgia and locally in the Gulf of Mexico, and red porgy, Pagrus pagrus, is the most important species in headboat catches in the Atlantic north of Florida. The red porgy is also common locally in the Gulf of Mexico, as on Florida's Middle Grounds (Smith 1976), but it is not a major component of the catch and is perhaps replaced in the environment in part by red snapper. At seasonally cooled, shallow (40-60 m) inshore reefs of the South Atlantic from Cape Hatteras to St. Augustine and off the northeastern Gulf of Mexico, black sea bass, Centropristis striata, is abundant and allows large catches.

The true coral region of southeast Florida produces diverse catches. Prominent in the catch are yellowtail snapper, Ocyurus chrysurus, mutton snapper, L. analis, lane snapper, L. synagris, red, vermilion, and other snappers, groupers including gag, scamp, red grouper, and black grouper, M. bonaci, rock and red hinds, E. adscensionis and E. guttatus, and Nassau grouper, E. striatus, as well as porgies, Calamus calamus and C. nodosus, grunts, Haemulon plumieri, H. album, H. sciurus, and others, and the large wrasse, Lachnolaimus maximus (hogfish).

Deep reefs of the region produce mostly groupers including snowy, E. niveatus, yellowedge, E. flavolimbatus, and Warsaw, E. nigritus, and a few snappers, especially silk snapper and very large red snapper. Tilefishes, Caulolatilus spp. (100-200 m) and Lopholatilus chamaeleonticeps (>200 m), occur at the deepest extent of grouper distribution.

Fisheries

Fishing practices vary little with region, habitat, or species. In the Atlantic and probably the Gulf, most of the commercial catch results from hook-and-line fishing with powered reels. Bottom longlining, as described earlier, is increasingly popular for deep reef fishing and produces most of the grouper from the Gulf of Mexico. Trawling with roller gear and "high rise" trawls (Ulrich et al. 1976) is sporadically attempted and produces some large catches in the South Atlantic north of Cape Canaveral. Finally, traps are very popular in the FCZ of the Atlantic and were used on reefs under state jurisdiction in southeast Florida before being banned in 1980. Sea basses and occasionally other reef fishes are trapped off southeast Florida. Some reef fish trapping occurs in the eastern Gulf of Mexico and a little off Texas.

The recreational catch, most of which is made with hook and line, is made from both private vessels and from those for hire. Headboats, usually carrying 20 or more passengers each of whom has paid separately, are popular throughout the region and allow virtually all of the recreational catch in the Atlantic north of Florida. There are about 100 headboats in the South Atlantic and 80 in the Gulf of Mexico. In Florida and through the Gulf of Mexico, private vessels, usually 7 to 10 m in length, allow a large but undetermined amount of reef fishing. Finally, charter vessels, those for hire at a daily rate and usually carrying six passengers or less, contribute a small and varying fraction of the reef fish catch.

The history of development of fisheries in the South Atlantic is very different from that in the Gulf. In the Gulf the snapper fishery, begun by relocated New England schooner and dory fishermen in the late 1800s (Camber 1955; Carpenter 1965), was first a commercial fishery; and recreational fishing did not begin until well into the 20th century. Conversely, in the South Atlantic north of Florida, the commercial snapper fishery is a modern development that began in earnest in the late 1970s. Recreational reef fishing has occurred in the area since the 1920s and was substantially developed by the early 1960s or sooner (Huntsman 1976a).

Obstacles to Management

As the two Councils shared, on the whole, similar habitats, faunas, and fisheries, so they also shared many of the same obstacles to achieving fishery management plans for reef fish. The foremost obstacle was lack of vital information. Fishery statistics were lacking or uninterpretable. Ostensible records of commercial catches for each area were fraught with flaws. Foremost among these was that the records presented location of landings rather than location of fishing. Thus catches made by the wide-ranging snapper fleet could not be attributed to the source waters. Landings accorded to Gulf ports came from the South Atlantic, Bahamas, northern South America, and, especially, Mexico's Campeche Banks; and apportionment of the catch to these areas was imprecise. In the South Atlantic, landings included fish from the Bahamas and elsewhere, but worse, some of the South Atlantic catch was attributed to Gulf ports because either vessels returned to the Gulf coast to unload or, commonly, fish were trucked to Gulf packing houses without recognition at the Atlantic port. In southeast Florida, a major fraction of the commercial catch is believed to be delivered directly to restaurants without establishment of a record.

A second major flaw was that species separations were either lacking, improper, or irregularly applied. For instance, in the Atlantic the category "red snapper" included, red, blackfin, and silk snapper, and depending on the year, may or may not have included vermilion snapper. In both the Atlantic and Gulf, the category "grouper" included over a dozen species of two genera.

Information on recreational catches was either totally lacking or so fragmented that it was useless. In the Atlantic, the South Atlantic Headboat Survey (Huntsman 1976b) created a measure of catch by species that reasonably estimated the total recreational catch for the Carolinas and Georgia, where few private boats were used for reef fishery. But in Florida, small private vessels are numerous in the reef fishery and produce an unrecorded but apparently large catch. There was no useful measure of the recreational catch in the Gulf.

The National Marine Recreational Fisheries Survey ([U.S.] Department of Commerce 1984), designed to allow reliable estimates of the catch of those species providing greater than 3% of the catch, was not useful for measuring reef fish catches, which even in aggregate are <3% of the total marine recreational fish catch.

As there were no fishery-dependent data upon which to base stock assessments, neither were there fishery-independent data. The distribution and abundance of various reef species are still imprecisely known. At least at the beginning of the planning process, life history research, especially growth, of South Atlantic and Gulf reef species was limited to three works, one of which was suspect (Moe 1969; Starck and Schroeder 1970; Manooch and Huntsman 1977). Fortunately, planning lasted long enough that numerous major works (Manooch 1986), especially on growth, were completed in time to support the management effort. Other than those provided by the headboat survey, few data on the size distribution of reef fishes existed. Only in the last year (1984) has a region-wide program to provide information on sizes of reef fishes in the commercial catch begun.

Little information on fishing effort existed. The South Atlantic headboat survey provided some information on recreational effort, and the commercial fisheries statistics program of the National Marine Fisheries Service, NOAA annually recorded the number of operating units for various vessel types.

Finally, almost no information on the economic and social aspects of the Atlantic and Gulf reef fisheries existed.

Thus the two Fishery Management Councils faced an awesome task—no doubt similar to the tasks of councils elsewhere—of attempting to prevent and manage problems in regionally important fisheries without access to the basic information needed to define those problems or the pathways to their solutions.

THE MECHANISM OF PLAN DEVELOPMENT

Despite the similarities of the resources and problems to be solved, the Gulf and South Atlantic Councils from the beginning chose divergent approaches to formulating management plans. Because of a large workload and small staff, the Gulf of Mexico Council contracted development of their first draft plant to an outside party, the Florida Sea Grant system; the Gulf plan was formulated by a team drawn almost entirely from the state university system of Florida. The South Atlantic Council chose to formulate the plan using a team headed by a staff member and consisting of State representatives and specialists from many sources. These teams, in turn, chose to define the manageable resource in different ways. The Gulf team, believing that life history information and catch data on most reef fishes were too sparse to be useful, included only 33 species, almost all of which were snappers and groupers. The South Atlantic team, however, believing that reef fishes of many families were important to the catch and to the functioning of the ecological system supporting the catch, and forced to cope with the species-rich south Florida fauna, included for management 69 species of 8 families.

Later versions of the Gulf plan document co-ccurrence of 17 other species of 7 families in the fishery and suggest the eventual admission of these to the management unit. Ironically, the Gulf Council document, focused on snappers and groupers, is entitled a reef fish resources plan, while the multispecies, multifamily treatment of the South Atlantic is labeled a snapper-grouper plan.

Faced with an apparent legal requirement for numerical estimates of the maximum sustainable yield (MSY) in their plans, the teams took virtually polar positions. The Gulf group, although recognizing the many flaws in the purported catch and effort data, provided MSY estimates through use of logistic, or surplus yield, models. To the best of their ability the team adjusted the catch and effort information to account for such major deficiencies as missing data on the recreational fishery, contributions to the catch from foreign waters, and very imprecise measurement of effort. Not all observers believe that such major flaws in the catch and effort data were obviated. Actually, logistic models constructed (no doubt in part from desperation) for aggregates of many species (i.e., all snappers, all groupers, all reef fish) may be more useful than originally suspected. Ralston's (1981) investigation of the use of logistic models for Hawaiian reef fisheries revealed that the best fits were obtained for models applied to community assemblages of species.

The Gulf team wisely did not attempt to draw detailed conclusions from their models, but did conclude that there was overfishing on those nearshore Gulf waters where both commercial and recreational fishing were intense. In offshore waters, harvest was believed to be approaching the MSY level. Recently Matheson and Huntsman (1984) have reported a similar situation in the Atlantic. From their observations the Gulf team derived the concept of a "stressed area" for which special restrictions would apply.

The South Atlantic team, eschewing the mathematical legerdemain necessary to produce MSY estimates with suspect data and perhaps inappropriate models, first attempted an unorthodox estimate and then wisely chose not to commit themselves to a numerical estimate of the MSY. Following a suggestion by researchers at the Southeast Fisheries Center Beaufort Laboratory (Huntsman et al. 1983), the team recognized a single general pattern of yield-per-recruit models for many reef species. (Many such models and the growth data on which they depended had become available since organization of the team.) This pattern indicated that there are numerous combinations of fishing effort and recruitment ages for reef species that produce a high percentage of the maximally available yield per recruit. Because commercial reef fisheries over much of the South Atlantic FCZ at that time (approximately 1978) were in the early stages of development, the team believed that most species were being recruited at the moderate ages needed but were enduring sufficient fishing mortality to produce near-maximum yield per recruit. And, further, because landings had not evidenced great annual fluctuations indicating highly variable recruitment, and because the contemporary literature of reef fishes (e.g., Erlich 1975) suggested reef fishery production was limited by habitat rather than recruitment, the team proposed that the current catch was near the maximal yield per recruit and that current catches estimated the MSY. Thus the perplexing problem of how to estimate MSY was resolved without having a series of valid catch and effort measurements. As a team member, Huntsman now realizes that the team should have been content at that stage. But, glowing with the optimism of all conquerors, the team surged into the quivering mire of catch statistics, and escape was not to come for some time.

The South Atlantic team proposed that if the then-current catches approximated MSY, then all that was necessary in order to know the MSY was to decide what that catch was. Of course, determining those catches had been and continues to be one of the greatest challenges facing both Councils. But the blood was hot, and the team proposed that not only could it estimate catches (including those elusive recreational values), but that it could also subdivide them into various geographical and water depth-fish community compartments and provide the Council with tidy quotas with which to regulate the fishery.

The South Atlantic Council, understandably reluctant to undertake effort restrictions, viewed the quota proposal as the only viable solution to the problem of maintaining the fishery. The team dove aggressively into the computation of quotas. The inshore fishery was divided into several latitudinal strata, some of which cleaved Florida waters. Records of landings by county were reviewed as the team attempted to sort out who caught what and where, and to translate the information into area quotas. But soon (and not as soon as they should have) several truths began to assert themselves: (1) that fishery statistics that were unusable at first were still unusable; (2) that recreational catches were still (as now) largely a mystery; and (3) that the fishery statistics system in existence at that time was the same as that which had created the useless statistics of former years. Thus, even if quotas could have been calculated and enacted, there was no immediate hope that the Council would be able to tell when the quota was attained. Fortunately, the pursuit of quotas had redemptive value, for the team had been introduced to yield-per-recruit models. It was another ready application of these, size limits, which was selected as the preferred management measure. The apparent utility and easy and democratic applicability of size limits led to their inclusion as a principal management tool in the approved plan. An appealing feature of minimum size limits, as revealed by the yield-per-recruit models, was that they would allow maintaining a high total annual yield despite great effort increases, if, as believed, recruitment remained sufficient and survival of released, undersized fish was high.

Virtually simultaneously, Connor Davis of the Gulf of Mexico Council staff began investigation of the usefulness of yield-per-recruit models and concluded that appreciable increases in yield per recruit of red snapper, the species of greatest concern, would result from a size limit. So after months of Mosaic trek through the wilderness of reef fishery stock assessment, the two teams finally converged at the oasis of size limits.

Convergence was only temporary, however, for the two groups had decidedly different opinions of what were the major problems of implementation of size limits. For the South Atlantic Council, the principal problem was estimating and evaluating the duration and magnitude of reduced catches resulting from initiation of size limits. The Gulf Council, in response to concern of its constituents and a threat of litigation, had explicit interest in the effect of imperfect survival of released, undersized fish on yield per recruit. The South Atlantic Council recognized the latter problem but accorded it secondary importance, while the Gulf Council did not address the question of reduced catches at all. Working to support both groups, we were required to provide two different kinds of analyses of the impacts of instituting size limits. It is these analyses that we will discuss in the remainder of this paper.

ANALYSES FOR THE SOUTH ATLANTIC COUNCIL

The South Atlantic Council's concern about reduced catch was justified because a size limit protects young fish that otherwise would have been caught and landed. Therefore, catches initially decline because fewer young fish are caught and catches of older fish remain relatively unchanged. Over time, catches gradually increase as the minimum size limit allows greater numbers of young fish to survive and be caught in future years as older and heavier fish (Figure 12.1).

The South Atlantic team first simplistically attempted to discern the magnitude of catch reduction by examining length frequencies from headboat catches to see what fraction of the contemporary catch would be excluded by various size limits, but soon realized that a more dynamic approach, based on modeling, would be necessary. Waters (Unpub.) created a model that estimated the change in yield per recruit (and catch in a steady state fishery) with time and allowed easy prediction of: (1) the initial reduction in yield per recruit; (2) the time until return to the initial yield per recruit; (3) the potential gain in annual yield per recruit; (4) the time until initial losses were replaced by gains resulting from the size limits; and (5) the time until yield per recruit

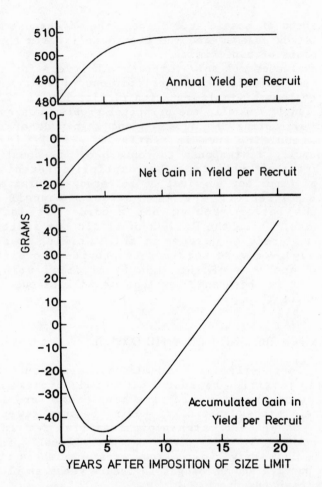

Figure 12.1   Predicted change in yield per
recruit after imposition of a 30.5 cm (12-inch)
(total length) size limit on red snapper in the
South Atlantic

stabilized.   This information was provided by a simple
model that calculated the theoretical transition between
population equilibria following adoption of a size limit
(Appendix A).   All of the estimates depended on the
initial state of the fishery, especially the first age or
size of entry of fish into the catch, and fishing
mortality rate, as well as life history parameters of the
species including growth coefficients and the natural
mortality rate.

While the biological model was of itself a powerful tool, Waters, an economist, further enhanced it by incorporating the internal rate of return as a statistic for evaluating the potential gain in yield per recruit against a discount rate. Using the common argument of economists that gains to be obtained in the future are worth less (by the chosen discount rate) than an equivalent gain obtained sooner, the discount rate analysis provided a useful tool to the South Atlantic Council for objectively deciding whether the gains provided by a size limit were worth the initial short-term losses.

The internal rate of return (IRR) is the average annual growth in yield per recruit as calculated from the time path of gains and losses in yield per recruit. Equation 1 evaluates the time sequence of net changes, ΔYPR_t, in yield per recruit and is solved iteratively for the IRR:

$$\sum_{t=1}^{T} \Delta YPR_t \, (1 + IRR)^{-t} = 0 \; . \tag{1}$$

The IRR does not have intrinsic properties allowing evaluation of a size limit. Instead, the IRR must be compared to some standard. The South Atlantic Council decided that for a size limit to be worthwhile it must exhibit an IRR of at least 3%, a value often used to discount future returns on investments of public resources. The Council established that the IRR should be determined over a period lasting from inception of the size limit to 20 years, or until the annual yield per recruit stabilized, whichever was longer. Evaluation over longer periods would increase the IRR, while shorter time periods would decrease it.

The magnitude of a size limit and resultant IRR are inversely related because the proportional growth in weight declines as fish mature. Consequently small size limits, which protect only younger, faster growing fish, usually produce a high IRR, while larger size limits protect additional older fish with lower growth rates. Hence, the average growth rate of all protected fish and the IRR are smaller with larger size limits. Attempts to maximize the IRR would lead to the choice of small size limits that do not protect older, relatively slower growing fish. A better procedure is to choose the largest size limit that yields an IRR greater than the predetermined minimally acceptable level, provided that the

548

resulting size limit does not exceed that necessary to maximize yield per recruit. In general, our analyses recommended the size limits that maximized yield per recruit.

An extremely important factor affecting the success of a size limit in increasing yields is the degree of survival of undersized fish that are taken and released. Imperfect survival of released fish reduces the expected increase in yield per recruit and the IRR resulting from any size limit. The Waters algorithm allows easy incorporation of rates of survival (Appendix A). When the Council had estimates of survival rates from experimentation, these were used; but for species lacking other estimates, 60% was used.

Through establishment of standards (e.g., 3% IRR and minimum survival rate of 60%) and use of innovative models, the South Atlantic Council mechanized the decision process about implementation of the management measure, size limits. These mechanized decisions by and large could be completed by their staff in a nonpolitical and nonemotional environment. Eventually the Council evaluated size limits for 17 species from 4 families and choose to implement 5 size limits, for: black sea bass, red grouper, Nassau grouper, red snapper, and yellowtail snapper; and 1 trawl mesh size limit for vermilion snapper.

However, some fishermen and biologists believed that more, and more restrictive, size limits were needed. Both the data and the process used to measure the benefits could have resulted in disapproval of some proposed limits, or imposition of limits substantially smaller than those required for maximization of yield per recruit. Determination of the value of a size limit depended upon accurate knowledge of the contemporary state of the fishery. If extant fishing mortality or growth rates were understated, or if natural mortality rate, mortality at release, or recruitment age were overstated, estimated increased yields from proposed size limits would be underestimated. Estimates of the independent variables better than the ones used might have resulted in approval of more, and more stringent, size limits. In addition, attempts to maximize the IRR would lead to the choice of small size limits that do not protect older, relatively slower-growing fishes. And, certainly, use of a study period that is less than infinitely long could, in some instances, lead to the choice of size limits smaller than those needed to maximize yield per recruit.

ANALYSES FOR THE GULF COUNCIL

Rather than concern about short-term losses, the Gulf
Council had far more explicit interest in the effect of
imperfect survival of released, undersized fish on yield
per recruit. This interest sponsored two research efforts
by the Southeast Fisheries Center. The first was field
experimentation to estimate the actual survival rate of
released red snapper. The second, of greater consequence
to our discussion, was the development of a yield-per-
recruit model incorporating incomplete survival of
released fish but allowing the generation of yield isopleths. The model used by the South Atlantic team, while
incorporating and combining the concepts of yield per
recruit and imperfect survival of released fish, generates
solutions in response to only one value of each of the
independent variables (fishing mortality and recruitment
age) at a time. Generation of yield isopleths with this
model is cumbersome and requires repetitive computations
using different independent variables. The model used for
the Gulf Council introduced the probability of survival of
released fish into the traditional Beverton and Holt
(1957) yield-per-recruit model and allows easy examination
of the interaction of age at recruitment to the gear, age
at the size limit, and fishing mortality rate with a
single survival rate of released fish (Waters and Huntsman
In press). Computation of the model is necessary for each
survival rate of interest and, as in the original Beverton
and Holt model, for each estimate of natural mortality
rate and growth parameters.

The essential feature of the model is a new age
parameter, t_m, corresponding to the age at the proposed
minimum legal size (Appendix B). The fishing mortality
coefficient for fish between the age at first capture, t_c,
and age t_m is $F (1 - P_s)$ where P_s is the probability of
survival of a released fish. At ages greater than t_m,
fish experience the full fishing mortality, F. The
instantaneous rates of change in population numbers,
dN/dt, are defined as follows:

$$\frac{dN}{dt} = - MN \qquad\qquad t < t_c$$

$$\frac{dN}{dt} = - (M + F(1 - P_s))N \qquad t_c \leq t < t_m$$

$$\frac{dN}{dt} = - (M + F)N \qquad\qquad t_m \leq t$$

The use of an unmodified Beverton and Holt model implies
that $P_S = 1.0$ and that $F = 0$ until age is greater than t_m.
The possibility that released fish may not survive merely
reduces the number of recruits remaining in the population
at age t_m. Therefore, the coefficient $F(1-P_S)$ overstates
catch and release mortality if fish congregate by size as
red snapper do, and fishermen minimize the capture of
undersized fish by avoiding those areas. By specifying
that undersized fish are caught at the same time as those
without a size limit, we either correctly estimate or
underestimate the potential gains in yield per recruit.
We assumed that fishermen release all undersized fish.

Application of the model for red snapper and several
other reef fishes from the Gulf of Mexico revealed that
the shape of yield isopleths changed markedly as the
probability of survival of released fish decreased (Figures 12.2 and 12.3). In the traditional yield-per-recruit
model (where, by definition, $P_S = 1$), the yields become

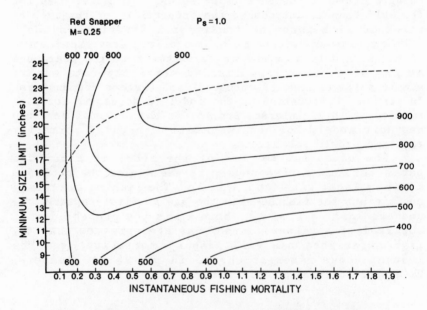

Figure 12.2 Beverton and Holt (1957) yield-per-
recruit model for red snapper in the Gulf of
Mexico with the rate of survival of released,
undersized fish equal to 1.0. Dotted line
indicates maximum yield per recruit for each
fishing mortality coefficient

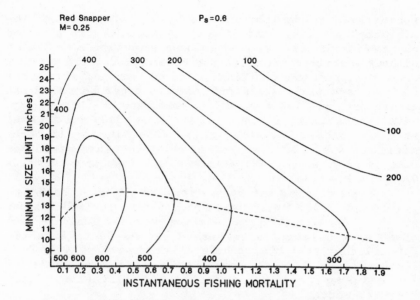

Figure 12.3   Beverton and Holt (1957) yield-per-
recruit model for red snapper in the Gulf of
Mexico with the rate of survival of released,
undersized fish equal to 0.6.   Dotted line
indicates maximum yield per recruit for each
fishing mortality coefficient

approximately constant for any given recruitment age, and
the upper and lower limbs of any isopleth are approximately parallel at F greater than about 0.3. But in the
model with imperfect survival (P_S <1), isopleths are
closed loop contours with a maximum yield per recruit that
shifts toward the origin as P_S declines.   Our result
corroborates the common sense notion that catch and
release mortality reduces the potential effectiveness of
any minimum size limit, especially when the probability of
survival, P_S, is low and when many undersized fish are
caught and released (i.e., when F and ($t_m - t_c$) are large).
     Management implications of the models with imperfect
survival include the ideas that size limits can be of
value in increasing yield per recruit despite fairly great
mortality (P_S is greater than about 0.6) of released fish,
but that if high levels of mortality are expected, the
management body must limit fishing mortality to maintain
yields because size limits alone are not effective.   If
there is a great deal of time between the age at first

recruitment to the gear and the age of attainment of the minimum legal size, and if fishing mortality is high and probability of survival upon release low, then size limits without effort restrictions are counterproductive.

To support the Gulf Council's one proposed size limit (for red snapper), we calculated yield per recruit with growth data published by Nelson and Manooch (1982), survival probabilities ranging from 0.2 to 1.0, and several natural mortality coefficients. The 330-mm (13-inch) minimum size limit is predicted to increase yield per recruit if P_S exceeds 0.5 when $M = 0.25$, and if P_S exceeds 0.6 when $M = 0.35$.

Interestingly, the suggestion that P_S must be 0.6 or greater for a 330-mm limit to be of value for red snapper (if $M = 0.35$) exactly parallels the standard (used in lieu of other knowledge) established by the South Atlantic Council that size limits be evaluated at $P_S = 0.6$. Preliminary field work suggests that P_S is approximately 0.8 for red snapper in 90 m depths off Galveston, Texas (Parker Unpub.).

CONCLUSION

Having begun with similar resources and problems, the planning of the two Councils diverged then reconverged on the same management strategy, increasing yield per recruit through minimum size limits. The strategy was especially appropriate to reef fishes for at least two reasons. First, there had been no evidence of recruitment overfishing. Small fish seemed to remain abundant even where heavy fishing had removed the large individuals. Second, yield-per-recruit management is especially appropriate to animals like reef fishes (or shellfish), which become essentially permanent residents of a site after initial recruitment. The site-specific populations do not necessarily reproduce themselves, and managers only need to maximize the harvest from those populations. It appears the site residency of reef fishes would allow convenient geographic subdivision of the resource with different management in each subdivision.

It is our opinion that size limits that maximize yield per recruit for gonochoristic (bisexual) species would probably allow continued adequate reproduction of that species regardless of fishing mortality if release-related mortality is low. Protection of reproduction occurs because the size limit that maximizes yield per recruit appears mathematically related to the downward inflection of the von Bertalanffy growth curve. The inflection usually occurs at the initial age of sexual maturity when the fish's energy is partially diverted from somatic growth to reproduction. Thus, size limits that maximize yield per recruit usually allow attainment of sexual maturity.

Size limits for those species with relatively small P_S, and for the protogynous species (apparently all groupers and some porgies), may not allow adequate reproduction if fishing mortality becomes very high. Small size limits, most desirable for species with low P_S and high fishing mortality, would result in killing a large fraction of the population before they spawned. Similarly, high fishing mortality imposed on protogynous species, even with a relatively great minimum size limit, might still allow an insufficient number of fish to become males to provide adequate spawning and recruitment. In a model of the interaction of fishing and protogyny, for the graysby, Epinepheulus cruentatus, the size limit which maximized yield per recruit allowed the protogynous population to produce the same number of fertilized eggs as a gonochoristic population experiencing the same fishing mortality (Huntsman and Schaaf Unpub.). Fortunately, the Gulf Council has acted to establish a framework for a bag limit if restriction of fishing mortality appears necessary, and the South Atlantic Council considered area closures and quotas to accomplish the same purpose. Thus, both Councils are aware that minimum sizes alone may not protect yield.

Certainly, experimentation with size limits for reef fishes in the southeastern United States is not over. The South Atlantic Council established in its plan a team to monitor the fishery and to evaluate species for application of size limits if growth overfishing appears imminent, and the Gulf Council established a framework for adding and changing minimum sizes by plan amendment.

The results of the present size limits (instituted in the Atlantic in September 1983 and in the Gulf in November 1984) cannot yet be determined. Certainly these results, or the lack thereof, will result in adjustments of the present limits. Moreover, we expect even greater use of size limits as information improves on growth and mortality of reef species, and as fishing continues to intensify on Gulf and South Atlantic reefs.

Although size limits are readily applied and seem especially appropriate to reef fishery management, we are aware of a major conceptual flaw in their present use. The flaw is that size limits are currently developed for a single species at a time. Although the growth and mortality data on which the limits are based represent the interaction of the single species with other fishes in its community, there is no guarantee that the aggregate result of imposing size limits simultaneously on several sympatric species will be the same as if the species were reacting completely independently. Indeed, the evidence available (Ralston 1981; Ogden 1982; Powers and Crow 1982) suggests that species interactions are likely and probably strong. Thus, current yield-per-recruit models may be only crude indicators of the true response of fish species in the wild.

In this discourse, we did not presume to tell the full tale of the reef fish management plans of the southeast United States. We have ignored issues like regulations on fish traps and on poisons and explosives that are at least politically important and well worth describing. But we wanted to focus on what we regard as the essence of the plans, the schemes for stock assessment, and on the principal management devices resulting from those assessments.

Our chase is not over, but we have sighted our quarry. It appears for now that both our grail and our beast are size limits. And while a size limit may not heal, by faith, all our fishery ills, it just might, like the Beast Glatisant, leave about some fewmets, droppings of the beast pursued by which we can tell "whether (the device) is a warrantable beast or otherwise, and what state it is in." And we leave you like Pellinore, and now us, to "carry fewmets (of reef fish management) about practically all the time. 'Insanitary habit', added the king" (White 1939).

BIBLIOGRAPHY

Beverton, R. J. H., and S. J. Holt. 1957. On the dynamics of exploited fish populations. Fish. Invest., Ser. II, Mar. Fish., G. B., Minist. Agric. Fish. Food 19:1-533.

Bright, T. J., and L. H. Pequegnat (editors). 1974. Biota of the West Flower Garden Bank. Gulf Publishing Co., Houston, 435 p.

Camber, C. I. 1955. A survey of the red snapper fishery of the Gulf of Mexico with special reference to the

Campeche Banks. Fla. Board Conserv. Mar. Res. Lab. Tech. Ser. 12, 61 p.

Carpenter, J. S. 1965. A review of the Gulf of Mexico red snapper fishery. U.S. Fish Wildl. Serv. Circ. 208, 35 p.

Chester, A. J., G. R. Huntsman, P. A. Tester, and C. S. Manooch, III. 1984. South Atlantic Bight reef fish communities as represented in hook-and-line catches. Bull. Mar. Sci. 34:267-279.

Ditton, R. B., and J. M. Falk. 1981. Obsolete petroleum platforms as artificial reef material. In D. Y. Aska (editor), Artificial reefs: Conference proceedings, p. 96-105. Fla. Sea Grant Coll. Rep. 141.

Erlich, P. L. 1975. The population biology of coral reef fishes. Annu. Rev. Ecol. Syst. 6:211-247.

Gilbert, C. R. 1972. Characteristics of the western Atlantic fish fauna. Q. J. Fla. Acad. Sci. 35:130-144.

Grimes, C. B., C. S. Manooch, III, and G. R. Huntsman. 1982. Reef and rock outcropping fishes of the outer continental shelf of North Carolina and South Carolina, and ecological notes on the red porgy and vermilion snapper. Bull. Mar. Sci. 32:277-289.

Huntsman, G. R. 1976a. Offshore bottom fisheries of the United States South Atlantic coast. In H. R. Bullis, Jr. and A. C. Jones (editors), Proceedings: Colloquium on snapper-grouper fishery resources of the western central Atlantic Ocean, p. 192-221. Texas A&M Univ. Sea Grant Coll. and Mississippi-Alabama Sea Grant Consortium. Fla. Sea Grant Coll. Rep. 17.

_____. 1976b. Offshore headboat fishing in North Carolina and South Carolina. Mar. Fish. Rev. 38(3):13-23.

Huntsman, G. R., and I. G. Macintyre. 1971. Tropical coral patches in Onslow Bay. Am. Littoral Soc. Spec. Publ. 7(2):32-34.

Huntsman, G. R., C. S. Manooch, III, and C. B. Grimes. 1983. Yield per recruit models of some reef fishes of the U.S. South Atlantic Bight. Fish. Bull., U.S. 81:679-695.

Huntsman, G. R., and W. E. Schaaf. Unpub. Interaction of fishing and protogyny for the graysby, Epinephelus cruentatus. Southeast Fish. Cent. Beaufort Lab., Natl. Mar. Fish. Serv., NOAA, Beaufort, NC 28516-9722.

Manooch, C. S., III. 1986. A review of age and growth of the Lutjanidae and Serranidae. In J. J. Polovina and S. Ralston (editors), Tropical snappers and groupers: Biology and fisheries management. Westview Press, Inc., Boulder. [See this volume.]

Manooch, C. S., III, and G. R. Huntsman. 1977. Age, growth, and mortality of the red porgy, Pagrus pagrus. Trans. Am. Fish. Soc. 106:26-33.

Matheson, R. H., III, and G. R. Huntsman. 1984. Growth, mortality, and yield-per-recruit models for speckled hind and snowy grouper from the United States South Atlantic Bight. Trans. Am. Fish. Soc. 113:607-616.

Miller, G. C., and W. J. Richards. 1980. Reef fish habitat, faunal assemblages, and factors determining distributions in the South Atlantic Bight. Proc. 32d Gulf Caribb. Fish. Inst. p. 114-130.

Moe, M. A., Jr. 1969. Biology of the red grouper Epinephelus morio (Valenciennes) from the eastern Gulf of Mexico. Fla. Dep. Nat. Resour., Mar. Res. Lab. Prof. Pap. Ser. 10:1-95.

Nelson, R. S., and C. S. Manooch, III. 1982. Growth and mortality of red snapper, Lutjanus campechanus, in the west central Atlantic and northern Gulf of Mexico. Trans. Am. Fish. Soc. 111:465-475.

Nelson, W. R., and J. S. Carpenter. 1968. Bottom longline explorations in the Gulf of Mexico. Commer. Fish. Rev. 30(8):57-62.

Ogden, J. C. 1982. Fisheries management and the structure of coral reef fish communities. In G. R. Huntsman, W. R. Nicholson, and W. W. Fox, Jr. (editors), The biological bases for reef fishery management, p. 147-159. U.S. Dep. Commer., NOAA Tech. Memo. NMFS, NOAA-TM-NMFS-SEFC-80.

Parker, R. O., Jr. Unpub. Survival of released red snapper. Southeast Fish. Cent. Beaufort Lab., Natl. Mar. Fish. Serv., NOAA, Beaufort, NC 28516-9722.

Parker, R. O., Jr., D. R. Colby, and T. D. Willis. 1983. Estimated amount of reef habitat on a portion of the U.S. South Atlantic and Gulf of Mexico Continental Shelf. Bull. Mar. Sci. 33:935-940.

Powers, J. E. and M. E. Crow. 1982. Towards models of reef exploitation. In G. R. Huntsman, W. R. Nicholson, W. W. Fox, Jr. (editors), The biological bases for reef fishery management, p. 185-201. U.S. Dep. Commer., NOAA Tech. Memo. NMFS, NOAA-TM-NMFS-SEFC-80.

Ralston, S. 1981. A study of the Hawaiian deep-sea handline fishery with special reference to the population

557

dynamics of opakapaka, Pristipomoides filamentosus
(Pisces: Lutjanidae). Ph.D. Dissertation, Univ.
Wash., Seattle, 204 p.

Smith, G. B. 1976. Ecology and distribution of eastern
Gulf of Mexico reef fishes. Fla. Dep. Nat. Resour.,
Mar. Res. Publ. 19, 78 p.

Starck, W. A., II. 1968. A list of fishes of Alligator
Reef, Florida, with comments on the nature of the
Florida reef fish fauna. Undersea Biol. 1(1):1-40.

Starck, W. A., II, and R. E. Schroeder. 1970. Investigations on the gray snapper, Lutjanus griseus. Stud.
Trop. Oceanogr. (Miami) 10, 224 p., 44 figs. (Copyright 1971.)

Struhsaker, P. 1969. Demersal fish resources: Composition, distribution, and commercial potential of the
continental shelf stocks off southeastern United
States. Fish. Ind. Res. 4:261-300.

Tennyson, A. 1939. Idylls of the king. C. W. French (editor). The Macmillan Co., N.Y., 397 p.

Ulrich, G. F., R. J. Rhodes, and K. J. Roberts. 1976.
Status report on the commercial snapper-grouper
fisheries off South Carolina. Proc. Gulf Caribb.
Fish. Inst. 29:102-125.

[U.S.] Department of Commerce. 1984. Marine recreational
fishery statistics survey, Atlantic and Gulf coasts,
1979 (revised)-1980. U.S. Natl. Mar. Fish. Serv.,
NOAA, Curr. Fish. Stat. 8322, 239 p.

Waters, J. R. Unpub. Dynamic yield per recruit analyses
for establishing minimum size limits in the South
Atlantic snapper-grouper fishery. Southeast Fish.
Cent. Beaufort Lab., Natl. Mar. Fish. Serv., NOAA,
Beaufort, NC 28516-9722.

Waters, J. R., and G. R. Huntsman. In press. Incorporating mortality from catch and release into yield-per-
recruit analyses of minimum size limits. N. Am. J.
Fish. Manage.

Wenner, C. 1983. Species associations and day-night
variability of trawl-caught fishes from the inshore
sponge-coral habitat, South Atlantic Bight. Fish.
Bull., U.S. 81:537-552.

White, T. H. 1939. The once and future king. G. B.
Putnam's & Sons, N.Y., 677 p.

APPENDIX A DYNAMIC YIELD-PER-RECRUIT MODEL

The dynamic model calculates the change in catch over time following the adoption of a minimum size limit. To correspond as closely as possible to the traditional yield-per-recruit model, we specify an initial population that is in equilibrium and as constant recruitment of one fish per year. A more rigorous analysis could relax these assumptions.

The model follows the growth and survival of fish in each of $i = 1, 2, \ldots I$ cohorts. Weight at age a for fish in cohort i at time t, $W(a_{it})$, increases according to the von Bertalanffy relationship

$$W(a_{it}) = W_\infty \, (1 - \exp(-K(a_{it} - t_0)))^3 \quad .$$

Parameters K and t_0 define the rate at which weight asymptotically approaches W_∞.

A simplified Leslie matrix defines survival rates for each age class.

$$S = \begin{bmatrix} 1 & 0 & 0 & \ldots & 0 \\ S^1 & 0 & 0 & \ldots & 0 \\ 0 & S^2 & 0 & \ldots & 0 \\ 0 & 0 & S^3 & \ldots & 0 \\ \cdot & \cdot & \cdot & & \cdot \\ 0 & 0 & 0 & \ldots & S_{I-1} \end{bmatrix}$$

where

$$
\begin{aligned}
&= \exp(-M\Delta a_{it}) && \text{for } a_r \leq a_{it} \leq a_c \\
s_i &= \exp(-(M+F(1-P_s))\Delta a_{it}) && \text{for } a_c < a_{it} \leq a_m \\
&= \exp(-M+F)\Delta a_{it}) && \text{for } a_m < a_{it} \leq a_\lambda
\end{aligned}
$$

and

a_r = age at recruitment
a_c = age when fish are first caught
a_m = age corresponding to a minimum size limit
a_λ = maximum age in fishery
Δa_{it} = change in age of cohort i during year t
M = instantaneous natural mortality coefficient
F = instantaneous fishing mortality coefficient
P_s = probability of survival for released, undersized fish

Yield is calculated as the sum over all age classes of biomass landed per recruit

$$YPR = C\ N$$

where YPR is yield per recruit in grams, N is a column vector of population numbers at the beginning of year t and C is a row vector with elements defined as

$$C_i = 0 \qquad \text{for } a_r \le a_{it} \le a_m$$

$$C_i = F\ W_\infty \sum_{j=0}^{3} \frac{G(j)\ \exp(-jK(a_{it} - t_0))}{(M + F + jK)}\ (1 - \exp(-(M + F + jK)\ (a_{it+1} - a_{it})))$$

$$\text{for } a_m < a_{it} \le a_\lambda$$

where $G(0) = 1$, $G(1) = -3$, $G(2) = 3$, $G(3) = -1$. The catch, C_i, from age class i during year t is determined following Beverton and Holt (1957) as the sum of the instantaneous catches between birthdays a_{it} and a_{it+1}.

Elements C_i and survival rates S_i are adjusted whenever a_r, a_c, a_m, or a_λ fall between birthdays a_{it} and a_{it+1}. For example, if $a_{it} < a_m < a_{it+1}$, then

$$S_i = \exp(-(M + F(1 - P_s))\ (a_m - a_{it}) - (M + F)\ (a_{it+1} - a_m))$$

$$= \exp(-(M + F)\ (a_{it+1} - a_{it}) + FP_s(a_m - a_{it}))$$

$$C_i = F\ W_\infty\ \exp(-(M + F(1 - P_s))\ (a_m - a_{it}))$$

$$x \sum_{j=0}^{3} \frac{G(j)\ \exp(-jK(a_m - t_0))}{(M + F + jK)}\ (1 - \exp(-(M + F + jK)\ (a_{it+1} - a_m)))\ .$$

APPENDIX B   INCORPORATING CATCH AND RELEASE MORTALITY INTO THE BEVERTON AND HOLT YIELD–PER–RECRUIT MODEL

An analytical solution for yield per recruit in the presence of catch and release mortality was derived in the manner of Beverton and Holt (1957:35–38) by integrating catch in biomass from ages t_m to t_λ.

$$YPR = \int_{t_m}^{t_\lambda} F\, N(t)\, W(t)\, dt$$

$$= F\, W_\infty\, N(t_m) \sum_{j=0}^{3} \frac{G(j)\, \exp(-jK(t_m - t_0))}{(F+M+jK)} (1-\exp(-(M+F+jK)\,(t_\lambda - t_m)))$$

where
YPR = yield per recruit in grams
$N(t)$ = fraction of a recruit surviving at age t
$N(t_m)$ = $N(t_r)\, \exp(-M(t_c - t_r))\, \exp(-(M+F(1-P_s))(t_m - t_c))$
$N(t_r)$ = 1.0
t_r = age at recruitment
t_c = average age when fish are first caught
t_m = age corresponding to a minimum size limit
t_λ = maximum age in the fishery
M = instantaneous natural mortality coefficient
F = instantaneous fishing mortality coefficient
P_s = probability that undersized fish would
        survive if caught and released
$W(t)$ = weight (grams) per fish at age t
     = $W_\infty(1 - \exp(-K(t-t_0)))^3$
W_∞ = maximum attainable weight.
K = growth parameter in von Bertalanffy equation
t_0 = age parameter in von Bertalanffy equation
$G(0)$ = 1, $G(1) = -3$, $G(2) = 3$, $G(3) = -1$

Catch and release mortality affects yield per recruit by reducing recruitment to the legal minimum size

$$N(t_m) = \exp(-M(t_m - t_r))\, \exp(-F(1-P_s)(t_m - t_c)) \qquad (2)$$

where the term $\exp(-F(1-P_s)(t_m - t_c))$ represents the fraction of a recruit that survives the catch and release process. Therefore

$$YPR(P_s < 1) = YPR(P_s = 1)\, \exp(-F(1-P_s)(t_m - t_c)) \ .$$

13
Reproductive Strategies and the Management of Snappers and Groupers in the Gulf of Mexico and Caribbean

Scott Bannerot, William W. Fox, Jr.
University of Miami, Rosenstiel School
of Marine and Atmospheric Science
Miami, Florida 33149

and

Joseph E. Powers
Southeast Fisheries Center Miami Laboratory
National Marine Fisheries Service, NOAA
Miami, Florida 33149

ABSTRACT

Fisheries for tropical reef species, particularly snappers and groupers, in the tropical western Atlantic region are described. The efforts and methodology to determine the status of those species are reviewed along with current management practices. The effects of reproductive strategies on assessment techniques and management measures are investigated. Snappers have a gonochoristic reproductive strategy while groupers have a protogynic hermaphroditic reproductive strategy. The exploitation responses of populations with these reproductive strategies are compared using mathematical models. Generally, there are parametric regions where hermaphroditism is more resilient to exploitation than is gonochorism; this parametric region is increased if hermaphrodites exercise some social behavior during spawning which decreases randomness in gamete encounters.

DESCRIPTION OF FISHERIES

History of Exploitation

Snappers and groupers are captured in the Gulf of Mexico and Caribbean together with numerous other members of the highly diverse reef fish community in which they are typically important predators (Hobson 1965, 1982; Bohnsack 1982). Historical data on fisheries for reef species, however, are scant compared to those for the more traditional temperate demersal and pelagic fisheries of the world. Commercial exploitation off the Gulf coast of the United States began in the 1800s (Gulf of Mexico Fishery Management Council (GMFMC 1984)), while recreational reef fisheries of some importance began in the early 1900s. Reef fishing around the Caribbean has traditionally been smaller scale and more artisanal (Salmon 1958; Hess 1961), and recreational effort has been traditionally low. Munro (1983) reviewed fishing gears used to exploit snappers, groupers, and other reef fish. These included traps, hook and line, beach seines, gill nets, cast nets, spears, dynamite, and poisons. In recent years bottom longlines and roller-rigged trawls have been used extensively on shallow, subtropical hard bottom and deep reefs in the Gulf of Mexico region of the U.S. Fishery Conservation Zone (FCZ).

Species composition of catches varies considerably between areas in both the Gulf of Mexico and Caribbean. Thompson and Munro (1983a, 1983b) listed the snappers and groupers typical of many Caribbean island fisheries. Species diversity of Caribbean catches exceeds that typical of continental shelf areas. In general these catches tend to be less dominated by one or several species.

Munro (1983) reviewed historical landings for the Caribbean over the period 1965-1973. Unreliable reporting makes the information difficult to interpret. More detailed data from Bermuda and Puerto Rico are presented later in this chapter. Bermuda has experienced severe declines in grouper landings over the past decade, almost certainly due to overfishing with traps. Data from Puerto Rico are less reliable, but indicate a declining trend in nominal catch per unit effort (CPUE) with increasing effort for shallow-water reef fishes. If a generalization can be made, it is that catches are chronically low from narrow, small island shelves and increase for more extensive shelves.

The extremes of this spectrum of catches and shelf areas in the Caribbean region are Monserrat (9,000 ha of shelf area) and the Bahamas (18,311,000 ha of shelf area). In the Bahamas considerable commercial fishing effort for snappers and groupers has been expended over the past decade by large (up to 20 m (65 ft)) diesel-powered vessels based in Spanish Wells and Great Abaco Island, a number of which have on-board refrigeration. Remaining at sea for 3 to 4 weeks has consistently resulted in a few thousand pounds or more of groupers, snappers, and spiny lobsters per trip. This is not typical elsewhere in the Caribbean.

The GMFMC (1984) reviewed the history of landings in the Gulf region of the United States. Updates were provided by several contributions to the Stock Assessment Workshop (SAW) (1984). The magnitude of annual catches of reef fishes from these areas is considerably larger than that from locations in the Caribbean. Overall landings have increased over the past 10 years, partly because of the development of bottom longline fisheries for yellowedge and red groupers. Long lifespans, relatively high ages of sexual maturation, slow growth rates, and in some cases the alternative reproductive strategies of the groupers cast considerable doubt on how long the high catches can be sustained. Fisheries for yellowedge groupers in some areas of the Gulf of Mexico have already ceased because of sharp declines in catch rate (W. Nelson Pers. com., Southeast Fisheries Center Mississippi Laboratories, Pascagoula Facility, National Marine Fisheries Service, NOAA, Pascagoula, MS 39567, 1984). Other recent commercial fishing trends have included the introduction of roller-rigged trawls in both the Gulf and Atlantic, and increased numbers of fish traps directed at snappers and groupers. The proportion of total landings attributed to recreational effort has increased considerably, particularly in the Gulf of Mexico. Richards and Bohnsack (1982) discussed some of the present conflicts resulting from these trends.

Species Composition of the Catch

Habitat suitable for colonization by snappers and groupers in the Gulf of Mexico and Caribbean includes both well-developed coral reefs and subtropical hard bottom which consists of lower-relief, rocky ledges with minor scleractinian coral growth, sponges, and octocorals. The southwestern Gulf of Mexico and Caribbean regions are characterized by clear, warm waters and well-developed coral aggregations. From Texas to southern Florida, the Gulf of Mexico features more turbid, cooler, subtropical oceanographic conditions with the exception of scattered offshore banks. Thus exploited snappers and groupers in this region reside within a continental reef fish fauna, while farther south the communities are typically insular.

Table 13.1 lists snappers and groupers commonly taken in the Gulf of Mexico and Caribbean. Red snappers are easily the most important lutjanid, in terms of total weight and value, taken in the Gulf. Among the serranid fishes the gags, scamp, and red groupers have historically been the object of sustained high-volume fisheries on the continental shelf of the Gulf. More recently, yellowedge groupers were taken in large numbers in deeper waters (over 70 m). Jewfish are caught occasionally, either by spearing or by hook-and-line fishing in the vicinity of wrecks and ledges. Warsaw groupers are found primarily between 80 and 300 m and, like jewfish, large (over 50 kg) individuals infrequently enter the catch. The smaller sea basses are important to recreational fisheries and small scale commercial interests. Speckled hinds and snowy groupers sometimes enter the catches from deeper water.

In the Caribbean, lane and yellowtail snappers are taken more frequently than other lutjanids from shallow insular shelf waters. Mutton, gray, dog, mahogany, and occasional cubera snappers, and schoolmasters are also caught. Rock hinds, red hinds, graysbys, and coneys are small groupers, often mixed with snappers in shallow water Caribbean catches. Nassau, yellowfin, and black and tiger groupers are larger species found both on top of and in deeper waters off the edge of insular shelves. Red groupers and jewfish are also taken, but less frequently. Yellowmouth groupers are caught along the shelf break, while misty groupers replace the warsaw grouper in catches from deeper tropical waters. Deepwater snappers, taken from the drop-offs and ledges at insular shelf breaks, include vermilion, black, queen, blackfin, and silk snappers and wenchman. Of these, silk snappers are caught in greatest numbers.

TABLE 13.1
List of species of snappers and groupers
commonly taken in the Gulf of Mexico and
Caribbean

SERRANIDAE - groupers

Bank sea bass	Centropristis ocyurus
Rock sea bass	C. philadelphica
Black sea bass	C. striata
Rock hind	Epinephelus adscensionis
Graysby	E. cruentatus
Speckled hind	E. drummondhayi
Yellowedge grouper	E. flavolimbatus
Coney	E. fulvus
Red hind	E. guttatus
Jewfish	E. itajara
Red grouper	E. morio
Misty grouper	E. mystacinus
Warsaw grouper	E. nigritus
Snowy grouper	E. niveatus
Nassau grouper	E. striatus
Black grouper	Mycteroperca bonaci
Yellowmouth grouper	M. interstitialis
Gag	M. microlepis
Scamp	M. phenax
Tiger grouper	M. tigris
Yellowfin grouper	M. venenosa

LUTJANIDAE - snappers

Black snapper	Apsilus dentatus
Queen snapper	Etelis oculatus
Mutton snapper	Lutjanus analis
Schoolmaster	L. apodus
Blackfin snapper	L. buccanella
Red snapper	L. campechanus
Cubera snapper	L. cyanopterus
Gray snapper	L. griseus
Mahogany snapper	L. mahogoni
Dog snapper	L. jocu
Lane snapper	L. synagris
Silk snapper	L. vivanus
Yellowtail snapper	Ocyurus chrysurus
Wenchman	Pristipomoides aquilonaris
Wenchman	P. macrophthalmus
Vermilion snapper	Rhomboplites aurorubens

A REVIEW OF STOCK ASSESSMENT AND MANAGEMENT

Background

Worldwide, the majority of reef habitat exists in the euphotic zone (above approximately 70 m depth), although snappers and groupers may occur in significant numbers considerably below this depth both on continental shelves and off the edge of abrupt insular shelf breaks common to many oceanic islands. Shallow depths and warm, clear water make extensive reef areas readily accessible to humans which, in turn, has led to the establishment of a large number of marine sanctuaries in tropical seas throughout the world (see Randall 1982). Predictably, these conditions have attracted the attention of mostly descriptive biologists and ecologists, who have created a large volume of literature on various aspects of the systematics, life history, and field ecology of snappers, groupers, and other reef fishes. Longley and Hildebrand (1941), Bohlke and Chaplin (1968), and Starck (1968), for example, published major works on the systematics of reef fishes in Florida and the Bahamas. Smith (1961), Randall (1963), Collette and Talbot (1972), Smith and Tyler (1973a, 1973b), and Manooch and Huntsman (1977) are among many authors who have contributed papers on the life history or descriptive ecology of reef fishes. Goldman and Talbot (1976), Sale (1976, 1977, 1978, 1980), Molles (1978), and Bohnsack (1979) dealt with theoretical aspects of factors influencing community structure of coral reef fishes.

Despite the abundance of literature, little work has been done on specific aspects of population dynamics critical to conservation and proper management. Analysis and prediction of population responses to exogenous mortality represents a major gap in our knowledge of and ability to manage snapper and grouper resources.

Two reasons for the lack of knowledge about snapper and grouper population dynamics are: (1) lack of appropriate empirical data and (2) biological complexities of reef fish in general at both the ecosystem/community and population/species levels. Lack of attention to these barriers derives largely from the small scale, artisanal nature of many of the fisheries for reef fishes and the location of many such fisheries within the jurisdiction of developing countries. More recently, interest in stock assessment of reef fish has grown as both developed and developing nations seek to manage the living resources within their FCZs.

A number of data limitations, which create practical obstacles to stock assessment, result directly from biological qualities of reef fish systems and species. Fisheries for reef fish have the following general attributes: (1) many species enter the catch; (2) fishing effort is diffuse, unevenly distributed in space, and often artisanal, employing a variety of gears; and (3) catch is often landed at many small ports. These attributes, in turn, lead to typical limitations in data from reef fisheries: (1) data on catch and effort, when they exist, are incomplete by geographical area; (2) data on effort are particularly difficult both to collect and to quantify by gear type; and (3) several species are often reported in combined categories. These limitations often thwart efforts to assess the biological status of the exploited populations.

Two biological characteristics, the first of the reef fish systems and the second of certain reef fish species, pose problems for more theoretical aspects of stock assessment: (1) interspecific interaction and (2) alternative reproductive strategy. Perturbation of one or several species may have positive or negative impacts on populations of ecologically related species (Bohnsack 1982). Hermaphroditic populations may respond differently to perturbation than gonochoristic (sexes separate) populations (Fox 1972; Smith 1982).

The interaction of these biological and ecological characteristics of snappers, groupers, and other reef fish with socioeconomic conditions associated with fishing produces a challenging set of circumstances for stock assessment. Two complementary analytical techniques most often applied to the assessment of fish stocks are: (1) production models and (2) yield-per-recruit (YPR) models. These two assessment techniques are often termed standard yield models. When catch-at-age data are complete, cohort or virtual population analysis (VPA) may be used to estimate necessary parameters.

These approaches (including VPA) were largely developed in the 1950s and 1960s and applied mostly to single species, gonochoristic populations. Although some theoretical work has been done to incorporate rudimentary inter- and intraspecific competition, mixing of populations, effects of a protandrous hermaphroditic life history strategy, and interactions of multiple gears, the complex suite of characteristics typical of most snapper and grouper fisheries has not yet been sufficiently addressed.

In the interim, management advice for snappers and groupers in the Gulf of Mexico and Caribbean has at best been generated by cursory application of the two standard yield models without consideration of reproductive strategy-specific or multispecies effects. Yield-per-recruit models have been fit using sexes-pooled size-at-age data on groupers, ignoring the possibility of growth patterns specifically associated with protogyny. Production models have been fit to species-pooled catch data on snappers and groupers, assuming that the multispecies complex behaves as a single species. Regions of potential instability over the range of equilibrium predictions from both models, specific to protogynous populations, have until recently been uninvestigated.

Population Parameters

Estimates of age, growth, and mortality of snappers and groupers in the Gulf of Mexico, Caribbean, and nearby regions are scattered through both published literature and several National Marine Fisheries Service (NMFS) reports still in preparation. Some of these were summarized in South Atlantic Fishery Management Council (SAFMC) (1983), and again in SAW (1984). Huntsman et al. (1983) provided a table of some parameters from the South Atlantic Bight. Bannerot (1984) listed age, growth, and mortality parameters by species, reference, and geographical area for the Gulf, Caribbean, and western tropical Atlantic.

In general, growth rates for snappers and groupers in the tropical Western Hemisphere are relatively low. Deeper-dwelling groupers, such as snowy groupers and speckled hinds, exhibit lower growth rates than groupers inhabiting more shallow depths in the region. Scamp are the only species common in shallow depths that are estimated to grow as slowly as their deepwater counterparts. However, the parameter estimates for scamp are suspected to be biased (Matheson et al. 1984). Depth-related trends in the growth of snappers are not apparent, and growth estimates show no systematic relationship with geographic area.

Theoretically, smaller species of each group should be more vulnerable to predation (Menge and Sutherland

1976). Smaller groupers, for example, red hinds, coneys, and graysbys, apparently experience greater mortality than larger species. However, size-related mortality is not apparent for snappers.

Considerably more variable estimates of total mortality, Z, for snappers and groupers of the South Atlantic Bight have been made based on catch curves assuming stable age distributions (Witzig and Huntsman 1984). Total effort in the fishery is believed to have increased over the time these data were collected, however, increasing the likelihood that this assumption does not hold. If catches of older age-classes are inflated through spatial or temporal expansion of effort, resulting in removal of large proportions of standing crops, Z will be biased downward. The annual Z estimates vary widely in both directions through time, though, so that an overall trend is not clear.

Similar problems are present for estimates of Z for scamp, speckled hinds, and snowy groupers. The Z from catch curves for scamp was quite different when estimated from commercial compared to recreational data (Matheson et al. 1984). Difficulty in aging older fishes contributes to the uncertainty of estimates of Z for all three species.

The current information on population parameters of exploited snappers and groupers in the Gulf, Caribbean, and elsewhere in the tropical Western Hemisphere, with all its limitations, is still probably more complete than for other exploited reef fish fauna in the world. This information has three main applications for management: (1) it provides a basis for sensitivity analysis of standard yield model parameters; (2) it provides a basis for extrapolation to reef fisheries operating in less-studied areas of the world, following, for example, the methods of Pauly (1980a, 1980b); and (3) it provides a basis for selecting parameters for population estimation and simulation models.

An Overview of Assessment and Management

Management measures for snapper and grouper resources have not been widely employed in the Gulf of Mexico and Caribbean. For the Caribbean nations, with the exception of Bermuda, restrictions on spearfishing and prohibition of fishing with poisons or explosives commonly constitute the only regulations. Spearing regulations range from complete prohibition (Bonaire of the Netherlands Antilles) to restrictions on techniques, such as disallowing the use of scuba gear, spear guns, and power heads (Bahamas). The U.S. FCZ around Puerto Rico and the U.S. Virgin Islands, under the jurisdiction of the Caribbean Fishery Management Council, presently has no regulations governing fishing for snappers and groupers. This Council is now developing a fishery management plan (FMP) for reef fish. The GMFMC implemented an FMP governing reef fishes within federal waters of the United States (GMFMC 1984). The states bordering the Gulf had several regulations already in place, but these regulations were seldom based on quantitative assessments.

States bordering the Gulf of Mexico, particularly Florida, have minimum size limits for several species of groupers and a few snappers. The GMFMC (1984) defines several stressed areas in which power heads, traps, and roller trawls are prohibited. Also, the design and use of fish traps is regulated and a minimum size limit is imposed for red snappers.

The State of Florida has banned the use of fish traps and roller trawls in State waters, has a 45.7-cm (18-in.) minimum size limit for red, black, yellowfin, and Nassau groupers, gags, and jewfish, has a 30.5-cm (12-in.) minimum size limit for red, mutton, and yellowtail snappers, and prohibits the use of power heads for taking groupers (poisons and explosives are also prohibited).

Thus, minimum sizes and various area and gear restrictions are the only current management strategies in the Gulf of Mexico and Caribbean. Fishing seasons, bag limits, and limited entry were rejected at the federal level in the United States essentially because of the lack of well-defined spawning periods, difficulty of enforcement, and political unpalatability, respectively. Caribbean Council staff and the NMFS are considering a novel system of rotating area closures, which amounts to a pulse fishing strategy, but little data are available to predict its effectiveness. The Government of Bermuda has taken the strongest recent reef fish management action in the region by imposing a system of limited entry.

Stock assessments were the basis for few of these regulations. The GMFMC (1984) aggregated catches of all snappers and groupers, estimated gross effort, and fitted a simple parabolic production model. The Caribbean Council used the same procedure in the course of work on its reef fish FMP, except it combines all species of reef fish. Current management strategies have not considered potential problems described earlier for assessment of snappers and groupers: (1) the potentially different responses of gonochoristic (for example, snappers) and protogynic hermaphrodite species (such as groupers) to exploitation, and differences in population dynamics specific to reproductive strategy that could lead to general, recognizable errors in the predictions obtained from standard yield models and (2) the utility of production models applied to multispecies complexes. Bannerot (1984) addressed these problems using computer simulation. Some of those results are summarized in the following section.

RECENT DEVELOPMENTS

A Comparison of Gonochoristic and Protogynic Hermaphroditic Reproductive Strategies

The species of sea basses and groupers inhabiting the Gulf of Mexico and Caribbean are all either known or suspected to be protogynous hermaphrodites (PH), where individuals mature as females and undergo a sexual transition to become males. Snappers, on the other hand, are gonochorists (G). Many snappers and groupers in the Gulf and Caribbean, however, have similar estimated age, growth, and mortality parameters (Huntsman et al. 1983; SAFMC 1983; Bannerot 1984; SAW 1984). A suspected greater vulnerability of groupers to fishing is based on the premise that overfishing of larger, older males may result in lower rates of fertilization of eggs produced by the population (Smith 1972; Shapiro 1984), due to some combination of insufficient sperm and social disruption. If this is true, lower sex ratios (all sex ratios in this chapter are males divided by females, M/F) should be associated with higher fishing mortality. Scattered empirical data support this association (Bannerot 1984).

The critical question, from an evolutionary perspective, is when female bias becomes a detriment to success of fertilization of eggs produced by the population. Since the sex of an individual is genetically determined, the reproductive strategy and associated sex ratios are theoretically predictable at equilibrium. Charnov (1982) used this theoretical approach to explain and predict the general patterns of protogyny and gonochorism. For gonochorism, Charnov stated that the early work of Fisher (1930), and later work by Shaw and Mohler (1953) and

Werren and Charnov (1978), generally conclude that the optimal sex ratio is 1.0. In the case of protogyny, female-biased sex ratios were predicted to be optimal.

Bannerot (1984) adapted static and dynamic population simulation models whose behavior was consistent with the previously described theoretical and empirical observations and compared: (1) population resiliency of PH and G populations and (2) potential effects of reproductive strategy on the predictions from standard yield models. The purpose of the static representation of reproduction, which ignores transitional population states and age-specific fecundity, was to produce a framework of preliminary expectations for the more comprehensive second step of dynamic simulation. This latter step involved the use of an age-structured exploited population simulation model to compare the dynamics of responses through time of the two types of populations as mortality increased under a variety of recruitment and mating hypotheses. Both steps used models originally by Fox (1972, 1973) for protandry that were converted to a protogynous reproductive strategy. Yield model predictions were then evaluated for both PH and G reproductive strategies by comparing results between forecasted and realized dynamics of simulated populations.

Figure 13.1 summarizes the predictions of the static reproductive model. Sex ratio (S) is a hyperbolic function of total mortality (Z) and time spent as a sexually mature female (T). The 1.0 sex ratio is the solid curve between the 0.5 and 2.0 isopleths of S and is believed to be optimal for gonochorists (Charnov 1982). According to the model in Bannerot (1984), this particular hyperbola also represents the lower left-hand bound for the ratio of PH to G females fertilized (mated female ratio or MFR) to be >1, in which case the hermaphroditic reproductive capacity exceeds that of the gonochorists. The dashed line represents the upper right-hand bound for MFR being >1, which is deflected away from the origin (arrow) as either the rate of contact between mates or the length of spawning season increases. When PH sex ratios fall between the 1.0 and dashed curves, the hermaphrodites should be reproductively superior to a G population with sex ratio 1.0. It is interesting to note that this range of values lies well within the range of empirical observations for groupers given in Bannerot (1984). This result is inconsistent with the hypothesis that groupers in the Gulf and Caribbean may be more vulnerable to overexploitation than snappers simply as a result of protogyny.

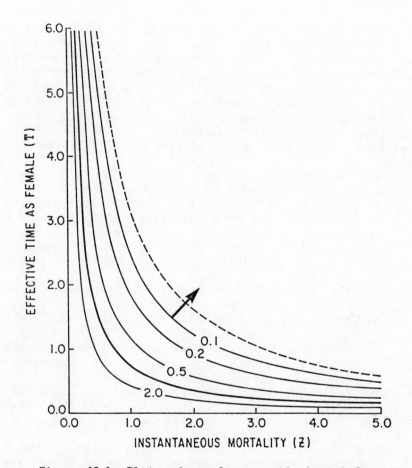

Figure 13.1 Plots of equal sex ratio hyperbolae as functions of T and Z. Sex ratios are number of males divided by number of females. The solid line between the 0.5 and 2.0 isopleths represents sex ratio 1.0, the lower left hand bound for MFR > 1 (protogynous reproductive superiority). The upper right hand bound for MFR > 1 is illustrated by the dashed line, which is deflected away from the origin for increasing rate of contact between mates or duration of spawning season (arrow)

As with all mathematical models, the resemblance of results and predictions to reality is at the mercy of, among other things, imperfectly met assumptions. This warrants consideration of the assumptions implicit to the static model and their applicability to groupers, particularly since the same assumptions listed below are implicit to the reproductive sector of the dynamic population simulator GXPOPS if random mating (sperm limitation) is assumed. Fox (1973) discussed five assumptions implicit to the models:

1. Instantaneous rate of mating per female is linear and proportional to the number of males.
2. The rate of fertilization (controlled by a coefficient in the model which represents instantaneous rate of contact between sexes and fraction of contacts resulting in fertilization of eggs) is independent of the age of males and females.
3. The rate of fertilization is independent of population or size.
4. A single mating results in fertilization of all or some constant fraction of the eggs.
5. Multiple matings, if they occur, do not alter the fraction of total eggs fertilized of an individual female during the spawning season.

Bannerot (1984) presented an examination of the applicability of these assumptions to groupers, concluding that they may provide a reasonable approximation of reproduction based on current knowledge.

The simulation of dynamic population responses required the selection of a set of biological parameters representative of groupers. Reasonably extensive information on the various parameters required for GXPOPS (growth, mortality, maturation, fecundity, etc.) were available for only four Gulf and Caribbean groupers: gags, red groupers, red hinds, and graysbys. Of these, gags were selected for simulation because they: (1) comprised an important component of commercial and recreational catch in the FCZ, and (2) exhibited a continental life history, perhaps increasing the chance that populations in, for example, the South Atlantic Bight may behave essentially as a unit stock. Parameter values were selected from McErlean (1963), McErlean and Smith (1964), and Manooch and Haimovici (1978).

Program GXPOPS1, an enhanced version of Fox's (1972, 1973) population simulator GXPOPS, was utilized to simulate gags and a gonochoristic (snapper-like) counterpart (identical in all respects except reproductive strategy) under a variety of different exogenous mortality schedules, growth rates, recruitment schedules, and different degrees of sperm limitation, varied according to a factorial experimental design. Additional simulation experiments incorporated compensatory schedules of growth, contact between mates, and sexual transition. Bannerot (1984) discussed in detail the model and the execution of baseline experiments and sensitivity analyses. The general conclusion was that populations with the life history characteristics of groupers were predicted to be reproductively superior to their G counterparts over a broad range of female-biased sex ratios, given that spawning success remained high (approximately 95% or more of all females are mated) through, for example, social behavior or rapid sex transition. If availability of sperm becomes a problem, for example, through high exogenous mortality applied to older age groups without the social behavior or rapid sex transition, then gonochorists are predicted to be relatively more resilient to exploitation.

Utility of Standard Yield Models
Applied to Simulated Populations with
Parameters of Snappers and Groupers

Two standard yield models, YPR and stock production models, are the techniques most often used to assess the status of fish stocks and to produce the management decision environment (Ricker 1975). The effects of protogyny are likely to be manifested in two key ways regarding standard yield models (1) in judging the balance of growth against fishing mortality rates and (2) in judging the effects of fishing mortality on stock productivity. Growth rates, sizes at age, and weights at a given length may differ between the sexes among economically important groupers (Moe 1969; Burnett-Herkes 1975; Nagelkerken 1979; Thompson and Munro 1983a). Since males develop sequentially from females, it is not a simple matter of constructing a pair of sex-specific growth curves as for G species, especially considering that the time allocated to the female stage may be influenced by fishing mortality rates applied to the population. With regard to stock production, it has already been shown that PH populations are either more or less productive than G populations, depending on population characteristics.

Thus with all other parameters equal, data points from the PH population might be expected to deviate from the yield curve of the G population. Furthermore, depending on the nature of the differences, production models might produce generic errors in predictions that are related to reproductive strategy. These hypotheses were tested by comparing yield model predictions with yield realized by simulated PH and G populations.

Two primary hypotheses were tested regarding the ability of YPR models to describe accurately PH and G populations with parameters exemplifying snappers and groupers: (1) that predictions of equilibrium yield would be made in instances where the population was actually unstable and declining, and that some of these errors would be reproductive strategy-specific, and (2) that if groupers experience a period of more rapid growth following sexual transition, equilibrium yield predictions will represent misestimates of realized yield. The primary value of this part of the investigation was the specification of the patterns and extent of the predicted errors, and the implications these have for the degree of conservatism of resulting management advice.

The first test consisted of separately comparing predicted with realized equilibrium YPR for PH (designated EHM2) and G (EGM2) for populations under the assumptions of both random (sperm limitation) and nonrandom (no sperm limitation) mating. Equilibrium yield predictions were based on growth and mortality parameters identical to those of the simulated populations from which realized YPR was derived. Program YPER (W. W. Fox, Jr. Pers. com., Rosenstiel School of Marine and Atmospheric Science, University of Miami, Miami, Fla., 1983) computed all equilibrium YPR values from the Beverton and Holt (1966) short form.

Figure 13.2 shows predicted equilibrium YPR over a range of F for gags when length at entry is 510 mm (the mean length at age 3). Figures 13.3 and 13.4 illustrate realized equilibrium YPR from simulation of random and nonrandom mating EHM2 and EGM2 populations, where age of first full availability to fishing was 3. The absolute values of YPR are not comparable between Figure 13.2 and Figures 13.3 and 13.4, since the realized YPR values from GXPOPS1 are computed from the Beverton and Holt (1957) long form. Also, these values are derived from the different levels of recruitment and different age structures realized by simulated populations at equilibrium for specific values of F. The relationships of YPR

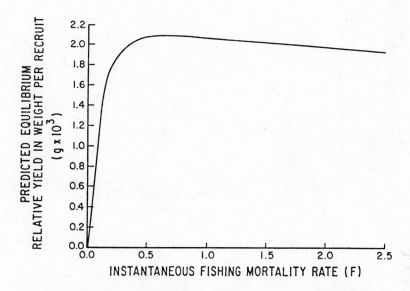

Figure 13.2 Predicted equilibrium yield per recruit (YPR) over a range of F for gags when length at entry is 510 mm (the mean length at age 3). Program YPER (Fox Unpub.), which computes YPR from the Beverton and Holt short form, calculated the plotted values

to F, however, are comparable between predicted (Figure 13.2) and realized (Figures 13.3 and 13.4) plots in terms of deriving management advice from their results.

The YPR (Figure 13.2) is predicted to increase rapidly over a low range of F (0 to 0.5), attaining a maximum at F = 0.632 (F_{Ymax}) and remaining high and relatively constant thereafter. The lack of a distinct dome is characteristic of relatively high M/K ratios (here M/K = 2.459). Since these YPR calculations are based on the assumption of constant recruitment, the actual maximum sustainable F cannot be predicted.

Figures 13.3 and 13.4 show that realized F_{Ymax} was less than that predicted by the YPR model for all populations. Additionally, random mating populations could not sustain F greater than 0.5 (Figure 13.3), and nonrandom mating populations became unstable beyond F = 1.0 (Figure 13.4). For random mating, the EGM2 population was relatively more resilient than the EHM2 population. For nonrandom mating the reverse was true. Since the

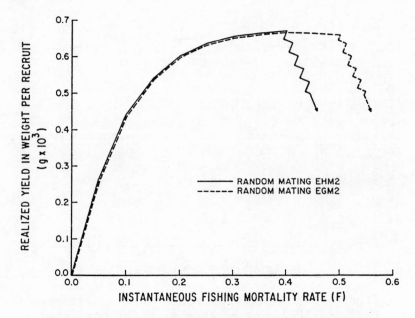

Figure 13.3 Realized equilibrium yield per recruit (YPR) from a simulation of random mating EHM2 and EGM2 populations. Plotted values were calculated by dividing yield in weight from GXPOPS1, which computes yield based on the Beverton and Holt long form, by recruitment realized from populations with stable age distributions

random mating populations destabilized exactly at realized F_{Ymax} (0.40), management of F based on an equilibrium YPR model could result in recruitment overfishing for those kinds of populations. In the case of nonrandom mating, management by predicted F_{Ymax} would cause growth over-fishing in populations EHM2 and EGM2. Furthermore, the EGM2 and EHM2 populations would become recruitment-overfished at F = 0.8 and F = 1.0 (Figure 13.4).

The general conclusion of this test is that equilibrium YPR models may overestimate the true F_{Ymax}. The effect of management based on controlling F may differ between PH and G species, depending on the conditions. Specifically, the error for PH species is predicted to be greater than that for G species when sperm becomes limiting.

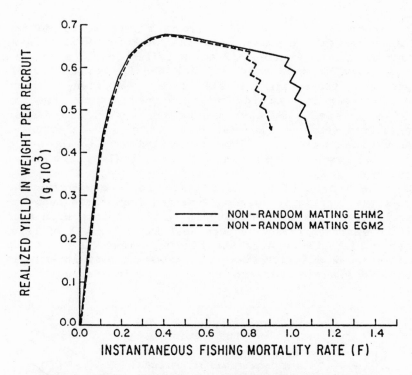

Figure 13.4 Realized equilibrium yield per recruit (YPR) from a simulation of nonrandom mating EHM2 and EGM2 populations. Plotted values were calculated by dividing yield in weight from GXPOPS1, which computes yield based on the Beverton and Holt long form, by recruitment realized from populations with stable age distributions

The "transition growth spurt hypothesis," forming the basis for the second YPR test, is consistent with the premise that protogyny should be selected for when size confers enhanced reproductive success on males (Ghiselin 1969; Charnov 1982). No published empirical data clearly demonstrate an increase in growth following sexual transition. However, both Moe (1969) and Nagelkerken (1979) plotted sex-specific growth curves for groupers and found distinct discontinuities between equal-aged individuals of different sexes, with male size larger than that of females. C. S. Manooch (Pers. com., Southeast

580

Fisheries Center Beaufort Laboratory, National Marine
Fisheries Service, NOAA, Beaufort, NC 28516-9722, 1984),
suspects a similar trend in sex-specific length at age in
gags based on data from Manooch and Haimovici (1978).
Because of the apparent plasticity of transition size and
age in groupers, combined data on growth over time for
large, unsexed samples could easily mask the proposed
inflection point and general form of the growth curve of
individuals over time. Thus calculated equilibrium yield
in weight per recruit could be chronically biased for
groupers.

The degree of bias was examined by comparing the
predicted equilibrium yield resulting from three hypothetical growth curves featuring inflection points with that
of the empirically-derived von Bertalanffy growth of gags.
Figure 13.5 illustrates the four relationships of weight
with age. Equilibrium yield with constant recruitment was
computed via piecewise integration of yield curves using

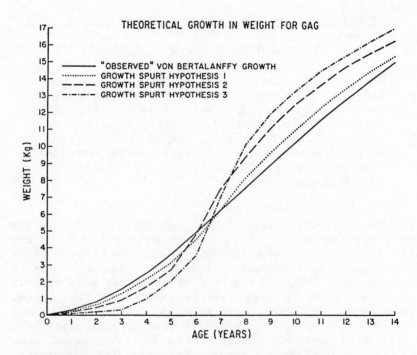

Figure 13.5 Growth in weight of gags according
to the empirically-fit von Bertalanffy curve and
three transition growth spurt hypotheses

the program YIELD 2 (P. K. Tomlinson Pers. com., Inter-American Tropical Tuna Commission, c/o Scripps Institution of Oceanography, La Jolla, Calif., 1984). The computations are summarized by Bannerot (1984) from Tomlinson's unpublished program description.

Results of the transition growth spurt examination for a length of first capture of 510 mm are summarized in Figure 13.6. The equilibrium yield varied substantially and systematically according to the hypothetical growth curves in Figure 13.5. The yield at each F was inversely related to the magnitude of the transition growth spurt. In addition, the relative decline in yield at high F increases with the magnitude of the hypothetical growth spurt at transition.

A potentially more serious error resulting from a transition growth spurt is the misestimation of $F_{Y_{max}}$.

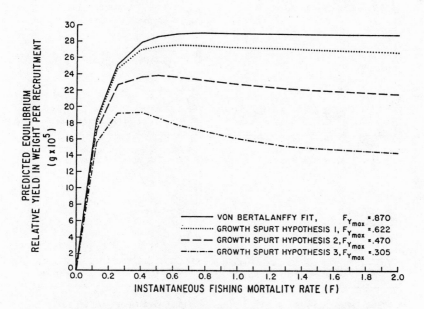

Figure 13.6 Equilibrium yield with constant recruitment corresponding to each of four theoretical growth curves: (1) growth of gags predicted by the von Bertalanffy equation fitted to a large, sexes-lumped sample; and (2) hypothesized growth patterns 1, 2, and 3 corresponding to small, intermediate, and large increases in growth rate after sexual transition

F_{Ymax} is inversely related to the growth spurt magnitude and the F_{Ymax} associated with the von Bertalanffy growth curve exceeded that predicted for all growth spurt curves. Therefore, an increased growth rate after transition, if masked by mathematical descriptions of growth obtained through fits to sexes-lumped samples, could lead to an overestimation of F_{Ymax}.

Tests of the utility of production models applied to PH and G populations consisted of comparing model fits to equilibrium and transitional catch histories created by GXPOPS1 for gags (EHM2) and their G counterparts (EGM2). Both random and nonrandom mating (sperm-limited and nonsperm-limited, respectively) EHM2 and EGM2 populations were simulated according to a slow- and a fast-developing

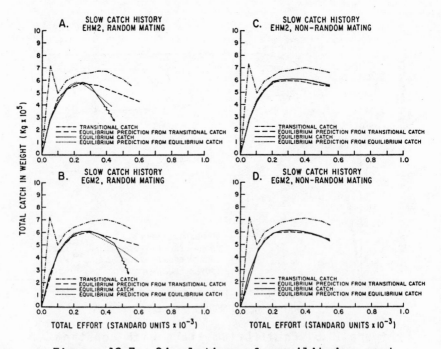

Figure 13.7 Simulation of equilibrium and transitional slow-developing catch histories, each consisting of 45 levels of F between 0.0 and 0.5463. Fits of the generalized production model to both equilibrium and transitional catches are plotted for random and nonrandom mating EHM2 and EGM2 populations

catch history. Program PRODFIT (Fox 1975) was used to obtain a least-squares fit of the generalized production model to the simulated data. Resulting management advice was then compared among the four populations and two catch histories to test the hypothesis of reproductive strategy-specific errors, as well as errors of a more general nature.

Figure 13.7 depicts the simulated equilibrium and transitional slow-developing catch histories for each of the four populations and the fits of the generalized production model. Equilibrium yields correspond to the annual catch after 130 years of fishing at each of 45 values of F distributed between 0.0 and 0.5463, while transitional data were generated by a sequence of a single

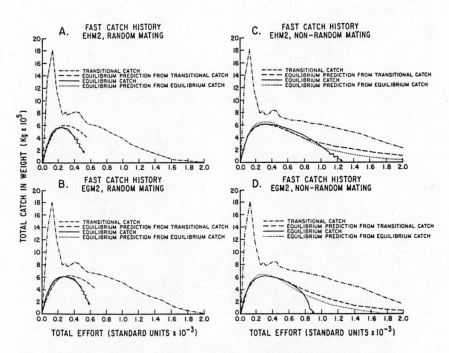

Figure 13.8 Simulation of equilibrium and transitional fast-developing catch histories, each consisting of 32 levels of F between 0.0 and 1.97. Fits of the generalized production model to both equilibrium and transitional catches are plotted for random and nonrandom mating EHM2 and EGM2 populations

year of fishing at each F value. Figure 13.8 presents the same information except that the catch history is fast-developing, consisting of 32 levels of F betwen 0.0 and 1.97. The simulated populations throughout this study usually required 12 to 30 or more years to achieve equilibrium after any change in F.

The transitional yield trajectories depicted in Figure 13.8 represent a fairly rapid development of fishing on grouper populations, resulting in a very high state of disequilibrium and eventual population crash. An empirical example of this kind of trajectory is the Bermuda grouper fishery, where an intensive shallow water trap fishery for six species of groupers led to severe decreases in yield over the last 7 years of the fishery. The empirical yield trajectories for tiger, black, yellowfin, yellowmouth, and Nassau groupers, and red hinds are shown in Figure 13.9. The similarity of the empirical and simulated trajectories is striking, particularly in the presence of the yield pulse following the period of initial decline. Effort in the Bermuda fishery is known to have increased over the period 1975-1981, although the specific pattern and magnitudes of changes in effort between years have not been estimated. Alternative explanations for this pulse in the empirical data might include, for example, increased data collection effort in 1979. This particular explanation is believed not to be the case (B. E. Luckhurst Pers. com., Bermuda Department of Agriculture and Fisheries, 1984). It is also interesting to note that the yield pulse is most pronounced for congenerics of the gag (tiger, yellowfin, yellowmouth, and black groupers), and least apparent for red hinds.

Under equilibrium conditions and with nonrandom mating, the protogynous population (EHM2) is more productive and resilient to exploitation than the gonochoristic population (EGM2), i.e., the maximum sustainable yield, Y_{max}, the level of fishing effort producing Y_{max}, and the maximum level of sustainable fishing effort are all higher (Figures 13.7 and 13.8, solid curves; and Tables 13.2 and 13.3). The reverse is true under random mating, i.e., the gonochoristic population is more resilient to exploitation. However, the trajectories of the transitional catches are nearly identical between the EHM2 and EGM2 populations (Figures 13.7 and 13.8, dash-dot curves) in each comparison; the advantages of each reproductive strategy noted at equilibrium are barely discernible.

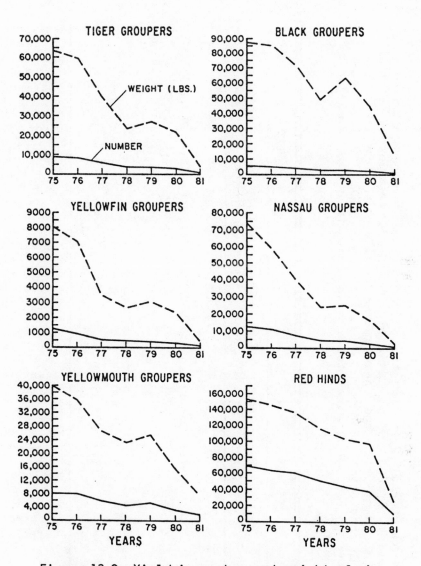

Figure 13.9 Yield in number and weight of six groupers exploited by an intensive shallow-water trap fishery during the years 1975-1981 in Bermuda. The pulses of yield apparent in the weight data are similar to yield pulses produced by the fast-developing catch history of gags simulated by GXPOPS1 (Figure 13.8)

586

TABLE 13.2
Performance of PRODFIT in predicting values critical to management from equilibrium (Equil.) and transitional (Trans.) slow-developing catch histories of both random and nonrandom EHM2 and EGM2 populations. Percent error in predictions of maximum sustainable yield (Y_{max}) and effort producing Y_{max} (f_{opt}) were computed based on comparisons with simulated values of Y_{max} and f_{opt}

	EHM2					EGM2				
	Simu-lated	Equil. Test	% Error	Trans. Est.	% Error	Simu-lated	Equil. Test	% Error	Trans. Est.	% Error
Random Mating										
f_{opt}	238.6	220.421	−7.6	257.39	+7.9	282.0	252.809	−10.4	289.229	+2.6
Y_{max}	577500	570955	−1.1	575059	−0.4	604400	600677	− 0.6	589225	−2.5
Nonrandom Mating										
f_{opt}	323.0	318.535	−1.4	313.615	−2.9	307.0	298.837	− 8.2	305.841	−0.4
Y_{max}	616200	617030	+0.1	594869	−3.5	615600	613302	− 0.4	597654	−2.9

TABLE 13.3

Performance of PRODFIT in predicting values critical to management from equilibrium (Equil.) and transitional (Trans.) fast-developing catch histories of both random and nonrandom EHM2 and EGM2 populations. Percent error in predictions of maximum sustainable yield (Y_{max}) and effort producing Y_{max} (f_{opt}) were computed based on comparisons with simulated values of Y_{max} and f_{opt}

	EHM2					EGM2				
	Simu-lated	Equil. Test	% Error	Trans. Est.	% Error	Simu-lated	Equil. Test	% Error	Trans. Est.	% Error
					Random Mating					
f_{opt}	250.0	224.447	-10.2	290.126	+16.1	290.0	248.245	-14.4	334.135	+15.2
Y_{max}	577500	575163	- 0.4	607007	+ 5.1	604200	603948	- 0.04	625239	+ 3.5
					Nonrandom Mating					
f_{opt}	330.0	303.498	- 8.0	301.368	- 8.7	305.0	283.362	- 7.1	312.766	+ 2.5
Y_{max}	616100	658331	+6.9	604032	- 2.0	615500	644747	+ 4.8	615851	+ 0.06

Using equilibrium data, the generalized production model as fit by PRODFIT describes the equilibrium relationship between yield and fishing effort reasonably well up to and in the vicinity of f_{opt} (dotted versus solid curves in Figures 13.7 and 13.8). At levels of fishing effort much beyond f_{opt}, the generalized production model represents neither the precipitous collapse which occurs under random mating nor the concave-downward shape of the yield curve for populations under nonrandom mating. However, the management criteria of Y_{max} and f_{opt} are reasonably well estimated.

The aspects of general production model fitting found in this study are common to the technique itself. No discernible departures could be ascribed to the protogynous reproductive strategy that would invalidate the use of this approach to serve as a simple model for developing properly qualified management advice.

Utility of Production Models Applied to Multispecies Complexes

The most commonly practiced method of analyzing species-lumped data from a sustained yield perspective has been termed the "total biomass Schaefer model." All species are lumped and treated as a single species. The approach has been widely applied to tropical multispecies fisheries (Pauly 1979), and has recently been applied to catch data on groupers from the Gulf of Mexico (GMFMC 1984).

The potential interactions between species are ignored by the total biomass approach, the implicit assumption being either that: (1) fishing effort on the complex affects each species structurally in a consistent manner (availability, age-specific catchability, and fishing mortality, etc.) or, alternatively, (2) interspecific interactions are such that despite increases and decreases in relative contribution of particular species, total yield is conserved through time. If reef fish ecosystems are resilient, flexible, and "evolutionarily opportunistic" enough, the latter assumption may not be severely violated. The problem of interspecific interaction as it relates to fishing has been considered by numerous authors (Larkin 1963, 1966; Paulik et al. 1967; Saila and Parrish 1972; Garrod 1973; Marten 1979a, 1979b; May et al. 1979; Bohnsack 1982; Nisbet and Gurney 1982; Powers and Crow 1982; Saila 1982). Primary templates for competition are food (Silliman 1968) and space (Smith and Tyler 1972; Sale 1975). Development of a solvable system of differential equations that incorporates interaction between species, however, results in gross oversimplification of the system (May et al. 1979; Nisbet and Gurney 1982; Powers and Crow 1982). More complex analytical formulations, on the other hand, have so far defied solution. The total biomass approach is an empirically-based response to what has been an intractable analytical problem.

The ability of the total biomass approach to predict sustained yields of multispecies assemblages has not been tested. Also, most applications to date have fit the simple, parabolic Schaefer model to the data. We used GXPOPS1 to simulate equilibrium and transitional catch histories of four groupers from the Gulf and Caribbean. Biological parameters were drawn from the literature as described in Bannerot (1984). The generalized production model was then fit to each of these simulated yield curves to check for species-specific errors in fits and to derive four separate predictions of f_{opt} and Y_{max}. Then, both equilibrium and transitional data from all four species were combined to form two aggregated data sets similar to existing species-lumped empirical data, and the production model was fitted: (1) to compare equilibrium and transitional fits and (2) to compare f_{opt} and Y_{max} to their "true" or separate component counterparts. Last, the generalized production model was fit to an empirical, species-lumped data set from a multispecies trap fishery for groupers in Puerto Rico, and the results were compared to those of the simulation fitting experiment.

Simulated catch histories of individual grouper species and corresponding production model fits are plotted in Figure 13.10. Equilibrium simulations were run for the number of years equal to 10 times the lifespan of each species, and transitional data were generated sequentially by 1 year of fishing at each F. The fast-developing fishing effort history from the preceding section was used for all simulations.

The general shape and relationship of transitional yield curves in Figure 13.10 and their equilibrium counterparts are similar to those in Figure 13.8. The expected initial spike of high yield from exploiting a virgin standing crop is evident for all species. The transitional yield curve for red hinds more closely approximates equilibrium than the other curves because of a short lifespan (8 years) and the high, almost constant,

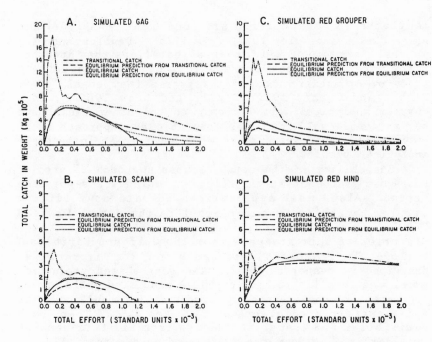

Figure 13.10 Plots of equilibrium and transitional simulated catch histories for scamp, gags, red groupers, and red hinds. Predictions of PRODFIT based on equilibrium and transitional data are plotted for each species. The vertical axis scale for red hinds is kg x 10[4]

recruitment chosen by Bannerot (1984). Red hind cohorts enter and pass through the population at 1.6 to 3 times the rate of passage for the other species, so the same effort history applied to red hinds represents a slower relative acceleration of effort. At the other extreme, the initial high transitional yields of red groupers persisted the longest because of their 25-year lifespan.

Table 13.4 summarizes the performance of the generalized production model fitted with PRODFIT to each species separately in estimating the simulation model results for f_{opt} and Y_{max}. The results for gags are those of the EHM2 nonrandom mating population from the preceding section. Except for red hinds, predictions based on equilibrium-simulated data tended to underestimate f_{opt}

TABLE 13.4

Performance of PRODFIT in predicting values critical to management from equilibrium (Equil.) and transitional (Trans.) fast-developing catch histories of gags, scamp, red groupers, and red hinds. Percent error in predictions of maximum sustainable yield (Y_{max}) and effort producing Y_{max} (f_{opt}) were computed based on comparisons with simulated values of Y_{max} and f_{opt}

	Simu-lated	Equil. Test	% Error	Trans. Est.	% Error	Simu-lated	Equil. Test	% Error	Trans. Est.	% Error
			Gag					Scamp		
f_{opt}	330.0	303.498	-8.0	301.368	- 8.7	455.0	367.809	-19.2	404.285	-11.1
Y_{max}	616100	658331	+6.9	604032	- 2.0	186300	199024	+ 6.8	145849	-21.7
		Red Grouper						Red Hind		
f_{opt}	175.0	174.776	-0.1	160.149	- 8.5	697.0	784.601	+12.6		--
Y_{max}	179700	188770	+5.0	133599	-25.7	34190	34773.7	+ 1.7	33490.9	- 2.0

592

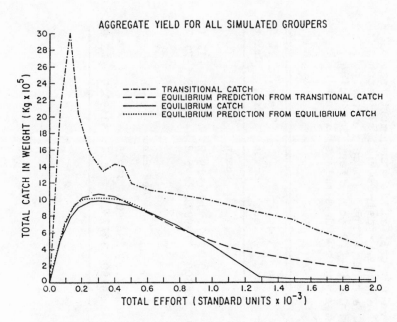

Figure 13.11 Equilibrium and transitional yield
curves for the aggregated data of four simulated
grouper species, with equilibrium estimates of
the generalized production model made by PRODFIT

and overestimate Y_{max}, while those from transitional data
underestimated both f_{opt} and Y_{max}.

Figure 13.11 shows the equilibrium and transitional
yield curves formed by aggregating the respective catch
curves for all four species, along with the corresponding
production model fits. The assumption implicit in this
approach, of course, is that there are no interspecific
effects. The maximum of the aggregated equilibrium yields
is 9.8×10^5, as compared with 10.2×10^5 for the sum of
the individual species' Y_{max} values, and it occurs at 305
effort units. The estimates from PRODFIT are slightly
high for Y_{max} and slightly low for f_{opt}. The value for
f_{opt} is a midrange value of individually estimated f_{opt}
values. Thus the aggregate model estimates an f_{opt} that
would fish gags at f_{opt}, overfish red groupers, underfish
red hinds, and slightly underfish scamp. In our case,
gags dominate the multispecies catch (Figures 13.10 and
13.11), but the general expectation is that the aggregate
f_{opt} will be significantly influenced by the manner in

which effort is directed among the species (Paulik et al. 1967).

Our results imply that the total biomass approach may provide a reasonable initial prediction of Y_{max}. If the assumption of a consistent relationship of constant catchability among species does not hold, however, the predicted Y_{max} might not be realized over time. For example, the sequential overexploitation of a number of species would sustain some overall yield until all species were depleted while providing time-varying estimates of Y_{max}.

Our calculations do not address the broader question of interspecific interaction. Larkin (1963, 1966) and later May et al. (1979) described the problem for simple systems using differential equations. These demonstrations indicated how removal of components of multispecies communities can, through competitive relationships, lead to predictable shifts in the relative abundance of different species. Marten (1979a, 1979b) and Bohnsack (1982) provided empirical observations of fishing-induced changes in community composition.

In the context of the aggregated grouper fishery simulated in this section, fishing according to the f_{opt} predicted by the total biomass approach results in overfishing the red groupers and an overall Y_{max} less than the sum of that for the individual species. If, however, the removal of red groupers created an ecological benefit for gags or other species, these populations might expand to fill the void, causing Y_{max} to approximate the individual sum. Alternatively, some other species with food and habitat requirements similar to those of red groupers might invade the community and become a part of Y_{max}. Conversely, the community could be destabilized by the selective removal of one or several species. Higher-level predators may play a key role in stabilizing diverse communities by opportunistically cropping a variety of prey species (Ricklefs 1973). If red groupers were important in this sense, and if gags, scamp, or red hinds were not able to fulfill the function of red groupers, the community might undergo large changes affecting the total yield of the large predators. Management decisions based on the total biomass approach are, therefore, subject to considerable uncertainty as to the ultimate effect of effort on the yields from the fishery.

An empirical example, a multispecies trap fishery for groupers in Puerto Rico, was addressed by Bannerot (1984).

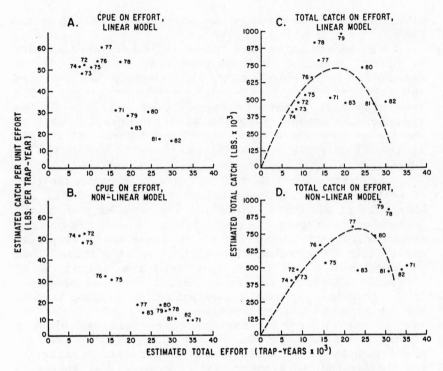

Figure 13.12 Plots of catch per unit effort
(CPUE) on fishing effort and of total catch on
fishing effort for the linear and nonlinear
estimations for a multispecies trap fishery.
Data represent an aggregation of all grouper
species caught per year in Puerto Rico for the
years 1971 to 1983

Figure 13.12 shows the plots of CPUE on fishing effort and
total catch on fishing effort. The totals were estimated
from partial landings data according to two different
hypotheses, a linear and nonlinear model. The data were
fit to the generalized production model by PRODFIT using
various effort-averaging times (i.e., the number of year-
classes contributing significantly to the catch). The
dashed curves in Figure 13.12 illustrate the fits obtained
with the intermediate effort-averaging time of 3 years.
The estimates of Y_{max} and f_{opt} significantly decreased as
the effort-averaging time increased. For example, Y_{max}
estimated from the nonlinearly adjusted data decreased
from 369 metric tons (MT) (811,000 lb) to 358 to 318 MT

(788,000 to 700,000 lb) as the averaging time increased
from 1 to 3 to 6 years, respectively. The corresponding
estimates for f_{opt} decreased from 25,000 traps to 23,700
to 21,400. Based on this parameter instability, the short
data set, the incompleteness of the basic data set, and
the aforementioned dynamics of grouper populations and
their communities, actual management advice in the Puerto
Rican grouper fishery should be very conservative.

SUMMARY AND DISCUSSION OF MANAGEMENT IMPLICATIONS

Snappers and groupers form an ecologically and
economically important component of reef fish communities
in the Gulf of Mexico and Caribbean. The term "reef fish"
applies to a diverse category of co-occurring demersal and
semipelagic fish species often exploited as a multispecies
complex. Most literature on the biology and ecology of
snappers, groupers, and other reef fish concentrates on:
(1) those species inhabiting well-developed coral reefs
and (2) commercially important species that may be found
over a wider range of subtropical demersal habitats. A
review of this literature revealed a paucity of knowledge
about aspects of reef fish population dynamics important
for management.

Exploitation of Gulf and Caribbean reef fish communities has increased over the past 20 years in most areas,
in some cases resulting in sharp declines in yield.
However, management measures on reef resources in the
region often have not been implemented. Few existing
regulations are based on a quantitative stock assessment,
and none have explicitly considered the effects of either
interspecific interaction or the hermaphroditic reproductive strategy.

Static and dynamic computer simulation techniques
were used to investigate the potential effects of
protogynous hermaphroditic reproduction on the responses
to exploitation of populations with the parameters of
groupers as compared to those of gonochoristic control
populations. Results from the static model predicted
that: (1) protogynous hermaphrodites should be reproductively superior to gonochorists, all other factors being
equal, if sperm is not limiting; (2) as increasing mortality disrupts the ability of mates to come into contact,
the reproductive success of protogynous hermaphrodites
relative to that of gonochorists declines; (3) protracted
spawning activity and shortened time spent in the female

stage enhances reproductive contact between mates; and (4) when sperm becomes limiting, gonochoristic reproduction is superior at the highest levels of mortality. Results from the dynamic model were consistent with those from the static model in predicting relatively greater resiliency to exploitation of PH when sperm is not limiting.

These simulations highlighted the need for several critical field studies on reproduction. Populations under exploitation should be monitored to deduce whether or not a significant proportion of eggs go unfertilized as exogenous mortality increases, and to follow any change in population sex ratio over a range of exploitation levels. Specific research is needed to characterize population compensatory mechanisms for avoiding sperm limitation, and to determine the time required for hermaphroditic individuals to change sex and the range of sizes capable of changing sex. In addition to these parameters, studies of mating strategies, as indicated by spawning behavior and gonad condition over time, would be valuable for making inferences about potential fishing-induced disruption of spawning. Until field data show otherwise, the predictions of both the static and dynamic models indicate that the management decision environment of exploited grouper populations should be conservative.

The effects of protogynous hermaphroditic reproduction and grouper population parameters on the predictions from the standard YPR and stock production models were also examined. The results indicated a definite risk if grouper populations are managed strictly by YPR models at high fishing mortality and in the absence of knowledge about population compensation mechanisms for sperm limitation. In addition, the potential influence of accelerated growth following sexual transformation was overestimation of the optimum fishing mortality rate for a given age at first capture. The calculations demonstrated some potential effects of the hypothesized growth pattern, and they indicate the need for data on sex-specific growth for groupers over a range of exploitation levels. Fitting of the generalized production model to individual grouper populations provided reasonably accurate estimates of the shapes of the equilibrium yield curves and the key management criteria of maximum sustainable yield (MSY), and the corresponding level of fishing effort within the general limitations of this approach. No differences between protogynous hermaphroditic and gonochoristic reproductive strategies were evident.

The generalized production model applied to data aggregated for several grouper species appears to be a reasonable approach but only under very restrictive assumptions. With no interspecific interactions, the MSY of aggregated catches from a common level of fishing mortality is less than the sum of the individual maxima as has been demonstrated for other species assemblages. Only direct knowledge of interspecific interaction will lead to an improvement of management advice for these mixed fisheries.

ACKNOWLEDGMENT

This article was developed largely under the auspices of the Florida Sea Grant College Program with support from the National Oceanic and Atmospheric Administration (NOAA), Office of Sea Grant, U.S. Department of Commerce, Grant No. NA80AA-D-00038. Additional support was provided by NOAA Cooperative Agreement No. NA80-RAH-00001 and NA84-WC-H-06098. The U.S. Government is authorized to produce and distribute reprints for governmental purposes notwithstanding any copyright notation that may appear hereon. Finally, we are grateful to the Bermuda Department of Agriculture and Fisheries, especially the cooperation and assistance of Brian Luckhurst.

BIBLIOGRAPHY

Bannerot, S. P. 1984. The dynamics of exploited groupers (Serranidae): An investigation of the protogynous hermaphroditic reproductive strategy. Ph.D. Dissertation, Univ. Miami, Coral Gables, 393 p.

Beverton, R. H. H., and S. J. Holt. 1957. On the dynamics of exploited fish populations. Fish. Invest. Ser. II, Mar. Fish., G. B. Minist. Agric. Fish. Food 19:1-533.

_____. 1966. Manual of methods for fish stock assessment. Part 2. Tables of yield functions. FAO Fish. Tech. Pap. 38:1-67.

Bohlke, J. E., and C. C. G. Chaplin. 1968. Fishes of the Bahamas and adjacent tropical waters. Livingston Publishing Co., Wynnewood, Penn., 771 p.

Bohnsack, J. A. 1979. The ecology of reef fishes on isolated coral heads: An experimental approach with emphasis on island biogeographic theory. Ph.D. Dissertation, Univ. Miami, Coral Gables, 269 p.

_____. 1982. Effects of piscivorous predator removal on coral reef fish community structure. In G. Caillet and C. A. Simensted (editors), Gutshop 81: Fish food habits studies, p. 258-267. Wash. Sea Grant Prog., Seattle.

Burnett-Herkes, J. 1975. Contribution to the biology of the red hind, Epinephelus guttatus, a commercially important serranid fish from the tropical western Atlantic. Ph.D. Dissertation, Univ. Miami, Coral Gables, 154 p.

Charnov, E. L. 1982. The theory of sex allocation. Monogr. Popul. Biol. 18, 335 p.

Collette, B. B., and F. H. Talbot. 1972. Activity patterns of coral reef fishes with emphasis on nocturnal-diurnal changeover. In B. B. Collette and S. A. Earle (editors), Results of the Tektite program: Ecology of coral reef fishes, p. 98-124. Los Ang. Cty. Nat. Hist. Mus. Sci. Bull. 14.

Fisher, R. A. 1930. The genetical theory of natural selection. Oxford University Press, Dover, 291 p.

Fox, W. W., Jr. 1972. Dynamics of exploited pandalid shrimps and an evaluation of management models. Ph.D. Dissertation, Univ. Wash., Seattle, 194 p.

_____. 1973. A general life history exploited population simulator with pandalid shrimp as an example. Fish. Bull., U.S. 71:1019-1028.

_____. 1975. Fitting the generalized stock production model by least-squares and equilibrium approximation. Fish. Bull., U.S. 73:23-37.

Garrod, D. J. 1973. Management of multiple resources. J. Fish. Res. Board Can. 30:1977-1985.

Ghiselin, M. T. 1969. The evolution of hermaphroditism among animals. Q. Rev. Biol. 44:189-208.

Goldman, B. and F. Talbot. 1976. Aspects of the ecology of coral reef fishes. In O. A. Jones and R. Endean (editors), Biology and geology of coral reefs, p. 125-154. Vol. 3, Biol. 2, Acad. Press, N.Y.

Gulf of Mexico Fishery Management Council (GMFMC). 1984. Environmental impact statement and fishery management plan for the reef fish resources of the Gulf of Mexico. Prepared by Fla. Sea Grant Coll., Gainesville and GMFMC, Tampa.

Hess, E. 1961. The fisheries of the Caribbean Sea. In G. Borgstrom and A. J. Heighway (editors), Atlantic

Ocean fisheries, p. 213–222. Fishing News (Books) Ltd., Lond.

Hobson, E. S. 1965. Diurnal–nocturnal activity of some inshore fishes in the Gulf of California. Copeia 1965:291–302.

_____. 1982. The structure of fish communities on warm–temperate and tropical reefs. In G. R. Huntsman, W. R. Nicholson, and W. W. Fox, Jr. (editors), The biological bases for reef fishery management, p. 160–166. U.S. Dep. Commer., NOAA Tech. Memo. NMFS, NOAA–TM–NMFS–SEFC–80.

Huntsman, G. R., C. S. Manooch, III, and C. B. Grimes. 1983. Yield per recruit models of some reef fishes of the U.S. South Atlantic Bight. Fish. Bull, U.S. 81:679–696.

Larkin, P. A. 1963. Interspecific competition and exploitation. J. Fish. Res. Board Can. 29:647–648.

_____. 1966. Exploitation in a type of predator–prey relationship. J. Fish. Res. Board Can. 23:349–356.

Longley, W. H., and S. F. Hildebrand. 1941. Systematic catalogue of the fishes of Tortugas, Florida with observations on color, habits, and local distribution. Pap. Tortugas Lab. 34:1–331.

Manooch, C. S., III, and M. Haimovici. 1978. Age and growth of the gag, Mycteroperca microlepis, and size–age composition of the recreational catch off the southeastern United States. Trans. Am. Fish. Soc. 107:234–240.

Manooch, C. S., III, and G. R. Huntsman. 1977. Age, growth, and mortality of the red porgy, Pagrus pagrus. Trans. Am. Fish. Soc. 106:26–33.

Marten, G. G. 1979a. Predator removal: Effect on fisheries yields in Lake Victoria (East Africa). Science 203:646–648.

_____. 1979b. Impact of fishing on the inshore fishery of Lake Victoria (East Africa). J. Fish. Res. Board Can. 36:891–900.

Matheson, R. H., III, G. R. Huntsman, and C. S. Manooch III. 1984. Age, growth, mortality, foods and reproduction of the scamp, Mycteroperca phenax, collected off North Carolina and South Carolina. Second Southeast Stock Assessment Workshop, June 4–8, 1984, Miami. Southeast Fish. Cent., Natl. Mar. Fish. Serv., NOAA, SAW/84/RFR/8, 38 p.

May, R. M., J. R. Beddington, C. W. Clark, S. J. Holt, and R. M. Laws. 1979. Management of multispecies fisheries. Science 205:267-277.

McErlean, A. J. 1963. A study of the age and growth of the gag, Mycteroperca microlepis Goode and Bean (Pisces: Serranidae) on the west coast of Florida. Fla. Board Conserv., Mar. Res. Lab. Tech. Ser. 41:1-29.

McErlean, A. J., and C. L. Smith. 1964. The age of sexual succession in the protogynous hermaphrodite, Mycteroperca microlepis. Trans. Am. Fish. Soc. 93:301-302.

Menge, B. A., and J. P. Sutherland. 1976. Species diversity gradients: Synthesis of the roles of predation, competition, and temporal heterogeneity. Am. Nat. J. 110:351-369.

Moe, M. A., Jr. 1969. Biology of the red grouper Ephinephelus morio (Valenciennes) from the eastern Gulf of Mexico. Fla. Dep. Nat. Resour., Mar. Res. Lab. Prof. Pap. Ser. 10:1-95.

Molles, M. C., Jr. 1978. Fish species diversity on model and natural reef patches: Experimental insular biogeography. Ecol. Monogr. 48:289-305.

Munro, J. L. 1983. Coral reef fish and fisheries of the Caribbean Sea. In J. L. Munro (editor) Caribbean coral reef fishery resources, p. 1-9. ICLARM Stud. Rev. 7, Manila.

Nagelkerken, W. P. 1979. Biology of the graysby, Epinephelus cruentatus, of the coral reef of Curacao. Stud. Fauna Curacao Other Caribb. Isl. 60:1-118.

Nisbet, R. M., and W. S. C. Gurney. 1982. Modelling fluctuating populations. John Wiley & Sons, N.Y., 379 p.

Paulik, G. J., A. S. Hourston, and P. A. Larkin. 1967. Exploitation of multiple stocks by a common fishery. J. Fish. Res. Board Can. 24:2527-2537.

Pauly, D. 1979. Theory and management of tropical multispecies stocks: A review with emphasis on the Southeast Asian demersal fisheries. ICLARM Stud. Rev. 1, Manila, 35 p.

_____. 1980a. On the relationships between natural mortality, growth parameters, and mean environmental temperature in 175 fish stocks. J. Cons. Cons. Int. Explor. Mer 39:175-192.

_____. 1980b. A new methodology for rapidly acquiring basic information on tropical fish stocks: growth, mortality and stock recruitment relationships. In S. B. Saila and P. M. Roedel (editors), Stock assessment for tropical small-scale fisheries, p. 154-172. Int. Cent. Mar. Resour. Dev., Univ. Rhode Island, Kingston.

Powers, J. E., and M. E. Crow. 1982. Towards models of reef fish exploitation. In G. R. Huntsman, W. R. Nicholson, and W. W. Fox, Jr. (editors), The biological bases for reef fishery management, p. 185-201. U.S. Dep. Commer., NOAA Tech. Memo. NMFS, NOAA-TM-NMFS-SEFC-80.

Randall, J. E. 1963. An analysis of the fish populations of artificial and natural reefs in the Virgin Islands. Caribb. J. Sci. 3(1):31-47.

_____. 1982. Tropical marine sanctuaries and their significance in reef fisheries research. In G. R. Huntsman, W. R. Nicholson, and W. W. Fox, Jr. (editors), The biological bases for reef fishery management, p. 167-178. U.S. Dep. Commer., NOAA Tech. Memo. NMFS, NOAA-TM-NMFS-SEFC-80.

Richards, W. J., and J. A. Bohnsack. 1982. The conflicts and controversies surrounding the use of reef-fish resources. Mar. Recreational Fish. 7:45-56.

Ricker, W. E. 1975. Computation and interpretation of biological statistics of fish populations. Bull. Fish. Res. Board Can. 191, 382 p.

Ricklefs, R. E. 1973. Ecology. Chiron Press, Portland, 861 p.

Saila, S. B. 1982. Markov models in fish community studies - some basic concepts and suggested applications. In G. R. Huntsman, W. R. Nicholson, and W. W. Fox, Jr. (editors), The biological bases for reef fishery management, p. 202-210. U.S. Dep. Commer., NOAA Tech. Memo. NMFS, NOAA-TM-NMFS-SEFC-80.

Saila, S. B., and J. D. Parrish. 1972. Exploitation effects upon interspecific relationships in marine ecosystems. Fish. Bull., U.S. 70:383-393.

Sale, P. F. 1975. Patterns of use of space in a guild of territorial reef fishes. Mar. Biol. (Berl.) 29:89-97.

_____. 1976. Reef fish lottery. Nat. Hist. 85:60-65.

_____. 1977. Maintenance of high diversity in coral reef fish communities. Am. Nat. 111:337-359.

_____. 1978. Coexistence of coral reef fishes--a lottery for living space. Environ. Biol. Fishes 3:85-102.

_____. 1980. Assemblages of fish on patch reefs - predictable or unpredictable? Environ. Biol. Fishes 5:243-249.

Salmon, G. C. 1958. Report on the fisheries industry in the countries served by the Caribbean commission. FAO Fish. Rep. 781, 86 p.

Shapiro, D. Y. 1984. Detrimental effects of intensive fishing over spawning aggregations of a commercially important grouper. Sea Grant Proj. R/LR-06-1 Annu. Rep., 12 p.

Shaw, R. F., and J. D. Mohler. 1953. The selective advantage of the sex ratio. Am. Nat. 87:337-342.

Silliman, R. P. 1968. Interaction of food level and exploitation in experimental fish populations. Fish. Bull., U.S. 66:425-439.

Smith, C. L. 1961. Synopsis of biological data on groupers (Ephinephelus and allied genera) of the western North Atlantic. FAO Fish. Biol. Synop. 23, 61 p.

_____. 1972. A spawning aggregation of Nassau grouper, Epinephelus striatus (Bloch). Trans. Am. Fish. Soc. 101:257-261.

_____. 1982. Patterns of reproduction in coral reef fishes. In G. R. Huntsman, W. R. Nicholson, and W. W. Fox, Jr. (editors), The biological bases for reef fishery management, p. 49-66. U.S. Dep. Commer., NOAA Tech. Memo. NMFS, NOAA-TM-NMFS-SEFC-80.

Smith, C. L., and J. C. Tyler. 1972. Space resource sharing in a coral reef fish community. Los Ang. Cty. Mus. Contrib. Sci. Bull. 14:125-170.

_____. 1973a. Direct observations of resource sharing in coral reef fish. Helgol. Wiss. Meeresunters. 24:264-275.

_____. 1973b. Population ecology of a Bahamian suprabenthic shore fish assemblage. Am. Mus. Novit. 2528:1-38.

South Atlantic Fishery Management Council (SAFMC). 1983. Source document, fishery management plan, regulatory impact review, and environmental impact statement for the snapper-grouper fishery of the South Atlantic region. Prepared by the SAFMC, Charleston, South Carolina, in cooperation with NMFS.

Starck, W. A., II. 1968. A list of fishes of Alligator Reef, Florida with comments on the nature of the Florida reef fish fauna. Undersea Biol. 1:5-40.

Stock Assessment Workshop (SAW). 1984. Reef fisheries reports. Second Southeast Stock Assessment Workshop,

4-8 June 1984, Miami. Southeast Fish. Cent., Natl. Mar. Fish. Serv., NOAA, SAW/84/RFR.

Thompson, R., and J. L. Munro. 1983a. The biology, ecology, and bionomics of the hinds and groupers, Serranidae. In J. L. Munro (editor), Caribbean coral reef fishery resources, p. 59-81. ICLARM Stud. Rev. 7, Manila.

_____. 1983b. The biology, ecology, and bionomics of the snappers, Lutjanidae. In J. L. Munro (editor), Caribbean coral reef fishery resources, p. 94-109. ICLARM Stud. Rev. 7, Manila.

Werren, J. H., and E. L. Charnov. 1978. Facultative sex ratios and population dynamics. Nature 171:349-350.

Witzig, J., and G. R. Huntsman. 1984. Mortality rates of South Atlantic reef fishes as determined from samples from the headboat fishery. Second Southeast Stock Assessment Workshop, 4-8 June 1984, Miami, Fla. Southeast Fish. Cent., Natl. Mar. Fish. Serv., NOAA, Contrib. No. SAW/84/RFR/6, 24 p.

14
Demand Considerations in Fisheries Management-- Hawaii's Market for Bottom Fish

Samuel G. Pooley
Southwest Fisheries Center Honolulu Laboratory
National Marine Fisheries Service, NOAA
Honolulu, Hawaii 96822-2396

ABSTRACT

Fisheries management decisions are usually predicated on affecting the supply of fish at the point of harvest. However, changes in supply may have significant impacts on processors, wholesalers, and the final consumer.

Examination of Hawaii's market for bottom fish shows some price volatility in the short run, and quality premiums in both the short and long run. Long-term demand has been significantly positive, most closely associated with increasing population, tourist arrivals, and exports. Fisheries management decisions must take into account the impact of changing supply conditions on the availability and price of fresh bottom fish in the market.

INTRODUCTION

Fisheries management frequently affects not only the total volume of fish that reaches a market but also the timing and composition of supply. All three factors can affect the ex-vessel price of fish and thus commercial fishing incomes and, through the marketing chain, wholesale and processor incomes and consumer budgets. Once the nature of demand is determined, any management scheme (e.g., supply constraint) can be evaluated with respect to its effect on prices and income. This paper describes the market for fresh snappers and groupers in the U.S. as a whole (primarily the east coast) but emphasizes Hawaii in particular. Then the demand for fresh bottom fish in Hawaii is estimated through price flexibility functions. Finally, some management implications that derive from market demand estimation are explored.

DESCRIPTION OF THE MARKETS

International Markets

Fresh snappers are a high-value seafood product throughout their range: the east and gulf coasts of the mainland United States, Hawaii, the Caribbean, Australia, and New Zealand. Groupers are also an important seafood product in a number of these places, while jacks appear to be marginal commercial species but are valued for their sports fishing appeal. These species constitute the bottom fish management complex in Hawaii.

Annual landings of snappers on the mainland U. S. (primarily Florida) have declined recently to 4,200 metric tons (MT) valued at $15 million in 1984. Landings of grouper and sea bass have been growing, with 1984 landings of 7,800 MT with an ex-vessel value of $21 million ([U.S.] National Marine Fisheries Service (NMFS) 1985).

Hawaii's snapper-grouper market has always been considered marginal from a national perspective, but recent harvest records may change that assessment. There is, however, almost no competition between east coast and Hawaii snappers in either market area at this time, nor has there been substantial competition from imports. Imports of snappers and groupers to the U. S. have been relatively erratic in volume and appear to have a minimal impact on price determination for domestic species (Keithly and Prochaska 1984). Imports of snappers (and associated species) to the southeastern U. S. in 1984 were 3,800 MT, a record (Vondruska and Cunningham 1985).

In the U.S., snappers and groupers have a relatively low volume compared with apparently similar fish (e.g., west coast rockfish) and command considerably higher prices. The handline-harvested product is treated with considerably more respect than trawl-caught fish (although trawling for snappers has been instituted on the mainland U.S.) and receives appropriately higher prices. For example, April 1985 **wholesale** prices for red snapper at the Fulton Street Market in New York were in the range of $3-$5 a pound (roughly equivalent to Norwegian salmon), while sole and flounder were at $1.50. In Hawaii the **ex-**

vessel price for all bottom fish averaged $2.47 a pound (about $3.50 **wholesale**) in 1984, a year of record supply, and prices for individual species reached over $10 a pound during peak buying season for some species.

Economic studies of snappers and groupers emphasize the localized nature of their harvest and their primary markets. Cato and Prochaska (1976) reported a highly inelastic demand for fresh red snapper from Florida, indicating that there are relatively few substitutes for this species. Keithly and Prochaska (1984) found continued dominance of red snapper in the fresh market through 1982, with average prices for red snapper about double those for groupers. The primary source for growth in the price for snappers was growing total personal disposable income. More recent information shows that red snapper prices have been relatively constant over the past 4 years, while prices for other snappers and groupers have risen. This suggests that the market is broadening and that premiums for red snapper may diminish (Vondruska and Cunningham 1985). Rockfish from the west coast is already being marketed as snapper (at a substantially lower price) in some areas. Since harvests of red snapper may have already reached their biological limits in the United States, substitution of less heavily harvested species may be desirable, although this will have an unwanted income effect on commercial harvesters concentrating on red snappers.

It appears that the market for snappers in general is relatively independent of the demand for other seafood. It makes up a small percentage of average family household consumption (Keithly and Prochaska 1984), but the restaurant market for snappers may be relatively more important. Fluctuations in the price of snappers appear to be determined primarily by an exogenous domestic supply.

Snappers are also an important commercial sports fish on the east and gulf coasts (Huntsman et al. 1983), but this is not so in Hawaii (Samples et al. 1984). Huntsman points out that sports fishers prize large snappers, but that the commercial market has developed a niche for smaller fish, which may reduce the availability of larger, older snappers. One might conjecture that the development of the trawl fishery on the east coast, with its lower size selectivity, led to this development. In Hawaii, small snappers are also caught extensively by small-scale fishing vessel operators (part-time commercial and ostensibly recreational) for direct sale to households. Management problems appear to exist in both areas in terms of allocation between groups of fishers, i.e., between full-time and part-time commercial fishers and with recreational fishers.

Hawaii Market

Hawaii's overall seafood market is well-known for relatively high prices based on local preference for a limited number of species of fresh fish. Included in this consumption bundle are a number of snappers, groupers, and jacks of which opakapaka, *Pristipomoides filamentosus*, is the most important. A fisheries management problem has developed because bottom fish and reef fish stocks in the main Hawaiian Islands (MHI) appear to be at or near maximum sustainable yields while market demand for bottom fish (especially in "up-scale" restaurants) has grown substantially in the past 5 to 10 years. The household market for small bottom and reef fish also continues to grow.

Hawaii's overall seafood market has been surveyed a number of times and is depicted in Figure 14.1. This diagram shows the market channels for all types of seafood in Hawaii. The bottom fish market, including fresh bottom and reef fishes and imported frozen snapper, follows these channels. Hawaii's retail market for fresh and frozen bottom fish and reef fish has been estimated at 2,750 MT ($13.7 million), which constitutes approximately 11% of the final retail market. Frozen snapper imports to Hawaii (mainland U. S. and foreign) are estimated at 800 MT (1.8 million lb), $2.5 million wholesale value (Higuchi and Pooley 1985; Pooley Unpub.; data from an unpublished 1981-1982 NMFS survey).

Figure 14.2 depicts retail outlets for all varieties of seafood in Hawaii and is representative for bottom fish. The Hawaii wholesale seafood business has three major components: (1) 10 major wholesale dealers who predominate in the fresh fish market; (2) 50 smaller fresh fish dealers who sell wholesale and retail; and (3) 50 wholesalers and brokers who handle frozen seafood imported from the U.S. mainland and foreign sources. The fresh bottom fish market operates around an auction in Honolulu, although sizable market channels exist outside the auction. The latter channels are based on bilateral exchange with negotiated pricing, typical of other fresh fish markets in the U.S. (Wilson 1980). The overall market might be termed one of contestable competition

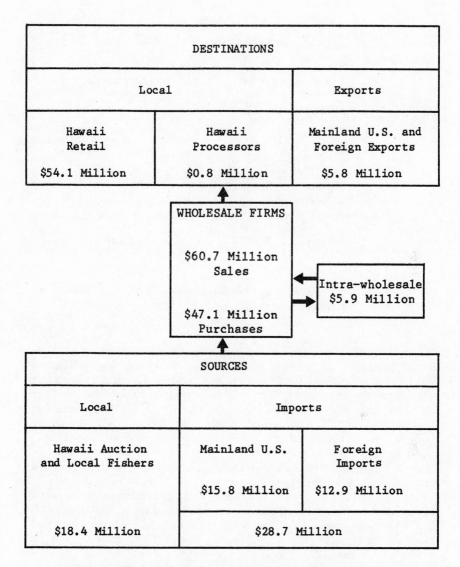

Figure 14.1   Market channels for Hawaii seafood
sales, 1979 (millions of dollars)

610

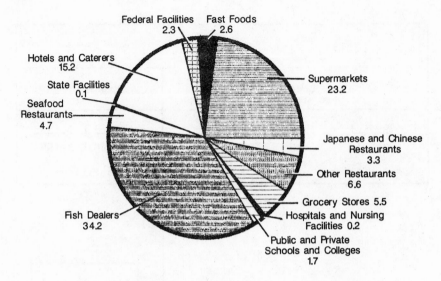

Figure 14.2 Retail outlets for all types of seafood in Hawaii (percentage of total revenue)

(Baumol 1982) in which a relatively small number of wholesale dealers of fresh and frozen seafood are able to generate economies of scale and scope in their product exchange functions. This reduces transactions and information costs while maintaining product heterogeneity, including an abundance of high quality, fresh seafood (Cooper and Pooley 1983). Retail prices are competitive.

Retail sales to Hawaii consumers include two components: regular purchases within a household's weekly food budget and a strong seasonal demand based on a cultural interest in large, red snappers for ceremonial occasions such as New Year's. This cultural demand also includes nonseasonal events such as weddings and birthdays. Favored fish in this category include the opakapaka, onaga, Etelis coruscans, and uku, Aprion virescens. The regular household component can be served by small bottom and reef fishes, by fillets of larger bottom fish, and by frozen snappers imported from the mainland United States and New Zealand. Although consumer substitution between product forms occurs, the frozen product is considered an inferior alternative for local bottom fish consumers. The price differential is substantial. In 1981 frozen snappers from New Zealand were entering Hawaii as fillets at $1.40 per pound. During that year the average price for whole

bottom fish was $2.30 per pound and for opakapaka alone,
it was $2.80 (NMFS unpublished wholesale market survey
1981-1982).

Restaurant demand for fresh bottom fish is centered on
fresh opakapaka and is based on catering to "up-scale"
tourist preferences (Takenaka et al. 1984; Monaghan 1985).
Successful market promotion and a fairly regular supply of
this species in large sizes has led to its introduction on
restaurant menus as a high quality item. Substitution of
other bottom fish and reef species has begun to occur, but
this is not a preferred practice.

Exports of opakapaka and a few other large bottom
fish have followed the growth of the tourist restaurant
market, much as a market for red snapper moved north from
Florida to New York years ago, but exports are still a
fairly small component of the demand for local bottom
fish. Fresh bottom fish is imported increasingly from
American Samoa, Guam, Fiji, and Micronesia.

HAWAII PRODUCTION

From the production side, the bottom fish market is
served by two types of Hawaii-based commercial fishing
vessels as well as by import brokerage. Relatively large-
scale (12-20 m, i.e., 45-65 ft), full-time commercial fishing boats ply the waters of the relatively distant (500-
1,000 nmi) Northwestern Hawaiian Islands (NWHI). These
modern vessels have the capacity to flood the fresh market
at the conclusion of their 2- to 3-week trips, landing up
to 7,000 kg of mixed bottom fish, but their boats have not
developed an effective market for frozen product. This
limits not only their catch total but their fishing range
(Hau 1984). Opakapaka is the major catch of the NWHI
fishery.

On the other hand, the MHI are the site of a mixed
commercial and part-time fishery of relatively small
vessels. Their catches fill a niche with smaller bottom
and reef fishes. Their boats land <1,000 kg and usually
much less. The MHI vessels are frequently operated on
extra-economic rationales and are faced with substantial
resource pressure. Both the NWHI and the MHI vessels
compete in the same fresh fish market, although size
composition tends to allocate the larger fish of the NWHI
catch to restaurants and the smaller fish of the MHI catch
to the household market (Table 14.1). This competition
between large- and small-scale vessels, each representing

TABLE 14.1
Hawaii bottom fish sales, 1984 (numbers in pounds rounded). Scientific names are given in the text. MHI = Main Hawaiian Islands; NWHI = Northwestern Hawaiian Islands. (Source: Western Pacific Regional Fishery Management Council 1985:152)

Group/ Species	Landings		Prices		Total Revenue
	MHI	NWHI	MHI	NWHI	
Group 1					
Uku	146,100	10,600	$2.30	$2.50	$362,500
Ulua	59,700	80,300	1.90	1.05	197,700
Subtotal	205,800	90,900	2.18	1.22	560,200
Group 2					
Opakapaka	211,600	331,900	3.35	2.70	1,605,000
Gindai	4,600	2,800	2.20	2.95	18,400
Hapuupuu	55,300	98,100	1.80	1.65	261,400
Lehi	16,300	0	2.30	0.00	37,500
Subtotal	87,800	432,800	2.97	2.46	1,922,300
Group 3					
Onaga	190,700	6,500	4.00	2.95	782,000
Ehu	36,800	5,000	2.75	2.10	111,700
Kalekale	23,800	2,500	2.20	1.60	56,400
Subtotal	251,300	14,000	3.65	2.40	950,100
Other	165,000	8,600	1.25	1.10	215,700
Total	909,900	546,300	2.65	2.25	$3,595,900

small business enterprises, has increased pressure for government regulation, including limited entry (Western Pacific Regional Fishery Management Council (Council) 1985; Pooley Unpub.).

Such institutional factors should be considered in fisheries management planning but generally are not. Since the supply of fish is the major variable affected by fishery management plans, its effect on the market needs to be investigated. In the next section, the demand for fresh bottom fish in Hawaii is estimated with a view toward understanding the relationship between fisheries production and marketing. The final section examines the economic impact of regulated changes in supply.

ECONOMIC DEMAND

The demand for fresh bottom fish represents a specific behavioral relationship: Consumers are said to determine the quantity demanded of a particular type of fish based on a number of demand determinants (characteristics). The primary determinant is the price of the fish, but other determinants include the price of substitutes, the size and quality of the fish, and seasonal considerations. Long-term characteristics include per capita disposable income and the size of the market, i.e., the population. The data available for estimating the demand for Hawaii's bottom fish are based on wholesale purchases of fresh product in the round. Therefore, in this paper a short-run price formation function of the following general form is utilized.

$$P_f = f(Q_f, Q_a, SD, CD)$$

where P_f is the ex-vessel price per pound of a particular type of bottom fish, Q_f is the market quantity of that type of fish, Q_a is the market quantity of substitute (alternative) species, SD is a dummy variable representing product quality based on the source of the product, and CD is a dummy variable representing seasonal consumer demand. In the short run, population and income are assumed to be fixed. Wholesale buyers make their offer prices to harvesters based on expectations of conditions in the final consumer markets. This offer is not significantly affected by inventories in a fresh fish market. Therefore, the price formation curve is mathematically equivalent to the inverse of the demand curve.

The price-quantity relationship can be depicted as a linear or logarithmic relationship and through two summary measures: (1) elasticity, which is not directly applicable to wholesale market analysis, and (2) its inverse, a price flexibility coefficient, F_p, which measures the percentage rate of change of a product's price relative to the rate of change of the product's quantity sold, i.e.,

$$F_p = -\frac{\%dP_f}{\%dQ_f} * 100$$

A logarithmic transformation of the price and quantity variables translates regression coefficients directly into estimates of elasticity or price flexibility, depending on the form of the equation.

The problem of explanation for seafood market price-quantity relationships is not trivial and is not unlike problems in understanding population dynamics and other features of fish stocks where observable phenomena have an uncertain relationship to underlying forces. The seafood market is a complex institution embedded in a network of social structures. The quantitative measures of market behavior are limited and interpretation of market forces is frequently contested. Previous explanations of seafood markets in Hawaii have explored the social side of fresh fish auctioning (Peterson 1973), the nature of market channels (Garrod and Chong 1978), the econometrics of a fresh fish cooperative (Hudgins 1980), industrial structure (Adams 1981), and characteristics of market transactions (Cooper and Pooley 1983). This paper builds on those explanations but does not completely "explain" the demand for fresh bottom fish. Although microeconomic theory of price determination has been developed in great detail (it is probably the most elaborate theoretical structure within economics), it is a relational theory of static aggregations of interpersonal interactions in an implicitly formulated general equilibrium framework. Therefore, the best that econometric analysis of market price can hope to accomplish is to reveal the pattern of exchange characteristics that can be directly observed, i.e., the variations in price and quantity.

None of the characteristics that describe the seafood market has causal properties in and of itself; each is a manifestation of underlying human activity. On one side, commercial fishers require monetary equivalents for their harvest; on another side there is the institutional arrangement of wholesale dealers in transacting commodity exchange; and on a third side are the preferences of consumers concerning their consumption expenditures. Econometric analysis of the wholesale market for fresh bottom fish distills this behavior and social structure into a limited number of quantitative variables, but it is examination of, and experience with, the particular characteristics of this market, and the existence of a lengthy intellectual tradition pertaining to microeconomic analysis, that make this distillation practical and informative.

Assuming a competitive equilibrium market, price and quantity data represent the intersection of supply and demand where only the point of equality is revealed. Therefore, a time series is subject to an identification problem: What is being discovered, the demand or the supply relationship? This problem is solved in short-term analysis of a highly perishable product like fresh seafood by the prior restriction that supply be independent of price. Demand is considered stable over a year. The exogenous determination of quantity supplied to the market allows statistical determination of the demand curve from market data.

MARKET DATA

Basic data for this analysis come from two sources. The only publicly available long-term source of price and quantity information is the State of Hawaii's landing records. The Hawaii Division of Aquatic Resources (HDAR) requires all commercial fishers in Hawaii to report their sales of fish on a monthly basis. These data are summarized and provide a monthly time series of market volume and price by individual species. The HDAR data were

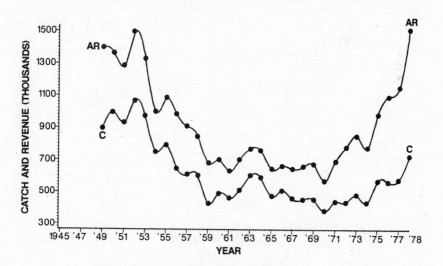

Figure 14.3 Bottom fish landings in Hawaii, 1949-1978 (AR = adjusted revenue in 1981 prices; L = catch in 1,000s of pounds)

TABLE 14.2
Hawaii fresh fish market: Monthly summary
statistics, 1965-1982. N = 216

Variable Description	Variable Name	Average	Standard Deviation	Coefficient of Variation (%)	Logarithmic Mean
Pounds Sold					
Bottom fish	QBTTM	37,000	15,000	41	3.53
Group 1	QBTTM-G1	14,000	7,000	49	2.52
Group 2	QBTTM-G2	16,000	9,000	60	2.57
Group 3	QBTTM-G3	7,000	4,000	51	1.86
Tunas	QTUNA	825,000	621,000	75	6.46
Mahimahi and wahoo	QMAHI/ONO	21,000	15,000	71	2.75
Average Monthly Prices	**Inflation-Adjusted Prices Per Pound (December 1982 Price Level)**				
Bottom fish	PBTTM[R]	$2.09	0.42	20	0.72
Group 1	PBTTM-G1[R]	1.65	0.35	21	0.48
Group 2	PBTTM-G2[R]	2.01	0.59	29	0.66
Group 3	PBTTM-G3[R]	3.14	0.54	17	1.13
All fresh fish	PFISH[R]	1.11	0.44	40	0.02
Fresh fish, excluding skipjack tuna	PFISH-SJ[R]	1.55	0.35	23	1.55
Hawaii Demographics					
Defacto population	POP	900,000	95,000	11	6.79
Resident population	RES	841,000	31,000	53	6.73

(Continued)

TABLE 14.2 (Cont.)

Variable Description	Variable Name	Average	Standard Deviation	Coefficient of Variation (%)	Logarithmic Mean
Average daily visitor census					
	VISIT	59,000	--	--	3.91
Real disposable personal income per capita (monthly)					
	RDINC	$876	$112	13	6.77
Consumer dummy: 1=Jan., Dec., Mar., or Apr.; 0=normal demand					
	CD	0.25	--	--	--

available for bottom fish through December 1982. This analysis uses the data beginning in 1965, the year in which Hawaii's overall commercial fishery "bottomed out" following much higher sales following World War II. Figure 14.3 presents bottom fish landings in the postwar period and Table 14.2 presents average monthy values. The HDAR revenue figures are "adjusted" for inflation by basing all prices on the December 1982 consumer price index for Honolulu.

For the long-term analysis, monthly Hawaii population and tourist arrival information was obtained from regular State of Hawaii Department of Planning and Economic Development reports. Hawaii has experienced considerable growth in population and visitor arrivals (averaging roughly 2.5% annually since 1965), and the variables are highly correlated ($r = 0.92$). Data on real disposable personal income per capita (RDINC) were obtained from U.S. Bureau of the Census and Hawaii Department of Planning and Economic Development sources. The RDINC has declined since 1976 due to structural and cyclical economic factors in Hawaii's economy.

The source of short-term market information is the Council, which has a regular monitoring program of wholesale bottom fish purchases from Hawaii's commercial

fishery.   These data represent a large proportion of the
entire fresh fish market in Hawaii and were collected
throughout 1984. However, to protect the confidentiality
of their source, the quantity data have been scaled to
levels approximate to an estimate of the overall market
volume.   The data were aggregated into weekly quantities
and prices, and summaries appear in Table 14.3.

TABLE 14.3
Hawaii fresh bottom fish market: Weekly, 1984.
(MHI = main Hawaiian Islands; NWHI = Northwestern
Hawaiian Islands)

Variable Description	Variable Name	Average	Standard Deviation	Coefficient of Variation (%)	Logarithmic Mean
Pounds Sold					
Bottom fish	QBTTM	24,700	11,200	45	9.9
Group 1	QBTTM-G1	5,700	3,900	68	8.42
Group 2	QBTTM-G2	13,900	7,500	54	9.34
Group 3	QBTTM-G3	5,100	3,500	69	8.25
MHI	QMHI	14,300	8,000	56	9.38
NWHI	QNWHI	10,300	7,000	68	8.98
Average Weekly Prices			**Price Per Pound**		
Bottom fish	PBTTM	$2.91	0.74	25	1.04
Group 1	PBTTM-G1	2.12	0.75	35	0.69
Group 2	PBTTM-G2	2.95	0.80	27	1.05
Group 3	PBTTM-G3	4.03	0.89	22	1.37
MHI	PMHI	3.31	0.88	27	1.16
NWHI	PNWHI	2.45	0.74	30	0.86
Consumer dummy: 1=peak season; 0=normal demand	CD	0.17	--	--	--

For both the long-term and short-term analysis, a consumer dummy variable takes on a value of 1 during peak demand periods (Christmas, New Year's, and Easter) and 0 otherwise.

METHODOLOGY

The basic question is: How do seafood consumers (or wholesale dealers acting on expectations of consumer behavior) react to changes in the supply of fresh bottom fish? If consumers have a number of substitutes for fresh bottom fish, then we can expect the price formation function to be relatively flat as consumers adjust their purchases to price. On the other hand, if consumers accept few substitutes, we would expect a steep demand curve and high price flexibility. It appears that the former is the case, but the purchase decision appears to be a "limited choice" decision, i.e., there is little likelihood of substitution to apparently comparable fresh fish when prices rise, and the range of purchases is limited.

With the assumption that the quantity supplied to the market by the commercial fishery is independent of price, at least in the short run, a simple linear model using ordinary least squares regression techniques can be applied to the price and quantity data to estimate the price formation curve. Although this is a rudimentary technique, it appears to be viable in this case.

Previous analysis of similar data indicated a problem with serial correlation of the residuals from regression analysis of the time series (Higuchi and Pooley Unpub.). Therefore, the data are transformed through an autoregressive lag technique called the Hildreth-Lu procedure, which corrects for such serial correlation. The autoregressive factor, g, is indicated for each equation. The equations are in the appendix.

Price flexibility coefficients are calculated from the regression coefficients of the price equations. Logarithmic conversion of the data provides continuous estimates of price flexibility from the regression coefficients. The logarithmic form also deals with some nonlinearities in the demand function. Although it is unlikely that consistency of the price flexibility parameter across the entire range of quantity applies, the results of the logarithmic and the linear models (equations not shown) showed no significant differences.

Substitution is examined for three groups of Hawaii's bottom fish taken from depth-groupings (Ralston 1979). All but two of the species are snappers.

Group 1: uku, _Aprion virescens_
          ulua, _Caranx_ spp. (jacks)

Group 2: gindai, _Pristipomoides zonatus_
          hapuupuu, _Epinephelus quernus_ (sea bass)
          lehi, _Aphareus rutilans_
          opakapaka, _P. filamentosus_

Group 3: ehu, _Etelis marshi_
          kalekale, _P. sieboldii_
          onaga, _E. carbunculus_

These groups, based on depth habitats, reflect neither commercial harvest nor market comparability characteristics. A simple factor analysis of prices and quantities for the nine species could find no stronger relationships, and an alternative specification of groups showed no stronger overall average bottom fish price-quantity relationship than the groups chosen, although individual group prices were better explained in some cases.

RESULTS

Short Run Demand, 1984

The weekly data for 1984 show a statistically significant negative price-quantity relationship for fresh bottom fish sales in Hawaii. The average weekly price of all bottom fish is negatively correlated with the weekly quantity supplied, and the relationship is statistically significant at the 99% confidence level (Equation 1). The same is true for monthly aggregations (Equation 2). The consumer dummy variable is also significant in both situations. Variation in quantity supplied and in the consumer dummy variable statistically explains half the price variation (R^2 = 53% for the weekly data and R^2 = 59% for the monthly data). The weekly price-quantity relationship, corrected for seasonal effects, is plotted in Figure 14.4. Interestingly, the price-quantity relationship for weekly bottom fish sales in 1984 is almost exactly the

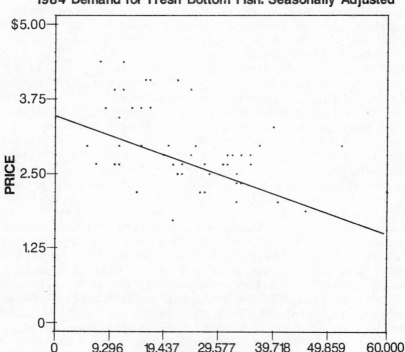

1984 Demand for Fresh Bottom Fish: Seasonally Adjusted

Figure 14.4   Demand for fresh bottom fish, 1984

same as a previous analysis based on 1976–1977 weekly
sales (Higuchi and Pooley Unpub.).

The price flexibility coefficent calculated from the
regression equation on weekly data is 23%, while the
monthly coefficient is 42% (calculated from Equations 1
and 2) . This means that price does not vary as much as
quantity. The average weekly market sales are 11 MT
(25,000 lb) with a standard deviation of 5 MT (11,000 lb).
A change in landings of one standard deviation raises or
lowers price a predicted 30 cents, approximately 10%.
Price volatility is occasionally much greater than predicted by this simple statistical technique. In most
cases, wholesalers ride out reductions in the quantity
supplied in the short run through short-term "inventories." However, if quantity is suppressed or increased
for several weeks, then such discounting cannot be main-

tained and price will fluctuate more widely. This is shown by the higher price flexibility coefficient for monthly aggregations. The range in actual prices (one standard deviation) was $\pm\$1.13$, or a price flexibility of 100%.

Central to the fresh bottom fish market in Hawaii are quality premiums: Fish handled carefully and those caught closer to the Honolulu market have longer shelf life and commensurately higher prices. Although this price formation behavior can be observed at the Honolulu auction, specification of a quality factor is extremely difficult because it is only reflected in the judgment of bidders and final users. Fish caught in the MHI are caught nearer to the market (thus have longer shelf life) and are caught in smaller numbers (thus maximizing the potential for individual handling). This advantage is offset by the fact that NWHI fish are generally larger and thus have a larger yield and because the NWHI vessels have better refrigeration. Smaller fish are valued by many local consumers because they can be used as single meals, but larger fish are prized by restaurants for their fillets.

Using the 1984 market sample and discriminating between fish landed from the MHI and the NWHI, the conflicting effects of quantity and quality are revealed. A pooled cross-section time-series approach was used to test for price differences based on location of catch. Average weekly sales for each species group were divided into MHI and NWHI and pooled together into a data set where a dummy variable was used to specify the MHI fish. The source dummy is statistically significant (Equation 3) and indicates that fish landed from the MHI can expect approximately a 50% price "bonus" because of quality consideration. However, some fish from the NWHI are handled well and receive comparable prices and paradoxically, the more fish landed from the NWHI (variable QN:Q), the higher the average price. (This is explained by short-run supply effects whereby NWHI vessel operators attempt to land during peak demand periods or when rough weather restricts the smaller MHI vessels from fishing.)

Breaking quantity sold into species groups substantially improves the price formation function (Equation 4). The strongest simple correlation comes from the shallow water group (ulua and uku), which receives the lowest average price. Price flexibility for each of the species groups is also estimated (Equations 5-7).

One expects the determination of price to be improved by examining the market by species group. However, this leads to another interesting question: To what extent do landings of other species affect the price of a particular species? This relationship is termed cross-elasticity, and its effect is represented by the statistical significance of the regression coefficient for the quantity supplied of the alternative species group. These results (Equations 8-10) show a fair degree of separability for the high-priced groups (opakapaka and onaga), since the cross-elasticities are not large.

Examination of data for 1976-1977 shows almost no cross effects with other types of fresh seafood in Hawaii, e.g., tuna, mahimahi, and wahoo (Higuchi and Pooley Unpub.). Landings of one bottom fish group have some effect on the prices in the other bottom fish groups. However, landings in the rest of the fishery (i.e., tunas, mahimahi, wahoo, and marlins, etc.) seem to have no noticeable influence in the short-term price formation for bottom fish, which supports the idea that their short-term demand is relatively independent (see also Equation 14).

Another question important to Hawaii's commercial fishery is: To what extent is market price determined by relative landings from the two main harvesting areas? The strongest correlation with overall market price is with NWHI landings, which is not surprising since they provide larger fluctuations in volume (Equation 11). However, a price determination equation for the MHI alone shows that NWHI landings appear to have little causal effect on MHI prices, compared with the effect of MHI landings and the consumer dummy variable (Equation 12). Because landings from the MHI are considered of higher quality, their volume appears to determine their own price level independently of NWHI landings.

Long-Term Demand, 1965 to 1982

In the short run, one can assume that consumer demand for a product, such as fresh bottom fish, is rather stable, since consumer preferences are themselves relatively stable. However, in the long run, a number of factors will affect the market demand for a product. First, the size of the market may change through population growth or expansion into new markets such as restaurants, retail promotion, and exports. Second, the characteristics of consumers may change through a change in their disposable income (income after taxes), or their basic preference structures may change through advertising, perceived health effects, generational shifts, etc. Summary statistics for this period appear in Table 14.2.

Not surprisingly, the statistical information suggests that the strongest long-term impact on the price for bottom fish is the growth of Hawaii's de facto population (resident and tourist combined). The simple correlation between the resident population and the inflation-adjusted price for fresh bottom fish was statistically significant, r = 0.441. Relationships with actual landings, the seasonal dummy variable, and real disposable income per capita were much weaker. However, when placed in a linear regression format, seafood volume and the consumer seasonal dummy variable, as well as resident population, are highly significant, while real disposable income per capita is not (Equation 13). These variables "explain" 60% of the variation in the inflation-adjusted price of bottom fish over the period 1965-1982.

I also investigated the cross effect of other species groups on bottom fish prices and somewhat surprisingly found a strong negative relationship between local landings of tuna (ahi--yellowfin and bigeye tunas, and aku--skipjack tuna) and the price of bottom fish (Equation 14). A regression on the price of bottom fish with bottom fish, tuna, and mahimahi or wahoo landings (using the logarithmic transformations as before) as well as the consumer dummy variable "explains" 34% of the monthly variation in price over the 18-year period. The negative effect of tuna on bottom fish price suggests some substitution, while the positive effect of mahimahi and wahoo indicates the parallel marketing of these white-fleshed species (Takenaka et al. 1984). A 22,700 kg (50,000 lb) increase in the total supply of tuna reduces bottom fish prices by only 1.8 cents; however, this change in supply is <10% of the standard deviation for tuna landings.

Finally, although prices for fresh fish in Hawaii track together to a certain extent (Equation 15), the relationship is weaker than one might expect. Over the long term, the price of bottom fish rose more rapidly than the price of all fresh fish (Figure 14.5) except skipjack tuna, which increasingly shifted from the cannery to the fresh market in Hawaii. The nonskipjack tuna prices rose at an annual rate of 1.5%, of which bottom fish prices rose by 3.1% after adjustment for inflation. In terms of the three species groups, prices tracked quite closely for the two groups with the highest percentage of catch in the NWHI, i.e., the ulua-uku and opakapaka groups (Table 14.4). The opakapaka group had the strongest time-trend

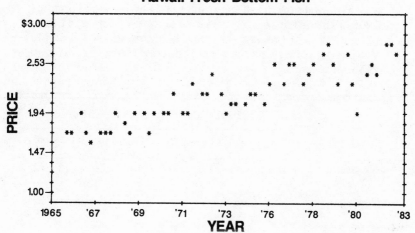

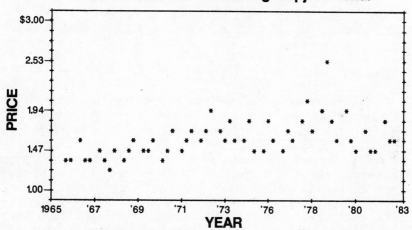

Figure 14.5 Inflation-adjusted prices for fresh bottom fish and all species, excluding skipjack tuna, Hawaii 1965-1982

(r = 0.809) and the onaga-ehu group had the lowest (r = 0.302). This also suggests the importance of the restaurant market, which has promoted opakapaka, compared with the traditional home market, which prizes onaga, for growth in the demand for fresh bottom fish in Hawaii.

TABLE 14.4
Hawaii bottom fish prices (inflation-adjusted)
1965-1982 simple correlations. All correlations
are significant at the 99.9% confidence level.
Monthly average prices for bottom fish and bottom
fish groups

	Simple Correlation Coefficients			
	PBTTM	PBTTM-G1	PBTTM-G2	PBTTM-G3
PBTTM[R]	1			
PBTTM-G1 [R]	0.888	1		
PBTTM-G2 [R]	0.864	0.731	1	
PBTTM-G3 [R]	0.643	0.454	0.523	1
Month (1-216)	0.664	0.596	0.809	0.302

CONCLUSION

The evidence obtained from examining the interaction
of pounds sold and prices in Hawaii's fresh fish market
suggests that factors affecting the supply of fresh bottom
fish and exogenous changes in Hawaii's markets, especially
in the growth of the domestic and export markets, may have
important effects on prices. As a result, to the extent
that wholesale prices are parallel to ex-vessel prices,
the incomes available to the commercial fishery will be
affected. The commercial fishers in Hawaii have long
worried about large swings in the price for fresh fish,
particularly on the "down" side, such that the total
revenue to the vessel (and hence its captain, crew, and
owner) is actually reduced despite increased landings. In
particular, MHI vessel operators worry that landings from
the larger vessels which ply the NWHI and make less
frequent landings will flood the market and reduce income
for the MHI fishery. The same problem also affects the
NWHI vessel operators who depend on some type of price
stability to rationalize their fishing schedules.
The average "swing" in the Hawaii bottom fish market
in terms of pounds sold, prices, and gross revenues is

substantial: pounds and revenue vary by 45% weekly, while prices vary by 25% (Table 14.3, coefficient of variation). In other words, although prices and quantities tend to be negatively related, there are sufficiently large exogenous effects on the market so that the income effects of "swings" may be considerable. Thus not only are Hawaii's commercial fisheries related in terms of the resource, they are linked in the market.

A particularly visible example is the effect of the newly developed NWHI bottom fishery. Using somewhat hypothetical cost and catch rate data, one NWHI vessel unloads a total of 4,500 kg (10,000 lb) of mixed bottom fish at the end of a normal trip, based on 1984 data. The captain can expect an average price of $2.45 per pound for the catch, $25,000 in gross revenue, a crew share of some $10,000, and a net income (after all expenses) of approximately $1,500 (Hau 1984; and unpublished vessel simulators by Pooley). At the same time, some 20-40 MHI vessels (fishing relatively full-time) can expect a price of $3.31 based on their total landings of 6,400 kg (14,000 lb). This would represent weekly crew incomes of $400 per person and net vessel incomes of $300 per vessel after expenses (data from NMFS cost-earnings surveys (Lyman and Hawaii Opinion 1984) and unpublished vessel simulators).

If an **additional** NWHI vessel off-loaded during a particular week, total landings would increase by 4,500 kg (10,000 lb), increasing total market volume by 42%. Average prices would fall approximately 10%: for the NWHI vessels to approximately $2.20 and for MHI vessels to $3.00 (using Equation 1 and Table 14.3). The effect on gross sales is still positive: Gross sales increase from $70,800 to $86,000, or 17.5%. However, the effect on the individual vessels is, of course, negative: Each NWHI vessel gets $2,500 less than otherwise and each MHI vessel gets $150 less. This translates into smaller crew shares and net returns per vessel. Similar effects could occur from other factors which would increase landings for one sector of the overall fishery and not another, such as increased sales by "recreational" fishers.

These competitive effects are well known and are a substantial reason why the fishing industry favors some form of management. Fishery managers, however, usually concentrate on the biological effects of overfishing on fish stocks without as much attention to the overall economic effect of such decisions. Yet simply by affecting the **timing** of total landings (optimized at whatever long-run level), fishery managers can have substantial

effects on short-run liquidity and long-run profitability
for harvesters and processors.

Seasonal closures and quotas (including the currently
popular share system known as "individual fishermen's
quotas"), which tend to "clump" landings early in the
quota period, may depress incomes for vessels landing any
species subject to price flexibility. (There are of course
other effects.) Consumers, on the other hand, would be
faced with higher prices during the off-season, during
which MHI vessels would receive relatively higher prices.
While such price effects are frequently not relevant for
"industrial" fisheries such as tuna, shrimp, and rockfish,
it is certainly the case for fresh snappers.

For example, in Hawaii's fishery, a 2-month closure
of the NWHI with no effect on total annual landings
(implying increased effort during the "on-season" and no
shifting of effort into the MHI) would increase weekly
landings during the on-season by 910 kg (2,000 lb). This
would have only a marginal impact on prices, which might
be expected to decline by 5 cents. However, for the NWHI
vessels, which are incurring larger costs during the on-
season, this will affect total net income, reducing their
annual gross sales by $27,500. During the off-season, the
amount of bottom fish available in the Hawaii market would
decline by 4,800 kg (10,500 lb) per week. This would
increase prices by 28 cents per pound, on average, and
thus increase the value of the MHI catch during the off-
season by a total of $40,000. The net gross sales effect
of the price changes in the two seasons would be almost
exactly offset for the MHI fleet.

The Council calculates that the maximum sustainable
yield (MSY) for the NWHI fishery is approximately 320,000
kg (700,000 lb) of mixed bottom fish (Council 1985). This
is approximately 30% more than was landed in 1984 as the
fishery was still developing. This increase in landings
might be expected to depress market prices until additional export markets are found: The price effect would
be 19 cents, so that gross revenue would increase by only
20%.

If the fishery stabilizes at MSY over the long term,
and Hawaii's domestic market grows because of population
effects, then there would be a positive price effect. The
State projection of population in 1990 is for a 10%
increase. The price effect of a growing market would be
45 cents (15.6%), raising gross revenue on the MSY level
of landings by $300,000.

The market for fresh bottom fish in Hawaii appears to be much as the markets for snappers are throughout the world--a market for a product highly valued with significant quality premiums. Short-run (weekly) fluctuations in landings are reflected in price but perhaps less than the commercial fishers might expect. Medium-run (monthly) fluctuations are greater and indicate the kind of problems that might arise with management measures affecting the scheduling of landings (such as annual catch quotas or seasonal closures). At the same time, the market seems capable of domestic expansion, which increases the potential biological pressure on fish stocks. Proposals for managing Hawaii's bottom fish may have to reflect the quality premiums that exist for fish coming from the MHI as well as the weak substitutability between species, especially in the case of opakapaka (Pooley 1985). Whether a high-quality frozen product would be acceptable in Hawaii and whether it would compete with the MHI catch or with frozen snapper imports is another important issue.

The total income effects shown in this section are not dramatic because of the relatively low short-term price flexibilities and small landings volume in Hawaii's fishery. However, for this small-scale industry, which is similar to other snapper fisheries throughout the world, the individual effects are important. Perhaps the state of fisheries science is not sufficiently precise to emphasize the effect of the market on the impact of fisheries regulations and development, but a general awareness of such effects would seem to be an important contribution to obtaining the highest level of social value from these unique resources.

NOTES

Appreciation but neither blame nor responsibility to three reviewers: L. Hudgins, D. Squires, and J. Waters.

1. The recorded supply of fresh bottom and reef fish in Hawaii is only some 1,250 MT (2.5-3 million lb). The discrepancy with the retail survey is not explained but may relate to double counting on the retail side (i.e., resale) and undercounting on the harvest side (through "back door" sales).

2. Disequilibrium models are not applicable to fresh fish markets.

3. Data manipulation was assisted by Jim Baxter, computer aid, and Wesley K. Higuchi, mathematics aid.

4. Kurt Kawamoto of the Western Pacific Regional Fishery Management Council was responsible for this data collection.

5. A value of -1.0 on the regression coefficient for quantity purchased (Qd) indicates price and quantity changes are strictly (negatively) proportional and the price flexibility coefficient is 100%. A value less than -1 indicates an inelastic demand where price changes relatively more than pounds sold. A coefficient of -2.0 translates into a price flexibility of 200%. A value between 0 and -1 indicates an elastic demand where pounds sold change relatively more than price. A coefficient of 0 shows a price flexibility of 0 and a coefficient of -0.50 translates into a price flexibility of 50%. However, translation of elasticities into price flexibilities, especially between ex-vesssel and retail levels, is somewhat suspect (Manderscheid 1964; Houck 1965).

BIBLIOGRAPHY

Adams, M. F. 1981. Competition and market structure in the Hawaii fish industry. Southwest Fish. Cent. Honolulu Lab., Natl. Mar. Fish. Serv., NOAA, Honolulu, HI 96822-2396, Admin. Rep. H-81-5, 20 p.

Baumol, W. R. 1982. Contestable markets: An uprising in the theory of industry structure. Am. Econ. Rev. 72-1:1-15.

Cato,J. C., and F. J. Prochaska. 1976. The Gulf of Mexico commercial and recreational red snapper-grouper fishery: An economic analysis of production, marketing, and prices. In H. R. Bullis, Jr. and A. C. Jones (editors), Proceedings: Colloquium on snapper-grouper fishery resources of the western central Atlantic Ocean, p. 95-128. Texas A&M Univ. Sea Grant Coll. and Mississippi-Alabama Sea Grant Consortium. Fla. Sea Grant Coll. Rep. 17.

Cooper, J. C., and S. G. Pooley. 1983. Characteristics of Hawaii's wholesale seafood market. Southwest Fish. Cent. Honolulu Lab., Natl. Mar. Fish. Serv., NOAA, Honolulu, HI 96822-2396, Admin. Rep. H-83-22, 33 p.

Garrod, P. V., and K. C. Chong. 1978. The fresh fish market in Hawaii. Dep. Pap. 23, Hawaii Agric. Exp. Stn., Coll. Trop. Agric., Univ. Hawaii, 24 p.

Hau, S. 1984. Economic analysis of deep bottom fishing in the Northwestern Hawaiian Islands. In R. W. Grigg and K. Y. Tanoue (editors), Proceedings of the Second

Symposium on Resource Investigations in the Northwestern Hawaiian Islands, Vol. 1, May 25-27, 1983, Univ. Hawaii, Honolulu, Hawaii, p. 265-282. UNIHISEAGRANT-MR-84-01.

Higuchi, W. K., and S.G. Pooley. 1985. Hawaii's retail seafood volume. Southwest Fish. Cent. Honolulu Lab., Natl. Mar. Fish. Serv., NOAA, Honolulu, HI 96822-2396, Admin. Rep. H-85-6, 16 p.

_____. Unpub. Market responsiveness in Hawaii's commercial fishery. Southwest Fish. Cent. Honolulu Lab., Natl. Mar. Fish. Serv., NOAA, Honolulu, HI 96822-2396.

Houck, J. P. 1965. The relationship of direct price flexibilities to direct price elasticities. J. Farm Econ. 47(3):789-792.

Hudgins, L. L. 1980. Economic model of a fisheries market with endogenous supply: The Hawaii skipjack tuna case. Ph.D. Dissertation, Univ. Hawaii, Honolulu, 114 p.

Huntsman, G. R., C. S. Manooch III, and C. B. Grimes. 1983. Yield per recruit models of some reef fishes of the U.S. South Atlantic Bight. Fish. Bull., U.S. 81:679-695.

Keithly, W. R., and F. J. Prochaska. 1984. The demand for major reef fish species in the Gulf and South Atlantic regions of the United States. Louisiana State Univ. Working Pap., 14 p.

Lyman, A. L. Inc., and Hawaii Opinion, Inc. 1984. Economic and financial analysis of Hawaii's longline and handline fisheries. Southwest Fish. Cent. Honolulu Lab., Natl. Mar. Fish. Serv., NOAA, Honolulu, HI 96822-2396, Admin. Rep. H-84-17C, var. pag.

Manderscheid, L. V. 1964. Some observations on interpreting measured demand elasticities. J. Farm Econ. 46(1):128-136.

Monaghan, C. 1985. Seafood heaven. United 30:10:86-184.

Peterson, S. B. 1973. Decisions in a market: A study of the Honolulu fish auction. Ph.D. Dissertation, Univ. Hawaii, Honolulu, 287 p.

Pindyck, R. S., and D. L. Rubinfeld. 1981. Econometric models and economic forecasts. McGraw-Hill Book Co., N.Y., 630 p.

Pooley, S. G. 1985. The hopelessness of the invisible hand: Small versus large fishing vessels in Hawaii. Southwest Fish. Cent. Honolulu Lab., Natl. Mar. Fish. Serv., NOAA, Honolulu, HI 96822-2396, Admin. Rep. H-85-2, 16 p.

_____. Unpub. Competitive markets and bilateral exchanges: The wholesale seafood market in Hawaii. Southwest Fish. Cent. Honolulu Lab., Natl. Mar. Fish. Serv., NOAA, Honolulu, HI 96822-2396.

Ralston, S. 1979. A description of the bottom fish fisheries of Hawaii, American Samoa, Guam, and the Northern Marianas. A report submitted to the Western Pacific Regional Fishery Management Council, January 1979, 102 p.

Samples, K. C., J. N. Kusakabe, and J. T. Sproul. 1984. A description and economic appraisal of charter boat fishing in Hawaii. Southwest Fish. Cent. Honolulu Lab., Natl. Mar. Fish. Serv., NOAA, Honolulu, HI 96822-2396, Admin. Rep. H-84-6C, 130 p.

Takenaka, B., L. Torricer, J. C. Cooper, and S. G. Pooley. 1984. Trends in the market for mahimahi and ono in Hawaii. Southwest Fish. Cent. Honolulu Lab., Natl. Mar. Fish. Serv., NOAA, Honolulu, HI 96822-2396, Admin. Rep. H-84-9, 20 p.

[U.S.] National Marine Fisheries Service. 1985. Fisheries of the United States. Current Fishery Statistics No. 8360, 121 p.

Vondruska, G., and F. Cunningham. 1985. Southeast finfish situation and outlook--1984. Southeast Region, Natl. Mar. Fish. Serv., NOAA, St. Petersburg, FL 33720, 16 p.

Western Pacific Regional Fishery Management Council. 1985. Combined draft fishery management plan, environmental assessment and regulatory impact review for the bottom fish and seamount groundfish fisheries of the Western Pacific Region, var. pag.

Wilson, J. A. 1980. Adaptation to uncertainty and small numbers exchange: The New England fresh fish market. Bell J. Econ. 11-2:491-504.

APPENDIX EQUATIONS

All equations involve logarithmic transformation of
the continuous variables. The variables are also transformed to account for significant levels of serial correlation (determined by the Durbin-Watson test) through the
Hildreth-Lu procedure (Pindyck and Rubinfeld 1981). The
regression estimates are calculated using ordinary least
squares techniques.

The results are given in the following form: The
first line presents the equation number, a brief description, and the data source. The second line presents the
dependent variable on the left and the independent variables on the right; the third line presents the beta
coefficients of the regression; the fourth line presents
the t-statistics; the fifth line presents summary information on the equation, including the coefficient of multiple determination (R^2), the resultant Durbin-Watson (DW)
statistic for serial-correlation, the Hildreth-Lu serial-
correlation correction factor (g), and the number of
observations. Abbrevations for each variable are introduced below the equation. The quantity data are in pounds
and prices by per pound. Statistical significance is
represented by an asterisk (*), corresponding to a 95%
confidence level.

**All values are in natural logarithms except for the
consumer dummy variable.**

Equation 1: Hawaii bottom fish demand--1984 weekly
wholesale data

PBTTM   =   CNST   QBTTM   CD

Beta   3.24   −0.23   0.42
t-statistic −4.73*   5.14*

R^2 = 48.5%, DW = 1.93, g = 0.2, N = 51

BTTM: The average price per pound of bottom fish,
              natural logarithms
QBBTM: The average quantity of bottom fish sold in
              pounds per period, natural logarithms
CNST: The constant
CD: A consumer dummy variable taking the value
              of 1 for the high demand season and the
              value of 0 for the low demand season

*Significant at the 95% confidence level.

Equation 2: Hawaii bottom fish demand—1984 monthly wholesale data

PBTTM	=	CNST	QBTTM	CD
Beta		5.68	-0.42	1.04
t-statistic			-3.33*	2.21

R^2 = 55.9%, DW = 2.07, g = 0.8, N = 12

Equation 3: Hawaii bottom fish demand by source of supply—pooled 1984 MHI and NWHI weekly data

PB:N:M	=	CNST	QBTTM	QN:Q	CD	M:N:S
Beta		2.62	-0.20	0.34	0.29	0.36
t-statistic			-4.00*	2.91*	4.29*	6.92*

R^2 = 45.3%, DW = 1.88*, g = 0, N = 104

PB:M:N: Average weekly price of bottom fish landed either from the MHI or NWHI, natural log

QN:Q: Ratio of NWHI landings to total landings for the week

M:N:S: A dummy variable valued 1 for MHI landings and 0 for NWHI landings

Equation 4: Hawaii bottom fish demand by group—1984 weekly wholesale data

PBTTM	=	CNST	QBTTMG1	QBTTMG2	QBTTMG3	CD
Beta		2.99	-0.13	-0.13	0.04	0.35
t-statistic			-3.30*	-2.90*	0.97	4.11*

R^2 = 54.5%, DW = 1.91*, g = 0.2, N = 50

QBTTMG1: Quantity for bottom fish group 1 (uku and ulua), natural log (equivalently for other groups)

Equation 5: Hawaii bottom fish demand group 1 (ulua and uku)--1984 weekly wholesale data

PBTTMG1	=	CNST	QBTTMG1	CD
Beta		1.52	-0.11	0.47
t-statistic			-1.64	3.87*

R^2 = 30.9%, DW = 1.84*, g = 0, N = 52

Equation 6: Hawaii bottom fish demand group 2 (opakapaka, et al.)--1984 weekly wholesale data

PBTTMG2	=	CNST	QBTTMG2	CD
Beta		3.04	-0.22	0.41
t-statistic			-6.19*	6.06*

R^2 = 57.5%, DW = 1.77*, g = 0, N = 52

Equation 7: Hawaii bottom fish demand group 3 (onaga, et al.)--1984 weekly wholesale data

PBTTMG3	=	CNST	QBTTMG2	CD
Beta		3.31	-0.11	0.31
t-statistic			-3.48*	1.96

R^2 = 29.8%, DW = 1.96*, g = 0.6, N = 52

Equation 8: Hawaii bottom fish group 1 (ulua and uku) cross effects--1984 weekly wholesale data

PBTTMG1	=	CNST	QBTTMG1	QBTTM2&3	CD
Beta		2.98	-0.08	-0.18	0.54
t-statistic			-1.25	-2.85*	4.70*

R^2 = 40.9%, DW = 2.17*, g = 0, N = 52

QBTTM2&3:   Quantity for groups 2 and 3 combined, natural log (equivalently for other groups)

Equation 9: Hawaii bottom fish group 2 (opakapaka, et al.) cross effects—1984 weekly wholesale data

PBTTMG2 =	CNST	QBTTMG2	QBTTM1&3	CD
Beta	3.43	−0.19	−0.08	0.39
t—statistic		−4.36*	−1.26	5.77*

R^2 = 57.5%, DW = 1.75*, g = 0, N = 52

Equation 10: Hawaii bottom fish group 3 (onaga, et al.) cross effects—1984 weekly wholesale data

PBTTMG3 =	CNST	QBTTMG3	QBTTM1&2	CD
Beta	3.58	−0.10	−0.03	0.32
t—statistic		−2.65*	−0.53	1.97

R^2 = 23.9%, DW = 2.03*, g = 0.6, N = 50

Equation 11: Hawaii bottom fish demand by source—1984 weekly wholesale data

PBTTM84 =	CNST	QMHI	QNWHI	CD
Beta	2.12	−0.10	−0.03	0.43
t—statistic		−2.04*	−0.88	4.08*

R^2 = 32.9%, DW = 2.02, g = 0.2, N = 47

QMHI: Quantity landed from main Hawaiian Islands, natural log
QNWHI: Quantity landed from Northwestern Hawaiian Islands, natural log

Equation 12:   Main Hawaiian Islands bottom fish prices--
1984 weekly wholesale data

PMHI	=	CONST	QMHI	QNWHI	CD
Beta		2.29	-0.16	0.03	0.38
t-statistic			-3.43*	1.21	3.84*

R^2 = 15.53%, DW = 1.98*, g = 0.2, N = 44

PMHI: Average price for bottom fish landed from
the main Hawaiian Islands, natural log

Equation 13:   Hawaii commercial landings, bottom fish
demand--HDAR monthly data, 1965-1982 (prices
adjusted by the December 1982 consumer price
index for Honolulu)

PBTTM[R]	=	CNST	RES	RDINC	QBTTM	CD
Beta		-9.29	1.56	0.05	-0.23	0.145
t-statistic			11.30*	0.67	-8.45*	4.25*

R^2 = 44.9%, DW = 2.12, g = 0.4, N = 214

PBTTM[R]:   Inflation-adjusted price of bottom fish,
natural log
QBTTM: Quantity of bottom fish (1,000s lb), natural
log
RES: Resident population in Hawaii (1,000s),
natural log
RDINC: Real disposable income per capita in Hawaii,
(inflation-adjusted), natural log

Equation 14: Hawaii commercial landings, cross effects—HDAR monthly data, 1965–1982 (prices adjusted by the December 1982 consumer price index for Honolulu)

PBTTM[R] =	CNST	QBTTM	QTUNA	QMAHI	CD
Beta	1.78	−0.18	−0.13	0.13	0.12
t–statistic		−5.98*	−7.02*	6.65*	3.03*

R^2 = 33.5%, DW = 1.88*, g = 0.4, N = 214

QTUNA: Quantity of fresh market tuna (1,000s 1b), natural log

QMAHI: Quantity of mahimahi and wahoo (1,000s 1b), natural log

Equation 15: Hawaii bottom fish price trends—HDAR monthly data, 1965–1982 (prices adjusted by the December 1982 consumer price index for Honolulu)

PBTTM[R] =	CNST	PFISH[R]
Beta	0.71	0.29
t–statistic		8.85*

R^2 = 25.7%, DW = 2.08*, g = 0.4, N = 214

PFISH[R]:   Price of all species, inflation–adjusted, natural log

15
Workshop Synthesis and Directions for Future Research[1]

John L. Munro
International Center for Living Aquatic Resources
Management, South Pacific Office
Townsville, Qld 4810, Australia

ABSTRACT

The proceedings of the workshop are reviewed
and the major points arising from the presentations
and discussions are summarized under the headings of
taxonomy and systematics, reproduction, larval and
juvenile stages, age and growth, mortality, feeding,
stock assessment, and management. Future research
needs are identified and some recommendations made
on research methods.

INTRODUCTION

The task confronting this contributor was twofold:
(1) to draw together the conclusions of this meeting
(without being unduly repetitive); and (2) to formulate
some opinions on future research needs and priorities, if
effective mechanisms for regulation and management of
fisheries for snappers and groupers are to be developed.
A basic dichotomy must be recognized in what is
covered by the term "tropical snappers and groupers."
Many of the species of principal interest to commercial
fishermen on a worldwide basis are those which occupy the
so-called "deep reefs" or "outer slopes" in depths of 60
to 250 m. These tend to be relatively large and abundant
fishes, and a few species usually represent the major
portion of the aquatic biomass at those depths. In
contrast, other snappers and groupers and associated
groups such as the lethrinids and plectorhynchids occupy
relatively shallow, often coralline, tropical shelves.
With some notable exceptions, most of these fishes are

639

relatively small and usually are a minor (although economically important) component of the total exploited fish community. Thus, while it is possible to conceive of management schemes for each of the deep-dwelling species or species groups, the management of the shallow-dwelling species must be effected as part of some overall scheme for the whole exploited fish community.

Management schemes will also vary among countries. For example, in Australia the target species in shelf waters of the Great Barrier Reef are the coral trout (_Plectropomus_ spp.) and a small selection of other groupers, snappers, plectorhynchids, and lethrinids. There are limited markets for any other species of reef fishes. In contrast, in the developing countries to the north of Australia, which have similar fish communities, a very wide range of shallow-dwelling tropical fishes and other organisms are marketable, and the above-mentioned groups are merely a highly desirable component of the catch. Additionally, in many developing countries the deep-dwelling snappers and groupers are not currently exploited because of technological deficiencies or high operating costs combined with limited markets for large fishes. Thus management problems will tend to be country-specific. In contrast, biological and ecological problems have broad international overtones, and many species have very wide distributions over the Indo-Pacific or Caribbean faunal provinces.

There are few research problems that pertain exclusively to snappers and groupers as opposed to other harvestable reef fishes. In many areas snappers and groupers are the most valuable and sought-after components in reef fisheries, occupy the topmost trophic levels in fish communities, and exert a major influence over the other parts of the fish community (Goeden 1982). The degree to which these families influence their prey species is not yet quantified and our knowledge of mortality rates in reef communities is minimal, as is our understanding of the degree to which these will change under the influence of fishing.

TAXONOMY AND SYSTEMATICS

Although taxonomic questions will no doubt continue to arise for many years, the syntheses offered in the first three chapters of this book will serve to clarify the identity and status of the snappers (Lutjanidae) and groupers (Serranidae: Epinephelinae). Being generally large species, a problem common to these groups is the lack of adequate size ranges of samples, and greater efforts are needed to secure both very large specimens and very small individuals, particularly of the serranids. It also appeared to the workshop that the systematics of the "red snapper" group in the Indo-Pacific was not yet fully resolved and would continue to be a source of uncertainty for some time.

REPRODUCTION

Problems of reproductive life histories are fundamentally different in the lutjanids and serranids. The lutjanids are, without known exception, gonochoristic and often appear to be sexually dimorphic in size, but no clear pattern of which sex is usually the larger is apparent. It seems highly likely that all epinepheline serranids are protogynous hermaphrodites. While the groups are properly treated separately, common problems include a scarcity of data on the seasonality of reproduction and recruitment and difficulties in interpreting results of studies of the seasonality of gonad maturation.

Details of the seasonality of reproduction are only available for a few species, and contradictions emerge when generalizations are made. In the case of the groupers a particular question relates to why Caribbean groupers appear, with few exceptions, to spawn over a limited period in the winter months (Thompson and Munro 1974; Olsen and LaPlace 1979; Munro 1983a) whereas Indo-Pacific species appear to spawn in summer (Goeden 1978; Chen et al. 1980; Loubens 1980). Grimes (1986) has suggested that snappers exhibit two distinct spawning patterns, irrespective of latitude, in which insular stocks spawn year-round, usually with spring or fall peaks, while continental stocks have an extended summer spawning season. A possible alternative interpretation of the available data is that snappers are summer spawners in higher latitudes but tend towards spring and fall spawning in lower latitudes, where most of the islands are located. Studies of reproductive patterns in subtropical islands such as Hawaii and Bermuda might clarify this. The data of Loubens (1980) indicate that the snappers of New Caledonia (at lat. 23° S) have a single, midsummer spawning peak.

However, the important point is that the main part of the problem lies in the interpretation of what is observed in the gonads of specimens (which are perhaps selectively caught), what is observed by divers, and what arrives on the nursery grounds. All too often there is poor agreement between these phenomena in reef fish in general. The possibility emerges that many species of tropical reef fish, including the snappers (but probably not the groupers), spawn over very extended periods in the equatorial regions, but that the survival of their larvae is predicated by environmental factors (often on a local or subregional scale), leading to major periods of recruitment being observed over a much shorter time period than observed spawning activity. This "survival window" concept (Sharp 1981; Bakun et al. 1982) requires careful examination. Studies of seasonality of gonad maturation in fishes, covering the full size range of the species and taken from the full range of depths and habitats occupied, should be combined with monitoring of recruitment in a number of different sites in the distributional range of the species in question and, for those species living in relatively shallow water, routine observation of spawning activity by divers.

The problem of managing fisheries for hermaphroditic species occupied more time than any other topic during the meeting but was not resolved (Bannerot et al. 1986; Shapiro 1986). In particular, the question of whether or not sex change in groupers is behaviorally induced, merely occurs at a certain size, or cannot be induced below a certain size is unresolved but is vital to developing management techniques for these fishes. Future research appears to require histological studies on a wider range of grouper species, particularly on Indo-Pacific species, and comparisons of size frequencies of male and female groupers and sex ratios in stocks exploited at different intensities (Bannerot et al. 1986). The essence of the unresolved debate is that if sex change is under behavioral control, then heavily exploited stocks of groupers may still be reproductively functional because females will transform into males at a progressively smaller size. If this does not occur, grouper stocks will tend towards reproductive disfunctionality as the numbers of fishes surviving to the size at transformation is diminished as a result of exploitation. Bannerot et al. (1986) predict that protogynous hermaphrodites such as groupers will be reproductively superior to gonochorists over a broad range of female biased sex ratios, provided that reproductive success is not limited by the availability of sperm. That is, provided that the surviving males are able to release appreciable quantities of sperm in the vicinity of most spawning females and the density of sperm in the water column is sufficient to ensure fertilization of virtually all eggs, there will be no diminution of reproductive success. Furthermore, by virtue of most animals being females, there will be an actual gain in the numbers of eggs produced.

However, a better understanding is required of the possible evolutionary benefits or disadvantages of gonochorism over sequential hermaphroditism and of protogyny over protandry. Why, for example, are the groupers protogynous hermaphrodites while the lethrinids are protandrous hermaphrodites and the snappers, which have similar ecological and morphological characteristics to the lethrinids, are bisexual gonochorists?

LARVAL AND JUVENILE STAGES

The problem of larval survival and subsequent recruitment to reef fish stocks has been discussed by a number of authors (Munro et al. 1973; Sale 1980; Williams 1980; Doherty 1981; Munro 1983a; Munro and Williams 1985) and it is not expected that snappers and groupers will differ in any significant respects from other reef fish. In essence, the current evidence suggests that isolated habitats such as reefs can be chronically recruitment-limited because the fraction of the tropical oceans that is actually covered by reefs is very small and most of the pelagic larvae that survive to metamorphosis therefore perish as a result of being remote from suitable habitats when they reach metamorphosis.

Research on the pelagic phases of the life histories of snappers and groupers has been faced with the vexing problem of the very low abundances of larvae in the plankton. This places severe limits on the numbers of specimens of each stage available for taxonomic purposes and leads to extremely limited possibilities for statistical treatment of samples.

Grouper and snapper larvae are found mostly in coastal waters (Leis 1986). It would, therefore, appear likely that the spawning strategies of the two groups are fundamentally similar and that spawning occurs in areas where the larvae are likely to be entrained in coastal eddies and have some chance of recruiting to the same areas in which they were spawned. The retention of eggs and larvae in eddies is a fundamental part of the recruitment problem. As these are local events, it can be expected that recruitment limitation will be area-specific and that areas favored by consistent gyres of the right magnitude will always receive more recruits than other areas and, if space and food are not limiting factors, support larger stocks per unit area.

A major research problem is to identify settlement periods for snappers and groupers. In some, if not most cases, this will also entail identifying the settlement and early juvenile habitats. It is often extremely difficult to find juveniles of many of the larger, commonly exploited reef fish species, and some fairly sophisticated and relatively expensive programs need to be mounted to solve these problems.

The role of sea grass beds as nursery grounds for members of these families needs to be investigated, as there is some evidence that such areas might be of major importance in the tropics. However, this also raises the problem of the location of alternative nursery grounds in those reef areas which do not harbor sea grasses.

AGE AND GROWTH

The paucity of information on the growth of prerecruit snappers and groupers is perhaps best high-lighted by the fact that the topic was barely mentioned during the course of the meeting. Indeed, it seems that the only information presently available is from a few studies in which limited numbers of otoliths of a few species have been examined for daily rings (Brothers and McFarland 1981; Brothers 1982; Brothers et al. 1983; Brouard et al. 1984). Additionally, there might be information on the growth of hatchery-reared groupers in Southeast Asia. There appears to be a good opportunity here for use of daily rings in otoliths to clarify aspects of the life history as has been done by Brothers and McFarland (1981) in the case of the grunt, Haemulon flavolineatum.

In the case of adult snappers and groupers the evidence presented to the workshop suggests that as a general case the von Bertalanffy growth function (VBGF) is an adequate descriptor of growth. However, the use of this function is still bedevilled by problems of interpretation of the parameters. Some of the discussions of the workshop centered on the possible magnitudes of values of the growth coefficient K and of L_∞, and there was some criticism of the tendency to equate a low value of K, with "slow" growth. The rate at which fishes increase in mass is very much a function of the values both of K and of the asymptotic weight and is more dependent upon the latter value. Compared with most other species or groups of reef fishes, the snappers and groupers are rapid-growing simply by virtue of their relatively large sizes. However, compared with the smaller reef fishes, they are slow to attain maturity; this can be an important factor in their management because by virtue of their rapid growth they are usually recruited to the fisheries at a relatively early, immature age.

It is clear that a better understanding is needed of the range of possible values of the parameters of the VBGF within species or within families. Linear relationships between the log of the VBGF growth parameter (K) and the log of the asymptotic weight or length have been estimated from a data set composed of a diverse group of species (Munro and Pauly 1983; Pauly and Munro 1984). These relationships are more than just empirical equations but have a biological basis.

Following this approach, Manooch (1986) presents a relationship between growth parameter K and the asymptotic length L_∞ estimated from a pooled data set of just snappers and groupers as follows:

$$Log_{10}(K) = 1.098 - 0.658 \, Log_{10}(L_\infty).$$

This relationship can be used to obtain a preliminary estimate of K for a snapper or grouper from an estimate of the asymptotic length.

MORTALITY

By far the best information on the value of the coefficient of natural mortality (M) is that derived from sampling virgin stocks. However, as the fisheries for the deep-living snappers and groupers develop throughout the tropics, the opportunities to gather such data are diminishing and there is an urgent need to acquire samples from such stocks before the opportunity is irretrievably lost. The criticality of reliable estimates of M in stock assessments is well illustrated by the work of Sainsbury (1986).

It was suggested by Ralston (1986) that, as a general case, the ratios of the coefficients of natural mortality and growth (M/K) are close to 2.0 in snappers and groupers, even if sufficient data have not yet been gathered to precisely define the value. The fact that this ratio can be derived from size-frequency distributions of unexploited stocks (or the ratio of Z/K in the case of exploited stocks) where Z is the coefficient of total mortality (Beverton and Holt 1956) without any knowledge of the growth rates (Munro and Thompson 1973; Jones 1984) is of the greatest importance. If the values of M/K, L_∞, and W_∞ are known, preliminary stock assessments can be made using the Beverton and Holt (1957) yield per recruit model (Munro 1983b). If generalizations about family-specific values of M/K can be substantiated, then the value of the ratio of the coefficient of fishing mortality, F, to the growth coefficient, K, can be established for exploited populations merely by subtracting M/K from Z/K values derived from length-frequency distributions. One important qualification needs to be made in respect of the foregoing. It is usually assumed that M will be a constant throughout the lives of the fishes or at least through the exploited phase. However, if predation is a major source of mortality then the natural mortality rates of prey species must change in response to exploitation of their predators or any other factor which reduces the abundance of the predators. It would therefore appear that the M/K ratios are ecologically determined and might vary within a certain range in response to changes in the community that are brought about by exploitation of multispecies stocks.

The most important developments in fisheries science in recent years have probably been the advances in length-frequency-based stock assessment methodologies (Pauly 1982; Pauly and Morgan In press), particularly the development of length-converted catch curves, which enable mortality rates to be directly estimated from length-frequency data provided that the growth parameters are known and samples have been accumulated in a statistically satisfactory manner over, at least, a full year. The latter proviso is essential in the case of relatively fast-growing fishes but less so in the case of slow-growing animals.

The methodologies for construction of length-frequency-based catch curves now include: (1) that developed by Pauly (1982, 1983); (2) an iterative modification of Pauly's method by Sparre (Pauly 1984:64); (3) that of Jones and Van Zalinge (1981); and (4) a recent development by Wetherall et al. (In press). All of these

methods except Pauly's assume that the coefficient of
mortality, Z, is constant and mortality estimates are,
therefore, neither length- nor age-specific. The most
important feature of the catch curves is that they enable
fisheries scientists to monitor Z in exploited stocks
without recourse to data on actual fishing effort (Munro
1983b).

FEEDING

The detailed review by Parrish (1986) quite clearly
shows the basic predatory habits of the two families and
emphasizes the importance of fish, shrimp, and crabs in
diets, with more variety in the diet of snappers,
including the liberal utilization of pelagic urochordates.
The latter is a manifestation of the fact that the energy
flow in reef systems is partly governed by the reef acting
as a giant plankton net (Munro and Williams 1985).

The recognition that the components of multispecies
stocks cannot be managed individually has led to the
development of ecosystem models (e.g., Polovina 1984) that
offer insights into the flow of energy in exploited
ecosystems. This has generated a need for much more
information about the food consumed by tropical species.
In particular, more information is required on electivity
(Ivlev 1961) together with more systematic or consistent
methods for reporting food items.

STOCK ASSESSMENT

Despite all of the efforts at modeling fish stocks,
the fallback positions are still (1) the Beverton and Holt
(1957) constant recruitment model; (2) various surplus
production models (Schaefer 1954, 1957; Fox 1970; Gulland
1971; Munro and Thompson 1973; Schnute 1977; Csirke and
Caddy 1983; (3) cohort or virtual population analyses
(VPA) (Gulland 1965; Pope 1972; Jones and Van Zalinge
1981).

All of the models have acknowledged deficiencies in
the form of assumptions of constant parameters or stock-
recruitment relationships, and all are basically intended
for single species assessments. As species interactions
are still very difficult to quantify, the choice is one of
either simply summing the yield curves for single species,
or empirically regressing catch per unit of effort,

against effort, for all or parts of exploited communities
if applying the existing methodologies to multispecies
stocks. Ralston and Polovina (1982) used cluster analysis
to aggregate species in the Hawaiian deep-sea handline
fishery into three groups to which a stock production
model was applied.

In almost all cases, catch statistics are inadequate
and cohort analyses or VPAs have not yet been published
for any stocks of snappers or groupers. Contributions to
this volume utilize both length-based and age-based
assessment methods. Both methodologies are applicable to
snappers and groupers, but in tropical latitudes age
estimation is very difficult and time-consuming and, in
many countries, skilled technicians are not available. It
is important to recognize that length- and age-based
methodologies are complementary.

A particular research opportunity that to date has
only been pursued by Ralston et al. (In press) involves
the possible amalgamation of the visual census techniques
developed by reef fish ecologists (Brock 1954; Craik 1981;
Brock 1982; Sale and Sharp 1983; Bell et al. 1985; Russ
1985) with catch rate data derived from test fishing or
monitoring of catches. Visual census data yield estimates
of numbers, and if data on average sizes are available, on
total biomass. The catch rate of a particular gear
divided by the mean biomass at that time leads directly to
an estimate of the catchability coefficient, q, defined as
the average amount of mortality generated by one unit of
fishing effort. If the total fishing effort (f) on a reef
is known, the fishing mortality (F) can be calculated as $F
= qf$. In exploited stocks, the total mortality rate (Z)
can be independently estimated from the size-frequency
distributions of catches, and natural mortality rates (M)
could be estimated by deduction ($M = Z - F$).

The intensive fishing technique adopted by Polovina
(1986) for assessing the fisheries of the Mariana Archipelago also leads to estimates of catchability (q) and
virgin biomass ($B\infty$) and concurrently yields size frequency
samples which can give some indication of the natural
mortality coefficient (M).

These approaches should, in theory, give all of the
data required for complete single-species stock assessments, as is demonstrated by Polovina (1986).

The methods could also be combined with the Csirke
and Caddy (1983) model in which catch rates are regressed
against the coefficient of total mortality, Z. The latter
can be derived from routine length-frequency analysis and

the catch rates could be obtained from routine test fishing or from monitoring selected vessels (Munro 1983b).

MANAGEMENT

Several contributors alluded to the fact that catches of snappers and groupers usually decline drastically relative to other components of the reef community and the species can even become virtually extinct. This is attributed to low M/K ratios, high catchability, and high demand--perhaps coupled in the case of groupers with protogynous hermaphroditism. In the absence of effective management of snapper and grouper fisheries, it appears to be inevitable that this will happen.

One of the basic items of information for which adequate estimates are still lacking is the harvests that can be expected per unit area or linear measure of an isobath. The estimates given by Polovina (1986) suggest that harvests from the community of snappers and jacks in the Marianas would be in the range 165-280 kg/nmi of the 200 m isobath when F is set at 1.0, while the maximum sustainable yield (MSY) in the Hawaiian Islands is conservatively estimated at 272 kg/nmi. These are very low values in comparison with the yields of 15 metric tons (MT)/km^2, which appear to be possible on intensively harvested coralline shelves in depths of <30 m (Munro 1984; Munro and Williams 1985), and they highlight the fact that, even if the estimates eventually prove to be somewhat conservative, the resources, principally snapper, available from around the steep outer reefs of oceanic islands are unlikely to be very large.

Great care must be taken to avoid overcapitalizing such fisheries in which the accumulated virgin stocks are substantial. The initial catch rates will be relatively high but can be expected to decline quite rapidly. High initial profits should be regarded as an opportunity to pay off capital and not to further capitalize the fishery. A knowledge of the likely harvests at F_{opt} makes it possible to calculate the numbers of boats that the fishery will be able to support, given data on the area or length of the 200-m isobath available to the fishery and the catch rates necessary to profitably sustain the operations of the proposed vessels.

On the basis of observations in exploited communities, it has been suggested (Clark and Brown 1977; Munro and Smith 1985; Munro and Williams 1985; Russ 1985) that a sequence of changes in the composition of exploited fish communities will occur in response to exploitation, and that the larger fishes such as snappers and groupers will be among the first species to decline to negligible levels as a result of exploitation. This means that in fisheries in which the large species are the principal target species (for example, in the United States and Australia), effort needs to be constrained to far lower levels than would be regarded as optimal in fisheries where all species of reef fishes can be marketed.

Management options mentioned during the workshop included limitations on entry to the fishery, area closures, catch limits or quotas, and size limits. Limitations on entry are, it appears, anathema to United States fishermen, and only the paper describing the somewhat atypical trawl fishery of the Northwest Australian Shelf (Sainsbury 1986) deals with effort regulation as a management tool. In that particular context this raises few problems, as only licensed foreign vessels are active in the fishery. Elsewhere in the world, one can expect that limitations on entry to the fisheries will be more readily adopted and the major difficulty facing U.S. fisheries will not be encountered.

In the U.S. portions of the Gulf of Mexico and the waters off the southeastern United States, the move has been towards the imposition of size limits based upon single-species assessments (Huntsman and Waters 1986). As most of the fishes in question are taken by hook and line, the survival of undersized fish that are returned to the sea after capture is critical if yield is to be optimized or maximized. Studies described in this volume suggest that survival might well be sufficiently high for a benefit to be realized by the fisheries. However, there must be some doubts over whether the same survival rates will be realized when fish are unhooked by amateur anglers or commercial fishermen. There is extremely little information on gear selectivity for any of the snapper and grouper fisheries, and this would appear to be a topic deserving of more attention. Although Ralston (1982) found that hooks within the usual size range used by Hawaiian fishermen have little effect on the size composition of catches, significant changes in size compositions in response to hook sizes have been found by others (McCracken 1963; Satersdal 1963) in temperate water fisheries. It might, therefore, be worthwhile investigating the selectivity of hooks covering a wider size range than those used by Ralston (1982), in order to define more clearly the selective effects. The likely situation would be that hooks have flattened, bell-shaped selection curves and that while small hooks will often capture large fishes, the converse will be much less common. Well-publicized information on optimum hook sizes might be effective in reducing catches of undersized fish, even if the use of recommended sizes is purely voluntary.

There are some indications that in virgin stocks or lightly exploited stocks, the size at first capture by the fisheries will be larger than in heavily exploited stocks, simply because the larger fishes are more aggressive and less cautious in taking baits or entering traps (e.g., Thompson and Munro 1974). This raises the possibility that, to some degree at least, the mean length at first capture, ℓ_c, will be an inverse function of the fishing intensity. If this is true, and it needs to be validated, this factor will also have to be inserted into analytical models of fisheries in which ℓ_c is not regulated.

In connection with size limits, the conclusion reached by Polovina (1986) that:

$$\text{if } \ell_c > \ell_m , \quad F_{opt} <= 2M$$
$$\text{or}$$
$$\text{if } \ell_c <= \ell_m , \quad F_{opt} <= M$$

(in which ℓ_m is the mean length at maturity, F_{opt} is the "optimum" fishing effort and M is the coefficient of natural mortality), is another of those useful rules of thumb that will need to be applied in the interim before snapper and grouper fisheries can be properly managed.

It would appear that in the U.S. context, the reduction of effort by seasonal or areal closures is the only mechanism available for reducing effort. While such measures can be inflicted upon the angling communities without undue hardship (although not without some complaints), application of the same restrictions to the professional and party-boat operators would undoubtedly cause severe economic disruptions.

In the shallow-reef areas from which the bulk of the world's snapper and grouper catches are taken by myriads of artisanal fishermen, management problems are likely to remain intractable. In contrast to the deep-reef fisheries, in which only a few interacting species are harvested, the shallow-reef fisheries harvest hundreds of species of fishes including dozens of species of snappers and groupers. The fisheries for the higher-priced and more desirable snappers and groupers cannot be regulated as separate entities as these fish merely number in the top predatory components of a highly complex ecosystem. Depending upon price differentials between the most-valued and lesser-valued species, it might not be worth endeavoring to maintain predatory species at high levels if this merely maintains high natural mortality rates in the prey species and thus reduces the harvests available to the fishermen.

However, our knowledge of species interactions is simply inadequate for attempts to be made to develop dynamic models of these communities, even though the "equilibrium" model ECOPATH (Polovina 1984), represents a major step towards an understanding of how such communities might respond to selective exploitation.

In the interim we need to accept management plans based on empirical approaches to assessment such as the various forms of total biomass surplus yield curves (Munro and Thompson 1973; Brown et al. 1976), which while lacking in any finesse still appear to be the only tools available that can immediately be applied to a wide range of fisheries.

The need to conserve spawning stocks was also recognized, and the possibility of having areas permanently closed to fishing to serve as reservoirs of spawning stock was discussed. Artificial reefs and environmental enhancement were also mentioned, but it was noted that the cost-effectiveness of artificial reefs has yet to be demonstrated.

An approach which needs to be investigated involves the artificial stocking of reefs with selected species of snappers and groupers or other desirable species of reef fishes (Munro and Williams 1985). This is feasible only if reef fish stocks are recruitment-limited and space and food resources are not limiting factors.

Although the fisheries covered by the workshop were principally those of the United States, it needs to be recognized that the problems of assessing and managing these stocks are not unique to the United States. Many useful deductions can be made by examining these topics over the widest possible geographic range. Examples of changes in species composition in the absence of effective management can be seen in the fisheries of Southeast Asia and of the Caribbean. Much can be learned by seeking analogies in the lightly and selectively exploited fisheries of the Great Barrier Reef.

Finally, a detailed look at the deepwater snapper market in Hawaii (which appears similar to other U.S.

markets for snappers and groupers) indicates that it is primarily a fresh fish market, highly valued, with significant quality premiums. It was noted that in this type of market, management measures such as annual catch quotas or seasonal landings which could produce fluctuations in landings would result in price fluctuations which would adversely affect fishermen (Pooley 1986).

NOTE

1. ICLARM Contribution No. 266.

BIBLIOGRAPHY

Bakun, A., J. Beyer, D. Pauly, J. G. Pope, and G. D. Sharp. 1982. Ocean sciences in relation to living resources. Can. J. Fish. Aquat. Sci. 39:1059-1070.

Bannerot, S. P., W. W. Fox, Jr., and J. E. Powers. 1986. Reproduction strategies and the management of snappers and groupers in the Gulf of Mexico and Caribbean. In J. J. Polovina and S. Ralston (editors), Tropical snappers and groupers: Biology and fisheries management. Westview Press, Inc., Boulder. [See this volume.]

Bell, J. D., G. J. S. Craik, D. A. Pollard, and B. C. Russell. 1985. Estimating length frequency distributions of large reef fish underwater. Coral Reefs 4:41-44.

Beverton, R. J. H., and S. J. Holt. 1956. A review of methods for estimating mortality rates in fish populations with special reference to sources of bias in catch sampling. Rapp. P.-V. Reun. Cons. Int. Explor. Mer 140:67-83.

_____. 1957. On the dynamics of exploited fish populations. Fish. Invest. Ser. II, Mar. Fish., G. B. Minist. Agric. Fish. Food 19:1-533.

Brock, R. E. 1982. A critique of the visual census method for assessing coral reef fish populations. Bull. Mar. Sci. 32:269-276.

Brock, V. 1954. A preliminary report on a method of estimating reef fish populations. J. Wildl. Manage. 18:297-308.

Brothers, E. B. 1982. Aging reef fishes. In G. R. Huntsman, W. R. Nicholson, and W. W. Fox (editors),

The biological bases for reef fishery management, p. 3-23. U.S. Dep. Commer., NOAA Tech. Memo. NMFS, NOAA-TM-NMFS-SEFC-80.

Brothers, E. B., and W. N. McFarland. 1981. Correlations between otolith microstructure, growth, and life history transitions in newly recruited French grunts [Haemulon flavolineatum (Desmarest), Haemulidae]. Rapp. P.-V. Reun. Cons. Int. Explor. Mer 178:369-374.

Brothers, E. B., D. McB. Williams, and P. F. Sale. 1983. Length of larval life in twelve families of fishes at "One Tree Lagoon," Great Barrier Reef, Australia. Mar. Biol. (Berl.) 76:319-324.

Brouard, F., R. Grandperrin, M. Kulbicki, and J. Rivaton. 1984. Note on observations of daily rings on otoliths of deepwater snappers. ICLARM Transl. 3, 8 p.

Brown, B. E., J. A. Brennan, M. D. Grosslein, E. G. Heyerdahl, and R. C. Hennemuth. 1976. The effect of fishing on the marine finfish biomass in the northwest Atlantic from the Gulf of Maine to Cape Hatteras. Int. Comm. Northwest Atl. Fish. Res. Bull. 12:49-68.

Chen, C.-P., H. L. Hsieh, and K.-H. Chang. 1980. Some aspects of the sex change and reproductive biology of the grouper, Epinephelus diacanthus (Cuvier et Valenciennes). Bull. Inst. Zool. Acad. Sin. (Taipei) 18:11-17.

Clark, S. H., and B. E. Brown. 1977. Changes in biomass of finfishes and squids from the Gulf of Maine to Cape Hatteras, 1963-74, as determined from research vessel survey data. Fish. Bull., U.S. 75:1-21.

Craik, W. 1981. Underwater survey of coral trout Plectropomus leopardus (Serranidae) populations in the Capricornia section of the Great Barrier Reef Marine Park. In E. D. Gomez, C. E. Birkeland, R. W. Buddemeier, R. E. Johannes, J. A. Marsh, Jr., and R. T. Tsuda (editors), Proc. 4th Int. Coral Reef Symp., Manila 1:53-58.

Csirke, J., and J. F. Caddy. 1983. Production modeling using mortality estimates. Can. J. Fish. Aquat. Sci. 40:43-51.

Doherty, P. J. 1981. Coral reef fishes: Recruitment-limited assemblages? In E. D. Gomez, C. E. Birkeland, R. W. Buddemeier, R. E. Johannes, J. A. Marsh, Jr., and R. T. Tsuda (editors), Proc. 4th Int. Coral Reef Symp., Manila 2:465-470.

Fox, W. W., Jr. 1970. An exponential surplus-yield model for optimizing exploited fish populations. Trans. Am. Fish. Soc. 99:80-88.

Goeden, G. B. 1978. A monograph of the coral trout Plectropomus leopardus Lacepède. Queensl. Fish. Serv. Res. Bull. 1:1-42.

_____. 1982. Intensive fishing and a keystone predator species: Ingredients for community instability. Biol. Conserv. 22:273-281.

Grimes, C. B. 1986. Reproductive biology of the Lutjanidae: A review. In J. J. Polovina and S. Ralston (editors), Tropical snappers and groupers: Biology and fisheries management. Westview Press, Inc., Boulder. [See this volume.]

Gulland, J. A. 1965. Estimation of mortality rates. Annex to Arctic Fishery Working Group Rep. ICES CM 1965(3):9.

_____ (compiler and editor). 1971. The fish resources of the ocean. Fishing News (Books) Ltd., Surrey, Engl., 255 p.

Huntsman, G. R., and J. R. Waters. 1986. Development of management plans for reef fishes--Gulf of Mexico and United States South Atlantic. In J. J. Polovina and S. Ralston (editors), Tropical snappers and groupers: Biology and fisheries management. Westview Press, Inc., Boulder. [See this volume.]

Ivlev, V. S. 1961. Experimental ecology of the feeding of fishes. Yale Univ. Press, New Haven, 302 p. (Transl. from Russ. by D. Scott.)

Jones, R. 1984. Assessing the effects of changes in exploitation pattern using length composition data (with notes on VPA and cohort analysis). FAO Fish. Tech. Pap. 256:1-118.

Jones, R., and N. P. Van Zalinge. 1981. Estimates of mortality rate and population size for shrimps in Kuwait waters. Kuwait Bull. Mar. Sci. 2:273-288.

Leis, J. M. 1986. Review of the early life history of tropical groupers (Serranidae) and snappers (Lutjanidae). In J. J. Polovina and S. Ralston (editors), Tropical snappers and groupers: Biology and fisheries management. Westview Press, Inc., Boulder. [See this volume.]

Loubens, G. 1980. Biologie de quelques especes de poissons du lagon Neo-Caledonien. II. Sexualite et reproduction. Cah. l'Indo-Pac. 2(1):41-72.

Manooch, C. S., III. 1986. Age and growth of snappers and groupers. In J. J. Polovina and S. Ralston (editors), Tropical snappers and groupers: Biology and fisheries management. Westview Press, Inc., Boulder. [See this volume.]

McCracken, F. D. 1963. Selection by codend meshes and hooks on cod, haddock, flatfish and redfish. In The selectivity of fishing gear, p. 131-155. Proc. Joint ICNAF/ICES/FAO Spec. Sci. Meet., Lisbon, 1957, Vol. 2. Spec. Publ. 5, Int. Comm. Northwest Atl. Fish., Dartmouth N.S., Can.

Munro, J. L. 1983a. Epilogue: Progress in coral reef fisheries research, 1973-1982. In J. L. Munro (editor), Caribbean coral reef fishery resources, p. 249-265. ICLARM Stud. Rev. 7.

_____. 1983b. A cost-effective data acquisition system for assessment and management of tropical multispecies, multi-gear fisheries. Fishbyte [ICLARM] 1(1):7-12.

_____. 1984. Yields from coral reef fisheries. Fishbyte [ICLARM] 2(3):13-15.

Munro, J. L., V. C. Gaut, R. Thompson, and P. H. Reeson. 1973. The spawning seasons of Caribbean reef fishes. J. Fish Biol. 5:69-84.

Munro, J. L., and D. Pauly. 1983. A simple method for comparing the growth of fishes and invertebrates. Fishbyte [ICLARM] 1(1):5-6.

Munro, J. L., and I. R. Smith. 1985. Management strategies in multispecies complexes in artisanal fisheries. Proc. 36th Gulf Caribb. Fish. Inst.

Munro, J. L., and R. Thompson. 1973. The Jamaican fishing industry, the area investigated and the objectives and methodology of the ODA/UWI fisheries ecology research project. Res. Rep. Zool. Dep., Univ. West Indies 3(II):1-44. (Reprinted 1983 In J. L. Munro (editor), Caribbean coral reef fishery resources, in Chapter 2: The Jamaican fishing industry, p. 10-14, and in Chapter 3: Areas investigated, objectives and methodology, p. 15-25. ICLARM Stud. Rev. 7.)

Munro, J. L., and D. McB. Williams. 1985. Assessment and management of coral reef fisheries: Biological, environmental and socio-economic aspects. Proc. 5th Int. Coral Reef Congr., Tahiti 4:543-565.

Olsen, D. A., and J. A. LaPlace. 1979. A study of a Virgin Islands grouper fishery based on a breeding aggregation. Proc. 31st Annu. Gulf Caribb. Fish. Inst., p. 130-144.

Parrish, J. D. 1986. The trophic biology of snappers and groupers. In J. J. Polovina and S. Ralston (editors), Tropical snappers and groupers: Biology and fisheries management. Westview Press, Inc., Boulder. [See this volume.]

Pauly, D. 1982. Studying single species dynamics in a tropical multispecies context. In D. Pauly and G. I. Murphy (editors), Theory and management of tropical fisheries, p. 33–70. Proceedings of the ICLARM/CSIRO Workshop on the Theory and Management of Tropical Multispecies Stocks, 12–21 January 1981, Cronulla, Australia. ICLARM Conf. Proc. 9.

_____. 1983. Some simple methods for the assessment of tropical fish stocks. FAO Fish. Tech. Pap. 234:1–52.

_____. 1984. Fish population dynamics in tropical waters: A manual for use with programmable calculators. ICLARM Stud. Rev. 8, 325 p.

Pauly, D., and G. R. Morgan (editors). In press. Length-methods in fishery research. The ICLARM/KISR Conference on the Theory and Application of Length-Based Methods for Stock Assessment, Sicily, Italy, 11–16 February 1985.

Pauly, D., and J. L. Munro. 1984. Once more on the comparison of growth in fish and invertebrates. Fishbyte [ICLARM] 2(1):21.

Polovina, J. J. 1984. Model of a coral reef ecosystem. I. The ECOPATH model and its application to French Frigate Shoals. Coral Reefs 3:1–11.

_____. 1986. Assessment and management of deepwater bottom fishes in Hawaii and the Marianas. In J. J. Polovina and S. Ralston (editors), Tropical snappers and groupers: Biology and fisheries management. Westview Press, Inc., Boulder. [See this volume.]

Pooley, S. G. 1986. Demand considerations in fisheries management—Hawaii's market for bottom fish. In J. J. Polovina and S. Ralston (editors), Tropical snappers and groupers: Biology and fisheries management. Westview Press, Inc., Boulder. [See this volume.]

Pope, J. G. 1972. An investigation of the accuracy of virtual population analysis using cohort analysis. Int. Comm., Northwest Atl. Fish. Res. Bull. 9:65–74.

Ralston, S. 1982. Influence of hook size in the Hawaiian deep-sea handline fishery. Can. J. Fish. Aquat. Sci. 39:1297–1302.

_____. 1986. Mortality rates of snappers and groupers. In J. J. Polovina and S. Ralston (editors), Tropical snappers and groupers: Biology and fisheries management. Westview Press, Inc., Boulder. [See this volume.]

Ralston, S., R. M. Gooding, and G. M. Ludwig. In press. An ecological survey and comparison of bottom fish resource assessments (submersible versus handline fishing) at Johnston Atoll. Fish. Bull., U.S. 84(1).

Ralston, S., and J. J. Polovina. 1982. A multispecies analysis of the commercial deep-sea handline fishery in Hawaii. Fish. Bull., U.S. 80:435-448.

Russ, G. 1985. Effects of protective management on coral reef fishes in the central Philippines. Proc. 5th Int. Coral Reef Congr., Tahiti 4:219-224.

Sainsbury, K. J. 1986. Assessment and management of the demersal fishery on the continental shelf of northwestern Australia. In J. J. Polovina and S. Ralston (editors), Tropical snappers and groupers: Biology and fisheries management. Westview Press, Inc., Boulder. [See this volume.]

Sale, P. F. 1980. The ecology of fishes on coral reefs. Oceanogr. Mar. Biol. Annu. Rev. 18:367-421.

Sale, P., and B. J. Sharp. 1983. Correction for bias in visual transect censuses of coral reef fishes. Coral Reefs 2:37-42.

Satersdal, G. 1963. Selectivity of long lines. In The selectivity of fishing gear, p. 189-192. Spec. Publ. ICNAF/ICES/FAO Spec. Sci. Meet., Lisbon, 1957, Vol. 2. Spec. Publ. 5, Int. Comm. Northwest Atl. Fish., Dartmouth N.S., Can.

Schaefer, M. B. 1954. Some aspects of the dynamics of populations important to the management of the commercial marine fisheries. Inter-Am. Trop. Tuna Comm. Bull. 1:27-56.

_____. 1957. A study of the dynamics of the fishery for yellowfin tuna in the eastern tropical Pacific Ocean. [In Engl. and Span.] Inter-Am. Trop. Tuna Comm. Bull. 2:247-285.

Schnute, J. 1977. Improved estimates from the Schaefer production model: Theoretical considerations. J. Fish. Res. Board Can. 34:583-603.

Shapiro, D. Y. 1986. Reproduction in groupers. In J. J. Polovina and S. Ralston (editors), Tropical snappers and groupers: Biology and fisheries management. Westview Press, Inc., Boulder. [See this volume.]

Sharp, G. D. 1981. Report of the workshop on the effects of environmental variation on survival of larval pelagic fishes. In G. D. Sharp (editor), IOC Workshop Rep. 28, p. 15–104. UNESCO, Paris.

Thompson, R., and J. L. Munro. 1974. The biology, ecology and bionomics of Caribbean reef fishes: Serranidae (hinds and groupers). Res. Rep. Zool. Dep., Univ. West Indies, 3(V.b.):1–82. (Reprinted 1983 In J. L. Munro (editor), Caribbean coral reef fishery resources, in Chapter 7: The biology, ecology and bionomics of the hinds and groupers, Serranidae, p. 59–81. ICLARM Stud. Rev. 7.)

Wetherall, J. A., J. J. Polovina, and S. Ralston. In press. Estimating growth and mortality in steady state fish stocks from length–frequency data. In D. Pauly and G. R. Morgan (editors), Length-based methods in fishery research. The ICLARM/KISR Conference on the Theory and Application of Length-Based Methods for Stock Assessments, Sicily, Italy, 11–16 February 1985. Vol. 1.

Williams, D. McB. 1980. Dynamics of the pomacentrid community on small patch reefs in One Tree Lagoon (Great Barrier Reef). Bull. Mar. Sci. 30:159–170.